# 苏州统计年鉴

# SUZHOU STATISTICAL YEARBOOK

# 2013

苏州市统计局
SUZHOU STATISTICS BUREAU
国家统计局苏州调查队 编
STATE STATISTICS BUREAU SUZHOU INVESTIGATION TEAM

总期25期 NO:25

©中国统计出版社 **2013**
版权所有。未经许可，本书的任何部分不得以任何方式在世界任何地区以任何文字翻印、拷贝、仿制或转载。

©2013 China Statistics Press
All rights reserved. No part of the publication may be reproduced or transmitted in any form or by any means, electronic or mechanical, including photocopying, recording, or any information storage and retrieval system, without written permission from the publisher.

图书在版编目（C I P）数据

苏州统计年鉴. 2013 / 苏州市统计局, 国家统计局苏州调查队编. -- 北京 : 中国统计出版社, 2013.7
ISBN 978-7-5037-6828-6

Ⅰ.①苏… Ⅱ.①苏… Ⅲ.①统计资料－苏州市－2013－年鉴 Ⅳ.①C832.533-54

中国版本图书馆CIP数据核字(2013)第124035号

**苏州统计年鉴-2013**

**作　　者** / 苏州市统计局 国家统计局苏州调查队
**责任编辑** / 陈越月
**封面设计** / 苏州文汇雅聚文化交流有限公司
**出版发行** / 中国统计出版社
**通信地址** / 北京市西城区月坛南街57号　邮政编码/100826
**办公地址** / 北京市丰台区西三环南路甲6号　邮政编码/100073
**电　　话** / 邮购（010）63376909 书店（010）68783171
**网　　址** / http://csp.stats.gov.cn
**印　　刷** / 苏州印刷总厂有限公司
**经　　销** / 新华书店
**开　　本** / 880mm×1230mm 1/16
**字　　数** / 1340千字
**印　　张** / 44印张
**版　　别** / 2013年7月第1版
**版　　次** / 2013年7月第1次印刷
**定　　价** / 350.00元

**本书附同版本CD-ROM一张，光盘内容以书面文字为准。**
**如有印装差错，由本社发行部调换。**

## 《苏州统计年鉴—2013》编辑委员会

●名誉主任

周伟强

●主　任

黄正栋

●副主任

张建兴　张善祥　俞冠群　沈爱萍

葛惠龙　吴　盛　王　娴

●编　委（以姓氏笔划为序）

平荣祺　华伟民　朱桂萍　朱曹坚

许忠贵　孙　忆　陈　霞　陈　彤

张旦初　吴　蔚　吴建保　吴国军

诸葛明　盛彩英　盛冠球　章金弟

傅信忻

## 《苏州统计年鉴—2013》编辑部

●主　编

程玉珍

●副主编

马露露　张　鸣

●编辑部成员（以姓氏笔划为序）

马凤玲　王　坚　王佳荣　王晓蓉　尤　珏

刘春辉　刘玲慧　关羽茜　朱震平　孙新研

严国峰　陆　杰　陆　婷　陈春燕　陈　乾

陈　彧　吴　政　宋　莹　邹海峰　汪　栋

张　娴　张　睿　欧志弘　金苏明　房海峰

赵　发　俞　洋　费　玮　徐　浩　徐　静

钱苏芸　程　瑜　蒋　舟　詹　欣　戴　梦

●英文翻译

徐　鹏　费　玮　陈　彧

●统计制图

薛　蕴

## EDITORIAL BOARD

**Honorary Chairperson**

*Zhou Weiqiang*

**Chairman**

*Huang Zhengdong*

**Vice chairman**

*Zhang Jianxing　Zhang Shanxiang　Yu Guanqun　Shen Aiping*

*Ge Huilong　Wu Sheng　Wang Xian*

**Editorial Board** (*In order of strokes of Chinese surname*)

*Ping Rongqi　Hua Weimin　Zhu Guiping　Zhu Caojian*

*Xu Zhonggui　Sun Yi　Chen Xia　Chen Tong*

*Zhang Danchu　Wu Wei　Wu Jianbao　Wu Guojun*

*Zhuge Ming　Sheng Caiying　Sheng Guanqiu　Zhang Jindi*

*Fu Xinxin*

## EDITORIAL DEPARTMENT

**Editor in Chief**

*Cheng Yuzhen*

**Deputy Editor in Chief**

*Ma Lulu　Zhang Ming*

**Editorial Staff** (*In order of strokes of Chinese surname*)

*Ma Fengling　Wang Jian　Wang Jiarong　Wang Xiaorong　You Jue*

*Liu Chunhui　Liu Linhui　Guan Yuqian　Zhu Zhenping　Sun Xinyan*

*Yan Guofeng　Lu Jie　Lu Ting　Chen Chunyan　Chen Qian*

*Chen Yu　Wu Zheng　Song Ying　Zou Haifeng　Wang Dong*

*Zhang Xian　Zhang Rui　Ou Zhiqiang　Jin Suming　Fang Haifeng*

*Zhao Fa　Yu Yang　Fei Wei　Xu Hao　Xu Jing*

*Qian Suyun　Chen Yu　Jiang Zhou　Zhan Xin　Dai Meng*

**English Translator**

*Xu Peng　Fei Wei　Chen Yu*

**Statical Cartgraphy**

*Xue Yun*



编　辑：苏州市统计局
国家统计局苏州调查队
出　版：中国统计出版社
印　刷：苏州印刷总厂有限公司

**Edited By:** Suzhou Statistics Bureau
State Statistics Bureau Suzhou Investigation Team
**Published By:** China Statistics Press
**Printed By:** Suzhou General Printing House Co.,Ltd.

# 《苏州统计年鉴-2013》祝贺单位

(排名不分先后)

江苏省苏州地方税务局
苏州工业园区唯亭街道办事处
苏州市农业发展集团有限公司
中国建设银行股份有限公司苏州分行
中铁二十局集团第一工程有限公司
苏州市规划设计研究院有限责任公司
苏州相城经济开发区管理委员会
苏州市土地储备中心
苏州市民防局
苏州市水利(水务）局
中国银行股份有限公司苏州分行
中国农业银行股份有限公司苏州分行
渭塘镇人民政府
苏州市公安局
苏州市交通运输局
苏州质量技术监督局
江苏省电力公司苏州供电公司
苏州市轨道交通集团有限公司
恒丰银行股份有限公司苏州分行
苏州工业园区胜浦街道
江苏省太湖渔业管理委员会
中国人寿财产保险股份有限公司苏州市中心支公司
苏州市吴中区木渎镇人民政府
江苏常熟服装城管理委员会
江南嘉捷电梯股份有限公司
苏州信托有限公司
中国人寿保险股份有限公司苏州分公司
莱克电气股份有限公司
苏州市苏房集团有限公司
中海发展（苏州）有限公司
苏州市南环桥市场发展股份有限公司
华夏银行苏州分行
苏州新港建设集团有限公司
晋合置业(苏州）有限公司
苏州华成投资有限公司
江苏苏南万科房地产有限公司
江苏省广电信息网络股份有限公司苏州分公司
苏州石川制铁有限公司
苏州国发创业投资控股有限公司
苏州永新置地有限公司
江苏省吴中经济技术发展总公司
金科集团苏州房地产开发有限公司
苏州东瑞制药有限公司

## 编　者　说　明

1.《苏州统计年鉴-2013》以大量统计数据，全面、系统地反映2012年苏州经济、科技、社会各方面的发展情况。

2.本年鉴内容包括：发展成果图，综合，人口、劳动力，农业，工业，建筑业，运输、邮电业，贸易餐饮业，对外经济、国际旅游，能源消费，固定资产投资，企业调查，财政、金融、保险，物价指数，人民生活，科技，教育、文化，卫生、体育，民政、司法，城市建设、环境保护，城市比较等二十一个部分。

3.本年鉴辑入的统计数据以2012年为主，主要指标还列示了建国以来主要历史年份的统计数据。资料主要来自苏州市统计局、国家统计局苏州调查队的各项定期统计报表和抽样调查资料，部分资料来自苏州各主管部门。

4.根据国家统计制度的变化,部分历史数据作相应的调整,读者在使用历史资料时,凡以往年鉴与本年鉴有出入的,均以本年鉴为准。

5.2012年9月吴江撤市设区,原沧浪区、平江区、金阊区合并设立姑苏区。本年鉴表内全市数据包括姑苏区,吴中区,相城区,虎丘区、高新区,工业园区，吴江区，常熟市，张家港市，昆山市，太仓市，市区中包含吴江区数据(气象、水文、物价指数、城市居民家庭相关调查数据除外)。

6.本年鉴中的符号说明：

"..."　　表示数据不足本表最小单位数；

"空格"　表示该项统计数据不详；

"-"　　表示无该项统计数据；

"#"　　表示其中数。

《苏州统计年鉴》公开出版以来，受到社会各界的关注和支持，不少读者对年鉴的内容和编辑工作提出了许多宝贵的意见，对此，我们深表感谢。欢迎读者一如既往地对年鉴的不足之处批评指正，帮助我们进一步提高编辑水平。

## Complier's Note

Ⅰ.***Suzhou Statistical Yearbook 2013*** is a publication which provides comprehensive and systematic data covering the economic, technological and social development in Suzhou Municipality in 2012.

Ⅱ.This yearbook is comprised of 21 parts including Achievement Graphs and Charts, General Survey, Population and Labor Force, Agriculture, Industry, Construction, Transportation, Post and Telecommunication, Wholesale, Retail Sales and Catering Business, Export-Oriented Economy and International Tourism, Consumption of Energy, Investment in Fixed Assets, Enterprises Survey, Finance, Banking and Insurance, Price Indices, People's Livelihood, Science and Technology, Education and Culture, Public Health and Sports, Civil Administration, Judiciary and Other Items, Urban Construction and Environmental Protection, Cities Compare.

Ⅲ. The statistics in the yearbook are mainly the statistics in 2012, and the main indicators also list the statistical data in the key years since the founding of the People's Republic of China. The data mainly comes from the periodic statistical reports and sample survey data of Suzhou Municipal Bureau of Statistics and Suzhou Investigation Team of National Bureau of Statistics, and some of the information comes from administrative departments of Suzhou municipal government.

Ⅳ. According to the changes of the national statistical system, some historical data is adjusted accordingly, and in the use of historical data, when the data in previous yearbooks is different from that in this yearbook, the data in this yearbook is to be used.

Ⅴ. In September, 2012 Wujiang City was changed into Wujiang District, and the original Changlang District、Pingjiang Dictrict and Jinchang District were merged to become Gusu District. The whole city's data in the yearbook includes the data of Gusu District, Wuzhong District, Xiangcheng District, Huqiu District、 Suzhou New District, Suzhou Industrial Park, Wujiang District, Changshu City, Zhangjiagang City, Kunshan City and Taicang city, and the data of the central city includes that of Wujiang District (except the data of meteorology, price indices, hydrology and investigation of urban households).

Ⅵ. Explanations on symbols used in this yearbook:

"…" indicates that the data are not large enough to be rounded into the minimal unit,

"space" indicates that the data is unknown and indicates the data not available,

" – " indicates the data not available,

" # " indicates the component items.

Here we'd like to express our sincere thanks to the readers who have provided us so many invaluable suggestions on content selection and compilation of the yearbook. Our thanks also go to those friends in all circles of society who have shown their support and care to the publication of the yearbook. We welcome any suggestions and comments from readers at large so as to help us to further improve our work of compilation.

# 实力增强结构优化

CHART OF ACHIEVEMENTS

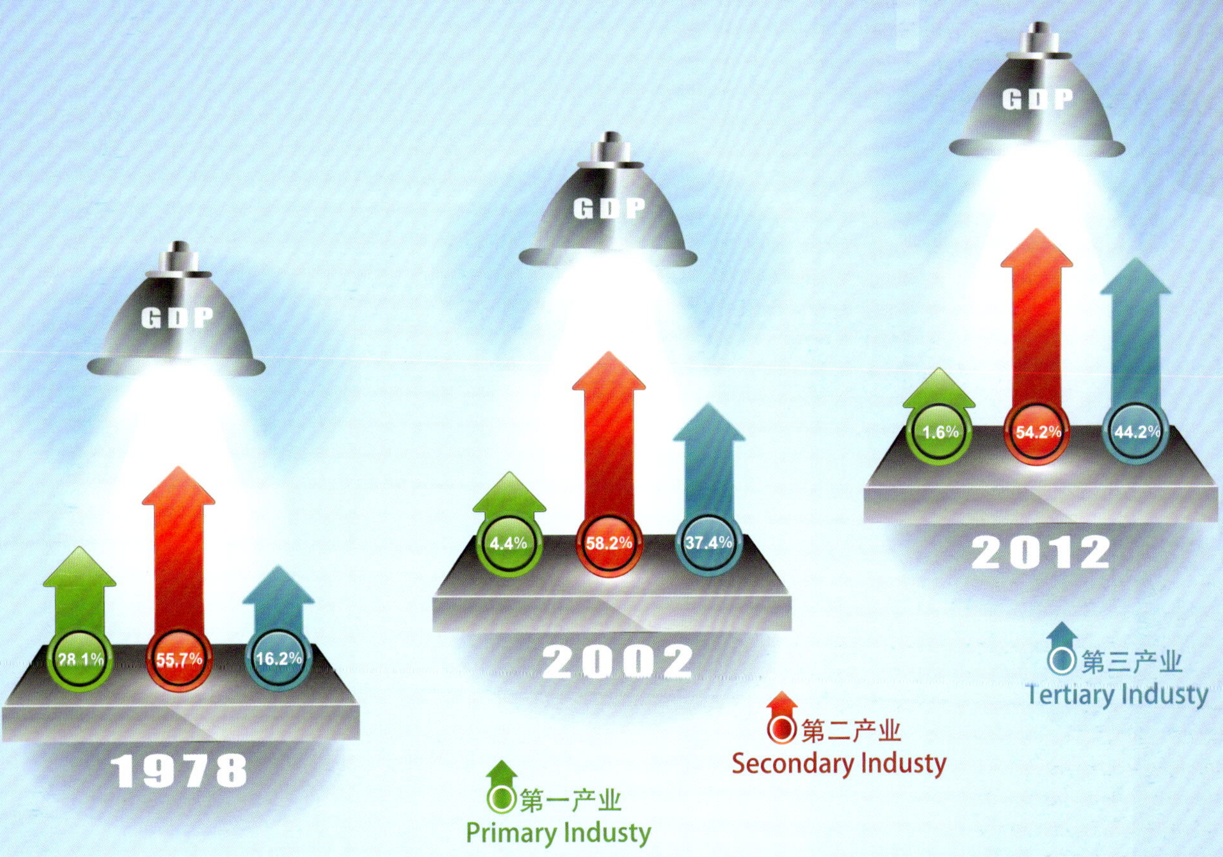

## 农林牧渔业总产值（亿元）
Gross Output Value of Agriculture (100 million yuan)

## 农林牧渔业总产值构成（%）
Composition of Gross Output Value of Agriculture(%)

# 工业经济持续增长
CHART OF ACHIEVEMENTS

## 工业总产值（亿元）
Output Value of Industry (100 million yuan)

## 规模以上工业总产值（亿元）
Output Value of Industrial Enterprises Above Designated Size(100 million yuan)

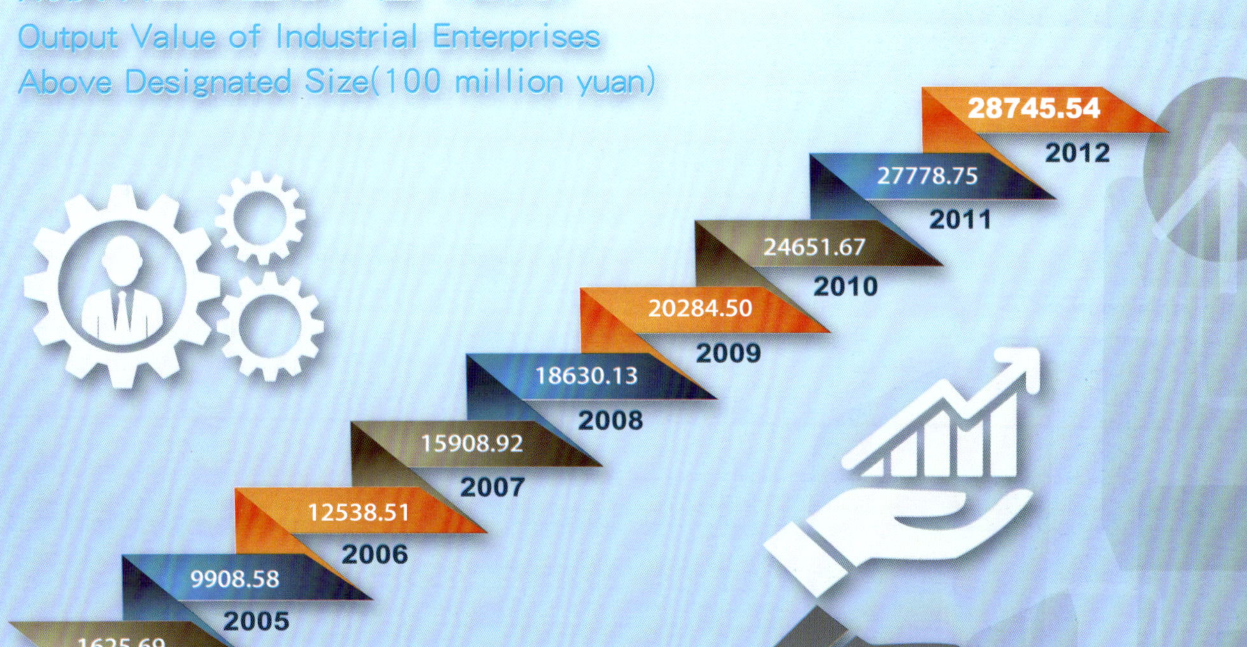

## 社会消费品零售总额（亿元）
Total Retail Sales of Consumer Goods (100 million yuan)

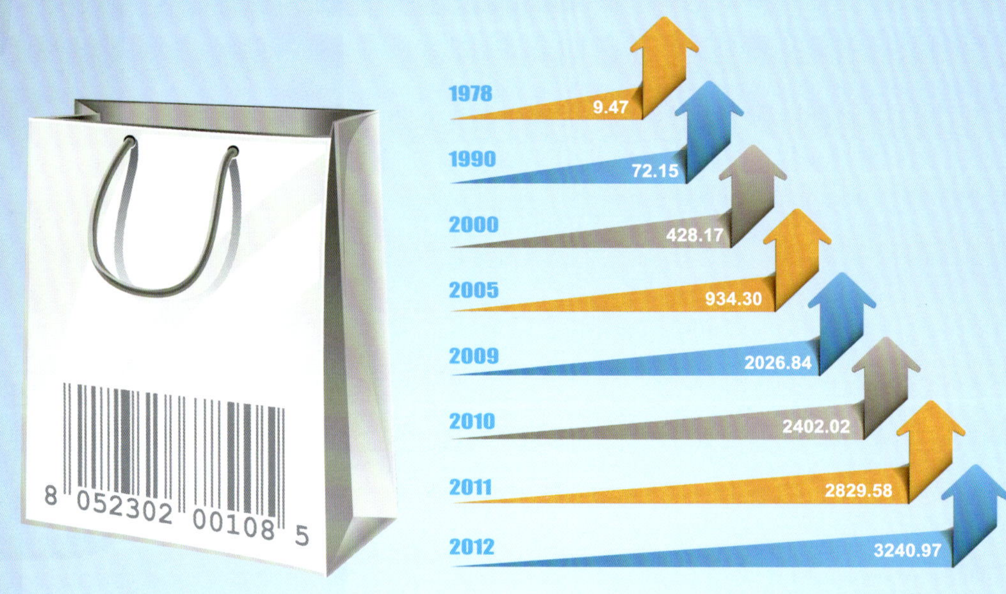


## 2012年限额以上批发和零售业商品零售额构成(%)
The Proportion of Wholesale and Retail Trade above Designated Size

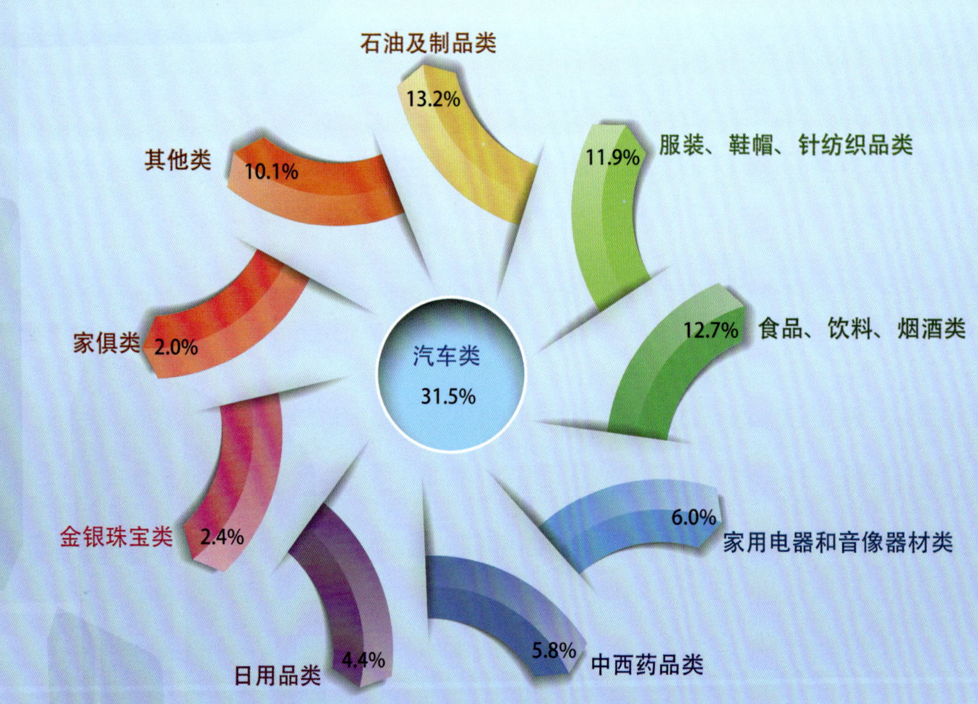

# 对外开放程度提高

CHART OF ACHIEVEMENTS

## 进出口总额（亿美元）

Import and Export Value (USD 100 million)

## 实际利用外资（亿美元）

Foreign Capital Actually Used (USD 100 million)

## 接待境外旅游者（万人次）

Received Foreign Tourists(10 000 person-times)

# 投资规模不断扩大

CHART OF ACHIEVEMENTS

## 全社会固定资产投资（亿元） Total Fixed Assets Investment (100 million yuan)

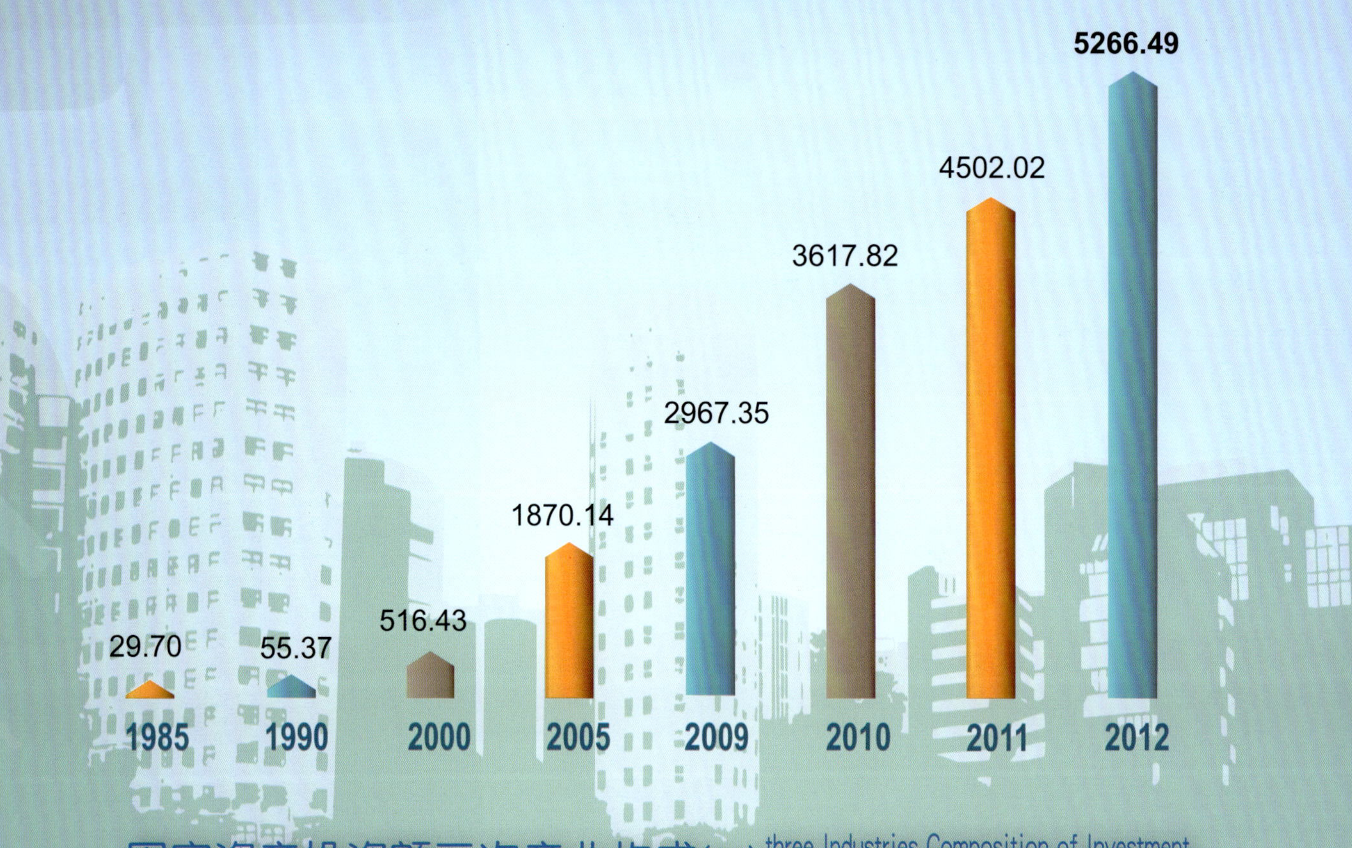


## 固定资产投资额三次产业构成(%) three Industries Composition of Investment in Fixed Assets(%)

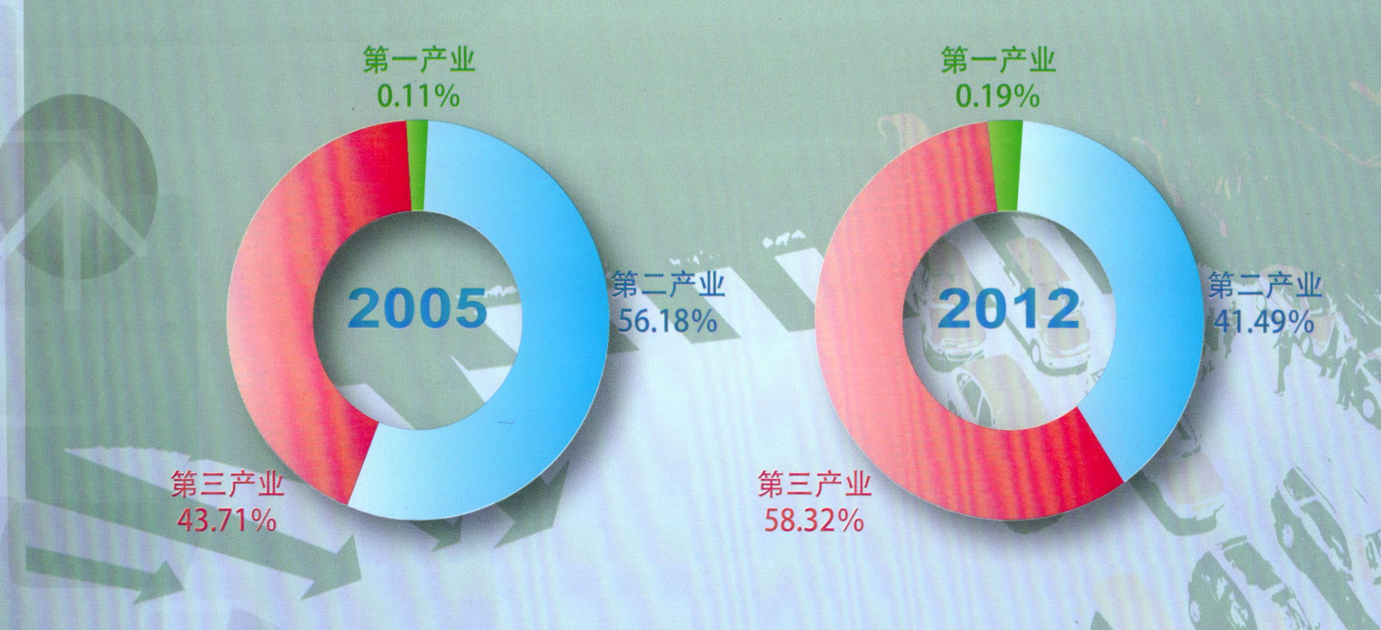

# 财政金融形势稳定
CHART OF ACHIEVEMENTS

## 财政收支（亿元）Financial Revenue and Expend iture(100 million yuan)

公共财政预算支出 Public Finance Budgetary Expenditure

| 2000 | 2005 | 2006 | 2007 | 2008 | 2009 | 2010 | 2011 | 2012 |
|---|---|---|---|---|---|---|---|---|
| 78.11 | 335.28 | 386.20 | 496.94 | 622.37 | 686.78 | 825.67 | 1002.63 | 1113.47 |

公共财政预算收入 Public Finance Budgetary Revenue

| 2000 | 2005 | 2006 | 2007 | 2008 | 2009 | 2010 | 2011 | 2012 |
|---|---|---|---|---|---|---|---|---|
| 80.39 | 316.78 | 400.23 | 541.82 | 668.91 | 745.18 | 900.55 | 1100.88 | 1204.33 |

## 金融机构存贷款余额（亿元）Savings and Loans Balances of Bank (100 million yuan)

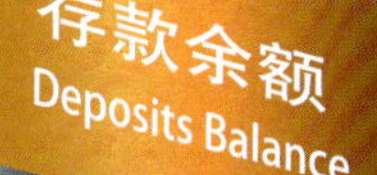


| | 1978 | 1990 | 2000 | 2005 | 2008 | 2009 | 2010 | 2011 | 2012 |
|---|---|---|---|---|---|---|---|---|---|
| 存款余额 Deposits Balance | 7.37 | 132.20 | 1477.01 | 4730.05 | 8340.79 | 10950.25 | 13570.35 | 15180.78 | 17663.50 |
| 贷款余额 Loans Balance | 15.45 | 134.10 | 970.60 | 3478.34 | 6301.81 | 8505.33 | 10133.15 | 11873.89 | 13626.86 |

# 基础设施更加完善

CHART OF ACHIEVEMENTS

建成区面积（平方公里）
Build up Area (sq.km)

| 2005 | 2006 | 2007 | 2008 | 2009 | 2010 | 2011 | 2012 |
|---|---|---|---|---|---|---|---|
| 432.8 | 500.4 | 532.9 | 623.4 | 641.8 | 660.4 | 698.9 | **719.9** |

建成区绿化覆盖率（%）
Coverage Rate of Green Areas in Developed Areas (%)

| 2005 | 2006 | 2007 | 2008 | 2009 | 2010 | 2011 | 2012 |
|---|---|---|---|---|---|---|---|
| 42.51 | 45.27 | 46.39 | 44.95 | 43.01 | 42.84 | 42.46 | **42.58** |

人均拥有道路面积（平方米）
Per Capita Area of Roads (sq.m)

| 2005 | 2006 | 2007 | 2008 | 2009 | 2010 | 2011 | 2012 |
|---|---|---|---|---|---|---|---|
| 21.5 | 27.6 | 28.6 | 29.0 | 29.8 | 30.4 | 31.3 | **31.3** |

# 科教文卫全面进步
CHART OF ACHIEVEMENTS

## 专业技术人员（万人） Scientific and Technical Personnel(10 000 persons)

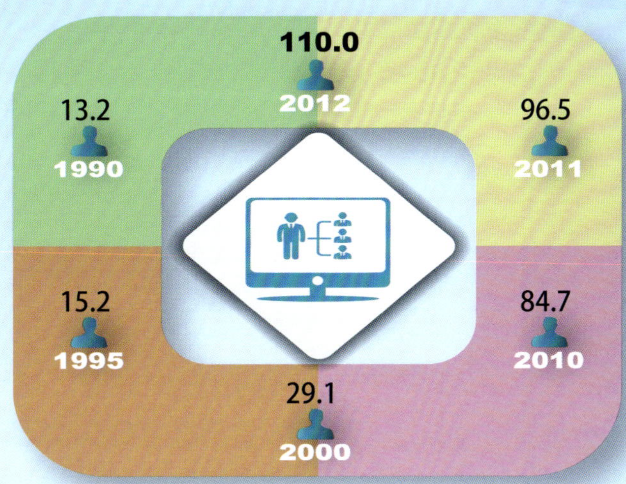


## 高校在校学生人数（万人）
Student Enrollment of Higher Education (10 000 persons)

| 1978 | 1990 | 2000 | 2010 | 2011 | 2012 |
|---|---|---|---|---|---|
| 0.65 | 1.63 | 4.77 | 18.78 | 18.88 | 19.22 |

## 专利申请授权量（件）
Patent Applications and Patent Granted (unit)

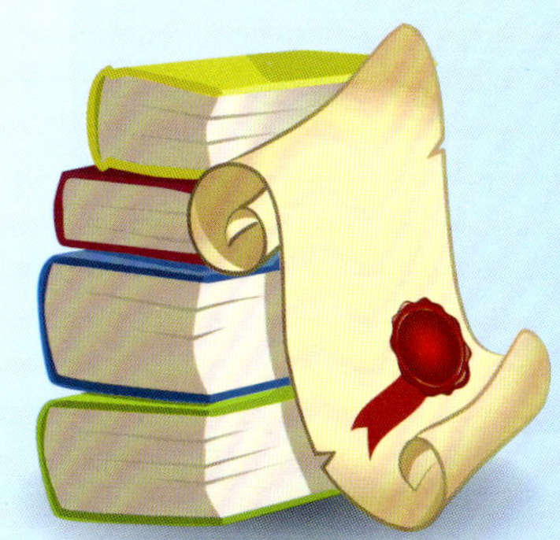

| 专利申请量（件） | | 专利授权量（件） | |
|---|---|---|---|
| 2011 | 2012 | 2011 | 2012 |
| 102164 | 139965 | 77281 | 98276 |

## 卫生机构床位数（张） Number of Beds in Health Institutions (unit)

| 1978 | 1990 | 2000 | 2010 | 2011 | 2012 |
|---|---|---|---|---|---|
| 14470 | 18424 | 19504 | 39204 | 42972 | 46070 |

# 居民增收物价稳定

CHART OF ACHIEVEMENTS

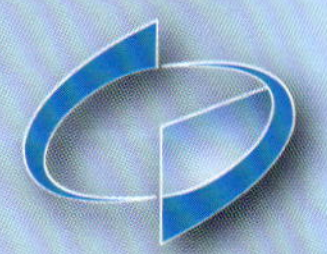

## 市区居民消费价格总指数（以上年价格为100） Residents Consumer Price Indices (Preceding Year is Taken as 100)

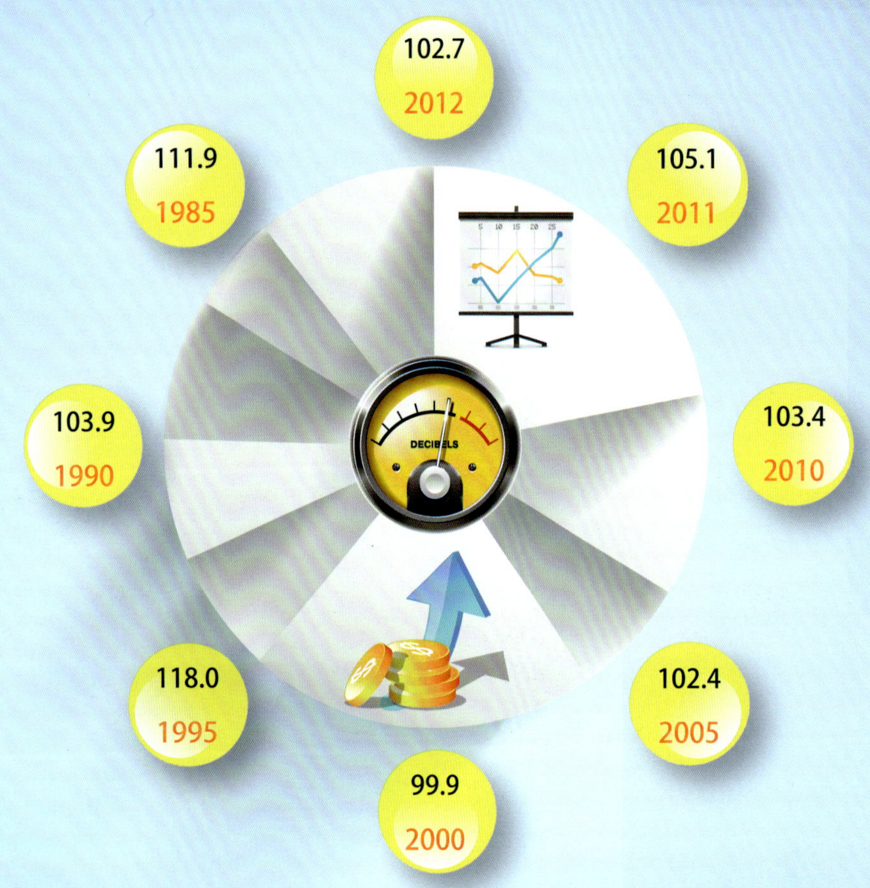


## 城乡居民收入（元） Income of Urban and Rural Residents (yuan)

**农村居民家庭人均纯收入**
Per Capital Annual Net Income of Rural Households

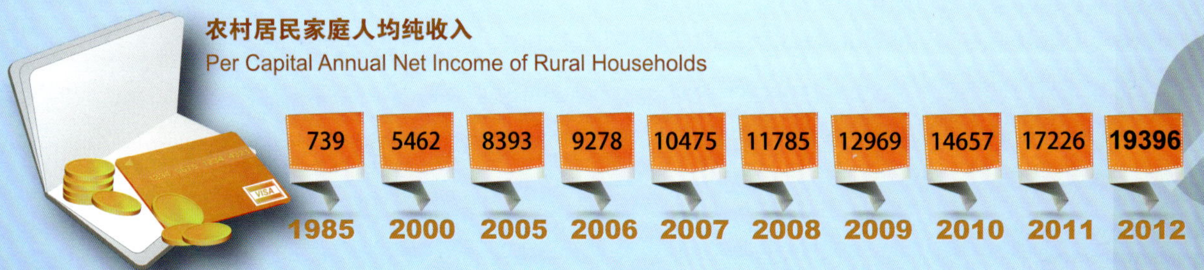


| 1985 | 2000 | 2005 | 2006 | 2007 | 2008 | 2009 | 2010 | 2011 | 2012 |
|---|---|---|---|---|---|---|---|---|---|
| 918 | 9274 | 16276 | 18532 | 21260 | 23867 | 26320 | 29219 | 33243 | 37531 |

**市区居民家庭人均可支配收入**
Per Capital Annual Disposable Income of Urban Households

# 目　　录
# CONTENTS

**二、人口、劳动力**

**POPULATION AND LABOR FORCE**

## 三、农　业

## AGRICULTURE

**四、工　业**

**INDUSTRY**

**五、建 筑 业**

**CONSTRUCTION**



**六、运输、邮电业**

**TRANSPORTATION, POST AND TELECOMMUNICATION**

**七、贸易餐饮业**

**TRADE AND CATERING BUSINESS**

## 八、对外经济、国际旅游

## FOREIGN TRADE ECONOMY AND INTERNATIONAL TOURISM

**九、能源消费**

**CONSUMPTION OF ENERGY**

**十、固定资产投资**

**INVESTMENT IN FIXED ASSETS**

**十一、企业调查**

**ENTERPRISES SURVEY**



**十二、财政、金融、保险**

**FINANCE, BANKING AND INSURANCE**

**十三、物价指数**

**PRICE INDICES**

**十四、人民生活**

**PEOPLE'S LIVELIHOOD**

## 十五、科　技

## SCIENCE AND TECHNOLOGY

**十六、教育、文化**

**EDUCATION AND CULTURE**

**十七、卫生、体育**

**PUBLIC HEALTH AND SPORTS**

**十九、城市建设、环境保护**

**URBAN CONSTRUCTION AND ENVIRONMENTAL PROTECTION**

**二十、城市比较**

**CITIES COMPARE**

# 2012年苏州市国民经济和社会发展概况

2012年，面对严峻复杂的国内外经济形势，全市围绕建设“三区三城”的总目标，以科学发展为主题、以转变发展方式为主线，认真贯彻“稳中求进、转中求好”的工作导向，突出“加快转型、稳定外贸、兴盛文化、广惠民生”等工作重点，努力克服和化解宏观经济运行的下行压力，有效加强经济运行调节，积极强化要素保障，全方位转变发展方式，高起点推进转型升级，大力度发展创新型经济，全年经济社会保持了平稳发展态势，主要指标稳中有增，结构调整步伐加快，城乡一体协调发展，民生质量持续改善，现代化建设取得了新进展。

**综合经济**

经济保持平稳增长。全市实现地区生产总值1.2万亿元，比上年增长10.1%；人均地区生产总值（按常住人口计算）超过11万元，按现行汇率折算超过1.8万美元。

全年实现地方公共财政预算收入1204.3亿元，比上年增长9.4%。其中各项税收收入1023.9亿元，增长10.2%。全年地方公共财政预算支出1113.47亿元，比上年增长11.1%。其中教育支出 180.7亿元，增长19.5%；科学技术支出66.59亿元，增长24.2%；社会保障和就业支出101.6亿元，增长20.1%。全市各级财政用于民生方面的支出605.4亿元，占财政支出的54.4%。

**农业生产**

农业生产提质增效。全市实现农林牧渔业总产值337.7亿元，比上年增长4.1%。粮食总产量116.5万吨，比上年增长1.3%，其中夏粮总产量36.7万吨，增长5.1%；秋粮总产量79.8万吨，下降0.4%。粮食连续实现三年增产。

农业现代化建设稳步推进。全市新增设施农业（渔业）面积9.15千公顷，累计达到41.25千公顷。新建高标准农田20千公顷，累计达到106.7千公顷。全市农业适度规模经营比重达到86.8%。规模以上农业龙头企业年销售收入1050亿元，比上年增长13.6%。全年新增无公害农产品、绿色食品和有机食品121只，累计达到1722只。

**农村建设**

农田水利设施改造升级加快。全市完成农田水利总土方3121万立方米，疏浚整治各级河道1691公里，加高加固圩堤356公里，增砌护岸159公里。农业综合机械化率达到87%。

城乡一体化综合配套改革取得新进展。全市新增农村社区股份合作、土地股份合作、农业专业合作组织431家，累计

3928家，持股农户占农户总数的比重达96%。农村集体资产突破1200亿元，村均集体收入582万元，分别比上年增长14%和15.7%。全市90%的农村工业企业进入工业园，88%的承包耕地实现规模经营，48%的农民实现集中居住。

## 工　业

工业经济努力克服市场需求放缓、生产成本上升、经营难度加大的不利影响，以强化要素保障实现稳定增长，以加快结构调整促进提档升级。全市实现工业总产值34528亿元，其中规模以上工业总产值28746亿元，分别比上年增长3.5%和5.2%。全市规模以上工业中，私营工业产值4868亿元，增长4.3%；外资工业产值18870亿元，增长4.0%。重工业产值21354亿元，轻工业产值7392亿元，分别比上年增长6.1%和2.5%。全市新产品产值4627亿元，比上年增长20.5%。

主导产业稳定发展。通信设备和计算机及其他电子设备制造业、黑色金属冶炼及压延加工业、电气机械及器材制造业、纺织业、化学原料及化学制品制造业、通用设备制造业六大支柱行业实现产值19420亿元，比上年增长6.1%，占规模以上工业总产值的比重达67.6%。

新兴产业成为亮点。全市制造业领域新兴产业实现产值12367亿元，比上年增长11%，占规模以上工业产值的43%，比上年提高5.0个百分点。新兴产业创造利税、利润分别占全市规模以上工业的45.3%和47.8%。其中新材料、新型平板显示、高端装备制造业产值分别达到3426亿元、2780亿元、2371亿元，占新兴产业产值的69.4%。

重点企业贡献度提升。全市百强工业企业完成产值12406亿元，比上年增长13.7%，占规模以上工业产值的43.2%。百强工业企业中产值超百亿元的企业28家，完成工业产值8207亿元，比上年增长16.1%。

高耗能行业有效抑制。钢铁、纺织、化工、造纸、建材、电力等六大高耗能行业产值增长2.8%，六大行业产值占规模以上工业总产值的比重为24.3%，比上年下降1.6个百分点。

受市场环境制约，工业企业经营效益有所下降，但降幅逐步收窄。全年规模以上工业企业实现主营业务收入28999亿元，比上年增长3.6%；利税总额1816.4亿元，比上年下降5.7%，其中利润总额1251.6亿元，下降10.4%；规模以上工业产销率达到99.3%。

## 建筑业

建筑业实现平稳发展。全市完成建筑业总产值1745亿元，比上年增长13.9%。全市资质以上建筑业企业房屋施工面积11014万平方米，比上年增长9.4%，其中新开工面积4574万平方米，下降12%。建筑业企业在外省完成建筑业产值300亿元，比上年增长16.1%。年末拥有总承包和专业承包资质的建筑企业1477家，实现利润73亿元，比上年增长17.4%；上缴税金71亿元，增长13.8%。

## 运输邮电业

全市以加快基础设施建设、提高运输服务能力、构筑现代物流体系为重点，推进现代交通运输产业发展。

交通基础设施不断完善。全市完成交通基础设施投资116.1亿元，其中公路建设投资60.7亿元，港口建设投资35亿元。年末公路总里程13090公里，其中高速公路535公里。

客货运量稳定增长。全市完成公路、水路客运量6.9亿人次，旅客周转量307.74亿人公里，分别比上年增长8.2%和

12.1%；完成货运量1.73亿吨，货物周转量170.51亿吨公里，分别增长11.0%和13.8%。

港口运输能力增强。苏州港港口货物吞吐量4.28亿吨，比上年增长12.6%;集装箱运量586万标箱，比上年增长25.2%。苏州港新增万吨级以上码头泊位9个。太仓港年吞吐量突破400万标箱，太仓港在全国内河港中第一个获批享受海港待遇。

邮电通信平稳发展。全市邮政系统发送函件2.92亿件、特快专递2313万件、报刊3.1亿份。年末邮政储蓄余额433.8亿元，比年初增加60.86亿元。全市电信业务总收入187.35亿元，比上年增长10.8%。年末移动电话用户1555万户，互联网宽带用户达到283.57万户。

私家汽车保有量继续增加。年末拥有机动车239.27万辆，其中汽车177.90万辆，分别比上年增长7.1%和18.1%。私家汽车保有量144.54万辆，比上年增长20.6%。

## 国内贸易

积极改善提升消费环境，加快优化城乡商贸布局，大力发展新型消费业态，突出扩大消费需求对经济增长的贡献。全年实现社会消费品零售总额3241亿元，比上年增长14.5%。其中城镇消费品市场实现零售额2831.4亿元，增长14.3%；农村消费品市场实现零售额409.6亿元，增长16.3%。批发和零售业零售额2830亿元，增长14.3%；住宿和餐饮业零售额383亿元，增长19.1 %。全市家电下乡产品销售额12.38亿元。

全市限额以上批发零售贸易业零售额中，服装、鞋帽、针纺织品类增长28.1%；食品、饮料、烟酒类增长23.1%；日用品类增长21.7%；通讯器材类增长20.7%；文化办公用品类增长11.1%；汽车类增长4.1%；金银珠宝类增长0.4%；体育、娱乐用品类增长0.1%；家用电器和音像器材类下降3.6%。

商业载体建设稳步推进。全市拥有国家级特色（著名）商业街13条。国家级、省级商业示范社区21家。年末全市共有商品交易市场625个，其中亿元以上市场90个，实现成交额4855亿元。新型流通业态以及现代经营方式较快发展。网络购物、无店铺销售、仓储式销售等新兴业态发展迅猛。吴中区金枫电子商务产业园成为国家电子商务示范基地。

## 金融业

货币信贷总量平稳增长，金融业态多元发展，对实体经济支持力度加大。年末金融机构人民币存、贷款余额分别为1.77万亿元和1.36万亿元，分别比年初增加2483亿元和1754亿元。各项存款中，储蓄存款余额5788亿元；单位存款余额10758亿元。各项贷款中，短期贷款余额5717亿元，比年初增加1073亿元；中长期贷款余额7504亿元，比年初增加626亿元。年末金融机构本外币存、贷款余额分别为1.88万亿元和1.49万亿元，比年初分别增加2793亿元和2102亿元。

年末全市共有证券营业部60家，证券交易开户总数121万户。证券机构托管市值总额1283亿元，比上年增长10.9%。全年各类证券交易额10476亿元，比上年下降26.8%。期货市场交易额34901亿元，比上年下降8.6%。

保险业稳健运行。注册资本20亿元、国内首家在地级市设立的寿险法人总部机构——东吴人寿保险股份有限公司获准开业。全年新增保险机构5家，年末全市保险机构共68家。全年保费收入237亿元，比上年增长13.3%，其中财产险收入105亿元，增长19.4%；人身险收入133亿元，增长8.9%。

**房地产业**

在国家房地产政策调控的总基调下，房地产开发投资、施工面积增速放缓，市场销售总体保持稳定，刚性需求有所释放，住房供给和需求结构得到调整。全年完成房地产开发投资额1263.36亿元，比上年增长5.4%，占全社会固定资产投资的比重为24%。商品房新开工面积2060.5万平方米，比上年增长0.5%；商品房施工面积8404万平方米，增长5.8%；竣工面积1828万平方米，增长20.7%。商品房销售面积1466.29万平方米，增长21.1%，其中住宅销售面积1263.11万平方米，增长28.4%。市区存量房交易面积312万平方米，交易金额316亿元，分别比上年增长28%和29%。

**旅游业**

着力提升文化旅游城市影响力，以项目开发、优化品质、树立品牌、提升服务为重点，全面促进旅游产业融入经济社会发展。全市实现旅游总收入1376.24亿元，比上年增长15.1%；接待境外游客321.87万人次，比上年增长8.1%。入境游客中，外国游客230.18万人次，港澳台同胞91.69万人次。旅游外汇收入16.47亿美元，比上年增长12.1%。全市景区接待游客11503万人次，比上年增长13.6%。

年末全市拥有星级饭店144家，其中四星级及以上饭店75家。金鸡湖景区成功创建国家5A级景区，全市共有5A级景区点4家，4A级景区点28家，3A级景区点20家。苏州被确定为全国智慧旅游试点城市。

**现代服务业**

积极推进金融创新发展。新增上市公司12家，年末拥有境内外上市公司82家，累计募集资金661亿元。发行企业债券174亿元。新增批准开业小额贷款公司11家，累计83家。股权创业投资快速发展。年末拥有备案创投企业102家，创投机构管理资金规模超过750亿元。全社会新增融资规模近4000亿元。

全市以服务业税收“营改增”试点、省级服务业综合改革试点为契机，加快发展现代服务业。年末全市省、市级服务业集聚区达到70个，集聚区从业人员超过80万人，年销售（营业）收入超6000亿元，比上年增长20%以上。新增制造业企业分离发展现代服务业企业260家，累计达到1042家。全年服务外包接包合同额和离岸接包执行额56亿美元和30.6亿美元，分别比上年增长56.8%和51.9%。

**民营经济**

全市优化发展环境，激活民间资本，民营经济发展量增质升，对经济的贡献份额不断提高。全年私营企业、个体户新登记注册户数11.23万户。年末全市私营个体登记注册户数64.46万户，其中私营企业22.96万户、个体工商户41.50万户，分别比上年增长9.1%、10.4%和 8.4%。年末私营个体注册资金8716.11亿元，比上年增长16.1%。年末注册资金超1000万元的私营企业15967户，比上年增加1773户；其中超亿元的企业1424户，增加252户。全市民间投资占固定资产投资的比重达56.1%，民营工业产值占规模以上工业产值的比重达31.9%。

## 对外贸易

在欧债危机和主要发达经济体复苏进程缓慢的影响下，外贸增长减缓。全市实现进出口总额3056.92亿美元，其中出口1746.89亿美元，分别比上年增长1.6%和4.5%，增幅分别比上年回落8.2和4.7个百分点。外资企业进出口2273.51亿美元，比上年下降7.5%。积极推进加工贸易转型升级，大力发展一般贸易、保税物流贸易和服务贸易，外贸方式加快转变。全市加工贸易增值率由上年的77.1%提升至83.8%。一般贸易出口占出口总额的比重达25.3%，比上年提高1.6个百分点。保税物流园区进出口贸易增长59%。新兴市场增势强劲。全市对东盟、非洲和俄罗斯的出口额分别比上年增长13.8%、14.0%和10.7%。成功举办第一届中国国际进口产品博览会。

## 招商引资

积极推进高端引资，鼓励企业增资扩股，推动利用外资稳量提质。全年实际利用外资91.65亿美元，比上年增长2.8%，其中服务业利用外资30.24亿美元，增长3.1%，占实际利用外资比重达33%。新兴产业和高新技术项目利用外资35.14亿美元，占实际利用外资的比重达38.3%。新增外资地区性总部及功能性总部机构45家，累计达180家。43家企业被认定为首批省级跨国公司地区总部和功能性机构。世界500强企业中有145家落户苏州。

## 对外经济合作

全年新批境外投资中方协议投资额12.22亿美元，比上年增长74.4%，规模实现全省九连冠。全年新签对外劳务承包合同额10.26亿美元，完成营业额8.37亿美元，分别比上年增长7.9%和8.9%。年末境外投资涉及的国家和地区达到80多个。

## 开发区建设

开发区载体功能再拓展。全市共有省级以上开发区17家，其中国家级开发区11家。全市开发区实际利用外资76.09亿美元，出口总额1511亿美元，实现地方公共财政预算收入689亿元，占全市的比重分别为83.0%、86.5%和57.2%。吴中经济开发区升格为国家级开发区，张家港保税港区汽车整车进口口岸获得国务院批准，苏州高新区成为全国首个国家知识产权服务业集聚发展区。

## 固定资产投资

全市坚持扩内需、稳投资的发展方针，着力扩大基础设施、重点项目、民生工程、新兴产业的投入力度，有效引导投资结构，夯实经济发展基础。全年完成全社会固定资产投资5266.49亿元，比上年增长17%。其中国有经济完成投资1226.61亿元，增长9.4%；私营个体投资1586.95亿元，增长14.2%。投资结构继续优化，第一产业完成投资10.01亿元，增长13.7%；第二产业完成投资2184.89亿元，增长15.6%，其中工业投资2176.43亿元，增长15.9%；第三产业完成投资3071.59亿元，增长18%，占全社会投资的比重达到58.3%，比上年提高0.5个百分点。新兴产业投入快速增长。全市新兴产业在建项目完成投资1133.34亿元，比上年增长31.8%。

**城乡规划与建设**

围绕建设“一核四城”的发展目标，实施部分行政区划重大调整，撤销平江、沧浪、金阊三个区，设立姑苏区、苏州国家历史文化名城保护区；吴江撤市设区。中心城市首位度得到提升。苏州市区面积由3254.7平方公里扩大到4474.4平方公里（含水域面积）。农村生态环境进一步改善，新增林地、绿地面积13.3千公顷。村庄环境整治达标率超过95%。基础设施建设全面提速。全年完成基础设施投资908亿元，比上年增长19%。轨道交通1号线建成投运，苏州成为国内首个运营轨道交通的地级市。轨道交通2号线实现“轨通”，4号线及支线、2号线延伸段、太仓港疏港高速公路、常嘉高速公路昆山至吴江段开工建设。苏虞张快速通道北段改建完成通车。中环快速路工程全面启动，东环、南环快速路延伸加快建设。±800千伏锦苏特高压输电线路及同里换流站、胥门变电站建成启用。新增人防设施72万平方米。

**公用事业**

多元化公共交通服务得到新提升。市区新辟公交线路20条，年末市区营运车辆达到3826辆，营运线路285条，线路总长达到6488公里；市区公交运客总量6.26亿人次，比上年增长10.6%。年末城市轨道交通运营里程25.2公里。轨道1号线自开通运营到年底，运客量达到2595万人次。新增电调专用出租车300辆，市区年末营运出租汽车4303辆。市区新购公交车506辆，国III以上排放标准的公交车比例达到91.7%。新建公共自行车网点151个。全年新增农村客运（公交）班线19条，行政村农村客运班车通达率保持100%，城乡客运一体化覆盖率达到90%。

公用事业投入不断加大。市区新建、改建公共卫生间25座，新建、改建垃圾中转站2座，新、扩建城镇污水处理厂11座，建设配套截污管网798.74公里，新增污水日处理能力（含扩建）20.75万吨。

市区管道天然气供气总量7.43亿立方米，人工煤气供气总量4449万立方米。城乡居民生活用电86.49亿千瓦时，比上年增长 12.1%。

市区新增绿地450万平方米，市区人均公共绿地面积14.94平方米，市区建成区绿化覆盖率42.4%。

**节能降耗与环境保护**

以绿色发展、低碳发展、可持续发展为目标，妥善处理节能减排与稳定经济发展的关系，改善优化生态环境，全力构筑生态宜居地区。

全年万元地区生产总值能耗为0.637吨标准煤，比上年下降4.61%。全年全社会用电量1189.93亿千瓦时，比上年增长5.2%。其中工业用电量982.66亿千瓦时，增长3.9%。全年规模以上工业综合能源消费量5015万吨标准煤，比上年增长2.8%，其中消耗的主要能源品种为：原煤5005万吨，下降1.1%；天然气37亿立方米，增长8.5%；电力807亿千瓦时，增长5.5%。

全社会环保投入达到445亿元，增长14.9%，占GDP的比重达到3.7%。全市环境质量综合指数93.26。市区空气质量优良以上天数达到339天。集中式饮用水源地水质达标率为100%。功能区环境噪声达标率100%。推动实施PM2.5监测。全市建成55个环境优美镇，其中50个为国家级生态镇；新增省级生态村25个，省级以上生态村累计达到526个，占行政村总数的48.4%。

扎实开展“能效之星”创建活动，实施“万家企业节能低碳行动”，实现节能100万吨标准煤。全年实施减排项目174个，全年主要污染物二氧化硫和化学需氧量排放总量分别比上年下降3.7%和3.0%以上，氨氮削减率和氮氧化物削减率均超过3%。

## 科技事业

围绕结构调整和产业转型升级，着力提升科技进步对经济增长的贡献度，全力打造以增强自主创新能力为核心的区域创新体系。全市研究与试验发展经费支出占地区生产总值的比重达到2.5%。全年落实企业研发费加计扣除金额42.47亿元。

全市新增省级以上高新技术企业588家、累计达到1864家。新认定省级以上高新技术产品2367个，累计达10031个。新增省级以上企业技术中心43家，累计176家。新增省级以上工程技术研究中心109家，累计337家。全市80%的本土大中型企业建立研发机构。高新技术产业实现产值11889亿元，占全市规模以上工业产值的比重达到41.3%。

全市专利申请量和授权量达到14万件和9.8万件，分别比上年增长37%和27.2%，专利申请量和授权量均列全国大中城市第一位。新增中国驰名商标17件，累计达75件。苏州成为首批国家知识产权示范城市，并顺利通过全国版权示范城市验收。

## 人才建设

人才强市战略深入实施，创新人才、领军人才、高层次人才和高技能人才的引进和培育力度不断增强。全年引进大专以上各类人才14.2万人。年末全市各类人才总量178万人，其中留学回国人员超过1.28万人，高层次人才突破11万人，高技能人才达到38万人。年末全市拥有各类专业技术人员110万人，比上年增长14%。新增入选国家“千人计划”人才51人，累计105人，居全国地级市第一；新增入选省“双创计划”人才96人，累计301人；新增入选市“姑苏计划”人才118人，累计347人。国家“千人计划”中，创业人才的比重达到70%。

## 教育事业

教育现代化稳步推进。年末全市拥有各级各类学校1097所（含幼儿园），在校学生125.28万人，毕业生30.78万人，教职工总数9.72万人，其中专任教师7.95万人。在苏州的普通高等院校20所，独立二级学院5所。普通高等学校在校学生19.22万人，毕业生4.97万人；成人高等学校在校学生3.4万人，毕业生1.94万人。 各类教育均衡发展。学前三年幼儿入学率达99.9%，义务教育阶段学生入学率、巩固率继续保持在100%，全市初中毕业生升学率为99.7%。全市高等教育毛入学率达到64.3%。苏州独墅湖科教创新区被教育部确定为高等教育国际化示范区。

## 文化事业

文化事业加快发展。年末全市有艺术表演团体14个，文化馆12个，博物馆36个，公共图书馆12个。镇（街道）以上公益性文化设施实现全覆盖，行政村公益性文化设施覆盖率达90%。文艺精品新作连创佳绩。滑稽戏《青春跑道》入选国家文化部建国以来优秀保留剧目大奖。

大力发展文化产业。全市文化产业营业收入2600亿元。年末拥有国家级文化产业示范基地7个，省级文化产业示范基地5个、市级基地28个。

文化保护和传承加强。全市累计6个项目列入联合国人类非物质文化遗产代表作名录，29个项目列入国家级非物质文化遗产代表作名录，39人列入国家级非物质文化遗产代表性传承人。大运河苏州段成功列入中国大运河首批申遗名单，昆曲遗产保护、传承、弘扬工程顺利通过国家级文化创新工程验收。

**卫生事业**

公共卫生服务能力和医疗卫生服务水平不断提高。年末全市有各类卫生机构2992个，其中医院、卫生院251个，卫生防疫、防治机构13个，妇幼保健机构7个。年末卫生机构拥有床位4.61万张，拥有卫生技术人员5.72万人，其中医生2.32万人，分别比上年增长7.2%、12.4%和18.8%。城乡社区卫生服务机构覆盖率达100%。建成国家级示范卫生服务中心2个，镇村卫生机构均达到省定建设标准。

**体育事业**

全民健身活动长效化，竞技体育取得丰硕成果。成功举办市第13届体育运动会。苏州健儿在伦敦奥运会上勇夺2枚金牌、1枚银牌。新增4名世界冠军，苏州世界冠军总数达23人。全年共承办省级以上体育竞赛68项次，其中国际、洲际比赛23项次，全国比赛40项次，省级比赛5项，办赛数量在全省各市保持领先。体育设施进一步完善。市区新建、更新全民健身路径169条。体育彩票销售创新高，实现总销量33亿元，位居全国地级市第一，全国大中城市第二位。

**人口与就业**

人口规模保持稳定。全市户籍人口出生6.8万人，出生率为10.56‰，人口自然增长率为3.58‰。年末全市户籍总人口647.81万人，比上年增加5.48万人，其中市区户籍人口248.51万人，比上年增加 3.26万人。

就业形势保持平稳。全市新增就业16.8万人，开发公益性岗位9500个。苏州籍高校毕业生就业率达到96.6%。全年免费培训城乡劳动力43.8万人。城乡基层就业公共服务平台加快建设。

**社会保障**

城乡社会保障一体化稳步推进。实现养老保险、医疗保险城乡并轨，成为全国首个全面实现社保城乡并轨的地区。年末全市城镇职工养老保险缴费人数472.88万人，职工医疗保险参保人员541.56万人，城镇职工失业、工伤、生育参保缴费人数分别为375.74万人、404.07万人和403.97万人。城镇职工五大社会保险覆盖率和社会保障基金征缴率均保持在99%以上。城乡居民养老保险和居民医疗保险覆盖率均达到99%以上。城乡老年居民享受社会养老保险待遇覆盖率达到100%。企业退休人员月人均增加基本养老金165.5元。城乡居民最低生活保障标准由每人每月500元提高至570元。苏州社会保障·市民卡顺利发放，市区发放量超过250万张。

### 社会福利与救助

年末全市拥有各类养老机构205个，床位总数46223张，收养人数32500人。新增养老床位8355张、日间照料中心87个，助餐点142个。全市27711户、56911人纳入低保范围，累计发放保障金2.06亿元。全年社会救助支出达18.3亿元，惠及困难群众16.8万人次。

### 人民生活

全市积极实施城乡居民收入六年倍增计划，居民收入稳步增加。市区居民人均可支配收入37531元，农民人均纯收入19396元，分别增长12.9%和12.6%。收入结构进一步优化，非工资性收入保持较快增长。

市区居民家庭月人均可支配收入分组表：

| 组 别 | 各组所占比重(%) | 全年人均可支配收入(元) |
|---|---|---|
| 1000元以下 | 2.7 | 9991 |
| 1000-1500元 | 11.3 | 15221 |
| 1500-2000元 | 17.0 | 21198 |
| 2000-2500元 | 18.3 | 26591 |
| 2500-3000元 | 12.3 | 32802 |
| 3000-4000元 | 16.0 | 40767 |
| 4000-5000元 | 8.7 | 53051 |
| 5000元以上 | 13.7 | 97676 |

保障性住房建设规模扩大，住房保障覆盖范围稳步提高。全市新开工建设保障性住房37454套、竣工25420套，为4894户困难家庭发放廉租住房租赁补贴。市区完成113万平方米老住宅小区、16万平方米零星居民楼综合整治任务，解危修缮直管公房4.5万平方米。实施城区居民家庭改厕8739户，改造城中村（无地队）17个。新增住房公积金缴存人数52.64万人，职工使用住房公积金188亿元。全市新建、改建城乡农贸市场47家，市区开设农产品直供网点46家，新建农产品平价直销网点102个。

### 市场物价

在大宗商品价格震荡下行、全球通胀压力有所缓解的大背景下，居民消费价格指数逐步回落。全年市区居民消费价格总水平比上年上升2.7%，八大类消费价格“六升二降”：食品类、烟酒类、衣着类、家庭设备用品及维修服务类、医疗健和个人用品类、居住类价格分别比上年上升5.1%、1.7%、4.4%、5.3%、2.1%和2.7%；交通及通信类、娱乐教育文化用品及服务类价格比上年下降1.5%、0.2%。

**市区居民消费价格指数（以上年价格为100）：**

| 类　别 | 2012年 | 2011年 |
|---|---|---|
| 居民消费价格总指数 | 102.7 | 105.1 |
| 1. 食　品 | 105.1 | 114.6 |
| #粮　食 | 101.7 | 109.8 |
| 油　脂 | 102.9 | 107.5 |
| 肉禽及其制品 | 103.7 | 118.2 |
| 蛋 | 100.3 | 115.4 |
| 水产品 | 107.3 | 112.6 |
| 菜 | 111.7 | 99.8 |
| 2. 烟　酒 | 101.7 | 101.6 |
| 3. 衣　着 | 104.4 | 104.0 |
| 4. 家庭设备用品及维修服务 | 105.3 | 102.8 |
| 5. 医疗保健和个人用品 | 102.1 | 102.9 |
| 6. 交通和通信 | 98.5 | 100.6 |
| 7. 娱乐教育文化用品及服务 | 99.8 | 97.2 |
| 8. 居　住 | 102.7 | 103.1 |

2012年在紧运行环境下，苏州经济结构调整和转型升级取得新进展，内生发展动力进一步增强，惠民措施得到有效落实，城市功能和基础设施进一步完善，社会事业、生态环境协调发展，城乡统筹和区域发展得到新提升，但受宏观环境影响，开放型经济和实体经济面临一定的困难。2013年要充分估计经济形势的严峻性，以提高经济增长质量和效益为中心，突出创新引领、聚焦转型、生态优先、民生为本，扎实推进稳定增长、科技创新、经济国际化、社会建设等重点工作，以更大力度、更实举措，努力实现经济社会持续健康发展。

**注：本文中市区数据不包含吴江区。**

# An Overview of the 2012 Economic and Social Development of Suzhou Municipality

In 2012, in the face of the severe and complicated economic situation at home and abroad, and with the building of the "three districts and three towns" as the overall objective, the scientific development as the theme and the change of the development mode as the main line, the city conscientiously implemented the task orientation of "maintaining stability ahead and changing in the pursuit of the better ", focused on the tasks of "speeding up the change of the development mode, stabling foreign trade, making culture flourished, and widely benefiting people's lives", made efforts to overcome and resolve the downward pressure of the macroeconomic performance, effectively improved the economic regulation, actively strengthened the security of elements, changed the development mode in an all-round way, promoted the transformation and upgrading from a higher starting point, and made great efforts to develop an innovation-based economy. In the year the economy and society maintained a stable development trend, the main indicators steadily increased, the pace of structural adjustment speeded up, the urban and rural integration underwent coordinated development, the quality of people's lives continued to improve, and the construction of modernization made new progress.

**General economy**

The economy maintained steady growth. The city realized GDP of 1.2 trillion yuan, an increase of 10.1% over the previous year; per capita GDP was more than 110,000 yuan (resident population), or over $18,000 at the current exchange rate.

In the year the local public budget revenue reached 120.43 billion yuan, an increase of 9.4% over the previous year. Of it the tax revenue was 102.39 billion yuan, an increase of 10.2%. In the year the local public budget expenditure was 111.347 billion yuan, an increase of 11.1% over the previous year. Of it the education spending was 18.07 billion yuan, an increase of 19.5%; the science and technology spending 6.659 billion yuan, an increase of 24.2%; and the social security and employment expenditure 10.16 billion yuan, an increase of 20.1%. The financial expenditure for people's lives by the city's departments at all levels was 60.54 billion yuan, accounting for 54.4% of the total financial expenditure.

**Agricultural production**

The quality of agricultural production was improved and its efficiency increased. The city's total output value of agriculture, forestry, animal husbandry and fishery reached 33.77 billion yuan, an increase of 4.1% over the previous year. The total grain output was 1.165 million tons, an increase of 1.3% over the previous year, of which the total summer grain output was 0.367 million tons, an increase of 5.1% and the total autumn grain output 0.798 million tons, down 0.4%. The grain output increased for three consecutive years.

Agricultural modernization was steadily advanced. The city's new facilities-agriculture (fisheries) area reached 9,150 hectares with a total of 41,250 hectares. The city's new high-standard farmland reached 20,000 hectares with a total of 106,700 hectares. The city's scale-management agriculture accounted for 86.8%. The year's sales income of the leading agricultural enterprises above designated size reached 105 billion yuan, an increase of 13.6% over the previous year. The year saw 121 new pollution-free agricultural, green food and organic food products, with a total of 1,722.

**Rural development**

The upgrading of irrigation and water conservancy facilities was accelerated. The city completed 31.21 million cubic meters of irrigation and water conservancy earthworks, dredging 1,691 kilometers of rivers at all levels, heightening and consolidating 356 kilometers of levee, and building 159 kilometers of new revetment. The rate of comprehensive agricultural mechanization reached 87%.

The comprehensive reform of the integration of urban and rural areas made new progress. The city saw 431 new rural community shares cooperatives, land stock cooperatives, and farmer cooperatives, with a total of 3,928, and the cumulative shareholding farmers accounted for 96% of the total number of households. The rural collective assets exceeded 120 billion yuan, and the average village collective income was 5.82 million yuan, an increase of 14% and 15.7% respectively over the previous year. 90% of the city's rural industrial enterprises entered the industrial parks, 88% of the contracted arable land achieved scaled operation, and 48% of the farmers lived together.

**Industry**

The industrial economy made efforts to overcome the adverse influence of slowdown in market demand, rising production costs, and management being more difficult, to strengthen the security of elements in order to achieve steady growth, and to speed up structural adjustment in order to promote the upgrading. The city achieved a total industrial output value of 3,452.8 billion yuan, of which the above-scale industrial output value was 2,874.6 billion yuan, an increase of 3.5% and 5.2% respectively over the previous year. Of the city's above-scale industries, the private industrial output value was 486.8 billion yuan, an increase of 4.3%; the foreign industrial output value 1,887 billion yuan, an increase of 4.0%. The output value of the heavy industry was 2,135.4 billion yuan and that of the light industry 739.2 billion yuan, an increase of 6.1% and 2.5% respectively over the previous year. The output value of the city's new products was 462.7 billion yuan, an increase of 20.5% over the previous year.

The leading industries steadily developed. The output value of the six pillar industries of communications equipment and computers and other electronic equipment manufacturing industry, ferrous metal smelting and rolling processing industry, electrical machinery and equipment manufacturing industry, textile industry, chemical raw materials and chemical products manufacturing industry, and general equipment manufacturing industry was 1,942 billion yuan , an increase of 6.1% over the previous year, and accounting for 67.6% of the total output value of the industrial enterprises above designated size .

The emerging industries became a bright spot. The output value of the emerging industries of the city's manufacturing sector was 1,236.7 billion yuan, an increase of 11% over the previous year, and accounting for 43% of the above-scale industrial output value, an increase of 5 percentage points over the previous year. The taxes and profits created by the emerging industries accounted for 45.3% and 47.8% of those by the city's above-scale industries. The output value of the new materials industry, the new flat panel display industry and the high-end equipment manufacturing industry reached 342.6 billion yuan, 278 billion yuan and 237.1 billion yuan respectively, accounting for 69.4% of the output value of the emerging industries.

The key enterprises made greater contributions. The output value of city's top 100 industrial enterprises was 1,240.6 billion yuan, an increase of 13.7% over the previous year, and accounting for 43.2% of that of the above-scale industries. The number of the top 100 industrial enterprises with an output value of over ten billion yuan each was 28, which achieved an output value of 820.7 billion yuan, an increase of 16.1% over the previous year.

The high energy-consuming industries were effectively controlled. The output value of the six high energy-consuming industries of iron and steel, textiles, chemicals, paper, building materials, and electricity was up 2.8%, and the output value of the six industries accounted for 24.3% of that of the above-scale industries, 1.6 percentage points lower than the previous year.

By the constraints of the market environment, the operating efficiency of industrial enterprises has declined, but the decline narrowed. The above-scale industrial enterprises realized 2,899.9 billion yuan of main business income, an increase of 3.6% over the previous year; and 181.64 billion yuan of total profits and taxes, a decrease of 5.7% over the previous year and of them the total profits were 125.16 billion yuan, down 10.4%; and the production and sales rate of large-scale industries reached 99.3%.

**Construction**

The construction achieved stable development. The total output value of the city's construction reached 174.5 billion yuan, an increase of 13.9% over the previous year. The city's housing construction area by qualified building enterprises was 110.14 million square meters, an increase of 9.4% over the previous year, of which the new construction area was 45.74 million square meters, down 12%. The construction output value in other provinces achieved by the city's building enterprises was 30 billion yuan, an increase of 16.1% over the previous year. At the end of the year there were 1,477 building enterprises with general contracting and professional contracting qualifications, which realized 7.3 billion yuan of profits, an increase of 17.4% over the previous year; and paid 7.1 billion yuan of taxes, an increase of 13.8%.

**Transportation, post and telecommunication**

Focusing on speeding up infrastructure construction, improving the capacity of transport services, and building a modern logistics system, the city promoted the development of modern transportation industry.

Transport infrastructure was constantly improved. The city invested 11.61 billion yuan in transport infrastructure, including 6.07 billion yuan in highway construction and 3.5 billion yuan in port construction. At the end of the year the city's total mileage was 13,090 kilometers, including 535 kilometers of expressways.

Passenger and cargo traffic steadily grew. The city's road and waterway passenger capacity was 690 million passengers, and the passenger turnover 30.774 billion person-kilometers, an increase of 8.2% and 12.1% respectively over the previous year; the city's cargo completed was 173 million tons, and the cargo turnover 17.051 billion tons km, an increase of 11.0% and 13.8 % respectively.

Port capacity was enhanced. Suzhou port cargo throughput was 428 million tons, an increase of 12.6% over the previous year; and the container traffic 5.86 million TEUs, an increase of 25.2% over the previous year. There appeared 9 new above-one-million-ton berths in Suzhou ports. Taicang Port's throughput was over 4 million TEUs, and Taicang Port became the first to have been approved to enjoy the seaport treatment among the river ports in the country.

Post and telecommunications developed smoothly. The city's postal system sent 292 million letters, 23.13 million speed post matters, and 310 million copies of newspapers and periodicals. At the end of the year the postal savings balance was 43.38 billion yuan, an increase of 6.086 billion yuan over the beginning of the year. The city's telecom business income was 18.735 billion yuan, an increase of 10.8% over the previous year. At the end of the year there were 15.55 million mobile phone subscribers and 2.8357 million broadband Internet subscribers.

Private car ownership continued to increase. At the end of the year there were 2.3927 million motor vehicles, including 1.779 million cars, an increase of 7.1% and 18.1% respectively over the previous year. There were 1.4454 million private cars, an increase of 20.6% over the previous year.

**Domestic trade**

The consumption environment was actively improved, the optimization of the layout of urban and rural commerce and trade accelerated, new consumer format vigorously developed, and the contributions of the expansion of consumer demand to economic growth highlighted. The year's total retail sales of the society's consumer goods were 324.1 billion yuan, an increase of 14.5% over the previous year, including 283.14 billion yuan in the urban consumer goods markets, an increase of 14.3%; 40.96 billion yuan in the rural consumer goods markets, an increase of 16.3%. The wholesale and retail sales were 283 billion yuan, an increase of 14.3%; and the accommodation and catering retail sales 38.3 billion yuan, an increase of 19.1%. The city's sales of home appliances products sent to the countryside were 1.238 billion yuan.

Of the retail sales of the city's above designated wholesale and retail trade, those of clothing, footwear and textile products were up 28.1%, those of food, beverages, tobacco and alcohol up 23.1%; those of daily necessities up 21.7%; those of communications equipment up 20.7%; those of cultural and office supplies up 11.1%; those of motor vehicles up 4.1%; and those of gold, silver and jewelry up 0.4%; and those of sports and recreational goods up 0.1%; and those of household appliances and audiovisual equipment down 3.6%.

Commerce-related construction was steadily promoted. In the city there were 13 national (famous) commercial streets with characteristics, and 21 national or provincial business model communities. At the end of the year, in the city there were 625 commodity trading markets, including 90 over-one-million-yuan markets, with a turnover of 485.5 billion yuan. New circulation types and modern management methods were rapidly developed. New business types such as online shopping, non-store sales and warehouse sales were rapidly developed. Jinfeng E-commerce Industrial Park of Wuzhong District became a national e-commerce demonstration base.

**Financial sector**

The total amount of money credit steadily grew, financial format diversified and the real economy was greatly supported. At the end of the year, the RMB deposits and loans of the city's financial institutions were 1,770 billion yuan and 1,360 billion yuan, an increase of 248.3 billion yuan and 175.4 billion yuan respectively, compared with the beginning of the year. Of the various deposits, the savings deposits were 578.8 billion yuan, and the unit deposits 1,075.8 billion yuan. Of the various loans, the short-term loans were 571.7 billion yuan, an increase of 107.3 billion yuan over the beginning of the year; the medium-or-long-term loans were 750.4 billion yuan, an increase of 62.6 billion yuan over the beginning of the year. At the end of the year the deposits and loans of national and foreign currencies of the city's financial institutions were 1,880 billion yuan and 1,490 billion yuan, an increase of 279.3 billion yuan and 210.2 billion yuan respectively, compared with the beginning of the year.

At the end of the year, there were 60 securities business departments in the city, and the total number of securities trading accounts was 1,210,000. The total hosting market capitalization of the city's securities institutions was 128.3 billion yuan, an increase of 10.9% over the previous year. In the year the amount of transactions of the various types of securities was 1,047.6 billion yuan, a decrease of 26.8% over the previous year. Futures market transactions amounted to 3,490.1 billion yuan, down 8.6% over the previous year.

The insurance industry was stably operated. The registered capital was 2 billion yuan. Dongwu Life Insurance Co., Ltd. the first life insurance corporate headquarters institution established in the prefecture-level city was allowed to open. The year saw 5 new insurance agencies, and at the end of the year there were 68 insurance agencies in the city. The year's premium income was 23.7 billion yuan, an increase of 13.3% over the previous year, of which the property insurance income was 10.5 billion yuan, an increase of 19.4%; the life insurance income 13.3 billion yuan, an increase of 8.9%.

**Real estate**

Under the general tone of the national housing policy control, the growth of investment in real estate development and of construction area slowed down, the market remained stable overall, rigid demand was released, housing supply and demand structure was adjusted. The year's investment in real estate development was 126.336 billion yuan, an increase of 5.4% over the previous year, and accounting for 24% of the society's investment in fixed assets. The new construction area of commercial housing was 20.605 million square meters, an increase of 0.5% over the previous year; the area of commercial housing under construction 84.04 million square meters, an increase of 5.8%; the area of completed commercial housing 18.28 million square meters, up

20.7%. The area of sold commercial housing was 14,662,900 square meters, an increase of 21.1%, including 12,631,100 square meters of sold residential housing, an increase of 28.4%. The trading area of reserved housing in the city proper was 3.12 million square meters, and the transaction amount was 31.6 billion yuan, an increase of 28% and 29% respectively over the previous year.

**Tourism**

The city made efforts to enhance the influence of the cultural and tourist city, focused on project development, optimizing the quality, establishing brands and improving service, and fully promoted the integration of the tourism industry into the economic and social development. The city's total tourism income was 137.624 billion yuan, an increase of 15.1% over the previous year; the tourists received from outside mainland China were 3,218,700, an increase of 8.1% over the previous year. Of the inbound tourists, foreign tourists were 2,301,800, and Hong Kong, Macao and Taiwan compatriots 916,900. Tourism foreign exchange earnings were $1.647 billion, an increase of 12.1% over the previous year. The city's scenic tourists were 115.03 million, an increase of 13.6% over the previous year.

At the end of the year there were 144 star hotels in the city, including 75 four-star-and-above hotels. Jinji Lake scenic spot successfully became a national 5A-level scenic spot, and there were 4 5A-level scenic spots, 28 4A-level scenic spots and 20 3A-level scenic spots in the city. Suzhou was identified as a wisdom tourism pilot city.

**Modern service industry**

The development of financial innovation actively promoted. The city saw 12 new listed companies, and at the end of the year there were 82 domestic and foreign listed companies with total proceeds of 66.1 billion yuan. Corporate bonds of 17.4 billion yuan were issued. 11 new small loan companies were approved to open, with a total of 83. Equity venture capital was rapidly developed. At the end of the year there were 102 venture capital companies put on record, and the venture capital institutions managed more than 75 billion yuan of funds. The new scale of financing in society as a whole was nearly 400 billion yuan.

With "sales tax replaced by VAT" as a pilot tax scheme in services, and the pilot comprehensive reform of provincial services as an opportunity, the city accelerated the development of modern service industry. At the end of the year there were 70 gathering areas of provincial and municipal services employing more than 800,000 people, and in the year the sales (business) revenue was over 600 billion yuan, an increase of more than 20% over the previous year. There were 260 new modern service enterprises isolated and developed from the manufacturing enterprises, totaling 1,042. In the service outsourcing the year's access package contract amount and offshore access package execution amount were $5.6 billion and $3.06 billion, an increase of 56.8% and 51.9% respectively over the previous year.

**Private economy**

With the optimization of the development environment and the activation of private capital, the private economy developed with an increase in volume and a rise in quality, and continuously made greater contributions to the economy. In the year 112,300 private enterprises and individual industrial and commercial households were newly registered. At the end of the year there were 644,600 registered private enterprises and individual industrial and commercial households, an increase of 9.1% over the previous year, of which 229,600 were private enterprises and 415,000 individual industrial and commercial households, up 10.4% and 8.4% respectively over the previous year. At the end of the year the registered capital of the private enterprises and individual industrial and commercial households was 871.611 billion yuan, an increase of 16.1% over the previous year. At the end of the year there were 15,967 private enterprises with over-10 million-yuan registered capital each, an increase of 1,773 over the previous year, including 1,424 enterprises with over-0.1 billion-yuan each, an increase of 252 enterprises. The city's private investment accounted for 56.1% of the total investment in fixed assets, and the private industrial output value accounted for 31.9% of the above-scale industrial output value.

**Foreign trade**

Under the impact of the Euro debt crisis and the slow recovery process of the major developed economies, foreign trade growth slowed down. The city's total imports and exports were $305.692 billion, of which exports were $174.689 billion, an increase of 1.6% and 4.5% respectively over the previous year, and an increase of 8.2 percentage points and 4.7 percentage points lower than the previous year respectively. The imports and exports of the foreign-funded enterprises were $227.351 billion, a decrease of 7.5% over the previous year. The transformation and upgrading of processing trade was actively promoted, general trade, bonded logistics trade and trade in services vigorously developed, and the transformation of the ways of foreign trade accelerated. The city's processing trade value-added rate increased to 83.8% from 77.1% in the previous year. The general trade exports accounted for 25.3% of the total exports, 1.6 percentage points higher than the previous year. The import and export trade of the Bonded Logistics Park was up 59%. Emerging markets were strong. The city's exports to ASEAN, Africa and Russia were up13.8%, 14.0% and 10.7% respectively over the previous year. The city successfully held the First China International Import Expo.

**Investment**

The city actively promoted high-end foreign capital, encouraged enterprises to increase their investment, and promoted the use of foreign capital to stable the quantity and improve the quality. The year's foreign capital actually utilized was $9.165 billion, an increase of 2.8% over the previous year, of which the foreign capital utilized by services was $3.024 billion, an increase of 3.1% and accounting for 33% of the city's foreign capital actually utilized. The foreign capital utilized by emerging industries and high-tech projects was $3.514 billion, accounting for 38.3% of the foreign capital actual utilized. There were 45 new foreign regional headquarters and functional agencies at headquarters with a total of 180. 43 companies were identified as the first provincial-level regional headquarters of multinationals and functional agencies. 145 of the Fortune 500 companies had settled in Suzhou.

**Foreign economic cooperation**

The year's newly approved Chinese overseas investment was $1.222 billion, an increase of 74.4% over the previous year, and the city's overseas investment was the first in scale in the province for nine consecutive years. The year's amount of newly-signed foreign labor service contracts was $1.026 billion and the completed turnover $0.837 billion, an increase of 7.9% and 8.9% respectively over the previous year. At the end of the year there were more than 80 countries and regions involved in overseas investment.

**Construction of development zones**

The vector function of the development zones was expanded. In the city there were 17 development zones above the provincial level, including 11 national development zones. The foreign capital actually utilized by the city's development zones was $7.609 billion, their total exports $151.1 billion, and their local public budget revenue 68.9 billion yuan, accounting for the city's 83.0%, 86.5% and 57.2% respectively. Wuzhong Economic Development Zone was upgraded to a national development zone, the automobile import port of Zhangjiagang Bonded Port Area obtained the approval of the State Council, and Suzhou New Zone became the country's first concentrated development area of national intellectual property service industries.

### Investment in fixed assets

The city adhered to the development policy of expanding domestic demand and stabling investment, made efforts to expand investment in infrastructure, key projects, livelihood projects and emerging industries, effectively guided the investment structure, and laid a solid basis for economic development. The year's total fixed asset investment was 526.649 billion yuan, an increase of 17% over the previous year. Of the total investment 122.661 billion yuan was invested by state-owned economy, an increase of 9.4%; and 158.695 billion yuan by private enterprises and individual industrial and commercial households, an increase of 14.2%. Investment structure continued to optimize, the primary industry invested 1.001 billion yuan, an increase of 13.7%; the secondary industry 218.489 billion yuan, an increase of 15.6%, including 217.643 billion yuan of industrial investment, an increase of 15.9%; the tertiary industry invested 307.159 billion yuan , an increase of 18%, and accounting for 58.3% of the society's total investment and 0.5 percentage points higher than the previous year. The increase of investment in emerging industries accelerate. The emerging industrial projects under construction in the city completed an investment of 113.334 billion yuan, an increase of 31.8% over the previous year.

### Urban and rural planning and construction

Focusing on the development goal of building "one core and four towns", the city implemented a major adjustment of some administrative divisions, revoked the three districts of Pingjiang, Changlang and Jinchang, and established Gusu District and the protected area of Suzhou national historical and cultural city; Wujiang City was made to be Wujiang District. The importance of the central city was raised. The urban area of Suzhou was expanded from 3,254.7 square kilometers to 4,474.4 square kilometers (including water area). Ecological environment in rural areas was further improved with 13,300 hectares of new woodland and green area. The village environment compliance rate was more than 95%.The speed of infrastructure construction was comprehensively improved. The city's investment in infrastructure was 90.8 billion yuan, an increase of 19% over the previous year. Rail Transit Line No.1 was put into operation, and Suzhou became the first domestic prefecture-level city with the operation of rail transportation. The track of Rail Transit Line No.2 was completed, and the construction of Line No.4 and its extension, the extension of Line No.2, Taicang Harbor Expressway and the Kunshan-Wujiang section of Changshu-Jiaxing Expressway started. The reconstruction of the northern section of SuYuZhang (Suzhou-Changshu-Zhangjiagang) fast-track was completed and it was opened to traffic. The construction of the project of the Central Ring Expressway started, and the construction of the extension of the East Ring Expressway and that of the South Ring Expressway speeded up. The construction of ± 800 KV Jingsu high-voltage transmission line and Tongli Converter Station, and Xumen Transformer Substation was completed and they started to be used. New air defense facilities were 720,000 square meters.

### Utilities

Diversified public transport services were upgraded. 20 new bus lines were put into operation in the urban area, and at the end of the year there were 3,826 buses and 285 lines in operation with a total line length of 6,488 kilometers in the urban area; the urban area's total number of bus transport passengers was 626 million, an increase of 10.6% over the previous year. At the end of the year urban rail transit operating mileage was 25.2 kilometers. From the beginning of its operation to the end of the year the number of passengers on Track Line No.1 reached 25.95 million. 300 new phone-called taxis were put into operation, and at the end of the year there were 4,303 working taxis in the urban area. 506 new buses were bought in the urban area, and the buses above the national III emission standard accounted for 91.7%. 151 new public bicycle network points were set up. The year saw 19 new rural passenger transport (bus) lines, 100% of the administrative villages had access to rural passenger transport, and the coverage rate of the integration of urban and rural passenger transport reached 90%.

Investment in utilities continued to increase. In the urban area 25 public toilets and 2 garbage transfer stations were built or renovated, and 11 urban sewage treatment plants built or expanded, 798.74 kilometers of supporting sewage interception pipe network newly installed and the daily new sewage treatment capacity (including expansion) was 207,500 tons.

In the urban area the total pipeline natural gas supply was 743 million cubic meters, and the total artificial coal gas supply 44.49 million cubic meters. Urban and rural residential electricity consumption was 8.649 billion kwh, an increase of 12.1% over the previous year.

There appeared 4.5 million square meters of urban new green space, urban per capita public green area was 14.94 square meters, and the urban green coverage was 42.4%.

**Energy saving and environmental protection**

With green development, low-carbon development and sustainable development as the goal, the city properly handled the relationship between energy saving and stable economic development, improved and optimized the ecological environment, and made efforts to build eco-livable areas.

It is estimated that the year's energy consumption of 10,000-yuan GDP was 0.637 tons of standard coal, a decrease of 4.61% over the previous year. The year's total electricity consumption was 118.993 billion kwh, an increase of 5.2% over the previous year, of which the industrial electricity consumption was 98.266 billion kwh, an increase of 3.9%. In the year the comprehensive energy consumption of the above-scale industries was 50.15 million tons of standard coal, an increase of 2.8% over the previous year, and the main varieties of energy consumed were: 50.05 million tons of raw coal, down 1.1%; 3.7 billion cubic meters of natural gas, up 8.5%; 80.7 billion kwh of electricity, up 5.5%.

The whole society's environmental investment reached 44.5 billion yuan, an increase of 14.9% and accounting for 3.7% of the city's GDP. The comprehensive index of the city's environmental quality was 93.26. The number of air fine days in the urban area was 339. The water quality compliance rate in the centralized sources of drinking water was 100%. The environmental noise compliance rate in the functional area was 100%. The implementation of the PM2.5 monitoring was promoted. The city built 55 beautiful environment towns, including 50 state-level eco-towns; there were 25 new provincial eco-villages, with a total of 526 eco-villages at or above the provincial level, accounting for 48.4% of the total number of administrative villages.

The city solidly carried out the activities of creating "energy efficiency stars", implemented the "energy-saving and low-carbon action in ten thousand enterprises", and saved energy of 1 million tons of standard coal. In the year 174 emission reduction projects were implemented, the year's total emissions of the major pollutants sulfur dioxide and chemical oxygen demand decreased by 3.7% and 3.0% respectively over the previous year, and the ammonia reduction rate and nitrogen oxides reduction rate both exceeded 3%.

**Science and technology**

Centering the structural adjustment and industrial restructuring and upgrading, and making efforts to enhance the contribution of scientific and technological progress to economic growth, the city created a regional innovation system in order to enhance the capability of independent innovation as the core. The city's expenditures on research and experimental development have accounted for 2.5% of its GDP. 4.247 billion yuan of corporate R & D costs was fulfilled.

In the city there were 588 new high-tech enterprises above the provincial level with a total of 1,864. There were 2,367 newly-identified above-the-provincial-level high-tech products with a total of 10,031. There were 43 new above-the-provincial-level enterprise technical centers with a total of 176. There were 109 new above-the-provincial-level engineering technology research centers with a total of 337. 80% of the city's local large and medium-sized enterprises established R & D institutions. The high-tech industrial output value was 1,188.9 billion yuan, which accounted for 41.3% of the city's industrial output value.

The city's patent applications were 140,000 and granted 98,000, an increase of 37% and 27.2% respectively over the previous year, and the volume of patent applications and licensing both ranked the first in the large and medium-sized cities in our country. There were 17 new well-known trademarks in China with a total of 75. Suzhou became the first national IPR demonstration city, and passed the acceptance as the National Copyright demonstration city.

**Personnel development**

The strategy of making the city stronger with talented people was implemented in depth, and the efforts to introduce and cultivate creative talents, leading talents, high-level personnel and highly-skilled talents enhanced. The year saw the introduction of 142,000 junior-college-or-above graduates of all kinds. At the end of the year the city's total number of talents of all kinds was 1.78 million, including over 12,800 returned students, over 110,000 high-level personnel, and 380,000 highly-skilled personnel. At the end of the year there were 1.1 million professional and technical personnel of all kinds in the city, an increase of 14% over the previous year. 51 people were newly selected to enter the national "Thousand-talent Program" with a total of 105 people, which ranked the first in the prefecture-level cities in our country; 96 people were newly selected to enter the provincial "Double Innovation Program" with a total of 301 people; 118 people were newly selected to enter the City's "Gusu Program" with a total of 347 people. In the national "Thousand-talent Program" the proportion of the entrepreneurial talents reached 70%.

**Education**

The modernization of education was steadily promoted. At the end of the year in the city there were 1,097 schools of all levels and types (including kindergartens), 1,252,800 students in the school, 307,800 graduates, and 97,200 faculty and staff members in all, of which 79,500 were full-time teachers. There were 20 colleges and universities, and 5 independent colleges in Suzhou. There were 192,200 college and university students in the school, and 49,700 graduates; there were 34,000 students in the adult institutions of higher learning and 19,400 graduates. All types of education were developed in a balanced way. The city's pre-school children enrollment rate was 99.9%, the enrollment rate and consolidation rate of students receiving compulsory education continued to maintain 100%, and the rate of the city's junior high school graduates entering middle schools was 99.7%. The city's higher education gross enrollment rate was 64.3%. Suzhou Dushu Lake Science and Education Innovation Zone was identified by the Ministry of Education as a demonstration zone of the internationalization of higher education.

**Cultural undertakings**

The development of cultural undertakings was accelerated. At the end of the year there were 14 performing arts groups, 12 cultural centers, 36 museums, and 12 public libraries in the city. Non-profit cultural facilities achieved full coverage in the towns (streets) and above, and 90% of the administrative villages enjoyed nonprofit cultural facilities. New and fine literary and artistic works continuously created success. The burlesque *Youth Track* was selected for the awards for the Ministry of Culture excellent repertoire since the founding of the People's Republic of China.

The cultural industry was vigorously developed. The operating income of the city's cultural industry was estimated to exceed 260 billion yuan. At the end of the year there were 7 national cultural industry demonstration bases, 5 provincial cultural industry model bases, and 28 municipal bases.

The protection of cultural heritage was strengthened. The city had a total of 6 projects included in the United Nations Human Intangible Cultural Heritage Representative List, 29 projects included in the national intangible cultural heritage representative list, and 39 people included as national intangible cultural heritage representative inheritors. Suzhou section of the Grand Canal was successfully included in the first batch of sections of China's Grand Canal to be applied in the World Heritage list, and the project of protecting, inheriting and promoting Kunqu heritage passed the acceptance as a national cultural innovation project.

**Health services**

Public health services and medical and health services continuously improved. At the end of the year in the city there were 2,992 health institutions of all kinds, including 251 hospitals and health centers, 13 centers for disease control and prevention, and 7 maternal and child health agencies. At the end of the year there were 46,100 beds in the health institutions, and 57,200 health workers, including 23,200 doctors, an increase of 7.2%, 12.4% and 18.8% respectively over the previous year. The urban and rural community health services coverage was 100%. 2 national model health service centers were built, and the town and village health institutions were all up to the provincial construction standards.

**Sports**

People's fitness activities were long-term-oriented and the results of competitive sports fruitful. The 13th Municipal Sports Meeting was successfully held. Suzhou athletes won 2 gold medals and 1 silver medal in London Olympic Games. There were 4 new world champions in the city, with a total of 23 world champions. In the year the city hosted a total of 68 sports competitions at or above the provincial level, including 23 international or continental, 40 national and 5 provincial competitions, and the number of competitions hosted stayed ahead of the municipalities in the province. Sports facilities were further improved. In the urban area 169 people's fitness routes were newly built or updated. The sports lottery sales hit a new high, and the total sales volume reached 3.3 billion yuan, ranking the first among the prefecture-level cities and the second among the large and medium-sized cities.

**Population and employment**

The size of the population remained stable. In the city 68,000 babies were born from registered household population, the birth rate was 10.56 ‰, and the natural population growth rate was 3.58 ‰. At the end of the year the city's total registered household population was 6,478,100, an increase of 54,800 over the previous year, of which the registered urban household population was 3,289,900 million, an increase of 35,600 over the previous year.

The employment situation remained stable. In the city 168,000 people were newly employed, and 9,500 public service jobs created. The employment rate of college graduates from registered Suzhou households reached 96.6%. In the year 438,000 people of the urban and rural labor force received free training. The construction of urban and rural grass-roots public employment service platform was accelerated.

**Social security**

The integration of urban and rural social security was steadily promoted. The city realized the merger of urban and rural pension insurance and medical insurance, and became the first city where the unification of urban and rural social security was fully realized. At the end of the year in the city there were 4,728,800 urban workers paying pension premiums, 5,415,600 workers participating in medical insurance, and 3,757,400 urban workers paying unemployed insurance, 4,040,700 work injury insurance, and 4,039,700 maternity insurance. The urban workers' top five social insurance coverage and social security fund collection rates both maintained above 99%. The coverage of pension insurance and medical insurance for urban and rural residents both reached more than 99%. The coverage of urban and rural elderly residents enjoying the social old-age insurance benefits reached 100%. The retirees from the enterprises enjoyed 165.5 yuan increase per capita monthly in the basic pension. The minimum living standard of urban and rural residents was raised from 500 yuan per person per month to 570 yuan. The Suzhou Social Security • Citizen Cards were issued smoothly, and in the urban area more than 2.5 million cards were issued.

**Social welfare and relief**

At the end of the year in the city there were 205 nursing institutions of various types, a total of 46,223 beds, and 32,500 very old people admitted. There were 8,355 new nursing beds and 87 day-care centers, and 142 meal-assistant places. In the city 27,711 households and 56,911 people were put in the minimum range of security, and the total security payments issued were 206 million yuan. The social relief of the year amounted to 1.83 billion yuan, and 168,000 people benefited from it.

**People's lives**

The plan to double the city's urban and rural residents' income in six years was actively implemented, and the residents' income steadily increased. In the urban area the residents' disposable income per capita was 37,531 yuan, and the farmers' net income per capita about 19,396 yuan, an increase of 12.9% and 12.6% respectively. The income structure was further optimized, and non-wage income maintained rapid growth.

**A grouping table of urban household monthly disposable income per capita:**

| Groups | Proportion (%) | Annual disposable income per capita (￥) |
| --- | --- | --- |
| Less than 1,000 yuan | 2.7 | 9,991 |
| 1,000-1,500 yuan | 11.3 | 15,221 |
| 1,500-2,000 yuan | 17.0 | 21,198 |
| 2,000-2,500 yuan | 18.3 | 26,591 |
| 2,500-3,000 yuan | 12.3 | 32,802 |
| 3,000-4,000 yuan | 16.0 | 40,767 |
| 4,000-5,000 yuan | 8.7 | 53,051 |
| More than 5,000 yuan | 13.7 | 97,676 |

The scale of construction of affordable housing was expanded, and the coverage of housing security steadily improved. In the city 37,454 units of affordable housing were under construction, and 25,420 units completed, and low-rent housing rental subsidies were issued to 4,894 needy families. In the urban area the comprehensive remediation tasks of 1.13 million square meters of old residential areas and 160,000 square meters of sporadic residential buildings were completed, and 45,000 square meters of dilapidated housing repaired. In the urban area the transformation of toilets of 8,739 households and of 17 villages in the city (landless team) was implemented. 526,400 more people deposited housing provident fund, and 18.8 billion yuan of housing fund was used by workers. In the city 47 farmers' markets in urban and rural areas were newly built or converted, and in the urban area 46 direct supply outlets of agricultural produce were opened and 102 parity direct sales outlets of agricultural products newly built.

**Market prices**

In the context of shock downstream in commodity prices and ease in global inflationary pressures, the consumer price index fell gradually. In the year the total level of urban consumer prices rose by 2.7% over the previous year, the consumer prices of the eight major categories, "six rose and two fell": the prices of food, alcohol and tobacco, clothing, household equipment and maintenance services, healthcare and personal products, and housing prices rose by 5.1%, 1.7%, 4.4%, 5.3%, 2.1% and 2.7% respectively over the previous year; the prices of transport and communications, and entertainment and educational products and services fell by 1.5% and 0.2% over the previous year.

**The urban consumer price index (preceding year = 100):**

| Category | 2012 | 2011 |
|---|---|---|
| The consumer price index | 102.7 | 105.1 |
| 1. Food | 105.1 | 114.6 |
| # Grain | 101.7 | 109.8 |
| Oil Lipid | 102.9 | 107.5 |
| Meat and poultry | 103.7 | 118.2 |
| Eggs | 100.3 | 115.4 |
| Aquatic products | 107.3 | 112.6 |
| Vegetables | 111.7 | 99.8 |
| 2. Alcohol and tobacco | 101.7 | 101.6 |
| 3. Clothing | 104.4 | 104.0 |
| 4. Household equipment and maintenance services | 105.3 | 102.8 |
| 5. Healthcare and personal products | 102.1 | 102.9 |
| 6. Transport and communications | 98.5 | 100.6 |
| 7. Entertainment and educational products and services | 99.8 | 97.2 |
| 8. Housing | 102.7 | 103.1 |

In 2012, in the tight running environment, the restructuring, and transformation and upgrading of Suzhou economy made new progress, the endogenous development momentum further increased, the measures beneficial to the people were effectively implemented, the urban functions and infrastructure were further improved, social undertakings and ecological environment underwent coordinated development, and the co-ordination of urban and rural areas and regional development were improved, but affected by the macroeconomic environment, an open economy and the real economy were faced with certain difficulties. In 2013, we should fully estimate the seriousness of the economic situation, center on the improvement of the quality and efficiency of economic growth, highlight the innovation lead, focus on transformation, consider ecology to be a priority and take the people's lives as a fundamental, solidly advance such key tasks as stable growth, scientific and technological innovation, internationalization of the economy, and social construction, and make efforts to achieve sustainable and healthy development of the economy and society with greater intensity and more practical initiatives.

**Note: The data of urban area in this overview does not include Wujiang District.**

# 一、综 合

# CHAPTER 1
# GENERAL SURVEY

# 综　合
# GENERAL SURVEY

## 从统计数字看2012年的苏州
## SUZHOU IN STATISTICS OF 2012

### 苏州在全国的地位
### POSITION OF SUZHOU IN THE COUNTRY

| | | | |
|---|---|---|---|
| 地区生产总值 | Gross Domestic Product | 居全国第 6 位 | 6th Place in the Country |
| 地方公共财政预算收入 | General Budgetary Revenue | 居全国第 6 位 | 6th Place in the Country |
| 进出口总额 | Total Value of Imports and Exports | 居全国第 4 位 | 4th Place in the Country |

### 苏州在全省的地位
### POSITION OF SUZHOU IN JIANGSU PROVINCE

| | | | |
|---|---|---|---|
| 地区生产总值 | Gross Domestic Product | 居全省第 1 位 | First Place in Jiangsu |
| 财政收入 | Financial Revenue | 居全省第 1 位 | First Place in Jiangsu |
| 进出口总额 | Total Value of Imports and Exports | 居全省第 1 位 | First Place in Jiangsu |

### 苏州的人口
### POPULATION OF SUZHOU

| | | | | |
|---|---|---|---|---|
| 年末户籍总人口 | Year-end Registered Population | 647.81 | 万人 | 10 000 persons |
| 年末户籍总户数 | Year-end Registered Households | 214.04 | 万户 | 10 000 households |
| 户籍人口密度 | Density of Registered Population | 763 | 人/平方公里 | person/sq.km |
| 年末常住总人口 | Year-end Permanent Population | 1 054.91 | 万人 | 10 000 persons |
| 常住人口密度 | Density of Permanent Population | 1 243 | 人/平方公里 | person/sq.km |

### 苏州的经济发展
### ECONOMIC DEVELOPMENT OF SUZHOU

| | | 2012年 | 1979-2012年平均增长(%) Average Growth Rate |
|---|---|---|---|
| 地区生产总值 (亿元) | Gross Domestic Product (100 million yuan) | 12 011.65 | 14.1 |
| #第三产业 | Tertiary Industry | 5 314.32 | 15.5 |
| 财政收入 | Financial Revenue | 2 561.67 | 18.4 |
| 工业总产值 | Gross Industrial Output Value | 34 528.10 | 22.7 |
| 社会消费品零售总额 | Total Retail Sales of Consumer Goods | 3 240.97 | 18.7 |
| 进出口总额 (亿美元) | Total Exports and Imports (USD 100 million) | 3 056.92 | - |
| 实际利用外资 | Actual Utilization of Foreign Capital | 91.65 | - |
| 全社会固定资产投资 (亿元) | Total Value of Investment in Fixed Assets (100 million yuan) | 5 266.49 | 27.4 |

## 苏州的人均水平
## PER CAPITA LEVEL OF SUZHOU

| | | | | |
|---|---|---|---|---|
| 地区生产总值 | Gross Domestic Product | 186 207 | 元 | yuan |
| 社会消费品零售总额 | Total Retail Sales of Consumer Goods | 50 242 | | |
| 财政收入 | Financial Revenue | 39 712 | | |
| 在岗职工工资 | Wage of Staff and Works | 57 622 | | |
| 市区居民可支配收入 | Disposable Income of Urban Residents | 37 531 | | |
| 农民纯收入 | Net Income of Rural Residents | 19 396 | | |
| 市区居民住房建筑面积 | Per Capita Floor Space of Residential Buildings of Urban Residents | 34.10 | 平方米 | sq.m |
| 市区拥有道路面积 | Per Capita Area of Roads of Urban Residents | 31.39 | 平方米 | sq.m |
| 每万人拥有医生数 | Number of Doctors Serving Per 10000 Persons | 35.80 | 人 | person |

## 苏州的一天
## ONE DAY IN SUZHOU

| | | | | |
|---|---|---|---|---|
| 地区生产总值 | Gross Domestic Product | 333 657 | 万元 | 10 000 yuan |
| # 第三产业 | Tertiary Industry | 147 620 | | |
| 工业总产值 | Gross Industrial Output Value | 959 114 | | |
| 社会消费品零售总额 | Total Retail Sales of Consumer Goods | 90 027 | | |
| 进出口总额 | Total Exports and Imports | 84 914 | 万美元 | USD 10 000 |
| 实际利用外资 | Actual Utilization of Foreign Capital | 2 546 | | |
| 全社会固定资产投资额 | Total Investment in Fixed Assets | 146 291 | 万元 | 10 000 yuan |
| 财政收入 | Financial Revenue | 71 158 | | |
| 邮寄函件 | Letters Delivered | 81.02 | 万件 | 10 000 pcs |

# 行政区划及自然概况

## 行政区划

苏州简称苏。下辖4个县级市：常熟市，张家港市，昆山市，太仓市；6个区：姑苏区，吴中区，相城区，高新区、虎丘区，工业园区和吴江区。2012年末, 全市共有镇55个、街道40个、行政村1068个、居委会931个。

## 位 置

苏州位于长江三角洲中部，在北纬30度47分至32度零2分，东经119度55分至121度20分之间，东邻上海，南连浙江省嘉兴、湖州两市，西傍太湖，与无锡相接，北枕长江。

苏州地理位置优越。沪宁铁路、沪宁高速铁路、沪宁和沿江高速公路贯穿东西，京杭大运河和苏嘉杭高速公路连接南北，境内河港密布，公路四通八达。横卧北侧的长江是重要水运干道。位于长江下游南岸的苏州港是国家一类口岸。

## 地 势

苏州地处太湖为中心的浅碟形平原的底部，地形以平原为主，全市地势低平，一般高程为海拔3.5至5米。东南部地势低洼，最低点低洼地在海拔2米以下。西南部多小山丘，穹窿山主峰“箬帽峰”，海拔341.7米，有“吴中之巅”之称。

## 面 积

苏州全市总面积8488.42平方公里，其中丘陵面积为225平方公里，占总面积的2.7%；水域面积为3609平方公里，占总面积的42.5%。市区建成区面积为436.53平方公里。

## 河 流

苏州是著名的江南水乡，拥有各级河道2万多条，大小湖泊300多个，著名的有太湖、阳澄湖、长江、京杭运河等。

## 气 候

苏州属亚热带湿润性季风海洋性气候，四季分明，气候温和，雨量充沛。年平均气温在17摄氏度左右，年降水量1000毫米左右。

# ADMINISTRATIVE DIVISIONS & NATURAL CONDITIONS

**Administrative Divisions**

Suzhou is called Su in short. It includes four county-level cities: Changshu city, Zhangjiagang city, Kunshan city and Taicang city, and six districts: Gusu District, Wuzhong District,Xiangcheng District, New & Hi-tech, Huqiu District , Industrial Park and Wujiang

**Location**

Suzhou lies in the center of Yangtse River Delta, between 30°47′—32°02′E and 119°55′—121°20′N. It borders on Shanghai on the east, Jiaxing and Huzhou of Zhejiang on the south, Taihu Lake and Wuxi on the west and Yangtse on the north.

Suzhou enjoys strategic geographical location. Hu-Ning Railway, Hu-Ning Expressway and the riparian highway runs from east to west; Beijing-Hangzhou Grand Canal and Su-Jia-Hang expressway connect south and north. Suzhou abounds in waterways and highways. Yangtse Rive that lies on the north of the city is a key waterway artery. suzhou Port on the south bank of the lower reaches

**Typography**

Suzhou, at the bottom of a shallow saucer-shaped plain with Lake Tai at its center, is low and even. Average height is 3.5m-5m above sea level. The southeast part is relatively lower, with the lowest point 2m below sea level. The southwest is a hilly area, with the highest point, the peak of Qionglong Hill, 341.7m above sea level.

**Area**

The total area of Suzhou is 8488.42 sq.km, 2.7% of it, i. e. 225 sq.km is hilly area; 42.5% of it, i. e. 3609 sq.km, is water area. Built -up Urban Area covers 436.53 sq.km.

**Rivers & Lakes**

Suzhou is a famous water country region to the south of Yangtse River. It has over 20 000 rivers and over 300 lakes of various size. Famous among them are Taihu Lake, Yangcheng Lake, Yangtse River & Beijing-Hongzhou Canal, etc.

**Climate**

Suzhou's climate belongs to monsoon of subtropical moist marine climate zone, with distinct four seasons, Suzhou has a mild climate with plenty rainfall. Average temperature of the year is around 17℃ and annual precipitation is around 1000 millimeter.

表1-1

# 行政区划和土地面积（2012年末）
# ADMINISTRATIVE DIVISION AND LAND AREA (END OF 2012)

单位：个 (unit)

| 地 区 | Region | 镇 Town | 村 Village | 街 道 Subdistrict | 居委会 Neighborhood Committee | 土地面积 (平方公里) Area of Land (sq.km) |
|---|---|---|---|---|---|---|
| **全 市** | **Whole Municipality** | **55** | **1 068** | **40** | **931** | **8 488.42** |
| **市 区** | **Urban Area** | **22** | **455** | **37** | **527** | **2 742.62** |
| 姑苏区 | Gusu District | - | 10 | 17 | 155 | |
| 吴中区 | Wuzhong District | 7 | 84 | 8 | 86 | |
| 相城区 | Xiangcheng District | 4 | 77 | 4 | 66 | |
| 高新区、虎丘区 | New & Hi-tech Zone, Huqiu District | 3 | 34 | 3 | 49 | |
| 工业园区 | Industrial Park | - | - | 4 | 110 | |
| 吴江区 | Wujiang District | 8 | 250 | 1 | 61 | 1 092.90 |
| **县级市** | **Cities at County Level** | **33** | **613** | **3** | **404** | **3 351.30** |
| 常 熟 | Changshu | 9 | 219 | 2 | 93 | 1 094.00 |
| 张家港 | Zhangjiagang | 8 | 165 | - | 92 | 772.40 |
| 昆 山 | Kunshan | 10 | 153 | - | 149 | 864.90 |
| 太 仓 | Taicang | 6 | 76 | 1 | 70 | 620.00 |

注：全市土地面积中含太湖、阳澄湖、淀山湖等大型湖泊水域面积，分地区土地面积中未包括。

Note:The land area of the whole municipality includes water area of Taihu Lake,Yangcheng Lake and Dianshan Lake,while land area of regions do not.

表1-2

# 市区分月气象情况（2012年）
# MONTHLY CLIMATE CONDITIONS OF URBAN AREA (2012)

| 月 份 | Month | 平均气温 (摄氏度) Average Temperature (℃) | 降水量 (毫米) Precipitation (mm) | 日照时数 (小时) Sunshine Hours (hours) | 平均相对湿度 (%) Average Relative Humidity (%) | 平均风力 (米/秒) Average Wind Force (m/second) |
|---|---|---|---|---|---|---|
| **全 年** | **Annual Total** | **16.9** | **1 308.1** | **1 928.7** | **71** | **2.3** |
| 1月 | Jan. | 4.3 | 71.6 | 84.7 | 71 | 1.9 |
| 2月 | Feb. | 4.1 | 85.3 | 77.8 | 75 | 2.0 |
| 3月 | Mar. | 9.6 | 147.9 | 131.5 | 73 | 2.2 |
| 4月 | Apr. | 18.0 | 56.5 | 189.4 | 70 | 2.4 |
| 5月 | May | 21.9 | 133.4 | 190.6 | 71 | 2.3 |
| 6月 | Jun. | 25.2 | 110.8 | 136.5 | 80 | 2.3 |
| 7月 | Jul. | 29.9 | 154.0 | 261.5 | 74 | 2.4 |
| 8月 | Aug. | 29.1 | 215.5 | 213.2 | 69 | 3.3 |
| 9月 | Sept. | 23.8 | 92.1 | 185.2 | 59 | 2.4 |
| 10月 | Oct. | 19.7 | 37.3 | 200.1 | 66 | 2.0 |
| 11月 | Nov. | 11.9 | 117.6 | 149.0 | 70 | 2.1 |
| 12月 | Dec. | 5.7 | 86.1 | 109.2 | 71 | 2.3 |

注：本表数据不含吴江区。 Note: The data in this table does not include Wujiang.

表1-3

# 分地区气象、水文情况（2012年）
# CLIMATE AND HYDROLOGIC CONDITIONS BY REGION (2012)

| 地 区 | Region | 年平均气温(摄氏度) Annual Average Temperature (℃) | 年极端最高气温(摄氏度) Highest Temperature of the Year (℃) | 年极端最低气温(摄氏度) Lowest Temperature of the Year (℃) | 年降水量(毫米) Annual Precipitation (mm) | 年降水日(天) Raining Days of the Year (day) | 年平均气压(百帕) Annual Average Pressure (hPa) |
|---|---|---|---|---|---|---|---|
| 市 区 | Urban Area | 16.9 | 37.7 | -4.1 | 1 308.1 | 147 | 1 015.7 |
| 吴江区 | Wujiang District | 16.9 | 37.8 | -4.1 | 1 257.1 | 178 | 1 015.0 |
| 常 熟 | Changshu | 16.4 | 37.5 | -4.7 | 1 037.7 | 139 | 1 014.8 |
| 张家港 | Zhangjiagang | 16.1 | 37.8 | -6.0 | 1 111.7 | 134 | 1 015.0 |
| 昆 山 | Kunshan | 16.7 | 37.4 | -4.4 | 1 084.5 | 144 | 1 015.1 |
| 太 仓 | Taicang | 16.4 | 37.9 | 5.6 | 1 124.8 | 145 | 1 015.2 |

表1-3 续表 Continued

| 地 区 | Region | 年无霜期(天) Annual frost-free period (day) | 年日照时间(小时) Annual Sunshine Hours (hours) | 年平均相对湿度(%) Annual Average Relative Humidity (%) | 最高水位(米) Highest Water Level (m) | 最低水位(米) Lowest Water Level (m) | 年平均水位(米) Average Water Level of the Year (m) |
|---|---|---|---|---|---|---|---|
| 市 区 | Urban Area | 244 | 1 928.7 | 71 | 3.65 | 2.86 | 3.18 |
| 吴江区 | Wujiang District | 250 | 1 863.7 | 72 | 3.83 | 2.85 | 3.20 |
| 常 熟 | Changshu | 228 | 1 776.4 | 76 | 3.82 | 3.00 | 3.29 |
| 张家港 | Zhangjiagang | 228 | 1 771.3 | 73 | 4.52 | 2.87 | 3.61 |
| 昆 山 | Kunshan | 228 | 1 731.8 | 74 | 3.50 | 2.47 | 2.87 |
| 太 仓 | Taicang | 231 | 1 877.5 | 72 | 3.75 | 2.73 | 3.22 |

注：本表市区数据不含吴江区。 Note: The data in this table does not include Wujiang.

表1-4

# 重要年份国民经济主要指标

| 指　　标 | | Item | | 1952年 | 1970年 |
|---|---|---|---|---|---|
| **人　口** | | **Population** | | | |
| 年末户籍总人口 | (万人) | Year-end Population | (10 000 persons) | 352.32 | 468.02 |
| 年末户籍总户数 | (万户) | Total Number of Households (year–end) | (10 000 households) | 88.33 | 120.31 |
| **劳动力** | | **Labor Force** | | | |
| 年末从业人员 | (万人) | Employed Persons (year-end) | (10 000 persons) | 158.87 | 260.61 |
| # 在岗职工 | | Staff and Workers | | | 38.39 |
| **地区生产总值** | (亿元) | **Gross Domestic Product** | (100 million yuan) | 4.38 | 15.03 |
| # 第三产业 | | Tertiary Industry | | 1.29 | 2.62 |
| **农　业** | | **Agriculture** | | | |
| 1.农林牧渔业总产值 | | Gross Output Value of Farming, Forestry, Animal Husbandry and Fishery | | | |
| 2.主要农产品产量 | | Output of Major Farm Products | | | |
| 粮　食 | (万吨) | Grain | (10 000 tons) | 133.41 | 223.62 |
| 棉　花 | (吨) | Cotton | (ton) | 14 810 | 35 880 |
| 油　料 | (万吨) | Oil-bearing Crops | (10 000 tons) | 2.50 | 5.71 |
| 蚕　茧 | (吨) | Silkworm Cocoons | (ton) | 3 047 | 4 520 |
| 水产品 | (万吨) | Aquatic Products | (10 000 tons) | 2.15 | 4.48 |
| 猪出栏数 | (万头) | Slaughtered Fattened Hogs | (10 000 heads) | 22.16 | 117.68 |
| 猪年末存栏数 | | Hogs in Stock at Year–end | | 37.98 | 214.19 |
| **工　业** | | **Industry** | | | |
| 1.工业总产值 | (亿元) | Gross Industrial Output Value | (100 million yuan) | | |
| 2.主要工业产品产量 | | Output of Major Industrial Products | | | |
| 纱 | (吨) | Yarn | (ton) | 11 743 | 23 749 |
| 布 | (万米) | Cloth | (10 000 m) | 5 498 | 12 941 |
| 饮料酒 | (万升) | Beverage, Drinks | (10 000 liters) | 1 004 | 2 454 |
| 机制纸及纸板 | (万吨) | Machine-made Paper and Paperboards | (10 000 tons) | 1.99 | 5.02 |
| 彩色电视机 | (万台) | Color Television Sets | (10 000 units) | – | – |
| 电风扇 | | Electric Fans | | – | 1.04 |
| 电冰箱 | | Refrigerators | | – | – |
| 生　铁 | (万吨) | Pig Iron | (10 000 tons) | – | 9.58 |
| 粗　钢 | | Raw Steel | | – | 0.16 |
| 钢　材 | | Steel Products | | – | 2.81 |
| 硫　酸 | | Sulfuric Acid | | – | 6.40 |

# MAJOR NATIONAL ECONOMICAL INDICATORS OF IMPORTANT YEARS

| 1978年 | 1980年 | 1990年 | 1995年 | 2000年 | 2005年 | 2010年 | 2011年 | 2012年 |
|---|---|---|---|---|---|---|---|---|
| | | | | | | | | |
| 506.27 | 518.62 | 561.02 | 572.91 | 578.17 | 607.31 | 637.66 | 642.33 | 647.81 |
| 137.42 | 142.33 | 173.36 | 187.83 | 198.18 | 206.83 | 211.79 | 213.24 | 214.04 |
| | | | | | | | | |
| 301.15 | 317.17 | 346.74 | 324.45 | 313.89 | 393.72 | 554.15 | 575.45 | 588.27 |
| 60.91 | 70.30 | 95.43 | 96.62 | 74.09 | 100.44 | 126.97 | 129.83 | 130.40 |
| 31.95 | 40.68 | 202.14 | 903.11 | 1 540.68 | 4 138.21 | 9 228.91 | 10 716.99 | 12 011.65 |
| 5.18 | 6.8 | 43.9 | 279.33 | 579.62 | 1 364.97 | 3 819.31 | 4 581.50 | 5 314.32 |
| | | | | | | | | |
| 18.75 | 11.42 | 58.12 | 141.62 | 169.30 | 162.87 | 271.29 | 309.86 | 337.72 |
| 294.26 | 254.31 | 283.50 | 265.67 | 193.95 | 110.76 | 114.43 | 115.00 | 116.46 |
| 36 330 | 35 180 | 36 932 | 40 210 | 11 722 | 4 605 | 1 685 | 1 508 | 1 292 |
| 9.13 | 8.16 | 14.01 | 14.56 | 12.61 | 6.96 | 3.45 | 2.89 | 2.59 |
| 3 325 | 4 784 | 9 785 | 12 435 | 7 291 | 2 771 | 638 | 558 | 495 |
| 8.22 | 8.71 | 21.73 | 28.41 | 34.51 | 31.65 | 27.70 | 28.41 | 28.84 |
| 185.66 | 310.14 | 193.54 | 177.46 | 198.50 | 139.91 | 117.70 | 118.49 | 113.44 |
| 264.31 | 250.34 | 154.62 | 111.73 | 104.75 | 73.85 | 83.51 | 85.34 | 84.97 |
| | | | | | | | | |
| 48.51 | 73.71 | 563.73 | 1 962.74 | 3 620.74 | 12 123.09 | 28 483.69 | 33 347.37 | 34 528.10 |
| 37 770 | 53 988 | 120 599 | 84 218 | 167 776 | 804 971 | 730 896 | 632 629 | 793 212 |
| 17 699 | 24 171 | 35 943 | 34 986 | 29 782 | 68 437 | 77 094 | 57 434 | 90 334 |
| 2 753 | 6 391 | 18 159 | 29 130 | 23 074 | 34 439 | 50 005 | 45 773 | 45 160 |
| 5.37 | 8.15 | 15.34 | 19.70 | 40.59 | 182.54 | 549.35 | 509.76 | 582.99 |
| – | – | 24.29 | 33.27 | 97.47 | 132.52 | 1 158.32 | 994.39 | 1 141.23 |
| 8.05 | 38.09 | 505.20 | 1 359.19 | 144.49 | 112.98 | 239.48 | 143.21 | 112.64 |
| 0.0006 | 0.40 | 33.33 | 4.25 | 91.80 | 141.56 | 187.14 | 188.50 | 175.49 |
| 16.62 | 17.84 | 29.38 | 46.26 | 59.10 | 1 031.79 | 1 974.20 | 1 964.93 | 2 229.74 |
| 6.33 | 9.94 | 38.82 | 79.59 | 183.14 | 1 358.33 | 2 227.06 | 2 539.82 | 2 662.19 |
| 11.10 | 23.41 | 54.51 | 211.18 | 480.54 | 1 336.64 | 3 279.65 | 3 704.24 | 4 059.41 |
| 7.60 | 8.92 | 16.03 | 22.19 | 43.54 | 48.69 | 189.22 | 219.24 | 206.09 |

表1-4 续表 1

| 指 标 | | Item | | 1952年 | 1970年 |
|---|---|---|---|---|---|
| 烧 碱 | (吨) | Caustic Soda | (ton) | 112 | 4 576 |
| 农用化肥 | (万吨) | Chemical Fertilizers for Agricultural Use | (10 000 tons) | - | 2.05 |
| 水 泥 | | Cement | | 0.03 | 6.94 |
| 交流电动机 | (万千瓦) | Alternating Current Motor | (10 000 kw) | - | 15.85 |
| **运输邮电** | | **Transportation and Postal** | | | |
| 1.全社会公路水运货运量 | (万吨) | Total Freight Traffic of Highways and Waterways | (10 000 tons) | 209 | 926 |
| 2.全社会公路水运客运量 | (万人次) | Total Passenger Traffic of Highways and Waterways | (10 000 person-times) | 383 | 1 724 |
| 3.邮电业务总收入 | (万元) | Postal and Telecommunications Business Volume | (10 000 yuan) | 402 | 1 096 |
| 4.函 件 | (万件) | Letters Delivered | (10 000 pcs) | 781 | 1 417 |
| 5.报刊累计数 | (万份) | Number of Newspapers and Magazines Circulation | (10 000 copies) | 941 | 7 471 |
| **国内贸易** | | **Domestic Trade** | | | |
| 社会消费品零售总额 | (亿元) | Total Retail Sales of Consumer Goods | (100 million yuan) | 3.12 | 5.14 |
| **对外经济和国际旅游** | | **Foreign Trade Economy and International Tourism** | | | |
| 1.进出口总额 | (亿美元) | Total Exports and Imports | (USD 100 million) | - | - |
| # 出口总额 | | Exports | | - | - |
| 2.利用外资 | | Utilization of Foreign Capital | | | |
| 新签合同数 | (个) | Number of Projects for Utilization of Foreign Capital in the Signed Agreements & Contracts | (unit) | - | - |
| 合同外资金额 | (万美元) | Amount of Foreign Capital to Be Utilized in the Signed Agreements & Contracts | (USD 10 000) | - | - |
| 实际利用外资 | | Amount of Foreign Capital Actually Utilized | | - | - |
| 3.国际旅游 | | International Tourism | | | |
| 接待境外旅游者人数 | (万人次) | Number of Foreign Tourists | (10 000 person-times) | - | - |
| **电 力** | | **Electricity** | | | |
| 全社会用电量 | (亿千瓦时) | Electricity Consumption of the Whole Society | (100 million kwh) | 0.45 | 5.78 |
| **固定资产投资** | | | | | |
| 全社会固定资产投资 | (亿元) | Total Value of Investment in Fixed Assets | (100 million yuan) | | |
| # 城镇投资 | | Investment in Fixed Assets Collective Units | | | |
| 房地产开发投资 | | Value of Investment in Real Estate Development | | | |

Continued 1

| 1978年 | 1980年 | 1990年 | 1995年 | 2000年 | 2005年 | 2010年 | 2011年 | 2012年 |
|---|---|---|---|---|---|---|---|---|
| 13 202 | 18 611 | 36 972 | 50 600 | 75 030 | 91 630 | 364 776 | 355 197 | 573 857 |
| 7.70 | 10.59 | 13.02 | 14.25 | 28.74 | 46.38 | 54.70 | 41.89 | 45.57 |
| 47.93 | 73.08 | 207.33 | 512.55 | 526.00 | 958.88 | 1 219.33 | 915.99 | 863.88 |
| 42.40 | 37.14 | 52.24 | 325.49 | 28.06 | 157.60 | 543.12 | 503.96 | 538.46 |
| | | | | | | | | |
| 2 195 | 2 712 | 3 211 | 8 561 | 7 816 | 10 393 | 13 417 | 15 602 | 17 325 |
| 3 296 | 4 813 | 6 764 | 18 945 | 18 559 | 30 707 | 56 475 | 63 793 | 68 998 |
| 1 774 | 2 300 | 12 818 | 141 415 | 441 910 | 986 846 | 1 726 867 | 2 036 508 | 2 076 637 |
| 1 732 | 2 245 | 3 051 | 7 229 | 5 476 | 11 128 | 27 841 | 29 694 | 29 167 |
| 7 234 | 9 977 | 16 246 | 23 151 | 30 461 | 23 964 | 30 438 | 32 102 | 32 157 |
| | | | | | | | | |
| 9.47 | 15.67 | 72.15 | 242.31 | 428.17 | 934.30 | 2 402.02 | 2 829.58 | 3 240.97 |
| | | | | | | | | |
| – | – | 1.88 | 45.92 | 200.70 | 1 405.89 | 2 740.76 | 3 008.63 | 3 056.92 |
| – | – | 1.55 | 23.35 | 104.81 | 727.75 | 1 531.08 | 1 672.33 | 1 746.89 |
| – | – | 164 | 905 | 943 | 2 181 | 1 537 | 1 516 | 1 189 |
| – | – | 14 361 | 565 119 | 467 787 | 1 533 971 | 1 691 980 | 1 702 391 | 1 516 828 |
| – | – | 6 954 | 237 779 | 288 338 | 511 607 | 853 511 | 891 222 | 916 490 |
| – | 8.37 | 27.84 | 33.72 | 71.41 | 156.02 | 265.15 | 297.75 | 321.87 |
| | | | | | | | | |
| 13.88 | 20.53 | 50.77 | 99.85 | 190.04 | 566.04 | 1 024.10 | 1 131.63 | 1 189.93 |
| | | | | | | | | |
| 1.40 | 2.87 | 55.37 | 334.10 | 516.43 | 1 870.14 | 3 617.82 | 4 502.02 | 5 266.49 |
| 1.40 | 2.87 | 16.85 | 137.64 | 266.37 | 819.43 | 1 657.54 | 2 180.60 | 2 649.90 |
| | | 1.65 | 58.65 | 61.18 | 414.33 | 935.80 | 1 199.13 | 1 263.36 |

表1-4 续表 2

| 指 标 | Item | 1952年 | 1970年 |
|---|---|---|---|
| **财 政** | **Public Finance** | | |
| 财政收入 (亿元) | Financial Revenue (100 million yuan) | 1.13 | 4.12 |
| 财政支出 | Financial Expenditures | 0.10 | 0.57 |
| **金 融** | **Finance** | | |
| 金融机构人民币存款余额 | Deposit Balance of Financial Institutions | 0.26 | 4.66 |
| 金融机构人民币贷款余额 | Loans Balance of Financial Institutions | 0.11 | 5.57 |
| **物价指数**(以上年价格为100) | **Price Indices** (The Price of Preceding Year is Taken as 100) | | |
| 市区居民消费价格总指数 | General Consumer Price Index of Urban Residents | | |
| 市区商品零售价格总指数 | General Retail Price Index of Urban Area | | |
| **人民生活** | **People's Livelihood** | | |
| 在岗职工工资总额 (亿元) | Total Wages of Staff and Workers (100 million yuan) | 0.47 | 1.11 |
| 在岗职工平均工资 (元) | Average Wages of Staff and Workers (yuan) | 455 | 524 |
| 农民人均纯收入 | Per Capita Net Income of Rural Residents | | 133 |
| 市区居民人均可支配收入 | Per Capita Disposable Income of Urban Households | | |
| 城乡居民人民币储蓄存款余额 (亿元) | Amount of Saving Deposits in Urban and Rural Areas (100 million yuan) | | 0.66 |
| **教 育** | **Education** | | |
| 1.在校学生数 (万人) | Students Enrollment (10 000 persons) | 33.93 | 83.91 |
| #高等学校 (人) | Institutions of Higher Education (person) | 2 349 | 37 |
| 中等职业教育学校 | Secondary Vocational Education Schools | | |
| 技工学校 | Skilled Workers' Schools | | |
| 普通中学 (万人) | Regular Secondary Schools (10 000 persons) | 3.40 | 17.12 |
| 小 学 | Primary Schools | 29.42 | 66.76 |
| 2.毕业生数 | Graduates | 2.20 | 13.51 |
| **卫 生** | **Health Care** | | |
| 卫生机构数 (所) | Number of Health Institutions (unit) | 238 | 675 |
| #医院、卫生院 | Hospitals | 16 | 169 |
| 床位数 (张) | Number of Beds (bed) | 1 372 | 9 001 |
| #医院、卫生院 | Hospitals | | |
| 卫生技术人员 (人) | Number of Medical Personnel (person) | 3 256 | 7 593 |
| #医 生 | Doctors | 2 363 | 3 999 |

Continued 2

| 1978年 | 1980年 | 1990年 | 1995年 | 2000年 | 2005年 | 2010年 | 2011年 | 2012年 |
|---|---|---|---|---|---|---|---|---|
| | | | | | | | | |
| 8.28 | 9.46 | 21.47 | 53.86 | 158.27 | 718.10 | 1 950.63 | 2 311.62 | 2 561.67 |
| 1.35 | 1.67 | 7.99 | 24.73 | 79.91 | 409.86 | 1 095.75 | 1 284.81 | 1 479.59 |
| | | | | | | | | |
| 7.37 | 15.68 | 132.20 | 566.65 | 1 477.01 | 4 730.05 | 13 570.35 | 15 180.78 | 17 663.50 |
| 15.45 | 21.19 | 134.10 | 424.07 | 970.60 | 3 478.34 | 10 133.15 | 11 873.89 | 13 626.86 |
| | | | | | | | | |
| | | 103.9 | 118.0 | 99.9 | 102.4 | 103.4 | 105.1 | 102.7 |
| | 104.2 | 103.2 | 113.3 | 98.5 | 101.1 | 103.1 | 104.7 | 101.9 |
| | | | | | | | | |
| 3.12 | 4.69 | 23.11 | 67.10 | 89.31 | 240.07 | 565.81 | 686.50 | 783.43 |
| 514 | 687 | 2 450 | 6 944 | 11 778 | 25 016 | 45 566 | 51 660 | 57 622 |
| 204 | 271 | 1 664 | 4 444 | 5 462 | 8 393 | 14 657 | 17 226 | 19 396 |
| | | 2 150 | 5 790 | 9 274 | 16 276 | 29 219 | 33 243 | 37 531 |
| 1.77 | 3.64 | 73.33 | 296.49 | 803.70 | 2 059.52 | 4 655.56 | 5 078.59 | 5 787.75 |
| | | | | | | | | |
| 96.81 | 81.28 | 71.13 | 78.95 | 87.69 | 95.69 | 95.85 | 97.26 | 98.91 |
| 6 502 | 8 819 | 16 280 | 23 182 | 47 701 | 113 090 | 187 829 | 188 750 | 192 206 |
| | | 25 293 | 57 999 | 60 185 | 115 541 | 74 828 | 71 409 | 64 706 |
| | | 5 866 | 10 844 | 12 346 | 27 215 | 32 158 | 29 371 | 27 244 |
| 32.76 | 22.86 | 21.73 | 27.08 | 30.47 | 33.82 | 27.25 | 26.54 | 26.18 |
| 62.96 | 56.79 | 44.56 | 42.26 | 44.84 | 35.99 | 38.84 | 41.50 | 44.04 |
| 26.27 | 18.44 | 14.15 | 18.19 | 19.26 | 24.71 | 24.19 | 23.15 | 22.42 |
| | | | | | | | | |
| 971 | 1 125 | 1 537 | 1 486 | 1 319 | 1 945 | 2 675 | 2 858 | 2 992 |
| 204 | 207 | 207 | 210 | 197 | 197 | 216 | 242 | 251 |
| 14 470 | 13 720 | 18 424 | 19 535 | 19 504 | 26 185 | 39 204 | 42 972 | 46 070 |
| 13 209 | 12 385 | 16 223 | 17 218 | 17 582 | 23 916 | 36 839 | 40 805 | 43 772 |
| 12 902 | 14 514 | 22 253 | 25 326 | 24 881 | 32 049 | 46 507 | 50 866 | 57 168 |
| 5 434 | 6 316 | 10 895 | 12 182 | 11 594 | 12 939 | 18 156 | 19 518 | 23 194 |

表1-5

# 重要年份国民经济主要指标发展速度

| 指　标 | Item | 2012年为 | |
|---|---|---|---|
| | | 1952年 | 1970年 |
| **人　口** | **Population** | | |
| 年末户籍总人口 | Year-end Population | 183.9 | 138.4 |
| 年末户籍总户数 | Total Number of Households (year–end) | 242.3 | 177.9 |
| **劳动力** | **Labor Force** | | |
| 年末从业人员 | Employed Persons (year–end) | 370.3 | 225.7 |
| # 职　工 | Staff and Workers | | 339.7 |
| **地区生产总值** | **Gross Domestic Product** | 687.0倍 | 250.1倍 |
| # 第三产业 | | | |
| **农　业** | **Agriculture** | | |
| 1.农林牧渔业总产值 | Gross Output Value of Farming, Forestry, Animal Husbandry and Fishery | | |
| 2.主要农产品产量 | Output of Major Farm Products | | |
| 粮　食 | Grain | 87.3 | 52.1 |
| 棉　花 | Cotton | 8.7 | 3.6 |
| 油　料 | Oil–bearing Crops | 103.6 | 45.4 |
| 蚕　茧 | Silkworm Cocoons | 16.2 | 11.0 |
| 水产品 | Aquatic Products | 13.2倍 | 634.6 |
| 猪出栏数 | Slaughtered Fattened Hogs | 511.9 | 96.4 |
| 猪年末存栏数 | Hogs in Stock at Year–end | 223.7 | 39.7 |
| **工　业** | **Industry** | | |
| 1.工业总产值 | Gross Industrial Output Value | | |
| 2.主要工业产品产量 | Output of Major Industrial Products | | |
| 纱 | Yarn | 67.5 倍 | 33.4倍 |
| 布 | Cloth | 16.4倍 | 698.0 |
| 饮料酒 | Beverages, Drinks | 45.0倍 | 18.4倍 |
| 机制纸及纸板 | Machine–made Paper and Paperboards | 293.0倍 | 116.1倍 |
| 彩色电视机 | Color Television Sets | – | – |
| 电风扇 | Electric Fans | – | 108.3倍 |
| 电冰箱 | Refrigerators | – | – |
| 生　铁 | Pig Iron | – | 232.7倍 |
| 粗　钢 | Raw Steel | – | 1.7万倍 |
| 钢　材 | Steel Products | – | 1 444.6倍 |
| 硫　酸 | Sulfuric Acid | – | 32.2倍 |

# GROWTH RATES OF MAJOR NATIONAL ECONOMICAL INDICATORS OF IMPORTANT YEARS

| 以下各年的% | % of the Following Years | | | | | | | 1979-2012年平均增长% Average Growth Rate |
|---|---|---|---|---|---|---|---|---|
| 1978年 | 1980年 | 1990年 | 1995年 | 2000年 | 2005年 | 2010年 | 2011年 | |
| | | | | | | | | |
| 128.0 | 124.9 | 115.5 | 113.1 | 112.0 | 106.7 | 101.6 | 100.9 | 0.7 |
| 155.8 | 150.4 | 123.5 | 114.0 | 108.0 | 103.5 | 101.1 | 100.4 | 1.3 |
| | | | | | | | | |
| 195.3 | 185.5 | 169.7 | 181.3 | 187.4 | 149.4 | 106.2 | 102.2 | 2.0 |
| 214.1 | 185.5 | 136.6 | 135.0 | 176.0 | 129.8 | 102.7 | 100.4 | 2.3 |
| 88.9倍 | 74.6倍 | 22.2倍 | 845.3 | 487.8 | 237.1 | 123.3 | 110.1 | 14.1 |
| 132.3倍 | 108.2倍 | 32.9倍 | 101.4 | 528.0 | 265.8 | 128.1 | 113.5 | 15.5 |
| | | | | | | | | |
| 13.3倍 | 21.9倍 | 430.0 | 176.4 | 147.6 | 135.5 | 108.3 | 104.1 | 7.9 |
| | | | | | | | | |
| 39.6 | 45.8 | 41.1 | 43.8 | 60.0 | 105.1 | 101.8 | 101.3 | -2.7 |
| 3.6 | 3.7 | 3.5 | 3.2 | 11.0 | 28.1 | 76.7 | 85.7 | -9.3 |
| 28.4 | 31.7 | 18.5 | 17.8 | 20.5 | 37.2 | 75.1 | 89.6 | -3.6 |
| 14.9 | 10.3 | 5.1 | 4.0 | 6.8 | 17.9 | 77.6 | 88.7 | -5.4 |
| 345.9 | 326.4 | 130.8 | 100.1 | 82.4 | 89.8 | 102.6 | 100.1 | 3.7 |
| 61.1 | 36.6 | 58.6 | 63.9 | 57.1 | 81.1 | 96.4 | 95.7 | -1.4 |
| 32.1 | 33.9 | 55.0 | 76.0 | 81.1 | 115.1 | 101.7 | 99.6 | -3.3 |
| | | | | | | | | |
| 1 052.2倍 | 692.4倍 | 90.5倍 | 17.5倍 | 947.9 | 283.1 | 121.2 | 103.5 | 22.7 |
| | | | | | | | | |
| 21.0倍 | 14.7倍 | 657.7 | 941.9 | 472.8 | 98.5 | 108.5 | 125.3 | 9.4 |
| 510.4 | 373.7 | 251.3 | 258.2 | 303.3 | 132.0 | 117.2 | 157.3 | 4.9 |
| 16.4倍 | 706.6 | 248.7 | 155.0 | 195.7 | 131.1 | 90.3 | 98.7 | 8.6 |
| 108.6倍 | 71.5倍 | 38.0倍 | 29.6倍 | 14.4倍 | 319.4 | 106.1 | 114.4 | 14.8 |
| - | - | 47.0倍 | 34.3倍 | 11.7倍 | 861.2 | 98.5 | 114.8 | - |
| 14.0倍 | 295.7 | 22.3 | 8.3 | 78.0 | 99.7 | 47.0 | 78.7 | 8.1 |
| 29.2万倍 | 438.7倍 | 526.5 | 41.3倍 | 191.2 | 124.0 | 93.8 | 93.1 | 44.8 |
| 134.2倍 | 125.0倍 | 75.9倍 | 48.2倍 | 37.7倍 | 216.1 | 112.9 | 113.5 | 15.5 |
| 420.6倍 | 267.8倍 | 68.6倍 | 33.4倍 | 14.5倍 | 196.0 | 119.5 | 104.8 | 19.4 |
| 365.7倍 | 173.4倍 | 74.5倍 | 19.2倍 | 844.8 | 303.7 | 123.8 | 109.6 | 19.0 |
| 27.1倍 | 23.1倍 | 12.9倍 | 928.8 | 473.3 | 423.3 | 108.9 | 94.0 | 10.2 |

表1-5 续表 1

| 指　　标 | Item | 2012年为 | |
|---|---|---|---|
| | | 1952年 | 1970年 |
| 烧　碱 | Caustic Soda | 5 123.7倍 | 125.4倍 |
| 农用化肥 | Chemical Fertilizers for Agricultural Use | - | 22.2倍 |
| 水　泥 | Cement | 2.9万倍 | 124.5倍 |
| 交流电动机 | Alternating Current Motor | - | 34.0倍 |
| **运输邮电** | **Transportation and Postal** | | |
| 1.全社会公路水运货运量 | Total Freight Traffic of Highways and Waterways | 98.8倍 | 22.3倍 |
| 2.全社会公路水运客运量 | Total Passenger Traffic of Highways and Waterways | 224.5倍 | 49.9倍 |
| 3.邮电业务总收入 | Postal and Telecommunications Business Volume | 5 165.8倍 | 1 894.7倍 |
| 4.函　件 | Letters Delivered | 37.3倍 | 20.6倍 |
| 5.报刊杂志累计数 | Number of Newspapers and Magazines Circulation | 34.2倍 | 430.4 |
| **国内贸易** | **Domestic Trade** | | |
| 社会消费品零售总额 | Total Retail Sales of Consumer Goods | 1 038.8倍 | 630.5倍 |
| **对外经济和国际旅游** | **Foreign Trade Economy and International Tourism** | | |
| 1.进出口总额 | Total Exports and Imports | - | - |
| # 出口总额 | Exports | - | - |
| 2.利用外资 | Utilization of Foreign Capital | | |
| 新签合同数 | Number of Projects for Utilization of Foreign Capital in the Signed Agreements & Contracts | - | - |
| 合同外资金额 | Amount of Foreign Capital to Be Utilized in the Signed Agreements & Contracts | - | - |
| 实际利用外资 | Amount of Foreign Capital Actually Utilized | - | - |
| 3.国际旅游 | International Tourism | | |
| 接待境外旅游者人数 | Number of Foreign Tourists | - | - |
| **电　力** | **Electricity** | | |
| 全社会用电量 | Electricity Consumption of the Whole Society | 2 644.3倍 | 205.9倍 |
| **固定资产投资** | | | |
| 全社会固定资产投资 | Total Value of Investment in Fixed Assets | | |
| # 城镇投资 | Investment in Fixed Assets Collective Units | | |
| 房地产开发投资 | Value of Investment in Real Estate Development | | |

注：全社会公路水运客、货运量的增长按同口径计算。

Continued 1

| 以下各年的% | % of the Following Years | | | | | | | 1979-2012年平均增长% Average Growth Rate |
|---|---|---|---|---|---|---|---|---|
| 1978年 | 1980年 | 1990年 | 1995年 | 2000年 | 2005年 | 2010年 | 2011年 | |
| 43.5倍 | 30.8倍 | 15.5倍 | 11.3倍 | 764.8 | 626.3 | 157.3 | 161.6 | 11.7 |
| 591.8 | 430.3 | 350.0 | 319.8 | 158.6 | 98.3 | 83.3 | 108.8 | 5.4 |
| 18.0倍 | 11.8倍 | 416.7 | 168.5 | 164.2 | 90.1 | 70.8 | 94.3 | 8.9 |
| 12.7倍 | 14.5倍 | 10.3倍 | 165.4 | 19.2倍 | 341.7 | 99.1 | 106.8 | 7.8 |
| | | | | | | | | |
| 940.8 | 761.5 | 643.1 | 241.2 | 264.2 | 198.7 | 129.1 | 111.0 | 6.8 |
| 26.1倍 | 17.9倍 | 12.7倍 | 453.8 | 463.3 | 278.0 | 122.2 | 108.2 | 10.1 |
| 1 170.6 倍 | 902.9倍 | 162.0倍 | 14.7倍 | 469.9 | 210.4 | 120.3 | 102.0 | 23.1 |
| 16.8倍 | 13.0倍 | 956.0 | 403.5 | 532.6 | 262.1 | 104.8 | 98.2 | 8.7 |
| 444.5 | 322.3 | 197.9 | 138.9 | 105.6 | 134.2 | 105.6 | 100.2 | 4.5 |
| | | | | | | | | |
| 342.2倍 | 206.8倍 | 44.9倍 | 13.4倍 | 756.9 | 346.9 | 134.9 | 114.5 | 18.7 |
| | | | | | | | | |
| - | - | 1 626.0倍 | 66.6倍 | 15.2倍 | 217.4 | 111.5 | 101.6 | - |
| - | - | 1 127.0倍 | 74.8倍 | 16.7倍 | 240.0 | 114.1 | 104.5 | - |
| | | | | | | | | |
| - | - | 725.0 | 131.4 | 126.1 | 54.5 | 77.4 | 78.4 | - |
| - | - | 105.6倍 | 268.4 | 324.3 | 98.9 | 89.6 | 89.1 | - |
| - | - | 299.7倍 | 876.4 | 722.7 | 179.2 | 107.3 | 102.8 | - |
| | | | | | | | | |
| - | 38.5倍 | 11.6倍 | 954.5 | 450.7 | 206.3 | 121.4 | 108.1 | - |
| | | | | | | | | |
| 85.7倍 | 58.2倍 | 23.4倍 | 11.9倍 | 626.1 | 210.2 | 116.2 | 105.2 | 14.0 |
| | | | | | | | | |
| 3 761.8倍 | 1 835.0倍 | 95.1倍 | 15.8倍 | 10.2倍 | 281.6 | 145.6 | 117.0 | 27.4 |
| 1 892.5倍 | 923.2倍 | 157.2倍 | 19.2倍 | 994.7 | 323.3 | 159.8 | 121.5 | 24.8 |
| | | 765.7倍 | 21.5倍 | 20.7倍 | 304.9 | 135.0 | 105.4 | - |

Note:Total of Passenger and Freight Traffic of Highways and Waterways calculated in accordance with the caliber.

表1-5 续表 2

| 指　标 | Item | 2012年为 | |
|---|---|---|---|
| | | 1952年 | 1970年 |
| **财　政** | **Public Finance** | | |
| 财政收入 | Financial Revenue | 2 267.0倍 | 621.8倍 |
| 财政支出 | Financial Expenditures | 1.5万倍 | 2 595.8倍 |
| **金　融** | **Finance** | | |
| 金融机构人民币存款余额 | Deposit Balance of Financial Institutions | 6.8万倍 | 3 790.5倍 |
| 金融机构人民币贷款余额 | Loans Balance of Financial Institutions | 12.4万倍 | 2 446.5倍 |
| **物价指数** | **Price Indices** | | |
| 市区居民消费价格总指数 | General Consumer Price Index of Urban Residents | | |
| 市区商品零售价格总指数 | General Retail Price Index of Urban Area | | |
| **人民生活** | **People's Livelihood** | | |
| 在岗职工工资总额 | Total Wages of Staff and Workers | 1 666.9倍 | 705.8倍 |
| 在岗职工平均工资 | Average Wages of Staff and Workers | 126.6倍 | 110.0倍 |
| 农民人均纯收入 | Per Capita Net Income of Rural Residents | | 145.8倍 |
| 市区居民人均可支配收入 | Per Capita Disposable Income of Urban Households | | |
| 城乡居民人民币储蓄存款余额 | Amount of Saving Deposits in Urban and Rural Areas | | 8 769.3倍 |
| **教　育** | **Education** | | |
| 1.在校学生数 | Students Enrollment | 291.5 | 117.9 |
| # 高等学校 | Institutions of Higher Education | 81.8倍 | 5 194.8倍 |
| 中等职业教育学校 | Secondary Vocational Education Schools | | |
| 技工学校 | Skilled Workers' Schools | | |
| 普通中学 | Regular Secondary Schools | 770.0 | 152.9 |
| 小　学 | Primary Schools | 149.7 | 66.0 |
| 2.毕业生数 | Graduates | 10.2倍 | 166.0 |
| **卫　生** | **Health Care** | | |
| 卫生机构数 | Number of Health Institutions | 12.6倍 | 443.3 |
| # 医院、卫生院 | Hospitals | 15.7倍 | 148.5 |
| 床位数 | Number of Beds | 33.6倍 | 511.8 |
| # 医院、卫生院 | Hospitals | | |
| 卫生技术人员 | Number of Medical Personnel | 17.6倍 | 752.9 |
| # 医　生 | Doctors | 981.5 | 580.0 |

Continued 2

| 以下各年的% | % of the Following Years | | | | | | | 1979-2012年 平均增长% Average Growth Rate |
|---|---|---|---|---|---|---|---|---|
| 1978年 | 1980年 | 1990年 | 1995年 | 2000年 | 2005年 | 2010年 | 2011年 | |
| | | | | | | | | |
| 309.4倍 | 270.8倍 | 119.3倍 | 47.6倍 | 16.2倍 | 356.7 | 131.3 | 110.8 | 18.4 |
| 1 096.0倍 | 886.0倍 | 185.2倍 | 59.8倍 | 18.5倍 | 361.0 | 135.0 | 115.2 | 22.9 |
| | | | | | | | | |
| 2 396.7倍 | 1 126.5倍 | 133.6倍 | 31.2倍 | 12.0倍 | 373.4 | 130.2 | 116.4 | 25.7 |
| 882.0倍 | 643.1倍 | 101.6倍 | 32.1倍 | 14.0倍 | 391.8 | 134.5 | 114.8 | 22.1 |
| | | | | | | | | |
| | | 315.1 | 147.3 | 134.4 | 124.2 | 107.9 | 102.7 | |
| 507.2 | 476.7 | 223.6 | 112.8 | 117.2 | 117.3 | 106.7 | 101.9 | 4.9 |
| | | | | | | | | |
| 251.1倍 | 167.0倍 | 33.9倍 | 11.7倍 | 877.2 | 326.3 | 138.5 | 114.1 | 17.6 |
| 112.1倍 | 83.9倍 | 23.5倍 | 829.8 | 489.2 | 230.3 | 126.5 | 111.5 | 14.9 |
| 95.1倍 | 71.6倍 | 11.7倍 | 436.5 | 355.1 | 231.1 | 132.3 | 112.6 | 14.3 |
| | | 19.1倍 | 707.5 | 441.7 | 230.6 | 128.4 | 112.9 | |
| 3 269.9倍 | 1 590.0倍 | 78.9倍 | 19.5倍 | 720.1 | 281.0 | 124.3 | 114.0 | 26.9 |
| | | | | | | | | |
| 102.2 | 121.7 | 139.1 | 125.3 | 112.8 | 103.4 | 103.2 | 101.7 | 0.1 |
| 29.6倍 | 21.8倍 | 11.8倍 | 829.1 | 402.9 | 170.0 | 102.3 | 101.8 | 10.5 |
| | | 255.8 | 111.6 | 107.5 | 56.0 | 86.5 | 90.6 | 9.7 |
| 23.1倍 | 15.5倍 | 464.4 | 251.2 | 220.7 | 100.1 | 84.7 | 92.8 | 9.7 |
| 79.9 | 114.5 | 120.5 | 96.7 | 85.9 | 77.4 | 96.1 | 98.6 | -0.7 |
| 69.9 | 77.5 | 98.8 | 104.2 | 98.2 | 122.4 | 113.4 | 106.1 | -1.0 |
| 85.3 | 121.6 | 158.4 | 123.3 | 116.4 | 90.7 | 92.7 | 96.8 | -0.5 |
| | | | | | | | | |
| 308.1 | 266.0 | 194.7 | 201.3 | 226.8 | 153.8 | 111.9 | 104.7 | 3.4 |
| 123.0 | 121.3 | 121.3 | 119.5 | 127.4 | 127.4 | 116.2 | 103.7 | 0.6 |
| 318.4 | 335.8 | 250.1 | 235.8 | 236.2 | 175.9 | 117.5 | 107.2 | 3.5 |
| 331.4 | 353.4 | 269.8 | 254.2 | 249.0 | 183.0 | 118.8 | 107.3 | 3.6 |
| 443.1 | 393.9 | 256.9 | 225.7 | 229.8 | 178.4 | 122.9 | 112.4 | 4.5 |
| 426.8 | 367.2 | 212.9 | 190.4 | 200.1 | 179.3 | 127.7 | 118.8 | 4.4 |

表1-6

# 部分年份国民经济主要比例关系
# MAJOR PROPORTIONS IN NATIONAL ECONOMY OF PARTIAL YEARS

单位：% (%)

| 指　标 | Item | 1978年 | 1990年 | 2000年 | 2010年 | 2011年 | 2012年 |
|---|---|---|---|---|---|---|---|
| **一、地区生产总值中三次产业比例** | **Ratio of GDP by Type of Industry** | | | | | | |
| 第一产业 | Primary Industry | 28.1 | 17.3 | 5.9 | 2.2 | 1.7 | 1.6 |
| 第二产业 | Secondary Industry | 55.7 | 61.0 | 56.5 | 64.8 | 55.6 | 54.2 |
| 第三产业 | Tertiary Industry | 16.2 | 21.7 | 37.6 | 33.0 | 42.7 | 44.2 |
| **二、农林牧渔业总产值中各业比例** | **Ratio in Total Output of Farming, Forestry, Animal Husbandry and Fishery** | | | | | | |
| 农　业 | Agriculture | 87.3 | 60.1 | 59.2 | 35.5 | 39.0 | 40.0 |
| 林　业 | Forestry | 0.3 | 0.9 | 0.7 | 3.9 | 5.8 | 6.0 |
| 牧　业 | Animal Husbandry | 10.1 | 20.5 | 13.6 | 13.3 | 13.3 | 11.9 |
| 渔　业 | Fishery | 2.3 | 18.5 | 26.5 | 36.5 | 31.6 | 31.6 |
| 农林牧渔服务业 | Farming, Forestry, Animal usanry, Fishery and Service Industry | – | – | – | 10.8 | 10.3 | 10.5 |
| **三、农作物播种面积比例** | **Ratio of Farm Crops Sown Area** | | | | | | |
| #粮食作物 | Grain | 76.6 | 73.7 | 59.6 | 54.6 | 60.0 | 60.7 |
| 经济作物 | Cash Crop | | 25.4 | 39.6 | 44.7 | 39.0 | 38.7 |
| #棉　花 | Cotton | 5.7 | 5.2 | 2.3 | 1.4 | 0.5 | 0.4 |
| 油　料 | Oil-bearing Crops | 5.8 | 11.6 | 12.6 | 10.7 | 4.4 | 3.8 |
| **四、规模以上工业总产值中轻、重工业比例** | **Ratio of Light and Heavy Industries in Total Industrial Output Above Designated Size** | | | | | | |
| 轻工业 | Light Industry | 55.9 | 67.6 | 47.7 | 33.6 | 26.5 | 24.5 |
| 重工业 | Heavy Industry | 44.1 | 32.4 | 52.3 | 66.4 | 73.5 | 75.5 |
| **五、全社会客运量比例** | **Ratio of Total Passenger Traffic** | | | | | | |
| 铁　路 | Railways | 9.8 | 10.0 | 4.8 | 5.1 | 3.4 | 3.6 |
| 公　路 | Highways | 67.8 | 86.7 | 94.6 | 94.9 | 96.4 | 96.3 |
| 水　运 | Waterways | 22.4 | 3.3 | 0.6 | … | 0.2 | 0.1 |

表1-6 续表　Continued

单位：%　(%)

| 指　标 | Item | 1978年 | 1990年 | 2000年 | 2010年 | 2011年 | 2012年 |
|---|---|---|---|---|---|---|---|
| **六、全社会货运量比例** | **Ratio of Freight Traffic** | | | | | | |
| 铁　路 | Railways | 3.8 | 3.5 | 2.0 | 0.7 | 0.6 | 0.5 |
| 公　路 | Highways | 14.4 | 22.4 | 57.3 | 94.5 | 94.3 | 94.4 |
| 水　运 | Waterways | 81.8 | 74.1 | 40.7 | 4.8 | 5.1 | 5.1 |
| **七、全社会固定资产投资额比例** | **Ratio of Total Fixed Assets Investment** | | | | | | |
| 城镇投资 | City &Town Collective Units | | 30.4 | 51.6 | 45.8 | 48.4 | 50.3 |
| 房地产开发 | Real Estate Development | | 3.0 | 11.8 | 25.9 | 26.6 | 24.0 |
| 农村投资 | Investment in Rural Area | | 24.1 | 31.4 | 28.3 | 25.0 | 25.7 |
| 城镇和工矿区私人建房 | Building Construction by Privates in Industrial and Mining Regions of Cities and Towns | | 4.1 | 0.6 | – | – | – |
| 农村私人建房 | Building Construction by Privates in Countryside | | 38.4 | 4.6 | – | – | – |
| **八、财政收入占地区生产总值比例** | **Proportion of Financial Revenue to GDP** | **25.9** | **10.6** | **10.3** | **21.1** | **21.6** | **21.3** |
| **九、年末从业人员中各种身份就业者比例** | **Proportion of Employee by Ownership at Year–end** | | | | | | |
| 职　工 | Staff and Workers | 20.2 | 27.5 | 23.6 | 22.9 | 22.6 | 22.2 |
| # 国有职工 | State–owned Units | 11.4 | 15.1 | 12.0 | 3.9 | 3.8 | 3.8 |
| 集体职工 | Collective–owned Units | 8.8 | 11.4 | 3.5 | 0.5 | 0.5 | 0.4 |
| 其他从业人员 | Other Employee | – | – | 1.0 | 0.7 | 0.6 | 0.6 |
| 农村劳动者 | Rural Laborers | 79.7 | 72.0 | 66.1 | 34.4 | 32.1 | 30.5 |
| 城镇私营及个体劳动者 | Township Private Enterprises and Self–employed Individuals | … | 0.5 | 9.3 | 42.0 | 44.8 | 46.8 |
| **十、年末从业人员中三次产业比例** | **Proportion of Employee by Type of Industry at Year–end** | | | | | | |
| 第一产业 | Primary Industry | 62.3 | 29.7 | 21.0 | 5.0 | 4.5 | 4.3 |
| 第二产业 | Secondary Industry | 27.1 | 51.3 | 49.8 | 59.6 | 58.4 | 56.9 |
| 第三产业 | Tertiary Industry | 10.6 | 19.0 | 29.2 | 35.4 | 37.1 | 38.7 |

表1-7

# 部分年份国民经济主要指标日均水平
# MAJOR DAILY INDICATORS OF NATIONAL ECONOMY OF PARTIAL YEARS

| 指　标 | Item | 1978年 | 1990年 | 2000年 | 2010年 | 2011年 | 2012年 |
|---|---|---|---|---|---|---|---|
| 地区生产总值 (万元) | Gross Domestic Product (10 000 yuan) | 888 | 5 615 | 42 797 | 256 359 | 297 694 | 333 657 |
| 农林牧渔业总产值 | Gross Output Value of Farming, Forestry, Animal Husbandry and Fishery | 521 | 1 614 | 4 703 | 7 536 | 8 607 | 9 381 |
| 工业总产值 | Gross Industrial Output Value | 1 348 | 15 659 | 100 576 | 791 214 | 926 316 | 959 114 |
| 财政收入 | Financial Revenue | 230 | 596 | 4 396 | 54 184 | 64 212 | 71 158 |
| 生　铁 (吨) | Pig Iron (ton) | 462 | 816 | 1 642 | 54 839 | 54 581 | 61 937 |
| 钢　材 | Steel Products | 308 | 1 514 | 13 348 | 91 101 | 102 896 | 112 761 |
| 水　泥 | Cement | 1 331 | 5 759 | 14 611 | 33 870 | 25 444 | 23 997 |
| 布 (万米) | Cloth (10 000 m) | 49.16 | 99.84 | 82.73 | 214.15 | 159.54 | 250.93 |
| 彩色电视机 (台) | Color Television Sets (unit) | – | 675 | 2 708 | 32 176 | 27 622 | 31 701 |
| 电风扇 | Electric Fans | 224 | 14 033 | 4 014 | 6 652 | 3 978 | 3 129 |
| 电冰箱 | Refrigerators | … | 926 | 2 550 | 5 198 | 5 236 | 4 875 |
| 社会消费品零售总额 (万元) | Total Retail Sales of Consumer Goods (10 000 yuan) | 263 | 2 004 | 11 894 | 66 723 | 78 599 | 90 027 |
| 全社会固定资产投资额 | Total Fixed Assets Investment |  | 1 538 | 14 345 | 100 495 | 125 056 | 146 291 |
| 竣工住宅建筑面积 (平方米) | Floor Space of Residential Buildings Completed (sq.m) | 591 | 2 661 | 11 278 | 42 258 | 39 741 | 49 548 |
| 进出口总额 (万美元) | Total Exports and Imports (USD 10 000) | – | 52 | 5 575 | 76 132 | 83 573 | 84 914 |
| # 出　口 | Exports | – | 43 | 2 911 | 42 530 | 46 454 | 48 525 |
| 全社会公路水运货运量(万吨) | Total Freight Traffic of Highways and Waterways (10 000 tons) | 6.10 | 8.92 | 21.71 | 37.27 | 43.34 | 48.13 |
| 全社会公路水运客运量(万人次) | Total Passenger Traffic of Highways and Waterways (10 000 person-times) | 9.16 | 18.79 | 51.55 | 156.88 | 177.20 | 191.66 |
| 市区公共汽车客运总数 | Passenger Traffic of Buses in Urban Area |  |  |  | 157.36 | 175.87 | 193.65 |
| 市区家庭煤气用量 (万立方米) | Household Coal Gas Consumption in Urban Area (10 000cu.m) | – | 3.99 | 13.61 | 12.69 | 16.86 | 9.79 |
| 市区家庭天然气用量 (万立方米) | Household Natural Gas Consumption in Urban Area (10 000cu.m) | – | – | – | 22.73 | 33.02 | 40.01 |
| 函　件 (万件) | Number of Letters (10 000 pcs) | 4.81 | 8.48 | 15.21 | 77.34 | 82.48 | 81.02 |
| 结　婚 (对) | Marriages (couple) |  | 154 | 113 | 154 | 173 | 174 |
| 离　婚 | Divorces |  | 10 | 30 | 43 | 44 | 46 |

表1-8

# 部分年份国民经济主要指标人均水平
# MAJOR PER CAPITA INDICATORS OF NATIONAL ECONOMY OF PARTIAL YEARS

| 指　标 | | Item | | 1978年 | 1990年 | 2000年 | 2010年 | 2011年 | 2012年 |
|---|---|---|---|---|---|---|---|---|---|
| 地区生产总值 | (元) | Gross Domestic Product | (yuan) | 634 | 3 617 | 26 692 | 145 229 | 167 454 | 186 207 |
| 农林牧渔业总产值 | | Gross Output Value of Farming, Forestry, Animal Husbandry and Fishery | | 372 | 1 040 | 2 933 | 4 269 | 4 842 | 5 235 |
| 工业总产值 | | Gross Industrial Output Value | | 963 | 10 088 | 62 730 | 448 228 | 521 057 | 535 262 |
| 主要农产品产量 | | Output of Major Farm Products | | | | | | | |
| 粮　食 | (公斤) | Grain | (kg) | 584 | 507 | 336 | 180 | 180 | 181 |
| 棉　花 | | Cotton | | 7.20 | 6.60 | 2.03 | 0.27 | 0.24 | 0.20 |
| 油　料 | | Oil-bearing Crops | | 18.10 | 25.10 | 21.80 | 5.42 | 4.52 | 4.01 |
| 蚕　茧 | | Silkworm Cocoons | | 0.70 | 1.80 | 1.30 | 0.10 | 0.09 | 0.08 |
| 水产品 | | Aquatic Products | | 16.30 | 38.90 | 59.80 | 43.60 | 44.39 | 44.71 |
| 牛　奶 | | Milk | | 0.50 | 2.90 | 7.60 | 14.43 | 14.47 | 14.34 |
| 猪出栏数 | (头) | Slaughtered Fattened Hogs | (head) | 0.40 | 0.30 | 0.30 | 0.19 | 0.19 | 0.18 |
| 猪年末存栏数 | | Hogs in Stock at Year-end | | 0.50 | 0.30 | 0.20 | 0.13 | 0.13 | 0.13 |
| 主要工业产品产量 | | Output of Major Industrial Products | | | | | | | |
| 生　铁 | (公斤) | Pig Iron | (kg) | 33 | 53 | 102 | 3 107 | 3 070 | 3 457 |
| 钢　材 | | Steel Products | | 22 | 98 | 833 | 5 161 | 5 788 | 6 293 |
| 水　泥 | | Cement | | 95 | 371 | 911 | 1 919 | 1 431 | 1 339 |
| 布 | (米) | Cloth | (m) | 35 | 64 | 52 | 121 | 90 | 140 |
| 彩色电视机 | (台) | Color Television Sets | (unit) | – | 0.04 | 0.17 | 1.82 | 1.55 | 1.77 |
| 电风扇 | | Electric Fans | | 0.02 | 0.90 | 0.25 | 0.38 | 0.22 | 0.17 |
| 电冰箱 | | Refrigerators | | – | 0.06 | 0.16 | 0.29 | 0.29 | 0.27 |
| 财政收入 | (元) | Financial Revenue | (yuan) | 164 | 384 | 2 742 | 30 696 | 36 119 | 39 712 |
| 社会消费品零售总额 | | Total Retail Sales of Consumer Goods | | 188 | 1 291 | 7 418 | 37 799 | 44 213 | 50 242 |
| 全社会固定资产投资额 | | Total Fixed Assets Investment | | | 991 | 8 947 | 56 931 | 70 345 | 81 642 |
| 进出口总额 | (美元) | Total Exports and Imports | (USD) | – | 34 | 3 477 | 43 129 | 47 010 | 47 389 |
| 人民生活 | | People's Livelihood | | | | | | | |
| 在岗职工工资 | (元) | Wage of Staff and Workers | (yuan) | 514 | 2 450 | 11 778 | 45 566 | 51 660 | 57 622 |
| 市区居民可支配收入 | | Per Capita Disposable Income of Urban Residents | | | 2 150 | 9 274 | 29 219 | 33 243 | 37 531 |
| 市区居民消费性支出 | | Per Capita Living Expenditures of Urban Residents | | | 1 805 | 7 027 | 17 879 | 21 046 | 23 092 |
| 农民纯收入 | | Per Capita Net Income of Rural Residents | | 204 | 1 664 | 5 462 | 14 657 | 17 226 | 19 396 |

表1-9

# 苏州市国民经济主要指标在全省的地位 (2012年)
# POSITION OF SUZHOU'S MAJOR NATIONAL ECONOMICAL INDICATORS IN THE PROVINCE (2012)

| 指　标 | Item | 苏　州<br>Suzhou City | 江　苏<br>Jiangsu Province | 苏州占江苏的比重(%)<br>Percentage of Suzhou in Jiangsu |
|---|---|---|---|---|
| 年末户籍总人口　(万人) | Total Population (year-end)　(10 000 persons) | 647.81 | 7 553.48 | 8.6 |
| 年末常住总人口 | Resident Population (year-end) | 1 054.91 | 7 920.00 | 13.3 |
| # 城镇人口 | Urban Population | 762.85 | 4 990.00 | 15.3 |
| 地区生产总值　(亿元) | Gross Domestic Product　(100 million yuan) | 12 011.65 | 54 058.22 | 22.2 |
| 第一产业 | Primary Industry | 195.08 | 3 418.29 | 5.7 |
| 第二产业 | Secondary Industry | 6 502.25 | 27 121.95 | 24.0 |
| 第三产业 | Tertiary Industry | 5 314.32 | 23 517.98 | 22.6 |
| 农林牧渔业总产值 | Gross Output Value of Farming, Forestry, Animal Husbandry and Fishery | 337.72 | 5 808.81 | 5.8 |
| 主要农产品产量 | Output of Major Farm Products | | | |
| 粮　食　(万吨) | Grain　(10 000 tons) | 116.46 | 3 372.48 | 3.5 |
| 棉　花 | Cotton | 0.13 | 22.04 | 0.6 |
| 油　料 | Oil-bearing Crops | 2.59 | 146.95 | 1.8 |
| 水产品 | Aquatic Products | 28.84 | 493.74 | 5.8 |
| 牛　奶 | Cow Milk | 9.25 | 61.30 | 15.1 |
| 主要工业产品产量 | Output of Major Industrial Products | | | |
| 发电量　(亿千瓦时) | Electricity　(100 million kwh) | 913.34 | 3 928.35 | 23.2 |
| 钢　材　(万吨) | Steel Products　(10 000 tons) | 4 059.41 | 10 989.18 | 36.9 |
| 粗　钢 | Raw Steel | 2 662.19 | 7 419.70 | 35.9 |
| 水　泥 | Cement | 863.88 | 16 777.87 | 5.1 |
| 农用化肥 | Agricultural Chemical Fertilizers | 45.57 | 267.15 | 17.1 |
| 硫　酸 | Sulfuric Acid | 206.09 | 397.27 | 51.9 |
| 纱 | Yarn | 79.32 | 451.31 | 17.6 |
| 布　(亿米) | Cloth　(100 million m) | 9.03 | 80.34 | 11.2 |

表1-9 续表　　Continued

| 指　　标 | Item | 苏　州 Suzhou City | 江　苏 Jiangsu Province | 苏州占江苏的比重(%) Percentage of Suzhou in Jiangsu |
|---|---|---|---|---|
| 全社会用电量　(亿千瓦时) | Electricity Consumption　(100 million kwh) | 1 189.93 | 4 580.90 | 26.0 |
| # 工　业 | Industry | 982.66 | 3 562.48 | 27.6 |
| 社会消费品零售总额　(亿元) | Total Retail Sales of Consumer Goods　(100 million yuan) | 3 240.97 | 18 331.30 | 17.7 |
| 进出口总额　(亿美元) | Total Exports and Imports　(USD 100 million) | 3 056.92 | 5 480.93 | 55.8 |
| 进口总额 | Total Imports | 1 310.03 | 2 195.55 | 59.7 |
| 出口总额 | Total Exports | 1 746.89 | 3 285.38 | 53.2 |
| 外商投资企业合同外资金额 | Amount of Signed Agreements & Contracts of Foreign Funded Enterprises | 151.68 | 571.41 | 26.5 |
| 外商投资企业实际利用外资 | Amount of Foreign Capital Actually Utilized of Foreign Funded Enterprises | 91.65 | 357.60 | 25.6 |
| 规模以上固定资产投资 (亿元) | Investment in Fixed Assets　(100 million yuan) | 5 142.51 | 31 706.58 | 16.2 |
| 地方公共财政预算收入 | General Budgetary Revenue | 1 204.33 | 5 860.69 | 20.5 |
| 地方公共财政预算支出 | General Budgetary Expenditure | 1 113.47 | 7 027.67 | 15.8 |
| 金融机构年末存款余额 | Deposit Balance of Financial Institutions at Year-end | 17 663.50 | 75 481.51 | 23.4 |
| 金融机构年末贷款余额 | Loans Balance of Financial Institutions at Year-end | 13 626.86 | 54 412.30 | 25.0 |
| 高等学校在校学生　(万人) | Students Enrollment of Institutions of Higher Education (10 000 persons) | 19.22 | 167.12 | 11.5 |
| 中等职业教育学校 | Specialized Secondary Schools | 6.47 | 88.45 | 7.3 |
| 普通中学在校学生 | Students Enrollment of Regular Secondary Schools | 26.18 | 317.89 | 8.2 |
| 小学在校学生 | Students Enrollment of Primary Schools | 44.04 | 422.76 | 10.4 |
| 卫生机构　(所) | Health Institutions　(unit) | 2 992 | 31 054 | 9.6 |
| # 医院、卫生院 | Hospitals | 251 | 2 543 | 9.9 |
| 卫生机构床位数　(万张) | Number of Beds in Health Institutions　(10 000 units) | 4.61 | 33.31 | 13.8 |
| 卫生技术人员　(万人) | Number of Medical Personnel　(10 000 persons) | 5.72 | 39.61 | 14.4 |
| # 医　生 | Doctors | 2.32 | 15.80 | 14.7 |
| 城镇居民人均可支配收入(元) | Per Capita Disposable Income of Town Residents (yuan) | 39 079 | 29 677 | - |
| 农民人均纯收入 | Per Capita Net Income of Rural Residents | 19 396 | 12 202 | - |

表1-10

# 历年地区生产总值
# GROSS DOMESTIC PRODUCT OVER THE YEARS

单位：亿元 (100 million yuan)

| 年 份<br>Year | 地 区<br>生产总值<br>Gross Domestic Product | 第一产业<br>Primary Industry | 第二产业<br>Secondary Industry | | | 第三产业<br>Tertiary Industry | 人 均<br>生产总值<br>（元）<br>Per Capita GDP (yuan) |
|---|---|---|---|---|---|---|---|
| | | | | 工 业<br>Industry | 建筑业<br>Construction | | |
| 1952 | 4.38 | 2.01 | 1.09 | 1.06 | 0.03 | 1.29 | 126 |
| 1957 | 5.58 | 2.46 | 1.72 | 1.64 | 0.08 | 1.41 | 147 |
| 1962 | 7.15 | 2.97 | 2.40 | 2.34 | 0.06 | 1.78 | 180 |
| 1965 | 10.78 | 4.95 | 3.74 | 3.56 | 0.18 | 2.10 | 254 |
| 1970 | 15.03 | 6.26 | 6.16 | 5.61 | 0.55 | 2.62 | 325 |
| 1975 | 23.32 | 8.18 | 10.98 | 10.08 | 0.91 | 4.15 | 471 |
| 1978 | 31.95 | 8.97 | 17.79 | 16.69 | 1.10 | 5.18 | 634 |
| 1980 | 40.68 | 10.03 | 23.85 | 22.61 | 1.24 | 6.80 | 787 |
| 1985 | 91.91 | 18.07 | 56.67 | 52.59 | 4.08 | 17.17 | 1 714 |
| 1990 | 202.14 | 35.00 | 123.24 | 112.52 | 10.71 | 43.90 | 3 617 |
| 1991 | 235.10 | 35.76 | 147.22 | 134.46 | 12.76 | 52.11 | 4 178 |
| 1992 | 359.69 | 40.56 | 230.77 | 209.80 | 20.97 | 88.35 | 6 360 |
| 1993 | 525.96 | 50.16 | 336.06 | 305.05 | 31.01 | 139.74 | 9 258 |
| 1994 | 720.90 | 68.46 | 442.89 | 404.88 | 38.01 | 209.55 | 12 639 |
| 1995 | 903.11 | 80.37 | 543.41 | 499.12 | 44.29 | 279.33 | 15 784 |
| 1996 | 1 002.14 | 88.18 | 567.96 | 513.36 | 54.60 | 346.00 | 17 474 |
| 1997 | 1 132.59 | 88.16 | 636.42 | 577.12 | 59.30 | 408.01 | 19 713 |
| 1998 | 1 250.01 | 88.01 | 701.95 | 632.48 | 69.47 | 460.05 | 21 733 |
| 1999 | 1 358.43 | 88.14 | 764.07 | 691.54 | 72.53 | 506.22 | 23 592 |
| 2000 | 1 540.68 | 90.96 | 870.10 | 790.83 | 79.27 | 579.62 | 26 692 |
| 2001 | 1 760.28 | 91.41 | 999.89 | 912.11 | 87.78 | 668.98 | 30 384 |
| 2002 | 2 080.37 | 91.72 | 1 211.52 | 1 106.87 | 104.65 | 777.13 | 35 733 |
| 2003 | 2 801.56 | 75.75 | 1 771.86 | 1 586.61 | 185.25 | 953.95 | 47 693 |
| 2004 | 3 450.00 | 77.00 | 2 268.00 | 2 068.00 | 200.00 | 1 105.00 | 57 992 |
| 2005 | 4 138.21 | 91.71 | 2 681.54 | 2 520.33 | 161.21 | 1 364.97 | 68 618 |
| 2006 | 4 900.63 | 104.15 | 3 152.03 | 2 978.55 | 173.48 | 1 644.45 | 80 116 |
| 2007 | 5 850.11 | 115.18 | 3 632.03 | 3 442.20 | 189.83 | 2 102.91 | 94 318 |
| 2008 | 7 078.09 | 133.60 | 4 257.90 | 4 025.30 | 232.60 | 2 686.59 | 112 872 |
| 2009 | 7 740.20 | 142.82 | 4 547.12 | 4 265.47 | 281.65 | 3 050.26 | 122 565 |
| 2010 | 9 228.91 | 155.79 | 5 253.81 | 4 916.49 | 337.32 | 3 819.31 | 145 229 |
| 2011 | 10 716.99 | 177.75 | 5 957.74 | 5 555.33 | 402.41 | 4 581.50 | 167 454 |
| 2012 | 12 011.65 | 195.08 | 6 502.25 | 6 055.10 | 447.15 | 5 314.32 | 186 207 |

注：2005年开始数据根据经济普查已作调整，下同。
Note: From 2005, the statistics data has been adjusted in accord with the economic general investigation, same as the following.

表1-11

# 历年地区生产总值构成
# PROPORTIONS IN GROSS DOMESTIC PRODUCT OVER THE YEARS

单位：% (%)

| 年 份<br>Year | 地 区<br>生产总值<br>Gross Domestic Product | 第一产业<br>Primary Industry | 第二产业<br>Secondary Industry | 工 业<br>Industry | 建筑业<br>Construction | 第三产业<br>Tertiary Industry |
|---|---|---|---|---|---|---|
| 1952 | 100.0 | 45.9 | 24.8 | 24.2 | 0.6 | 29.3 |
| 1957 | 100.0 | 44.0 | 30.7 | 29.3 | 1.4 | 25.3 |
| 1962 | 100.0 | 41.6 | 33.5 | 32.7 | 0.8 | 24.9 |
| 1965 | 100.0 | 45.9 | 34.6 | 33.0 | 1.6 | 19.5 |
| 1970 | 100.0 | 41.6 | 41.0 | 37.3 | 3.6 | 17.4 |
| 1975 | 100.0 | 35.1 | 47.1 | 43.2 | 3.9 | 17.8 |
| 1978 | 100.0 | 28.1 | 55.7 | 52.2 | 3.4 | 16.2 |
| 1980 | 100.0 | 24.7 | 58.6 | 55.6 | 3.0 | 16.7 |
| 1985 | 100.0 | 19.7 | 61.6 | 57.2 | 4.4 | 18.7 |
| 1990 | 100.0 | 17.3 | 61.0 | 55.7 | 5.3 | 21.7 |
| 1991 | 100.0 | 15.2 | 62.6 | 57.2 | 5.4 | 22.2 |
| 1992 | 100.0 | 11.3 | 64.2 | 58.3 | 5.8 | 24.5 |
| 1993 | 100.0 | 9.5 | 63.9 | 58.0 | 5.9 | 26.6 |
| 1994 | 100.0 | 9.5 | 61.4 | 56.2 | 5.3 | 29.1 |
| 1995 | 100.0 | 8.9 | 60.2 | 55.3 | 4.9 | 30.9 |
| 1996 | 100.0 | 8.8 | 56.7 | 51.2 | 5.5 | 34.5 |
| 1997 | 100.0 | 7.8 | 56.2 | 51.0 | 5.2 | 36.0 |
| 1998 | 100.0 | 7.0 | 56.2 | 50.6 | 5.6 | 36.8 |
| 1999 | 100.0 | 6.5 | 56.2 | 50.9 | 5.3 | 37.3 |
| 2000 | 100.0 | 5.9 | 56.5 | 51.3 | 5.2 | 37.6 |
| 2001 | 100.0 | 5.2 | 56.8 | 51.8 | 5.0 | 38.0 |
| 2002 | 100.0 | 4.4 | 58.2 | 53.2 | 5.0 | 37.4 |
| 2003 | 100.0 | 2.7 | 63.2 | 56.6 | 6.6 | 34.1 |
| 2004 | 100.0 | 2.2 | 65.7 | 59.9 | 5.8 | 32.1 |
| 2005 | 100.0 | 2.2 | 64.8 | 60.9 | 3.9 | 33.0 |
| 2006 | 100.0 | 2.1 | 64.3 | 60.8 | 3.5 | 33.6 |
| 2007 | 100.0 | 2.0 | 62.1 | 58.8 | 3.3 | 35.9 |
| 2008 | 100.0 | 1.8 | 60.2 | 56.9 | 3.3 | 38.0 |
| 2009 | 100.0 | 1.8 | 58.8 | 55.1 | 3.7 | 39.4 |
| 2010 | 100.0 | 1.7 | 56.9 | 53.2 | 3.7 | 41.4 |
| 2011 | 100.0 | 1.7 | 55.6 | 51.8 | 3.8 | 42.7 |
| 2012 | 100.0 | 1.6 | 54.2 | 50.5 | 3.7 | 44.2 |

表1-12

# 历年地区生产总值指数
# INDICES OF GROSS DOMESTIC PRODUCT OVER THE YEARS

单位：% (%)

| 年 份 Year | 地 区 生产总值 Gross Domestic Product | 第一产业 Primary Industry | 第二产业 Secondary Industry | | | 第三产业 Tertiary Industry | 人均生产总值 Per Capita GDP |
|---|---|---|---|---|---|---|---|
| | | | | 工 业 Industry | 建筑业 Construction | | |
| 1979 | 104.0 | 86.2 | 107.0 | 106.6 | 113.4 | 124.1 | 102.6 |
| 1980 | 114.5 | 103.9 | 124.1 | 126.1 | 96.4 | 98.5 | 113.2 |
| 1981 | 107.5 | 94.7 | 110.5 | 109.9 | 121.8 | 112.7 | 106.4 |
| 1982 | 107.5 | 115.6 | 106.8 | 105.9 | 120.9 | 101.6 | 106.3 |
| 1983 | 111.2 | 95.6 | 113.0 | 112.2 | 124.3 | 123.1 | 110.5 |
| 1984 | 126.3 | 135.3 | 126.5 | 126.0 | 132.5 | 117.4 | 126.1 |
| 1985 | 130.0 | 96.3 | 138.8 | 139.4 | 131.9 | 132.9 | 129.6 |
| 1986 | 108.1 | 111.1 | 106.5 | 105.0 | 126.9 | 112.2 | 107.2 |
| 1987 | 116.4 | 100.1 | 120.4 | 118.1 | 146.0 | 114.2 | 115.2 |
| 1988 | 116.8 | 99.4 | 121.7 | 120.2 | 135.6 | 109.3 | 115.7 |
| 1989 | 95.5 | 96.4 | 94.0 | 95.7 | 80.5 | 101.7 | 94.6 |
| 1990 | 113.5 | 108.6 | 116.3 | 117.7 | 103.9 | 104.9 | 112.5 |
| 1991 | 111.9 | 98.7 | 114.3 | 114.4 | 112.9 | 109.2 | 111.2 |
| 1992 | 145.8 | 109.6 | 147.7 | 147.9 | 145.1 | 156.7 | 145.0 |
| 1993 | 125.1 | 101.6 | 126.0 | 128.2 | 102.4 | 130.3 | 124.5 |
| 1994 | 112.1 | 101.0 | 109.0 | 109.3 | 105.2 | 125.0 | 111.7 |
| 1995 | 114.8 | 111.8 | 114.5 | 114.9 | 108.6 | 116.5 | 114.4 |
| 1996 | 106.3 | 106.3 | 102.5 | 101.5 | 119.8 | 115.7 | 106.0 |
| 1997 | 114.2 | 103.4 | 114.4 | 114.8 | 108.6 | 116.5 | 114.0 |
| 1998 | 113.1 | 100.2 | 114.6 | 114.4 | 117.4 | 112.8 | 113.0 |
| 1999 | 112.1 | 106.2 | 113.2 | 113.7 | 105.1 | 111.0 | 112.0 |
| 2000 | 112.6 | 104.1 | 112.7 | 113.1 | 106.7 | 113.8 | 112.3 |
| 2001 | 112.3 | 101.2 | 112.6 | 112.9 | 109.6 | 113.6 | 111.9 |
| 2002 | 114.5 | 101.1 | 116.3 | 116.3 | 116.3 | 113.8 | 114.0 |
| 2003 | 118.0 | 94.5 | 121.7 | 120.3 | 133.5 | 115.0 | 117.0 |
| 2004 | 117.6 | 99.5 | 120.4 | 122.5 | 105.9 | 114.5 | 116.1 |
| 2005 | 115.3 | 100.2 | 115.3 | 115.6 | 110.3 | 116.7 | 113.8 |
| 2006 | 115.8 | 103.4 | 115.8 | 116.3 | 107.2 | 116.8 | 114.2 |
| 2007 | 116.1 | 104.2 | 115.6 | 116.1 | 107.5 | 117.8 | 114.5 |
| 2008 | 113.2 | 103.6 | 112.2 | 112.7 | 102.0 | 115.8 | 112.0 |
| 2009 | 111.5 | 104.3 | 110.0 | 109.5 | 119.3 | 114.5 | 110.7 |
| 2010 | 113.3 | 104.1 | 113.3 | 113.3 | 112.0 | 113.7 | 112.5 |
| 2011 | 112.0 | 104.1 | 111.5 | 111.7 | 108.1 | 112.9 | 111.2 |
| 2012 | 110.1 | 104.4 | 107.8 | 107.4 | 113.5 | 113.5 | 109.3 |

表1-13

# 全市生产总值
# GROSS DOMESTIC PRODUCT IN THE WHOLE CITY

| 项 目 | Item | 2011年 | 2012年 | 增长%（可比价）Increased (%) (at comparable prize) |
|---|---|---|---|---|
| **全市生产总值** (亿元) | **Gross Domestic Product** (100 million yuan) | **10 716.99** | **12 011.65** | **10.1** |
| **第一产业** | **Primary Industry** | **177.75** | **195.08** | **4.4** |
| **第二产业** | **Secondary Industry** | **5 957.74** | **6 502.25** | **7.8** |
| 工 业 | Industry | 5 555.33 | 6 055.10 | 7.4 |
| 建筑业 | Construction | 402.41 | 447.15 | 13.5 |
| **第三产业** | **Tertiary Industry** | **4 581.50** | **5 314.32** | **13.5** |
| 交通运输、仓储和邮政业 | Transportation, Logistics and Postal | 350.82 | 387.47 | 10.8 |
| 信息传输、软件和信息技术服务业 | Information transmission, software and information technology services | 209.51 | 230.54 | 9.8 |
| 批发和零售业 | Wholesale and Retail Trade Services | 1 476.02 | 1 645.12 | 10.7 |
| # 零售业 | Retail Trade Services | 274.88 | 325.73 | 16.1 |
| 住宿和餐饮业 | Accommodation and Catering Services | 260.57 | 313.50 | 13.5 |
| # 餐饮业 | Catering Services | 223.28 | 269.72 | 13.0 |
| 金融业 | Financial Industries | 633.26 | 819.57 | 29.6 |
| 房地产业 | Real Estate | 581.15 | 657.51 | 12.2 |
| # 房地产开发经营业 | Real Estate Development | 249.82 | 301.25 | 12.6 |
| 租赁和商务服务业 | Leasing and Business Services | 313.08 | 389.85 | 16.6 |
| 科学研究和技术服务业 | Scientific Research and Technical Services | 65.22 | 89.22 | 30.7 |
| 水利、环境和公共设施管理业 | Water Conservancy, Environment and Public Facilities Management | 42.69 | 58.09 | 26.1 |
| 居民服务和其他服务业 | Community Service and Other Services | 63.28 | 72.35 | 3.9 |
| 教 育 | Education | 153.16 | 179.61 | 4.8 |
| 卫生和社会工作 | Health Care and Social Work | 96.88 | 114.47 | 4.4 |
| 文化、体育和娱乐业 | Culture, Sports and Entertainment | 73.18 | 74.88 | 1.0 |
| 公共管理和社会组织 | Public Administration and Social Organizations | 262.68 | 282.14 | 4.7 |
| **人均生产总值**(户籍人口) (元) | **Per Capita GDP** (Household Register Population) (yuan) | **167 454** | **186 207** | **9.3** |
| **人均生产总值**(常住人口) | **Per Capita GDP** (The Resident Population) | **102 129** | **114 029** | **9.7** |

表1-14

# 分地区生产总值（2012年）

| 项　目 | | Item | | 市　区 Urban Area |
|---|---|---|---|---|
| **绝对值** | | **Absolute Value** | | |
| **地区生产总值** | (亿元) | **Gross Domestic Product** | (100 million yuan) | **6 047.99** |
| 第一产业 | | Primary Industry | | 72.47 |
| 第二产业 | | Secondary Industry | | 3 221.30 |
| # 工　业 | | Industry | | 2 965.65 |
| 第三产业 | | Tertiary Industry | | 2 754.22 |
| 人均地区生产总值(户籍人口) | (元) | Per Capita GDP (Household Register Population) | (yuan) | 184 835 |
| 人均地区生产总值(常住人口) | | Per Capita GDP (The Resident Population) | | 111 628 |
| **构　成** | (%) | **Composition** | (%) | |
| **地区生产总值** | | **Gross Domestic Product** | | **100.0** |
| 第一产业 | | Primary Industry | | 1.2 |
| 第二产业 | | Secondary Industry | | 53.3 |
| # 工　业 | | Industry | | 49.0 |
| 第三产业 | | Tertiary Industry | | 45.5 |
| **比上年增长** | (%) | **Increase Over Last Year** | (%) | |
| **地区生产总值** | | **Gross Domestic Product** | | **10.3** |
| 第一产业 | | Primary Industry | | 4.3 |
| 第二产业 | | Secondary Industry | | 7.8 |
| # 工　业 | | Industry | | 7.3 |
| 第三产业 | | Tertiary Industry | | 13.7 |
| 人均地区生产总值(户籍人口) | | Per Capita GDP (Household Register Population) | | 9.2 |
| 人均地区生产总值(常住人口) | | Per Capita GDP (The Resident Population) | | 9.2 |

# GROSS DOMESTIC PRODUCT BY REGION (2012)

| # 吴江区 Wujiang District | 常　熟 Changshu | 张家港 Zhangjiagang | 昆　山 Kunshan | 太　仓 Taicang |
|---|---|---|---|---|
| **1 321.49** | **1 870.19** | **2 050.58** | **2 725.32** | **955.12** |
| 34.27 | 37.02 | 27.53 | 24.46 | 33.61 |
| 750.14 | 996.95 | 1 175.51 | 1 631.25 | 520.36 |
| 709.22 | 952.62 | 1 129.98 | 1 551.28 | 491.55 |
| 537.08 | 836.22 | 847.54 | 1 069.61 | 401.15 |
| 164 502 | 175 195 | 225 577 | 373 022 | 202 585 |
| 103 044 | 123 882 | 164 441 | 165 291 | 134 439 |
| **100.0** | **100.0** | **100.0** | **100.0** | **100.0** |
| 2.6 | 2.0 | 1.3 | 0.9 | 3.5 |
| 56.8 | 53.3 | 57.4 | 59.9 | 54.5 |
| 53.7 | 50.9 | 55.1 | 56.9 | 51.5 |
| 40.6 | 44.7 | 41.3 | 39.2 | 42.0 |
| **10.9** | **10.2** | **10.9** | **11.2** | **10.3** |
| 4.6 | 4.8 | 4.9 | 4.7 | 4.2 |
| 8.0 | 8.3 | 8.0 | 9.1 | 8.1 |
| 7.5 | 8.2 | 7.8 | 8.9 | 7.9 |
| 15.9 | 12.9 | 15.2 | 15.2 | 14.0 |
| 10.6 | 10.1 | 10.5 | 9.2 | 9.9 |
| 10.4 | 10.3 | 11.2 | 11.5 | 10.7 |

表1-15

# 私营企业户数 (2012年末)

单位：户

| 项　　目 | Item | 全　市 Whole Municipality |
|---|---|---|
| **私营企业** | **Private Enterprises** | **229 618** |
| 农、林、牧、渔业 | Farming , Forestry ,Animal Husbandry and Fishery | 1 296 |
| 采矿业 | Mining and Quarrying | 12 |
| 制造业 | Manufacturing | 76 453 |
| 电力、燃气及水的生产和供应业 | Power, Gas and Water Production and Supply | 129 |
| 建筑业 | Construction | 14 504 |
| 交通运输、仓储和邮政业 | Transportation, Logistics and Postal | 5 759 |
| 信息传输、计算机服务和软件业 | Information Transmission, Computer Services and Software Industries | 4 627 |
| 批发和零售业 | Wholesale and Retail Trade Services | 82 390 |
| 住宿和餐饮业 | Accommodation and Catering Services | 1 785 |
| 金融业 | Financial Industries | 617 |
| 房地产业 | Real Estate | 5 495 |
| 租赁和商务服务业 | Leasing and Business Services | 19 977 |
| 科学研究、技术服务和地质勘查业 | Scientific Research, Technological Services and Geological Prospecting | 9 230 |
| 水利、环境和公共设施管理业 | Water Conservancy, Environment and Public Facilities Management | 985 |
| 居民服务和其他服务业 | Community Service and Other Services | 4 879 |
| 教　育 | Education | 72 |
| 卫生、社会保障和社会福利业 | Health Care, Social Security and Social Welfare | 329 |
| 文化、体育和娱乐业 | Culture, Sports and Entertainment | 1 074 |
| 其他行业 | Others | 5 |

# NUMBER OF PRIVATE ENTERPRISES ( END OF 2012)

(household)

| 市　区 Urban Area | # 吴江区 Wujiang District | 常　熟 Changshu | 张家港 Zhangjiagang | 昆　山 Kunshan | 太　仓 Taicang | 本年开业 Opened in This Year | 本年注销 Cancelled in This Year |
|---|---|---|---|---|---|---|---|
| **125 980** | **27 025** | **22 257** | **24 697** | **43 905** | **12 779** | **33 326** | **5 339** |
| 796 | 223 | 179 | 96 | 144 | 81 | 304 | 25 |
| 7 | 2 | 1 | 2 | 1 | 1 | – | 1 |
| 37 965 | 12 231 | 9 912 | 10 094 | 12 635 | 5 847 | 6 497 | 1 089 |
| 64 | 21 | 18 | 28 | 12 | 7 | 9 | 6 |
| 8 129 | 1 097 | 857 | 894 | 3 921 | 703 | 2 286 | 353 |
| 3 069 | 336 | 486 | 696 | 922 | 586 | 945 | 151 |
| 3 196 | 324 | 244 | 275 | 742 | 170 | 875 | 116 |
| 44 371 | 9 823 | 6 809 | 9 978 | 17 813 | 3 419 | 12 844 | 2 072 |
| 1 083 | 133 | 222 | 69 | 346 | 65 | 960 | 68 |
| 323 | 43 | 163 | 48 | 54 | 29 | 77 | 13 |
| 3 000 | 483 | 478 | 222 | 1 437 | 358 | 649 | 228 |
| 13 892 | 1 306 | 1 290 | 894 | 3 220 | 681 | 4 683 | 753 |
| 5 907 | 358 | 513 | 814 | 1 574 | 422 | 2 100 | 206 |
| 448 | 78 | 162 | 50 | 277 | 48 | 93 | 38 |
| 2 917 | 353 | 722 | 447 | 608 | 185 | 717 | 180 |
| 46 | 8 | 7 | 6 | 9 | 4 | 8 | 2 |
| 122 | 7 | 57 | 36 | 75 | 39 | 64 | 15 |
| 640 | 198 | 137 | 48 | 115 | 134 | 213 | 22 |
| 5 | 1 | – | – | – | – | 2 | 1 |

表1-16

# 个体劳动者户数 (2012年末)

单位：户

| 项　　目 | Item | 全　市 Whole Municipality |
|---|---|---|
| **个体劳动者** | **Self-employed Individuals** | **415 023** |
| 农、林、牧、渔业 | Farming, Forestry, Animal Husbandry and Fishery | 1 443 |
| 采矿业 | Mining and Quarrying | 11 |
| 制造业 | Manufacturing | 54 883 |
| 电力、燃气及水的生产和供应业 | Power, Gas and Water Production and Supply | 65 |
| 建筑业 | Construction | 1 713 |
| 交通运输、仓储和邮政业 | Transportation, Logistics and Postal | 7 946 |
| 信息传输、计算机服务和软件业 | Information Transmission, Computer Services and Software Industries | 532 |
| 批发和零售业 | Wholesale and Retail Trade Services | 273 364 |
| 住宿和餐饮业 | Accommodation and Catering Services | 29 585 |
| 金融业 | Financial Industries | - |
| 房地产业 | Real Estate | 1 269 |
| 租赁和商务服务业 | Leasing and Business Services | 4 500 |
| 科学研究、技术服务和地质勘查业 | Scientific Research, Technological Services and Geological Prospecting | 1 550 |
| 水利、环境和公共设施管理业 | Water Conservancy, Environment and Public Facilities Management | 178 |
| 居民服务和其他服务业 | Community Service and Other Services | 35 285 |
| 教　育 | Education | 52 |
| 卫生、社会保障和社会福利业 | Health Care, Social Security and Social Welfare | 412 |
| 文化、体育和娱乐业 | Culture, Sports and Entertainment | 2 228 |
| 其他行业 | Others | 7 |

# NUMBER OF SELF-EMPLOYED INDIVIDUALS ( END OF 2012)

(household)

| 市 区<br>Urban Area | # 吴江区<br>Wujiang District | 常 熟<br>Changshu | 张家港<br>Zhangjiagang | 昆 山<br>Kunshan | 太 仓<br>Taicang | 本年开业<br>Opened in This Year | 本年注销<br>Cancelled in This Year |
|---|---|---|---|---|---|---|---|
| **197 327** | **44 826** | **74 428** | **50 300** | **63 528** | **29 440** | **78 964** | **37 240** |
| 663 | 210 | 156 | 197 | 262 | 165 | 288 | 70 |
| 3 | – | – | 4 | 4 | – | – | 2 |
| 22 632 | 4 970 | 11 416 | 6 992 | 8 216 | 5 627 | 9 380 | 5 728 |
| 20 | 5 | 24 | 7 | 9 | 5 | 6 | 1 |
| 415 | 76 | 180 | 226 | 507 | 385 | 371 | 81 |
| 793 | 150 | 2 866 | 3 443 | 422 | 422 | 1 502 | 343 |
| 172 | 30 | 57 | 151 | 82 | 70 | 190 | 34 |
| 134 114 | 31 498 | 49 977 | 28 718 | 42 596 | 17 959 | 52 014 | 24 227 |
| 14 248 | 3 085 | 4 046 | 4 445 | 4 992 | 1 854 | 7 386 | 2 754 |
| – | – | – | – | – | – | – | – |
| 560 | 8 | 48 | 26 | 409 | 226 | 170 | 109 |
| 2 494 | 430 | 356 | 478 | 859 | 313 | 1 102 | 322 |
| 850 | 154 | 178 | 165 | 234 | 123 | 275 | 141 |
| 35 | 1 | 43 | 13 | 72 | 15 | 35 | 10 |
| 18 544 | 3 956 | 4 784 | 5 173 | 4 615 | 2 169 | 5 872 | 3 206 |
| 25 | 4 | 1 | 2 | 19 | 5 | 12 | 4 |
| 279 | 40 | 10 | 47 | 54 | 22 | 54 | 22 |
| 1 475 | 208 | 286 | 213 | 174 | 80 | 306 | 186 |
| 5 | 1 | – | – | 2 | – | 1 | – |

表1-17

# 私营企业从业人员 (2012年末)

单位：人

| 项　　目 | Item | 全　市 Whole Municipality |
|---|---|---|
| **私营企业** | **Private Enterprises** | **3 067 910** |
| 农、林、牧、渔业 | Farming, Forestry, Animal Husbandry and Fishery | 13 436 |
| 采矿业 | Mining and Quarrying | 111 |
| 制造业 | Manufacturing | 1 654 674 |
| 电力、燃气及水的生产和供应业 | Power, Gas and Water Production and Supply | 3 110 |
| 建筑业 | Construction | 218 294 |
| 交通运输、仓储和邮政业 | Transportation, Logistics and Postal | 60 441 |
| 信息传输、计算机服务和软件业 | Information Transmission, Computer Services and Software Industries | 40 426 |
| 批发和零售业 | Wholesale and Retail Trade Services | 586 661 |
| 住宿和餐饮业 | Accommodation and Catering Services | 40 159 |
| 金融业 | Financial Industries | 9 134 |
| 房地产业 | Real Estate | 76 529 |
| 租赁和商务服务业 | Leasing and Business Services | 184 581 |
| 科学研究、技术服务和地质勘查业 | Scientific Research, Technological Services and Geological Prospecting | 95 249 |
| 水利、环境和公共设施管理业 | Water Conservancy, Environment and Public Facilities Management | 13 815 |
| 居民服务和其他服务业 | Community Service and Other Services | 53 839 |
| 教　育 | Education | 678 |
| 卫生、社会保障和社会福利业 | Health Care, Social Security and Social Welfare | 7 724 |
| 文化、体育和娱乐业 | Culture, Sports and Entertainment | 9 020 |
| 其他行业 | Others | 29 |

# EMPLOYMENT OF PRIVATE ENTERPRISES ( END OF 2012)

(person)

| 市　区 Urban Area | # 吴江区 Wujiang District | 常　熟 Changshu | 张家港 Zhangjiagang | 昆　山 Kunshan | 太　仓 Taicang | 附：注册资金 (万元) Registered Capital (10 000 yuan) |
|---|---|---|---|---|---|---|
| **1 515 540** | **340 124** | **450 336** | **449 310** | **464 044** | **188 680** | **84 646 807** |
| 6 790 | 1 989 | 1 873 | 1 239 | 2 330 | 1 204 | 303 656 |
| 55 | 16 | 3 | 39 | 6 | 8 | 5 953 |
| 732 615 | 220 274 | 306 744 | 292 043 | 209 278 | 113 994 | 26 543 563 |
| 1 585 | 371 | 522 | 595 | 151 | 257 | 259 341 |
| 106 620 | 12 845 | 28 595 | 20 967 | 51 437 | 10 675 | 5 019 522 |
| 31 308 | 3 447 | 5 062 | 8 773 | 8 405 | 6 893 | 1 877 052 |
| 28 154 | 1 772 | 2 521 | 2 930 | 5 200 | 1 621 | 854 191 |
| 312 964 | 69 152 | 56 195 | 84 506 | 103 125 | 29 871 | 15 427 061 |
| 25 192 | 3 425 | 4 779 | 3 348 | 5 861 | 979 | 402 699 |
| 5 308 | 349 | 2 434 | 653 | 539 | 200 | 3 346 113 |
| 40 657 | 5 747 | 7 371 | 4 675 | 18 224 | 5 602 | 6 593 399 |
| 122 751 | 10 187 | 12 371 | 9 009 | 33 335 | 7 115 | 19 179 022 |
| 58 203 | 4 115 | 8 178 | 10 404 | 12 696 | 5 768 | 3 611 237 |
| 5 913 | 871 | 2 461 | 909 | 3 681 | 851 | 415 517 |
| 29 151 | 3 835 | 9 222 | 6 247 | 7 188 | 2 031 | 534 490 |
| 443 | 116 | 86 | 39 | 50 | 60 | 4 993 |
| 2 505 | 140 | 664 | 2 484 | 1 613 | 458 | 63 103 |
| 5 297 | 1 471 | 1 255 | 450 | 925 | 1 093 | 205 142 |
| 29 | 2 | – | – | – | – | 753 |

表1-18

# 个体劳动者从业人员 (2012年末)

单位：人

| 项　　目 | Item | 全　市<br>Whole Municipality |
|---|---|---|
| **个体劳动者** | **Self-employed Individuals** | **806 147** |
| 农、林、牧、渔业 | Farming, Forestry, Animal Husbandry and Fishery | 3 527 |
| 采矿业 | Mining and Quarrying | 27 |
| 制造业 | Manufacturing | 190 696 |
| 电力、燃气及水的生产和供应业 | Power, Gas and Water Production and Supply | 139 |
| 建筑业 | Construction | 4 512 |
| 交通运输、仓储和邮政业 | Transportation, Logistics and Postal | 9 244 |
| 信息传输、计算机服务和软件业 | Information Transmission, Computer Services and Software Industries | 916 |
| 批发和零售业 | Wholesale and Retail Trade Services | 407 499 |
| 住宿和餐饮业 | Accommodation and Catering Services | 91 836 |
| 金融业 | Financial Industries | – |
| 房地产业 | Real Estate | 1 969 |
| 租赁和商务服务业 | Leasing and Business Services | 8 558 |
| 科学研究、技术服务和地质勘查业 | Scientific Research, Technological Services and Geological Prospecting | 3 239 |
| 水利、环境和公共设施管理业 | Water Conservancy, Environment and Public Facilities Management | 504 |
| 居民服务和其他服务业 | Community Service and Other Services | 75 751 |
| 教　育 | Education | 139 |
| 卫生、社会保障和社会福利业 | Health Care, Social Security and Social Welfare | 1 074 |
| 文化、体育和娱乐业 | Culture, Sports and Entertainment | 6 511 |
| 其他行业 | Others | 6 |

# EMPLOYMENT OF SELF-EMPLOYED INDIVIDUALS ( END OF 2012)

(person)

| 市 区<br>Urban Area | # 吴江区<br>Wujiang District | 常 熟<br>Changshu | 张家港<br>Zhangjiagang | 昆 山<br>Kunshan | 太 仓<br>Taicang | 附：注册资金<br>(万元)<br>Registered Capital<br>(10 000 yuan) |
|---|---|---|---|---|---|---|
| **409 501** | **83 765** | **133 135** | **92 354** | **128 322** | **42 835** | **2 514 328** |
| 1 768 | 601 | 399 | 437 | 684 | 239 | 32 163 |
| 12 | – | – | 8 | 7 | – | 88 |
| 86 850 | 16 343 | 43 235 | 22 271 | 24 375 | 13 965 | 527 747 |
| 43 | 7 | 41 | 23 | 21 | 11 | 578 |
| 1 095 | 186 | 612 | 816 | 1 210 | 779 | 17 652 |
| 1 279 | 368 | 3 319 | 3 595 | 556 | 495 | 41 983 |
| 329 | 57 | 79 | 252 | 182 | 74 | 2 293 |
| 212 899 | 46 886 | 62 679 | 40 392 | 71 438 | 20 091 | 1 324 038 |
| 50 522 | 9 122 | 10 888 | 11 989 | 15 147 | 3 290 | 272 871 |
| – | – | – | – | – | – | – |
| 848 | 11 | 65 | 39 | 776 | 241 | 4 788 |
| 5 031 | 813 | 687 | 730 | 1 705 | 405 | 37 904 |
| 1 902 | 271 | 322 | 367 | 513 | 135 | 8 146 |
| 112 | 10 | 108 | 65 | 185 | 34 | 2 467 |
| 42 120 | 8 423 | 9 878 | 10 241 | 10 654 | 2 858 | 203 172 |
| 64 | 23 | 1 | 4 | 56 | 14 | 380 |
| 787 | 161 | 19 | 72 | 165 | 31 | 4 754 |
| 3 836 | 482 | 803 | 1 053 | 646 | 173 | 33 270 |
| 4 | 1 | – | – | 2 | – | 34 |

# 主 要 统 计 指 标 解 释

**行政区划** 指国家对行政区域的划分。根据有关法规规定，我国的行政区域划分如下：(1)全国分为省、自治区、直辖市；(2)省、自治区分为自治州、地区、自治县、市；(3)自治州分为县、自治县、市；(4)县、自治县分为乡、民族乡、镇；(5)直辖市和较大的市分为区、县；(6)国家在必要时设立的特别行政区。

**气温** 指空气的温度，我国一般以摄氏度(℃)为单位表示。气象观测的温度表是放在离地面约1.5米处通风良好的百叶箱里测量的，因此，通常说的气温指的是离地面1.5米处百叶箱中的温度。

**相对湿度** 指空气中实际所含水蒸气密度和同温度下饱和水蒸气密度的百分比值。

**降水量** 指从天空降落到地面的液态或固态(经融化后)水，未经蒸发、渗透、流失而在地面上积聚的深度。

**日照时数** 指太阳实际照射地面的时间。

**国内生产总值(GDP)** 指按市场价格计算的一个国家(或地区)所有常住单位在一定时期内生产活动的最终成果。在国家层面上叫国内生产总值，在地区层面上叫地区生产总值。国内生产总值有三种表现形态，即价值形态、收入形态和产品形态。从价值形态看，它是所有常住单位在一定时期内生产的全部货物和服务价值超过同期投入的全部非固定资产货物和服务价值的差额，即所有常住单位的增加值之和；从收入形态看，它是所有常住单位在一定时期内创造并分配给常住单位和非常住单位的初次收入之和；从产品形态看，它是所有常住单位在一定时期内最终使用的货物和服务价值减去货物和服务进口价值。在实际核算中，国内生产总值有三种计算方法，即生产法、收入法和支出法。三种方法分别从不同的方面反映国内生产总值及其构成。

**三次产业** 三次产业的划分是世界上较为常用的产业结构分类，但各国的划分不尽一致。我国的三次产业划分是：

第一产业是指农业、林业、畜牧业、渔业和农林牧渔服务业。

第二产业是指采矿业，制造业，电力、煤气及水的生产和供应业，建筑业。

第三产业是指除第一、二产业以外的其他行业。

# EXPLANATORY NOTES ON MAIN STATISTICAL INDICATORS

**Divisions of Administrative Areas** refers to the division of administrative areas by the State. The relative laws stipulate that 1) the whole country is divided into provinces, autonomous regions and municipalities directly under the Central Government; 2) provinces and autonomous regions are further divided into autonomous prefectures, counties, autonomous counties and cities; 3) autonomous prefectures are further divided into counties, autonomous counties and cities; 4) counties and autonomous counties are further divided into townships, ethnic townships and towns; 5) municipalities and large cities are divided into districts and counties, 6) the State shall, when necessary, establish special administrative regions.

**Temperature** refers to the air temperature. China uses centigrade as the unit. The thermometry used for weather observation is put in a breezy shutter, which is 1.5 meters high from the ground. Therefore, the commonly used temperature refers to the temperature in the breezy shutter 1.5 meters away from the ground.

**Relative Humidity** refers to the ratio of actual water vapour pressure to the saturation water vapour density under the current temperature.

**Volume of Precipitation** refers to the deepness of liquid state or solid state (thawed) water falling from the sky to the ground that has not been evaporated, infiltrated or run off.

**Sunshine Hours** refer to the actual hours of sun irradiating the earth. The calculation method is the same as that of the precipitation.

**Gross Domestic Product (GDP)** refers to the final products at market prices produced by all resident units in a country (or a region) during a certain period of time. Gross domestic product is expressed in three different perspectives, namely value, income, and products respectively. GDP in its value perspective refers to the total value of all goods and services produced by all resident units during a certain period of time, minus the total value of input of goods and services of the nature of non-fixed assets; in other words, it is the sum of the value-added of all resident units. GDP from the perspective of income includes the primary income created by all resident units and distributed to resident and non-resident units. GDP from the perspective of products refers to the value of all goods and services for final consumption by all resident units minus the net exports of goods and services during a given period of time. In the practice of national accounting, gross domestic product is calculated from three approaches, namely production approach, income approach and expenditure approach, which reflect gross domestic product and its composition from different angles.

**Three Strata of Industry** Classification of economic activities into three strata of industry is a common practice in the world, although the grouping varies to some extent form country to country. In China economic activities are categorized into the following three strata of industry:

Primary industry refers to agriculture, forestry, animal husbandry and fishery and services in support of these industries.

Secondary industry refers to mining and quarrying, manufacturing, production and supply of electricity, water and gas, and construction.

Tertiary industry refers to all other economic activities not included in the primary or secondary industries.

# 二、人口 劳动力

# CHAPTER 2
# POPULATION AND LABOR FORCE

# 人口　劳动力
# POPULATION AND LABOR FORCE

## 主要统计指标
## MAJOR STATISTICAL INDICATORS

| | | | | |
|---|---|---|---|---|
| 2012年末常住总人口 | Total Resident Population | 1 054.91 | 万人 | 10 000 persons |
| 城镇人口比重 | Proportion of Urban Population | 72.31 | % | |
| 2012年末户籍总户数 | Total Households | 214.04 | 万户 | 10 000 households |
| 比上年增长 | Increase Over Last Year | 0.4 | % | |
| 2012年末户籍总人口 | Total Household Population | 647.81 | 万人 | 10 000 persons |
| 比上年增长 | Increase Over Last Year | 0.9 | % | |
| 2012年户籍人口中: | In the Household Population | | | |
| 出生人数 | Birth Population | 68 097 | 人 | persons |
| 出生率 | Birth Rate | 10.56 | ‰ | |
| 死亡人数 | Death Population | 45 010 | 人 | persons |
| 死亡率 | Death Rate | 6.98 | ‰ | |
| 自然增长人数 | Natural Growth Population | 23 087 | 人 | persons |
| 自然增长率 | Natural Growth Rate | 3.58 | ‰ | |
| 2012年末从业人员 | Number of Employed Persons | 588.27 | 万人 | 10 000 persons |
| 比上年增长 | Increase Over Last Year | 2.2 | % | |
| 2012年在岗职工平均工资 | Average Wage of Staff and Workers | 57 622 | 元 | yuan |
| 比上年增长 | Increase Over Last Year | 11.5 | % | |

表2-1

# 全市历次人口普查主要数据
# MAIN DATA OF THE PREVIOUS CENSUS

| 指　标 | | Item | | 1982年 “三普” The Third Census in 1982 | 1990年 “四普” The Fourth Census in 1990 | 2000年 “五普” The Fifth Census in 2000 | 2010年 “六普” The Sixth Census in 2010 |
|---|---|---|---|---|---|---|---|
| **总人口** | (万人) | **Total Population** | (10 000 persons) | **527.53** | **564.36** | **679.22** | **1 045.99** |
| 男 | | Male | | 264.87 | 282.77 | 336.41 | 533.45 |
| 女 | | Female | | 262.66 | 281.59 | 342.82 | 512.54 |
| 性别比(女性为100) | | Sex Ratio (Female = 100) | | 100.84 | 100.42 | 98.13 | 104.08 |
| **家庭户规模** | (人/户) | **Family Size** | (person/household) | **3.50** | **3.51** | **3.15** | **2.84** |
| **各年龄组人口** | (万人) | **Population by Age Group** | (10 000 persons) | | | | |
| 0-14岁 | | Aged 0—14 | | 126.08 | 105.07 | 97.88 | 96.31 |
| 15-64岁 | | Aged 15—64 | | 367.23 | 413.75 | 516.25 | 860.77 |
| 65岁及以上 | | Aged 65 and Over | | 34.22 | 45.54 | 65.09 | 88.91 |
| **劳动适龄人口** | (万人) | **Working Age Population** | (10 000 persons) | **326.88** | **370.77** | **469.16** | **779.41** |
| 男（16-59岁） | | Male (Aged 15—59) | | 172.01 | 194.75 | 241.46 | 414.93 |
| 女（16-54岁） | | Female (Aged 15—54) | | 154.87 | 176.02 | 227.70 | 364.48 |
| **民族人口** | (万人) | **Population by Ethnicity** | (10 000 persons) | | | | |
| 汉族 | | Han Nationality | | 527.25 | 563.79 | 677.56 | 1 038.70 |
| 占总人口比重 | (%) | Proportion | (%) | 99.94 | 99.89 | 99.76 | 99.30 |
| 少数民族 | | Minority Nationalities | | 0.28 | 0.57 | 1.66 | 7.29 |
| 占总人口比重 | (%) | Proportion | (%) | 0.06 | 0.11 | 0.24 | 0.70 |
| **各种受教育程度的人口** | (万人) | **Population with Various Education Attainments** | (10 000 persons) | **342.56** | **411.63** | **596.41** | **975.11** |
| 小学 | | Primary School | | 191.98 | 199.25 | 219.89 | 226.64 |
| 初中 | | Junior Secondary School | | 108.69 | 149.02 | 249.88 | 402.38 |
| 高中、中专 | | Senior Secondary School and Technical Secondary School | | 37.71 | 52.82 | 94.41 | 199.79 |
| 大专及以上 | | Junior College and Above | | 4.18 | 10.55 | 32.23 | 146.30 |
| #大学专科 | | Junior College | | | | 20.32 | 88.49 |
| 大学本科 | | Undergraduate College | | | | 11.39 | 53.21 |
| 研究生 | | Graduate College | | | | 0.52 | 4.60 |
| **城乡人口** | (万人) | **Population by Residence** | (10 000 persons) | | | | |
| 城镇人口 | | Urban Population | | 108.24 | 146.01 | 387.73 | 732.95 |
| 乡村人口 | | Rural Population | | 419.29 | 418.35 | 291.49 | 313.04 |

表2-2

# 分地区常住人口
# RESIDENT POPULATION BY REGION

单位：万人 (10 000 persons)

| 地 区 | Region | 2011年末 End of 2011 | | 2012年末 End of 2012 | |
|---|---|---|---|---|---|
| | | 常住总人口 Total Population | 城镇人口比重 (%) Proportion of Urban Population (%) | 常住总人口 Total Population | 城镇人口比重 (%) Proportion of Urban Population (%) |
| **全 市** | **Whole Municipality** | **1 051.87** | **71.31** | **1 054.91** | **72.31** |
| **市 区** | **Urban Area** | **538.15** | **77.33** | **545.45** | **78.34** |
| 姑苏区 | Gusu District | 95.77 | 100.00 | 94.96 | 100.00 |
| 吴中区 | Wuzhong District | 115.97 | 67.26 | 113.83 | 68.33 |
| 相城区 | Xiangcheng District | 69.81 | 66.12 | 70.94 | 67.14 |
| 高新区、虎丘区 | New & Hi-tech Zone , Huqiu District | 57.53 | 82.74 | 60.81 | 83.74 |
| 工业园区 | Industrial Park | 71.32 | 95.53 | 76.17 | 96.42 |
| 吴江区 | Wujiang District | 127.75 | 63.02 | 128.74 | 64.16 |
| **县级市** | **Cities at County Level** | | | | |
| 常 熟 | Changshu | 151.22 | 63.09 | 150.71 | 64.05 |
| 张家港 | Zhangjiagang | 125.22 | 62.98 | 124.18 | 64.00 |
| 昆 山 | Kunshan | 165.87 | 69.30 | 163.89 | 69.88 |
| 太 仓 | Taicang | 71.41 | 62.72 | 70.68 | 63.67 |

注:常住人口是根据当年人口变动情况抽样调查数据推算。
Note:Resident population is calculated according to the change of the population sample survey data.

表2-3

# 历年年末户籍户数、人口数
# YEAR-END HOUSEHOLDS AND POPULATION OVER THE YEARS

单位：人 (person)

| 年 份 Year | 全市总人口 Total Population of Whole Municipality | 按地区分 | | | | | |
|---|---|---|---|---|---|---|---|
| | | 市 区 Urban Area | # 吴江区 Wujiang District | 常熟市 Changshu | 张家港市 Zhangjiagang | 昆山市 Kunshan | 太仓市 Taicang |
| 1949 | 3 386 027 | 1 613 652 | 468 631 | 681 358 | 484 098 | 304 813 | 302 106 |
| 1952 | 3 523 189 | 1 671 208 | 490 870 | 693 474 | 497 929 | 348 754 | 311 824 |
| 1957 | 3 851 040 | 1 839 466 | 539 483 | 750 452 | 538 305 | 382 491 | 340 326 |
| 1962 | 3 996 505 | 1 912 708 | 541 890 | 773 606 | 569 442 | 389 084 | 351 665 |
| 1965 | 4 295 134 | 2 057 262 | 585 879 | 820 204 | 618 233 | 427 467 | 371 968 |
| 1970 | 4 680 237 | 2 199 896 | 657 381 | 894 054 | 698 071 | 483 290 | 404 926 |
| 1975 | 4 926 040 | 2 319 193 | 693 119 | 939 340 | 735 534 | 509 228 | 422 745 |
| 1978 | 5 062 702 | 2 392 332 | 708 187 | 964 437 | 756 618 | 521 320 | 427 995 |
| 1980 | 5 186 167 | 2 490 995 | 716 057 | 980 263 | 762 715 | 523 532 | 428 662 |
| 1985 | 5 351 145 | 2 597 103 | 733 017 | 998 031 | 782 712 | 537 940 | 435 359 |
| 1990 | 5 610 165 | 2 732 375 | 764 187 | 1 032 888 | 834 070 | 564 610 | 446 222 |
| 1991 | 5 642 658 | 2 749 861 | 768 762 | 1 036 704 | 840 124 | 568 430 | 447 539 |
| 1992 | 5 668 940 | 2 765 013 | 772 150 | 1 039 279 | 844 139 | 572 051 | 448 458 |
| 1993 | 5 692 841 | 2 780 361 | 774 819 | 1 041 416 | 846 435 | 575 519 | 449 110 |
| 1994 | 5 714 296 | 2 795 173 | 776 921 | 1 042 992 | 848 767 | 578 269 | 449 095 |
| 1995 | 5 729 088 | 2 805 659 | 777 226 | 1 043 573 | 850 486 | 580 504 | 448 866 |
| 1996 | 5 741 163 | 2 813 076 | 776 458 | 1 043 391 | 851 988 | 583 364 | 449 344 |
| 1997 | 5 749 902 | 2 818 180 | 775 609 | 1 043 260 | 853 567 | 585 155 | 449 740 |
| 1998 | 5 753 485 | 2 820 759 | 773 308 | 1 041 785 | 853 979 | 587 509 | 449 453 |
| 1999 | 5 762 287 | 2 830 054 | 771 085 | 1 039 978 | 854 137 | 588 865 | 449 253 |
| 2000 | 5 781 689 | 2 843 674 | 771 822 | 1 039 064 | 854 953 | 594 592 | 449 406 |
| 2001 | 5 805 252 | 2 864 844 | 770 320 | 1 037 618 | 853 597 | 600 279 | 448 914 |
| 2002 | 5 838 599 | 2 893 397 | 769 423 | 1 036 229 | 852 718 | 606 936 | 449 319 |
| 2003 | 5 909 656 | 2 940 849 | 772 186 | 1 037 962 | 860 195 | 619 534 | 451 116 |
| 2004 | 5 988 510 | 2 985 027 | 777 509 | 1 043 132 | 868 640 | 637 157 | 454 554 |
| 2005 | 6 073 101 | 3 034 158 | 783 094 | 1 047 659 | 879 033 | 654 603 | 457 648 |
| 2006 | 6 160 814 | 3 089 935 | 788 438 | 1 054 825 | 887 804 | 666 809 | 461 441 |
| 2007 | 6 244 311 | 3 146 191 | 793 172 | 1 061 410 | 893 039 | 679 846 | 463 825 |
| 2008 | 6 297 530 | 3 177 364 | 795 254 | 1 065 018 | 898 430 | 690 435 | 466 283 |
| 2009 | 6 332 903 | 3 199 301 | 797 240 | 1 066 417 | 900 132 | 699 885 | 467 168 |
| 2010 | 6 376 558 | 3 224 328 | 799 569 | 1 066 908 | 905 085 | 711 333 | 468 904 |
| 2011 | 6 423 336 | 3 254 268 | 801 784 | 1 067 183 | 907 868 | 723 644 | 470 373 |
| 2012 | 6 478 054 | 3 289 922 | 804 868 | 1 067 798 | 910 208 | 737 565 | 472 561 |

表2-3 续表 Continued

单位：人 (person)

| 年 份<br>Year | 按性别分 By Sex | | 年平均人口<br>Average Person Per Year | 总户数(户)<br>Total Number of Households (household) | 平均每户人口<br>Average Person | 人口密度(人/平方公里)<br>Density of Population (person/sq.km) |
|---|---|---|---|---|---|---|
| | 男<br>Male | 女<br>Female | | | | |
| 1949 | 1 685 685 | 1 700 342 | 3 384 031 | 815 858 | 4.15 | 399 |
| 1952 | 1 768 903 | 1 754 286 | 3 467 676 | 883 279 | 3.99 | 415 |
| 1957 | 1 910 677 | 1 940 363 | 3 818 428 | 950 301 | 4.05 | 453 |
| 1962 | 1 977 577 | 2 018 928 | 3 966 800 | 1 080 214 | 3.70 | 471 |
| 1965 | 2 143 538 | 2 151 596 | 4 294 262 | 1 081 437 | 3.97 | 506 |
| 1970 | 2 330 843 | 2 349 394 | 4 642 755 | 1 203 088 | 3.89 | 551 |
| 1975 | 2 461 171 | 2 464 869 | 4 904 225 | 1 269 739 | 3.88 | 580 |
| 1978 | 2 534 209 | 2 528 493 | 5 036 822 | 1 374 222 | 3.68 | 596 |
| 1980 | 2 598 646 | 2 587 521 | 5 167 938 | 1 423 285 | 3.64 | 611 |
| 1985 | 2 685 217 | 2 665 928 | 5 335 524 | 1 556 308 | 3.44 | 630 |
| 1990 | 2 812 685 | 2 797 480 | 5 588 121 | 1 733 612 | 3.24 | 661 |
| 1991 | 2 827 843 | 2 814 815 | 5 626 412 | 1 758 717 | 3.21 | 665 |
| 1992 | 2 839 282 | 2 829 658 | 5 655 799 | 1 800 124 | 3.15 | 668 |
| 1993 | 2 851 356 | 2 841 485 | 5 680 891 | 1 823 304 | 3.12 | 671 |
| 1994 | 2 860 771 | 2 853 525 | 5 703 569 | 1 843 579 | 3.10 | 673 |
| 1995 | 2 866 058 | 2 863 030 | 5 721 692 | 1 878 344 | 3.05 | 675 |
| 1996 | 2 867 616 | 2 873 547 | 5 735 126 | 1 911 529 | 3.00 | 676 |
| 1997 | 2 868 569 | 2 881 333 | 5 745 533 | 1 938 413 | 2.97 | 677 |
| 1998 | 2 867 134 | 2 886 351 | 5 751 693 | 1 935 432 | 2.97 | 678 |
| 1999 | 2 867 598 | 2 894 689 | 5 757 886 | 1 948 501 | 2.96 | 679 |
| 2000 | 2 873 897 | 2 907 792 | 5 771 988 | 1 981 783 | 2.92 | 681 |
| 2001 | 2 882 853 | 2 922 399 | 5 793 471 | 1 994 777 | 2.91 | 684 |
| 2002 | 2 900 486 | 2 938 113 | 5 821 926 | 2 019 150 | 2.89 | 688 |
| 2003 | 2 927 836 | 2 981 820 | 5 874 128 | 2 049 073 | 2.88 | 696 |
| 2004 | 2 963 235 | 3 025 275 | 5 949 083 | 2 058 936 | 2.91 | 705 |
| 2005 | 3 003 445 | 3 069 656 | 6 030 805 | 2 068 264 | 2.93 | 715 |
| 2006 | 3 045 120 | 3 115 694 | 6 116 958 | 2 072 444 | 2.97 | 726 |
| 2007 | 3 085 728 | 3 158 583 | 6 202 563 | 2 087 038 | 2.99 | 736 |
| 2008 | 3 110 084 | 3 187 446 | 6 270 921 | 2 096 473 | 3.00 | 742 |
| 2009 | 3 125 028 | 3 207 875 | 6 315 217 | 2 106 918 | 3.01 | 746 |
| 2010 | 3 144 153 | 3 232 405 | 6 354 731 | 2 117 941 | 3.01 | 751 |
| 2011 | 3 164 805 | 3 258 531 | 6 399 947 | 2 132 385 | 3.01 | 757 |
| 2012 | 3 189 087 | 3 288 967 | 6 450 695 | 2 140 419 | 3.03 | 763 |

表2-4

# 历年人口自然变动情况
# NATURAL CHANGE OF POPULATION OVER THE YEARS

| 年 份 Year | 出 生 Birth | | 死 亡 Death | | 自然增长 Natural Growth | |
|---|---|---|---|---|---|---|
| | 人数(人) Population (person) | 出生率(‰) Birth Rate (‰) | 人数(人) Population (person) | 死亡率(‰) Death Rate (‰) | 人数(人) Population (person) | 自然增长率(‰) Natural Growth Rate(‰) |
| 1949 | 112 250 | 33.17 | 36 481 | 10.78 | 75 769 | 22.39 |
| 1952 | 128 700 | 37.11 | 32 286 | 9.31 | 96 414 | 27.80 |
| 1957 | 151 343 | 39.63 | 42 553 | 11.14 | 108 790 | 28.49 |
| 1962 | 123 893 | 31.23 | 45 428 | 11.45 | 78 465 | 19.78 |
| 1965 | 138 504 | 32.59 | 36 606 | 8.61 | 101 898 | 23.98 |
| 1970 | 119 799 | 25.80 | 31 297 | 6.74 | 88 502 | 19.06 |
| 1975 | 67 435 | 13.75 | 31 667 | 6.46 | 35 768 | 7.29 |
| 1978 | 73 308 | 14.55 | 32 800 | 6.51 | 40 508 | 8.04 |
| 1980 | 60 835 | 11.77 | 33 726 | 6.53 | 27 109 | 5.24 |
| 1985 | 55 305 | 10.37 | 36 219 | 6.79 | 19 086 | 3.58 |
| 1990 | 67 998 | 13.32 | 37 402 | 6.69 | 30 596 | 6.63 |
| 1991 | 61 920 | 11.01 | 36 996 | 6.58 | 24 924 | 4.43 |
| 1992 | 58 354 | 10.32 | 39 454 | 6.98 | 18 900 | 3.34 |
| 1993 | 54 750 | 9.64 | 38 638 | 6.80 | 16 112 | 2.84 |
| 1994 | 54 341 | 9.53 | 39 915 | 7.00 | 14 426 | 2.53 |
| 1995 | 48 803 | 8.53 | 40 073 | 7.00 | 8 730 | 1.53 |
| 1996 | 45 040 | 7.85 | 40 319 | 7.03 | 4 721 | 0.82 |
| 1997 | 40 304 | 7.01 | 39 898 | 6.94 | 406 | 0.07 |
| 1998 | 40 487 | 7.04 | 42 125 | 7.32 | -1 638 | -0.28 |
| 1999 | 38 122 | 6.62 | 39 396 | 6.84 | -1 274 | -0.22 |
| 2000 | 44 002 | 7.62 | 40 677 | 7.05 | 3 325 | 0.58 |
| 2001 | 36 694 | 6.33 | 38 930 | 6.72 | -2 236 | -0.39 |
| 2002 | 40 068 | 6.88 | 41 634 | 7.15 | -1 566 | -0.27 |
| 2003 | 42 786 | 7.28 | 42 308 | 7.20 | 478 | 0.08 |
| 2004 | 47 501 | 7.98 | 40 814 | 6.86 | 6 687 | 1.12 |
| 2005 | 48 477 | 8.04 | 41 385 | 6.86 | 7 092 | 1.18 |
| 2006 | 46 325 | 7.57 | 39 111 | 6.39 | 7 214 | 1.18 |
| 2007 | 48 552 | 7.83 | 40 503 | 6.53 | 8 049 | 1.30 |
| 2008 | 47 772 | 7.62 | 41 743 | 6.66 | 6 029 | 0.96 |
| 2009 | 49 663 | 7.86 | 41 427 | 6.56 | 8 236 | 1.30 |
| 2010 | 58 402 | 9.19 | 42 866 | 6.75 | 15 536 | 2.44 |
| 2011 | 58 732 | 9.18 | 41 956 | 6.56 | 16 776 | 2.62 |
| 2012 | 68 097 | 10.56 | 45 010 | 6.98 | 23 087 | 3.58 |

表2-5

# 分地区户籍户数与人口情况(2012年末)
# HOUSEHOLDS AND POPULATION BY REGION (END OF 2012)

| 地　　区 | Region | 总户数(户) Total Number of Households (household) | 总人口(人) Total Population (person) | 按性别分(人) By Sex (person) | |
|---|---|---|---|---|---|
| | | | | 男 Male | 女 Female |
| **全　市** | **Whole Municipality** | **2 140 419** | **6 478 054** | **3 189 087** | **3 288 967** |
| **市　区** | **Urban Area** | **1 077 162** | **3 289 922** | **1 625 144** | **1 664 778** |
| 姑苏区 | Gusu District | 280 535 | 751 246 | 370 917 | 380 329 |
| 吴中区 | Wuzhong District | 186 269 | 609 191 | 298 688 | 310 503 |
| 相城区 | Xiangcheng District | 124 769 | 387 189 | 189 563 | 197 626 |
| 高新区、虎丘区 | New & Hi-tech Zone , Huqiu District | 103 585 | 345 702 | 172 536 | 173 166 |
| 工业园区 | Industrial Park | 125 763 | 391 726 | 195 811 | 195 915 |
| 吴江区 | Wujiang District | 256 241 | 804 868 | 397 629 | 407 239 |
| **县级市** | **Cities at County Level** | **1 063 257** | **3 188 132** | **1 563 943** | **1 624 189** |
| 常　熟 | Changshu | 331 867 | 1 067 798 | 519 464 | 548 334 |
| 张家港 | Zhangjiagang | 336 570 | 910 208 | 447 898 | 462 310 |
| 昆　山 | Kunshan | 248 528 | 737 565 | 367 419 | 370 146 |
| 太　仓 | Taicang | 146 292 | 472 561 | 229 162 | 243 399 |

表2-5 续表 1　Continued 1

| 地　　区 | Region | 年平均人口(人) Average Person Per Year (person) | 平均预期寿命 e°x (岁) Average Life-span (age) | | |
|---|---|---|---|---|---|
| | | | 合　计 Total | 男 Male | 女 Female |
| **全　市** | **Whole Municipality** | **6 450 695** | **81.77** | **79.37** | **84.18** |
| **市　区** | **Urban Area** | **3 272 095** | **81.99** | **79.78** | **84.23** |
| 姑苏区 | Gusu District | 752 982 | 82.91 | 80.78 | 85.12 |
| 吴中区 | Wuzhong District | 606 231 | 81.51 | 79.56 | 83.41 |
| 相城区 | Xiangcheng District | 384 371 | 81.21 | 79.01 | 83.35 |
| 高新区、虎丘区 | New & Hi-tech Zone , Huqiu District | 343 192 | 81.99 | 79.29 | 84.71 |
| 工业园区 | Industrial Park | 381 994 | 82.31 | 79.99 | 84.60 |
| 吴江区 | Wujiang District | 803 326 | 81.55 | 79.20 | 84.02 |
| **县级市** | **Cities at County Level** | **3 178 600** | **81.55** | **78.96** | **84.13** |
| 常　熟 | Changshu | 1 067 491 | 81.12 | 78.56 | 83.60 |
| 张家港 | Zhangjiagang | 909 038 | 81.64 | 78.88 | 84.47 |
| 昆　山 | Kunshan | 730 605 | 81.67 | 79.18 | 84.18 |
| 太　仓 | Taicang | 471 467 | 82.31 | 79.62 | 84.94 |

表2-5 续表 2 Continued 2

| 地 区 | Region | 出生人数（人）Birth Population (person) | 出生率（‰）Birth Rate (‰) | 死亡人数（人）Death Population (person) | 死亡率（‰）Death Rate (‰) |
|---|---|---|---|---|---|
| **全 市** | **Whole Municipality** | **68 097** | **10.56** | **45 010** | **6.98** |
| **市 区** | **Urban Area** | **38 881** | **11.88** | **21 386** | **6.54** |
| 姑苏区 | Gusu District | 6 568 | 8.72 | 5 512 | 7.32 |
| 吴中区 | Wuzhong District | 7 671 | 12.65 | 3 741 | 6.17 |
| 相城区 | Xiangcheng District | 5 141 | 13.37 | 2 601 | 6.77 |
| 高新区、虎丘区 | New & Hi-tech Zone , Huqiu District | 4 718 | 13.75 | 1 802 | 5.25 |
| 工业园区 | Industrial Park | 6 922 | 18.12 | 1 652 | 4.33 |
| 吴江区 | Wujiang District | 7 861 | 9.79 | 6 078 | 7.57 |
| **县级市** | **Cities at County Level** | | | | |
| 常 熟 | Changshu | 8 053 | 7.54 | 8 648 | 8.10 |
| 张家港 | Zhangjiagang | 8 214 | 9.04 | 6 797 | 7.48 |
| 昆 山 | Kunshan | 9 311 | 12.74 | 4 418 | 6.05 |
| 太 仓 | Taicang | 3 638 | 7.72 | 3 761 | 7.98 |

表2-5 续表 3 Continued 3

| 地 区 | Region | 自然增长人数（人）Natural Growth Population (person) | 自然增长率（‰）Natural Growth Rate (‰) | 迁入人数（人）Number of the Transferred From Outside (person) | 迁出人数（人）Number of the Transferred to Outside (person) |
|---|---|---|---|---|---|
| **全 市** | **Whole Municipality** | **23 087** | **3.58** | **65 857** | **32 548** |
| **市 区** | **Urban Area** | **17 495** | **5.35** | **39 975** | **22 303** |
| 姑苏区 | Gusu District | 1 056 | 1.40 | 8 101 | 7 418 |
| 吴中区 | Wuzhong District | 3 930 | 6.48 | 6 452 | 4 555 |
| 相城区 | Xiangcheng District | 2 540 | 6.61 | 3 261 | 692 |
| 高新区、虎丘区 | New & Hi-tech Zone , Huqiu District | 2 916 | 8.50 | 6 201 | 4 328 |
| 工业园区 | Industrial Park | 5 270 | 13.80 | 12 727 | 3 698 |
| 吴江区 | Wujiang District | 1 783 | 2.22 | 3 233 | 1 612 |
| **县级市** | **Cities at County Level** | | | | |
| 常 熟 | Changshu | -595 | -0.56 | 4 088 | 2 401 |
| 张家港 | Zhangjiagang | 1 417 | 1.56 | 5 119 | 2 710 |
| 昆 山 | Kunshan | 4 893 | 6.70 | 12 942 | 3 966 |
| 太 仓 | Taicang | -123 | -0.26 | 3 733 | 1 168 |

表2-6

# 婚姻登记情况（2012年）
# CONDITIONS OF MARRIAGE REGISTRATION (2012)

| 地　区 | Region | 准予结婚登记(对) Marriage Legally Registered (couple) | 初　婚(人) First Married (person) | 再　婚(人) Re-married (person) | 女性晚婚率(%) Rate of Marriage at Mature Age for Female (%) | 离　婚(对) Divorced (couple) |
|---|---|---|---|---|---|---|
| **全　　市** | **Whole Municipality** | **62 460** | **108 825** | **16 095** | **73.81** | **16 666** |
| **市　区** | **Urban Area** | **33 032** | **58 908** | **7 156** | **74.29** | **8 652** |
| 姑苏区 | Gusu District | 7 850 | 13 137 | 2 563 | 86.51 | 2 387 |
| 吴中区 | Wuzhong District | 5 511 | 9 508 | 1 514 | 68.39 | 1 304 |
| 相城区 | Xiangcheng District | 3 714 | 6 601 | 827 | 60.84 | 922 |
| 高新区、虎丘区 | New & Hi-tech Zone , Huqiu District | 3 908 | 7 710 | 106 | 73.04 | 929 |
| 工业园区 | Industrial Park | 5 054 | 8 225 | 1 883 | 87.51 | 1 321 |
| 吴江区 | Wujiang District | 6 995 | 13 727 | 263 | 69.26 | 1 789 |
| **县级市** | **Cities at County Level** | | | | | |
| 常　熟 | Changshu | 8 307 | 13 912 | 2 702 | 67.05 | 2 150 |
| 张家港 | Zhangjiagang | 9 429 | 15 893 | 2 965 | 75.07 | 2 402 |
| 昆　山 | Kunshan | 7 905 | 13 160 | 2 650 | 73.49 | 2 347 |
| 太　仓 | Taicang | 3 787 | 6 952 | 622 | 69.08 | 1 115 |

表2-7

# 计划生育情况（2012年）
# CONDITIONS OF BIRTH CONTROL (2012)

| 地　区 | Region | 育龄妇女年末人数（万人） Number of Woman of Child-bearing Age (10 000 persons) | 计划生育率(%) Family Planning Rate (%) | 独生子女证有效领证率(%) Only-child Certificate Rate (%) | 节育率(%) Contraceptive Rate (%) | 总和生育率(%) Total Fertility Rate(%) |
|---|---|---|---|---|---|---|
| **全　　市** | **Whole Municipality** | **166.14** | **99.83** | **20.11** | **83.71** | **1.10** |
| **市　区** | **Urban Area** | **83.71** | **99.74** | **18.90** | **85.33** | **1.12** |
| 姑苏区 | Gusu District | 15.51 | 99.98 | 24.25 | 89.29 | 0.72 |
| 吴中区 | Wuzhong District | 16.56 | 99.47 | 17.82 | 84.33 | 1.25 |
| 相城区 | Xiangcheng District | 10.16 | 99.68 | 9.24 | 83.67 | 1.31 |
| 高新区、虎丘区 | New & Hi-tech Zone , Huqiu District | 8.95 | 99.66 | 28.97 | 86.72 | 1.28 |
| 工业园区 | Industrial Park | 11.26 | 99.92 | 14.15 | 88.15 | 0.96 |
| 吴江区 | Wujiang District | 21.27 | 99.83 | 16.80 | 82.40 | 1.25 |
| **县级市** | **Cities at County Level** | | | | | |
| 常　熟 | Changshu | 26.36 | 99.99 | 20.66 | 85.20 | 1.01 |
| 张家港 | Zhangjiagang | 23.95 | 99.94 | 25.40 | 80.26 | 0.99 |
| 昆　山 | Kunshan | 19.93 | 99.93 | 25.25 | 83.57 | 1.29 |
| 太　仓 | Taicang | 12.19 | 99.88 | 11.40 | 76.34 | 0.93 |

表2-8

# 历年按三次产业划分的年末从业人员及构成
# NUMBER AND COMPOSITION OF EMPLOYED PERSONS BY INDUSTRY OVER THE YEARS

| 年 份<br>Year | 年末从业人员<br>(万人)<br>Number of Employed Persons<br>(10 000 persons) | | | | 构 成<br>(%)<br>Composition<br>(%) | | | |
|---|---|---|---|---|---|---|---|---|
| | | 第一产业<br>Primary Industry | 第二产业<br>Secondary Industry | 第三产业<br>Tertiary Industry | | 第一产业<br>Primary Industry | 第二产业<br>Secondary Industry | 第三产业<br>Tertiary Industry |
| 1952 | 158.87 | 128.58 | 13.55 | 16.74 | 100.0 | 80.9 | 8.5 | 10.6 |
| 1957 | 177.69 | 144.40 | 17.95 | 15.34 | 100.0 | 81.3 | 10.1 | 8.6 |
| 1970 | 260.61 | 213.62 | 30.40 | 16.59 | 100.0 | 81.9 | 11.7 | 6.4 |
| 1975 | 282.34 | 213.12 | 45.49 | 23.73 | 100.0 | 75.5 | 16.1 | 8.4 |
| 1978 | 301.15 | 187.70 | 81.57 | 31.88 | 100.0 | 62.3 | 27.1 | 10.6 |
| 1980 | 317.17 | 184.93 | 98.85 | 33.39 | 100.0 | 58.3 | 31.2 | 10.5 |
| 1985 | 349.44 | 128.37 | 168.49 | 52.58 | 100.0 | 36.7 | 48.2 | 15.1 |
| 1990 | 346.74 | 103.13 | 177.84 | 65.77 | 100.0 | 29.7 | 51.3 | 19.0 |
| 1991 | 345.29 | 101.01 | 178.69 | 65.59 | 100.0 | 29.3 | 51.7 | 19.0 |
| 1992 | 344.12 | 93.09 | 181.84 | 69.19 | 100.0 | 27.1 | 52.8 | 20.1 |
| 1993 | 334.71 | 82.15 | 179.49 | 73.07 | 100.0 | 24.6 | 53.6 | 21.8 |
| 1994 | 328.57 | 67.36 | 181.67 | 79.54 | 100.0 | 20.5 | 55.3 | 24.2 |
| 1995 | 324.45 | 65.08 | 178.98 | 80.39 | 100.0 | 20.0 | 55.2 | 24.8 |
| 1996 | 323.84 | 66.21 | 174.15 | 83.48 | 100.0 | 20.4 | 53.8 | 25.8 |
| 1997 | 320.47 | 66.96 | 167.69 | 85.82 | 100.0 | 20.9 | 52.3 | 26.8 |
| 1998 | 307.52 | 68.40 | 153.87 | 85.25 | 100.0 | 22.3 | 50.0 | 27.7 |
| 1999 | 311.29 | 68.50 | 151.72 | 91.07 | 100.0 | 22.0 | 48.7 | 29.3 |
| 2000 | 313.89 | 65.90 | 156.27 | 91.72 | 100.0 | 21.0 | 49.8 | 29.2 |
| 2001 | 321.96 | 66.29 | 158.98 | 96.69 | 100.0 | 20.6 | 49.4 | 30.0 |
| 2002 | 323.75 | 61.66 | 161.38 | 100.71 | 100.0 | 19.0 | 49.9 | 31.1 |
| 2003 | 346.19 | 55.02 | 195.31 | 95.86 | 100.0 | 15.9 | 56.4 | 27.7 |
| 2004 | 358.82 | 48.61 | 211.11 | 99.10 | 100.0 | 13.6 | 58.8 | 27.6 |
| 2005 | 393.72 | 43.38 | 231.68 | 118.66 | 100.0 | 11.0 | 58.9 | 30.1 |
| 2006 | 429.46 | 35.94 | 263.71 | 129.81 | 100.0 | 8.4 | 61.4 | 30.2 |
| 2007 | 483.40 | 33.64 | 307.23 | 142.53 | 100.0 | 7.0 | 63.5 | 29.5 |
| 2008 | 495.53 | 32.11 | 303.86 | 159.56 | 100.0 | 6.5 | 61.3 | 32.2 |
| 2009 | 518.66 | 29.45 | 311.04 | 178.17 | 100.0 | 5.7 | 60.0 | 34.3 |
| 2010 | 554.15 | 27.83 | 330.14 | 196.19 | 100.0 | 5.0 | 59.6 | 35.4 |
| 2011 | 575.45 | 26.02 | 335.87 | 213.56 | 100.0 | 4.5 | 58.4 | 37.1 |
| 2012 | 588.27 | 25.34 | 334.98 | 227.95 | 100.0 | 4.3 | 56.9 | 38.8 |

注：本表从业人员数据不包括灵活就业人员。 Note: Employed persons in this table do not include flexible obtain employees.

表2-9

# 历年按就业者身份划分的年末从业人员
# NUMBER OF YEAR-END EMPLOYED PERSONS BY IDENTITY OVER THE YEARS

单位：万人 (10 000 persons)

| 年 份 Year | 年末从业人员 Number of Employed Persons | 职工人数 Number of Staff and Workers | 农村劳动者 Rural Laborers | 城镇私营与个体 Township Private & Self-Employed Individuals | 其他从业人员 Other Employed Persons |
|---|---|---|---|---|---|
| 1952 | 158.87 | | | - | - |
| 1957 | 177.69 | | | - | - |
| 1970 | 260.61 | 38.39 | 222.22 | - | - |
| 1975 | 282.34 | 50.34 | 232.00 | - | - |
| 1978 | 301.15 | 60.91 | 240.13 | 0.11 | - |
| 1980 | 317.17 | 70.30 | 246.69 | 0.18 | - |
| 1985 | 349.44 | 85.84 | 262.64 | 0.96 | - |
| 1990 | 346.74 | 95.43 | 249.77 | 1.54 | - |
| 1991 | 345.29 | 97.70 | 246.00 | 1.59 | - |
| 1992 | 344.12 | 98.50 | 243.65 | 1.97 | - |
| 1993 | 334.71 | 97.33 | 232.44 | 2.61 | 2.33 |
| 1994 | 328.57 | 96.30 | 227.50 | 3.08 | 1.69 |
| 1995 | 324.45 | 96.62 | 221.57 | 4.24 | 2.02 |
| 1996 | 323.84 | 94.51 | 221.94 | 5.22 | 2.17 |
| 1997 | 320.47 | 93.69 | 217.76 | 6.78 | 2.24 |
| 1998 | 307.52 | 78.88 | 216.43 | 10.45 | 1.76 |
| 1999 | 311.29 | 76.24 | 213.09 | 19.15 | 2.81 |
| 2000 | 313.89 | 74.09 | 207.54 | 29.01 | 3.25 |
| 2001 | 321.96 | 73.45 | 205.60 | 39.87 | 3.04 |
| 2002 | 323.75 | 74.16 | 204.18 | 41.04 | 4.37 |
| 2003 | 346.19 | 81.09 | 202.70 | 56.92 | 5.48 |
| 2004 | 358.82 | 87.18 | 200.76 | 67.23 | 3.65 |
| 2005 | 393.72 | 100.44 | 207.20 | 83.78 | 2.30 |
| 2006 | 429.46 | 111.39 | 206.90 | 108.47 | 2.70 |
| 2007 | 483.40 | 122.97 | 205.49 | 151.89 | 3.05 |
| 2008 | 495.53 | 118.08 | 205.94 | 168.46 | 3.05 |
| 2009 | 518.66 | 115.80 | 199.99 | 199.48 | 3.39 |
| 2010 | 554.15 | 126.97 | 190.42 | 232.87 | 3.89 |
| 2011 | 575.45 | 129.83 | 184.77 | 257.60 | 3.25 |
| 2012 | 588.27 | 130.40 | 179.54 | 275.08 | 3.25 |

注：1998年起职工指标为在岗职工口径。 Note:From 1998, the statistics about workers refers to those workers being employed.

表2-10

# 历年分经济类型职工人数
# NUMBER OF STAFF AND WORKERS BY OWNERSHIP OVER THE YEARS

单位：万人 (10 000 persons)

| 年 份<br>Year | 职工人数<br>Number of Staff and Workers | 国有经济<br>State-owned Units | 城镇集体<br>Urban Collective-owned Units | 其他经济<br>Other Ownership Units |
|---|---|---|---|---|
| 1949 | | 6.73 | | - |
| 1952 | | 10.34 | | - |
| 1957 | | 14.71 | | - |
| 1962 | | 17.72 | | - |
| 1965 | 36.64 | 17.81 | 18.83 | - |
| 1970 | 38.39 | 22.30 | 16.09 | - |
| 1975 | 50.34 | 26.43 | 23.91 | - |
| 1978 | 60.91 | 34.47 | 26.44 | - |
| 1980 | 70.30 | 40.32 | 29.98 | - |
| 1985 | 85.84 | 45.74 | 38.36 | 1.74 |
| 1990 | 95.43 | 52.49 | 39.43 | 3.51 |
| 1991 | 97.70 | 53.67 | 40.28 | 3.75 |
| 1992 | 98.50 | 54.11 | 39.64 | 4.75 |
| 1993 | 97.33 | 55.33 | 35.87 | 6.13 |
| 1994 | 96.30 | 55.33 | 33.85 | 7.12 |
| 1995 | 96.62 | 54.14 | 33.57 | 8.91 |
| 1996 | 94.51 | 53.72 | 30.76 | 10.03 |
| 1997 | 93.69 | 53.19 | 29.13 | 11.37 |
| 1998 | 78.88 | 44.87 | 19.62 | 14.39 |
| 1999 | 76.24 | 40.91 | 15.55 | 19.78 |
| 2000 | 74.09 | 37.53 | 11.07 | 25.49 |
| 2001 | 73.45 | 34.32 | 8.29 | 30.84 |
| 2002 | 74.16 | 29.84 | 6.64 | 37.68 |
| 2003 | 81.09 | 25.53 | 4.95 | 50.61 |
| 2004 | 87.18 | 22.58 | 3.97 | 60.63 |
| 2005 | 100.44 | 22.63 | 3.20 | 74.61 |
| 2006 | 111.39 | 21.14 | 2.43 | 87.82 |
| 2007 | 122.97 | 20.78 | 2.84 | 99.35 |
| 2008 | 118.08 | 20.83 | 2.71 | 94.54 |
| 2009 | 115.80 | 21.19 | 2.58 | 92.03 |
| 2010 | 126.97 | 21.57 | 2.54 | 102.86 |
| 2011 | 129.83 | 22.14 | 2.77 | 104.91 |
| 2012 | 130.40 | 22.61 | 2.50 | 105.29 |

表2-11

# 历年分地区职工人数
# NUMBER OF STAFF AND WORKERS BY REGION OVER THE YEARS

单位：万人 (10 000 persons)

| 年 份<br>Year | 全 市<br>Whole Municipality | 市 区<br>Urban Area | # 吴江区<br>Wujiang District | 常 熟<br>Changshu | 张家港<br>Zhangjiagang | 昆 山<br>Kunshan | 太 仓<br>Taicang |
|---|---|---|---|---|---|---|---|
| 1975 | 50.34 | 33.41 | 4.74 | 5.96 | 4.80 | 2.97 | 3.20 |
| 1976 | 53.26 | 35.25 | 5.09 | 6.38 | 4.84 | 3.37 | 3.42 |
| 1977 | 62.10 | 40.96 | 5.64 | 7.12 | 5.41 | 4.86 | 3.75 |
| 1978 | 60.91 | 40.90 | 5.56 | 7.20 | 5.32 | 3.77 | 3.72 |
| 1979 | 65.95 | 44.82 | 5.95 | 7.67 | 5.48 | 3.95 | 4.03 |
| 1980 | 70.30 | 47.52 | 6.43 | 8.22 | 5.88 | 4.27 | 4.41 |
| 1985 | 85.84 | 56.78 | 8.60 | 9.88 | 8.07 | 5.28 | 5.83 |
| 1990 | 95.43 | 60.91 | 9.51 | 11.98 | 9.50 | 6.21 | 6.83 |
| 1991 | 97.70 | 61.59 | 9.61 | 12.37 | 9.86 | 6.82 | 7.06 |
| 1992 | 98.50 | 61.13 | 9.58 | 12.59 | 10.13 | 7.26 | 7.39 |
| 1993 | 97.33 | 60.46 | 9.50 | 12.57 | 10.44 | 7.64 | 6.22 |
| 1994 | 96.30 | 59.26 | 9.07 | 12.51 | 10.17 | 8.18 | 6.18 |
| 1995 | 96.62 | 58.05 | 8.88 | 12.89 | 11.05 | 8.48 | 6.15 |
| 1996 | 94.51 | 56.40 | 8.68 | 12.70 | 10.33 | 8.90 | 6.18 |
| 1997 | 93.69 | 55.33 | 8.12 | 12.88 | 10.00 | 9.28 | 6.20 |
| 1998 | 78.88 | 44.12 | 6.91 | 11.31 | 8.82 | 9.04 | 5.59 |
| 1999 | 76.24 | 42.42 | 6.31 | 10.50 | 8.56 | 9.12 | 5.64 |
| 2000 | 74.09 | 39.53 | 5.77 | 10.34 | 8.17 | 10.65 | 5.40 |
| 2001 | 73.45 | 38.90 | 7.14 | 10.03 | 8.08 | 11.23 | 5.21 |
| 2002 | 74.16 | 38.22 | 6.79 | 9.66 | 8.12 | 12.67 | 5.49 |
| 2003 | 81.09 | 42.92 | 7.54 | 9.59 | 8.45 | 13.53 | 6.60 |
| 2004 | 87.18 | 46.19 | 7.76 | 9.70 | 9.33 | 14.16 | 7.80 |
| 2005 | 100.44 | 54.35 | 8.37 | 10.64 | 10.15 | 16.02 | 9.28 |
| 2006 | 111.39 | 62.37 | 8.50 | 10.42 | 11.57 | 16.89 | 10.14 |
| 2007 | 122.97 | 68.73 | 9.13 | 11.12 | 12.71 | 18.69 | 11.72 |
| 2008 | 118.08 | 65.77 | 9.04 | 10.92 | 12.45 | 17.34 | 11.60 |
| 2009 | 115.80 | 65.28 | 9.14 | 11.18 | 12.27 | 16.17 | 10.90 |
| 2010 | 126.97 | 72.68 | 11.04 | 11.62 | 13.07 | 18.32 | 11.28 |
| 2011 | 129.83 | 71.92 | 11.36 | 12.37 | 13.88 | 19.58 | 12.08 |
| 2012 | 130.40 | 72.60 | 11.50 | 12.22 | 14.47 | 19.21 | 11.90 |

表2-12

# 历年分地区职工工资总额
# TOTAL WAGES OF STAFF AND WORKERS BY REGION OVER THE YEARS

单位：万元 (10 000 yuan)

| 年 份 Year | 全 市 Whole Municipality | 市 区 Urban Area | # 吴江区 Wujiang District | 常 熟 Changshu | 张家港 Zhangjiagang | 昆 山 Kunshan | 太 仓 Taicang |
|---|---|---|---|---|---|---|---|
| 1975 | 23 949 | 16 682 | 2 062 | 2 558 | 1 808 | 1 394 | 1 507 |
| 1976 | 24 962 | 17 203 | 2 201 | 2 744 | 1 916 | 1 519 | 1 580 |
| 1977 | 28 687 | 20 021 | 2 409 | 3 066 | 2 158 | 1 757 | 1 685 |
| 1978 | 31 197 | 21 666 | 2 719 | 3 408 | 2 378 | 1 852 | 1 893 |
| 1979 | 36 217 | 25 137 | 3 112 | 3 894 | 2 833 | 2 086 | 2 267 |
| 1980 | 46 852 | 32 564 | 3 983 | 5 073 | 3 618 | 2 713 | 2 884 |
| 1985 | 92 421 | 61 406 | 8 154 | 11 077 | 8 321 | 5 498 | 6 119 |
| 1990 | 231 139 | 151 569 | 22 586 | 29 206 | 20 107 | 14 678 | 15 579 |
| 1991 | 255 829 | 167 002 | 25 476 | 32 376 | 21 554 | 17 528 | 17 369 |
| 1992 | 334 485 | 214 504 | 30 999 | 41 984 | 32 287 | 23 569 | 22 141 |
| 1993 | 415 192 | 261 936 | 37 961 | 53 514 | 43 624 | 31 832 | 24 286 |
| 1994 | 568 591 | 346 889 | 47 427 | 77 518 | 58 455 | 49 541 | 36 188 |
| 1995 | 670 992 | 403 802 | 55 915 | 91 302 | 79 038 | 57 524 | 39 326 |
| 1996 | 735 361 | 438 338 | 60 967 | 100 661 | 80 922 | 69 966 | 45 474 |
| 1997 | 792 260 | 470 743 | 61 837 | 109 806 | 83 198 | 78 380 | 50 133 |
| 1998 | 775 708 | 453 420 | 61 116 | 107 056 | 80 212 | 83 000 | 52 020 |
| 1999 | 823 530 | 491 426 | 61 270 | 104 897 | 81 597 | 87 916 | 57 694 |
| 2000 | 893 130 | 525 793 | 62 711 | 106 415 | 83 744 | 114 221 | 62 957 |
| 2001 | 1 019 144 | 602 077 | 82 884 | 116 638 | 95 202 | 136 022 | 69 205 |
| 2002 | 1 181 670 | 682 747 | 92 970 | 131 853 | 111 718 | 177 482 | 77 870 |
| 2003 | 1 554 557 | 905 495 | 121 785 | 172 936 | 142 183 | 228 013 | 105 930 |
| 2004 | 1 884 564 | 1 074 788 | 140 895 | 197 994 | 188 852 | 278 174 | 144 756 |
| 2005 | 2 400 711 | 1 375 498 | 178 977 | 242 456 | 233 333 | 351 649 | 197 775 |
| 2006 | 3 019 484 | 1 792 932 | 213 552 | 260 280 | 300 205 | 413 471 | 252 596 |
| 2007 | 3 770 329 | 2 209 925 | 276 620 | 314 091 | 365 878 | 534 871 | 345 564 |
| 2008 | 4 485 105 | 2 650 264 | 345 465 | 370 660 | 414 075 | 627 940 | 422 166 |
| 2009 | 4 610 823 | 2 715 599 | 377 850 | 412 108 | 443 766 | 619 106 | 420 244 |
| 2010 | 5 658 128 | 3 386 088 | 490 381 | 475 838 | 545 841 | 744 934 | 505 427 |
| 2011 | 6 864 959 | 4 027 396 | 595 017 | 590 805 | 683 053 | 949 273 | 614 432 |
| 2012 | 7 834 273 | 4 483 308 | 671 892 | 695 556 | 860 183 | 1 101 498 | 693 728 |

表2-13

# 历年分地区职工平均工资
# AVERAGE WAGE OF STAFF AND WORKERS BY REGION OVER THE YEARS

单位：元 (yuan)

| 年份 Year | 全市 Whole Municipality | 市区 Urban Area | # 吴江区 Wujiang District | 常熟 Changshu | 张家港 Zhangjiagang | 昆山 Kunshan | 太仓 Taicang |
|---|---|---|---|---|---|---|---|
| 1975 | 489 | 505 | 452 | 450 | 415 | 469 | 502 |
| 1976 | 481 | 499 | 448 | 442 | 398 | 464 | 478 |
| 1977 | 502 | 513 | 476 | 440 | 421 | 448 | 464 |
| 1978 | 514 | 537 | 498 | 472 | 443 | 496 | 522 |
| 1979 | 574 | 590 | 548 | 473 | 550 | 531 | 575 |
| 1980 | 687 | 704 | 643 | 586 | 654 | 638 | 693 |
| 1985 | 1 106 | 1 107 | 987 | 1 156 | 1 079 | 1 068 | 1 100 |
| 1990 | 2 450 | 2 512 | 2 393 | 2 474 | 2 183 | 2 352 | 2 327 |
| 1991 | 2 643 | 2 728 | 2 663 | 2 656 | 2 224 | 2 576 | 2 545 |
| 1992 | 3 395 | 3 488 | 3 241 | 3 364 | 3 251 | 3 272 | 3 021 |
| 1993 | 4 256 | 4 311 | 3 994 | 4 257 | 4 177 | 4 160 | 4 003 |
| 1994 | 5 918 | 5 838 | 5 172 | 6 192 | 5 826 | 6 180 | 5 950 |
| 1995 | 6 944 | 6 917 | 6 319 | 7 196 | 7 163 | 6 818 | 6 452 |
| 1996 | 7 742 | 7 681 | 7 006 | 7 920 | 7 806 | 7 919 | 7 570 |
| 1997 | 8 443 | 8 462 | 7 687 | 8 472 | 8 214 | 8 598 | 8 353 |
| 1998 | 9 616 | 9 947 | 8 613 | 9 325 | 8 907 | 9 235 | 9 272 |
| 1999 | 10 583 | 11 258 | 9 468 | 9 801 | 9 436 | 9 591 | 10 211 |
| 2000 | 11 778 | 12 898 | 10 324 | 10 246 | 10 156 | 10 658 | 11 006 |
| 2001 | 13 670 | 15 231 | 11 478 | 11 500 | 11 777 | 12 271 | 12 114 |
| 2002 | 15 924 | 17 902 | 13 605 | 13 590 | 13 702 | 14 383 | 13 334 |
| 2003 | 19 790 | 22 024 | 16 919 | 18 063 | 17 081 | 17 602 | 16 084 |
| 2004 | 22 510 | 24 991 | 19 157 | 20 327 | 20 226 | 20 099 | 18 564 |
| 2005 | 25 016 | 26 905 | 22 236 | 22 994 | 23 330 | 22 928 | 22 078 |
| 2006 | 28 010 | 29 775 | 25 911 | 25 411 | 26 042 | 25 989 | 25 503 |
| 2007 | 31 404 | 32 952 | 30 740 | 28 732 | 29 089 | 29 704 | 30 111 |
| 2008 | 36 090 | 37 826 | 35 440 | 33 420 | 33 538 | 33 735 | 34 716 |
| 2009 | 40 261 | 42 513 | 40 303 | 37 095 | 36 597 | 37 394 | 38 718 |
| 2010 | 45 566 | 47 780 | 44 393 | 41 784 | 42 518 | 41 669 | 45 120 |
| 2011 | 51 660 | 54 011 | 49 281 | 47 917 | 50 041 | 46 749 | 51 045 |
| 2012 | 57 622 | 59 692 | 55 949 | 53 982 | 56 591 | 53 461 | 57 037 |

表2-14 各行业按就业者身份划分的从业人员（2012年末）

单位：人

| 行　　业 | Sector | 从业人员 Total Employment |
|---|---|---|
| **总　　计** | **Total** | **5 882 745** |
| **第一产业** | **Primary Industry** | **253 453** |
| **第二产业** | **Secondary Industry** | **3 349 828** |
| 采矿业 | Mining and Quarrying | 85 |
| 制造业 | Manufacturing | 3 013 678 |
| 电力、燃气及水的生产和供应业 | Power, Gas and Water Production and Supply | 13 820 |
| 建筑业 | Construction | 322 245 |
| **第三产业** | **Tertiary Industry** | **2 279 464** |
| 交通运输、仓储和邮政业 | Transportation, Logistics and Postal | 138 762 |
| 信息传输、软件和信息技术服务业 | Information transmission, software and information technology services | 60 795 |
| 批发和零售业 | Wholesale and Retail Trade Services | 970 434 |
| 住宿和餐饮业 | Accommodation and Catering Services | 177 587 |
| 金融业 | Financial Industries | 56 781 |
| 房地产业 | Real Estate | 97 481 |
| 租赁和商务服务业 | Leasing and Business Services | 172 546 |
| 科学研究和技术服务业 | Scientific Research and Technical Services | 98 098 |
| 水利、环境和公共设施管理业 | Water Conservancy, Environment and Public Facilities Management | 21 455 |
| 居民服务和其他服务业 | Community Service and Other Services | 213 836 |
| 教　育 | Education | 87 454 |
| 卫生和社会工作 | Health Care and Social Work | 60 836 |
| 文化、体育和娱乐业 | Culture, Sports and Entertainment | 29 619 |
| 公共管理和社会组织 | Public Administration and Social Organizations | 93 780 |

# NUMBER OF EMPLOYED PERSONS BY SECTOR AND IDENTITY (END OF 2012)

(person)

| 在岗职工<br>Fully Employed Staff and Workers | 农村劳动者<br>Rural Laborers | 城镇私营与个体<br>Township Private & Self-employed Individuals | 其他从业人员<br>Other Employed Persons |
|---|---|---|---|
| **1 304 025** | **1 795 400** | **2 750 860** | **32 460** |
| **661** | **242 200** | **10 592** | **-** |
| **923 338** | **1 171 200** | **1 241 815** | **13 475** |
| - | - | 85 | - |
| 871 810 | 1 068 400 | 1 062 477 | 10 991 |
| 11 501 | - | 2 052 | 267 |
| 40 027 | 102 800 | 177 201 | 2 217 |
| **380 026** | **382 000** | **1 498 453** | **18 985** |
| 27 069 | 56 200 | 55 220 | 273 |
| 14 051 | 9 800 | 36 931 | 13 |
| 36 691 | 103 000 | 829 741 | 1 002 |
| 15 823 | 44 500 | 115 738 | 1 526 |
| 41 448 | 7 700 | 5 970 | 1 663 |
| 9 222 | 25 500 | 62 144 | 615 |
| 7 887 | - | 164 379 | 280 |
| 7 893 | 2 000 | 87 556 | 649 |
| 11 007 | - | 8 943 | 1 505 |
| 908 | 103 100 | 109 807 | 21 |
| 72 469 | 8 700 | 780 | 5 505 |
| 49 065 | - | 7 894 | 3 877 |
| 6 153 | 9 500 | 13 350 | 616 |
| 80 340 | 12 000 | - | 1 440 |

表2-15

# 分地区分行业从业人员 (2012年末)

单位：人

| 行　业 | Sector | 全　市 Whole Municipality |
|---|---|---|
| **总　　计** | **Total** | **5 882 745** |
| **第一产业** | **Primary Industry** | **253 453** |
| **第二产业** | **Secondary Industry** | **3 349 828** |
| 采矿业 | Mining and Quarrying | 85 |
| 制造业 | Manufacturing | 3 013 678 |
| 电力、燃气及水的生产和供应业 | Power, Gas and Water Production and Supply | 13 820 |
| 建筑业 | Construction | 322 245 |
| **第三产业** | **Tertiary Industry** | **2 279 464** |
| 交通运输、仓储和邮政业 | Transportation, Logistics and Postal | 138 762 |
| 信息传输、软件和信息技术服务业 | Information transmission, software and information technology services | 60 795 |
| 批发和零售业 | Wholesale and Retail Trade Services | 970 434 |
| 住宿和餐饮业 | Accommodation and Catering Services | 177 587 |
| 金融业 | Financial Industries | 56 781 |
| 房地产业 | Real Estate | 97 481 |
| 租赁和商务服务业 | Leasing and Business Services | 172 546 |
| 科学研究和技术服务业 | Scientific Research and Technical Services | 98 098 |
| 水利、环境和公共设施管理业 | Water Conservancy, Environment and Public Facilities Management | 21 455 |
| 居民服务和其他服务业 | Community Service and Other Services | 213 836 |
| 教　育 | Education | 87 454 |
| 卫生和社会工作 | Health Care and Social Work | 60 836 |
| 文化、体育和娱乐业 | Culture, Sports and Entertainment | 29 619 |
| 公共管理和社会组织 | Public Administration and Social Organizations | 93 780 |

# NUMBER OF EMPLOYED PERSONS BY SECTOR AND REGION (END OF 2012)

(person)

| 市 区 Urban Area | # 吴江区 Wujiang District | 常 熟 Changshu | 张家港 Zhangjiagang | 昆 山 Kunshan | 太 仓 Taicang |
|---|---|---|---|---|---|
| **2 856 412** | **720 008** | **885 569** | **811 893** | **908 107** | **420 764** |
| **123 246** | **43 830** | **40 275** | **35 333** | **21 110** | **33 489** |
| **1 507 007** | **429 755** | **552 609** | **499 208** | **523 314** | **267 690** |
| 29 | 16 | 3 | 42 | 3 | 8 |
| 1 350 958 | 400 522 | 491 776 | 454 039 | 466 771 | 250 134 |
| 6 145 | 1 790 | 3 129 | 1 904 | 1 030 | 1 612 |
| 149 875 | 27 427 | 57 701 | 43 223 | 55 510 | 15 936 |
| **1 226 159** | **246 423** | **292 685** | **277 352** | **363 683** | **119 585** |
| 62 478 | 12 972 | 22 043 | 27 616 | 16 285 | 10 340 |
| 41 371 | 5 255 | 3 916 | 5 700 | 6 956 | 2 852 |
| 513 161 | 113 332 | 118 101 | 122 371 | 174 342 | 42 459 |
| 96 541 | 18 956 | 22 408 | 23 688 | 29 080 | 5 870 |
| 33 812 | 5 174 | 7 218 | 5 539 | 5 934 | 4 278 |
| 43 627 | 7 697 | 13 868 | 8 272 | 25 633 | 6 081 |
| 117 161 | 10 070 | 12 074 | 8 076 | 28 727 | 6 508 |
| 61 125 | 4 173 | 7 618 | 10 396 | 13 962 | 4 997 |
| 10 482 | 2 546 | 3 279 | 2 270 | 3 955 | 1 469 |
| 111 669 | 35 173 | 42 608 | 24 704 | 22 805 | 12 050 |
| 44 074 | 11 591 | 11 941 | 12 029 | 12 426 | 6 984 |
| 27 528 | 6 169 | 8 129 | 10 306 | 10 296 | 4 577 |
| 15 497 | 3 120 | 5 405 | 3 681 | 3 350 | 1 686 |
| 47 633 | 10 195 | 14 077 | 12 704 | 9 932 | 9 434 |

表2-16

# 分地区分行业城镇单位在岗职工人数 (2012年末)
# NUMBER OF URBAN STAFF AND WORKERS EMPLOYED BY SECTOR AND REGION (END OF 2012)

单位：人 (person)

| 地区或行业 | Region or Sector | 职工人数 Number of Staff & Workers | 国有经济 State-owned Units | 城镇集体 Urban Collective-owned Units | 其他经济 Other Ownership Units |
|---|---|---|---|---|---|
| **总　计** | **Total** | **1 304 025** | **226 108** | **25 052** | **1 052 865** |
| **一、按地区分** | **Grouped by Region** | | | | |
| 市　区 | Urban Area | 726 008 | 117 369 | 10 335 | 598 304 |
| # 吴江区 | Wujiang District | 114 989 | 23 916 | 3 316 | 87 757 |
| 常　熟 | Changshu | 122 211 | 29 779 | 3 490 | 88 942 |
| 张家港 | Zhangjiagang | 144 678 | 33 286 | 2 859 | 108 533 |
| 昆　山 | Kunshan | 192 135 | 26 306 | 6 453 | 159 376 |
| 太　仓 | Taicang | 118 993 | 19 368 | 1 915 | 97 710 |
| **二、按企业、事业、机关分** | **Grouped by Character of the Units** | | | | |
| 企　业 | Enterprises | 1 088 925 | 31 527 | 7 209 | 1 050 189 |
| 事　业 | Institutions | 152 739 | 132 220 | 17 843 | 2 676 |
| 机　关 | Government Agencies | 62 361 | 62 361 | - | - |
| **三、按行业分** | **Grouped by Sector** | | | | |
| 农、林、牧、渔业 | Farming, Forestry, Animal Husbandry and Fishery | 661 | 127 | 152 | 382 |
| 采矿业 | Mining and Quarrying | - | - | - | - |
| 制造业 | Manufacturing | 871 810 | 2 656 | 814 | 868 340 |
| 电力、燃气及水的生产和供应业 | Power, Gas and Water Production and Supply | 11 501 | 2 575 | 60 | 8 866 |
| 建筑业 | Construction | 40 027 | 573 | 39 | 39 415 |
| 交通运输、仓储和邮政业 | Transportation, Logistics and Postal | 27 069 | 6 866 | 2 882 | 17 321 |
| 信息传输、软件和信息技术服务业 | Information transmission, software and information technology services | 14 051 | 948 | 48 | 13 055 |
| 批发和零售业 | Wholesale and Retail Trade Services | 36 691 | 2 478 | 596 | 33 617 |
| 住宿和餐饮业 | Accommodation and Catering Services | 15 823 | 3 995 | 917 | 10 911 |
| 金融业 | Financial Industries | 41 448 | 5 612 | - | 35 836 |
| 房地产业 | Real Estate | 9 222 | 2 092 | 185 | 6 945 |
| 租赁和商务服务业 | Renting and Labor Services | 7 887 | 2 426 | 642 | 4 819 |
| 科学研究和技术服务业 | Scientific Research and Technical Services | 7 893 | 3 373 | 282 | 4 238 |
| 水利、环境和公共设施管理业 | Water Conservancy, Environment and Public Facilities Management | 11 007 | 7 299 | 2 694 | 1 014 |
| 居民服务和其他服务业 | Residents Service and Other Service Trades | 908 | 459 | 268 | 181 |
| 教　育 | Education | 72 469 | 70 776 | 554 | 1 139 |
| 卫生和社会工作 | Health Care and Social Work | 49 065 | 30 159 | 13 494 | 5 412 |
| 文化、体育和娱乐业 | Culture, Sports and Entertainment | 6 153 | 4 457 | 341 | 1 355 |
| 公共管理和社会组织 | Public Administration and Social Organizations | 80 340 | 79 237 | 1 084 | 19 |

表2-17

# 市区分行业城镇单位在岗职工人数 (2012年末)
# NUMBER OF URBAN STAFF AND WORKERS EMPLOYED BY SECTOR IN URBAN AREA (END OF 2012)

单位：人 (person)

| 行业 | Sector | 职工人数 Number of Staff & Workers | 国有经济 State-owned Units | 城镇集体 Urban Collective-owned Units | 其他经济 Other Ownership Units |
|---|---|---|---|---|---|
| **总计** | **Total** | **726 008** | **117 369** | **10 335** | **598 304** |
| **一、按企业、事业、机关分** | **Grouped by Character of the Units** | | | | |
| 企业 | Enterprises | 615 424 | 16 972 | 1 443 | 597 009 |
| 事业 | Institutions | 77 445 | 67 258 | 8 892 | 1 295 |
| 机关 | Government Agencies | 33 139 | 33 139 | - | - |
| **二、按行业分** | **Grouped by Sector** | | | | |
| 农、林、牧、渔业 | Farming, Forestry, Animal Husbandry and Fishery | 348 | 104 | 152 | 92 |
| 采矿业 | Mining and Quarrying | - | - | - | - |
| 制造业 | Manufacturing | 488 786 | 1 260 | 5 | 487 521 |
| 电力、燃气及水的生产和供应业 | Power, Gas and Water Production and Supply | 4 834 | 621 | 60 | 4 153 |
| 建筑业 | Construction | 15 794 | 303 | 18 | 15 473 |
| 交通运输、仓储和邮政业 | Transportation, Logistics and Postal | 14 742 | 2 583 | - | 12 159 |
| 信息传输、软件和信息技术服务业 | Information transmission, software and information technology services | 10 757 | 11 | - | 10 746 |
| 批发和零售业 | Wholesale and Retail Trade Services | 24 991 | 1 882 | 300 | 22 809 |
| 住宿和餐饮业 | Accommodation and Catering Services | 10 172 | 2 239 | 225 | 7 708 |
| 金融业 | Financial Industries | 26 389 | 3 639 | - | 22 750 |
| 房地产业 | Real Estate | 5 822 | 1 669 | 89 | 4 064 |
| 租赁和商务服务业 | Renting and Labor Services | 5 433 | 1 807 | 476 | 3 150 |
| 科学研究和技术服务业 | Scientific Research and Technical Services | 4 182 | 1 478 | - | 2 704 |
| 水利、环境和公共设施管理业 | Water Conservancy, Environment and Public Facilities Management | 6 671 | 4 708 | 1 367 | 596 |
| 居民服务和其他服务业 | Residents Service and Other Service Trades | 248 | 218 | 30 | - |
| 教育 | Education | 38 658 | 37 636 | 472 | 550 |
| 卫生和社会工作 | Health Care and Social Work | 22 800 | 13 523 | 6 497 | 2 780 |
| 文化、体育和娱乐业 | Culture, Sports and Entertainment | 3 486 | 2 235 | 221 | 1 030 |
| 公共管理和社会组织 | Public Administration and Social Organizations | 41 895 | 41 453 | 423 | 19 |

表2-18

# 分地区、分行业城镇单位在岗职工工资总额 (2012年)
# TOTAL WAGES OF EMPLOYED URBAN STAFF AND WORKERS BY SECTOR AND REGION (2012)

单位：万元 (10 000 yuan)

| 地区或行业 | Region or Sector | 工资总额 Total Wage | 国有经济 State-owned Units | 城镇集体 Urban Collective-owned Units | 其他经济 Other Ownership Units |
|---|---|---|---|---|---|
| **总　计** | **Total** | **7 834 273** | **1 977 589** | **155 963** | **5 700 721** |
| **一、按地区分** | **Grouped by Region** | | | | |
| 市　区 | Urban Area | 4 483 308 | 1 036 334 | 73 511 | 3 373 463 |
| # 吴江区 | Wujiang District | 671 892 | 227 104 | 27 214 | 417 574 |
| 常　熟 | Changshu | 695 556 | 234 730 | 16 836 | 443 990 |
| 张家港 | Zhangjiagang | 860 183 | 274 914 | 13 009 | 572 260 |
| 昆　山 | Kunshan | 1 101 498 | 269 305 | 41 420 | 790 773 |
| 太　仓 | Taicang | 693 728 | 162 306 | 11 187 | 520 235 |
| **二、按企业、事业、机关分** | **Grouped by Character of the Units** | | | | |
| 企　业 | Enterprises | 5 969 712 | 252 583 | 35 225 | 5 681 904 |
| 事　业 | Institutions | 1 223 592 | 1 084 037 | 120 738 | 18 817 |
| 机　关 | Government Agencies | 640 969 | 640 969 | - | - |
| **三、按行业分** | **Grouped by Sector** | | | | |
| 农、林、牧、渔业 | Farming, Forestry, Animal Husbandry and Fishery | 3 504 | 990 | 1 598 | 916 |
| 采矿业 | Mining and Quarrying | - | - | - | - |
| 制造业 | Manufacturing | 4 464 145 | 18 999 | 2 790 | 4 442 356 |
| 电力、燃气及水的生产和供应业 | Power, Gas and Water Production and Supply | 95 104 | 20 003 | 305 | 74 796 |
| 建筑业 | Construction | 161 452 | 3 337 | 202 | 157 913 |
| 交通运输、仓储和邮政业 | Transportation, Logistics and Postal | 147 676 | 42 527 | 14 165 | 90 984 |
| 信息传输、软件和信息技术服务业 | Information transmission, software and information technology services | 113 943 | 10 294 | 598 | 103 051 |
| 批发和零售业 | Wholesale and Retail Trade Services | 172 974 | 21 680 | 2 624 | 148 670 |
| 住宿和餐饮业 | Accommodation and Catering Services | 61 694 | 15 151 | 2 707 | 43 836 |
| 金融业 | Financial Industries | 533 735 | 72 983 | - | 460 752 |
| 房地产业 | Real Estate | 80 793 | 16 655 | 1 176 | 62 962 |
| 租赁和商务服务业 | Renting and Labor Services | 41 179 | 16 947 | 4 114 | 20 118 |
| 科学研究和技术服务业 | Scientific Research and Technical Services | 82 699 | 35 615 | 2 052 | 45 032 |
| 水利、环境和公共设施管理业 | Water Conservancy, Environment and Public Facilities Management | 61 447 | 46 945 | 8 613 | 5 889 |
| 居民服务和其他服务业 | Residents Service and Other Service Trades | 5 775 | 2 936 | 1 627 | 1 212 |
| 教　育 | Education | 585 304 | 573 860 | 3 831 | 7 613 |
| 卫生和社会工作 | Health Care and Social Work | 384 838 | 257 667 | 100 841 | 26 330 |
| 文化、体育和娱乐业 | Culture, Sports and Entertainment | 43 442 | 33 158 | 2 214 | 8 070 |
| 公共管理和社会组织 | Public Administration and Social Organizations | 794 569 | 787 842 | 6 506 | 221 |

表2-19

# 市区分行业城镇单位在岗职工工资总额 (2012年)
# TOTAL WAGES OF EMPLOYED URBAN STAFF AND WORKERS BY SECTOR IN URBAN AREA (2012)

单位：万元 (10 000 yuan)

| 行 业 | Sector | 工资总额 Total Wage | 国有经济 State-owned Units | 城镇集体 Urban Collective-owned Units | 其他经济 Other Ownership Units |
|---|---|---|---|---|---|
| **总 计** | **Total** | **4 483 308** | **1 036 334** | **73 511** | **3 373 463** |
| **一、按企业、事业、机关分** | **Grouped by Character of the Units** | | | | |
| 企 业 | Enterprises | 3 522 695 | 151 376 | 8 368 | 3 362 951 |
| 事 业 | Institutions | 612 256 | 536 601 | 65 143 | 10 512 |
| 机 关 | Government Agencies | 348 357 | 348 357 | - | - |
| **二、按行业分** | **Grouped by Sector** | | | | |
| 农、林、牧、渔业 | Farming, Forestry, Animal Husbandry and Fishery | 2 795 | 857 | 1 598 | 340 |
| 采矿业 | Mining and Quarrying | - | - | - | - |
| 制造业 | Manufacturing | 2 572 719 | 7 597 | 75 | 2 565 047 |
| 电力、燃气及水的生产和供应业 | Power, Gas and Water Production and Supply | 37 944 | 5 207 | 305 | 32 432 |
| 建筑业 | Construction | 68 373 | 1 816 | 100 | 66 457 |
| 交通运输、仓储和邮政业 | Transportation, Logistics and Postal | 89 266 | 18 457 | - | 70 809 |
| 信息传输、软件和信息技术服务业 | Information transmission, software and information technology services | 84 955 | 189 | - | 84 766 |
| 批发和零售业 | Wholesale and Retail Trade Services | 118 745 | 16 141 | 1 555 | 101 049 |
| 住宿和餐饮业 | Accommodation and Catering Services | 41 576 | 8 474 | 649 | 32 453 |
| 金融业 | Financial Industries | 352 645 | 53 341 | - | 299 304 |
| 房地产业 | Real Estate | 60 118 | 14 495 | 607 | 45 016 |
| 租赁和商务服务业 | Renting and Labor Services | 27 037 | 12 530 | 3 231 | 11 276 |
| 科学研究和技术服务业 | Scientific Research and Technical Services | 55 134 | 19 310 | - | 35 824 |
| 水利、环境和公共设施管理业 | Water Conservancy, Environment and Public Facilities Management | 38 341 | 29 418 | 4 348 | 4 575 |
| 居民服务和其他服务业 | Residents Service and Other Service Trades | 1 315 | 1 043 | 272 | - |
| 教 育 | Education | 300 501 | 293 946 | 3 347 | 3 208 |
| 卫生和社会工作 | Health Care and Social Work | 179 496 | 111 431 | 53 983 | 14 082 |
| 文化、体育和娱乐业 | Culture, Sports and Entertainment | 22 699 | 14 743 | 1 352 | 6 604 |
| 公共管理和社会组织 | Public Administration and Social Organizations | 429 649 | 427 339 | 2 089 | 221 |

表2-20

# 分地区、分行业城镇单位在岗职工平均工资（2012年）
# AVERAGE WAGE OF EMPLOYED URBAN STAFF AND WORKERS BY REGION AND SECTOR (2012)

单位：元 (yuan)

| 地区或行业 | Region or Sector | 平均工资 Average Wages | 国有经济 State-owned Units | 城镇集体 Urban Collective-owned Units | 其他经济 Other Ownership Units |
|---|---|---|---|---|---|
| **总　计** | **Total** | **57 622** | **88 459** | **63 844** | **51 284** |
| **一、按地区分** | **Grouped by Region** | | | | |
| 市　区 | Urban Area | 59 692 | 89 262 | 72 877 | 53 986 |
| # 吴江区 | Wujiang District | 55 949 | 96 182 | 83 786 | 44 789 |
| 常　熟 | Changshu | 53 982 | 79 413 | 48 590 | 46 333 |
| 张家港 | Zhangjiagang | 56 591 | 83 576 | 45 856 | 49 218 |
| 昆　山 | Kunshan | 53 461 | 104 678 | 67 394 | 45 404 |
| 太　仓 | Taicang | 57 037 | 84 179 | 59 064 | 51 789 |
| **二、按企业、事业、机关分** | **Grouped by Character of the Units** | | | | |
| 企　业 | Enterprises | 52 026 | 79 916 | 50 896 | 51 238 |
| 事　业 | Institutions | 81 413 | 83 321 | 68 962 | 70 108 |
| 机　关 | Government Agencies | 103 631 | 103 631 | - | - |
| **三、按行业分** | **Grouped by Sector** | | | | |
| 农、林、牧、渔业 | Farming, Forestry, Animal Husbandry and Fishery | 54 326 | 76 767 | 107 289 | 24 935 |
| 采矿业 | Mining and Quarrying | - | - | - | - |
| 制造业 | Manufacturing | 47 716 | 71 883 | 34 365 | 47 659 |
| 电力、燃气及水的生产和供应业 | Power, Gas and Water Production and Supply | 83 461 | 78 565 | 50 933 | 85 102 |
| 建筑业 | Construction | 43 565 | 57 630 | 50 375 | 43 334 |
| 交通运输、仓储和邮政业 | Transportation, Logistics and Postal | 55 336 | 62 119 | 53 755 | 52 880 |
| 信息传输、软件和信息技术服务业 | Information transmission, software and information technology services | 83 628 | 108 585 | 122 041 | 81 605 |
| 批发和零售业 | Wholesale and Retail Trade Services | 47 350 | 84 556 | 43 949 | 44 552 |
| 住宿和餐饮业 | Accommodation and Catering Services | 38 173 | 37 587 | 29 300 | 39 115 |
| 金融业 | Financial Industries | 133 104 | 132 336 | - | 133 227 |
| 房地产业 | Real Estate | 87 438 | 79 766 | 64 273 | 90 345 |
| 租赁和商务服务业 | Renting and Labor Services | 53 479 | 71 626 | 66 566 | 42 660 |
| 科学研究和技术服务业 | Scientific Research and Technical Services | 107 583 | 103 775 | 75 701 | 113 032 |
| 水利、环境和公共设施管理业 | Water Conservancy, Environment and Public Facilities Management | 55 846 | 64 037 | 31 758 | 61 346 |
| 居民服务和其他服务业 | Residents Service and Other Service Trades | 63 677 | 63 699 | 61 415 | 66 934 |
| 教　育 | Education | 82 032 | 82 352 | 71 606 | 67 249 |
| 卫生和社会工作 | Health Care and Social Work | 80 180 | 87 594 | 76 424 | 48 885 |
| 文化、体育和娱乐业 | Culture, Sports and Entertainment | 67 519 | 72 955 | 64 168 | 52 268 |
| 公共管理和社会组织 | Public Administration and Social Organizations | 99 952 | 100 444 | 62 618 | 110 900 |

表2-21

# 市区分行业城镇单位在岗职工平均工资（2012年）
# AVERAGE WAGE OF EMPLOYED URBAN STAFF AND WORKERS BY SECTOR IN URBAN AREA (2012)

单位：元 (yuan)

| 行业 | Sector | 平均工资 Average Wages | 国有经济 State-owned Units | 城镇集体 Urban Collective-owned Units | 其他经济 Other Ownership Units |
|---|---|---|---|---|---|
| **总计** | **Total** | **59 692** | **89 262** | **72 877** | **53 986** |
| **一、按企业、事业、机关分** | **Grouped by Character of the Units** | | | | |
| 企业 | Enterprises | 54 864 | 88 431 | 59 139 | 53 933 |
| 事业 | Institutions | 80 317 | 81 037 | 75 118 | 78 276 |
| 机关 | Government Agencies | 106 313 | 106 313 | - | - |
| **二、按行业分** | **Grouped by Sector** | | | | |
| 农、林、牧、渔业 | Farming, Forestry, Animal Husbandry and Fishery | 84 432 | 81 648 | 107 289 | 44 000 |
| 采矿业 | Mining and Quarrying | - | - | - | - |
| 制造业 | Manufacturing | 49 587 | 60 871 | 107 571 | 49 559 |
| 电力、燃气及水的生产和供应业 | Power, Gas and Water Production and Supply | 78 902 | 85 498 | 50 933 | 78 337 |
| 建筑业 | Construction | 50 371 | 58 568 | 55 278 | 50 172 |
| 交通运输、仓储和邮政业 | Transportation, Logistics and Postal | 60 766 | 71 929 | - | 58 404 |
| 信息传输、软件和信息技术服务业 | Information transmission, software and information technology services | 81 837 | 171 727 | - | 81 742 |
| 批发和零售业 | Wholesale and Retail Trade Services | 47 756 | 81 398 | 51 833 | 44 747 |
| 住宿和餐饮业 | Accommodation and Catering Services | 39 510 | 37 364 | 27 974 | 40 450 |
| 金融业 | Financial Industries | 137 940 | 149 457 | - | 136 072 |
| 房地产业 | Real Estate | 102 573 | 85 871 | 68 202 | 110 226 |
| 租赁和商务服务业 | Renting and Labor Services | 51 697 | 71 807 | 72 273 | 37 118 |
| 科学研究和技术服务业 | Scientific Research and Technical Services | 136 876 | 125 880 | - | 143 640 |
| 水利、环境和公共设施管理业 | Water Conservancy, Environment and Public Facilities Management | 57 217 | 62 208 | 31 280 | 78 613 |
| 居民服务和其他服务业 | Residents Service and Other Service Trades | 52 367 | 47 190 | 90 500 | - |
| 教育 | Education | 79 021 | 79 385 | 73 397 | 58 974 |
| 卫生和社会工作 | Health Care and Social Work | 80 419 | 84 143 | 85 701 | 50 693 |
| 文化、体育和娱乐业 | Culture, Sports and Entertainment | 60 147 | 63 167 | 60 637 | 54 266 |
| 公共管理和社会组织 | Public Administration and Social Organizations | 103 991 | 104 461 | 53 966 | 110 900 |

表2-22

# 分地区、分行业城镇单位其他从业人员及劳动报酬情况 (2012年)
# OTHER URBAN EMPLOYED PERSONS AND REMUNERATION BY REGION AND SECTOR (2012)

| 地区或行业 | Region or Sector | 其他从业人员(人) Other Employed Persons (person) | 劳动报酬(万元) Laborers' Remuneration (10 000 yuan) | 平均劳动报酬(元) Average Remuneration (yuan) |
|---|---|---|---|---|
| **总　计** | **Total** | **32 460** | **273 340** | **85 746** |
| **一、按地区分** | **Grouped by Region** | | | |
| 市　区 | Urban Area | 17 207 | 167 376 | 98 509 |
| # 吴江区 | Wujiang District | 1 595 | 9 504 | 58 344 |
| 常　熟 | Changshu | 2 875 | 14 377 | 51 200 |
| 张家港 | Zhangjiagang | 3 845 | 19 118 | 50 576 |
| 昆　山 | Kunshan | 5 337 | 46 201 | 89 763 |
| 太　仓 | Taicang | 3 196 | 26 268 | 83 337 |
| **二、按企业、事业、机关分** | **Grouped by Character of the Units** | | | |
| 企　业 | Enterprises | 20 386 | 227 251 | 111 853 |
| 事　业 | Institutions | 11 281 | 43 762 | 40 660 |
| 机　关 | Government Agencies | 793 | 2 327 | 29 154 |
| **三、按行业分** | **Grouped by Sector** | | | |
| 农、林、牧、渔业 | Farming, Forestry, Animal Husbandry and Fishery | - | - | - |
| 采矿业 | Mining and Quarrying | - | - | - |
| 制造业 | Manufacturing | 10 991 | 187 107 | 170 236 |
| 电力、燃气及水的生产和供应业 | Power, Gas and Water Production and Supply | 267 | 3 440 | 79 439 |
| 建筑业 | Construction | 2 217 | 7 963 | 37 812 |
| 交通运输、仓储和邮政业 | Transportation, Logistics and Postal | 273 | 1 002 | 35 049 |
| 信息传输、软件和信息技术服务业 | Information transmission, software and information technology services | 13 | 116 | 88 846 |
| 批发和零售业 | Wholesale and Retail Trade Services | 1 002 | 3 586 | 36 410 |
| 住宿和餐饮业 | Accommodation and Catering Services | 1 526 | 4 031 | 27 517 |
| 金融业 | Financial Industries | 1 663 | 6 853 | 44 130 |
| 房地产业 | Real Estate | 615 | 4 666 | 74 891 |
| 租赁和商务服务业 | Renting and Labor Services | 280 | 1 363 | 47 495 |
| 科学研究和技术服务业 | Scientific Research and Technical Services | 649 | 3 349 | 46 572 |
| 水利、环境和公共设施管理业 | Water Conservancy, Environment and Public Facilities Management | 1 505 | 4 545 | 30 301 |
| 居民服务和其他服务业 | Residents Service and Other Service Trades | 21 | 45 | 21 381 |
| 教　育 | Education | 5 505 | 21 415 | 41 358 |
| 卫生和社会工作 | Health Care and Social Work | 3 877 | 17 895 | 48 339 |
| 文化、体育和娱乐业 | Culture, Sports and Entertainment | 616 | 1 317 | 21 733 |
| 公共管理和社会组织 | Public Administration and Social Organizations | 1 440 | 4 647 | 18 669 |

表2-23

# 市区各区城镇单位从业人员 (2012年末)
# URBAN EMPLOYMENT BY DISTRICT (END OF 2012)

单位：人 (person)

| 地 区 | Region | 在岗职工 Fully Employed Staff and Workers | 国有经济 State-owned Units | 城镇集体 Urban Collective-owned Units | 其他经济 Other Ownership Units | 其他从业人员 Other Employed Persons |
|---|---|---|---|---|---|---|
| **市 区** | **Urban Area** | **726 008** | **117 369** | **10 335** | **598 304** | **17 207** |
| 姑苏区 | Gusu District | 119 325 | 51 278 | 713 | 67 334 | 6 530 |
| 吴中区 | Wuzhong District | 76 330 | 19 141 | 1 995 | 55 194 | 2 445 |
| 相城区 | Xiangcheng District | 54 761 | 8 280 | 2 370 | 44 111 | 396 |
| 高新区、虎丘区 | New & Hi-tech Zone, Huqiu District | 105 289 | 6 175 | 747 | 98 367 | 2 738 |
| 工业园区 | Industrial Park | 255 314 | 8 579 | 1 194 | 245 541 | 3 503 |
| 吴江区 | Wujiang District | 114 989 | 23 916 | 3 316 | 87 757 | 1 595 |

表2-24

# 分地区城镇单位劳务派遣人员情况表 (2012年)
# STATISTICS ON LABOR DISPATCH PERSONS OF URBAN UNITS BY REGION (2012)

单位：人 (person)

| 地 区 | Region | 劳务派遣人员 Labor Dispatch Persons | 国有经济 State-owned Units | 城镇集体 Urban Collective-owned Units | 其他经济 Other Ownership Units |
|---|---|---|---|---|---|
| **全 市** | **Whole Municipality** | **215 651** | **12 234** | **2 211** | **201 206** |
| 市 区 | Urban Area | 154 169 | 9 163 | 216 | 144 790 |
| 姑苏区 | Gusu District | 23 095 | 5 100 | 156 | 17 839 |
| 吴中区 | Wuzhong District | 11 914 | 345 | - | 11 569 |
| 相城区 | Xiangcheng District | 12 917 | 104 | 60 | 12 753 |
| 高新区、虎丘区 | New & Hi-tech Zone, Huqiu District | 31 903 | 1 028 | - | 30 875 |
| 工业园区 | Industrial Park | 63 616 | 616 | - | 63 000 |
| 吴江区 | Wujiang District | 10 724 | 1 970 | - | 8 754 |
| 常 熟 | Changshu | 14 547 | 793 | - | 13 754 |
| 张家港 | Zhangjiagang | 6 604 | 819 | - | 5 785 |
| 昆 山 | Kunshan | 34 307 | 762 | 1 991 | 31 554 |
| 太 仓 | Taicang | 6 024 | 697 | 4 | 5 323 |

# 主要统计指标解释

**人口数** 指一定时点、一定地区范围内有生命的个人总和。年度统计的年末人口数指每年12月31日24时的人口数。

**出生率**(又称粗出生率) 指在一定时期内(通常为一年)一定地区的出生人数与同期内平均人数(或期中人数)之比，用千分率表示。本资料中的出生率指年出生率，其计算公式为：

$$出生率=\frac{年出生人数}{年平均人数}\times 1000‰$$

式中：出生人数指活产婴儿，即胎儿脱离母体时(不管怀孕月数)，有过呼吸或其他生命现象。年平均人数指年初、年底人口数的平均数，也可用年中人口数代替。

**死亡率**(又称粗死亡率) 指在一定时期内(通常为一年)一定地区的死亡人数与同期内平均人数(或期中人数)之比，用千分率表示。本资料中的死亡率指年死亡率，其计算公式为：

$$死亡率=\frac{年死亡人数}{年平均人数}\times 1000‰$$

**人口自然增长率** 指在一定时期内(通常为一年)人口自然增加数(出生人数减死亡人数)与该时期内平均人数(或期中人数)之比，用千分率表示。计算公式为：

$$人口自然增长率=\frac{本年出生人数-本年死亡人数}{年平均人数}\times 1000‰$$

$$=人口出生率-人口死亡率$$

**从业人员** 指在16周岁及以上，从事一定社会劳动并取得劳动报酬或经营收入的人员。这一指标反映了一定时期内全部劳动力资源的实际利用情况，是研究我国基本国情国力的重要指标。

**单位从业人员** 指在各级国家机关、政党机关、社会团体及企业、事业单位中工作，取得工资或其他形式的劳动报酬的全部人员。包括在岗职工、再就业的离退休人员、民办教师以及在各单位中工作的外方人员和港澳台方人员、兼职人员、借用的外单位人员和第二职业者。不包括离开本单位仍保留劳动关系的职工。各单位的就业人员反映了各单位实际参加生产或工作的全部劳动力。

**城镇私营和个体就业人员** 城镇私营就业人员指在工商管理部门注册登记，其经营地址设在县城关镇(含县城关镇)以上的私营企业就业人员，包括私营企业投资者和雇工。城镇个体就业人员指在工商管理部门注册登记，并持有城镇户口或在城镇长期居住，经批准从事个体工商经营的就业人员，包括个体经营者和在个体工商户劳动的家庭帮工和雇工。

**职工** 指在国有、城镇集体、联营、股份制、外商和港、澳、台投资、其他单位及其附属机构工作，并由其支付工资的各类人员。不包括下列人员：(1)乡镇企业就业人员；(2)私营企业就业人员；(3)城镇个体劳动者；(4)离休、退休、退职人员；(5)再就业的离、退休人员；(6)民办教师；(7)在城镇单位中工作的外方及港、澳、台人员；(8)其他按有关规定不列入职工统计范围的人员。(1998年及以后的数据均为在岗职工数据，其他相关指标如职工工资总额，职工平均工资等指标也从1998年按此口径进行了相应调整)。

**国有单位** 指资产归国家所有的经济组织。包括按《中华人民共和国企业法人登记管理条例》规定登记注册的非公司制的经济组织，以及中央、地方各级国家机关、事业单位和社会团体。

**集体单位** 指生产资料归集体所有，并按《中华人民共和国企业法人登记管理条例》规定登记注册的经济组织。

**其他单位** 包括股份合作单位、联营单位、有限责任公司、股份有限公司、港澳台商投资单位以及外商投资单位等其他登记注册类型单位。

**在岗职工**　指在本单位工作并由单位支付工资的人员，以及有工作岗位，但由于学习、病伤产假等原因暂未工作，仍由单位支付工资的人员。

**工资总额**　指各单位在一定时期内直接支付给本单位全部职工的劳动报酬总额。工资总额的计算原则应以直接支付给职工的全部劳动报酬为依据。各单位支付给职工的劳动报酬以及其他根据有关规定支付的工资，不论是计入成本的还是不计入成本的，不论是按国家规定列入计征奖金税项目的，还是未列入计征奖金税项目的，不论是以货币形式支付的还是以实物形式支付的，均包括在工资总额内。

**平均工资**　指企业、事业、机关单位的职工在一定时期内平均每人所得的货币工资额。它表明一定时期职工工资收入的高低程度，是反映职工工资水平的主要指标。计算公式为:

$$平均工资=\frac{报告期实际支付的全部职工工资总额}{报告期全部职工平均人数}$$

**城镇单位就业人员劳动报酬**　指各单位在一定时期内直接支付给本单位全部就业人员的劳动报酬总额。包括职工工资总额和其他就业人员劳动报酬总额。

**平均劳动报酬**　指企业、事业、机关等单位的全部就业人员在一定时期内平均每人所得的劳动报酬。

计算公式为：

$$平均劳动报酬=\frac{\begin{array}{c}报告期实际支付的全部\\就业人员劳动报酬\end{array}}{报告期全部就业人员平均人数}$$

**劳务派遣人员**　根据《中华人民共和国劳动合同法》规定，指与劳务派遣单位签订劳动合同，并被劳务派遣单位派遣到实际用工单位工作，且劳务派遣单位与实际用工单位签订《劳务派遣协议》的人员。

注意：无论用工单位是否直接支付劳动报酬，劳务派遣人员均由实际用工单位填报，而劳务派遣单位(派出单位)不填报这些人员。

# EXPLANATORY NOTES ON MAIN STATISTICAL INDICATORS

**Total Population** refers to the total number of people alive at a certain point of time within a given area. The annual statistics on total population is taken at midnight, the 31st of December.

**Birth Rate (or Crude Birth Rate)** refers to the ratio of the number of births to the average population (or mid-period population) during a certain period of time (usually a year), expressed in ‰. Birth rate in the chapter refers to annual birth rate. The following formula is used:

$$\text{Birth Rate} = \frac{\text{Number of Births}}{\text{Annual Average Population}} \times 1000‰$$

Number of births in the formula refers to live births, i.e. when a baby has breathed or showed any vital phenomena regardless of the length of pregnancy.

Annual average population is the average of the number of population at the beginning of the year and that at the end of the year. Sometimes it is substituted by the mid-year population.

**Death Rate (or Crude Death Rate)** refers to the ratio of the number of deaths to the average population (or mid-period population) during a certain period of time (usually a year), expressed in ‰. Death rate in the chapter refers to annual death rate. The following formula is used:

$$\text{Death Rate} = \frac{\text{Number of Deaths}}{\text{Annual Average Population}} \times 1000‰$$

**Natural Growth Rate of Population** refers to the ratio of natural increase in population (number of births minus number of deaths) in a certain period of time (usually a year) to the average population (or mid-period population) of the same period, expressed in ‰. The following formula is applied:

= Birth Rate-Death Rate

$$\text{Natural Growth Rate of Population} = \frac{\text{Number of Births - Number of Deaths}}{\text{Annual Average Population}} \times 1000‰$$

**Employed Persons** refer to persons aged 16 and over who are engaged in gainful employment and thus receive remuneration payment or earn business income. This indicator reflects the actual utilization of total labor force during a certain period of time and is often used for the research on China's economic situation and national power.

**Persons Employed in Various Units** refer to all the persons working in government agencies of various levels, political and party organizations, social organizations, enterprises and institutions, and receiving wages or other forms of payment. They include fully-employed staff and workers, re-employed retirees, teachers in the schools run by the local people, foreigners and Chinese compatriots from Hong Kong, Macao, and Taiwan working in various units, part-time employees, employees of other units working temporarily at current posts, and employees holding the second job, but do not include persons who have left their working units while keeping their labor contract (employment relation) unchanged. This indicator reflects the total number of laborers actually engaged in production or other operations in various units.

**Persons Employed in Private Enterprises and Self-Employed Individuals in Urban Areas** Persons employed in private enterprises refer to the persons employed in the private enterprises which have been registered at the departments of industrial and commercial administration for which the business operation are situated at a county town (i.e. a town where the county government is located), or at urban areas with administrative hierarchy higher than a county town. The self-employed individuals in urban areas refer to persons who hold the certificates of residence in urban areas or have resided in the urban areas for a long time and have been registered at the departments of industrial and commercial administration and approved to be engaged in individual industrial or commercial business, including self-employed persons as well as helpers and hired labourers who work in individual households.

**Staff and Workers** refer to persons working in, and receive payment from units of state ownership, collective ownership, joint ownership, share holding ownership, foreign ownership, and ownership by entrepreneurs from Hong Kong, Macao, and Taiwan, and other types of ownership and their affiliated units. They do not include 1) persons employed in township enterprises, 2) persons employed in private enterprises, 3) urban self-employed persons, 4) retirees, 5) re-employed retirees, 6) teachers in the schools run by the local people, 7) foreigners and persons from Hong Kong, Macao and Taiwan who work in urban units, and 8) other persons not to be included by relevant regulations. (Data since 1998 refer to fully employed staff and workers. Other related statistics indicators, such as total wage bill and average wage are adjusted since 1998 accordingly).

**State-owned Units** refer to economic units whose assets are owned by the state, including non-corporation units registered according to *Regulation of the People's Republic of China on the Registration of Enterprises and Corporations*, state organs, institutions and social organizations at the central-level and local levels.

**Collective-owned Units** refer to economic units registered according to *Regulation of the People's Republic of China on the Registration of Enterprises and Corporations* where the means of production are collectively owned.

**Units of Other Types of Ownership** refer to units registered with other types of ownership, including cooperative units, joint ownership units, limited liability corporations, share holding corporations, units funded by entrepreneurs from Hong Kong, Macao, and Taiwan, and foreign- funded units.

**Employed Staff and Workers** refer to persons who work in, and receive wages from their working units, including persons who have their work posts but are temporarily absent from work for reasons of study or on sick, injury or maternal leave and still receive wages from their working units.

**Total Wage Bill** refers to the total remuneration payment to staff and workers in various units during a certain period of time. The calculation of total wage bill is based on the total remuneration payment to the staff and workers. Therefore, all the wages and salaries and other payments to staff and workers are included in the total wage bill regardless of sources, reckoning the cost of production or not, category, listing as items of premium taxation or not, and forms, paying in cash or in kind.

**Average Wage** refers to the average wage in money terms per person during a certain period of time for staff and workers in enterprises, institutions, and government agencies, which reflects the general level of wage income during a certain period of time and is calculated as follows:

$$\text{Average Wage} = \frac{\text{Total Wage Bill of Staff and Workers at Reference Time}}{\text{Average Number of Staff and Workers at Reference Time}}$$

**Earning** refer to total remuneration payment to all employees in various units in urban areas (did not include urban private units and self-employed individuals) during a certain period of time, including staff and workers and other employees (i.e., reemployed retirees or those who are from Hong Kong, Macao, Taiwan province or other countries).

**Average Earning** refer to average earning level in money terms per employee in the enterprise, institution and government organ during a certain period of time, it is calculated as follows:

$$\text{Average Earning Of Employees} = \frac{\text{Total Earnings of Employees at Reference Period}}{\text{Average Number of Employees at Reference Period}}$$

**Labor Dispatch Persons** According to the *Labor Contract Law of the People's Republic of China*, refer to persons who sign labor contracts with labor dispatch units, and was sent to the actual employment units, and the labor dispatch units and actual employment units had signed *Labor Dispatch Agreement.*

Note: regardless of whether the actual employment units paid labor remuneration, labor dispatch persons were filled by the actual employment units, while the labor dispatch units ( sending units ) didn't fill these persons.

# 三、农 业

# CHAPTER 3
# AGRICULTURE

# 农 业
# AGRICULTURE

## 主要统计指标
## MAJOR STATISTICAL INDICATORS

| | | | | |
|---|---|---|---|---|
| 2012年末乡村实有从业人员 | Rural Real Employed persons | 179.54 | 万人 | 10 000 persons |
| 比上年增长 | Increase Over Last Year | -2.8 | % | |
| 2012年农作物播种面积 | Sown Areas Of Farm Crops | 263.07 | 千公顷 | |
| 比上年增长 | Increase Over Last Year | -1.2 | % | |
| 2012年农林牧渔业总产值 | Gross Output Value of Farming, Forestry, Animal Husbandry and Fishery | 337.72 | 亿元 | 100 million yuan |
| 比上年增长 | Increase Over Last Year | 9.0 | % | |
| 2012年农林牧渔业总产值(可比价格) | Gross Output Value of Farming, Forestry, Animal Husbandry and Fishery (at Comparable Price) | 322.67 | 亿元 | 100 million yuan |
| 比上年增长 | Increase Over Last Year | 4.1 | % | |
| 2012年农林牧渔业增加值 | Value Added of Farming, Forestry, Animal Husbandry and Fishery | 195.08 | 亿元 | 100 million yuan |
| 比上年增长 | Increase Over Last Year | 4.5 | % | |
| 2012年粮食总产量 | Total Yield of Grain Crops | 116.46 | 万吨 | 10 000 tons |
| 比上年增长 | Increase Over Last Year | 1.3 | % | |

表3-1

# 部分年份农村基本情况
# BASIC CONDITIONS OF COUNTRYSIDE OF PARTIAL YEARS

| 项　目 | Item | 1990年 | 2000年 | 2010年 | 2011年 | 2012年 |
|---|---|---|---|---|---|---|
| **农村组织 (个)** | **Village Units (unit)** | | | | | |
| 镇政府 | Town Governments | 166 | 130 | 60 | 58 | 55 |
| 村民委员会 | Number of Villagers' Committees | 3 371 | 2 833 | 1 097 | 1 097 | 1 068 |
| 村民小组 | Villager Group | 38 156 | 36 465 | 28 512 | 27 932 | 27 514 |
| **乡村户数、人口** | **Households and Rural Population** | | | | | |
| 乡村总户数 (万户) | Number of Households (10 000 households) | 127.32 | 119.79 | 97.63 | 94.11 | 91.42 |
| 乡村总人口 (万人) | Rural Population (10 000 persons) | 433.04 | 377.49 | 319.37 | 305.02 | 296.41 |
| **年末乡村实有从业人员** | **Rural Employees of year-end** | | | | | |
| 合　计 | Total | 260.51 | 213.75 | 190.42 | 184.77 | 179.54 |
| 1.按性别分 | Grouped by Sex | | | | | |
| 男劳动力 | Male | 130.26 | 107.22 | 96.77 | 95.78 | 92.84 |
| 女劳动力 | Female | 130.25 | 106.53 | 93.65 | 88.99 | 86.70 |
| 2.按行业分 | Grouped by Sector | | | | | |
| 农林牧渔业 | Farming, Forestry, Animal Husbandry and Fishery | 100.44 | 64.16 | 26.82 | 24.97 | 24.22 |
| 农　业 | Farming | 84.28 | 53.01 | 17.24 | 15.91 | 15.40 |
| 林牧渔业 | Forestry, Animal Husbandry and Fishery | 16.16 | 11.15 | 9.58 | 9.06 | 8.82 |
| 工　业 | Industry | 104.08 | 92.82 | 111.90 | 109.50 | 106.84 |
| 建筑业 | Construction | 17.34 | 13.34 | 11.03 | 10.65 | 10.28 |
| 交通运输、邮电业 | Transportation, Postal and Telecommunications Services | 7.71 | 6.50 | 5.66 | 5.64 | 5.62 |
| 贸易、餐饮业 | Trade and Catering | 3.86 | 9.91 | 13.99 | 14.69 | 14.75 |
| 金融保险业 | Banking and Insurance | 0.16 | 0.25 | 0.58 | 0.70 | 0.77 |
| 房地产、社会服务业 | Real Estate and Social Services | 1.43 | 1.87 | 2.57 | 2.60 | 2.55 |
| 卫生、体育、社会福利业 | Health Care, Sporting and Social Welfare | 0.81 | 0.82 | 0.99 | 0.96 | 0.95 |
| 文、教、艺术和广播影视业 | Culture, Education and Arts, Radio, Film and Television | 1.04 | 0.65 | 0.78 | 0.84 | 0.87 |
| 科研和综合技术服务业 | Scientific Research and Polytechnical Services | 0.18 | 0.18 | 0.21 | 0.23 | 0.20 |
| 乡镇经济组织管理 | Rural Economic Management | 1.96 | 1.73 | 1.28 | 1.26 | 1.20 |
| 其　他 | Others | 21.50 | 21.52 | 14.61 | 12.73 | 11.29 |

表3-2

# 历年年末乡村实有从业人员

# RURAL REAL EMPLOYED PERSONS OVER THE YEARS (YEAR-END)

单位：万人 (10 000 persons)

| 年 份<br>Year | 全 市<br>Whole Municipality | 市 区<br>Urban Area | # 吴江区<br>Wujiang District | 常 熟<br>Changshu | 张家港<br>Zhangjiagang | 昆 山<br>Kunshan | 太 仓<br>Taicang |
|---|---|---|---|---|---|---|---|
| 1949 | 124.93 | 45.96 | 17.08 | 30.24 | 20.54 | 12.66 | 15.53 |
| 1952 | 130.35 | 48.80 | 17.87 | 30.47 | 20.79 | 14.74 | 15.55 |
| 1957 | 146.38 | 57.93 | 22.31 | 32.48 | 24.60 | 16.07 | 15.30 |
| 1962 | 150.22 | 60.28 | 20.73 | 33.87 | 23.51 | 15.72 | 16.84 |
| 1965 | 176.82 | 72.24 | 24.23 | 38.71 | 28.78 | 18.21 | 18.88 |
| 1970 | 222.22 | 92.13 | 32.71 | 48.02 | 36.45 | 23.91 | 21.71 |
| 1975 | 233.63 | 97.64 | 34.39 | 49.47 | 36.77 | 25.55 | 24.20 |
| 1978 | 244.55 | 98.51 | 34.76 | 52.83 | 41.78 | 26.30 | 25.13 |
| 1980 | 250.74 | 103.00 | 36.76 | 54.20 | 40.94 | 26.83 | 25.77 |
| 1985 | 269.24 | 112.57 | 39.61 | 57.10 | 44.62 | 30.19 | 24.76 |
| 1990 | 260.51 | 113.95 | 40.59 | 57.44 | 37.52 | 29.69 | 21.91 |
| 1991 | 255.26 | 111.91 | 40.13 | 55.34 | 36.85 | 29.43 | 21.73 |
| 1992 | 250.43 | 110.79 | 39.36 | 53.78 | 35.44 | 28.99 | 21.43 |
| 1993 | 238.98 | 102.69 | 38.93 | 52.56 | 34.42 | 28.20 | 21.11 |
| 1994 | 234.89 | 102.16 | 38.54 | 52.18 | 33.55 | 26.10 | 20.90 |
| 1995 | 230.96 | 101.07 | 37.77 | 50.02 | 32.96 | 26.29 | 20.62 |
| 1996 | 228.45 | 99.29 | 37.14 | 50.97 | 32.11 | 26.06 | 20.02 |
| 1997 | 224.83 | 98.27 | 36.06 | 49.43 | 32.05 | 25.36 | 19.72 |
| 1998 | 223.14 | 98.79 | 35.63 | 48.67 | 31.90 | 24.73 | 19.05 |
| 1999 | 219.42 | 96.90 | 34.56 | 50.43 | 31.40 | 23.19 | 17.50 |
| 2000 | 213.75 | 95.34 | 33.22 | 49.76 | 30.17 | 22.16 | 16.32 |
| 2001 | 212.22 | 95.50 | 32.13 | 49.47 | 30.16 | 21.52 | 15.57 |
| 2002 | 210.55 | 94.36 | 31.85 | 49.37 | 30.20 | 21.29 | 15.33 |
| 2003 | 209.42 | 92.50 | 30.88 | 49.96 | 30.35 | 21.33 | 15.28 |
| 2004 | 207.60 | 90.48 | 32.04 | 49.24 | 30.60 | 22.30 | 14.98 |
| 2005 | 207.20 | 89.88 | 31.99 | 48.83 | 30.54 | 23.14 | 14.81 |
| 2006 | 206.90 | 88.59 | 32.36 | 48.52 | 30.92 | 22.73 | 16.14 |
| 2007 | 205.49 | 89.90 | 32.81 | 44.63 | 31.14 | 22.96 | 16.86 |
| 2008 | 205.94 | 89.76 | 32.40 | 43.87 | 33.10 | 22.60 | 16.61 |
| 2009 | 199.99 | 84.68 | 32.25 | 42.92 | 33.49 | 22.47 | 16.43 |
| 2010 | 190.42 | 74.88 | 31.98 | 42.42 | 33.68 | 22.50 | 16.94 |
| 2011 | 184.77 | 73.31 | 32.67 | 40.89 | 32.55 | 21.39 | 16.63 |
| 2012 | 179.54 | 70.82 | 31.71 | 39.74 | 31.61 | 21.21 | 16.16 |

表3-3

# 历年农林牧渔业总产值
# GROSS OUTPUT VALUE OF FARMING, FORESTRY, ANIMAL HUSBANDRY AND FISHERY OVER THE YEARS

单位：万元 (10 000 yuan)

| 年 份 Year | 总产值 Gross Output Value | 农 业 Farming | # 种植业 Planting | 林 业 Forestry | 牧 业 Animal Husbandry | 渔 业 Fishery | 农林牧渔服务业 Farming,Forestry,Animal Husbandry,Fishery and Service Industry |
|---|---|---|---|---|---|---|---|
| 1978 | 187 469 | 163 707 | 163 015 | 557 | 18 837 | 4 368 | |
| 1979 | 193 422 | 162 903 | 162 044 | 582 | 25 343 | 4 594 | |
| 1980 | 114 163 | 83 915 | 82 812 | 720 | 23 600 | 5 928 | |
| 1981 | 145 188 | 114 309 | 112 962 | 740 | 22 036 | 8 103 | |
| 1982 | 182 166 | 132 412 | 129 889 | 1 866 | 34 782 | 13 106 | |
| 1983 | 186 438 | 137 668 | 133 575 | 2 239 | 34 090 | 12 441 | |
| 1984 | 253 046 | 190 348 | 170 909 | 3 075 | 43 058 | 16 565 | |
| 1985 | 274 220 | 171 637 | 148 084 | 3 091 | 62 215 | 37 277 | |
| 1986 | 325 440 | 202 286 | 169 216 | 3 791 | 63 300 | 56 063 | |
| 1987 | 375 729 | 226 423 | 179 219 | 4 275 | 82 410 | 62 621 | |
| 1988 | 477 125 | 284 236 | 226 902 | 4 399 | 104 269 | 84 221 | |
| 1989 | 502 225 | 300 561 | 245 598 | 4 019 | 111 139 | 86 506 | |
| 1990 | 581 222 | 349 554 | 290 067 | 5 025 | 119 400 | 107 243 | |
| 1991 | 586 831 | 364 221 | 298 524 | 4 698 | 115 081 | 102 831 | |
| 1992 | 687 303 | 443 730 | 324 601 | 7 740 | 123 611 | 112 222 | |
| 1993 | 867 634 | 560 735 | 410 256 | 7 712 | 154 676 | 144 511 | |
| 1994 | 1 274 976 | 804 597 | 618 022 | 9 990 | 248 916 | 211 473 | |
| 1995 | 1 416 173 | 918 417 | 697 111 | 9 834 | 233 110 | 254 812 | |
| 1996 | 1 625 939 | 1 077 094 | 779 714 | 6 725 | 242 010 | 300 110 | |
| 1997 | 1 650 915 | 1 071 369 | 751 572 | 9 011 | 231 268 | 339 267 | |
| 1998 | 1 654 137 | 1 047 069 | 693 739 | 8 789 | 239 493 | 358 786 | |
| 1999 | 1 647 033 | 1 012 489 | 630 165 | 11 583 | 224 721 | 398 240 | |
| 2000 | 1 692 982 | 1 001 634 | 610 779 | 11 740 | 231 251 | 448 357 | |
| 2001 | 1 734 596 | 962 669 | 562 869 | 27 485 | 247 416 | 497 026 | |
| 2002 | 1 744 598 | 901 031 | 516 749 | 43 046 | 245 472 | 555 049 | |
| 2003 | 1 562 657 | 561 773 | 561 773 | 38 031 | 232 988 | 547 683 | 182 182 |
| 2004 | 1 639 627 | 589 162 | 589 162 | 50 311 | 249 959 | 562 791 | 187 404 |
| 2005 | 1 628 655 | 577 417 | 577 417 | 63 554 | 217 068 | 594 059 | 176 557 |
| 2006 | 1 721 844 | 663 120 | 663 120 | 72 351 | 214 312 | 601 890 | 170 171 |
| 2007 | 1 810 817 | 663 883 | 663 883 | 86 189 | 274 583 | 609 590 | 176 572 |
| 2008 | 2 334 155 | 878 179 | 878 179 | 126 262 | 330 251 | 727 964 | 271 499 |
| 2009 | 2 489 315 | 940 627 | 940 627 | 147 646 | 347 466 | 785 044 | 268 532 |
| 2010 | 2 712 943 | 1 052 848 | 1 052 848 | 161 828 | 357 452 | 853 943 | 286 872 |
| 2011 | 3 098 576 | 1 210 220 | 1 210 220 | 179 825 | 411 440 | 978 319 | 318 772 |
| 2012 | 3 377 237 | 1 350 458 | 1 350 458 | 204 834 | 402 031 | 1 066 347 | 353 567 |

注：2008年数据根据农业普查、经济普查已作调整。 Note:The 2008 data were adjusted according to the agricultural census and the economic census.

表3-4

# 历年粮食、棉花、油料播种面积
# SOWN AREAS OF GRAIN CROPS, COTTON AND OIL-BEARING CROPS OVER THE YEARS

单位：千公顷 (1 000 hectares)

| 年 份 Year | 粮 食 Grain Crops | 夏 粮 Summer Grain | 秋 粮 Autumn Grain | 棉 花 Cotton | 油 料 Oil-bearing Crops | #油菜籽 Rapeseeds |
|---|---|---|---|---|---|---|
| 1949 | 527.02 | 193.56 | 333.46 | 44.58 | 39.95 | 39.25 |
| 1952 | 562.96 | 220.65 | 342.31 | 61.73 | 46.19 | 45.57 |
| 1957 | 593.95 | 238.15 | 355.80 | 46.05 | 45.46 | 44.81 |
| 1962 | 505.48 | 199.85 | 305.63 | 41.46 | 34.31 | 33.49 |
| 1965 | 499.19 | 188.97 | 310.22 | 47.56 | 37.92 | 37.41 |
| 1970 | 598.12 | 185.07 | 413.05 | 46.50 | 41.72 | 41.59 |
| 1975 | 644.58 | 181.05 | 463.53 | 48.30 | 46.23 | 46.19 |
| 1978 | 636.61 | 179.59 | 457.02 | 47.76 | 47.89 | 47.77 |
| 1980 | 600.83 | 178.75 | 422.08 | 47.39 | 51.46 | 51.38 |
| 1985 | 500.49 | 197.12 | 303.37 | 44.50 | 90.11 | 89.95 |
| 1990 | 471.29 | 197.89 | 273.40 | 33.21 | 74.23 | 74.05 |
| 1991 | 458.37 | 192.35 | 266.02 | 30.81 | 74.46 | 74.23 |
| 1992 | 444.77 | 187.66 | 257.11 | 30.92 | 73.20 | 72.98 |
| 1993 | 413.07 | 170.52 | 242.55 | 26.91 | 62.58 | 62.15 |
| 1994 | 407.58 | 161.96 | 245.62 | 25.33 | 63.86 | 63.59 |
| 1995 | 398.73 | 159.41 | 239.32 | 25.40 | 67.17 | 66.84 |
| 1996 | 399.25 | 157.88 | 241.37 | 21.06 | 68.06 | 67.78 |
| 1997 | 401.03 | 159.45 | 241.58 | 14.87 | 62.63 | 62.37 |
| 1998 | 371.31 | 145.58 | 225.73 | 16.22 | 61.84 | 61.55 |
| 1999 | 343.52 | 129.87 | 213.65 | 13.33 | 58.92 | 58.37 |
| 2000 | 290.33 | 105.93 | 184.40 | 11.29 | 61.56 | 60.82 |
| 2001 | 234.05 | 76.29 | 157.76 | 11.92 | 58.49 | 57.70 |
| 2002 | 219.07 | 75.52 | 143.55 | 7.63 | 52.43 | 51.69 |
| 2003 | 173.56 | 60.72 | 112.84 | 6.58 | 39.42 | 38.85 |
| 2004 | 167.61 | 51.21 | 116.40 | 6.35 | 31.64 | 31.12 |
| 2005 | 169.85 | 54.28 | 115.57 | 4.46 | 33.22 | 32.67 |
| 2006 | 163.26 | 58.63 | 104.63 | 2.97 | 27.86 | 27.41 |
| 2007 | 153.45 | 59.71 | 93.74 | 2.39 | 28.02 | 27.62 |
| 2008 | 162.43 | 65.21 | 97.22 | 2.37 | 17.70 | 17.11 |
| 2009 | 160.07 | 65.56 | 94.51 | 2.02 | 19.49 | 18.90 |
| 2010 | 161.72 | 70.10 | 91.62 | 1.59 | 14.47 | 13.95 |
| 2011 | 159.65 | 70.15 | 89.50 | 1.39 | 11.65 | 11.04 |
| 2012 | 159.66 | 71.31 | 88.35 | 1.18 | 10.09 | 9.53 |

表3-5

# 历年粮食、棉花、油料总产量
# TOTAL YIELD OF GRAIN CROPS, COTTON AND OIL-BEARING CROPS OVER THE YEARS

| 年份 Year | 粮食 (万吨) Grain Crops (10 000 tons) | 夏粮 Summer Grain | 秋粮 Autumn Grain | 棉花 (吨) Cotton (ton) | 油料 (吨) Oil-bearing Crops (ton) | # 油菜籽 Rapeseeds |
|---|---|---|---|---|---|---|
| 1949 | 84.01 | 8.98 | 75.03 | 4 450 | 14 420 | 14 130 |
| 1952 | 133.41 | 16.81 | 116.60 | 14 810 | 24 950 | 24 080 |
| 1957 | 135.69 | 20.73 | 114.96 | 16 490 | 26 410 | 25 430 |
| 1962 | 152.32 | 31.09 | 121.23 | 14 560 | 17 250 | 16 660 |
| 1965 | 210.32 | 40.55 | 169.77 | 40 820 | 41 120 | 39 360 |
| 1970 | 223.62 | 38.27 | 185.35 | 35 880 | 57 060 | 56 300 |
| 1975 | 241.87 | 42.96 | 198.91 | 37 350 | 55 780 | 55 460 |
| 1978 | 294.26 | 66.70 | 227.56 | 36 330 | 91 320 | 90 610 |
| 1980 | 254.31 | 75.64 | 178.67 | 35 180 | 81 620 | 81 120 |
| 1985 | 238.49 | 59.02 | 179.47 | 42 600 | 141 020 | 140 480 |
| 1990 | 283.50 | 75.74 | 207.76 | 36 932 | 140 129 | 139 760 |
| 1991 | 274.92 | 66.75 | 208.17 | 42 202 | 140 690 | 140 257 |
| 1992 | 282.55 | 80.38 | 202.17 | 35 415 | 149 597 | 149 026 |
| 1993 | 263.58 | 70.36 | 193.22 | 25 191 | 118 139 | 117 415 |
| 1994 | 262.88 | 64.19 | 198.69 | 35 945 | 89 575 | 88 731 |
| 1995 | 265.67 | 66.26 | 199.41 | 40 210 | 145 608 | 144 798 |
| 1996 | 279.10 | 70.06 | 209.04 | 36 594 | 146 606 | 145 861 |
| 1997 | 279.93 | 70.24 | 209.69 | 22 725 | 130 213 | 129 464 |
| 1998 | 239.63 | 36.57 | 203.06 | 24 284 | 56 462 | 55 702 |
| 1999 | 225.84 | 53.21 | 172.62 | 9 349 | 123 902 | 122 441 |
| 2000 | 193.95 | 40.61 | 153.34 | 11 722 | 126 066 | 123 917 |
| 2001 | 159.48 | 23.93 | 135.55 | 12 976 | 102 529 | 100 106 |
| 2002 | 146.42 | 22.30 | 124.12 | 7 527 | 78 093 | 75 896 |
| 2003 | 112.77 | 17.90 | 94.87 | 6 816 | 62 418 | 60 347 |
| 2004 | 117.71 | 20.44 | 97.27 | 7 450 | 69 234 | 67 387 |
| 2005 | 110.76 | 22.76 | 88.00 | 4 605 | 69 593 | 68 143 |
| 2006 | 111.21 | 24.38 | 86.83 | 3 117 | 63 019 | 61 779 |
| 2007 | 94.14 | 24.66 | 69.48 | 2 459 | 64 107 | 62 980 |
| 2008 | 113.22 | 31.39 | 81.83 | 2 525 | 42 571 | 40 884 |
| 2009 | 112.94 | 30.84 | 82.10 | 2 135 | 46 632 | 44 991 |
| 2010 | 114.43 | 33.12 | 81.31 | 1 685 | 34 468 | 33 052 |
| 2011 | 115.00 | 34.92 | 80.08 | 1 508 | 28 907 | 27 352 |
| 2012 | 116.46 | 36.71 | 79.75 | 1 292 | 25 882 | 24 354 |

表3-6

# 历年粮食、棉花、油料单产

# YIELD OF GRAIN CROPS, COTTON AND OIL-BEARING CROPS PER HECTARE OVER THE YEARS

单位：公斤/公顷 (kg/hectare)

| 年 份 Year | 粮 食 Grain Crops | 夏 粮 Summer Grain | 秋 粮 Autumn Grain | 棉 花 Cotton | 油 料 Oil-bearing Crops | # 油菜籽 Rapeseeds |
|---|---|---|---|---|---|---|
| 1949 | 1 594 | 464 | 2 250 | 100 | 361 | 360 |
| 1952 | 2 370 | 762 | 3 406 | 240 | 540 | 528 |
| 1957 | 2 285 | 870 | 3 231 | 358 | 581 | 568 |
| 1962 | 3 013 | 1 556 | 3 967 | 351 | 503 | 497 |
| 1965 | 4 213 | 2 146 | 5 473 | 858 | 1 084 | 1 052 |
| 1970 | 3 739 | 2 068 | 4 487 | 772 | 1 368 | 1 354 |
| 1975 | 3 752 | 2 373 | 4 291 | 773 | 1 261 | 1 201 |
| 1978 | 4 022 | 3 714 | 4 979 | 761 | 1 907 | 1 897 |
| 1980 | 4 233 | 4 232 | 4 233 | 742 | 1 586 | 1 579 |
| 1985 | 4 765 | 2 994 | 5 916 | 957 | 1 565 | 1 562 |
| 1990 | 6 015 | 3 825 | 7 605 | 1 112 | 1 888 | 1 887 |
| 1991 | 6 000 | 3 465 | 7 803 | 1 370 | 1 889 | 1 889 |
| 1992 | 6 353 | 4 283 | 7 863 | 1 145 | 2 044 | 2 042 |
| 1993 | 6 381 | 4 126 | 7 966 | 936 | 1 888 | 1 889 |
| 1994 | 6 450 | 3 964 | 8 089 | 1 419 | 1 403 | 1 395 |
| 1995 | 6 663 | 4 157 | 8 332 | 1 583 | 2 168 | 2 166 |
| 1996 | 6 990 | 4 437 | 8 661 | 1 738 | 2 154 | 2 152 |
| 1997 | 6 980 | 4 405 | 8 680 | 1 528 | 2 079 | 2 076 |
| 1998 | 6 454 | 2 512 | 8 996 | 1 497 | 913 | 905 |
| 1999 | 6 574 | 4 097 | 8 080 | 701 | 2 103 | 2 098 |
| 2000 | 6 680 | 3 833 | 8 316 | 1 038 | 2 048 | 2 037 |
| 2001 | 6 814 | 3 137 | 8 592 | 1 089 | 1 753 | 1 735 |
| 2002 | 6 684 | 2 953 | 8 646 | 987 | 1 489 | 1 468 |
| 2003 | 6 497 | 2 974 | 8 408 | 1 036 | 1 583 | 1 553 |
| 2004 | 7 023 | 3 991 | 8 356 | 1 173 | 2 188 | 2 165 |
| 2005 | 6 521 | 4 193 | 7 615 | 1 033 | 2 095 | 2 086 |
| 2006 | 6 812 | 4 159 | 8 299 | 1 051 | 2 262 | 2 254 |
| 2007 | 6 135 | 4 131 | 7 412 | 1 029 | 2 288 | 2 280 |
| 2008 | 6 970 | 4 813 | 8 417 | 1 065 | 2 405 | 2 389 |
| 2009 | 7 055 | 4 704 | 8 686 | 1 057 | 2 393 | 2 380 |
| 2010 | 7 076 | 4 725 | 8 874 | 1 060 | 2 382 | 2 369 |
| 2011 | 7 203 | 4 977 | 8 948 | 1 085 | 2 481 | 2 478 |
| 2012 | 7 294 | 5 148 | 9 027 | 1 095 | 2 565 | 2 556 |

表3-7

# 历年蚕桑、茶叶、水果生产情况
# STATISTICS ON SILKWORM COCOONS, TEA AND FRUITS OVER THE YEARS

| 年 份 Year | 蚕 桑 Silkworm Cocoons and Mulberry | | 茶 叶 Tea | | 水 果 Fruits | |
|---|---|---|---|---|---|---|
| | 桑园面积 (公顷) Mulberry Field Area (hectare) | 蚕茧产量 (吨) Output of Silkworm Cocoons (ton) | 茶园面积 (公顷) Tea Field Area (hectare) | 总产量 (吨) Total Output (ton) | 果园面积 (公顷) Area of Orchards (hectare) | 总产量 (吨) Total Output (ton) |
| 1949 | 7 051 | 1 797 | 117 | 66 | 1 096 | 6 785 |
| 1952 | 7 360 | 3 047 | 117 | 77 | 1 184 | 7 584 |
| 1957 | 7 191 | 2 510 | 121 | 47 | 1 321 | 8 257 |
| 1962 | 5 843 | 943 | 208 | 90 | 1 517 | 12 213 |
| 1965 | 5 745 | 1 917 | 212 | 137 | 1 599 | 16 236 |
| 1970 | 7 051 | 4 520 | 210 | 190 | 1 706 | 19 039 |
| 1975 | 7 046 | 4 340 | 314 | 261 | 2 098 | 23 357 |
| 1978 | 6 115 | 3 325 | 393 | 286 | 2 440 | 18 653 |
| 1980 | 6 065 | 4 784 | 401 | 286 | 2 778 | 17 407 |
| 1985 | 6 868 | 5 663 | 417 | 265 | 5 771 | 39 113 |
| 1990 | 7 973 | 9 785 | 360 | 369 | 4 853 | 42 280 |
| 1991 | 10 747 | 9 040 | 353 | 369 | 4 567 | 47 844 |
| 1992 | 11 795 | 12 077 | 353 | 337 | 6 558 | 37 098 |
| 1993 | 12 846 | 17 414 | 381 | 352 | 6 550 | 58 367 |
| 1994 | 12 301 | 16 356 | 410 | 288 | 6 947 | 45 467 |
| 1995 | 9 275 | 12 435 | 421 | 262 | 6 796 | 62 096 |
| 1996 | 7 092 | 9 805 | 422 | 274 | 6 070 | 56 155 |
| 1997 | 7 967 | 9 020 | 376 | 247 | 5 838 | 69 391 |
| 1998 | 7 583 | 8 669 | 411 | 253 | 5 862 | 44 250 |
| 1999 | 6 834 | 8 170 | 409 | 259 | 5 785 | 75 120 |
| 2000 | 6 188 | 7 291 | 469 | 258 | 6 080 | 59 203 |
| 2001 | 6 090 | 7 397 | 570 | 249 | 6 286 | 78 523 |
| 2002 | 5 333 | 5 785 | 679 | 235 | 6 523 | 67 918 |
| 2003 | 4 164 | 3 437 | 1 530 | 399 | 6 554 | 79 307 |
| 2004 | 3 918 | 3 512 | 1 815 | 315 | 6 191 | 73 084 |
| 2005 | 3 895 | 2 771 | 1 955 | 348 | 6 708 | 74 138 |
| 2006 | 3 881 | 3 008 | 2 106 | 381 | 7 029 | 76 023 |
| 2007 | 3 879 | 2 478 | 2 120 | 385 | 7 554 | 79 767 |
| 2008 | 3 853 | 1 654 | 2 207 | 397 | 8 712 | 91 102 |
| 2009 | 3 745 | 915 | 2 296 | 403 | 9 627 | 103 064 |
| 2010 | 3 618 | 638 | 2 344 | 338 | 10 214 | 96 953 |
| 2011 | 3 474 | 558 | 2 400 | 349 | 10 791 | 103 082 |
| 2012 | 3 601 | 495 | 2 416 | 375 | 10 866 | 105 993 |

表3-8

# 历年牧业、渔业生产情况
# STATISTICS ON LIVESTOCK AND FISHERY OVER THE YEARS

| 年 份 Year | 猪（万头）Hogs (10 000 heads) | | | 年末存栏 Livestock Being Raised at Year-end | | | 牛奶产量（吨）Output of Cow Milk (ton) | 水产品产量（吨）Output of Aquatic Products(ton) |
|---|---|---|---|---|---|---|---|---|
| | 年末存栏 Hog Being Raised at Year-end | 肉猪出栏 Slaughtered Hogs | 猪肉产量（吨）Output of Pork (ton) | 牛（万头）Cattle and Buffaloes (10 000 heads) | 羊（万只）Sheep and Goats (10 000 heads) | 家禽（万只）Poultry (10 000 heads) | | |
| 1949 | 23.21 | 11.80 | | 8.59 | 18.73 | 120.23 | | 14 977 |
| 1952 | 37.98 | 22.16 | | 10.18 | 26.86 | 178.32 | | 21 470 |
| 1957 | 81.58 | 40.40 | | 9.45 | 41.96 | 278.11 | | 30 998 |
| 1962 | 71.52 | 25.67 | | 6.69 | 58.40 | 162.37 | | 26 672 |
| 1965 | 155.04 | 120.68 | | 6.24 | 42.18 | 169.81 | | 32 817 |
| 1970 | 214.19 | 117.68 | | 6.20 | 49.28 | 203.55 | | 44 765 |
| 1975 | 245.64 | 178.35 | | 3.55 | 47.57 | 269.22 | 1 934 | 61 845 |
| 1978 | 264.31 | 185.66 | | 2.74 | 45.58 | 418.93 | 2 375 | 82 249 |
| 1980 | 250.34 | 310.14 | 129 457 | 2.43 | 48.53 | 453.57 | 4 110 | 87 119 |
| 1985 | 186.01 | 210.41 | 110 498 | 0.79 | 24.00 | 1 012.16 | 10 155 | 158 774 |
| 1990 | 154.62 | 193.54 | 101 418 | 0.62 | 41.00 | 1 048.48 | 16 069 | 217 276 |
| 1991 | 147.45 | 192.31 | 102 841 | 0.80 | 41.28 | 1 036.60 | 18 403 | 218 069 |
| 1992 | 147.14 | 187.30 | 101 049 | 0.68 | 40.72 | 919.43 | 20 530 | 229 075 |
| 1993 | 126.17 | 181.76 | 97 179 | 0.53 | 42.40 | | 21 088 | 232 838 |
| 1994 | 119.45 | 172.70 | 91 045 | 0.40 | 48.42 | 1 030.31 | 16 952 | 255 527 |
| 1995 | 111.73 | 177.46 | 104 321 | 0.34 | 49.38 | 1 008.51 | 12 316 | 284 097 |
| 1996 | 103.64 | 177.53 | 104 429 | 0.50 | 41.14 | 986.48 | 14 101 | 285 180 |
| 1997 | 103.32 | 178.19 | 116 098 | 0.48 | 39.63 | 696.20 | 16 605 | 301 319 |
| 1998 | 107.58 | 191.27 | 115 847 | 0.47 | 36.58 | 757.76 | 21 240 | 307 640 |
| 1999 | 97.15 | 186.14 | 106 825 | 0.59 | 33.23 | 816.41 | 28 293 | 321 206 |
| 2000 | 104.75 | 198.50 | 111 075 | 0.86 | 35.92 | 971.05 | 43 742 | 345 139 |
| 2001 | 98.71 | 204.74 | 115 631 | 1.89 | 36.16 | 1 109.73 | 80 453 | 354 308 |
| 2002 | 88.78 | 188.12 | 107 976 | 2.65 | 32.12 | 1 181.12 | 105 095 | 357 221 |
| 2003 | 75.89 | 178.49 | 93 809 | 2.47 | 27.05 | 1 067.30 | 100 266 | 338 707 |
| 2004 | 76.00 | 160.82 | 85 617 | 2.26 | 21.75 | 1 060.91 | 108 812 | 311 884 |
| 2005 | 73.85 | 139.91 | 86 274 | 2.40 | 13.08 | 1 202.80 | 94 651 | 316 523 |
| 2006 | 66.05 | 136.64 | 99 935 | 2.29 | 5.89 | 929.61 | 100 547 | 299 882 |
| 2007 | 70.87 | 122.24 | 92 499 | 2.30 | 4.67 | 1 050.83 | 98 129 | 292 785 |
| 2008 | 77.93 | 110.66 | 79 204 | 2.68 | 4.88 | 1 113.06 | 91 983 | 290 637 |
| 2009 | 82.37 | 117.34 | 88 876 | 2.32 | 6.49 | 1 120.89 | 91 019 | 273 498 |
| 2010 | 83.51 | 117.70 | 84 487 | 2.35 | 7.90 | 1 093.48 | 91 675 | 277 049 |
| 2011 | 85.34 | 118.49 | 86 164 | 2.34 | 7.77 | 991.09 | 92 577 | 284 083 |
| 2012 | 84.97 | 113.44 | 84 543 | 2.28 | 8.58 | 853.76 | 92 524 | 288 433 |

表3-9

# 农村基本情况 (2012年末)

| 项　　目 | | Item | | 全　市 Whole Municipality |
|---|---|---|---|---|
| **农村组织** | | **Village Units** | | |
| 镇政府 | (个) | Town Governments | (unit) | 55 |
| 村民委员会 | | Number of Villagers' Committees | | 1 068 |
| **乡村户数、人口** | | **Households and Rural Population** | | |
| 乡村总户数 | (万户) | Number of Households | (10 000 households) | 91.42 |
| 乡村总人口 | (万人) | Rural Population | (10 000 persons) | 296.41 |
| **年末乡村实有从业人员** | | **Rural Employees of year-end** | | |
| 合　计 | | Total | | 179.54 |
| 1.按性别分 | | Grouped by Sex | | |
| 男劳动力 | | Male | | 92.84 |
| 女劳动力 | | Female | | 86.70 |
| 2.按行业分 | | Grouped by Sector | | |
| 农林牧渔业 | | Farming, Forestry, Animal Husbandry and Fishery | | 24.22 |
| 工　业 | | Industry | | 106.84 |
| 建筑业 | | Construction | | 10.28 |
| 交通运输、仓储和邮政业 | | Transportation, Logistics and Postal | | 5.62 |
| 批发和零售业 | | Wholesale and Retail Trade Services | | 10.30 |
| 住宿和餐饮业 | | Accommodation and Catering Services | | 4.45 |
| 金融、保险业 | | Banking and Insurance | | 0.77 |
| 房地产、社会服务业 | | Real Estate and Social Services | | 2.55 |
| 卫生、体育、社会福利业 | | Health Care, Sporting and Social Welfare | | 0.95 |
| 文、教、艺术和广播影视业 | | Culture, Education and Arts, Radio, Film and Television | | 0.87 |
| 科研和综合技术服务业 | | Scientific Research and Polytechnical Services | | 0.20 |
| 乡镇经济组织管理 | | Rural Economic Management | | 1.20 |
| 其　他 | | Others | | 11.29 |

# BASIC CONDITIONS OF COUNTRYSIDE (END OF 2012)

| 市 区 Urban Area | # 吴江区 Wujiang District | 常 熟 Changshu | 张家港 Zhangjiagang | 昆 山 Kunshan | 太 仓 Taicang |
|---|---|---|---|---|---|
| | | | | | |
| 22 | 8 | 9 | 8 | 10 | 6 |
| 455 | 250 | 219 | 165 | 153 | 76 |
| | | | | | |
| 36.64 | 16.30 | 18.18 | 19.21 | 10.37 | 7.02 |
| 118.61 | 53.18 | 58.61 | 58.41 | 36.05 | 24.73 |
| | | | | | |
| 70.82 | 31.71 | 39.74 | 31.61 | 21.21 | 16.16 |
| | | | | | |
| 36.84 | 16.12 | 20.14 | 16.57 | 11.04 | 8.25 |
| 33.98 | 15.59 | 19.60 | 15.04 | 10.17 | 7.91 |
| | | | | | |
| 11.77 | 4.21 | 3.91 | 3.42 | 1.88 | 3.24 |
| 38.46 | 18.78 | 24.38 | 20.41 | 13.52 | 10.07 |
| 4.80 | 1.80 | 2.15 | 1.73 | 1.00 | 0.60 |
| 2.14 | 0.87 | 1.26 | 1.34 | 0.54 | 0.34 |
| 4.45 | 1.79 | 2.47 | 1.68 | 1.29 | 0.41 |
| 1.94 | 0.67 | 0.80 | 0.69 | 0.84 | 0.18 |
| 0.34 | 0.16 | 0.16 | 0.11 | 0.07 | 0.09 |
| 0.39 | 0.24 | 0.69 | 0.37 | 0.98 | 0.12 |
| 0.35 | 0.15 | 0.27 | 0.13 | 0.14 | 0.06 |
| 0.31 | 0.10 | 0.34 | 0.10 | 0.06 | 0.06 |
| 0.06 | 0.04 | 0.05 | 0.05 | 0.02 | 0.02 |
| 0.49 | 0.22 | 0.35 | 0.20 | 0.10 | 0.06 |
| 5.32 | 2.68 | 2.91 | 1.38 | 0.77 | 0.91 |

表3-10

# 农林牧渔业总产值 (2012年)
# GROSS OUTPUT VALUE OF FARMING, FORESTRY, ANIMAL HUSBANDRY AND FISHERY (2012)

单位：万元　　(可比价格　at Comparable Price)　　(10 000 yuan)

| 地　区 | Region | 总产值 Gross Output Value | 农　业 Farming | 林　业 Forestry | 牧　业 Animal Husbandry | 渔　业 Fishery | 农林牧渔服务业 Services |
|---|---|---|---|---|---|---|---|
| **全　市** | **Whole Municipality** | **3 226 739** | **1 265 659** | **196 013** | **409 818** | **1 013 638** | **341 611** |
| 市　区 | Urban Area | 1 214 671 | 371 660 | 58 580 | 128 101 | 513 993 | 142 337 |
| # 吴江区 | Wujiang | 551 209 | 232 809 | 18 170 | 63 923 | 218 713 | 17 594 |
| 常　熟 | Changshu | 597 611 | 306 923 | 19 904 | 68 502 | 135 232 | 67 050 |
| 张家港 | Zhangjiagang | 464 649 | 246 785 | 58 883 | 49 123 | 45 810 | 64 048 |
| 昆　山 | Kunshan | 396 186 | 112 036 | 36 845 | 23 980 | 204 359 | 18 966 |
| 太　仓 | Taicang | 554 334 | 229 099 | 21 801 | 140 112 | 114 049 | 49 273 |

注：由于各地所用缩减指数与全市有差异，因此分县区数据相加不等于全市数。
Note: As the deflators used by the local places are different from that of the whole city, the data of the counties and districts added up do not equal that of the whole city.

表3-11

# 农林牧渔业总产值 (2012年)
# GROSS OUTPUT VALUE OF FARMING, FORESTRY, ANIMAL HUSBANDRY AND FISHERY (2012)

单位：万元　　(10 000 yuan)

| 地　区 | Region | 总产值 Gross Output Value | 农　业 Farming | 林　业 Forestry | 牧　业 Animal Husbandry | 渔　业 Fishery | 农林牧渔服务业 Services |
|---|---|---|---|---|---|---|---|
| **全　市** | **Whole Municipality** | **3 377 237** | **1 350 458** | **204 834** | **402 031** | **1 066 347** | **353 567** |
| 市　区 | Urban Area | 1 271 484 | 396 561 | 61 216 | 125 667 | 540 721 | 147 319 |
| # 吴江区 | Wujiang | 581 300 | 247 942 | 19 169 | 63 092 | 232 711 | 18 386 |
| 常　熟 | Changshu | 626 774 | 327 180 | 20 800 | 67 200 | 142 264 | 69 330 |
| 张家港 | Zhangjiagang | 487 278 | 263 073 | 61 533 | 48 190 | 48 192 | 66 290 |
| 昆　山 | Kunshan | 416 501 | 119 654 | 38 503 | 23 524 | 215 190 | 19 630 |
| 太　仓 | Taicang | 575 200 | 243 990 | 22 782 | 137 450 | 119 980 | 50 998 |

表3-12

## 农林牧渔业增加值（2012年）
## VALUE ADDED OF FARMING, FORESTRY, ANIMAL HUSBANDRY AND FISHERY (2012)

单位：万元 (10 000 yuan)

| 项 目 | Item | 总产值 Gross Output Value | 中间消耗 Depreciation | 增加值 Value-added | 增加值率 (%) Value-adding Rate (%) |
|---|---|---|---|---|---|
| **总 计** | **Total** | **3 377 237** | **1 426 441** | **1 950 796** | **57.8** |
| 农 业 | Farming | 1 350 458 | 446 283 | 904 175 | 67.0 |
| 林 业 | Forestry | 204 834 | 96 934 | 107 900 | 52.7 |
| 牧 业 | Animal Husbandry | 402 031 | 227 835 | 174 196 | 43.3 |
| 渔 业 | Fishery | 1 066 347 | 487 336 | 579 011 | 54.3 |
| 农林牧渔服务业 | Services | 353 567 | 168 053 | 185 514 | 52.5 |

表3-13

## 分地区农林牧渔业增加值（2012年）
## VALUE ADDED OF FARMING, FORESTRY, ANIMAL HUSBANDRY AND FISHERY BY REGION (2012)

单位：万元 (10 000 yuan)

| 地 区 | Region | 增加值 Value-added | 农 业 Farming | 林 业 Forestry | 牧 业 Animal Husbandry | 渔 业 Fishery | 农林牧渔服务业 Services |
|---|---|---|---|---|---|---|---|
| **全 市** | **Whole Municipality** | **1 950 796** | **904 175** | **107 900** | **174 196** | **579 011** | **185 514** |
| 市 区 | Urban Area | 724 729 | 271 304 | 30 631 | 51 660 | 291 405 | 79 729 |
| # 吴江区 | Wujiang | 342 705 | 181 140 | 9 144 | 26 100 | 118 214 | 8 107 |
| 常 熟 | Changshu | 370 150 | 215 939 | 11 648 | 26 880 | 78 245 | 37 438 |
| 张家港 | Zhangjiagang | 275 271 | 167 568 | 30 397 | 21 201 | 26 937 | 29 168 |
| 昆 山 | Kunshan | 244 586 | 85 433 | 22 717 | 7 104 | 118 355 | 10 977 |
| 太 仓 | Taicang | 336 060 | 163 931 | 12 507 | 67 351 | 64 069 | 28 202 |

表3-14

# 农作物播种面积 (2012年)
# SOWN AREAS OF FARM CROPS (2012)

单位：千公顷 (1 000 hectares)

| 项　　目 | Item | 全　市 Whole Municipality | 市　区 Urban Area | #吴江区 Wujiang District | 常　熟 Changshu | 张家港 Zhang-jiagang | 昆　山 Kunshan | 太　仓 Taicang |
|---|---|---|---|---|---|---|---|---|
| **农作物总播种面积** | **Total Sown Area** | **263.07** | **57.37** | **38.89** | **74.67** | **55.81** | **25.23** | **49.99** |
| **一、粮食作物** | **Grain Crops** | **159.66** | **29.01** | **21.76** | **43.26** | **40.44** | **17.30** | **29.65** |
| （一）夏收粮食 | Summer Grain | 71.31 | 10.46 | 7.39 | 19.72 | 20.16 | 8.66 | 12.31 |
| 1.夏收谷物 | Summer Cereal | 69.63 | 10.41 | 7.39 | 19.09 | 19.94 | 8.50 | 11.69 |
| （1）小　麦 | Wheat | 69.63 | 10.41 | 7.39 | 19.09 | 19.94 | 8.50 | 11.69 |
| （2）元　麦 | Hull-less Barley | – | – | – | – | – | – | – |
| （3）大　麦 | Barley | – | – | – | – | – | – | – |
| 2.夏收豆类 | Summer Beans | 1.68 | 0.05 | – | 0.63 | 0.22 | 0.16 | 0.62 |
| （二）秋收粮食 | Autumn Grain | 88.35 | 18.55 | 14.37 | 23.54 | 20.28 | 8.64 | 17.34 |
| 1.秋收谷物 | Autumn Cereal | 84.89 | 18.52 | 14.37 | 22.90 | 19.12 | 8.25 | 16.10 |
| （1）稻　谷 | Rice | 83.14 | 18.52 | 14.37 | 22.36 | 18.93 | 8.01 | 15.32 |
| #单季晚稻 | Single Late Rice | 83.14 | 18.52 | 14.37 | 22.36 | 18.93 | 8.01 | 15.32 |
| （2）玉　米 | Corn | 1.75 | – | – | 0.54 | 0.19 | 0.24 | 0.78 |
| （3）其他谷物 | Others | – | – | – | – | – | – | – |
| 2.秋收豆类 | Autumn Beans | 2.68 | 0.01 | – | 0.36 | 1.02 | 0.34 | 0.95 |
| 大　豆 | Soybeans | 2.34 | 0.01 | – | 0.26 | 0.99 | 0.27 | 0.81 |
| 杂　豆 | Others | 0.34 | – | – | 0.10 | 0.03 | 0.07 | 0.14 |
| 3.秋收薯类 | Autumn Tubers | 0.78 | 0.02 | – | 0.28 | 0.14 | 0.05 | 0.29 |
| **二、油　料** | **Oil-bearing Crops** | **10.09** | **2.61** | **2.02** | **2.96** | **1.58** | **0.76** | **2.18** |
| #油菜籽 | Rapeseeds | 9.53 | 2.61 | 2.02 | 2.89 | 1.39 | 0.74 | 1.90 |
| **三、棉　花** | **Cotton** | **1.18** | – | – | **0.79** | **0.06** | **0.02** | **0.31** |
| **四、麻　类** | **Fiber Crops** | – | – | – | – | – | – | – |
| **五、糖　料** | **Sugar Crops** | **0.06** | – | – | – | **0.05** | – | **0.01** |
| **六、药　材** | **Crude Drugs** | **0.07** | – | – | – | **0.01** | **0.06** | – |
| **七、蔬菜、瓜类** | **Vegetables and Melon Crops** | **82.84** | **22.14** | **12.20** | **27.00** | **11.44** | **6.10** | **16.16** |
| **八、其他农作物** | **Others** | **9.17** | **3.61** | **2.91** | **0.66** | **2.23** | **0.99** | **1.68** |
| #青饲料 | Green Fodder | 2.32 | 1.75 | 1.50 | 0.11 | 0.03 | 0.17 | 0.26 |
| 绿　肥 | Green Manure | 1.54 | 1.42 | 1.41 | 0.04 | 0.08 | – | – |
| **附：常年蔬菜地** | **In Addition Vegetable Gardens** | **27.86** | **7.52** | **5.00** | **7.70** | **4.79** | **2.58** | **5.27** |

表3-15

# 农产品总产量 (2012年)
# TOTAL YIELD OF FARM CROPS (2012)

单位：吨 (ton)

| 项 目 | Item | 全 市 Whole Municipality | 市 区 Urban Area | # 吴江区 Wujiang District | 常 熟 Changshu | 张家港 Zhang-jiagang | 昆 山 Kunshan | 太 仓 Taicang |
|---|---|---|---|---|---|---|---|---|
| **一、粮食作物** | **Grain Crops** | **1 164 608** | **222 856** | **171 720** | **322 235** | **280 511** | **124 223** | **214 783** |
| （一）夏收粮食 | Summer Grain | 367 112 | 51 806 | 38 295 | 102 635 | 105 941 | 44 781 | 61 949 |
| 1.夏收谷物 | Summer Cereal | 361 040 | 51 708 | 38 295 | 99 826 | 105 426 | 44 164 | 59 916 |
| （1）小 麦 | Wheat | 361 040 | 51 708 | 38 295 | 99 826 | 105 426 | 44 164 | 59 916 |
| （2）元 麦 | Hull-less Barley | – | – | – | – | – | – | – |
| （3）大 麦 | Barley | – | – | – | – | – | – | – |
| 2.夏收豆类 | Summer Beans | 6 072 | 98 | – | 2 809 | 515 | 617 | 2 033 |
| （二）秋收粮食 | Autumn Grain | 797 496 | 171 050 | 133 425 | 219 600 | 174 570 | 79 442 | 152 834 |
| 1.秋收谷物 | Autumn Cereal | 782 580 | 170 925 | 133 425 | 215 444 | 170 808 | 77 285 | 148 118 |
| （1）稻 谷 | Rice | 769 592 | 170 925 | 133 425 | 210 363 | 169 587 | 75 123 | 143 594 |
| # 单季晚稻 | Single Late Rice | 769 592 | 170 925 | 133 425 | 210 363 | 169 587 | 75 123 | 143 594 |
| （2）玉 米 | Corn | 12 988 | – | – | 5 081 | 1 221 | 2 162 | 4 524 |
| （3）其他谷物 | Others | – | – | – | – | – | – | – |
| 2.秋收豆类 | Autumn Beans | 9 959 | 35 | – | 1 970 | 2 822 | 1 721 | 3 411 |
| 大 豆 | Soybeans | 8 438 | 35 | – | 1 335 | 2 744 | 1 408 | 2 916 |
| 杂 豆 | Others | 1 521 | – | – | 635 | 78 | 313 | 495 |
| 3.秋收薯类 | Autumn Tubers | 4 957 | 90 | – | 2 186 | 940 | 436 | 1 305 |
| **二、油 料** | **Oil-bearing Crops** | **25 882** | **6 529** | **5 301** | **8 012** | **4 041** | **1 756** | **5 544** |
| # 油菜籽 | Rapeseeds | 24 354 | 6 529 | 5 301 | 7 804 | 3 643 | 1 723 | 4 655 |
| **三、棉 花** | **Cotton** | **1 292** | – | – | **812** | **53** | **43** | **384** |
| **四、麻 类** | **Fiber Crops** | – | – | – | – | – | – | – |
| **五、糖 料** | **Sugar Crops** | **2 872** | – | – | – | **2 455** | – | **417** |

表3-16

# 农产品单产（2012年）
# YIELD OF FARM CROPS PER HECTARE (2012)

单位：公斤/公顷 (kg/hectare)

| 项　　目 | Item | 全　市 Whole Municipality | 市　区 Urban Area | #吴江区 Wujiang District | 常　熟 Changshu | 张家港 Zhang-jiagang | 昆　山 Kunshan | 太　仓 Taicang |
|---|---|---|---|---|---|---|---|---|
| **一、粮食作物** | **Grain Crops** | **7 294** | **7 682** | **7 892** | **7 449** | **6 936** | **7 181** | **7 244** |
| （一）夏收粮食 | Summer Grain | 5 148 | 4 953 | 5 182 | 5 205 | 5 255 | 5 171 | 5 032 |
| 1.夏收谷物 | Summer Cereal | 5 185 | 4 967 | 5 182 | 5 229 | 5 287 | 5 196 | 5 125 |
| （1）小　麦 | Wheat | 5 185 | 4 967 | 5 182 | 5 229 | 5 287 | 5 196 | 5 125 |
| （2）元　麦 | Hull-less Barley | – | – | – | – | – | – | – |
| （3）大　麦 | Barley | – | – | – | – | – | – | – |
| 2.夏收豆类 | Summer Beans | 3 614 | 1 960 | – | 4 459 | 2 341 | 3 856 | 3 279 |
| （二）秋收粮食 | Autumn Grain | 9 027 | 9 221 | 9 285 | 9 329 | 8 608 | 9 195 | 8 814 |
| 1.秋收谷物 | Autumn Cereal | 9 219 | 9 229 | 9 285 | 9 408 | 8 933 | 9 368 | 9 200 |
| （1）稻　谷 | Rice | 9 257 | 9 229 | 9 285 | 9 408 | 8 959 | 9 379 | 9 373 |
| # 单季晚稻 | Single Late Rice | 9 257 | 9 229 | 9 285 | 9 408 | 8 959 | 9 379 | 9 373 |
| （2）玉　米 | Corn | 7 422 | – | – | 9 409 | 6 426 | 9 008 | 5 800 |
| （3）其他谷物 | Others | – | – | – | – | – | – | – |
| 2.秋收豆类 | Autumn Beans | 3 716 | 3 500 | – | 5 472 | 2 767 | 5 062 | 3 591 |
| 大　豆 | Soybeans | 3 606 | 3 500 | – | 5 135 | 2 772 | 5 215 | 3 600 |
| 杂　豆 | Others | 4 474 | – | – | 6 350 | 2 600 | 4 471 | 3 636 |
| 3.秋收薯类 | Autumn Tubers | 6 355 | 4 500 | – | 7 807 | 6 714 | 8 720 | 4 500 |
| **二、油　料** | **Oil-bearing Crops** | **2 565** | **2 502** | **2 624** | **2 707** | **2 558** | **2 311** | **2 543** |
| # 油菜籽 | Rapeseeds | 2 556 | 2 502 | 2 624 | 2 700 | 2 621 | 2 328 | 2 450 |
| **三、棉　花** | **Cotton** | **1 095** | – | – | **1 028** | **883** | **2 150** | **1 239** |
| **四、麻　类** | **Fiber Crops** | – | – | – | – | – | – | – |
| **五、糖　料** | **Sugar Crops** | **47 867** | – | – | – | **49 100** | – | **41 700** |

表3-17

# 渔业生产情况（2012年）
# STATISTICS ON FISHERY (2012)

| 项 目 | Item | 全市 Whole Municipality | 市区 Urban Area | #吴江区 Wujiang District | 常熟 Changshu | 张家港 Zhang-jiagang | 昆山 Kunshan | 太仓 Taicang |
|---|---|---|---|---|---|---|---|---|
| **基本情况** | **Basic Conditions** | | | | | | | |
| 渔业村数 （个） | Number of Fishing Villages (unit) | 52 | 38 | 15 | – | 4 | 10 | – |
| 渔业户数 （户） | Number of Fishing Households (household) | 33 606 | 19 154 | 6 480 | 4 362 | 2 300 | 5 490 | 2 300 |
| #海 洋 | Seawater | 52 | – | – | 52 | – | – | – |
| 渔业人口 （人） | Population in Fishery (person) | 131 410 | 80 550 | 21 395 | 16 360 | 5 980 | 20 375 | 8 145 |
| 渔业劳动力 | Fishery Labor Force | 88 781 | 54 583 | 19 698 | 12 561 | 5 120 | 10 207 | 6 310 |
| #专业劳动力 | Specialized Labor Force | 68 869 | 41 057 | 13 274 | 11 073 | 2 980 | 9 358 | 4 401 |
| #捕捞专业 | Fish Catching | 8 825 | 5 093 | 1 658 | 835 | 287 | 1 562 | 1 048 |
| 养殖专业 | Aquaculture | 56 419 | 34 582 | 11 206 | 10 238 | 670 | 7 796 | 3 133 |
| **水产品产量** （吨） | **Output of Aquatic Products** (ton) | **288 433** | **140 777** | **79 178** | **38 008** | **17 756** | **53 232** | **38 660** |
| 海洋产品 | Seawater Aquatic Products | 22 224 | – | – | 1 920 | – | – | 20 304 |
| 淡水产品 | Freshwater Aquatic Products | 266 209 | 140 777 | 79 178 | 36 088 | 17 756 | 53 232 | 18 356 |
| 捕 捞 | Fish Catching | 18 075 | 12 094 | 2 431 | 812 | 900 | 1 033 | 3 236 |
| 养 殖 | Aquaculture | 248 134 | 128 683 | 76 747 | 35 276 | 16 856 | 52 199 | 15 120 |
| **渔 船** | **Fishing Boat** | | | | | | | |
| 机动渔船 （艘） | Motorized Fishing Boats (unit) | 11 560 | 10 098 | 2 740 | 359 | 90 | 767 | 246 |
| （吨） | (ton) | 56 779 | 42 724 | 9 306 | 3 754 | 901 | 2 636 | 6 764 |
| （千瓦） | (kw) | 134 380 | 101 415 | 34 637 | 8 839 | 2 213 | 8 172 | 13 741 |
| 非机动渔船 （艘） | Non-motorized Fishing Boats (unit) | 14 856 | 10 886 | 1 738 | 1 680 | 36 | 905 | 1 349 |
| （载吨） | (ton) | 40 394 | 32 992 | 6 578 | 2 530 | 40 | 2 668 | 2 164 |
| **淡水养殖面积** （千公顷） | **Freshwater Raise Areas**(1 000 hectares) | **76.99** | **44.94** | **22.01** | **11.21** | **3.04** | **13.37** | **4.43** |
| #池塘面积 | Pond Area | 40.94 | 20.80 | 10.15 | 6.73 | 2.39 | 8.33 | 2.69 |

表3-18

# 牧业生产情况（2012年）
# STATISTICS ON LIVESTOCK (2012)

| 项　目 | Item | 全　市 Whole Municipality | 市　区 Urban Area | #吴江区 Wujiang District | 常　熟 Changshu | 张家港 Zhang-jiagang | 昆　山 Kunshan | 太　仓 Taicang |
|---|---|---|---|---|---|---|---|---|
| **当年出栏数** | **Slaughtered Livestock of the Year** | | | | | | | |
| 牛　（万头） | Cattle and Buffaloes (10 000 heads) | – | – | – | – | – | – | – |
| 猪 | Hogs | 113.44 | 46.25 | 20.68 | 24.51 | 12.09 | 7.76 | 22.83 |
| 羊　（万只） | Sheep and Goats (10 000 heads) | 8.24 | 3.38 | 2.37 | 1.18 | 1.25 | 0.11 | 2.32 |
| #山　羊 | Goats | 2.53 | 0.04 | – | 0.27 | 1.21 | 0.04 | 0.97 |
| 家　禽 | Poultry | 2 900.22 | 300.66 | 181.00 | 233.87 | 192.96 | 32.73 | 2 140.00 |
| 兔 | Rabbit | 16.30 | 6.02 | 4.82 | 0.06 | 2.62 | – | 7.60 |
| **年末存栏数** | **Livestock Being Raised at Year-end** | | | | | | | |
| 牛　（万头） | Cattle and Buffaloes(10 000heads) | 2.28 | 0.67 | 0.02 | 0.42 | 0.43 | 0.27 | 0.49 |
| 猪 | Hogs | 84.97 | 29.03 | 14.99 | 21.82 | 10.02 | 4.72 | 19.38 |
| 羊　（万只） | Sheep and Goats (10 000 heads) | 8.58 | 3.80 | 2.75 | 1.14 | 0.97 | 0.19 | 2.48 |
| #山　羊 | Goats | 2.57 | 0.08 | – | 0.23 | 0.95 | 0.11 | 1.20 |
| 家　禽 | Poultry | 853.76 | 144.45 | 101.40 | 59.94 | 80.31 | 21.06 | 548.00 |
| 兔 | Rabbit | 7.59 | 4.34 | 3.92 | 0.13 | 0.82 | – | 2.30 |
| **产　量**　（吨） | **Output of Meat** (ton) | | | | | | | |
| 牛　肉 | Beef | – | – | – | – | – | – | – |
| 猪　肉 | Pork | 84 543 | 36 097 | 14 500 | 17 159 | 9 672 | 5 632 | 15 983 |
| 羊　肉 | Mutton | 1 538 | 696 | 452 | 301 | 186 | 17 | 338 |
| #山羊肉 | Goat Mutton | 366 | 8 | – | 37 | 181 | 5 | 135 |
| 禽　肉 | Poultry | 55 551 | 5 201 | 2 765 | 3 927 | 2 983 | 640 | 42 800 |
| 兔　肉 | Rabbit | 342 | 137 | 100 | 1 | 47 | – | 157 |
| 奶　类 | Milk | 92 524 | 29 269 | 723 | 12 476 | 18 269 | 16 639 | 15 871 |
| #牛　奶 | Cow Milk | 92 524 | 29 269 | 723 | 12 476 | 18 269 | 16 639 | 15 871 |
| 绵羊毛 | Sheep Wool | 61.99 | 40.00 | 40.00 | 21.00 | 0.99 | – | – |
| 蜂　蜜 | Honey | 197 | 21 | – | 45 | 33 | – | 98 |
| 禽　蛋 | Poultry Eggs | 44 854 | 9 662 | 7 280 | 3 907 | 7 494 | 1 060 | 22 731 |

表3-19

# 林业、蚕桑、茶叶、水果生产情况 (2012年)
# STATISTICS ON FISHERY, SILKWORM COCOONS, TEA AND FRUITS PRODUCTION (2012)

| 项 目 | Item | 全 市 Whole Municipality | 市 区 Urban Area | #吴江区 Wujiang District | 常 熟 Changshu | 张家港 Zhang-jiagang | 昆 山 Kunshan | 太 仓 Taicang |
|---|---|---|---|---|---|---|---|---|
| **林 业** | **Forestry** | | | | | | | |
| 造林面积 (公顷) | Build Forestry Areas (hectare) | 10 624 | 2 357 | | | | | |
| 四旁植树 (万株) | Planting (10 000 plants) | 350.40 | 98.60 | | | | | |
| 育苗面积 (公顷) | Raise Seedlings Areas (hectare) | 6 367 | 4 720 | 4 720 | 966 | - | 681 | - |
| 木材采伐 (万立方米) | Timber Cut (10 000 cu.m) | 0.08 | 0.04 | - | 0.03 | - | - | 0.01 |
| 竹材采伐 (万根) | Bamboo Cut (10 000 pieces) | 2 | 2 | - | - | - | - | - |
| 年末实有林地面积(公顷) | Actual Forestry Areas (year-end) (hectare) | 90 981 | 50 263 | | | | | |
| **蚕 桑** | **Silkworm Cocoons and Mulberry** | | | | | | | |
| 蚕茧产量 (吨) | Output of Silkworm Cocoons (ton) | 495 | 490 | 490 | - | - | - | 5 |
| 年末实有桑园面积 (公顷) | Mulberry Field Area(year-end) (hectare) | 3 601 | 3 568 | 3 565 | - | - | - | 33 |
| **茶 叶** | **Tea** | | | | | | | |
| 茶叶产量 (吨) | Output of Tea (ton) | 375 | 319 | - | 43 | 13 | - | - |
| #绿毛茶 | Green Tea | 375 | 319 | - | 43 | 13 | - | - |
| 年末实有茶园面积 (公顷) | Tea Field Area (year-end) (hectare) | 2 416 | 2 233 | - | 131 | 52 | - | - |
| **水 果** | **Fruits** | | | | | | | |
| 水果产量 (吨) | Output of Fruits (ton) | 105 993 | 42 088 | 10 930 | 18 004 | 26 425 | 11 653 | 7 823 |
| #柑 桔 | Citrus | 29 742 | 18 551 | 7 500 | 405 | 9 710 | 193 | 883 |
| 梨 | Pears | 7 980 | 3 785 | 1 150 | 948 | 1 182 | 1 800 | 265 |
| 葡 萄 | Grapes | 38 199 | 6 056 | 1 740 | 14 624 | 4 487 | 7 032 | 6 000 |
| 年末实有果园面积 (公顷) | Area of Orchards(year-end) (hectare) | 10 866 | 6 571 | 772 | 1 337 | 1 312 | 1 039 | 607 |
| #柑 桔 | Citrus | 2 224 | 1 836 | 467 | 35 | 229 | 25 | 99 |
| 梨 | Pears | 992 | 474 | 100 | 157 | 138 | 154 | 69 |
| 葡 萄 | Grapes | 2 500 | 478 | 105 | 774 | 316 | 628 | 304 |

表3-20 农业机械化、化学化及农田水利化情况 (2012年)

| 指标 | | Item | | 全市 Whole Municipality |
|---|---|---|---|---|
| **一、农业机械化情况** | | **Statistics on Agricultural Machinery** | | |
| （一）机耕面积 | (千公顷) | Area Ploughed by Tractors | (1 000 hectares) | 180.69 |
| （二）机播面积 | | Seeded Area by Tractors | | 140.49 |
| # 机插水稻面积 | | Rice Planted Area by Transplanters | | 68.57 |
| 机播水稻面积 | | Seeded Rice Area by Tractors | | 9.10 |
| 机播小麦面积 | | Wheat Area by Tractors | | 62.30 |
| （三）机械植保面积 | | Plant Protection Area by Tractors | | 175.73 |
| （四）机收面积 | | Harvest Area by Tractors | | 152.33 |
| # 机收水稻面积 | | Rice Harvest Area by Tractors | | 82.38 |
| 机收小麦面积 | | Wheat Harvest Area by Tractors | | 69.22 |
| （五）机械脱粒粮食数量 | (万吨) | Amount of Grain Crops Shelling by Thresher | (10 000 tons) | 104.02 |
| **二、农用化肥、农药施用量** | | **Use of Agricultural Fertilizers and Insecticides** | | |
| 化　肥（折纯量） | (吨) | Chemical Fertilizer (pure) | (ton) | 84 531 |
| 农　药 | | Agricultural Chemical Insecticides | | 4 141 |
| **三、农村用电量** | (万千瓦时) | **Electricity Consumed in Rural Area** | (10 000 kwh) | **5 560 864** |
| **四、农田水利建设情况** | | **Irrigation and Water Conservancy** | | |
| 有效灌溉面积 | (千公顷) | Effective Irrigation Area | (1 000 hectares) | 178.99 |

# STATISTICS ON AGRICULTURAL MACHINERY, CHEMICAL APPLICATION AND IRRIGATION OF FARMING LAND (2012)

| 市 区<br>Urban Area | # 吴江区<br>Wujiang District | 常 熟<br>Changshu | 张家港<br>Zhangjiagang | 昆 山<br>Kunshan | 太 仓<br>Taicang |
|---|---|---|---|---|---|
| | | | | | |
| 30.43 | 22.60 | 51.86 | 44.00 | 16.07 | 38.33 |
| 25.85 | 22.24 | 36.91 | 37.90 | 15.70 | 24.13 |
| 16.28 | 13.43 | 18.69 | 17.27 | 2.53 | 13.80 |
| 0.49 | 0.34 | 2.12 | 1.33 | 5.16 | - |
| 8.89 | 7.39 | 16.09 | 19.00 | 7.99 | 10.33 |
| 32.18 | 24.73 | 46.49 | 45.20 | 16.61 | 35.25 |
| 28.72 | 21.80 | 41.43 | 38.50 | 16.61 | 27.07 |
| 17.92 | 14.07 | 22.33 | 18.80 | 8.01 | 15.32 |
| 10.27 | 7.39 | 19.09 | 19.67 | 8.50 | 11.69 |
| 16.73 | 13.06 | 31.78 | 26.50 | 11.87 | 17.14 |
| | | | | | |
| 20 308 | 10 020 | 30 208 | 11 930 | 10 901 | 11 184 |
| 1 137 | 536 | 1 821 | 431 | 433 | 319 |
| **2 009 000** | **1 230 198** | **706 298** | **1 340 597** | **999 849** | **505 120** |
| | | | | | |
| 63.14 | 36.65 | 42.07 | 28.64 | 15.61 | 29.53 |

表3-21

# 主要农业机械拥有量 (2012年末)

| 项　目 | | Item | | 全 市 Whole Municipality |
|---|---|---|---|---|
| **农业机械总动力** | (万千瓦) | **Total Power of Agricultural Machinery** | (10 000 kw) | **168.98** |
| # 柴油机 | | Diesel Engines | | 96.03 |
| 电动机 | | Motor | | 57.45 |
| **主要农业机械** | | **Main Agricultural Machinery** | | |
| 1.大中型拖拉机 | (台) | Large and Medium Tractors | (unit) | 3 939 |
| | (万千瓦) | | (10 000 kw) | 16.30 |
| 2.小型拖拉机 | (台) | Mini-tractors | (unit) | 3 198 |
| | (万千瓦) | | (10 000 kw) | 2.85 |
| 3.机动水稻插秧机 | (台) | Rice Transplanters | (unit) | 3 813 |
| 4.农用排灌动力机械 | (万台) | Machinery for Agricultural Drainage and Irrigation | (10 000 units) | 4.31 |
| | (万千瓦) | | (10 000 kw) | 35.08 |
| # 柴油机 | (万台) | Diesel Engines | (10 000 units) | 0.64 |
| | (万千瓦) | | (10 000 kw) | 6.55 |
| 电动机 | (万台) | Motor | (10 000 units) | 3.51 |
| | (万千瓦) | | (10 000 kw) | 28.02 |
| 5.农用水泵 | (万台) | Agricultural Water Pump | (10 000 units) | 4.23 |
| 6.节水灌溉类机械 | (套) | Equipment in Water-saving Irrigation | (set) | 1 786 |
| 7.联合收割机 | (台) | Combine Harvesters | (unit) | 2 419 |
| 8.机动脱粒机 | | Motorized Huller | | 24 848 |
| 9.渔业机械 | | Machinery of Fishery | | 47 759 |
| | (万千瓦) | | (10 000 kw) | 15.98 |

# POSSESSION OF AGRICULTURAL MACHINERY (END OF 2012)

| 市 区<br>Urban Area | # 吴江区<br>Wujiang District | 常 熟<br>Changshu | 张家港<br>Zhangjiagang | 昆 山<br>Kunshan | 太 仓<br>Taicang |
|---|---|---|---|---|---|
| **63.89** | **40.10** | **35.50** | **33.15** | **17.90** | **18.54** |
| 35.08 | 18.08 | 17.71 | 22.98 | 10.16 | 10.10 |
| 20.00 | 15.29 | 16.53 | 6.62 | 6.99 | 7.31 |
| | | | | | |
| 717 | 502 | 981 | 943 | 434 | 864 |
| 2.57 | 1.71 | 4.15 | 4.24 | 1.90 | 3.44 |
| 803 | 624 | 1 410 | 342 | 546 | 97 |
| 0.75 | 0.57 | 1.20 | 0.33 | 0.48 | 0.09 |
| 783 | 681 | 1 325 | 1 056 | 149 | 500 |
| 1.53 | 1.13 | 1.14 | 0.70 | 0.19 | 0.75 |
| 16.08 | 11.81 | 7.54 | 4.79 | 3.05 | 3.62 |
| 0.42 | 0.29 | 0.19 | … | … | 0.02 |
| 4.13 | 3.23 | 2.15 | 0.02 | 0.06 | 0.19 |
| 1.10 | 0.84 | 0.95 | 0.54 | 0.19 | 0.73 |
| 11.96 | 8.58 | 5.38 | 4.26 | 2.99 | 3.43 |
| 1.38 | 0.87 | 1.37 | 0.58 | 0.19 | 0.71 |
| 624 | - | 350 | 443 | - | 369 |
| 253 | 191 | 719 | 698 | 267 | 482 |
| 3 737 | 2 237 | 18 938 | - | - | 2 173 |
| 24 851 | 19 543 | 6 986 | 2 861 | 10 117 | 2 944 |
| 9.13 | 7.21 | 1.53 | 0.38 | 2.68 | 2.26 |

表3-22

# 分乡、镇基本情况 (2012年)

| 乡、镇 Townships and Towns | | 年末人口(人) Population Year-end (person) | 乡镇从业人员(人) Rural Laborers (person) | #各类科技人员 Scientific and Technical Personnel of All Kinds | 年末耕地面积(公顷) Cultivated Area Year-end (hectare) | #有效灌溉面积 Effective Irrigation Area | 农机总动力(千瓦) Total Agricultural Machinery Power (kw) |
|---|---|---|---|---|---|---|---|
| **吴中区** | **Wuzhong District** | | | | | | |
| 甪　直 | Luzhi | 177 900 | 135 173 | 2 788 | 2 085 | 2 085 | 10 293 |
| 木　渎 | Mudu | 273 738 | 232 456 | 3 562 | 80 | 80 | 945 |
| 胥　口 | Xukou | 93 614 | 65 541 | 1 826 | 307 | 307 | 933 |
| 东　山 | Dongshan | 57 069 | 32 515 | 800 | 474 | 474 | 41 306 |
| 光　福 | Guangfu | 63 497 | 42 168 | 620 | 1 340 | 743 | 24 774 |
| 金　庭 | Jinting | 48 270 | 27 241 | 918 | 779 | 540 | 6 753 |
| 临　湖 | Linhu | 71 068 | 50 591 | 780 | 1 795 | 1 562 | 18 000 |
| **相城区** | **Xiangcheng District** | | | | | | |
| 望　亭 | Wangting | 76 643 | 49 822 | 563 | 1 563 | 1 378 | 13 450 |
| 黄　埭 | Huangdai | 139 540 | 88 742 | 1 414 | 948 | 821 | 23 896 |
| 渭　塘 | Weitang | 98 904 | 55 680 | 575 | 706 | 706 | 3 100 |
| 阳澄湖 | Yangchenghu | 65 827 | 43 205 | 340 | 1 701 | 171 | 21 876 |
| **高新区、虎丘区** | **New & Hi-tech Zone,Huqiu District** | | | | | | |
| 浒墅关 | Xushuguan | 51 080 | 20 930 | 610 | 700 | 444 | 1 500 |
| 通　安 | Tongan | 46 054 | 25 530 | 372 | 1 104 | 1 104 | 6 000 |
| 东　渚 | Dongzhu | 40 086 | 22 400 | 323 | 671 | 671 | 8 540 |
| **吴江区** | **WuJiang District** | | | | | | |
| 滨湖新城 | Binhuxincheng | 371 107 | 361 674 | 8 336 | 3 181 | 3 181 | 20 505 |
| 同　里 | Tongli | 53 827 | 33 260 | 2 430 | 2 928 | 2 928 | 25 451 |
| 平　望 | Pingwang | 95 934 | 58 951 | 3 459 | 4 342 | 4 220 | 19 693 |

# STATISTICS ON TOWNS AND TOWNSHIPS (2012)

| 农村用电量 (万千瓦时) Electricity Consumed in Rural Area (10 000 kwh) | 农作物播种面积 (公顷) Sown Area of Farm Crops (hectare) | # 粮食作物 Grain Crops | 粮食总产量 (吨) Total Output of Grain (ton) | 油料总产量 (吨) Total Output of Oil-bearing Crops (ton) | 水产品总产量 (吨) Total Output of Aquatic Products (ton) | 肉类总产量 (吨) Total Output of Meat (ton) | # 猪肉产量 Output of Pork | 农民人均纯收入(元) Per Capita Net Income of Rural Resident (yuan) |
|---|---|---|---|---|---|---|---|---|
| | | | | | | | | |
| 76 621 | 2 776 | 924 | 6 312 | 255 | 2 611 | 8 340 | 8 190 | 19 908 |
| 176 984 | 68 | 60 | 400 | – | 125 | 300 | 300 | 24 362 |
| 71 544 | 201 | 134 | 860 | 48 | 3 682 | 2 418 | 1 968 | 20 608 |
| 15 267 | 181 | 22 | 187 | – | 4 633 | 8 | 7 | 18 276 |
| 16 317 | 754 | 94 | 497 | – | 8 358 | 193 | 162 | 20 890 |
| 6 480 | 1 086 | 109 | 1 001 | 338 | 2 753 | 975 | 853 | 14 254 |
| 19 947 | 1 104 | 871 | 6 615 | 30 | 2 277 | 6 715 | 4 645 | 18 720 |
| | | | | | | | | |
| 36 722 | 1 128 | 961 | 6 828 | 33 | 458 | 198 | 198 | 19 647 |
| 75 100 | 1 466 | 1 341 | 9 607 | 102 | 3 032 | 5 164 | 4 430 | 19 600 |
| 54 845 | 230 | 22 | 144 | – | 2 101 | 770 | 470 | 20 528 |
| 17 074 | 307 | 111 | 809 | 72 | 8 031 | 5 047 | 3 955 | 19 649 |
| | | | | | | | | |
| 19 800 | 444 | 92 | 1 480 | 4 | 450 | 1 900 | 1 500 | 18 160 |
| 19 953 | 859 | 206 | 2 600 | 4 | 463 | 210 | 210 | 19 029 |
| 7 060 | 15 | – | – | 10 | 600 | 500 | 200 | 17 872 |
| | | | | | | | | |
| 358 790 | 2 633 | 1 611 | 12 781 | 932 | 24 480 | 1 688 | 1 160 | 21 664 |
| 70 255 | 3 575 | 1 447 | 9 234 | 877 | 18 760 | 9 018 | 3 555 | 19 800 |
| 236 180 | 5 247 | 4 069 | 32 940 | 724 | 1 940 | 2 088 | 1 853 | 20 420 |

表3-22 续表 1

| 乡、镇 Townships and Towns | | 地区生产总值 (万元) Gross Domestic Product (10 000 yuan) | 第一产业 Primary Industry | 第二产业 Secondary Industry | 第三产业 Tertiary Industry | 企业个数 (个) Number of Enterprises (unit) | 企业利税总额 (万元) Pre-tax Profits of Enterprises (10 000 yuan) |
|---|---|---|---|---|---|---|---|
| **吴中区** | **Wuzhong District** | | | | | | |
| 甪 直 | Luzhi | 914 047 | 19 328 | 456 608 | 438 111 | 2 184 | 151 187 |
| 木 渎 | Mudu | 1 139 998 | 6 067 | 548 678 | 585 253 | 7 210 | 261 756 |
| 胥 口 | Xukou | 856 945 | 18 594 | 534 593 | 303 758 | 1 842 | 262 742 |
| 东 山 | Dongshan | 200 518 | 27 351 | 102 536 | 70 631 | 475 | 34 237 |
| 光 福 | Guangfu | 251 420 | 16 049 | 126 758 | 108 613 | 411 | 45 180 |
| 金 庭 | Jinting | 158 332 | 20 990 | 32 271 | 105 071 | 94 | 9 655 |
| 临 湖 | Linhu | 413 500 | 28 400 | 181 700 | 203 400 | 832 | 79 900 |
| **相城区** | **Xiangcheng District** | | | | | | |
| 望 亭 | Wangting | 337 045 | 2 825 | 171 616 | 162 604 | 1 475 | 86 044 |
| 黄 埭 | Huangdai | 1 034 516 | 24 431 | 613 691 | 396 394 | 819 | 230 411 |
| 渭 塘 | Weitang | 483 805 | 5 315 | 266 425 | 212 065 | 1 420 | 195 684 |
| 阳澄湖 | Yangchenghu | 395 386 | 30 662 | 202 536 | 162 188 | 702 | 81 908 |
| **高新区、虎丘区** | **New & Hi-tech Zone,Huqiu District** | | | | | | |
| 浒墅关 | Xushuguan | 469 234 | 3 376 | 347 880 | 117 978 | 901 | 98 700 |
| 通 安 | Tongan | 228 390 | 9 555 | 119 764 | 99 071 | 1 110 | 124 240 |
| 东 渚 | Dongzhu | 32 102 | 2 266 | 21 025 | 8 811 | 230 | 7 830 |
| **吴江区** | **WuJiang District** | | | | | | |
| 滨湖新城 | Binhuxincheng | 4 809 345 | 39 580 | 3 158 409 | 1 611 356 | 7 110 | 1 689 668 |
| 同 里 | Tongli | 604 860 | 22 170 | 255 060 | 327 630 | 1 338 | 69 830 |
| 平 望 | Pingwang | 866 500 | 16 500 | 503 400 | 346 600 | 1 356 | 138 392 |

Continued 1

| 进出口总额（万美元）Total Imports and Exports (USD 10 000) | # 出口总额（万美元）Total Exports (USD 10 000) | 固定资产投资完成额(万元) Value of Investment in Fixed Assets (10 000 yuan) | 财政总收入(万元) Total Revenue (10 000 yuan) | 年末居民储蓄存款(万元) Amount of Year-end Savings Deposit of Residents (10 000 yuan) | 参加养老保险人数(人) Number of Persons Participating in Old Age Insurance (person) | 参加医疗保障人数(人) Number of Rural Residents Participating in Medical Welfare (person) |
|---|---|---|---|---|---|---|
| | | | | | | |
| 69 071 | 48 844 | 200 280 | 143 882 | 235 152 | 35 552 | 53 329 |
| 55 200 | 43 000 | 354 897 | 241 512 | 803 400 | 57 106 | 77 142 |
| 128 000 | 57 000 | 365 948 | 158 778 | 179 419 | 28 836 | 27 715 |
| 12 000 | 8 000 | 67 188 | 33 315 | 267 647 | 25 326 | 31 860 |
| 3 | 2 | 90 020 | 46 086 | 190 000 | 18 004 | 27 170 |
| 652 | 652 | 47 438 | 22 886 | 49 889 | 16 951 | 30 982 |
| 18 500 | 13 000 | 153 000 | 68 842 | 190 800 | 42 450 | 39 863 |
| | | | | | | |
| 14 277 | 7 345 | 222 330 | 62 200 | 226 675 | 31 882 | 35 701 |
| – | – | 431 618 | 140 145 | 284 000 | 42 345 | 46 715 |
| 18 200 | 12 200 | 332 000 | 107 826 | 47 510 | 27 400 | 23 850 |
| 14 156 | 14 156 | 328 124 | 54 379 | 228 500 | 23 110 | 31 009 |
| | | | | | | |
| – | – | 313 000 | 95 491 | 93 500 | 48 756 | 49 230 |
| 23 952 | 7 000 | 250 543 | 64 574 | 152 805 | 22 910 | 35 899 |
| – | – | 31 126 | 10 124 | 138 832 | 27 152 | 20 100 |
| | | | | | | |
| 1 768 294 | 945 015 | 2 592 718 | 874 510 | 4 110 591 | 156 020 | 185 433 |
| 39 923 | 32 932 | 370 288 | 71 922 | 243 958 | 39 198 | 43 474 |
| 43 907 | 22 569 | 536 279 | 101 169 | 389 073 | 67 189 | 52 530 |

表3-22 续表 2

| 乡、镇 Townships and Towns | | 年末人口 (人) Population Year-end (person) | 乡镇从业人员 (人) Rural Laborers (person) | #各类科技人员 Scientific and Technical Personnel of All Kinds | 年末耕地面积 (公顷) Cultivated Area Year-end (hectare) | #有效灌溉面积 Effective Irrigation Area | 农机总动力 (千瓦) Total Agricultural Machinery Power (kw) |
|---|---|---|---|---|---|---|---|
| 盛　泽 | Shengze | 200 323 | 145 732 | 4 536 | 4 429 | 4 429 | 47 600 |
| 七　都 | Qidu | 69 816 | 43 607 | 1 830 | 1 922 | 1 922 | 32 800 |
| 震　泽 | Zhenze | 78 793 | 46 599 | 3 476 | 2 985 | 2 985 | 45 520 |
| 桃　源 | Taoyuan | 77 397 | 45 081 | 1 940 | 1 035 | 1 035 | 19 800 |
| 汾　湖 | Fenhu | 174 538 | 104 673 | 28 652 | 8 473 | 8 473 | 99 360 |
| **常　熟** | **Chang Shu** | | | | | | |
| 虞　山 | Yushan | 294 016 | 220 558 | 51 925 | 3 876 | 3 876 | 21 640 |
| 梅　李 | Meili | 111 199 | 61 173 | 1 652 | 3 317 | 1 864 | 27 326 |
| 海　虞 | Haiyu | 135 906 | 96 879 | 2 031 | 3 868 | 3 022 | 20 668 |
| 古　里 | Guli | 105 303 | 86 152 | 2 133 | 2 630 | 2 630 | 33 139 |
| 沙家浜 | Shajiabang | 74 533 | 50 444 | 945 | 2 294 | 357 | 10 458 |
| 支　塘 | Zhitang | 109 800 | 52 147 | 1 450 | 5 598 | 5 598 | 37 022 |
| 董　浜 | Dongbang | 65 663 | 47 811 | 755 | 3 319 | 3 319 | 22 904 |
| 辛　庄 | Xinzhuang | 115 086 | 74 494 | 3 581 | 3 365 | 3 365 | 35 677 |
| 尚　湖 | Shanghu | 128 123 | 75 781 | 1 452 | 4 179 | 3 770 | 46 765 |
| **张家港** | **Zhang Jia Gang** | | | | | | |
| 杨　舍 | Yangshe | 276 598 | 228 551 | 22 950 | 3 756 | 3 756 | 39 553 |
| 塘　桥 | Tangqiao | 149 690 | 96 578 | 6 880 | 3 894 | 3 894 | 40 448 |
| 金　港 | JinGang | 296 894 | 203 603 | 19 250 | 3 951 | 3 951 | 32 967 |
| 锦　丰 | Jinfeng | 169 892 | 103 096 | 7 358 | 4 688 | 4 688 | 34 782 |
| 乐　余 | Leyu | 93 858 | 54 031 | 3 190 | 4 326 | 4 326 | 26 363 |

Continued 2

| 农村用电量(万千瓦时) Electricity Consumed in Rural Area (10 000 kwh) | 农作物播种面积(公顷) Sown Area of Farm Crops (hectare) | #粮食作物 Grain Crops | 粮食总产量(吨) Total Output of Grain (ton) | 油料总产量(吨) Total Output of Oil-bearing Crops (ton) | 水产品总产量(吨) Total Output of Aquatic Products (ton) | 肉类总产量(吨) Total Output of Meat (ton) | #猪肉产量 Output of Pork | 农民人均纯收入(元) Per Capita Net Income of Rural Resident (yuan) |
|---|---|---|---|---|---|---|---|---|
| 836 429 | 4 760 | 4 508 | 34 222 | 389 | 2 622 | 1 347 | 942 | 24 726 |
| 104 826 | 2 404 | 556 | 4 613 | 495 | 6 294 | 2 020 | 1 300 | 21 765 |
| 92 160 | 3 825 | 2 707 | 21 566 | 1 361 | 10 906 | 1 516 | 1 242 | 21 156 |
| 118 803 | 1 188 | 1 099 | 9 654 | 96 | 1 905 | 2 493 | 2 013 | 19 566 |
| 205 687 | 4 935 | 4 577 | 36 844 | 548 | 18 798 | 8 172 | 7 587 | 20 618 |
| | | | | | | | | |
| 257 144 | 7 977 | 7 014 | 49 222 | 446 | 2 543 | 5 750 | 4 849 | 22 118 |
| 163 290 | 5 264 | 3 227 | 24 241 | 1 686 | 830 | 2 729 | 2 495 | 21 728 |
| 94 473 | 7 678 | 6 345 | 46 162 | 1 051 | 1 310 | 932 | 817 | 21 733 |
| 136 138 | 5 246 | 4 942 | 36 543 | 498 | 7 065 | 5 830 | 5 347 | 21 703 |
| 69 590 | 813 | 654 | 4 264 | 19 | 11 059 | 1 537 | 1 537 | 21 620 |
| 59 778 | 9 563 | 7 263 | 55 584 | 933 | 4 613 | 7 080 | 4 522 | 20 455 |
| 51 629 | 8 896 | 1 530 | 10 743 | 291 | 1 713 | 3 618 | 3 206 | 21 194 |
| 61 978 | 4 314 | 3 421 | 24 054 | 148 | 11 328 | 2 579 | 2 347 | 21 266 |
| 60 868 | 8 558 | 7 738 | 52 197 | 495 | 4 847 | 3 814 | 3 260 | 21 415 |
| | | | | | | | | |
| 325 550 | 7 290 | 3 909 | 27 618 | 185 | 1 791 | 2 969 | 2 080 | 22 518 |
| 174 888 | 6 756 | 5 904 | 41 361 | 337 | 1 422 | 1 198 | 781 | 22 171 |
| 359 862 | 6 874 | 5 179 | 35 536 | 432 | 2 134 | 2 942 | 1 102 | 22 688 |
| 1 084 839 | 8 906 | 5 859 | 40 476 | 1 054 | 1 637 | 828 | 610 | 21 650 |
| 67 320 | 8 983 | 6 656 | 45 835 | 1 093 | 2 119 | 3 475 | 3 000 | 21 168 |

表3-22 续表 3

| 乡、镇 Townships and Towns | | 地区生产总值 (万元) Gross Domestic Product (10 000 yuan) | 第一产业 Primary Industry | 第二产业 Secondary Industry | 第三产业 Tertiary Industry | 企业个数 (个) Number of Enterprises (unit) | 企业利税总额 (万元) Pre-tax Profits of Enterprises (10 000 yuan) |
|---|---|---|---|---|---|---|---|
| 盛　泽 | Shengze | 3 025 008 | 15 350 | 1 607 249 | 1 402 409 | 16 183 | 1 011 100 |
| 七　都 | Qidu | 738 980 | 18 830 | 459 280 | 260 870 | 790 | 124 471 |
| 震　泽 | Zhenze | 956 480 | 35 220 | 563 020 | 358 240 | 1 331 | 181 953 |
| 桃　源 | Taoyuan | 632 039 | 13 355 | 358 885 | 259 799 | 1 216 | 112 258 |
| 汾　湖 | Fenhu | 1 792 369 | 37 693 | 1 041 770 | 712 906 | 4 648 | 650 218 |
| **常　熟** | **Chang Shu** | | | | | | |
| 虞　山 | Yushan | 7 429 501 | 24 045 | 2 121 977 | 5 283 479 | 7 380 | 1 506 746 |
| 梅　李 | Meili | 1 078 000 | 29 000 | 782 000 | 267 000 | 1 289 | 188 970 |
| 海　虞 | Haiyu | 857 438 | 23 290 | 608 122 | 226 026 | 1 196 | 196 801 |
| 古　里 | Guli | 1 222 175 | 23 552 | 957 462 | 241 161 | 1 342 | 381 061 |
| 沙家浜 | Shajiabang | 793 565 | 33 500 | 604 067 | 155 998 | 515 | 167 650 |
| 支　塘 | Zhitang | 653 860 | 30 300 | 370 200 | 253 360 | 1 885 | 61 825 |
| 董　浜 | Dongbang | 482 296 | 30 057 | 315 922 | 136 317 | 545 | 74 110 |
| 辛　庄 | Xinzhuang | 867 208 | 24 264 | 640 390 | 202 554 | 1 366 | 192 035 |
| 尚　湖 | Shanghu | 812 000 | 21 754 | 549 260 | 240 986 | 1 428 | 77 152 |
| **张家港** | **Zhang Jia Gang** | | | | | | |
| 杨　舍 | Yangshe | 5 798 935 | 44 709 | 2 208 811 | 3 545 415 | 6 711 | 1 445 333 |
| 塘　桥 | Tangqiao | 1 489 325 | 30 129 | 888 513 | 570 683 | 1 612 | 264 406 |
| 金　港 | JinGang | 5 538 246 | 34 046 | 3 040 022 | 2 464 178 | 11 053 | 751 139 |
| 锦　丰 | Jinfeng | 5 000 572 | 37 178 | 3 895 508 | 1 067 886 | 2 221 | 1 201 272 |
| 乐　余 | Leyu | 593 942 | 37 449 | 324 294 | 232 199 | 1 342 | 133 490 |

Continued 3

| 进出口总额（万美元）Total Imports and Exports (USD 10 000) | # 出口总额（万美元）Total Exports (USD 10 000) | 固定资产投资完成额(万元) Value of Investment in Fixed Assets (10 000 yuan) | 财政总收入(万元) Total Revenue (10 000 yuan) | 年末居民储蓄存款(万元) Amount of Year-end Savings Deposit of Residents (10 000 yuan) | 参加养老保险人数(人) Number of Persons Participating in Old Age Insurance (person) | 参加医疗保障人数(人) Number of Rural Residents Participating in Medical Welfare (person) |
|---|---|---|---|---|---|---|
| 242 468 | 118 337 | 1 151 200 | 623 814 | 1 253 216 | 146 239 | 132 516 |
| 20 684 | 12 050 | 394 061 | 85 481 | 270 000 | 34 580 | 37 960 |
| 25 299 | 17 384 | 336 968 | 90 624 | 501 300 | 43 360 | 35 890 |
| 20 555 | 19 034 | 276 619 | 84 891 | 227 825 | 31 257 | 38 388 |
| 113 300 | 81 137 | 750 885 | 344 294 | 780 000 | 93 918 | 71 247 |
| | | | | | | |
| 644 650 | 466 786 | 1 208 382 | 781 977 | 4 217 815 | 226 350 | 187 571 |
| 90 068 | 79 235 | 233 203 | 101 941 | 470 530 | 94 932 | 98 436 |
| 104 390 | 82 311 | 355 880 | 144 255 | 462 741 | 92 038 | 91 709 |
| 91 648 | 86 064 | 351 285 | 164 224 | 449 510 | 28 930 | 30 803 |
| 56 290 | 51 165 | 296 136 | 116 771 | 320 308 | 28 118 | 40 254 |
| 13 062 | 13 062 | 221 291 | 66 465 | 440 170 | 34 023 | 37 684 |
| 11 741 | 11 741 | 158 850 | 50 664 | 257 312 | 45 846 | 50 746 |
| 130 883 | 113 140 | 244 859 | 87 575 | 443 037 | 38 195 | 46 066 |
| 55 213 | 41 135 | 200 142 | 79 638 | 452 600 | 64 326 | 88 952 |
| | | | | | | |
| 620 987 | 491 133 | 1 774 000 | 735 928 | 3 476 882 | 210 343 | 276 598 |
| 630 467 | 72 000 | 357 000 | 162 977 | 614 735 | 60 257 | 94 289 |
| 1 438 194 | 284 145 | 1 513 572 | 713 881 | 1 270 249 | 149 856 | 165 387 |
| 607 200 | 208 100 | 1 436 500 | 449 341 | 723 134 | 110 166 | 131 378 |
| 35 420 | 32 500 | 247 600 | 77 528 | 412 856 | 68 320 | 85 650 |

表3-22 续表 4

| 乡、镇 Townships and Towns | 年末人口(人) Population Year-end (person) | 乡镇从业人员(人) Rural Laborers (person) | #各类科技人员 Scientific and Technical Personnel of All Kinds | 年末耕地面积(公顷) Cultivated Area Year-end (hectare) | #有效灌溉面积 Effective Irrigation Area | 农机总动力(千瓦) Total Agricultural Machinery Power (kw) |
|---|---|---|---|---|---|---|
| 凤 凰 Fenghuang | 102 968 | 63 461 | 8 580 | 2 525 | 2 525 | 43 709 |
| 南 丰 Nanfeng | 72 298 | 38 633 | 3 321 | 2 020 | 2 020 | 31 238 |
| 大 新 Daxin | 69 162 | 34 008 | 656 | 1 708 | 1 708 | 14 662 |
| **昆 山 Kun Shan** | | | | | | |
| 玉 山 Yushan | 203 189 | 141 082 | 23 654 | 895 | 895 | 9 834 |
| 巴 城 Bacheng | 91 045 | 73 969 | 5 730 | 1 138 | 1 138 | 42 388 |
| 周 市 Zhoushi | 140 228 | 102 192 | 29 591 | 544 | 544 | 14 991 |
| 陆 家 Lujia | 91 007 | 79 383 | 5 660 | 372 | 372 | 3 230 |
| 花 桥 Huaqiao | 111 825 | 83 877 | 5 710 | 534 | 534 | 4 878 |
| 淀山湖 Dianshanhu | 50 032 | 37 652 | 7 522 | 813 | 760 | 47 344 |
| 张 浦 Zhangpu | 133 088 | 98 711 | 9 995 | 2 398 | 1 807 | 24 840 |
| 周 庄 Zhouzhuang | 28 182 | 20 076 | 1 223 | 497 | 497 | 20 108 |
| 千 灯 Qiandeng | 149 690 | 94 742 | 1 560 | 1 283 | 1 283 | 13 012 |
| 锦 溪 Jinxi | 51 273 | 51 062 | 763 | 1 106 | 1 106 | 48 321 |
| **太 仓 Tai Cang** | | | | | | |
| 城 厢 Chengxiang | 327 649 | 204 578 | 13 540 | 3 926 | 3 582 | 33 502 |
| 沙 溪 Shaxi | 136 464 | 88 926 | 2 000 | 5 932 | 5 932 | 28 688 |
| 浏 河 Liuhe | 89 986 | 71 071 | 4 985 | 3 297 | 2 627 | 11 012 |
| 浮 桥 Fuqiao | 129 421 | 86 684 | 1 822 | 4 467 | 4 423 | 25 886 |
| 璜 泾 Huangjing | 88 509 | 57 315 | 1 792 | 4 436 | 4 049 | 28 549 |
| 双 凤 Shuangfeng | 57 177 | 41 021 | 1 508 | 2 678 | 2 671 | 17 995 |

注:2012年太仓陆渡镇数据并入城厢镇。

Continued 4

| 农村用电量 (万千瓦时) Electricity Consumed in Rural Area (10 000 kwh) | 农作物播种面积 (公顷) Sown Area of Farm Crops (hectare) | # 粮食作物 Grain Crops | 粮食总产量 (吨) Total Output of Grain (ton) | 油料总产量 (吨) Total Output of Oil-bearing Crops (ton) | 水产品总产量 (吨) Total Output of Aquatic Products (ton) | 肉类总产量 (吨) Total Output of Meat (ton) | # 猪肉产量 Output of Pork | 农民人均纯收入(元) Per Capita Net Income of Rural Resident (yuan) |
|---|---|---|---|---|---|---|---|---|
| 111 756 | 4 540 | 3 503 | 24 878 | 55 | 3 145 | 1 613 | 1 517 | 21 812 |
| 244 580 | 4 815 | 3 188 | 22 339 | 545 | 1 116 | 1 186 | 466 | 23 020 |
| 58 025 | 2 540 | 2 084 | 14 026 | 306 | 1 999 | 1 010 | 940 | 20 583 |
| | | | | | | | | |
| 208 557 | 2 792 | 2 220 | 16 204 | 91 | 7 108 | 350 | 322 | 25 520 |
| 70 681 | 2 681 | 1 265 | 8 685 | 347 | 7 626 | 1 896 | 1 781 | 24 276 |
| 122 041 | 2 008 | 1 228 | 9 504 | 197 | 3 101 | 543 | 467 | 24 273 |
| 127 838 | 1 169 | 711 | 5 170 | 8 | 278 | 120 | 116 | 24 682 |
| 73 117 | 1 042 | 822 | 5 893 | 133 | 298 | 224 | 224 | 24 282 |
| 36 058 | 1 851 | 1 545 | 11 443 | 3 | 7 427 | 2 333 | 2 301 | 22 790 |
| 165 290 | 4 521 | 2 886 | 20 607 | 221 | 11 621 | 3 259 | 2 872 | 24 250 |
| 9 319 | 985 | 772 | 5 455 | 131 | 7 570 | 210 | 199 | 21 906 |
| 114 551 | 3 511 | 2 134 | 15 568 | 73 | 3 761 | 696 | 680 | 24 598 |
| 28 966 | 2 247 | 1 854 | 13 569 | 114 | 3 673 | 1 209 | 1 169 | 21 256 |
| | | | | | | | | |
| 145 467 | 6 771 | 4 227 | 32 183 | 818 | 2 908 | 11 170 | 3 896 | 22 151 |
| 154 619 | 11 003 | 7 203 | 49 571 | 1 466 | 4 966 | 7 320 | 2 500 | 21 613 |
| 32 974 | 5 517 | 2 386 | 17 690 | 785 | 5 010 | 11 969 | 11 425 | 20 051 |
| 48 802 | 8 778 | 6 000 | 43 837 | 1 674 | 4 903 | 4 152 | 3 423 | 20 011 |
| 206 000 | 7 552 | 5 586 | 40 251 | 821 | 2 370 | 1 720 | 790 | 25 917 |
| 30 045 | 3 525 | 1 911 | 17 592 | 671 | 5 061 | 2 975 | 2 050 | 22 005 |

Note:Data of Ludu town in Taicang merged into Chengxiang town in 2012.

表3-22 续表 5

| 乡、镇 Townships and Towns | | 地区生产总值 (万元) Gross Domestic Product (10 000 yuan) | 第一产业 Primary Industry | 第二产业 Secondary Industry | 第三产业 Tertiary Industry | 企业个数 (个) Number of Enterprises (unit) | 企业利税总额 (万元) Pre-tax Profits of Enterprises (10 000 yuan) |
|---|---|---|---|---|---|---|---|
| 凤　凰 | Fenghuang | 879 846 | 32 057 | 547 103 | 300 686 | 1 635 | 243 627 |
| 南　丰 | Nanfeng | 816 090 | 21 211 | 627 187 | 167 692 | 469 | 341 327 |
| 大　新 | Daxin | 307 263 | 17 737 | 183 586 | 105 940 | 674 | 94 232 |
| **昆　山** | **Kun Shan** | | | | | | |
| 玉　山 | Yushan | 8 067 090 | 18 500 | 2 877 958 | 5 170 632 | 6 495 | 1 486 072 |
| 巴　城 | Bacheng | 1 220 793 | 40 023 | 570 183 | 610 587 | 1 878 | 217 561 |
| 周　市 | Zhoushi | 1 575 301 | 12 303 | 993 247 | 569 751 | 3 248 | 445 917 |
| 陆　家 | Lujia | 1 160 060 | 5 100 | 748 300 | 406 660 | 1 976 | 447 040 |
| 花　桥 | Huaqiao | 1 414 788 | 5 550 | 438 826 | 970 412 | 1 983 | 371 954 |
| 淀山湖 | Dianshanhu | 666 102 | 18 800 | 365 773 | 281 529 | 1 113 | 177 429 |
| 张　浦 | Zhangpu | 1 665 011 | 39 000 | 1 130 011 | 496 000 | 2 986 | 405 953 |
| 周　庄 | Zhouzhuang | 357 723 | 7 002 | 50 703 | 300 018 | 796 | 56 754 |
| 千　灯 | Qiandeng | 1 280 918 | 16 318 | 845 892 | 418 708 | 3 348 | 524 979 |
| 锦　溪 | Jinxi | 540 247 | 18 086 | 256 643 | 265 518 | 907 | 177 207 |
| **太　仓** | **Tai Cang** | | | | | | |
| 城　厢 | Chengxiang | 3 340 978 | 44 023 | 1 558 051 | 1 738 904 | 5 605 | 1 829 547 |
| 沙　溪 | Shaxi | 1 152 938 | 60 704 | 620 914 | 471 320 | 2 850 | 105 382 |
| 浏　河 | Liuhe | 703 000 | 46 500 | 306 247 | 350 253 | 1 052 | 70 542 |
| 浮　桥 | Fuqiao | 2 167 536 | 44 231 | 1 670 266 | 453 039 | 1 829 | 924 489 |
| 璜　泾 | Huangjing | 1 006 863 | 20 005 | 687 614 | 299 244 | 1 137 | 115 927 |
| 双　凤 | Shuangfeng | 271 636 | 33 140 | 122 816 | 115 680 | 1 005 | 30 179 |

Continued 5

| 进出口总额（万美元）Total Imports and Exports (USD 10 000) | # 出口总额（万美元）Total Exports (USD 10 000 | 固定资产投资完成额(万元) Value of Investment in Fixed Assets (10 000 yuan) | 财政总收入(万元) Total Revenue (10 000 yuan) | 年末居民储蓄存款(万元) Amount of Year-end Savings Deposit of Residents (10 000 yuan) | 参加养老保险人数(人) Number of Persons Participating in Old Age Insurance (person) | 参加医疗保障人数(人) Number of Rural Residents Participating in Medical Welfare (person) |
|---|---|---|---|---|---|---|
| 113 460 | 80 368 | 466 500 | 144 153 | 469 339 | 53 167 | 66 121 |
| 205 996 | 73 876 | 379 000 | 147 876 | 272 704 | 28 302 | 47 052 |
| 19 473 | 16 351 | 132 700 | 45 347 | 227 971 | 32 484 | 36 783 |
| | | | | | | |
| 661 311 | 421 050 | 1 220 434 | 1 120 797 | 3 299 265 | 117 542 | 171 985 |
| 108 306 | 68 327 | 471 931 | 291 078 | 487 726 | 82 280 | 91 045 |
| 183 900 | 105 900 | 538 400 | 371 704 | 507 596 | 128 565 | 140 228 |
| 170 014 | 122 950 | 422 440 | 227 919 | 329 000 | 77 358 | 90 765 |
| 131 249 | 62 140 | 1 151 892 | 498 054 | 340 632 | 101 560 | 110 930 |
| 73 500 | 60 000 | 313 127 | 150 966 | 173 986 | 43 205 | 49 932 |
| 204 371 | 83 487 | 490 621 | 323 511 | 460 785 | 72 983 | 95 492 |
| 13 336 | 11 064 | 132 564 | 56 799 | 113 527 | 19 559 | 22 280 |
| 169 500 | 108 400 | 459 536 | 297 210 | 416 500 | 128 655 | 148 201 |
| 91 996 | 61 636 | 241 873 | 155 315 | 159 875 | 39 621 | 43 123 |
| | | | | | | |
| 487 310 | 258 911 | 1 515 518 | 1 038 216 | 390 927 | 308 740 | 317 810 |
| 72 085 | 44 573 | 376 089 | 103 282 | 385 486 | 70 699 | 46 085 |
| 40 857 | 32 651 | 300 764 | 73 177 | 229 460 | 89 182 | 88 756 |
| 410 273 | 123 658 | 1 452 484 | 392 977 | 531 957 | 103 065 | 124 244 |
| 36 902 | 10 360 | 376 772 | 69 967 | 268 123 | 38 541 | 26 282 |
| 12 485 | 10 213 | 260 138 | 43 319 | 119 452 | 56 634 | 56 835 |

# 主要统计指标解释

**农林牧渔业总产值** 指以货币表现的农、林、牧、渔业全部产品和对农林牧渔业生产活动进行的各种支持性服务活动的价值总量，它反映一定时期内农林牧渔业生产总规模和总成果。1957年以前的农林牧渔业总产值中包括了厩肥和农民自给性手工业(如农民自制衣服、鞋、袜，自己从事粮食初步加工等)。1958年及以后，林业中增加了村及村以下竹木采伐产值；牧业中取消了厩肥产值；副业中取消了农民自给性手工业产值，增加了村及村以下办的工业产值； 渔业中增加了海洋捕捞水产品产值。1980年及以后，在副业中增加了农民家庭兼营工业商品部分的产值。从1984年起村及村以下工业产值划归工业。从1993年起取消副业，将野生动物的捕猎划入牧业，野生植物采集和农民家庭兼营商品性工业划归农业。从2003年起，执行新的国民经济行业分类标准，农林牧渔业总产值中包括了农林牧渔服务业产值。林业中增加了森林采运业产值。农业中取消了家庭兼营商品性工业产值，将野生林产品的采集划归林业。

农林牧渔业总产值的计算方法通常是按农、林、牧、渔业产品及其副产品的产量分别乘以各自单位产品价格求得；少数生产周期较长，当年没有产品或产品产量不易统计的，则采用间接方法匡算其产值；然后将四业产品产值及农林牧渔服务业产值相加即为农林牧渔业总产值。

**粮食产量** 指全社会的产量。包括国有经济经营的、集体统一经营的和农民家庭经营的粮食产量，还包括工矿企业办的农场和其他生产单位的产量。粮食除包括稻谷、小麦、玉米、高粱、谷子及其他杂粮外，还包括薯类和豆类。其产量计算方法，豆类按去豆荚后的干豆计算；薯类(包括甘薯和马铃薯，不包括芋头和木薯)1963年以前按每4公斤鲜薯折1公斤粮食计算，从1964年开始改为按5公斤鲜薯折1公斤粮食计算。城市郊区作为蔬菜的薯类(如马铃薯等)按鲜品计算，并且不作粮食统计。其他粮食一律按脱粒后的原粮计算。1989年以前全国粮食产量数据主要靠全面报表取得，1989年开始使用抽样调查数据。

**棉花产量** 指全社会的产量。包括春播棉和夏播棉。产量按皮棉计算。不包括木棉。

**油料产量** 指全部油料作物的生产量。包括花生、油菜籽、芝麻、向日葵籽、胡麻籽（亚麻籽）和其他油料。不包括大豆、木本油料和野生油料。花生以带壳干花生计算。

**水产品产量** 指人工养殖的水产品和天然生长的水产品的捕捞量。包括海水的鱼类、虾蟹类、贝类和藻类以及内陆水域的鱼类、虾蟹类和贝类，不包括淡水生植物。水产品产量是通过各级水产和统计部门逐级上报取得数据。1995年及以前，贝类中牡蛎按鲜肉计算；蚶、蛤、蛙按5斤鲜品折1斤计算。1996年以后则统一按鲜品计算。

**猪、牛、羊肉产量** 指当年出栏并已屠宰、除去头蹄下水后带骨肉(即胴体重)的重量。包括全社会范围内的产量。

**期初(末)畜禽存栏头(只)数** 指报告期初(末)农村各种合作经济组织和国营农场、农民个人、机关、团体、学校、工矿企业、部队等单位以及城镇居民饲养的大牲畜、猪、羊、家禽等畜禽的存栏数。

**农作物播种面积** 指实际播种或移植有农作物的面积。凡是实际种植有农作物的面积，不论种植在耕地上还是种植在非耕地上，均包括在农作物播种面积中。在播种季节基本结束后，因遭灾而重新改种和补种的农作物面积，也包括在内。它是反映我国耕地面积利用情况的一个重要指标。目前，农作物播种面积主要包括粮食、棉花、油料、糖料、麻类、烟叶、蔬菜和瓜类、药材和其他农作物九大类。

**有效灌溉面积** 指具有一定的水源，地块比较平整，灌溉工程或设备已经配套，在一般年景下，当年能够进行正常灌溉的耕地面积。在一般情况下，有效灌溉面积应等于灌溉工程或设备已经配备，能够进行正常灌溉的水田和水浇地面积之和。它是反映我国耕地抗旱能力的一个重要指标。

**农用化肥施用量** 指本年内实际用于农业生产的化肥数量，包括氮肥、磷肥、钾肥和复合肥。化肥施用量要求按折纯量计算数量。折纯量是指把氮肥、磷肥、钾肥分别按含氮、含五氧化二磷、含氧化钾的百分之百成份进行折算后的数量。复合肥按其所含主要成分折算。公式为：

折纯量=实物量×某种化肥有效成份含量的百分比

**农业机械总动力**　指主要用于农、林、牧、渔业的各种动力机械的动力总和。包括耕作机械、排灌机械、收获机械、农用运输机械、植物保护机械、牧业机械、林业机械、渔业机械和其他农业机械〔内燃机按引擎马力折成瓦(特)计算、电动机按功率折成瓦(特)计算〕。不包括专门用于乡、镇、村、组办工业、基本建设、非农业运输、科学试验和教学等非农业生产方面用的动力机械与作业机械。这个指标的统计数据主要来源于农机部门。

**乡村户数**　指长期(一年以上)居住在乡镇(不包括城关镇)行政管理区域内的住户，还包括居住在城关镇所辖行政村范围内的农村住户。户口不在本地而在本地居住一年及以上的住户也包括在本地农村住户内；有本地户口，但举家外出谋生一年以上的住户，无论是否保留承包耕地都不包括在本地农村住户范围内。不包括乡村地区内的国有经济的机关、团体、学校、企业、事业单位的集体户。

**乡村人口数**　指乡村地区常住居民户数中的常住人口数，即经常在家或在家居住6个月以上，而且经济和生活与本户连成一体的人口。外出从业人员在外居住时间虽然在6个月以上，但收入主要带回家中，经济与本户连为一体，仍视为家庭常住人口；在家居住，生活和本户连成一体的国家职工、退休人员也为家庭常住人口。但是现役军人、中专及以上(走读生除外)的在校学生、以及常年在外(不包括探亲、看病等)且已有稳定的职业与居住场所的外出从业人员，不应当作家庭常住人口。

**乡村从业人员**　指乡村人口中实际参加生产经营活动并取得实物或货币收入的人员，包括劳动年龄内经常参加劳动的人员，也包括超过劳动年龄但经常参加劳动的人员，但不包括户口在家的在外学生、现役军人和丧失劳动能力的人，也不包括待业人员和家务劳动者。从业人员按从事主业时间最长（时间相同按收入）分为农林牧渔业从业人员、工业从业人员、建筑业从业人员、交通运输业、仓储及邮电通信业从业人员、批零贸易业、餐饮业从业人员、其他非农行业从业人员。

# EXPLANATORY NOTES ON MAIN STATISTICAL INDICATORS

**Gross Output Value of Agriculture, Forestry, Animal Husbandry and Fishery** refers to the total value of products of agriculture, forestry, animal husbandry and fishery, and total value of services in support of agriculture, forestry, animal husbandry and fishery activities. It reflects the total scale and results of agricultural production during a given period. Prior to 1957, China's gross agricultural output value included barnyard manure and handicraft products for self-consumption (clothes, shoes, stockings, and initial grain processing undertaken by peasants). Since 1958, cutting and felling of bamboo and trees by villages and other cooperative organizations under villages have been included in forestry; value of barnyard manure has been excluded from animal husbandry; self consumed handicrafts have not been included from sideline occupations, while the output value of industries run by villages and cooperative organizations under village has been included in sideline occupations; and the output value of fish catches by motor fishing boats has been added to fishery. Since 1980, the value of handicraft products made for sale by individuals in households has been added to sideline occupations. Since 1984, industries run by villages and under villages have been included in the sector of industry. Since 1993, the subdivision of sideline occupations has been cancelled, and the hunting of wild animals has been classified into animal husbandry, and the gathering of wild plants and commodity industry run by rural household have been included in farming. A new industrial classification of economic activities was introduced in 2003. Under the new classification, value of services to agriculture, forestry, animal husbandry and fishery is included in the gross output value of agriculture, value of wood felling and transport is included in forestry, value of industrial output by rural households is not included in agriculture, and the collection of wild forest products is taken from agriculture and included in forestry.

Gross output value of agriculture is obtained by multiplying the output of each product or by-product by its price, resulting in the output value of each single item. For a small number of products, annual output of which is not available or difficult to get due to the long production (growing) process involved, the output value is estimated through an indirect approach. The sum of output values of all products of agriculture, forestry, animal husbandry and fishery and services in support to those industries is then equal to the gross output value of agriculture.

**Grain Output** refers to the total output in the whole country including grains produced by State farms, collective units, rural households, as well as by farms affiliated to industrial and mining enterprises and other production units. Grain includes rice, wheat, corn, sorghum, millet and other miscellaneous grains as well as tubers and beans. Output of beans refers to dry beans without pods. The output of tubers (sweet potatoes and potatoes, not including taros and cassava) are converted into that of grain at the ratio 4:1, i.e. 4 kilograms of fresh tubers were equivalent to 1 kilogram of grain up to 1963. Since 1964 the ratio for conversion has been 5:1. Tubers supplied as vegetables (such as potatoes) in cities and suburbs are calculated as fresh vegetables and their output is not included in the output of grain. Output of all other grains refers to husked grain. Data on grain production before 1989 were obtained through the Comprehensive Statistical Reporting System. Since 1989, data from sample surveys are used.

**Cotton Output** refers to cotton production in the whole country including cotton planted in spring and in autumn. Output is measured as the weight of ginned cotton. Ceiba is not included.

**Output of Oil-bearing Crops** refers to the total production of oil-bearing crops of various kinds, including peanuts (dry, in shell), rapeseeds, sesame, sunflower seeds, flax seeds, and other oil-bearing crops. Soybeans, oil-bearing woody plants, and wild oil-bearing crops are not included.

**Output of Aquatic Products** refers to catches of both artificially cultured and naturally grown aquatic products, including fish, shrimps, crabs and shellfish in sea and inland water as well as seaweed. Freshwater plants are not included.

**Output of Pork, Beef, and Mutton** refers to the meat of slaughtered hogs, cattle, sheep and goats with head, feet, and offal taken away. Data refers to the production of the whole country.

**Number of Livestock or Poultry in Stock at Beginning (or End) of Period** refers to the total number of large animals, pigs, sheep, fowls, etc. raised by rural cooperative organizations, State farms, rural individuals, government agencies, schools, industrial and mining enterprises, army, and urban residents at the beginning (or end) of the reference period.

**Sown Area of Crops** refers to area of land sown or transplanted with crops regardless of being in cultivated area or non-cultivated area. Area of land re-sown due to natural disasters is also included. This is an important indicator that can reflect the utilization condition of the cultivated land in China. At present, the sown area of crops mainly include the following 9 categories of crops: grain, cotton, oil-bearing crops, sugar crops, flax crops, tobacco, vegetables and melons, medicinal materials and other farm crops.

**Irrigated Area** refers to area of land that are effectively irrigated, i.e. relatively level land, where there are water sources or complete sets of irrigation facilities to lift and move adequate water for irrigation purpose under normal conditions. Under normal situations, irrigated area is the sum of watered fields and irrigated fields where irrigation systems or equipment have been installed for regular irrigation purpose. This important indicator reflects drought resistance capacity of the cultivated land in China.

**Consumption of Chemical Fertilizers in Agriculture** refers to the quantity of chemical fertilizers applied in agriculture in the year, including nitrogenous fertilizer, phosphate fertilizer, potash fertilizer, and compound fertilizer. The consumption of chemical fertilizers is calculated in terms of volume of effective components by means of converting the gross weight of the respective fertilizers into weight containing effective component (e.g. nitrogen content in nitrogenous fertilizer, phosphorous pentoxide contents in phosphate fertilizer, and potassium oxide contents in potash fertilizer). Compound fertilizer is converted in regard to its major components. The formula is:

Volume of effective component= physical quantity× effective component of certain chemical fertilizer (%)

**Total Power of Agricultural Machinery** refers to total mechanical power of machinery used in agriculture, forestry, animal husbandry and fishery, including machinery for ploughing, irrigation and drainage, harvesting, transport, plant protection, animal husbandry, forestry and fishery and other agricultural machineries. (For the power of internal combustion engines, it is converted from its horsepower into watts while for electric motors the output power is converted into watts.) Machinery employed for non-agricultural purposes, such as the machines used in township-run and village-run industry, construction, non-agricultural transport, scientific experiments and teaching, are not included. Data are mainly from agricultural machinery agencies.

**Number of Households in Villages** refers to households resident on a long term basis (i.e. 1 year or more) in administrative districts in townships (not including urban townships), including rural households resident in areas under the jurisdiction of urban townships. Households whose household registration is not in the locality yet resident for one year or more are included among the rural households. Households having local household registration yet the whole household having left for somewhere else for work for one year or more, whether still retaining contracted farmland, are not included among the local rural households. Also not included are collective households associated with institutions of the State economy, organizations, schools and enterprises.

**Number of Residents of Villages** refers to the number of usual residents in usual resident households in rural areas. These are persons who are regularly at home or are at home for 6 months or more and economically and socially integrated with the household. For persons who are away from home for employment for more than 6 months yet the main income is brought back home and thus economically integrated with the household, the person is still considered as a usual resident of the household. National employee and retired personnel who reside at home and whose living is integrated with the household are also considered as usual residents. However, serving military personnel, students at secondary technical level or above ( unless commuting between school and home), employed persons who are regularly elsewhere the year round ( except visiting relatives or receiving medical attention) and having a stable job and residence should not be considered as usual resident of the household.

**Rural Persons Engaged** refer to persons in the rural labour force aged over 16 years who are engaged in actual production and management activities and receive payment in kind or wages, including those covered within the labour force age bracket and regularly participating in production activities, and those who are out of the labour force age bracket yet also participating in production activities regularly. Students studying in other places with their permanent residence registered in local areas, servicemen and persons incapable of working are not included. Also not included are those who are waiting for jobs and those engaged in housework. Persons employed are classified as persons engaged in agriculture, forestry, animal husbandry or fishery activities; persons engaged in industrial activities; persons engaged in construction activities; persons engaged in transport, storage and telecommunications activities; persons engaged in wholesale and retail trade and catering activities; and persons engaged in other non-agriculture activities. In case the person is engaged in more than one type of work, classification is according to the industry in which he works most of the time (where time is the same income would be the criterion).

# 四、工 业

## CHAPTER 4
## INDUSTRY

# 工 业
# INDUSTRY

## 主 要 统 计 指 标
## MAJOR STATISTICAL INDICATORS

| | | | | |
|---|---|---|---|---|
| 2012年末工业企业单位数 | Number of Industrial Enterprises | 132 870 | 个 | unit |
| 比上年增长 | Increase Over Last Year | 9.0 | % | |
| 2012年工业总产值 | Gross Industrial Output Value | 34 528.10 | 亿元 | 100 million yuan |
| 比上年增长 | Increase Over Last Year | 3.5 | % | |
| 2012年规模以上工业总产值 | Gross Industrial Output Value Above Designated Size | 28 745.54 | 亿元 | 100 million yuan |
| 比上年增长 | Increase Over Last Year | 5.2 | % | |
| 按轻重工业分 | Grouped by Light and Heavy Industry | | | |
| 轻工业 | Light Industry | 7 391.61 | 亿元 | 100 million yuan |
| 重工业 | Heavy Industry | 21 353.93 | 亿元 | 100 million yuan |
| 按企业规模分 | Grouped by Size of Enterprises | | | |
| 大型企业 | Large | 15 757.95 | 亿元 | 100 million yuan |
| 中型企业 | Medium-sized | 5 597.08 | 亿元 | 100 million yuan |
| 小型企业 | Small | 6 974.37 | 亿元 | 100 million yuan |
| 微型企业 | Micro | 416.13 | 亿元 | 100 million yuan |

表4-1

# 历年工业企业单位数、工业总产值
# NUMBER AND OUTPUT VALUE OF INDUSTRIAL ENTERPRISES OVER THE YEARS

单位：万元 (10 000 yuan)

| 年 份 Year | 企业单位数 (个) Number of Enterprises (unit) | 工业总产值 Gross Industrial Output Value | | | | | | |
|---|---|---|---|---|---|---|---|---|
| | | 全 市 Whole Municipality | 市 区 Urban Area | # 吴江区 Wujiang District | 常 熟 Changshu | 张家港 Zhangjiagang | 昆 山 Kunshan | 太 仓 Taicang |
| 1978 | | 485 050 | 324 779 | 40 779 | 71 543 | 39 525 | 22 464 | 26 739 |
| 1979 | | 568 074 | 372 330 | 50 153 | 81 270 | 51 014 | 28 118 | 35 342 |
| 1980 | | 737 116 | 458 653 | 69 878 | 113 161 | 79 941 | 35 805 | 49 556 |
| 1981 | | 801 465 | 481 403 | 70 043 | 127 233 | 96 783 | 38 525 | 57 521 |
| 1982 | | 818 593 | 480 878 | 77 958 | 133 729 | 102 684 | 44 928 | 56 374 |
| 1983 | | 932 959 | 529 908 | 93 745 | 153 295 | 129 705 | 54 397 | 65 654 |
| 1984 | | 1 242 966 | 669 518 | 126 135 | 215 160 | 190 301 | 76 010 | 91 977 |
| 1985 | 31 046 | 1 891 164 | 943 476 | 185 526 | 348 644 | 315 300 | 128 362 | 155 382 |
| 1986 | 54 428 | 2 324 775 | 1 142 154 | 236 563 | 433 633 | 402 930 | 176 661 | 169 397 |
| 1987 | 67 299 | 3 036 865 | 1 454 227 | 320 836 | 565 274 | 535 849 | 249 480 | 232 035 |
| 1988 | 66 687 | 4 306 836 | 2 047 716 | 467 648 | 788 752 | 720 695 | 392 260 | 357 413 |
| 1989 | 59 818 | 5 058 307 | 2 453 367 | 563 709 | 874 586 | 807 090 | 509 303 | 413 961 |
| 1990 | 54 221 | 5 637 287 | 2 725 421 | 736 228 | 970 239 | 932 662 | 566 983 | 441 982 |
| 1991 | 53 443 | 6 598 757 | 3 104 843 | 818 394 | 1 139 318 | 1 030 910 | 724 593 | 599 093 |
| 1992 | 46 384 | 11 534 402 | 4 826 171 | 1 419 857 | 2 040 357 | 2 043 043 | 1 325 952 | 1 298 879 |
| 1993 | 58 995 | 17 826 171 | 7 338 941 | 2 303 254 | 3 046 051 | 3 410 930 | 1 940 525 | 2 089 724 |
| 1994 | 70 735 | 24 020 806 | 10 163 646 | 3 454 130 | 3 958 684 | 4 976 643 | 2 366 847 | 2 554 986 |
| 1995 | 75 854 | 19 627 449 | 8 944 876 | 2 696 328 | 3 235 916 | 4 200 560 | 1 802 991 | 1 443 106 |
| 1996 | 69 648 | 22 745 223 | 10 054 825 | 2 883 626 | 3 627 776 | 4 974 754 | 2 260 795 | 1 827 073 |
| 1997 | 77 201 | 24 224 588 | 10 824 895 | 3 028 394 | 3 621 599 | 4 993 214 | 2 700 890 | 2 083 990 |
| 1998 | 82 263 | 26 157 900 | 11 905 551 | 3 551 356 | 4 078 000 | 4 720 555 | 3 051 788 | 2 402 006 |
| 1999 | 83 978 | 30 062 835 | 14 275 058 | 3 731 020 | 4 497 008 | 4 966 329 | 3 659 803 | 2 664 637 |
| 2000 | 87 234 | 36 207 408 | 17 619 030 | 4 131 972 | 5 578 818 | 5 599 596 | 4 306 080 | 3 103 884 |
| 2001 | 89 439 | 40 758 099 | 19 095 203 | 4 550 114 | 6 602 696 | 6 811 218 | 5 128 749 | 3 120 233 |
| 2002 | 93 913 | 51 394 368 | 24 077 620 | 6 438 686 | 8 001 841 | 8 208 084 | 7 456 206 | 3 650 617 |
| 2003 | 103 517 | 70 107 652 | 33 693 949 | 9 011 620 | 10 384 361 | 11 009 185 | 10 672 258 | 4 347 899 |
| 2004 | 82 565 | 95 601 322 | 45 333 212 | 12 105 415 | 13 082 757 | 15 426 095 | 16 333 095 | 5 426 163 |
| 2005 | 85 581 | 121 230 937 | 54 565 875 | 14 853 547 | 16 502 812 | 20 021 799 | 23 332 394 | 6 808 057 |
| 2006 | 91 000 | 153 159 355 | 67 809 871 | 18 552 000 | 20 501 652 | 25 017 292 | 30 828 100 | 9 002 440 |
| 2007 | 99 812 | 190 601 250 | 81 482 095 | 23 300 000 | 25 603 688 | 32 201 183 | 40 306 451 | 11 007 833 |
| 2008 | 106 231 | 221 034 689 | 90 942 337 | 26 504 900 | 29 182 652 | 37 902 600 | 50 005 000 | 13 002 100 |
| 2009 | 112 468 | 237 045 579 | 93 827 939 | 25 122 500 | 30 106 215 | 40 021 014 | 58 032 212 | 15 058 199 |
| 2010 | 118 080 | 284 836 867 | 112 293 666 | 31 020 000 | 36 521 562 | 47 008 700 | 70 012 900 | 19 000 039 |
| 2011 | 121 928 | 333 473 737 | 132 940 095 | 37 000 125 | 42 753 862 | 54 555 010 | 80 015 670 | 23 209 100 |
| 2012 | 132 870 | 345 281 021 | 136 450 967 | 37 910 000 | 44 055 216 | 55 208 800 | 85 205 138 | 24 360 900 |

注：1995年起工业总产值按新口径计算。 Note:The total industrial output value from 1995 is calculated by the new method.

表4-2

# 历年分地区规模以上工业企业工业总产值
# OUTPUT VALUE OF INDUSTRIAL ENTERPRISES ABOVE DESIGNATED SIZE BY REGION OVER THE YEARS

单位：万元　　(10 000 yuan)

| 年 份 Year | 全 市 Whole Municipality | 市 区 Urban Area | # 吴江区 Wujiang District | 常 熟 Changshu | 张家港 Zhangjiagang | 昆 山 Kunshan | 太 仓 Taicang |
|---|---|---|---|---|---|---|---|
| 1998 | 16 256 934 | 7 336 488 | 1 665 121 | 2 101 273 | 3 072 288 | 2 420 098 | 1 326 787 |
| 1999 | 19 263 441 | 9 070 298 | 1 876 460 | 2 484 232 | 3 391 149 | 2 894 854 | 1 422 908 |
| 2000 | 23 965 052 | 11 659 000 | 2 318 918 | 3 096 625 | 4 007 507 | 3 559 366 | 1 642 554 |
| 2001 | 27 847 905 | 13 161 313 | 2 765 147 | 3 724 183 | 5 003 145 | 4 345 031 | 1 614 233 |
| 2002 | 34 658 727 | 15 930 828 | 3 290 451 | 4 352 008 | 6 219 393 | 6 173 313 | 1 983 185 |
| 2003 | 49 765 080 | 23 649 624 | 4 502 385 | 5 571 061 | 8 610 559 | 9 389 353 | 2 544 483 |
| 2004 | 73 075 445 | 35 517 607 | 8 469 680 | 7 520 464 | 12 470 707 | 14 101 475 | 3 465 192 |
| 2005 | 99 085 843 | 45 072 779 | 11 542 869 | 11 482 290 | 16 322 488 | 21 211 715 | 4 996 571 |
| 2006 | 125 385 124 | 54 348 374 | 14 684 833 | 15 582 685 | 20 499 187 | 27 986 607 | 6 968 271 |
| 2007 | 159 089 177 | 66 443 947 | 19 001 048 | 20 130 711 | 27 026 673 | 36 899 633 | 8 588 213 |
| 2008 | 186 301 295 | 76 343 404 | 21 784 723 | 22 907 113 | 31 537 806 | 45 548 614 | 9 964 358 |
| 2009 | 202 844 954 | 79 772 998 | 21 021 825 | 23 265 394 | 34 320 651 | 53 820 320 | 11 665 592 |
| 2010 | 246 516 665 | 97 355 621 | 26 216 173 | 28 832 743 | 39 579 760 | 65 908 022 | 14 840 519 |
| 2011 | 277 787 533 | 110 767 237 | 29 936 721 | 32 516 638 | 44 619 122 | 72 822 072 | 17 062 464 |
| 2012 | 287 455 409 | 111 570 697 | 29 863 062 | 33 692 100 | 47 005 617 | 76 868 173 | 18 318 822 |

注:2010年及以前规模以上工业企业为主营业务收入1000万元以上企业;2011年起规模以上工业企业调为主营业务收入2000万元以上企业。

Note: Before 2010, industrial enterprises above Designated Size refers to enterprise with main business income above 10 million yuan; In 2011, industrial enterprises above Designated Size refers to enterprise with main business income above 20 million yuan.

表4-3 历年规模以上工业企业单位数、总产值

单位：万元

| 年 份<br>Year | 企业单位数(个)<br>Number of Enterprises<br>(unit) | 工业总产值<br>Gross Industrial Output Value | 按轻重工业分<br>Grouped by Light and Heavy Industry | |
|---|---|---|---|---|
| | | | 轻工业<br>Light Industry | 重工业<br>Heavy Industry |
| 1998 | 2 994 | 16 256 934 | 8 893 282 | 7 363 652 |
| 1999 | 3 002 | 19 263 441 | 10 156 195 | 9 107 246 |
| 2000 | 3 112 | 23 965 052 | 11 436 139 | 12 528 913 |
| 2001 | 3 735 | 27 847 905 | 12 809 043 | 15 038 862 |
| 2002 | 4 112 | 34 658 727 | 15 444 514 | 19 214 212 |
| 2003 | 4 553 | 49 765 080 | 17 678 551 | 32 086 529 |
| 2004 | 5 044 | 73 075 445 | 23 975 758 | 49 099 687 |
| 2005 | 6 743 | 99 085 843 | 33 334 762 | 65 751 081 |
| 2006 | 7 485 | 125 385 124 | 41 050 258 | 84 334 866 |
| 2007 | 8 632 | 159 089 177 | 49 727 549 | 109 361 628 |
| 2008 | 9 959 | 186 301 295 | 53 942 361 | 132 358 934 |
| 2009 | 13 720 | 202 844 954 | 57 460 526 | 145 384 428 |
| 2010 | 13 538 | 246 516 665 | 67 657 641 | 178 859 024 |
| 2011 | 9 904 | 277 787 533 | 73 490 164 | 204 297 369 |
| 2012 | 10 444 | 287 455 409 | 73 916 098 | 213 539 311 |

注:2012年起企业规模按新标准划分为大型、中型、小型和微型。

# NUMBER AND OUTPUT VALUE OF INDUSTRIAL ENTERPRISES ABOVE DESIGNATED SIZE OVER THE YEARS

(10 000 yuan)

| 按企业规模分 Grouped by Size of Enterprises | | | |
|---|---|---|---|
| 大型企业 Large | 中型企业 Medium-sized | 小型企业 Small | 微型企业 Micro |
| 2 995 207 | 2 609 044 | 10 652 683 | |
| 3 414 152 | 2 716 347 | 13 132 942 | |
| 3 904 674 | 3 109 090 | 16 951 288 | |
| 7 135 751 | 8 218 624 | 12 493 530 | |
| 8 539 021 | 9 757 505 | 16 362 201 | |
| 16 870 145 | 19 628 859 | 13 266 076 | |
| 21 811 989 | 29 610 744 | 21 652 712 | |
| 35 539 278 | 38 002 461 | 25 544 104 | |
| 47 091 734 | 45 881 307 | 32 412 083 | |
| 60 631 093 | 56 618 033 | 41 840 051 | |
| 71 641 117 | 59 368 646 | 55 291 532 | |
| 85 074 954 | 61 423 155 | 56 346 845 | |
| 105 149 095 | 74 590 048 | 66 777 522 | |
| 124 795 596 | 83 096 116 | 69 895 821 | |
| 157 579 505 | 55 970 829 | 69 743 737 | 4 161 338 |

Note: From 2012, the enterprise size divide into large, medium-sized, small and micro by new standard.

表4-4

# 全市工业企业数与总产值 (2012年)

| 地　　区 | Region | 全部工业 Total Industry | 规模以上工业 Enterprises Above Designated | 按轻重工业 Grouped by Light and Heavy Industry | |
|---|---|---|---|---|---|
| | | | | 轻工业 Light Industry | 重工业 Heavy Industry |
| **工业企业单位数 (个)** | **Number of Industrial Enterprises (unit)** | **132 870** | **10 444** | **4 266** | **6 178** |
| 市　区 | Urban Area | 45 916 | 4 708 | 1 796 | 2 912 |
| 姑苏区 | Gusu District | 1 798 | 46 | 10 | 36 |
| 吴中区 | Wuzhong District | 10 212 | 922 | 306 | 616 |
| 相城区 | Xiangcheng District | 9 971 | 713 | 229 | 484 |
| 高新区、虎丘区 | New Hi-tech Zone & Huqiu District | 3 849 | 642 | 150 | 492 |
| 工业园区 | Industrial Park | 5 092 | 795 | 164 | 631 |
| 吴江区 | Wujiang District | 14 994 | 1 590 | 937 | 653 |
| 常　熟 | Changshu | 33 468 | 1 453 | 771 | 682 |
| 张家港 | Zhangjiagang | 17 235 | 1 242 | 570 | 672 |
| 昆　山 | Kunshan | 24 753 | 1 863 | 496 | 1 367 |
| 太　仓 | Taicang | 11 498 | 1 178 | 633 | 545 |
| **工业总产值 (万元)** | **Gross Industrial Output Value (10 000 yuan)** | **345 281 021** | **287 455 409** | **73 916 098** | **213 539 311** |
| 市　区 | Urban Area | 136 450 967 | 111 570 697 | 29 951 834 | 81 618 863 |
| 姑苏区 | Gusu District | 1 324 300 | 818 801 | 101 188 | 717 613 |
| 吴中区 | Wuzhong District | 16 010 901 | 11 870 617 | 3 404 172 | 8 466 445 |
| 相城区 | Xiangcheng District | 12 601 266 | 8 309 525 | 2 502 202 | 5 807 323 |
| 高新区、虎丘区 | New Hi-tech Zone & Huqiu District | 25 752 200 | 23 715 780 | 4 912 497 | 18 803 283 |
| 工业园区 | Industrial Park | 42 852 300 | 36 992 912 | 6 983 345 | 30 009 567 |
| 吴江区 | Wujiang District | 37 910 000 | 29 863 062 | 12 048 430 | 17 814 632 |
| 常　熟 | Changshu | 44 055 216 | 33 692 100 | 14 875 752 | 18 816 348 |
| 张家港 | Zhangjiagang | 55 208 800 | 47 005 617 | 11 578 596 | 35 427 021 |
| 昆　山 | Kunshan | 85 205 138 | 76 868 173 | 10 121 174 | 66 746 999 |
| 太　仓 | Taicang | 24 360 900 | 18 318 822 | 7 388 742 | 10 930 080 |

# NUMBER AND OUTPUT VALUE OF INDUSTRIAL ENTERPRISES OF THE WHOLE MUNICIPALITY (2012)

| 按经济类型分 Grouped by Ownership | | | | | 规模以下工业 Enterprises Below Designated Size |
|---|---|---|---|---|---|
| 国 有 State-owned | 民 营 Private and Individual | # 私 营 Private | 外商及港澳台 Enterprises with Investment from Foreign, Hong Kong, Macao and Taiwan | 其 他 Other | |
| **35** | **5 577** | **4 998** | **4 777** | **55** | **122 426** |
| 20 | 2 294 | 2 035 | 2 371 | 23 | 41 208 |
| 1 | 29 | 18 | 13 | 3 | 1 752 |
| 3 | 482 | 419 | 435 | 2 | 9 290 |
| 3 | 452 | 405 | 256 | 2 | 9 258 |
| 8 | 207 | 148 | 417 | 10 | 3 207 |
| 3 | 111 | 85 | 677 | 4 | 4 297 |
| 2 | 1 013 | 960 | 573 | 2 | 13 404 |
| 4 | 1 077 | 989 | 366 | 6 | 32 015 |
| 2 | 950 | 816 | 281 | 9 | 15 993 |
| 5 | 555 | 498 | 1 296 | 7 | 22 890 |
| 4 | 701 | 660 | 463 | 10 | 10 320 |
| **1 400 640** | **91 636 331** | **48 675 443** | **188 704 313** | **5 714 125** | **57 825 612** |
| 998 846 | 25 465 131 | 18 452 235 | 83 737 611 | 1 369 109 | 24 880 270 |
| 25 927 | 132 043 | 81 897 | 399 205 | 261 626 | 505 499 |
| 47 720 | 4 250 472 | 3 148 890 | 7 523 916 | 48 509 | 4 140 284 |
| 631 727 | 4 172 319 | 2 871 437 | 3 479 296 | 26 183 | 4 291 741 |
| 202 446 | 2 047 988 | 1 088 760 | 20 792 992 | 672 354 | 2 036 420 |
| 68 202 | 2 439 630 | 919 329 | 34 210 683 | 274 397 | 5 859 388 |
| 22 824 | 12 422 679 | 10 341 922 | 17 331 519 | 86 040 | 8 046 938 |
| 121 548 | 19 019 234 | 10 539 326 | 14 384 262 | 167 056 | 10 363 116 |
| 28 588 | 32 829 815 | 8 785 622 | 11 745 129 | 2 402 085 | 8 203 183 |
| 160 068 | 6 544 958 | 5 210 530 | 69 652 139 | 511 008 | 8 336 965 |
| 91 590 | 7 777 193 | 5 687 730 | 9 185 172 | 1 264 867 | 6 042 078 |

表4-5

# 规模以上工业企业主要经济指标 (2012年)

单位：万元

| 项　　目 | Item | 企业单位数(个) Number of Enterprises (unit) | # 亏损企业 Loss Making Enterprises |
|---|---|---|---|
| **总　　计** | **Total** | **10 444** | **2 449** |
| **一、按登记注册类型分** | **Grouped by Registration Status** | | |
| 国有企业 | State-owned Enterprises | 35 | 8 |
| 集体企业 | Collective-owned Enterprises | 36 | 9 |
| 股份合作企业 | Share-holding Cooperative Enterprises | 33 | 3 |
| 联营企业 | Joint Ownership Enterprises | 9 | 1 |
| 有限责任公司 | Limited Liability Corporations | 360 | 69 |
| 股份有限公司 | Share-holding Corporations Ltd. | 140 | 23 |
| 私营企业 | Private Enterprises | 4 998 | 940 |
| 其他企业 | Other Enterprises | 56 | 6 |
| 港澳台投资企业 | Enterprises with Investment from HongKong, Macao and Taiwan | 1 496 | 441 |
| 外商投资企业 | Enterprises with Foreign Investment | 3 281 | 949 |
| **二、按轻重工业分** | **Grouped by Light and Heavy Industry** | | |
| 轻工业 | Light Industry | 4 266 | 1 017 |
| 重工业 | Heavy Industry | 6 178 | 1 432 |
| **三、按企业规模分** | **Grouped by Size of Enterprises** | | |
| 大型企业 | Large | 422 | 58 |
| 中型企业 | Medium-sized | 1 742 | 437 |
| 小型企业 | Small | 7 787 | 1 803 |
| 微型企业 | Micro | 493 | 151 |
| **四、按行业类别分** | **Grouped by Sector** | | |
| 有色金属矿采选业 | Nonferrous Metals Mining and Processing | 1 | - |
| 非金属矿采选业 | Nonmetal  Minerals Mining and Dressing | 1 | - |
| 农副食品加工业 | Agricultural and Sideline Food Processing | 52 | 15 |
| 食品制造业 | Food Production | 48 | 14 |
| 酒、饮料和精制茶制造业 | Wine, beverage and refined tea manufacturing | 16 | 5 |
| 烟草制品业 | Manufacture of Tobacco | 1 | - |
| 纺织业 | Textile Industry | 1 521 | 333 |

# MAIN ECONOMIC INDICATORS OF INDUSTRIAL ENTERPRISES ABOVE DESIGNATED SIZE (2012)

(10 000 yuan)

| 工业总产值 Gross Industrial Output Value | 工业销售产值 Value of Industrial Products Sales | # 出口交货值 Delivery Value for Export | 资产合计 Total Assets | # 流动资产 Circulating Funds | # 应收帐款净额 Net Account Income | # 产成品 Manufactured Products |
|---|---|---|---|---|---|---|
| **287 455 409** | **285 382 454** | **125 865 028** | **233 314 843** | **141 547 251** | **45 880 180** | **12 319 612** |
| | | | | | | |
| 1 400 640 | 1 385 615 | 24 336 | 3 281 937 | 1 097 713 | 175 305 | 37 512 |
| 300 552 | 287 156 | – | 359 155 | 253 530 | 52 365 | 13 667 |
| 900 726 | 852 178 | 16 684 | 1 185 357 | 783 108 | 116 533 | 143 977 |
| 265 206 | 251 681 | 80 831 | 166 606 | 119 913 | 30 358 | 18 688 |
| 35 523 440 | 35 789 066 | 4 084 203 | 32 456 949 | 18 040 766 | 2 589 913 | 1 648 111 |
| 11 142 264 | 10 996 988 | 1 297 804 | 12 104 058 | 7 363 027 | 1 795 729 | 788 599 |
| 48 675 443 | 47 809 447 | 4 409 029 | 44 377 312 | 29 081 750 | 8 435 887 | 2 910 375 |
| 542 825 | 541 807 | 84 824 | 437 059 | 294 236 | 98 864 | 21 265 |
| 49 784 088 | 49 175 032 | 26 550 018 | 42 566 394 | 25 448 273 | 9 316 313 | 2 234 444 |
| 138 920 225 | 138 293 484 | 89 317 299 | 96 380 016 | 59 064 935 | 23 268 913 | 4 502 974 |
| | | | | | | |
| 73 916 098 | 73 087 158 | 22 537 357 | 65 881 125 | 38 693 018 | 9 441 356 | 4 267 042 |
| 213 539 311 | 212 295 296 | 103 327 671 | 167 433 718 | 102 854 233 | 36 438 824 | 8 052 570 |
| | | | | | | |
| 157 579 505 | 156 699 538 | 91 353 068 | 105 020 102 | 62 470 838 | 20 050 588 | 5 268 121 |
| 55 970 829 | 55 593 127 | 20 197 981 | 57 961 337 | 32 703 795 | 10 487 571 | 2 829 421 |
| 69 743 737 | 69 113 908 | 12 853 357 | 67 742 319 | 44 557 721 | 14 673 220 | 4 056 289 |
| 4 161 338 | 3 975 881 | 1 460 622 | 2 591 085 | 1 814 897 | 668 801 | 165 781 |
| | | | | | | |
| 5 025 | 5 490 | – | 27 018 | 14 379 | 397 | 276 |
| 16 813 | 16 581 | – | 37 763 | 10 067 | 1 421 | 1 042 |
| 3 007 093 | 3 079 590 | 61 803 | 1 868 607 | 1 367 972 | 183 755 | 129 020 |
| 1 674 431 | 1 553 076 | 165 705 | 1 229 079 | 535 977 | 167 112 | 83 525 |
| 362 874 | 357 781 | 5 374 | 505 827 | 195 163 | 34 819 | 15 437 |
| 13 332 | 10 787 | – | 41 521 | 15 980 | 883 | 2 258 |
| 14 431 325 | 14 169 332 | 2 346 979 | 14 669 961 | 9 011 696 | 1 795 765 | 1 155 016 |

表4-5 续表 1

单位：万元

| 项 目 | Item | # 固定资产 Fixed Assets | 固定资产原价 Original Value of Fixed Assets |
|---|---|---|---|
| **总 计** | **Total** | **69 866 801** | **115 155 060** |
| **一、按登记注册类型分** | **Grouped by Registration Status** | | |
| 国有企业 | State-owned Enterprises | 1 676 381 | 2 362 512 |
| 集体企业 | Collective-owned Enterprises | 77 803 | 104 311 |
| 股份合作企业 | Share-holding Cooperative Enterprises | 239 831 | 356 758 |
| 联营企业 | Joint Ownership Enterprises | 34 118 | 50 780 |
| 有限责任公司 | Limited Liability Corporations | 11 188 800 | 16 803 349 |
| 股份有限公司 | Share-holding Corporations Ltd. | 2 721 182 | 3 431 266 |
| 私营企业 | Private Enterprises | 9 779 382 | 14 237 070 |
| 其他企业 | Other Enterprises | 101 043 | 159 378 |
| 港澳台投资企业 | Enterprises with Investment from HongKong, Macao and Taiwan | 12 730 898 | 20 585 840 |
| 外商投资企业 | Enterprises with Foreign Investment | 31 317 363 | 57 063 796 |
| **二、按轻重工业分** | **Grouped by Light and Heavy Industry** | | |
| 轻工业 | Light Industry | 19 853 845 | 30 959 445 |
| 重工业 | Heavy Industry | 50 012 956 | 84 195 615 |
| **三、按企业规模分** | **Grouped by Size of Enterprises** | | |
| 大型企业 | Large | 32 294 125 | 57 143 070 |
| 中型企业 | Medium-sized | 19 702 110 | 30 966 379 |
| 小型企业 | Small | 17 314 502 | 26 374 697 |
| 微型企业 | Micro | 556 064 | 670 914 |
| **四、按行业类别分** | **Grouped by Sector** | | |
| 有色金属矿采选业 | Nonferrous Metals Mining and Processing | 12 639 | 4 803 |
| 非金属矿采选业 | Nonmetal Minerals Mining and Dressing | 19 109 | 30 467 |
| 农副食品加工业 | Agricultural and Sideline Food Processing | 332 795 | 548 354 |
| 食品制造业 | Food Production | 445 861 | 647 600 |
| 酒、饮料和精制茶制造业 | Wine, beverage and refined tea manufacturing | 269 502 | 368 456 |
| 烟草制品业 | Manufacture of Tobacco | 16 643 | 28 372 |
| 纺织业 | Textile Industry | 4 003 871 | 6 478 981 |

Continued 1

(10 000 yuan)

| 累计折旧 Accumulative Total Depreciation | 负债合计 Total Liabilities | 所有者权益合计 Total Creditors Equity | # 实收资本 Total Capital Hold | 国家资本 State Capital | 集体资本 Collective Capital | 法人资本 Corporate Capital | 个人资本 Personal Capital |
|---|---|---|---|---|---|---|---|
| **49 469 375** | **134 747 950** | **98 440 604** | **60 788 735** | **1 842 913** | **503 994** | **11 696 322** | **7 657 320** |
| | | | | | | | |
| 862 490 | 2 011 239 | 1 270 698 | 770 418 | 285 216 | 153 | 457 038 | 1 060 |
| 51 989 | 264 531 | 94 625 | 55 350 | 1 358 | 20 889 | 21 857 | 11 246 |
| 120 756 | 883 072 | 302 285 | 144 821 | 8 100 | 2 079 | 54 167 | 79 854 |
| 17 939 | 113 642 | 52 963 | 25 395 | 4 163 | 2 644 | 14 313 | 4 275 |
| 6 235 186 | 21 426 949 | 11 029 999 | 3 440 995 | 340 835 | 139 882 | 1 925 653 | 834 453 |
| 1 189 458 | 6 434 017 | 5 670 041 | 1 817 356 | 102 291 | 87 529 | 800 935 | 780 971 |
| 5 250 081 | 29 691 008 | 14 657 950 | 8 680 318 | 39 190 | 76 144 | 3 068 577 | 5 424 301 |
| 72 968 | 284 159 | 152 900 | 98 396 | 152 | 879 | 47 995 | 39 255 |
| 8 437 715 | 23 611 388 | 18 924 595 | 12 704 505 | 222 963 | 102 138 | 1 771 349 | 235 659 |
| 27 230 793 | 50 027 945 | 46 284 548 | 33 051 181 | 838 645 | 71 657 | 3 534 438 | 246 246 |
| | | | | | | | |
| 12 519 575 | 39 678 052 | 26 174 807 | 17 401 138 | 280 468 | 165 138 | 3 897 261 | 3 027 158 |
| 36 949 800 | 95 069 898 | 72 265 797 | 43 387 597 | 1 562 445 | 338 856 | 7 799 061 | 4 630 162 |
| | | | | | | | |
| 26 539 405 | 61 054 317 | 43 965 785 | 20 973 809 | 567 900 | 110 793 | 4 117 127 | 1 608 528 |
| 12 472 127 | 31 657 989 | 26 302 383 | 17 968 009 | 801 969 | 139 243 | 3 049 495 | 1 718 192 |
| 10 231 596 | 40 296 372 | 27 445 906 | 21 172 038 | 445 434 | 237 815 | 4 307 469 | 4 228 788 |
| 226 247 | 1 739 272 | 726 530 | 674 879 | 27 610 | 16 143 | 222 231 | 101 812 |
| | | | | | | | |
| 3 904 | 15 957 | 11 061 | 1 476 | 1 476 | – | – | – |
| 14 769 | 19 267 | 18 496 | 10 000 | – | – | 10 000 | – |
| 222 087 | 1 185 071 | 683 536 | 308 291 | 2 404 | 9 523 | 26 614 | 32 064 |
| 234 065 | 719 187 | 509 893 | 422 712 | 152 | 17 711 | 38 863 | 40 404 |
| 178 024 | 295 564 | 210 263 | 337 185 | – | – | 72 762 | 7 538 |
| 11 730 | 4 349 | 37 171 | 39 000 | – | – | 39 000 | – |
| 2 733 452 | 10 285 082 | 4 368 241 | 3 223 285 | 4 263 | 47 900 | 814 851 | 1 282 821 |

表4-5 续表 2

单位：万元

| 项　　目 | Item | 港澳台资本 Capital from Hong Kong, Macao and Taiwan | 外商资本 Foreign Invested Capital |
|---|---|---|---|
| **总　计** | **Total** | **9 924 500** | **29 163 687** |
| **一、按登记注册类型分** | **Grouped by Registration Status** | | |
| 国有企业 | State-owned Enterprises | 26 950 | - |
| 集体企业 | Collective-owned Enterprises | - | - |
| 股份合作企业 | Share-holding Cooperative Enterprises | - | 621 |
| 联营企业 | Joint Ownership Enterprises | - | - |
| 有限责任公司 | Limited Liability Corporations | 16 711 | 183 462 |
| 股份有限公司 | Share-holding Corporations Ltd. | 8 019 | 37 611 |
| 私营企业 | Private Enterprises | 52 309 | 19 797 |
| 其他企业 | Other Enterprises | 1 380 | 8 735 |
| 港澳台投资企业 | Enterprises with Investment from HongKong, Macao and Taiwan | 8 324 081 | 2 048 316 |
| 外商投资企业 | Enterprises with Foreign Investment | 1 495 050 | 26 865 145 |
| **二、按轻重工业分** | **Grouped by Light and Heavy Industry** | | |
| 轻工业 | Light Industry | 2 372 686 | 7 658 426 |
| 重工业 | Heavy Industry | 7 551 814 | 21 505 261 |
| **三、按企业规模分** | **Grouped by Size of Enterprises** | | |
| 大型企业 | Large | 3 863 561 | 10 705 900 |
| 中型企业 | Medium-sized | 3 122 497 | 9 136 613 |
| 小型企业 | Small | 2 795 959 | 9 156 574 |
| 微型企业 | Micro | 142 483 | 164 600 |
| **四、按行业类别分** | **Grouped by Sector** | | |
| 有色金属矿采选业 | Nonferrous Metals Mining and Processing | - | - |
| 非金属矿采选业 | Nonmetal Minerals Mining and Dressing | - | - |
| 农副食品加工业 | Agricultural and Sideline Food Processing | 12 738 | 224 949 |
| 食品制造业 | Food Production | 26 207 | 299 374 |
| 酒、饮料和精制茶制造业 | Wine, beverage and refined tea manufacturing | 6 055 | 250 830 |
| 烟草制品业 | Manufacture of Tobacco | - | - |
| 纺织业 | Textile Industry | 438 078 | 635 371 |

Continued 2

(10 000 yuan)

| 主营业务收入 Major Business Revenue | 主营业务成本 Major Business Cost | 主营业务税金及附加 Pre-tax and Related Payment of Major Business | 营业利润 Business Profits | 利润总额 Total Profits | 亏损企业亏损总额 Total Deficit of Loss-Making Enterprises | 利税总额 Total taxes and Profits | 应交增值税 Value Added Tax Payable |
|---|---|---|---|---|---|---|---|
| **289 987 963** | **256 573 705** | **782 517** | **12 997 143** | **12 515 742** | **2 218 631** | **18 163 524** | **4 865 266** |
| | | | | | | | |
| 1 375 857 | 1 104 148 | 7 500 | 103 738 | 117 478 | 8 293 | 198 571 | 73 593 |
| 281 569 | 242 182 | 1 504 | 11 253 | 12 365 | 3 378 | 21 486 | 7 617 |
| 844 377 | 731 820 | 2 097 | 56 298 | 60 694 | 531 | 74 493 | 11 702 |
| 299 053 | 272 220 | 1 170 | 14 275 | 15 134 | 1 203 | 24 527 | 8 223 |
| 37 671 125 | 34 131 876 | 90 263 | 968 049 | 944 276 | 147 933 | 1 731 235 | 696 696 |
| 11 191 614 | 9 210 744 | 43 815 | 900 963 | 875 617 | 32 459 | 1 166 148 | 246 716 |
| 47 992 195 | 42 662 492 | 150 985 | 1 546 593 | 1 598 841 | 288 192 | 2 711 199 | 961 373 |
| 548 301 | 480 802 | 1 371 | 23 278 | 28 403 | 6 591 | 42 089 | 12 315 |
| 49 935 851 | 44 385 297 | 138 059 | 2 277 434 | 2 288 937 | 448 304 | 3 369 461 | 942 465 |
| 139 848 021 | 123 352 124 | 345 753 | 7 095 262 | 6 573 997 | 1 281 747 | 8 824 315 | 1 904 566 |
| | | | | | | | |
| 74 578 751 | 65 063 841 | 234 834 | 2 925 505 | 2 763 157 | 518 672 | 4 529 494 | 1 531 503 |
| 215 409 212 | 191 509 864 | 547 683 | 10 071 638 | 9 752 585 | 1 699 959 | 13 634 030 | 3 333 763 |
| | | | | | | | |
| 160 459 079 | 144 668 032 | 295 645 | 7 553 223 | 6 904 412 | 474 568 | 9 263 783 | 2 063 726 |
| 56 108 809 | 47 654 527 | 218 353 | 2 960 085 | 3 048 255 | 637 610 | 4 512 081 | 1 245 473 |
| 69 472 939 | 60 483 547 | 263 724 | 2 499 129 | 2 566 856 | 1 003 305 | 4 344 401 | 1 513 821 |
| 3 947 136 | 3 767 599 | 4 795 | -15 294 | -3 781 | 103 148 | 43 259 | 42 246 |
| | | | | | | | |
| 5 827 | 3 804 | 115 | -198 | 255 | – | 1 056 | 686 |
| 16 581 | 10 460 | 215 | 315 | 610 | – | 2 652 | 1 827 |
| 3 126 740 | 2 791 811 | 4 023 | 79 439 | 60 533 | 10 842 | 95 523 | 30 967 |
| 1 574 056 | 1 162 037 | 9 145 | 68 715 | 70 029 | 3 221 | 148 786 | 69 613 |
| 356 167 | 272 321 | 17 730 | 21 498 | 22 132 | 9 938 | 58 383 | 18 521 |
| 10 787 | 9 352 | 34 | 266 | 294 | – | 526 | 198 |
| 14 177 928 | 12 899 088 | 36 295 | 279 484 | 286 845 | 103 571 | 615 016 | 291 876 |

表4-5 续表 3

单位：万元

| 项　目 | Item | 企业单位数（个）Number of Enterprises (unit) | # 亏损企业 Loss Making Enterprises |
|---|---|---|---|
| 纺织服装、服饰业 | Garments and Apparel Industry | 552 | 129 |
| 皮革、毛皮、羽毛及其制品和制鞋业 | Leather, Fur, Wool and Shoes Products | 97 | 32 |
| 木材加工及木、竹、藤、棕、草制品业 | Wood Processing, Wood, Bamboo, Rattan and Coir Products Straw Products | 49 | 8 |
| 家具制造业 | Furniture Manufacturing | 80 | 28 |
| 造纸及纸制品业 | Papermaking and Paper Products | 171 | 28 |
| 印刷业和记录媒介的复制 | Printing and Record Duplicating | 176 | 38 |
| 文教、工美、体育和娱乐用品制造业 | Stationary,Educational, Industrial arts, Sports and Entertainment products | 143 | 39 |
| 石油加工、炼焦及核燃料加工业 | Oil Processing, Coking and Nuclear Fuel Processing | 18 | 1 |
| 化学原料及化学制品制造业 | Raw Chemical Materials and Chemical Products | 700 | 133 |
| 医药制造业 | Medical and Pharmaceutical Products | 92 | 13 |
| 化学纤维制造业 | Chemical Fiber Manufacturing | 493 | 159 |
| 橡胶制品业塑料制品业 | Rubber and Plastic Products | 575 | 131 |
| 非金属矿物制品业 | Nonmetal Mineral Products | 321 | 80 |
| 黑色金属冶炼及压延加工业 | Smelting and Pressing of Ferrous Metals | 235 | 61 |
| 有色金属冶炼及压延加工业 | Smelting and Pressing of Nonferrous Metals | 257 | 68 |
| 金属制品业 | Metal Products | 665 | 137 |
| 通用设备制造业 | General Equipment Manufacture | 807 | 128 |
| 专用设备制造业 | Special Purposes Equipment Manufacturing | 653 | 131 |
| 汽车制造业 | Automobile Manufacturing | 269 | 62 |
| 铁路、船舶、航空航天和其他运输设备制造业 | Railway, Ship, Aerospace and other transportation equipment manufacturing | 132 | 38 |
| 电气机械及器材制造业 | Electric Equipment and Machinery Manufacturing | 760 | 182 |
| 计算机、通信和其他电子设备制造业 | Computer Telecommunications and Other Electronic Equipment Manufacture | 1 244 | 389 |
| 仪器仪表制造业 | Instruments, Meters Machinery | 159 | 28 |
| 其他制造业 | Other Products Manufacture | 12 | 6 |
| 废弃资源综合利用业 | Comprehensive Utilization of Waste Resources | 52 | 21 |
| 金属制品、机械和设备修理业 | Metal Products, Machinery and Equipment Repair | 2 | 1 |
| 电力、热力的生产和供应业 | Production and Supply of Electricity and Thermal Power | 47 | 6 |
| 燃气生产和供应业 | Production and Supply of Gas | 19 | 1 |
| 水的生产和供应业 | Production and Supply of Water | 24 | 4 |

Continued 3

(10 000 yuan)

| 工业总产值 Gross Industrial Output Value | 工业销售产值 Value of Industrial Products Sales | # 出口交货值 Delivery Value for Export | 资产合计 Total Assets | # 流动资产 Circulating Funds | # 应收帐款净额 Net Account Income | # 产成品 Manufactured Products |
|---|---|---|---|---|---|---|
| 6 869 114 | 6 768 104 | 1 660 794 | 5 666 646 | 3 736 893 | 823 979 | 520 204 |
| 762 382 | 761 745 | 473 996 | 676 379 | 493 328 | 125 526 | 45 677 |
| 549 939 | 557 748 | 74 114 | 819 156 | 560 101 | 131 099 | 60 791 |
| 947 993 | 940 068 | 681 573 | 816 363 | 504 106 | 126 849 | 49 109 |
| 4 832 050 | 4 786 925 | 550 900 | 6 622 749 | 3 407 522 | 842 704 | 166 152 |
| 1 876 497 | 1 866 929 | 489 288 | 1 959 241 | 1 165 325 | 455 071 | 67 097 |
| 2 013 536 | 1 992 998 | 940 257 | 1 662 606 | 982 062 | 248 725 | 136 181 |
| 1 173 258 | 1 152 934 | – | 599 048 | 487 557 | 133 200 | 78 328 |
| 15 605 716 | 15 388 931 | 2 695 303 | 15 990 828 | 9 043 469 | 2 836 408 | 841 890 |
| 2 440 230 | 2 342 163 | 468 920 | 2 590 001 | 1 511 773 | 367 507 | 176 801 |
| 11 649 633 | 11 585 839 | 765 922 | 10 814 712 | 5 675 598 | 731 456 | 888 944 |
| 7 130 361 | 7 066 956 | 2 528 279 | 6 519 164 | 3 879 570 | 1 511 067 | 440 693 |
| 5 005 336 | 4 949 580 | 644 797 | 7 046 503 | 4 217 293 | 1 587 465 | 306 613 |
| 26 296 206 | 26 325 117 | 2 493 328 | 21 138 258 | 11 551 618 | 947 316 | 1 023 420 |
| 6 250 555 | 6 507 179 | 568 841 | 3 919 171 | 2 675 601 | 786 276 | 222 016 |
| 7 714 587 | 7 543 456 | 1 523 237 | 6 889 875 | 4 351 716 | 1 530 925 | 424 902 |
| 17 078 082 | 16 893 664 | 6 883 304 | 14 759 358 | 9 917 124 | 3 395 516 | 1 029 946 |
| 9 554 594 | 9 567 416 | 3 616 621 | 10 547 984 | 6 890 261 | 2 274 544 | 666 346 |
| 7 142 944 | 7 110 011 | 1 643 646 | 5 918 107 | 3 552 480 | 1 469 276 | 299 623 |
| 2 194 613 | 2 131 916 | 862 332 | 2 176 209 | 1 509 282 | 480 355 | 137 419 |
| 22 762 024 | 22 380 003 | 9 053 887 | 20 352 999 | 13 133 793 | 5 041 926 | 1 148 446 |
| 98 024 492 | 97 607 592 | 83 549 574 | 50 981 824 | 33 524 597 | 16 027 747 | 1 883 169 |
| 3 173 838 | 3 137 288 | 958 482 | 3 536 294 | 2 307 237 | 773 500 | 155 622 |
| 58 188 | 57 998 | 17 942 | 68 995 | 36 834 | 12 091 | 2 939 |
| 1 635 579 | 1 532 722 | 3 890 | 1 634 408 | 1 485 744 | 580 775 | 155 951 |
| 24 806 | 25 542 | – | 13 657 | 6 321 | 2 258 | 295 |
| 3 754 916 | 3 803 255 | – | 6 640 697 | 1 816 965 | 340 996 | 145 |
| 1 029 306 | 1 018 532 | 135 940 | 1 743 851 | 1 144 372 | 98 546 | 1 281 |
| 393 741 | 387 206 | – | 2 829 984 | 827 475 | 12 925 | 3 038 |

表4-5 续表 4

单位：万元

| 项　　目 | Item | # 固定资产 Fixed Assets | 固定资产原价 Original Value of Fixed Assets |
|---|---|---|---|
| 纺织服装、服饰业 | Garments and Apparel Industry | 1 235 675 | 1 488 480 |
| 皮革、毛皮、羽毛及其制品和制鞋业 | Leather, Fur, Wool and Shoes Products | 122 680 | 229 507 |
| 木材加工及木、竹、藤、棕、草制品业 | Wood Processing, Wood, Bamboo, Rattan and Coir Products Straw Products | 147 765 | 282 798 |
| 家具制造业 | Furniture Manufacturing | 244 197 | 380 185 |
| 造纸及纸制品业 | Papermaking and Paper Products | 2 673 424 | 4 416 630 |
| 印刷业和记录媒介的复制 | Printing and Record Duplicating | 673 641 | 1 082 978 |
| 文教、工美、体育和娱乐用品制造业 | Stationary,Educational, Industrial arts, Sports and Entertainment products | 453 691 | 752 812 |
| 石油加工、炼焦及核燃料加工业 | Oil Processing, Coking and Nuclear Fuel Processing | 77 873 | 146 310 |
| 化学原料及化学制品制造业 | Raw Chemical Materials and Chemical Products | 5 220 619 | 7 736 972 |
| 医药制造业 | Medical and Pharmaceutical Products | 777 343 | 1 232 304 |
| 化学纤维制造业 | Chemical Fiber Manufacturing | 3 531 994 | 5 378 798 |
| 橡胶和塑料制品业 | Rubber and Plastic Products | 2 153 539 | 3 764 024 |
| 非金属矿物制品业 | Nonmetal Mineral Products | 1 982 348 | 3 367 056 |
| 黑色金属冶炼及压延加工业 | Smelting and Pressing of Ferrous Metals | 8 044 272 | 12 131 637 |
| 有色金属冶炼及压延加工业 | Smelting and Pressing of Nonferrous Metals | 852 763 | 1 429 155 |
| 金属制品业 | Metal Products | 1 867 729 | 2 724 233 |
| 通用设备制造业 | General Equipment Manufacture | 3 538 944 | 5 564 715 |
| 专用设备制造业 | Special Purposes Equipment Manufacturing | 2 855 735 | 4 065 786 |
| 汽车制造业 | Automobile Manufacturing | 1 930 833 | 2 921 515 |
| 铁路、船舶、航空航天和其他运输设备制造业 | Railway, Ship, Aerospace and other transportation equipment manufacturing | 526 452 | 813 405 |
| 电气机械及器材制造业 | Electric Equipment and Machinery Manufacturing | 4 395 968 | 6 365 929 |
| 计算机、通信和其他电子设备制造业 | Computer Telecommunications and Other Electronic Equipment Manufacture | 14 897 041 | 30 915 812 |
| 仪器仪表制造业 | Instruments, Meters Machinery | 898 673 | 1 384 064 |
| 其他制造业 | Other Products Manufacture | 29 541 | 48 855 |
| 废弃资源综合利用业 | Comprehensive Utilization of Waste Resources | 105 093 | 148 452 |
| 金属制品、机械和设备修理业 | Metal Products, Machinery and Equipment Repair | 6 116 | 15 986 |
| 电力、热力的生产和供应业 | Production and Supply of Electricity and Thermal Power | 3 564 984 | 5 828 843 |
| 燃气生产和供应业 | Production and Supply of Gas | 340 406 | 401 932 |
| 水的生产和供应业 | Production and Supply of Water | 1 617 042 | 2 028 854 |

Continued 4

(10 000 yuan)

| 累计折旧 Accumulative Total Depreciation | 负债合计 Total Liabilities | 所有者权益合计 Total Creditors Equity | # 实收资本 Total Capital Hold | | | | |
|---|---|---|---|---|---|---|---|
| | | | | 国家资本 State Capital | 集体资本 Collective Capital | 法人资本 Corporate Capital | 个人资本 Personal Capital |
| 573 423 | 3 627 553 | 2 030 090 | 935 728 | 10 598 | 5 260 | 221 625 | 338 976 |
| 112 274 | 369 877 | 306 807 | 179 868 | – | 628 | 26 253 | 35 297 |
| 142 788 | 395 887 | 423 269 | 226 245 | – | 4 000 | 40 462 | 28 701 |
| 142 152 | 431 017 | 385 346 | 330 461 | – | 5 858 | 40 221 | 38 433 |
| 1 786 534 | 3 325 194 | 3 297 555 | 2 733 200 | 6 000 | 1 303 | 431 307 | 54 459 |
| 448 537 | 993 991 | 965 250 | 568 123 | – | 11 080 | 132 516 | 115 240 |
| 339 735 | 903 897 | 758 709 | 537 151 | – | 18 977 | 115 696 | 59 400 |
| 69 883 | 325 131 | 273 917 | 93 410 | – | – | 25 940 | 10 902 |
| 2 809 442 | 8 004 330 | 7 980 293 | 4 962 043 | 93 808 | 27 853 | 751 943 | 406 675 |
| 530 246 | 1 334 305 | 1 255 696 | 930 932 | 12 906 | 780 | 184 108 | 31 290 |
| 1 966 800 | 7 127 400 | 3 685 350 | 2 205 786 | 27 746 | 4 419 | 904 586 | 642 243 |
| 1 696 358 | 2 896 235 | 3 622 920 | 2 509 738 | 1 852 | 6 881 | 262 814 | 210 506 |
| 1 465 927 | 4 305 588 | 2 740 915 | 1 925 108 | 67 193 | 26 499 | 507 625 | 262 103 |
| 4 515 059 | 14 215 118 | 6 920 732 | 2 498 429 | 115 738 | 29 550 | 890 919 | 597 800 |
| 633 369 | 2 421 356 | 1 497 816 | 1 193 253 | 78 550 | 975 | 173 594 | 196 013 |
| 988 042 | 3 824 419 | 3 062 064 | 2 085 455 | 22 817 | 28 057 | 467 256 | 436 357 |
| 2 239 288 | 7 328 068 | 7 428 268 | 3 856 922 | 75 111 | 11 123 | 804 139 | 662 264 |
| 1 435 998 | 5 361 906 | 5 183 625 | 2 872 923 | 46 298 | 5 129 | 534 138 | 359 756 |
| 1 154 865 | 3 164 236 | 2 753 871 | 1 777 166 | 32 213 | 9 706 | 159 829 | 160 034 |
| 356 706 | 1 244 273 | 931 936 | 542 522 | 2 766 | 585 | 57 475 | 78 947 |
| 2 214 923 | 11 948 173 | 8 397 922 | 4 597 637 | 24 340 | 29 646 | 1 310 640 | 863 606 |
| 16 696 616 | 28 132 079 | 22 775 149 | 15 442 994 | 572 095 | 43 842 | 1 575 648 | 527 533 |
| 535 053 | 1 790 668 | 1 745 626 | 828 399 | 518 | 5 404 | 154 836 | 101 091 |
| 20 363 | 43 411 | 25 581 | 43 298 | – | 5 999 | 1 200 | 10 751 |
| 49 519 | 1 433 395 | 201 013 | 216 518 | 19 999 | 46 972 | 40 200 | 23 860 |
| 9 879 | 5 494 | 8 164 | 12 708 | – | – | – | 350 |
| 2 397 284 | 4 268 768 | 2 371 929 | 1 518 533 | 364 024 | 56 503 | 622 010 | 35 343 |
| 111 445 | 1 234 648 | 509 202 | 162 489 | 27 725 | 9 000 | 79 507 | 5 663 |
| 628 836 | 1 767 056 | 1 062 928 | 659 747 | 232 321 | 32 831 | 177 745 | 900 |

表4-5 续表 5

单位：万元

| 项　　目 | Item | 港澳台资本 Capital from Hong Kong, Macao and Taiwan | 外商资本 Foreign Invested Capital |
|---|---|---|---|
| 纺织服装、服饰业 | Garments and Apparel Industry | 119 977 | 239 291 |
| 皮革、毛皮、羽毛及其制品和制鞋业 | Leather, Fur, Wool and Shoes Products | 33 522 | 84 168 |
| 木材加工及木、竹、藤、棕、草制品业 | Wood Processing, Wood, Bamboo, Rattan and Coir Products Straw Products | 15 470 | 137 612 |
| 家具制造业 | Furniture Manufacturing | 92 229 | 153 720 |
| 造纸及纸制品业 | Papermaking and Paper Products | 113 952 | 2 126 180 |
| 印刷业和记录媒介的复制 | Printing and Record Duplicating | 101 382 | 207 905 |
| 文教、工美、体育和娱乐用品制造业 | Stationary,Educational, Industrial arts, Sports and Entertainment products | 146 917 | 196 161 |
| 石油加工、炼焦及核燃料加工业 | Oil Processing, Coking and Nuclear Fuel Processing | – | 56 568 |
| 化学原料及化学制品制造业 | Raw Chemical Materials and Chemical Products | 821 528 | 2 860 236 |
| 医药制造业 | Medical and Pharmaceutical Products | 92 544 | 609 304 |
| 化学纤维制造业 | Chemical Fiber Manufacturing | 458 561 | 168 231 |
| 橡胶和塑料制品业 | Rubber and Plastic Products | 271 131 | 1 756 554 |
| 非金属矿物制品业 | Nonmetal Mineral Products | 247 699 | 813 991 |
| 黑色金属冶炼及压延加工业 | Smelting and Pressing of Ferrous Metals | 265 362 | 599 060 |
| 有色金属冶炼及压延加工业 | Smelting and Pressing of Nonferrous Metals | 165 256 | 578 865 |
| 金属制品业 | Metal Products | 335 126 | 795 842 |
| 通用设备制造业 | General Equipment Manufacture | 320 957 | 1 983 329 |
| 专用设备制造业 | Special Purposes Equipment Manufacturing | 398 960 | 1 528 642 |
| 汽车制造业 | Automobile Manufacturing | 67 478 | 1 347 906 |
| 铁路、船舶、航空航天和其他运输设备制造业 | Railway, Ship, Aerospace and other transportation equipment manufacturing | 77 586 | 325 163 |
| 电气机械及器材制造业 | Electric Equipment and Machinery Manufacturing | 776 529 | 1 592 875 |
| 计算机、通信和其他电子设备制造业 | Computer Telecommunications and Other Electronic Equipment Manufacture | 4 005 475 | 8 718 401 |
| 仪器仪表制造业 | Instruments, Meters Machinery | 68 191 | 498 360 |
| 其他制造业 | Other Products Manufacture | 7 822 | 17 526 |
| 废弃资源综合利用业 | Comprehensive Utilization of Waste Resources | 19 525 | 65 961 |
| 金属制品、机械和设备修理业 | Metal Products, Machinery and Equipment Repair | – | 12 358 |
| 电力、热力的生产和供应业 | Production and Supply of Electricity and Thermal Power | 379 389 | 61 264 |
| 燃气生产和供应业 | Production and Supply of Gas | 11 904 | 28 690 |
| 水的生产和供应业 | Production and Supply of Water | 26 950 | 189 000 |

Continued 5

(10 000 yuan)

| 主营业务收入 Major Business Revenue | 主营业务成本 Major Business Cost | 主营业务税金及附加 Pre-tax and Related Payment of Major Business | 营业利润 Business Profits | 利润总额 Total Profits | 亏损企业亏损总额 Total Deficit of Loss-Making Enterprises | 利税总额 Total taxes and Profits | 应交增值税 Value Added Tax Payable |
|---|---|---|---|---|---|---|---|
| 6 859 186 | 5 742 177 | 35 784 | 462 117 | 405 247 | 33 418 | 607 053 | 166 023 |
| 782 412 | 702 737 | 4 255 | 8 155 | 8 832 | 10 501 | 26 498 | 13 411 |
| 562 340 | 476 989 | 4 335 | 32 656 | 37 618 | 7 747 | 59 380 | 17 427 |
| 931 926 | 827 119 | 3 089 | 9 011 | 9 187 | 17 657 | 39 489 | 27 213 |
| 4 878 431 | 4 073 024 | 13 360 | 231 296 | 233 876 | 22 974 | 367 730 | 120 494 |
| 1 886 405 | 1 505 292 | 9 675 | 160 126 | 165 322 | 15 314 | 238 596 | 63 599 |
| 2 035 332 | 1 773 136 | 8 034 | 51 184 | 57 040 | 19 168 | 121 633 | 56 559 |
| 1 157 895 | 1 009 063 | 34 876 | 75 314 | 76 013 | 71 | 134 912 | 24 023 |
| 15 898 756 | 13 242 520 | 62 807 | 985 354 | 996 643 | 191 386 | 1 460 596 | 401 146 |
| 2 351 182 | 1 559 411 | 14 390 | 186 764 | 207 001 | 31 779 | 332 351 | 110 960 |
| 12 461 953 | 11 620 989 | 15 922 | 257 262 | 261 818 | 100 712 | 387 940 | 110 200 |
| 7 051 832 | 5 995 308 | 29 389 | 379 888 | 394 549 | 74 450 | 603 919 | 179 981 |
| 4 974 325 | 4 275 429 | 25 999 | 151 940 | 156 997 | 86 266 | 366 152 | 183 156 |
| 27 922 263 | 26 098 561 | 50 336 | 358 568 | 271 421 | 168 490 | 731 014 | 409 257 |
| 6 526 383 | 5 999 826 | 9 396 | 146 165 | 124 489 | 35 975 | 205 457 | 71 572 |
| 7 535 959 | 6 567 194 | 27 793 | 324 940 | 314 636 | 56 235 | 533 205 | 190 776 |
| 17 000 254 | 14 085 801 | 67 220 | 1 299 088 | 1 326 003 | 64 615 | 1 820 753 | 427 529 |
| 9 513 296 | 7 702 214 | 38 409 | 749 615 | 781 273 | 84 993 | 1 059 211 | 239 529 |
| 7 149 109 | 5 992 020 | 28 149 | 472 780 | 499 446 | 40 674 | 660 597 | 133 002 |
| 2 219 816 | 1 816 888 | 9 492 | 153 787 | 161 459 | 15 937 | 238 368 | 67 417 |
| 22 643 136 | 19 601 005 | 59 361 | 1 103 214 | 1 105 266 | 262 192 | 1 562 052 | 397 425 |
| 98 365 933 | 90 585 166 | 122 150 | 4 089 614 | 3 577 291 | 661 560 | 4 426 636 | 727 195 |
| 3 214 750 | 2 611 360 | 11 800 | 228 250 | 235 820 | 30 111 | 312 870 | 65 250 |
| 58 068 | 51 886 | 257 | -2 810 | -1 673 | 2 124 | 398 | 1 816 |
| 1 498 219 | 1 322 534 | 2 360 | -41 778 | -27 265 | 38 753 | 308 | 25 213 |
| 29 893 | 30 145 | 78 | -1 941 | -1 817 | 1 884 | -868 | 871 |
| 3 785 927 | 3 026 920 | 21 140 | 546 010 | 557 729 | 1 532 | 766 787 | 187 918 |
| 1 055 514 | 876 125 | 2 916 | 142 929 | 115 115 | 1 343 | 136 256 | 18 224 |
| 369 382 | 253 993 | 2 188 | -11 874 | 25 708 | 13 198 | 42 289 | 14 392 |

表4-6 规模以上国有及国有控股工业企业主要经济指标（2012年）

单位：万元

| 项 目 | Item | 企业单位数（个）Number of Enterprises (unit) | # 亏损企业 Loss Making Enterprises |
|---|---|---|---|
| **总 计** | **Total** | **113** | **26** |
| 有色金属矿采选业 | Nonferrous Metals Mining and Processing | 1 | - |
| 非金属矿采选业 | Nonmetal Minerals Mining and Dressing | 1 | - |
| 农副食品加工业 | Agricultural and Sideline Food Processing | 1 | - |
| 烟草制品业 | Manufacture of Tobacco | 1 | - |
| 纺织业 | Textile Industry | 2 | 1 |
| 造纸及纸制品业 | Papermaking and Paper Products | 2 | - |
| 文教、工美、体育和娱乐用品制造业 | Printing and Record Duplicating | 1 | - |
| 石油加工、炼焦及核燃料加工业 | Oil Processing, Coking and Nuclear Fuel Processing | 1 | - |
| 化学原料及化学制品制造业 | Raw Chemical Materials and Chemical Products | 10 | 2 |
| 医药制造业 | Medical and Pharmaceutical Products | 2 | - |
| 橡胶和塑料制品业 | Rubber and Plastic Products | 1 | - |
| 非金属矿物制品业 | Nonmetal Mineral Products | 12 | 4 |
| 黑色金属冶炼及压延加工业 | Smelting and Pressing of Ferrous Metals | 8 | 7 |
| 有色金属冶炼及压延加工业 | Smelting and Pressing of Nonferrous Metals | 4 | 1 |
| 金属制品业 | Manufacture of Metal Products | 2 | - |
| 通用设备制造业 | General Equipment Manufacture | 9 | 2 |
| 专用设备制造业 | For Special Purposes Equipment Manufacturing | 9 | - |
| 汽车制造业 | Automobile Manufacturing | 2 | 1 |
| 铁路、船舶、航空航天和其他运输设备制造业 | Transport Equipment Manufacturing | 1 | - |
| 电气机械及器材制造业 | Electric Equipment and Machinery Manufacturing | 3 | 1 |
| 计算机、通信和其他电子设备制造业 | Computer Telecommunications and Other Electronic Equipment Manufacture | 10 | 2 |
| 仪器仪表制造业 | Instruments, Meters Machinery | 2 | 1 |
| 废弃资源综合利用业 | Comprehensive Utilization of Waste Resources | 1 | 1 |
| 电力、热力的生产和供应业 | Production and Supply of Electricity and Thermal Power | 12 | - |
| 燃气生产和供应业 | Production and Supply of Gas | 5 | - |
| 水的生产和供应业 | Production and Supply of Water | 10 | 3 |

# MAIN ECONOMIC INDICATOR OF STATE-OWNED ENTERPRISES AND SHARE HOLDING INDUSTRIAL ENTERPRISES ABOVE DESIGNATED SIZE (2012)

(10 000 yuan)

| 工业总产值 Gross Industrial Output Value | 工业销售产值 Value of Industrial Products Sales | # 出口交货值 Delivery Value for Export | 资产合计 Total Assets | # 流动资产 Circulating Funds | # 固定资产 Fixed Assets | 累计折旧 Accumulative Depreciation | 负债合计 Total Liabilities |
|---|---|---|---|---|---|---|---|
| **10 773 640** | **11 102 774** | **1 445 695** | **14 431 900** | **6 866 568** | **5 729 222** | **3 415 356** | **9 760 429** |
| 5 025 | 5 490 | – | 27 018 | 14 379 | 12 639 | 3 904 | 15 957 |
| 16 813 | 16 581 | – | 37 763 | 10 067 | 19 109 | 14 769 | 19 267 |
| 1 787 958 | 1 753 343 | 17 824 | 1 102 456 | 886 921 | 157 183 | 137 626 | 716 806 |
| 13 332 | 10 787 | – | 41 521 | 15 980 | 16 643 | 11 730 | 4 349 |
| 125 842 | 126 867 | 74 480 | 81 789 | 60 006 | 15 166 | 4 653 | 65 398 |
| 118 091 | 122 819 | – | 135 344 | 72 379 | 57 696 | 109 006 | 28 393 |
| 25 203 | 25 050 | – | 27 248 | 14 826 | 7 089 | 10 007 | 10 202 |
| 314 122 | 319 490 | – | 132 486 | 98 546 | 25 394 | 13 224 | 66 678 |
| 986 392 | 974 454 | 222 567 | 1 073 918 | 539 198 | 367 591 | 245 967 | 597 978 |
| 79 773 | 76 271 | 165 | 106 339 | 67 325 | 27 116 | 12 298 | 84 487 |
| 5 660 | 5 426 | 1 113 | 7 656 | 4 122 | 3 532 | 2 974 | 5 725 |
| 273 277 | 265 589 | 30 561 | 531 278 | 193 898 | 124 750 | 47 000 | 303 972 |
| 846 979 | 879 843 | 108 889 | 1 466 597 | 802 375 | 406 415 | 241 374 | 1 281 343 |
| 1 364 349 | 1 643 071 | 36 215 | 302 198 | 203 284 | 82 381 | 22 119 | 203 240 |
| 42 628 | 41 224 | 12 803 | 123 959 | 71 514 | 32 409 | 9 232 | 72 484 |
| 202 461 | 201 304 | 15 265 | 335 281 | 216 412 | 59 231 | 32 339 | 178 619 |
| 384 790 | 402 614 | 15 713 | 574 204 | 326 375 | 200 571 | 52 248 | 405 797 |
| 51 975 | 67 577 | 2 006 | 89 274 | 50 203 | 28 690 | 31 658 | 95 467 |
| 9 373 | 9 373 | – | 17 506 | 16 877 | 165 | 265 | 12 157 |
| 49 167 | 50 085 | 311 | 53 849 | 39 679 | 8 654 | 4 862 | 48 003 |
| 1 370 032 | 1 368 378 | 904 154 | 1 912 714 | 821 758 | 855 688 | 674 881 | 1 369 182 |
| 23 857 | 25 009 | 3 629 | 24 010 | 17 671 | 5 646 | 4 449 | 10 453 |
| 36 368 | 35 425 | – | 141 011 | 124 797 | 2 785 | 252 | 121 393 |
| 2 072 392 | 2 123 893 | – | 3 336 193 | 922 305 | 2 165 550 | 1 259 834 | 2 110 670 |
| 384 962 | 375 297 | – | 955 201 | 768 611 | 96 460 | 52 469 | 766 301 |
| 182 819 | 177 514 | – | 1 795 087 | 507 060 | 950 669 | 416 216 | 1 166 108 |

表4-6 续表

单位：万元

| 项　　目 | Item | 所有者权益 Creditors Equity | # 实收资本 Total Capital Hold |
|---|---|---|---|
| **总　　计** | **Total** | **4 671 489** | **3 542 073** |
| 有色金属矿采选业 | Nonferrous Metals Mining and Processing | 11 061 | 1 476 |
| 非金属矿采选业 | Nonmetal Minerals Mining and Dressing | 18 496 | 10 000 |
| 农副食品加工业 | Agricultural and Sideline Food Processing | 385 651 | 104 288 |
| 烟草制品业 | Manufacture of Tobacco | 37 171 | 39 000 |
| 纺织业 | Textile Industry | 16 391 | 9 500 |
| 造纸及纸制品业 | Papermaking and Paper Products | 106 951 | 70 000 |
| 文教、工美、体育和娱乐用品制造业 | Printing and Record Duplicating | 17 046 | 5 691 |
| 石油加工、炼焦及核燃料加工业 | Oil Processing, Coking and Nuclear Fuel Processing | 65 808 | - |
| 化学原料及化学制品制造业 | Raw Chemical Materials and Chemical Products | 475 958 | 123 037 |
| 医药制造业 | Medical and Pharmaceutical Products | 21 852 | 17 720 |
| 橡胶和塑料制品业 | Rubber and Plastic Products | 1 931 | 3 631 |
| 非金属矿物制品业 | Nonmetal Mineral Products | 227 306 | 194 208 |
| 黑色金属冶炼及压延加工业 | Smelting and Pressing of Ferrous Metals | 185 254 | 428 405 |
| 有色金属冶炼及压延加工业 | Smelting and Pressing of Nonferrous Metals | 98 958 | 94 805 |
| 金属制品业 | Manufacture of Metel Products | 51 475 | 19 911 |
| 通用设备制造业 | General Equipment Manufacture | 156 663 | 59 194 |
| 专用设备制造业 | For Special Purposes Equipment Manufacturing | 168 407 | 125 721 |
| 汽车制造业 | Automobile Manufacturing | -6 193 | 34 600 |
| 铁路、船舶、航空航天和其他运输设备制造业 | Transport Equipment Manufacturing | 5 349 | 2 000 |
| 电气机械及器材制造业 | Electric Equipment and Machinery Manufacturing | 5 847 | 10 996 |
| 计算机、通信和其他电子设备制造业 | Computer Telecommunications and Other Electronic Equipment Manufacture | 543 532 | 1 068 713 |
| 仪器仪表制造业 | Instruments, Meters Machinery | 13 553 | 7 197 |
| 废弃资源综合利用业 | Comprehensive Utilization of Waste Resources | 19 619 | 20 000 |
| 电力、热力的生产和供应业 | Production and Supply of Electricity and Thermal Power | 1 225 523 | 797 673 |
| 燃气生产和供应业 | Production and Supply of Gas | 188 900 | 34 780 |
| 水的生产和供应业 | Production and Supply of Water | 628 980 | 259 527 |

Continued

(10 000 yuan)

| 主营业务收入 Major Business Revenue | 主营业务成本 Major Business Cost | 主营业务税金及附加 Pre-tax and Related Payment of Major Business | 营业利润 Business Profits | 利润总额 Total Profits | 亏损企业亏损总额 Total Deficit of Loss-Making Enterprises | 利税总额 Total taxes and Profits | 应交增值税 Value Added Tax Payable |
|---|---|---|---|---|---|---|---|
| **11 681 964** | **10 382 222** | **31 573** | **331 916** | **351 215** | **209 741** | **663 635** | **280 848** |
| 5 827 | 3 804 | 115 | -198 | 255 | – | 1 056 | 686 |
| 16 581 | 10 460 | 215 | 315 | 610 | – | 2 652 | 1 827 |
| 1 799 296 | 1 619 575 | 1 951 | 26 734 | 7 063 | – | 21 643 | 12 629 |
| 10 787 | 9 352 | 34 | 266 | 294 | – | 526 | 198 |
| 184 608 | 181 010 | 410 | -909 | -892 | 1 203 | 3 504 | 3 986 |
| 122 819 | 85 691 | 1 132 | 18 790 | 18 657 | – | 29 512 | 9 724 |
| 23 036 | 19 827 | 92 | 410 | 1 178 | – | 2 168 | 898 |
| 319 490 | 294 627 | 2 295 | 8 698 | 8 711 | – | 16 857 | 5 851 |
| 1 062 730 | 936 030 | 2 422 | 61 861 | 54 295 | 3 856 | 79 853 | 23 136 |
| 76 271 | 56 024 | 408 | 128 | 792 | – | 4 668 | 3 469 |
| 5 198 | 4 305 | 5 | 9 | 1 | – | 133 | 127 |
| 256 013 | 223 156 | 896 | -2 384 | 2 783 | 15 411 | 11 359 | 7 681 |
| 1 253 447 | 1 245 442 | 599 | -84 146 | -78 839 | 80 840 | -75 792 | 2 449 |
| 1 706 666 | 1 539 901 | 874 | 47 952 | 25 802 | 286 | 35 158 | 8 483 |
| 40 148 | 32 205 | 434 | 1 950 | 2 265 | – | 3 129 | 431 |
| 202 198 | 159 992 | 740 | 8 207 | 9 196 | 889 | 14 771 | 4 835 |
| 399 652 | 343 881 | 2 012 | 15 900 | 24 305 | – | 36 266 | 9 948 |
| 67 591 | 58 728 | 506 | -2 301 | -1 618 | 2 889 | 2 915 | 4 027 |
| 9 373 | 6 240 | 15 | 1 157 | 1 175 | – | 1 242 | 52 |
| 50 918 | 51 729 | 113 | -6 813 | -6 563 | 7 127 | -5 123 | 1 327 |
| 1 369 314 | 1 331 647 | 569 | -59 571 | -49 034 | 83 647 | -10 124 | 38 340 |
| 25 016 | 19 407 | 134 | -272 | 85 | 81 | 987 | 767 |
| 35 000 | 34 754 | 181 | -607 | -475 | 475 | 2 516 | 2 809 |
| 2 112 516 | 1 696 093 | 13 354 | 289 179 | 292 934 | – | 427 163 | 120 875 |
| 370 856 | 321 948 | 988 | 42 196 | 44 025 | – | 53 260 | 8 247 |
| 156 613 | 96 394 | 1 079 | -34 635 | -5 790 | 13 037 | 3 336 | 8 046 |

表4-7

# 规模以上民营工业企业主要经济指标 (2012年)

单位：万元

| 项　　目 | Item | 企业单位数（个）Number of Enterprises (unit) | # 亏损企业 Loss Making Enterprises |
|---|---|---|---|
| **总　　计** | **Total** | **5 577** | **1 045** |
| 农副食品加工业 | Agricultural and Sideline Food Processing | 27 | 5 |
| 食品制造业 | Food Production | 23 | 7 |
| 酒、饮料和精制茶制造业 | Wine, Beverage and Refined tea manufacturing | 4 | - |
| 纺织业 | Textile Industry | 1 239 | 247 |
| 纺织服装、服饰业 | Garments and Apparel Industry | 367 | 74 |
| 皮革、毛皮、羽毛及其制品和制鞋业 | Leather, Fur, Wool and Shoes Products | 50 | 14 |
| 木材加工及木、竹、藤、棕、草制品业 | Wood Processing, Wood, Bamboo, Rattan and Coir Products Straw Products | 27 | 1 |
| 家具制造业 | Furniture Manufacturing | 34 | 8 |
| 造纸及纸制品业 | Papermaking and Paper Products | 86 | 12 |
| 印刷业和记录媒介的复制 | Printing and Record Medium Reproduction | 112 | 21 |
| 文教、工美、体育和娱乐用品制造业 | Stationary,Educational, Industrial arts, Sports and Entertainment products | 60 | 9 |
| 石油加工、炼焦及核燃料加工业 | Petroleum Processing, Coking and Nucleus Fuel Machining Trade | 14 | 1 |
| 化学原料及化学制品制造业 | Raw Chemical Materials and Chemical Products | 320 | 39 |
| 医药制造业 | Medical and Pharmaceutical Products | 48 | 6 |
| 化学纤维制造业 | Chemical Fiber | 457 | 139 |
| 橡胶和塑料制品业 | Rubber and Plastic Products | 248 | 35 |
| 非金属矿物制品业 | Nonmetal Mineral Products | 184 | 39 |
| 黑色金属冶炼及压延加工业 | Smelting and Pressing of Ferrous Metals | 172 | 38 |
| 有色金属冶炼及压延加工业 | Smelting and Pressing of Nonferrous Metals | 164 | 40 |
| 金属制品业 | Metal Products | 428 | 71 |
| 通用设备制造业 | General Equipment Manufacture | 380 | 41 |
| 专用设备制造业 | Special Purposes Equipment Manufacturing | 297 | 42 |
| 汽车制造业 | Automobile Manufacturing | 64 | 12 |
| 铁路、船舶、航空航天和其他运输设备制造业 | Railway, Ship, Aerospace and other transportation equipment manufacturing | 42 | 13 |
| 电气机械及器材制造业 | Electric Equipment and Machinery Manufacturing | 384 | 67 |
| 计算机、通信和其他电子设备制造业 | Computer Telecommunications and Other Electronic Equipment Manufacture | 235 | 44 |
| 仪器仪表造业 | Instruments, Meters, Machinery | 48 | 8 |
| 其他制造业 | Other Industry | 3 | - |
| 废弃资源综合利用加工业 | Comprehensive Utilization of Waste Resources | 18 | 6 |
| 金属制品、机械和设备修理业 | Metal Products, Machinery and Equipment Repair | 1 | - |
| 电力、热力的生产和供应业 | Production and Supply of Electric Power and Heat Energy | 24 | 4 |
| 燃气生产和供应业 | Production and Supply of Gas | 7 | 1 |
| 水的生产和供应业 | Production and Supply of Water | 10 | 1 |

# MAIN ECONOMIC INDICATORS OF PRIVATE AND INDIVIDUAL INDUSTRIAL ENTERPRISES ABOVE DESIGNATED SIZE (2012)

(10 000 yuan)

| 工业总产值 Gross Industrial Output Value | 工业销售产值 Value of Industrial Products Sales | # 出口交货值 Delivery Value for Export | 资产合计 Total Assets | # 流动资产 Circulating Funds | # 固定资产 Fixed Assets | 累计折旧 Accumulative Depreciation | 负债合计 Total Liabilities |
|---|---|---|---|---|---|---|---|
| **91 636 331** | **90 446 370** | **9 653 808** | **83 902 432** | **52 159 849** | **21 546 972** | **11 346 681** | **54 215 798** |
| 564 135 | 559 411 | 32 181 | 272 504 | 183 850 | 49 827 | 25 682 | 187 228 |
| 371 983 | 374 255 | 33 198 | 279 471 | 160 574 | 72 285 | 69 227 | 131 171 |
| 121 083 | 115 223 | – | 142 130 | 67 435 | 50 145 | 16 665 | 84 332 |
| 10 942 768 | 10 755 431 | 1 439 913 | 10 340 458 | 6 223 190 | 2 853 629 | 1 841 456 | 7 446 112 |
| 5 463 245 | 5 361 899 | 794 061 | 4 479 000 | 2 931 266 | 965 283 | 358 901 | 2 977 311 |
| 312 598 | 311 596 | 142 188 | 228 889 | 173 020 | 32 103 | 23 475 | 146 523 |
| 302 857 | 299 128 | 3 948 | 414 991 | 252 220 | 69 839 | 51 807 | 197 543 |
| 215 633 | 208 365 | 81 114 | 210 953 | 154 475 | 43 412 | 24 841 | 148 100 |
| 640 296 | 636 974 | 20 397 | 455 661 | 325 712 | 98 446 | 58 587 | 326 988 |
| 784 015 | 780 450 | 57 476 | 825 330 | 503 401 | 267 282 | 172 101 | 517 290 |
| 593 639 | 566 745 | 141 421 | 562 233 | 315 101 | 149 240 | 93 859 | 375 764 |
| 389 001 | 383 994 | – | 215 321 | 176 350 | 19 458 | 9 177 | 150 571 |
| 4 921 794 | 4 842 002 | 546 952 | 4 500 959 | 2 950 124 | 909 461 | 484 261 | 2 287 444 |
| 845 538 | 827 186 | 163 672 | 745 845 | 380 860 | 230 712 | 98 336 | 441 306 |
| 8 511 117 | 8 289 403 | 399 000 | 7 031 901 | 4 328 637 | 1 775 835 | 1 231 058 | 4 843 165 |
| 1 656 314 | 1 636 985 | 240 860 | 1 309 120 | 897 431 | 284 714 | 156 198 | 791 059 |
| 2 084 214 | 2 027 105 | 75 614 | 3 228 209 | 2 348 454 | 488 446 | 381 068 | 2 369 389 |
| 21 828 068 | 21 945 726 | 1 869 514 | 17 145 006 | 9 388 748 | 6 642 231 | 3 511 354 | 11 485 066 |
| 2 736 127 | 2 701 018 | 190 162 | 1 815 202 | 1 285 502 | 276 665 | 161 534 | 1 326 718 |
| 4 655 180 | 4 513 859 | 457 631 | 3 656 269 | 2 415 313 | 841 409 | 343 407 | 2 409 590 |
| 4 360 497 | 4 261 424 | 701 317 | 4 673 968 | 2 988 534 | 1 063 560 | 494 553 | 2 575 889 |
| 2 337 993 | 2 335 236 | 376 849 | 2 890 422 | 1 933 200 | 655 516 | 277 485 | 1 708 824 |
| 1 968 823 | 1 979 575 | 284 578 | 1 585 244 | 1 048 403 | 361 326 | 148 822 | 1 061 847 |
| 314 299 | 302 559 | 12 491 | 558 143 | 374 847 | 138 018 | 37 103 | 366 504 |
| 8 982 765 | 8 764 944 | 830 933 | 9 677 031 | 6 136 784 | 1 651 250 | 587 167 | 5 876 336 |
| 4 016 552 | 3 976 393 | 699 144 | 3 940 981 | 2 614 457 | 838 948 | 304 298 | 2 273 241 |
| 859 488 | 836 134 | 54 867 | 1 375 520 | 905 638 | 269 297 | 85 409 | 737 982 |
| 19 704 | 19 648 | 3 317 | 16 552 | 7 137 | 8 737 | 2 460 | 6 499 |
| 188 534 | 190 653 | 1 010 | 147 224 | 110 404 | 23 988 | 9 800 | 114 331 |
| 12 213 | 12 213 | – | 5 322 | 4 792 | 412 | 88 | 4 499 |
| 366 197 | 363 390 | – | 592 429 | 186 506 | 252 381 | 206 201 | 408 034 |
| 130 981 | 129 996 | – | 222 595 | 143 249 | 60 049 | 13 908 | 167 742 |
| 138 680 | 137 450 | – | 357 549 | 244 235 | 103 068 | 66 393 | 271 400 |

表4-7 续表

单位：万元

| 项　　目 | Item | 所有者权益 Creditors Equity | # 实收资本 Total Capital Hold |
|---|---|---|---|
| **总　　计** | **Total** | **29 658 279** | **13 091 055** |
| 农副食品加工业 | Agricultural and Sideline Food Processing | 85 276 | 47 913 |
| 食品制造业 | Food Production | 148 300 | 114 269 |
| 酒、饮料和精制茶制造业 | Wine, Beverage and Refined tea manufacturing | 57 799 | 13 955 |
| 纺织业 | Textile Industry | 2 894 088 | 1 768 710 |
| 纺织服装、服饰业 | Garments and Apparel Industry | 1 492 217 | 520 049 |
| 皮革、毛皮、羽毛及其制品和制鞋业 | Leather, Fur, Wool and Shoes Products | 82 366 | 42 588 |
| 木材加工及木、竹、藤、棕、草制品业 | Wood Processing, Wood, Bamboo, Rattan and Coir Products Straw Products | 217 449 | 57 293 |
| 家具制造业 | Furniture Manufacturing | 62 853 | 62 508 |
| 造纸及纸制品业 | Papermaking and Paper Products | 128 673 | 75 323 |
| 印刷业和记录媒介的复制 | Printing and Record Medium Reproduction | 308 039 | 185 285 |
| 文教、工美、体育和娱乐用品制造业 | Stationary,Educational, Industrial arts, Sports and Entertainment products | 186 469 | 93 219 |
| 石油加工、炼焦及核燃料加工业 | Petroleum Processing, Coking and Nucleus Fuel Machining Trade | 64 750 | 36 842 |
| 化学原料及化学制品制造业 | Raw Chemical Materials and Chemical Products | 2 211 625 | 816 107 |
| 医药制造业 | Medical and Pharmaceutical Products | 304 539 | 221 173 |
| 化学纤维制造业 | Chemical Fiber | 2 186 774 | 1 020 617 |
| 橡胶和塑料制品业 | Rubber and Plastic  Products | 518 060 | 299 256 |
| 非金属矿物制品业 | Nonmetal Mineral Products | 858 820 | 443 246 |
| 黑色金属冶炼及压延加工业 | Smelting and Pressing of Ferrous Metals | 5 657 531 | 1 193 786 |
| 有色金属冶炼及压延加工业 | Smelting and Pressing of Nonferrous Metals | 488 483 | 337 975 |
| 金属制品业 | Metal Products | 1 243 287 | 745 946 |
| 通用设备制造业 | General Equipment Manufacture | 2 095 057 | 1 051 997 |
| 专用设备制造业 | Special Purposes Equipment Manufacturing | 1 181 598 | 580 982 |
| 汽车制造业 | Automobile Manufacturing | 523 397 | 247 649 |
| 铁路、船舶、航空航天和其他运输设备制造业 | Railway, Ship, Aerospace and other transportation equipment manufacturing | 191 640 | 109 691 |
| 电气机械及器材制造业 | Electric Equipment and Machinery Manufacturing | 3 794 748 | 1 604 413 |
| 计算机、通信和其他电子设备制造业 | Computer Telecommunications and Other Electronic Equipment Manufacture | 1 667 739 | 905 498 |
| 仪器仪表造业 | Instruments, Meters, Machinery | 637 538 | 204 689 |
| 其他制造业 | Other Industry | 10 048 | 9 500 |
| 废弃资源综合利用加工业 | Comprehensive Utilization of  Waste Resources | 32 893 | 33 600 |
| 金属制品、机械和设备修理业 | Metal Products, Machinery and Equipment Repair | 824 | 350 |
| 电力、热力的生产和供应业 | Production and Supply of Electric Power and Heat Energy | 184 395 | 140 564 |
| 燃气生产和供应业 | Production and Supply of Gas | 54 854 | 42 909 |
| 水的生产和供应业 | Production and Supply of Water | 86 150 | 63 153 |

Continued

(10 000 yuan)

| 主营业务收入 Major Business Revenue | 主营业务成本 Major Business Cost | 主营业务税金及附加 Pre-tax and Related Payment of Major Business | 营业利润 Business Profits | 利润总额 Total Profits | 亏损企业亏损总额 Total Deficit of Loss-Making Enterprises | 利税总额 Total taxes and Profits | 应交增值税 Value Added Tax Payable |
|---|---|---|---|---|---|---|---|
| **92 348 541** | **82 034 215** | **270 623** | **3 254 767** | **3 255 194** | **400 458** | **5 318 733** | **1 792 916** |
| 549 667 | 509 486 | 528 | 9 659 | 11 207 | 3 320 | 16 596 | 4 861 |
| 374 159 | 321 517 | 2 429 | 14 121 | 14 318 | 1 301 | 28 673 | 11 926 |
| 112 851 | 78 844 | 6 098 | 16 069 | 16 357 | – | 29 551 | 7 096 |
| 10 723 715 | 9 794 894 | 27 320 | 203 314 | 207 239 | 66 280 | 466 190 | 231 631 |
| 5 455 879 | 4 488 749 | 29 249 | 450 062 | 393 688 | 12 536 | 561 055 | 138 118 |
| 311 350 | 278 311 | 1 342 | 5 061 | 5 895 | 1 943 | 14 786 | 7 549 |
| 304 834 | 265 649 | 1 511 | 10 419 | 15 563 | 520 | 27 261 | 10 187 |
| 210 322 | 181 863 | 784 | 4 171 | 3 998 | 1 467 | 10 453 | 5 672 |
| 632 537 | 567 614 | 1 878 | 9 930 | 11 183 | 4 460 | 26 030 | 12 969 |
| 771 274 | 660 102 | 2 691 | 32 673 | 37 052 | 6 825 | 65 011 | 25 268 |
| 607 305 | 531 140 | 2 198 | 18 977 | 20 156 | 1 921 | 39 237 | 16 883 |
| 389 274 | 372 019 | 382 | 6 360 | 6 677 | 71 | 9 897 | 2 838 |
| 4 884 919 | 4 073 565 | 15 638 | 310 091 | 330 674 | 16 167 | 456 648 | 110 336 |
| 830 656 | 666 264 | 2 910 | 66 932 | 67 063 | 1 520 | 93 639 | 23 667 |
| 8 702 225 | 8 178 956 | 9 743 | 103 051 | 100 755 | 68 119 | 178 226 | 67 728 |
| 1 630 596 | 1 415 825 | 5 499 | 69 428 | 76 999 | 8 646 | 114 449 | 31 951 |
| 2 064 726 | 1 795 190 | 12 431 | 56 635 | 58 076 | 11 579 | 155 597 | 85 090 |
| 23 122 314 | 21 482 132 | 45 413 | 423 955 | 356 169 | 16 324 | 776 061 | 374 479 |
| 2 651 049 | 2 510 528 | 3 095 | 19 168 | 23 292 | 13 530 | 48 075 | 21 688 |
| 4 476 662 | 3 972 197 | 13 794 | 168 748 | 154 243 | 21 022 | 269 044 | 101 007 |
| 4 270 221 | 3 555 989 | 17 862 | 208 080 | 217 868 | 13 324 | 356 856 | 121 127 |
| 2 340 946 | 1 865 401 | 10 188 | 138 081 | 148 008 | 10 673 | 224 387 | 66 192 |
| 1 972 884 | 1 726 009 | 7 899 | 74 182 | 86 184 | 4 424 | 119 373 | 25 290 |
| 309 092 | 246 329 | 1 493 | 12 375 | 16 707 | 6 031 | 27 109 | 8 909 |
| 8 973 022 | 7 686 287 | 34 011 | 497 645 | 517 506 | 65 722 | 709 550 | 158 034 |
| 3 990 641 | 3 436 165 | 8 330 | 218 494 | 235 271 | 28 892 | 315 858 | 72 257 |
| 832 277 | 648 313 | 3 168 | 60 104 | 65 789 | 4 884 | 98 725 | 29 768 |
| 19 640 | 17 720 | 60 | 250 | 251 | – | 1 198 | 882 |
| 185 391 | 179 940 | 330 | -4 232 | -1 074 | 6 700 | 3 348 | 4 092 |
| 12 213 | 11 429 | 14 | 67 | 67 | – | 223 | 142 |
| 364 517 | 301 302 | 980 | 27 863 | 31 100 | 753 | 40 591 | 8 511 |
| 130 856 | 105 477 | 544 | 9 819 | 9 820 | 1 343 | 13 073 | 2 709 |
| 140 527 | 109 009 | 811 | 13 215 | 17 093 | 161 | 21 963 | 4 059 |

# 表4-8 规模以上外商和港澳台商投资工业企业主要经济指标 (2012年)

单位：万元

| 指　　标 | Item | 企业单位数(个) Number of Enterprises (unit) | # 亏损企业 Loss Making Enterprises |
|---|---|---|---|
| **总　　计** | **Total** | **4 777** | **1 390** |
| 农副食品加工业 | Agricultural and Sideline Food Processing | 25 | 10 |
| 食品制造业 | Food Production | 25 | 7 |
| 酒、饮料和精制茶制造业 | Wine, Beverage and Refined tea manufacturing | 12 | 5 |
| 纺织业 | Textile Industry | 280 | 85 |
| 纺织服装、服饰业 | Garments and Apparel Industry | 185 | 55 |
| 皮革、毛皮、羽毛及其制品和制鞋业 | Leather, Fur, Wool and Shoes Products | 47 | 18 |
| 木材加工及木、竹、藤、棕、草制品业 | Timber Processing, Bamboo, Cane, Palm Fiber and Straw Products | 22 | 7 |
| 家具制造业 | Furniture Manufacturing | 46 | 20 |
| 造纸及纸制品业 | Papermaking and Paper Products | 83 | 16 |
| 印刷业和记录媒介的复制 | Printing and Record Medium Reproduction | 64 | 17 |
| 文教、工美、体育和娱乐用品制造业 | Stationary,Educational, Industrial arts, Sports and Entertainment products | 83 | 30 |
| 石油加工、炼焦及核燃料加工业 | Petroleum Processing, Coking and Nucleus Fuel Machining Trade | 3 | – |
| 化学原料及化学制品制造业 | Raw Chemical Materials and Chemical Products | 372 | 93 |
| 医药制造业 | Medical and Pharmaceutical Products | 42 | 7 |
| 化学纤维制造业 | Chemical Fiber | 36 | 20 |
| 橡胶和塑料制品业 | Rubber and Plastic Products | 327 | 96 |
| 非金属矿物制品业 | Nonmetal Mineral Products | 126 | 38 |
| 黑色金属冶炼及压延加工业 | Smelting and Pressing of Ferrous Metals | 60 | 21 |
| 有色金属冶炼及压延加工业 | Smelting and Pressing of Nonferrous Metals | 91 | 28 |
| 金属制品业 | Metal Products | 235 | 66 |
| 通用设备制造业 | Ordinary Equipment Manufactory Trade | 419 | 85 |
| 专用设备制造业 | Special Purposes Equipment Manufacturing | 348 | 89 |
| 汽车制造业 | Automobile Manufacturing | 204 | 50 |
| 铁路、船舶、航空航天和其他运输设备制造业 | Railway, Ship, Aerospace and other transportation equipment manufacturing | 90 | 25 |
| 电气机械及器材制造业 | Electric Equipment and Machinery | 373 | 114 |
| 计算机、通信和其他电子设备制造业 | Computer Telecommunications and Other Electronic Equipment Manufacture | 1 004 | 345 |
| 仪器仪表制造业 | Instruments, Meters Machinery | 110 | 20 |
| 其他制造业 | Others Industry | 9 | 6 |
| 废弃资源综合利用业 | Comprehensive Utilization of Waste Resources | 33 | 14 |
| 电力、热力的生产和供应业 | Production and Supply of Electric Power and Heat Energy | 1 | 1 |
| 金属制品、机械和设备修理业 | Metal Products, Machinery and Equipment Repair | 11 | 2 |
| 燃气生产和供应业 | Production and Supply of Gas | 7 | – |
| 水的生产和供应业 | Production and Supply of Water | 4 | – |

# MAIN ECONOMIC INDICATORS OF INDUSTRIAL ENTERPRISES ABOVE DESIGNATED SIZE WITH FOREIGN INVESTMENT AND INVESTMENT FROM HONG KONG, MACAO AND TAIWAN (2012)

(10 000 yuan)

| 工业总产值 Gross Industrial Output Value | 工业销售产值 Value of Industrial Products Sales | # 出口交货值 Delivery Value for Export | 资产合计 Total Assets | # 流动资产 Circulating Funds | # 固定资产 Fixed Assets | 累计折旧 Accumulative Depreciation | 负债合计 Total Liabilities |
|---|---|---|---|---|---|---|---|
| **188 704 313** | **187 468 516** | **115 867 317** | **138 946 410** | **84 513 208** | **44 048 260** | **35 668 508** | **73 639 333** |
| 2 442 957 | 2 520 179 | 29 622 | 1 596 103 | 1 184 123 | 282 968 | 196 405 | 997 843 |
| 1 302 448 | 1 178 822 | 132 508 | 949 608 | 375 404 | 373 576 | 164 838 | 588 016 |
| 241 791 | 242 557 | 5 374 | 363 696 | 127 728 | 219 358 | 161 359 | 211 232 |
| 3 362 716 | 3 287 035 | 832 586 | 4 247 715 | 2 728 500 | 1 135 076 | 887 344 | 2 773 572 |
| 1 405 870 | 1 406 205 | 866 732 | 1 187 646 | 805 627 | 270 393 | 214 522 | 650 242 |
| 449 785 | 450 149 | 331 808 | 447 490 | 320 308 | 90 576 | 88 799 | 223 354 |
| 247 082 | 258 621 | 70 166 | 404 165 | 307 881 | 77 927 | 90 982 | 198 345 |
| 732 360 | 731 703 | 600 460 | 605 410 | 349 631 | 200 785 | 117 311 | 282 917 |
| 4 073 663 | 4 027 131 | 530 503 | 6 031 744 | 3 009 431 | 2 517 282 | 1 618 941 | 2 969 813 |
| 1 092 482 | 1 086 479 | 431 812 | 1 133 911 | 661 924 | 406 359 | 276 437 | 476 701 |
| 1 419 897 | 1 426 253 | 798 836 | 1 100 373 | 666 961 | 304 452 | 245 876 | 528 132 |
| 470 135 | 449 450 | – | 251 240 | 212 661 | 33 021 | 47 482 | 107 882 |
| 9 788 788 | 9 666 036 | 1 991 556 | 10 560 425 | 5 604 812 | 3 984 862 | 2 122 169 | 5 164 888 |
| 1 514 920 | 1 438 706 | 305 083 | 1 737 817 | 1 063 588 | 519 515 | 419 612 | 808 513 |
| 3 138 516 | 3 296 436 | 366 922 | 3 782 811 | 1 346 962 | 1 756 159 | 735 742 | 2 284 235 |
| 5 474 047 | 5 429 970 | 2 287 419 | 5 210 044 | 2 982 139 | 1 868 826 | 1 540 160 | 2 105 175 |
| 2 661 748 | 2 670 002 | 539 416 | 3 330 051 | 1 688 663 | 1 378 530 | 1 040 585 | 1 662 690 |
| 4 039 777 | 3 945 980 | 593 400 | 3 177 503 | 1 637 346 | 1 248 614 | 831 681 | 2 008 125 |
| 2 390 319 | 2 394 364 | 376 673 | 1 918 361 | 1 234 498 | 559 377 | 460 649 | 970 731 |
| 3 016 779 | 2 988 374 | 1 052 803 | 3 109 647 | 1 864 889 | 993 911 | 635 403 | 1 342 345 |
| 12 521 546 | 12 437 567 | 6 166 737 | 9 788 388 | 6 728 650 | 2 416 153 | 1 712 396 | 4 589 839 |
| 6 839 545 | 6 837 300 | 3 224 059 | 7 233 073 | 4 651 247 | 2 119 177 | 1 113 280 | 3 365 178 |
| 5 161 197 | 5 101 192 | 1 357 063 | 4 282 688 | 2 469 493 | 1 562 330 | 1 001 942 | 2 070 669 |
| 1 880 314 | 1 829 357 | 849 841 | 1 618 066 | 1 134 435 | 388 434 | 319 603 | 877 770 |
| 13 730 091 | 13 564 974 | 8 222 642 | 10 622 119 | 6 957 330 | 2 736 064 | 1 622 894 | 6 023 835 |
| 93 644 210 | 93 260 430 | 82 849 866 | 46 753 085 | 30 712 659 | 13 981 507 | 16 366 608 | 25 696 424 |
| 2 297 644 | 2 283 469 | 899 984 | 2 140 801 | 1 387 706 | 623 950 | 445 789 | 1 045 071 |
| 38 483 | 38 349 | 14 626 | 52 447 | 29 691 | 20 799 | 17 898 | 36 911 |
| 1 410 678 | 1 306 645 | 2 880 | 1 346 173 | 1 250 544 | 78 320 | 39 467 | 1 197 672 |
| 12 593 | 13 329 | – | 8 335 | 1 529 | 5 704 | 9 791 | 995 |
| 1 316 327 | 1 315 971 | – | 2 712 074 | 708 155 | 1 147 053 | 931 248 | 1 750 063 |
| 513 363 | 513 239 | 135 940 | 566 054 | 232 513 | 183 897 | 45 068 | 300 606 |
| 72 242 | 72 242 | – | 677 347 | 76 180 | 563 305 | 146 227 | 329 549 |

表4-8 续表

单位：万元

| 项　　目 | Item | 所有者权益 Creditors Equity | # 实收资本 Total Capital Hold |
| --- | --- | --- | --- |
| **总　计** | **Total** | **65 209 143** | **45 755 686** |
| 农副食品加工业 | Agricultural and Sideline Food Processing | 598 260 | 260 379 |
| 食品制造业 | Food Production | 361 592 | 308 443 |
| 酒、饮料和精制茶制造业 | Wine, Beverage and Refined tea manufacturing | 152 464 | 323 230 |
| 纺织业 | Textile Industry | 1 457 762 | 1 445 075 |
| 纺织服装、服饰业 | Garments and Apparel Industry | 537 874 | 415 679 |
| 皮革、毛皮、羽毛及其制品和制鞋业业 | Leather, Fur, Wool and Shoes Products | 224 442 | 137 279 |
| 木材加工及木、竹、藤、棕、草制品业 | Timber Processing, Bamboo, Cane, Palm Fiber and Straw Products | 205 820 | 168 952 |
| 家具制造业 | Furniture Manufacturing | 322 492 | 267 952 |
| 造纸及纸制品业 | Papermaking and Paper Products | 3 061 931 | 2 587 877 |
| 印刷业和记录媒介的复制 | Printing and Record Medium Reproduction | 657 211 | 382 838 |
| 文教、工美、体育和娱乐用品制造业 | Stationary,Educational, Industrial arts, Sports and Entertainment products | 572 240 | 443 932 |
| 石油加工、炼焦及核燃料加工业 | Petroleum Processing, Coking and Nucleus Fuel Machining Trade | 143 359 | 56 568 |
| 化学原料及化学制品制造业 | Raw Chemical Materials and Chemical Products | 5 391 223 | 4 064 199 |
| 医药制造业 | Medical and Pharmaceutical Products | 929 304 | 692 039 |
| 化学纤维制造业 | Chemical Fiber | 1 498 576 | 1 185 169 |
| 橡胶和塑料制品业 | Rubber and Plastic Products | 3 104 860 | 2 210 482 |
| 非金属矿物制品业 | Nonmetal Mineral Products | 1 667 361 | 1 304 501 |
| 黑色金属冶炼及压延加工业 | Smelting and Pressing of Ferrous Metals | 1 169 378 | 1 188 703 |
| 有色金属冶炼及压延加工业 | Smelting and Pressing of Nonferrous Metals | 947 630 | 806 417 |
| 金属制品业 | Metal Products | 1 767 302 | 1 319 598 |
| 通用设备制造业 | Ordinary Equipment Manufactory Trade | 5 198 549 | 2 766 731 |
| 专用设备制造业 | Special Purposes Equipment Manufacturing | 3 865 443 | 2 196 219 |
| 汽车制造业 | Automobile Manufacturing | 2 212 018 | 1 518 417 |
| 铁路、船舶、航空航天和其他运输设备制造业 | Railway, Ship, Aerospace and other transportation equipment manufacturing | 740 296 | 432 831 |
| 电气机械及器材制造业 | Electric Equipment and Machinery | 4 597 328 | 2 982 227 |
| 计算机、通信和其他电子设备制造业 | Computer Telecommunications and Other Electronic Equipment Manufacture | 20 982 066 | 14 461 330 |
| 仪器仪表制造业 | Instruments, Meters Machinery | 1 095 729 | 617 379 |
| 其他制造业 | Others Industry | 15 534 | 33 796 |
| 废弃资源综合利用业 | Comprehensive Utilization of Waste Resources | 148 501 | 162 924 |
| 电力、热力的生产和供应业 | Production and Supply of Electric Power and Heat Energy | 7 340 | 12 358 |
| 金属制品、机械和设备修理业 | Metal Products, Machinery and Equipment Repair | 962 011 | 580 296 |
| 燃气生产和供应业 | Production and Supply of Gas | 265 448 | 84 799 |
| 水的生产和供应业 | Production and Supply of Water | 347 799 | 337 067 |

Continued

(10 000 yuan)

| 主营业务收入 Major Business Revenue | 主营业务成本 Major Business Cost | 主营业务税金及附加 Pre-tax and Related Payment of Major Business | 营业利润 Business Profits | 利润总额 Total Profits | 亏损企业亏损总额 Total Deficit of Loss-Making Enterprises | 利税总额 Total taxes and Profits | 应交增值税 Value Added Tax Payable |
|---|---|---|---|---|---|---|---|
| **189 783 872** | **167 737 421** | **483 812** | **9 372 697** | **8 862 934** | **1 730 051** | **12 193 776** | **2 847 030** |
| 2 577 073 | 2 282 325 | 3 495 | 69 780 | 49 326 | 7 521 | 78 927 | 26 106 |
| 1 199 897 | 840 520 | 6 716 | 54 594 | 55 711 | 1 920 | 120 114 | 57 687 |
| 243 317 | 193 477 | 11 632 | 5 429 | 5 775 | 9 938 | 28 832 | 11 425 |
| 3 269 606 | 2 923 184 | 8 565 | 77 079 | 80 498 | 36 089 | 145 322 | 56 259 |
| 1 403 307 | 1 253 428 | 6 534 | 12 055 | 11 559 | 20 882 | 45 999 | 27 905 |
| 471 062 | 424 427 | 2 913 | 3 094 | 2 937 | 8 558 | 11 713 | 5 863 |
| 257 506 | 211 340 | 2 824 | 22 237 | 22 055 | 7 226 | 32 119 | 7 240 |
| 721 604 | 645 255 | 2 305 | 4 840 | 5 189 | 16 190 | 29 036 | 21 541 |
| 4 123 075 | 3 419 719 | 10 350 | 202 576 | 204 036 | 18 515 | 312 187 | 97 801 |
| 1 115 131 | 845 190 | 6 984 | 127 453 | 128 270 | 8 490 | 173 585 | 38 331 |
| 1 428 027 | 1 241 996 | 5 836 | 32 207 | 36 884 | 17 247 | 82 396 | 39 676 |
| 449 130 | 342 418 | 32 199 | 60 255 | 60 625 | – | 108 158 | 15 334 |
| 10 045 846 | 8 297 678 | 45 272 | 635 171 | 633 657 | 172 899 | 949 309 | 270 380 |
| 1 444 254 | 837 122 | 11 072 | 119 704 | 139 147 | 30 259 | 234 043 | 83 824 |
| 3 759 728 | 3 442 033 | 6 179 | 154 211 | 161 062 | 32 593 | 209 714 | 42 472 |
| 5 421 236 | 4 579 483 | 23 891 | 310 460 | 317 550 | 65 804 | 489 470 | 148 030 |
| 2 666 350 | 2 271 012 | 12 715 | 86 631 | 85 313 | 70 102 | 188 775 | 90 747 |
| 4 125 408 | 3 951 193 | 4 383 | -5 780 | -28 262 | 93 679 | 8 451 | 32 329 |
| 2 404 533 | 2 162 722 | 5 608 | 94 323 | 88 790 | 22 445 | 138 122 | 43 724 |
| 3 019 148 | 2 562 792 | 13 565 | 154 241 | 158 129 | 35 213 | 261 031 | 89 338 |
| 12 535 581 | 10 376 170 | 48 622 | 1 083 332 | 1 099 470 | 50 402 | 1 449 667 | 301 575 |
| 6 786 800 | 5 506 526 | 26 531 | 596 478 | 610 035 | 74 321 | 799 954 | 163 389 |
| 5 146 981 | 4 241 339 | 19 859 | 397 522 | 411 991 | 36 250 | 536 537 | 104 687 |
| 1 910 723 | 1 570 560 | 8 000 | 141 413 | 144 751 | 9 906 | 211 260 | 58 509 |
| 13 619 197 | 11 862 989 | 25 238 | 612 382 | 594 323 | 189 343 | 857 625 | 238 064 |
| 94 005 695 | 86 815 575 | 113 395 | 3 865 337 | 3 334 405 | 632 668 | 4 099 507 | 651 707 |
| 2 364 781 | 1 949 412 | 8 534 | 168 253 | 169 865 | 25 227 | 213 427 | 35 028 |
| 38 429 | 34 165 | 194 | -3 060 | -1 927 | 2 023 | -804 | 931 |
| 1 277 829 | 1 107 840 | 1 849 | -36 940 | -25 716 | 31 578 | -5 555 | 18 312 |
| 17 680 | 18 716 | 64 | -2 008 | -1 884 | 1 884 | -1 091 | 729 |
| 1 308 894 | 1 029 525 | 6 806 | 228 968 | 233 695 | 779 | 299 033 | 58 532 |
| 553 802 | 448 700 | 1 384 | 90 914 | 61 270 | – | 69 923 | 7 268 |
| 72 242 | 48 590 | 298 | 9 546 | 14 405 | – | 16 990 | 2 287 |

表4-9

# 规模以上工业高新技术产业主要经济指标（2012年）
# MAIN ECONOMIC INDICATORS OF HI-TECH MANUFACTURING INDUSTRY ABOVE THE DESIGNATED SIZE(2012)

| 项　　目 | Item | 全　市 Whole Municipality |
|---|---|---|
| 企业单位数 (个) | Number of Enterprises (unit) | 2 795 |
| 平均从业人员 (人) | Average Employees (person) | 1 475 123 |
| 工业总产值 (万元) | Gross Industrial Output Value Total (10 000 yuan) | 118 888 000 |
| 航空航天制造业 | Aviation and Aerospace | 298 713 |
| 电子计算机及办公设备制造业 | Computer and Manufacturing of Office Appliance | 21 835 870 |
| 电子及通讯设备制造业 | Electronics and Communications Equipment | 51 618 527 |
| 医药制造业 | Biomedical Manufacturing | 3 437 968 |
| 仪器仪表制造业 | Instrument Manufacturing | 1 973 205 |
| 智能电气设备制造业 | Electrical Equipment Manufacturing | 20 356 197 |
| 新材料制造业 | New Material Production Industry | 14 844 904 |
| 新能源制造业 | New Energy Manufacturing | 4 522 616 |
| 资产合计 | Total Assets | 87 726 156 |
| 负债合计 | Total Liabilities | 46 702 459 |
| 所有者权益合计 | Total Creditors Equity | 405 729 986 |
| # 实收资本 | Total Capital Hold | 253 834 737 |
| 主营业务收入 | Major Business Revenue | 116 540 771 |
| 利税总额 | Total Taxes and Profits | 7 363 907 |
| 利润总额 | Total Profits | 5 507 927 |
| 产销率 (%) | Proportion of Products Sold (%) | 98.37 |

表4-10

# 规模以上工业新兴产业主要经济指标（2012年）
# MAIN ECONOMIC INDICATORS OF EMERGING INDUSTRIES ABOVE THE DESIGNATED SIZE(2012)

| 项目 | Item | 全市 Whole Municipality |
|---|---|---|
| 企业单位数 (个) | Number of Enterprises (unit) | 2 048 |
| 平均从业人员 (人) | Average Employees (person) | 1 194 645 |
| 工业总产值 (万元) | Gross Industrial Output Value Total (10 000 yuan) | 123 668 289 |
| 新型平板显示 | New Flat Panel Displays | 27 796 051 |
| 新材料 | New Materials | 34 255 338 |
| 智能电网和物联网 | Smart Grid and Internet Of Things | 12 873 172 |
| 高端装备制造 | High-End Equipment Manufacturing | 23 711 280 |
| 节能环保 | Energy Saving and Environmental Protection | 9 232 206 |
| 新能源 | New Energy | 8 755 089 |
| 生物技术和新医药 | Biotechnology and New Medicines | 4 658 100 |
| 集成电路 | Integrated Circuit | 2 387 053 |
| 资产合计 | Total Assets | 103 244 869 |
| 负债合计 | Total Liabilities | 57 159 407 |
| 所有者权益合计 | Total Creditors Equity | 45 582 900 |
| # 实收资本 | Total Capital Hold | 27 441 051 |
| 主营业务收入 | Major Business Revenue | 120 295 596 |
| 利税总额 | Total Taxes and Profits | 8 220 023 |
| 利润总额 | Total Profits | 5 977 886 |
| 产销率 (%) | Proportion of Products Sold (%) | 98.06 |

表4-11 规模以上工业企业主要经济效益指标 (2012年)

单位：%

| 项　　目 | Item | 总资产贡献率 Total Assets Contribution Ratio |
| --- | --- | --- |
| **总　　计** | **Total** | **8.79** |
| **一、按轻重工业分** | **Grouped by Light and Heavy Industry** | |
| 轻工业 | Light Industry | 8.13 |
| 重工业 | Heavy Industry | 9.05 |
| **二、按行业类别分** | **Grouped by Sector** | |
| 有色金属矿采选业 | Nonferrous Metals Mining and Processing | 3.29 |
| 非金属矿采选业 | Nonmetal Minerals Mining and Dressing | 7.63 |
| 农副食品加工业 | Agricultural and Sideline Food Processing | 5.27 |
| 食品制造业 | Food Production | 12.71 |
| 酒、饮料和精制茶制造业 | Wine, Beverage and Refined tea manufacturing | 12.21 |
| 烟草制品业 | Manufacture of Tobacco | 0.42 |
| 纺织业 | Textile Industry | 6.03 |
| 纺织服装、服饰业 | Garments and Apparel Industry | 11.82 |
| 皮革、毛皮、羽毛及其制品和制鞋业 | Leather, Fur, Wool Products | 4.96 |
| 木材加工及木、竹、藤、棕、草制品业 | Wood Processing, Wood, Bamboo, Rattan and Coir Products Straw Products | 8.24 |
| 家具制造业 | Furniture Manufacturing | 5.30 |
| 造纸及纸制品业 | Papermaking and Paper Products | 6.80 |
| 印刷业和记录媒介的复制 | Printing and Record Duplicating | 12.91 |
| 文教、工美、体育和娱乐用品制造业 | Stationary,Educational, industrial arts, Sports and Entertainment products | 8.32 |
| 石油加工、炼焦及核燃料加工业 | Oil Processing, Coking and Nuclear Fuel Processing | 23.28 |

# MAIN INDICATORS OF ECONOMIC BENEFIT OF INDUSTRIAL ENTERPRISES ABOVE DESIGNATED SIZE (2012)

(%)

| 规模以上工业 Enterprises Above Designated Size | | | | # 民营工业 Private and Individual | |
|---|---|---|---|---|---|
| 成本费用利润率 Rate Between Profit and Cost | 资产负债率 Assets Liability Ratio | 固定资产净值率 New Value Added in Fixed Asset | 产销率 Proportion of Products Sold | 总资产贡献率 Total Assets Contribution Ratio | 成本费用利润率 Rate Between Profit and Cost |
| **4.47** | **57.75** | **57.04** | **99.28** | **8.06** | **3.57** |
| 3.78 | 60.23 | 59.56 | 98.99 | 8.10 | 3.22 |
| 4.71 | 56.78 | 56.11 | 99.42 | 8.03 | 3.77 |
| | | | | | |
| 3.95 | 59.06 | 18.72 | 109.25 | – | – |
| 3.35 | 51.02 | 51.52 | 98.62 | – | – |
| 2.00 | 63.42 | 59.50 | 102.41 | 7.60 | 2.06 |
| 4.59 | 58.51 | 63.86 | 92.75 | 10.93 | 3.98 |
| 6.70 | 58.43 | 51.68 | 98.60 | 23.38 | 17.29 |
| 2.81 | 10.48 | 58.66 | 80.91 | – | – |
| 1.95 | 70.11 | 57.81 | 98.18 | 6.51 | 1.83 |
| 6.30 | 64.02 | 61.48 | 98.53 | 13.66 | 7.82 |
| 1.14 | 54.68 | 51.08 | 99.92 | 8.56 | 1.92 |
| 6.78 | 48.33 | 49.51 | 101.42 | 7.75 | 5.28 |
| 0.99 | 52.80 | 62.61 | 99.16 | 6.25 | 1.91 |
| 4.92 | 50.21 | 59.55 | 99.07 | 7.48 | 1.78 |
| 9.54 | 50.73 | 58.58 | 99.49 | 9.29 | 4.98 |
| 2.82 | 54.37 | 54.87 | 98.98 | 8.75 | 3.42 |
| 7.23 | 54.27 | 52.24 | 98.27 | 6.08 | 1.73 |

表4-11 续表 1

单位：%

| 项　　目 | Item | # 民营工业<br>资产负债率<br>Assets Liability Ratio |
|---|---|---|
| **总　　计** | **Total** | **64.62** |
| **一、按轻重工业分** | **Grouped by Light and Heavy Industry** | |
| 轻工业 | Light Industry | 68.09 |
| 重工业 | Heavy Industry | 62.79 |
| **二、按行业类别分** | **Grouped by Sector** | |
| 有色金属矿采选业 | Nonferrous Metals Mining and Processing | - |
| 非金属矿采选业 | Nonmetal Minerals Mining and Dressing | - |
| 农副食品加工业 | Agricultural and Sideline Food Processing | 68.71 |
| 食品制造业 | Food Production | 46.94 |
| 酒、饮料和精制茶制造业 | Wine, Beverage and Refined tea manufacturing | 59.33 |
| 烟草制品业 | Manufacture of Tobacco | - |
| 纺织业 | Textile Industry | 72.01 |
| 纺织服装、服饰业 | Garments and Apparel Industry | 66.47 |
| 皮革、毛皮、羽毛及其制品业 | Leather, Fur, Wool Products | 64.01 |
| 木材加工及木、竹、藤、棕、草制品业 | Wood Processing, Wood, Bamboo, Rattan and Coir Products Straw Products | 47.60 |
| 家具制造业 | Furniture Manufacturing | 70.20 |
| 造纸及纸制品业 | Papermaking and Paper Products | 71.76 |
| 印刷业和记录媒介的复制 | Printing and Record Duplicating | 62.68 |
| 文教、工美、体育和娱乐用品制造业 | Stationary,Educational,Industrial arts, Sports and Entertainment products | 66.83 |
| 石油加工、炼焦及核燃料加工业 | Oil Processing, Coking and Nuclear Fuel Processing | 69.93 |

Continued 1

(%)

| Private and Individual | | # 外商和港澳台商 Enterprises with Investment from Foreign ,Hong Kong,Macao and Taiwan | | | | |
|---|---|---|---|---|---|---|
| 固定资产净值率 New Value Added in Fixed Asset | 产销率 Proportion of Products Sold | 总资产贡献率 Total Assets Contribution Ratio | 成本费用利润率 Rate Between Profit and Cost | 资产负债率 Assets Liability Ratio | 固定资产净值率 New Value Added in Fixed Asset | 产销率 Proportion of Products Sold |
| **63.44** | **98.70** | **9.31** | **4.88** | **53.00** | **54.06** | **99.35** |
| 59.95 | 98.12 | 8.41 | 4.29 | 56.63 | 58.96 | 99.50 |
| 65.35 | 99.03 | 9.61 | 5.05 | 52.79 | 52.54 | 99.30 |
| | | | | | | |
| – | – | – | – | – | – | – |
| – | – | – | – | – | – | – |
| 64.33 | 99.16 | 4.87 | 1.99 | 62.52 | 58.77 | 103.16 |
| 44.79 | 100.61 | 13.23 | 4.78 | 61.92 | 68.43 | 90.51 |
| 73.75 | 95.16 | 7.85 | 2.45 | 58.08 | 47.09 | 100.32 |
| – | – | – | – | – | – | – |
| 58.93 | 98.29 | 4.83 | 2.49 | 65.30 | 55.09 | 97.75 |
| 64.86 | 98.14 | 4.88 | 0.83 | 54.75 | 54.07 | 100.02 |
| 56.29 | 99.68 | 3.12 | 0.63 | 49.91 | 49.49 | 100.08 |
| 55.05 | 98.77 | 8.74 | 8.47 | 49.08 | 45.70 | 104.67 |
| 63.10 | 96.63 | 4.97 | 0.72 | 46.73 | 62.50 | 99.91 |
| 61.68 | 99.48 | 6.40 | 5.09 | 49.24 | 60.49 | 98.86 |
| 58.84 | 99.55 | 15.55 | 12.96 | 42.04 | 58.42 | 99.45 |
| 58.54 | 95.47 | 8.10 | 2.57 | 48.00 | 53.29 | 100.45 |
| 66.33 | 98.71 | 43.09 | 16.92 | 42.94 | 40.97 | 95.60 |

表4-11 续表 2

单位：%

| 项　　目 | Item | 总资产贡献率 Total Assets Contribution Ratio |
|---|---|---|
| 化学原料及化学制品制造业 | Raw Chemical Materials and Chemical Products | 10.31 |
| 医药制造业 | Medical and Pharmaceutical Products | 13.45 |
| 化学纤维制造业 | Chemical Fiber Manufacturing | 5.76 |
| 橡胶和塑料制品业 | Rubber and Plastic Products | 9.94 |
| 非金属矿物制品业 | Nonmetal Mineral Products | 6.30 |
| 黑色金属冶炼及压延加工业 | Smelting and Pressing of Ferrous Metals | 5.59 |
| 有色金属冶炼及压延加工业 | Smelting and Pressing of Nonferrous Metals | 6.88 |
| 金属制品业 | Metal Products | 8.91 |
| 通用设备制造业 | General Equipment Manufacture | 12.81 |
| 专用设备制造业 | Special Purposes Equipment Manufacturing | 10.58 |
| 汽车制造业 | Automobile Manufacturing | 11.88 |
| 铁路、船舶、航空航天和其他运输设备制造业 | Railway, Ship, Aerospace and other transportation equipment manufacturing | 11.71 |
| 电气机械及器材制造业 | Electric Equipment and Machinery Manufacturing | 8.60 |
| 计算机、通信和其他电子设备制造业 | Computer Telecommunications and Other Electronic Equipment Manufacture | 8.83 |
| 仪器仪表制造业 | Instruments, Meters Machinery | 9.69 |
| 其他制造业 | Other Products Manufacture | 2.65 |
| 废弃资源综合利用业 | Comprehensive Utilization of Waste Resources | 2.01 |
| 金属制品、机械和设备修理业 | Metal Products, Machinery and Equipment Repair | -4.19 |
| 电力、热力的生产和供应业 | Manufacture and Supply of Electricity and Thermal Power | 13.79 |
| 燃气生产和供应业 | Manufacture and Supply of Gas | 8.26 |
| 水的生产和供应业 | Manufacture and Supply of Water | 3.02 |

Continued 2

(%)

| 规模以上工业 Enterprises Above Designated Size | | | | # 民营工业 Private and Individual | |
|---|---|---|---|---|---|
| 成本费用利润率 Rate Between Profit and Cost | 资产负债率 Assets Liability Ratio | 固定资产净值率 New Value Added in Fixed Asset | 产销率 Proportion of Products Sold | 总资产贡献率 Total Assets Contribution Ratio | 成本费用利润率 Rate Between Profit and Cost |
| 6.56 | 50.06 | 63.69 | 98.61 | 11.67 | 7.03 |
| 9.48 | 51.52 | 56.97 | 95.98 | 13.80 | 8.68 |
| 2.11 | 65.90 | 63.43 | 99.45 | 5.05 | 1.15 |
| 5.87 | 44.43 | 54.93 | 99.11 | 10.00 | 4.85 |
| 3.25 | 61.10 | 56.46 | 98.89 | 6.26 | 2.88 |
| 0.97 | 67.25 | 62.78 | 100.11 | 6.81 | 1.54 |
| 1.96 | 61.78 | 55.68 | 104.11 | 5.09 | 0.87 |
| 4.27 | 55.51 | 63.73 | 97.78 | 9.01 | 3.50 |
| 8.35 | 49.65 | 59.76 | 98.92 | 8.72 | 5.30 |
| 8.64 | 50.83 | 64.68 | 100.13 | 8.94 | 6.66 |
| 7.39 | 53.47 | 60.47 | 99.54 | 8.42 | 4.47 |
| 7.75 | 57.18 | 56.15 | 97.14 | 7.45 | 5.58 |
| 5.07 | 58.70 | 65.21 | 98.32 | 8.50 | 6.01 |
| 3.79 | 55.18 | 45.99 | 99.57 | 9.02 | 6.20 |
| 7.76 | 50.64 | 61.34 | 98.85 | 8.55 | 8.40 |
| -2.75 | 62.92 | 58.32 | 99.67 | 8.72 | 1.30 |
| -1.96 | 87.70 | 66.64 | 93.71 | 4.87 | -0.56 |
| -5.71 | 40.22 | 38.20 | 102.97 | 7.32 | 0.55 |
| 16.95 | 64.28 | 58.87 | 101.29 | 10.63 | 8.77 |
| 11.80 | 70.80 | 72.27 | 98.95 | 6.13 | 8.07 |
| 6.08 | 62.44 | 69.01 | 98.34 | 6.54 | 12.92 |

表4-11 续表 3

单位：%

| 项　　目 | Item | # 民营工业<br>资产负债率<br>Assets Liability Ratio |
|---|---|---|
| 化学原料及化学制品制造业 | Raw Chemical Materials and Chemical Products | 50.82 |
| 医药制造业 | Medical and Pharmaceutical Products | 59.17 |
| 化学纤维制造业 | Chemical Fiber Manufacturing | 68.87 |
| 橡胶和塑料制品业 | Rubber and Plastic Products | 60.43 |
| 非金属矿物制品业 | Nonmetal Mineral Products | 73.40 |
| 黑色金属冶炼及压延加工业 | Smelting and Pressing of Ferrous Metals | 66.99 |
| 有色金属冶炼及压延加工业 | Smelting and Pressing of Nonferrous Metals | 73.09 |
| 金属制品业 | Metal Products | 65.90 |
| 通用设备制造业 | General Equipment Manufacture | 55.11 |
| 专用设备制造业 | Special Purposes Equipment Manufacturing | 59.12 |
| 汽车制造业 | Automobile Manufacturing | 66.98 |
| 铁路、船舶、航空航天和其他运输设备制造业 | Railway, Ship, Aerospace and other transportation equipment manufacturing | 65.66 |
| 电气机械及器材制造业 | Electric Equipment and Machinery Manufacturing | 60.72 |
| 计算机、通信和其他电子设备制造业 | Computer Telecommunications and Other Electronic Equipment Manufacture | 57.68 |
| 仪器仪表制造业 | Instruments, Meters Machinery | 53.65 |
| 其他制造业 | Other Products Manufacture | 39.28 |
| 废弃资源综合利用业 | Comprehensive Utilization of Waste Resources | 77.66 |
| 金属制品、机械和设备修理业 | Metal Products, Machinery and Equipment Repair | 84.53 |
| 电力、热力的生产和供应业 | Manufacture and Supply of Electricity and Thermal Power | 68.87 |
| 燃气生产和供应业 | Manufacture and Supply of Gas | 75.36 |
| 水的生产和供应业 | Manufacture and Supply of Water | 75.91 |

Continued 3

(%)

| Private and Individual | | # 外商和港澳台商 Enterprises with Investment from Foreign ,Hong Kong,Macao and Taiwan | | | | |
|---|---|---|---|---|---|---|
| 固定资产净值率 New Value Added in Fixed Asset | 产销率 Proportion of Products Sold | 总资产贡献率 Total Assets Contribution Ratio | 成本费用利润率 Rate Between Profit and Cost | 资产负债率 Assets Liability Ratio | 固定资产净值率 New Value Added in Fixed Asset | 产销率 Proportion of Products Sold |
| 63.24 | 98.38 | 9.98 | 6.71 | 48.91 | 64.25 | 98.75 |
| 67.38 | 97.83 | 13.72 | 10.48 | 46.52 | 52.93 | 94.97 |
| 57.97 | 97.40 | 7.09 | 4.43 | 60.38 | 69.96 | 105.03 |
| 62.95 | 98.83 | 9.93 | 6.18 | 40.41 | 53.92 | 99.19 |
| 54.58 | 97.26 | 6.57 | 3.31 | 49.93 | 56.06 | 100.31 |
| 63.99 | 100.54 | 1.71 | -0.67 | 63.20 | 59.85 | 97.68 |
| 59.82 | 98.72 | 8.13 | 3.77 | 50.60 | 53.67 | 100.17 |
| 69.21 | 96.96 | 9.01 | 5.42 | 43.17 | 59.51 | 99.06 |
| 65.76 | 97.73 | 15.00 | 9.50 | 46.89 | 57.51 | 99.33 |
| 68.85 | 99.88 | 11.32 | 9.48 | 46.52 | 63.57 | 99.97 |
| 66.52 | 100.55 | 13.18 | 8.58 | 48.35 | 59.36 | 98.84 |
| 73.66 | 96.26 | 13.17 | 8.12 | 54.25 | 52.48 | 97.29 |
| 72.16 | 97.58 | 8.78 | 4.52 | 56.71 | 61.77 | 98.80 |
| 72.14 | 99.00 | 8.84 | 3.69 | 54.96 | 44.93 | 99.59 |
| 75.25 | 97.28 | 10.49 | 7.58 | 48.82 | 56.71 | 99.38 |
| 76.66 | 99.71 | 0.73 | -4.65 | 70.38 | 53.27 | 99.65 |
| 69.79 | 101.12 | 1.70 | -2.22 | 88.97 | 65.07 | 92.63 |
| 82.39 | 100.00 | -11.53 | -9.58 | 11.93 | 36.77 | 105.84 |
| 54.01 | 99.23 | 12.26 | 21.14 | 64.53 | 55.11 | 99.97 |
| 71.58 | 99.25 | 13.62 | 12.54 | 53.11 | 78.19 | 99.98 |
| 47.41 | 99.11 | 3.81 | 19.85 | 48.65 | 75.05 | 100.00 |

表4-12

# 分地区规模以上工业企业主要经济指标 (2012年)

单位：万元

| 项　目 | Item | 企业单位数(个) Number of Enterprises (unit) | # 亏损企业 Loss Making Enterprises | 工业总产值 Gross Industrial Output Value |
|---|---|---|---|---|
| **总　计** | **Total** | **10 444** | **2 449** | **287 455 409** |
| **按地区分** | **Grouped by Region** | | | |
| 市　区 | Urban Area | 4 708 | 983 | 111 570 697 |
| 常　熟 | Changshu | 1 453 | 292 | 33 692 100 |
| 张家港 | Zhangjiagang | 1 242 | 364 | 47 005 617 |
| 昆　山 | Kunshan | 1 863 | 467 | 76 868 173 |
| 太　仓 | Taicang | 1 178 | 343 | 18 318 822 |
| **在市区中** | **In Urban Area** | | | |
| 姑苏区 | Gusu District | 46 | 11 | 818 801 |
| 吴中区 | Wuzhong District | 922 | 164 | 11 870 617 |
| 相城区 | Xiangcheng District | 713 | 139 | 8 309 525 |
| 高新区、虎丘区 | New Hi-tech Zone & Huqiu District | 642 | 181 | 23 715 780 |
| 工业园区 | Industrial Park | 795 | 187 | 36 992 912 |
| 吴江区 | Wujiang District | 1 590 | 301 | 29 863 062 |

# MAIN ECONOMIC INDICATORS OF INDUSTRIAL ENTERPRISES ABOVE DESIGNATED SIZE BY REGION (2012)

(10 000 yuan)

| 工业销售产值 Value of Industrial Products Sales | # 出口交货值 Delivery Value for Export | 资产合计 Total Assets | # 流动资产 Circulating Funds | # 固定资产 Fixed Assets | 累计折旧 Accumulative Depreciation |
|---|---|---|---|---|---|
| **285 382 454** | **125 865 028** | **233 314 843** | **141 547 251** | **69 866 801** | **49 469 375** |
| 110 864 464 | 56 141 852 | 98 295 095 | 61 195 200 | 27 687 302 | 20 626 502 |
| 33 045 925 | 9 535 576 | 32 395 480 | 19 166 209 | 9 195 408 | 5 070 941 |
| 47 027 673 | 6 078 782 | 40 598 239 | 22 880 799 | 14 264 094 | 8 159 725 |
| 76 543 045 | 51 376 673 | 44 640 347 | 28 612 076 | 12 871 820 | 12 471 449 |
| 17 901 347 | 2 732 145 | 17 385 682 | 9 692 967 | 5 848 177 | 3 140 758 |
| | | | | | |
| 867 096 | 192 509 | 1 442 785 | 1 033 480 | 258 840 | 190 905 |
| 11 749 699 | 5 059 890 | 10 884 417 | 6 936 672 | 2 886 385 | 1 808 965 |
| 8 292 635 | 2 140 688 | 8 814 279 | 5 301 815 | 2 452 469 | 1 464 658 |
| 23 543 610 | 15 491 647 | 18 267 587 | 12 051 005 | 4 714 108 | 4 318 528 |
| 36 858 078 | 22 460 612 | 30 740 322 | 19 044 237 | 9 644 336 | 8 620 736 |
| 29 553 346 | 10 796 506 | 28 145 705 | 16 827 991 | 7 731 164 | 4 222 710 |

表4-12 续表

单位：万元

| 项　　目 | Item | 负债合计 Total Liabilities | 所有者权益 Creditors Equity | # 实收资本 Total Capital Hold |
|---|---|---|---|---|
| **总　计** | **Total** | **134 747 950** | **98 440 604** | **60 788 735** |
| **按地区分** | **Grouped by Region** | | | |
| 市　区 | Urban Area | 54 121 705 | 44 089 418 | 29 146 224 |
| 常　熟 | Changshu | 19 894 470 | 12 489 538 | 7 901 136 |
| 张家港 | Zhangjiagang | 26 335 328 | 14 241 459 | 6 349 219 |
| 昆　山 | Kunshan | 23 993 914 | 20 637 089 | 12 839 330 |
| 太　仓 | Taicang | 10 402 533 | 6 983 100 | 4 552 826 |
| **在市区中** | **In Urban Area** | | | |
| 姑苏区 | Gusu District | 995 830 | 446 955 | 194 557 |
| 吴中区 | Wuzhong District | 5 818 984 | 5 046 228 | 3 575 167 |
| 相城区 | Xiangcheng District | 5 086 392 | 3 727 885 | 2 216 051 |
| 高新区、虎丘区 | New Hi-tech Zone & Huqiu District | 10 344 467 | 7 864 931 | 5 468 145 |
| 工业园区 | Industrial Park | 14 795 873 | 15 937 940 | 10 961 164 |
| 吴江区 | Wujiang District | 17 080 159 | 11 065 479 | 6 731 140 |

Continued

(10 000 yuan)

| 主营业务收入 Major Business Revenue | 主营业务成本 Major Business Cost | 主营业务税金及附加 Pre-tax and Related Payment of Major Business | 利税总额 Total taxes and Profits | 利润总额 Total Profits | 亏损企业亏损总额 Total Deficit of Loss-Making Enterprises | 应交增值税 Value Added Tax Payable |
|---|---|---|---|---|---|---|
| **289 987 963** | **256 573 705** | **782 517** | **18 163 524** | **12 515 742** | **2 218 631** | **4 865 266** |
| | | | | | | |
| 112 873 530 | 98 574 357 | 345 807 | 7 351 897 | 5 077 597 | 1 024 311 | 1 928 493 |
| 33 564 166 | 29 322 574 | 98 359 | 2 386 040 | 1 722 978 | 270 646 | 564 704 |
| 48 743 520 | 41 233 039 | 114 100 | 1 863 519 | 844 762 | 324 294 | 904 657 |
| 77 031 603 | 68 851 669 | 143 793 | 5 228 617 | 4 016 390 | 428 738 | 1 068 434 |
| 17 775 144 | 15 592 066 | 80 458 | 1 333 451 | 854 015 | 170 642 | 398 978 |
| | | | | | | |
| 925 734 | 803 539 | 2 939 | 85 442 | 68 182 | 4 999 | 14 322 |
| 11 639 415 | 9 957 837 | 43 458 | 779 314 | 492 721 | 144 237 | 243 135 |
| 8 672 217 | 7 535 333 | 25 767 | 559 880 | 355 197 | 42 667 | 178 916 |
| 23 871 051 | 21 099 851 | 61 370 | 1 151 876 | 722 024 | 316 113 | 368 482 |
| 37 477 085 | 31 940 205 | 135 135 | 2 990 520 | 2 220 105 | 316 708 | 635 279 |
| 30 288 028 | 27 237 592 | 77 138 | 1 784 865 | 1 219 368 | 199 587 | 488 359 |

表4-13

# 分地区、分经济类型规模以上工业企业主要经济效益指标 (2012年)

单位：%

| 项　　目 | Item | 经济效益综合指数 Comprehensive Index on Economic Return | 总资产贡献率 Ratio of Total Assets to Industrial Output Value |
|---|---|---|---|
| **总　　计** | **Total** | **203.53** | **8.79** |
| **按地区分** | **Grouped by Region** | | |
| 市　区 | Urban Area | 184.23 | 8.23 |
| 常　熟 | Changshu | 202.44 | 8.48 |
| 张家港 | Zhangjiagang | 249.48 | 6.61 |
| 昆　山 | Kunshan | 220.51 | 12.14 |
| 太　仓 | Taicang | 246.07 | 9.10 |
| **在市区中** | **In Urban Area** | | |
| 姑苏区 | Gusu District | 186.12 | 6.03 |
| 吴中区 | Wuzhong District | 154.99 | 7.80 |
| 相城区 | Xiangcheng District | 159.26 | 7.76 |
| 高新区、虎丘区 | New Hi-tech Zone & Huqiu District | 208.51 | 6.83 |
| 工业园区 | Industrial Park | 217.39 | 10.07 |
| 吴江区 | Wujiang District | 170.57 | 7.53 |
| **按经济类型分** | **Grouped by Ownership** | | |
| 国有经济 | State-owned | 323.63 | 7.53 |
| 民营经济 | Private and Individual | 191.43 | 8.06 |
| 外商及港澳台经济 | Enterprises with Investment from Foreign ,Hong Kong,Macao and Taiwan | 205.83 | 9.31 |

# MAIN INDICATORS OF ECONOMIC BENEFIT INDUSTRIAL ENTERPRISES ABOVE DESIGNATED SIZE BY REGIONAND AND OWNERSHIP (2012)

(%)

| 成本费用利润率<br>Rate Between Profit and Cost | 资产负债率<br>Assets Liability Ratio | 固定资产净值率<br>New Value Added in Fixed Asset | 产销率<br>Proportion of Products Sold | 资本保值增值率<br>Rate of the Preserved Value and Increased Value of Capital | 流动资产周转次数(次)<br>Number of Times of Turnover of Circulating Fund (time) |
|---|---|---|---|---|---|
| **4.47** | **57.75** | **57.04** | **99.28** | **108.34** | **2.08** |
| | | | | | |
| 4.67 | 55.06 | 55.80 | 99.37 | 109.97 | 1.86 |
| 5.31 | 61.41 | 61.89 | 98.08 | 111.09 | 1.79 |
| 1.73 | 64.87 | 62.51 | 100.05 | 101.37 | 2.22 |
| 5.49 | 53.75 | 49.29 | 99.58 | 107.31 | 2.72 |
| 4.93 | 59.83 | 64.41 | 97.72 | 111.61 | 1.88 |
| | | | | | |
| 7.46 | 69.02 | 57.53 | 105.90 | 130.04 | 0.93 |
| 4.39 | 53.46 | 60.47 | 98.98 | 108.42 | 1.70 |
| 4.25 | 57.71 | 61.72 | 99.80 | 110.93 | 1.65 |
| 3.13 | 56.63 | 51.26 | 99.27 | 103.07 | 2.00 |
| 6.23 | 48.13 | 51.24 | 99.64 | 110.35 | 1.99 |
| 4.15 | 60.68 | 62.55 | 98.96 | 114.53 | 1.82 |
| | | | | | |
| 8.95 | 61.28 | 63.49 | 98.93 | 121.32 | 1.29 |
| 3.57 | 64.62 | 63.44 | 98.70 | 109.12 | 1.83 |
| 4.88 | 53.00 | 54.06 | 99.35 | 107.95 | 2.27 |

表4-14

# 分地区大中型工业企业主要经济指标 (2012年)

| 项　目 | | Item | | 全　市<br>Whole Municipality |
|---|---|---|---|---|
| 企业单位数 | (个) | Number of Enterprises | (unit) | 2 164 |
| # 亏损企业 | | Loss Making Enterprises | | 495 |
| 工业总产值 | (万元) | Gross Industrial Output Value | (10 000 yuan) | 213 550 334 |
| 工业销售产值 | | Value of Industrial Products Sales | | 212 292 665 |
| # 出口交货值 | | Delivery Value for Export | | 111 551 049 |
| 年末资产合计 | | Total Assets (year-end) | | 162 981 439 |
| # 流动资产合计 | | Circulating Funds | | 95 174 633 |
| # 应收帐款 | | Net Account Income | | 30 538 159 |
| 产成品 | | Manufactured Products | | 8 097 542 |
| 固定资产合计 | | Fixed Assets | | 51 996 235 |
| 固定资产原价 | | Original Value of Fixed Assets | | 88 109 450 |
| 累计折旧 | | Accumulative Total Depreciation | | 39 011 532 |
| 固定资产净值 | | Net Value of Fixed Assets | | 49 097 918 |
| 负债合计 | | Total Liabilities | | 92 712 306 |
| 所有者权益合计 | | Total Creditors Equity | | 70 268 168 |
| 实收资本 | | Total Capital Hold | | 38 941 818 |
| 国家资本 | | State Capital | | 1 369 869 |
| 集体资本 | | Collective Capital | | 250 036 |
| 法人资本 | | Corporate Capital | | 7 166 622 |
| 个人资本 | | Personal Capital | | 3 326 720 |
| 港澳台资本 | | Capital from Hong Kong, Macao and Taiwan | | 6 986 058 |
| 外商资本 | | Foreign Capital | | 19 842 513 |
| 主营业务收入 | | Major Business Revenue | | 216 567 888 |
| 主营业务成本 | | Major Business Cost | | 192 322 559 |
| 主营业务税金及附加 | | Pre-tax and Related Payment of Major Business | | 513 998 |
| 营业利润 | | Business Profits | | 10 513 307 |
| 利税总额 | | Total Taxes and Profits | | 13 775 864 |
| # 利润总额 | | Total Profits | | 9 952 667 |
| 本年应交增值税 | | Value Added Tax Payable | | 3 309 200 |
| 成本费用利润率 | (%) | Rate Between Profit and Cost | (%) | 4.77 |
| 资产负债率 | | Assets Liability Ratio | | 56.89 |
| 工业产销率 | | Proportion of Products Sold | | 99.41 |
| 总资产贡献率 | | New Value Added in Fixed Asset | | 9.40 |

# MAIN INDICATORS OF ECONOMIC BENEFIT OF LARGE AND MEDIUM INDUSTRIAL ENTERPRISES BY REGION (2012)

| 市 区<br>Urban Area | # 吴江区<br>Wujiang District | 常 熟<br>Changshu | 张家港<br>Zhangjiagang | 昆 山<br>Kunshan | 太 仓<br>Taicang |
|---|---|---|---|---|---|
| 1 034 | 278 | 265 | 181 | 540 | 144 |
| 244 | 67 | 45 | 46 | 120 | 40 |
| 81 216 428 | 20 528 954 | 23 660 462 | 36 208 650 | 62 881 668 | 9 583 126 |
| 80 807 869 | 20 389 693 | 23 189 521 | 36 229 309 | 62 634 259 | 9 431 707 |
| 49 530 452 | 9 480 523 | 8 132 381 | 4 810 650 | 47 407 353 | 1 670 213 |
| 67 031 523 | 18 340 970 | 22 235 673 | 30 712 699 | 32 519 880 | 10 481 664 |
| 40 417 541 | 10 455 160 | 12 636 769 | 16 442 618 | 20 465 749 | 5 211 956 |
| 14 635 158 | 3 031 412 | 3 392 970 | 2 339 589 | 8 992 585 | 1 177 857 |
| 3 281 043 | 993 025 | 1 225 417 | 1 605 674 | 1 546 460 | 438 948 |
| 20 000 759 | 5 306 527 | 6 379 360 | 11 622 811 | 9 854 193 | 4 139 112 |
| 34 838 542 | 7 878 737 | 9 159 246 | 17 820 776 | 19 942 614 | 6 348 272 |
| 15 884 454 | 2 952 713 | 3 569 017 | 6 753 962 | 10 556 016 | 2 248 083 |
| 18 954 088 | 4 926 024 | 5 590 229 | 11 066 814 | 9 386 598 | 4 100 189 |
| 35 905 678 | 10 509 311 | 13 291 840 | 19 423 852 | 17 664 800 | 6 426 136 |
| 31 124 881 | 7 831 659 | 8 943 833 | 11 288 846 | 14 855 080 | 4 055 528 |
| 18 997 086 | 4 021 140 | 5 001 601 | 3 952 699 | 8 432 222 | 2 558 210 |
| 655 087 | 17 200 | 33 813 | 111 542 | 430 174 | 139 253 |
| 112 443 | 93 050 | 23 183 | 66 304 | 47 265 | 841 |
| 3 440 499 | 1 240 190 | 967 705 | 1 221 921 | 733 400 | 803 097 |
| 1 265 852 | 515 972 | 810 492 | 808 719 | 240 047 | 201 610 |
| 3 511 309 | 942 112 | 1 103 213 | 194 326 | 1 850 882 | 326 328 |
| 10 011 897 | 1 212 616 | 2 063 195 | 1 549 887 | 5 130 453 | 1 087 081 |
| 82 770 943 | 21 162 800 | 23 679 751 | 37 672 386 | 63 081 354 | 9 363 454 |
| 72 612 396 | 19 032 388 | 20 583 954 | 34 341 064 | 56 620 969 | 8 164 176 |
| 234 200 | 51 449 | 63 208 | 86 827 | 104 139 | 25 624 |
| 3 920 033 | 966 125 | 1 442 492 | 855 314 | 3 780 974 | 514 494 |
| 5 395 223 | 1 375 383 | 1 818 479 | 1 476 803 | 4 291 504 | 793 855 |
| 3 884 825 | 986 807 | 1 400 271 | 709 371 | 3 423 111 | 535 089 |
| 1 276 201 | 337 127 | 354 999 | 680 605 | 764 253 | 233 142 |
| 4.90 | 4.85 | 6.15 | 1.88 | 5.74 | 5.82 |
| 53.57 | 57.30 | 59.78 | 63.24 | 54.32 | 61.31 |
| 99.50 | 99.32 | 98.01 | 100.06 | 99.61 | 98.42 |
| 8.67 | 8.48 | 9.13 | 6.85 | 13.53 | 9.21 |

表4-15

# 规模以下工业企业及个体经营主要经济指标 (2012年)
# MAIN ECONOMIC INDICATORS OF INDUSTRIAL ENTERPRISES BELOW DESIGNATED SIZE AND THE INDIVIDUAL PROPRIETOR (2012)

单位：万元 (10 000yuan)

| 地区或类别 | Type | 企业单位数 (个) Number of Enterprises (unit) | 主营业务收入 Major Business Revenue | 年末资产总计 Total Assets at the Year end | 实收资本 Actual Capital Hold | 全部从业人员 (人) Total Employees (person) |
|---|---|---|---|---|---|---|
| **合　计** | **Total** | **122 426** | **53 653 108** | **34 340 190** | **12 779 085** | **1 558 929** |
| 市　区 | Urban Area | 41 208 | 23 545 633 | 13 534 114 | 6 338 286 | 666 726 |
| # 吴江区 | Wujiang District | 13 404 | 6 683 722 | 4 503 318 | 2 260 010 | 208 370 |
| 常　熟 | Changshu | 32 015 | 8 863 715 | 6 256 216 | 1 201 635 | 328 592 |
| 张家港 | Zhangjiagang | 15 993 | 8 156 430 | 6 317 235 | 1 679 265 | 188 738 |
| 昆　山 | Kunshan | 22 890 | 7 646 079 | 5 956 460 | 2 613 039 | 237 462 |
| 太　仓 | Taicang | 10 320 | 5 441 251 | 2 276 165 | 946 860 | 137 411 |
| **集体企业** | **Collective-owned Enterprises** | **186** | **114 469** | **208 128** | **67 338** | **6 433** |
| 市　区 | Urban Area | 62 | 32 939 | 75 887 | 21 717 | 1 705 |
| # 吴江区 | Wujiang District | - | - | - | - | - |
| 常　熟 | Changshu | 65 | 35 850 | 73 165 | 12 852 | 2 715 |
| 张家港 | Zhangjiagang | 29 | 18 357 | 17 574 | 6 385 | 979 |
| 昆　山 | Kunshan | 30 | 27 323 | 41 502 | 26 384 | 1 034 |
| 太　仓 | Taicang | - | - | - | - | - |
| **股份合作企业** | **Share-holding Cooperative Enterprises** | **553** | **274 585** | **184 157** | **61 409** | **5 601** |
| 市　区 | Urban Area | 514 | 251 568 | 165 346 | 53 426 | 4 497 |
| # 吴江区 | Wujiang District | 278 | 143 100 | 99 128 | 21 229 | 334 |
| 常　熟 | Changshu | - | - | - | - | - |
| 张家港 | Zhangjiagang | 37 | 20 422 | 15 241 | 6 594 | 952 |
| 昆　山 | Kunshan | 2 | 2 595 | 3 570 | 1 389 | 152 |
| 太　仓 | Taicang | - | - | - | - | - |
| **私营企业** | **Private Enterprises** | **57 869** | **33 248 553** | **19 143 415** | **7 484 252** | **955 690** |
| 市　区 | Urban Area | 25 845 | 14 100 264 | 8 189 215 | 3 564 860 | 413 305 |
| # 吴江区 | Wujiang District | 8 701 | 4 550 074 | 2 704 424 | 1 307 690 | 135 710 |
| 常　熟 | Changshu | 6 056 | 5 760 749 | 2 574 145 | 672 492 | 142 557 |

表4-15 续表　Continued

单位：万元　(10 000yuan)

| 地区或类别 | Type | 企业单位数(个) Number of Enterprises (unit) | 主营业务收入 Major Business Revenue | 年末资产总计 Total Assets at the Year end | 实收资本 Actual Capital Hold | 全部从业人员(人) Total Employees (person) |
|---|---|---|---|---|---|---|
| 张家港 | Zhangjiagang | 9 455 | 5 814 825 | 3 941 131 | 1 196 139 | 212 454 |
| 昆　山 | Kunshan | 12 611 | 4 957 959 | 3 436 723 | 1 601 081 | 122 145 |
| 太　仓 | Taicang | 3 902 | 2 614 756 | 1 002 201 | 449 680 | 65 229 |
| **联营企业** | **Joint Ownership Enterprises** | **54** | **16 383** | **17 801** | **14 372** | **668** |
| 市　区 | Urban Area | 7 | 2 931 | 4 823 | 3 543 | 72 |
| # 吴江区 | Wujiang District | - | - | - | - | - |
| 常　熟 | Changshu | - | - | - | - | - |
| 张家港 | Zhangjiagang | 2 | 502 | 953 | 689 | 20 |
| 昆　山 | Kunshan | 45 | 12 950 | 12 025 | 10 140 | 576 |
| 太　仓 | Taicang | - | - | - | - | - |
| **个体经营** | **Total of Self-employed Individuals** | **52 725** | **7 026 366** | **3 064 645** | **1 150 224** | **365 495** |
| 市　区 | Urban Area | 7 870 | 2 217 941 | 782 334 | 535 318 | 80 268 |
| # 吴江区 | Wujiang District | 3 740 | 710 042 | 377 012 | 255 450 | 37 380 |
| 常　熟 | Changshu | 24 653 | 2 114 015 | 788 896 | 93 759 | 164 562 |
| 张家港 | Zhangjiagang | 6 550 | 425 750 | 379 900 | 163 027 | 66 579 |
| 昆　山 | Kunshan | 8 021 | 204 400 | 209 117 | 85 294 | 13 296 |
| 太　仓 | Taicang | 5 631 | 2 064 260 | 904 398 | 272 826 | 40 790 |
| **外商及港澳台商投资企业** | **Enterprises with Foreign Investment or Investment from Hongkong, Macao and Taiwan** | **6 862** | **7 785 887** | **6 834 218** | **3 100 212** | **235 169** |
| 市　区 | Urban Area | 3 292 | 3 955 184 | 2 934 316 | 1 527 976 | 111 390 |
| # 吴江区 | Wujiang District | 574 | 779 247 | 657 056 | 597 591 | 29 078 |
| 常　熟 | Changshu | 235 | 251 652 | 1 116 215 | 355 862 | 10 211 |
| 张家港 | Zhangjiagang | 356 | 366 046 | 146 641 | 103 376 | 14 143 |
| 昆　山 | Kunshan | 2 192 | 2 450 770 | 2 267 480 | 888 644 | 68 033 |
| 太　仓 | Taicang | 787 | 762 235 | 369 566 | 224 354 | 31 392 |

表4-16

# 规模以上工业主要产品产量（2012年）

| 产品名称 | | Name of Products | | 全 市 Whole Municipality |
|---|---|---|---|---|
| 饲 料 | (吨) | Fodder | (ton) | 403 703 |
| 精制食用植物油 | | Refined Edible Vegetable Oil | | 914 872 |
| 乳制品 | | Dairy Products | | 122 981 |
| 大 米 | | Rice | | 47 604 |
| 饮料酒 | (千升) | Drinks | (1 000liters) | 451 604 |
| 纱 | (吨) | Yarn | (ton) | 793 212 |
| 布 | (万米) | Cloth | (10 000 m) | 90 334 |
| 绒线（毛线） | (吨) | Knitting Wool | (ton) | 63 834 |
| 毛机织物（呢绒） | (万米) | Wool Fabrics | (10 000 m) | 9 453 |
| 印染布 | | Printing and Dyeing Cloth | | 144 216 |
| 蚕丝及交织机织物(含蚕丝≥50%) | | Silk and Woven Fabrics (Including Silk ≥ 50%) | | 876 |
| 服 装 | (万件) | Garment | (10 000 pieces) | 80 090 |
| 皮革鞋靴 | (万双) | Leather Footwear | (10 000 pairs) | 1 737 |
| 人造板 | (立方米) | Artificial Board | (cu.m) | 938 707 |
| 家 具 | (件) | Furniture | (piece) | 10 146 991 |
| 机制纸及纸板 | (吨) | Machine Made Paper | (ton) | 5 829 941 |
| 焦 炭 | | Coke | | 5 792 448 |
| 硫酸（折100%） | | Sulfuric Acid (100%) | | 2 060 937 |
| 碳酸钠（纯碱） | | Soda Ash | | 1 021 697 |
| 合成氨 | | Synthetic Ammonia | | 630 055 |
| 农用氮、磷、钾化学肥料总计(折纯) | | Agricultural Chemical Fertilizers (Pure) | | 455 726 |
| 化学农药原药(折有效成分100%) | | Chemicals and Pesticides (Active Ingredient 100% Discount) | | 31 712 |
| 涂 料 | | Paint | | 308 539 |
| 纯 苯 | | Pure Benzene | | 2 639 |
| 初级形态的塑料(塑料树脂及共聚物) | | Primary form of Plastic | | 875 412 |

# MAJOR PRODUCTS OUTPUT OF INDUSTRIAL ENTERPRISES ABOVE DESIGNATED SIZE (2012)

| 市 区 Urban Area | # 吴江区 Wujiang District | 常 熟 Changshu | 张家港 Zhangjiagang | 昆 山 Kunshan | 太 仓 Taicang |
|---|---|---|---|---|---|
| 149 674 | – | 12 990 | 241 039 | – | – |
| 88 807 | 68 682 | 13 578 | 781 006 | 31 481 | – |
| 80 002 | – | – | 42 979 | – | – |
| – | – | – | 47 604 | – | – |
| 195 704 | – | 39 808 | 53 383 | 162 709 | – |
| 77 163 | 62 692 | 70 499 | 507 477 | 10 993 | 127 080 |
| 51 134 | 44 170 | 1 698 | 22 744 | 7 568 | 7 189 |
| 1 196 | 1 196 | 12 577 | 50 061 | – | – |
| 209 | – | 313 | 8 930 | – | – |
| 8 648 | – | 96 053 | 35 046 | 4 469 | – |
| 876 | 782 | – | – | – | – |
| 26 162 | 6 597 | 18 294 | 18 397 | 13 415 | 3 821 |
| 1 652 | 1 604 | – | – | 24 | 61 |
| 28 351 | – | 894 712 | 2 652 | – | 12 992 |
| 1 319 937 | 1 045 142 | 249 264 | 2 384 195 | 4 386 015 | 1 807 580 |
| 1 789 748 | – | 1 229 593 | 103 135 | 27 555 | 2 679 910 |
| 386 751 | – | – | 5 405 697 | – | – |
| – | – | 201 982 | 1 858 955 | – | – |
| – | – | – | 640 253 | 381 444 | – |
| – | – | – | 479 613 | 150 442 | – |
| – | – | – | 280 958 | 174 768 | – |
| 3 144 | – | – | – | – | 28 568 |
| 110 047 | – | 932 | 6 710 | 178 075 | 12 776 |
| – | – | 2 639 | – | – | – |
| 323 098 | 55 442 | 58 222 | 220 869 | 43 460 | 229 763 |

表4-16 续表 1

| 产品名称 | | Name of Products | | 全 市 Whole Municipality |
|---|---|---|---|---|
| 化学药品原药（化学原料药） | (吨) | Original Drug Chemicals (Chemical Medicine) | (ton) | 9 006 |
| 化学纤维 | | Chemical Fiber | | 6 638 359 |
| 橡胶轮胎外胎 | (条) | Tires | (piece) | 70 183 208 |
| 塑料制品 | (吨) | Plastic Products | (ton) | 901 060 |
| 水　泥 | | Cement | | 8 638 758 |
| 平板玻璃 | (重量箱) | Plate Glass | (wt.cases) | 52 797 066 |
| 生　铁 | (吨) | Pig Iron | (ton) | 22 297 401 |
| 粗　钢 | | Raw Steel | | 26 621 925 |
| 钢　材 | | Rolled Steel | | 40 594 120 |
| 金属切削机床 | (台) | Metal-cutting Machines | (unit) | 6 407 |
| # 数控金属切削机床 | | CNC Metal Cutting Machine | | 1 893 |
| 阀　门 | (吨) | Valves | (ton) | 66 959 |
| 滚动轴承 | (万套) | Rolling Bearing | (10 000 sets) | 198 953 |
| 模　具 | (套) | Mould | (set) | 1 793 194 |
| 汽　车 | (辆) | Trucks | (coach) | 23 768 |
| 改装汽车 | | Refit Trucks | | 41 148 |
| 两轮脚踏自行车 | | Two-wheel Pedal Bicycles | | 4 195 229 |
| 交流电动机 | (千瓦) | Alternating Current Motor | (kw) | 5 384 579 |
| 变压器 | (千伏安) | Transformer | (kva) | 17 040 284 |
| 通信及电子网络用电缆 | (对千米) | Communication Cables | (pair km) | 13 077 813 |
| 电力电缆 | (千米) | Electric Power Cables | (km) | 2 341 054 |
| 光　缆 | (芯千米) | Optic Fiber | (core kilometer) | 49 875 401 |
| 锂离子电池 | (只) | Lithium-Ion Batteries | (piece) | 262 764 555 |
| 家用电冰箱 | (台) | Household Refrigerator | (unit) | 1 754 891 |
| 家用冷柜（家用冷冻箱） | | Household Refrigerators (Household Freezers) | | 1 502 316 |

Continued 1

| 市 区<br>Urban Area | # 吴江区<br>Wujiang District | 常 熟<br>Changshu | 张家港<br>Zhangjiagang | 昆 山<br>Kunshan | 太 仓<br>Taicang |
|---|---|---|---|---|---|
| 4 754 | 290 | 1 622 | – | 2 005 | 625 |
| 4 385 799 | 3 390 882 | 412 145 | 885 865 | – | 954 550 |
| – | – | 15 130 802 | 5 498 463 | 49 553 943 | – |
| 306 874 | – | 56 561 | 286 472 | 200 569 | 50 583 |
| 2 728 068 | 1 919 270 | 117 152 | 3 011 518 | 981 844 | 1 800 176 |
| 4 284 206 | – | 6 194 995 | 30 356 996 | 11 041 224 | 919 645 |
| 504 947 | – | – | 21 792 454 | – | – |
| 548 140 | – | – | 26 073 785 | – | – |
| 1 150 991 | 116 995 | 5 039 051 | 34 348 541 | 55 537 | – |
| 4 075 | 283 | – | 1 118 | 1 214 | – |
| 1 367 | – | – | – | 526 | – |
| 59 409 | 7 486 | – | – | 7 550 | – |
| 20 613 |  | 4 406 | 132 359 | 17 259 | 24 316 |
| 1 245 550 | 1 242 283 | 520 703 | 14 875 | 12 066 | – |
| 23 768 | – | – | – | – | – |
| 260 | – | 1 802 | 5 191 | 33 895 |  |
| – | – | – | 213 719 | 2 842 578 | 1 138 932 |
| 1 337 944 | – | – | – | – | 4 046 635 |
| 17 029 949 | 16 695 679 | – | – | 10 335 | – |
| 12 218 507 | 12 083 648 | 189 489 | 669 341 | – | 476 |
| 1 636 478 | 80 092 | 638 396 | 45 826 | 20 354 | – |
| 46 033 418 | 46 033 418 | 3 841 983 | – | – | – |
| 140 478 237 | 58 786 527 | 75 861 456 | 7 993 292 | 38 431 570 | – |
| 1 592 195 | – | 162 696 | – | – | – |
| – | – | 1 502 316 | – | – | – |

表4-16 续表 2

| 产品名称 | | Name of Products | | 全 市 Whole Municipality |
|---|---|---|---|---|
| 房间空气调节器 | (台) | Room Air Conditioner | (unit) | 4 400 252 |
| 家用电风扇 | | Household Electric Fan | | 1 126 436 |
| 家用吸排油烟机 | | Household Smoke Absorbers | | 192 902 |
| 家用洗衣机 | | Household Washing Machines | | 3 401 948 |
| 家用吸尘器 | | Household Dust Catcher | | 34 804 107 |
| 家用燃气灶具 | | Household Gas Utensile | | 179 220 |
| 家用燃气热水器 | | Household Water Heater | | 173 538 |
| 程控交换机 | (线) | Program Control Exchanges | (line) | 46 389 |
| 移动通信手持机（手机） | (台) | Mobile Phone | (unit) | 7 118 182 |
| 微型计算机设备 | | Micro-Computer Equipment | | 87 520 423 |
| # 笔记本计算机 | | Laptop Computer | | 74 791 221 |
| 显示器 | | Monitors | | 19 442 395 |
| # 平板显示器 | | Flat Panel Displays | | 19 442 395 |
| 集成电路 | (万块) | Integrated Circuit | (10 000 piece) | 640 373 |
| 光电子器件 | (万只、片、套) | Optoelectronic Devices | (10 000 piece,set) | 1 241 196 |
| # 发光二极管(LED) | (万片) | Light Emitting Diode(LED) | (10 000 piece) | 954 064 |
| 电子元件 | (万只) | Electronic Components | | 12 359 088 |
| 印制电路板 | (平方米) | Printed Circuit Board | (sq.m) | 91 738 744 |
| 彩色电视机 | (台) | Color TV Sets | (unit) | 11 412 339 |
| # 液晶(LCD)电视机 | | Liquid Crystal (LCD) TV Sets | | 11 399 674 |
| 工业自动调节仪表与控制系统 | (台、套) | Industrial Automatically-Adjusting Instrumentation and Control System | (unit,set) | 557 278 |
| 照相机 | (台) | Cameras | (unit) | 15 345 746 |
| # 数码照相机 | | Digital Camera | | 13 305 909 |
| 发电量 | (万千瓦时) | Power Generation | (10 000 kwh) | 9 133 396 |
| 煤 气 | (万立方米) | Gas | (10 000 cu.m) | 10 108 |

Continued 2

| 市 区<br>Urban Area | # 吴江区<br>Wujiang District | 常 熟<br>Changshu | 张家港<br>Zhangjiagang | 昆 山<br>Kunshan | 太 仓<br>Taicang |
|---|---|---|---|---|---|
| 4 400 252 | 170 146 | – | – | – | – |
| 690 000 | – | – | – | 436 436 | – |
| – | – | – | – | 192 902 | – |
| 3 401 948 | – | – | – | – | – |
| 34 804 107 | – | – | – | – | – |
| – | – | – | – | 179 220 | – |
| – | – | – | – | 173 538 | – |
| 46 389 | – | – | – | – | – |
| 7 058 501 | 7 058 501 | – | – | 59 681 | – |
| 8 812 535 | – | – | – | 78 707 888 | – |
| 2 290 373 | – | – | – | 72 500 848 | – |
| 18 390 990 | 3 592 252 | – | – | 1 051 405 | – |
| 18 390 990 | 3 592 252 | – | – | 1 051 405 | – |
| 640 373 | 80 421 | – | – | – | – |
| 1 211 581 | 1 035 857 | – | 5 286 | 21 615 | 2 714 |
| 942 316 | 942 316 | – | – | 11 748 | – |
| 10 127 764 | 5 464 043 | 1 710 532 | 7 687 | 496 704 | 16 401 |
| 270 195 | 254 368 | 1 110 577 | – | 90 357 973 | – |
| 4 354 894 | 554 355 | – | – | 7 057 445 | – |
| 4 342 229 | 554 355 | – | – | 7 057 445 | – |
| 557 221 | 165 407 | – | – | – | 57 |
| 3 491 743 | 213 040 | – | – | 11 854 003 | – |
| 1 451 906 | 213 040 | – | – | 11 854 003 | – |
| 2 286 905 | 235 084 | 1 962 754 | 1 713 513 | 86 504 | 3 083 721 |
| 4 392 | – | – | – | – | 5 716 |

表4-17

# 全市工业主营业务收入百强企业（2012年）
# TOP 100 ENTERPRISES OF THE MAJOR BUSINESS REVENUE (2012)

| 序　号 No. | 企业名称 Name of Enterprises | 所在地区 Location | 序　号 No. | 企业名称 Name of Enterprises | 所在地区 Location |
|---|---|---|---|---|---|
| 1 | 江苏沙钢集团有限公司 | 张家港 | 26 | 富翔精密工业（昆山）有限公司 | 昆　山 |
| 2 | 仁宝信息技术（昆山）有限公司 | 昆　山 | 27 | 苏州乐轩科技有限公司 | 市　区 |
| 3 | 仁宝电子科技（昆山）有限公司 | 昆　山 | 28 | 江苏江南化纤集团有限公司 | 市　区 |
| 4 | 纬新资通（昆山）有限公司 | 昆　山 | 29 | 常熟市龙腾特种钢有限公司 | 常　熟 |
| 5 | 名硕电脑（苏州）有限公司 | 市　区 | 30 | 伟创力电脑（苏州）有限公司 | 市　区 |
| 6 | 江苏永钢集团有限公司 | 张家港 | 31 | 富士康（昆山）电脑接插件有限公司 | 昆　山 |
| 7 | 纬创资通（昆山）有限公司 | 昆　山 | 32 | 玖龙纸业（太仓）有限公司 | 太　仓 |
| 8 | 仁宝资讯工业（昆山）有限公司 | 昆　山 | 33 | 澳洋集团有限公司 | 张家港 |
| 9 | 苏州三星电子电脑有限公司 | 市　区 | 34 | 佳能（苏州）有限公司 | 市　区 |
| 10 | 达富电脑（常熟）有限公司 | 常　熟 | 35 | 博世汽车部件（苏州）有限公司 | 市　区 |
| 11 | 波司登股份有限公司 | 常　熟 | 36 | 苏州三星电子有限公司 | 市　区 |
| 12 | 华芳集团有限公司 | 张家港 | 37 | 阿特斯光伏电子（常熟）有限公司 | 常　熟 |
| 13 | 东海粮油工业（张家港）有限公司 | 张家港 | 38 | 南亚电子材料（昆山）有限公司 | 昆　山 |
| 14 | 瑞仪光电（苏州）有限公司 | 市　区 | 39 | 江苏骏马集团有限责任公司 | 张家港 |
| 15 | 纬智资通（昆山）有限公司 | 昆　山 | 40 | 江苏苏南特种装备集团有限责任公司 | 常　熟 |
| 16 | 张家港浦项不锈钢有限公司 | 张家港 | 41 | 伟创力电子技术（苏州）有限公司 | 市　区 |
| 17 | 康准电子科技（昆山）有限公司 | 昆　山 | 42 | 正新橡胶（中国）有限公司 | 昆　山 |
| 18 | 联建（苏州）科技有限公司 | 市　区 | 43 | 金龙联合汽车工业（苏州）有限公司 | 市　区 |
| 19 | 江苏恒力化纤有限公司 | 市　区 | 44 | 三一重机有限公司 | 昆　山 |
| 20 | 张家港市联合铜业有限公司 | 张家港 | 45 | 江苏隆力奇集团有限公司 | 常　熟 |
| 21 | 亨通集团有限公司 | 市　区 | 46 | 中达电子（江苏）有限公司 | 市　区 |
| 22 | 通鼎集团有限公司 | 市　区 | 47 | 苏州三星电子家电有限公司 | 市　区 |
| 23 | 苏州佳世达电通有限公司 | 市　区 | 48 | 江苏华昌（集团）有限公司 | 张家港 |
| 24 | 通力电梯有限公司 | 昆　山 | 49 | 牧田（昆山）有限公司 | 昆　山 |
| 25 | 江苏盛虹化纤有限公司 | 市　区 | 50 | 中利科技集团股份有限公司 | 常　熟 |

表4-17 续表 Continued

| 序 号<br>No. | 企业名称<br>Name of Enterprises | 所在地区<br>Location | 序 号<br>No. | 企业名称<br>Name of Enterprises | 所在地区<br>Location |
|---|---|---|---|---|---|
| 51 | 上海华电电力发展有限公司望亭发电厂 | 市 区 | 76 | 江苏苏南重工机械科技有限公司 | 常 熟 |
| 52 | 江苏梦兰集团有限公司 | 常 熟 | 77 | 群光电子（苏州）有限公司 | 市 区 |
| 53 | 攀华集团有限公司 | 张家港 | 78 | 索尼移动显示器（苏州）有限公司 | 市 区 |
| 54 | 苏州长城开发科技有限公司 | 市 区 | 79 | 苏州松下半导体有限公司 | 市 区 |
| 55 | 日立显示器（苏州）有限公司 | 市 区 | 80 | 江苏旋力集团股份有限公司 | 常 熟 |
| 56 | 亚旭电子科技（江苏）有限公司 | 市 区 | 81 | 江苏申久化纤有限公司 | 太 仓 |
| 57 | 香塘集团有限公司 | 太 仓 | 82 | 苏州协鑫光伏科技有限公司 | 市 区 |
| 58 | 舍弗勒（中国）有限公司 | 太 仓 | 83 | 苏州迅达电梯有限公司 | 市 区 |
| 59 | 江苏苏钢集团有限公司 | 市 区 | 84 | 苏州璨宇光学有限公司 | 市 区 |
| 60 | 四海电子（昆山）有限公司 | 昆 山 | 85 | 华润电力（常熟）有限公司 | 常 熟 |
| 61 | 金红叶纸业集团有限公司 | 市 区 | 86 | 苏州达方电子有限公司 | 市 区 |
| 62 | 江苏永恒钢铁实业有限公司 | 张家港 | 87 | 江苏永恒炉料实业有限公司 | 张家港 |
| 63 | 好孩子儿童用品有限公司 | 昆 山 | 88 | 三洋能源（苏州）有限公司 | 市 区 |
| 64 | 顺达电子科技（苏州）有限公司 | 市 区 | 89 | 张家港欣欣高纤股份有限公司 | 张家港 |
| 65 | 江苏腾晖电力科技有限公司 | 常 熟 | 90 | 华能太仓发电有限责任公司 | 太 仓 |
| 66 | 富港电子（昆山）有限公司 | 昆 山 | 91 | 夏普办公设备（常熟）有限公司 | 常 熟 |
| 67 | 诺基亚西门子通信（苏州）有限公司 | 市 区 | 92 | 江苏通润机电集团有限公司 | 常 熟 |
| 68 | 达研光电（常熟）有限公司 | 常 熟 | 93 | 雅鹿集团股份有限公司 | 太 仓 |
| 69 | 仁宝光电科技（昆山）有限公司 | 昆 山 | 94 | 卡特彼勒（苏州）有限公司 | 市 区 |
| 70 | 江苏国望高科纤维有限公司 | 市 区 | 95 | 辅讯光电工业（昆山）有限公司 | 昆 山 |
| 71 | 住友橡胶（常熟）有限公司 | 常 熟 | 96 | 长春化工（江苏）有限公司 | 常 熟 |
| 72 | 彩晶光电科技（昆山）有限公司 | 昆 山 | 97 | 芬欧汇川(中国)有限公司 | 常 熟 |
| 73 | 苏州维信电子有限公司 | 市 区 | 98 | 烨辉（中国）科技材料有限公司 | 常 熟 |
| 74 | 江苏鹰翔化纤股份有限公司 | 市 区 | 99 | 正鹏电子（昆山）有限公司 | 昆 山 |
| 75 | 苏州佳世达光电有限公司 | 市 区 | 100 | 辅讯光电工业（苏州）有限公司 | 市 区 |

表4-18

# 全市工业利税总额百强企业 (2012年)
# TOP 100 ENTERPRISES OF THE TOTAL TAXES AND PROFITS (2012)

| 序 号<br>No. | 企业名称<br>Name of Enterprises | 所在地区<br>Location | 序 号<br>No. | 企业名称<br>Name of Enterprises | 所在地区<br>Location |
|---|---|---|---|---|---|
| 1 | 江苏沙钢集团有限公司 | 张家港 | 26 | 阿特斯光伏电子（常熟）有限公司 | 常 熟 |
| 2 | 仁宝信息技术（昆山）有限公司 | 昆 山 | 27 | 南亚电子材料（昆山）有限公司 | 昆 山 |
| 3 | 仁宝电子科技（昆山）有限公司 | 昆 山 | 28 | 博世汽车部件（苏州）有限公司 | 市 区 |
| 4 | 纬新资通（昆山）有限公司 | 昆 山 | 29 | 正新橡胶（中国）有限公司 | 昆 山 |
| 5 | 纬创资通（昆山）有限公司 | 昆 山 | 30 | 江苏隆力奇集团有限公司 | 常 熟 |
| 6 | 江苏永钢集团有限公司 | 张家港 | 31 | 苏州三星电子家电有限公司 | 市 区 |
| 7 | 仁宝资讯工业（昆山）有限公司 | 昆 山 | 32 | 中达电子（江苏）有限公司 | 市 区 |
| 8 | 苏州三星电子电脑有限公司 | 市 区 | 33 | 金龙联合汽车工业（苏州）有限公司 | 市 区 |
| 9 | 波司登股份有限公司 | 常 熟 | 34 | 牧田（昆山）有限公司 | 昆 山 |
| 10 | 中粮东海粮油工业（张家港）有限公司 | 张家港 | 35 | 江苏苏南特种装备集团有限责任公司 | 常 熟 |
| 11 | 瑞仪光电（苏州）有限公司 | 市 区 | 36 | 中利科技集团股份有限公司 | 常 熟 |
| 12 | 纬智资通（昆山）有限公司 | 昆 山 | 37 | 上海华电电力发展有限公司望亭发电厂 | 市 区 |
| 13 | 华芳集团有限公司 | 张家港 | 38 | 江苏梦兰集团有限公司 | 常 熟 |
| 14 | 江苏恒力化纤股份有限公司 | 市 区 | 39 | 舍弗勒（中国）有限公司 | 太 仓 |
| 15 | 亨通集团有限公司 | 市 区 | 40 | 三一重机有限公司 | 昆 山 |
| 16 | 通鼎集团有限公司 | 市 区 | 41 | 中利腾晖光伏科技有限公司 | 常 熟 |
| 17 | 苏州佳世达电通有限公司 | 市 区 | 42 | 富港电子（昆山）有限公司 | 昆 山 |
| 18 | 通力电梯有限公司 | 昆 山 | 43 | 住友橡胶（常熟）有限公司 | 常 熟 |
| 19 | 江苏盛虹科技股份有限公司 | 市 区 | 44 | 苏州协鑫光伏科技有限公司 | 市 区 |
| 20 | 常熟市龙腾特种钢有限公司 | 常 熟 | 45 | 苏州迅达电梯有限公司 | 市 区 |
| 21 | 富士康（昆山）电脑接插件有限公司 | 昆 山 | 46 | 江苏旋力集团股份有限公司 | 常 熟 |
| 22 | 玖龙纸业（太仓）有限公司 | 太 仓 | 47 | 华润电力（常熟）有限公司 | 常 熟 |
| 23 | 澳洋集团有限公司 | 张家港 | 48 | 华能太仓发电有限责任公司 | 太 仓 |
| 24 | 佳能（苏州）有限公司 | 市 区 | 49 | 夏普办公设备（常熟）有限公司 | 常 熟 |
| 25 | 苏州三星电子有限公司 | 市 区 | 50 | 雅鹿集团股份有限公司 | 太 仓 |

表4-18 续表　Continued

| 序　号 No. | 企业名称 Name of Enterprises | 所在地区 Location | 序　号 No. | 企业名称 Name of Enterprises | 所在地区 Location |
|---|---|---|---|---|---|
| 51 | 卡特彼勒（苏州）有限公司 | 市　区 | 76 | 罗地亚飞翔精细化工有限公司 | 张家港 |
| 52 | 江苏通润机电集团有限公司 | 常　熟 | 77 | 三星电子（苏州）半导体有限公司 | 市　区 |
| 53 | 长春化工（江苏）有限公司 | 常　熟 | 78 | 安德鲁电信器材（苏州）有限公司 | 市　区 |
| 54 | 芬欧汇川(中国)有限公司 | 常　熟 | 79 | 沪士电子股份有限公司 | 昆　山 |
| 55 | 万都底盘部件（苏州）有限公司 | 市　区 | 80 | 国都化工（昆山）有限公司 | 昆　山 |
| 56 | 道康宁（张家港）有限公司 | 张家港 | 81 | 惠氏制药有限公司 | 市　区 |
| 57 | 江苏理文造纸有限公司 | 常　熟 | 82 | 金刚化工（昆山）有限公司 | 昆　山 |
| 58 | 捷安特（中国）有限公司 | 昆　山 | 83 | 艾默生环境优化技术（苏州）有限公司 | 市　区 |
| 59 | 太仓港协鑫发电有限公司 | 太　仓 | 84 | 康美包（苏州）有限公司 | 市　区 |
| 60 | 利乐包装（昆山）有限公司 | 昆　山 | 85 | 苏州纽威阀门股份有限公司 | 市　区 |
| 61 | 金华盛纸业（苏州）有限公司 | 市　区 | 86 | SEW-传动设备（苏州）有限公司 | 市　区 |
| 62 | 神华国华太仓发电有限公司 | 太　仓 | 87 | 中达光电工业（吴江）有限公司 | 市　区 |
| 63 | 埃克森美孚（太仓）石油有限公司 | 太　仓 | 88 | 昆山联滔电子有限公司 | 昆　山 |
| 64 | 莱克电气股份有限公司 | 市　区 | 89 | 常熟三爱富中昊化工新材料有限公司 | 常　熟 |
| 65 | 常熟市汽车饰件有限公司 | 常　熟 | 90 | 常熟开关制造有限公司 | 常　熟 |
| 66 | 张家港沙洲电力有限公司 | 张家港 | 91 | NGK（苏州）环保陶瓷有限公司 | 市　区 |
| 67 | 江苏常熟发电有限公司 | 常　熟 | 92 | 卫材（中国）药业有限公司 | 市　区 |
| 68 | 特灵空调系统（中国）有限公司 | 太　仓 | 93 | 碧辟（中国）工业油品有限公司 | 太　仓 |
| 69 | 鸿准精密模具（昆山）有限公司 | 昆　山 | 94 | 张家港保税区康得菲尔实业有限公司 | 张家港 |
| 70 | 克诺尔车辆设备（苏州）有限公司 | 市　区 | 95 | 可成科技（苏州）有限公司 | 市　区 |
| 71 | 德尔福电子（苏州）有限公司 | 市　区 | 96 | 江苏理文化工有限公司 | 常　熟 |
| 72 | 可利科技苏州工业园区有限公司 | 市　区 | 97 | 昆山三一机械有限公司 | 昆　山 |
| 73 | 张家港华兴电力有限公司 | 张家港 | 98 | 维益食品（苏州）有限公司 | 市　区 |
| 74 | 可胜科技（苏州）有限公司 | 市　区 | 99 | 江苏宝洁有限公司 | 太　仓 |
| 75 | 欧瑞康（中国）科技有限公司 | 市　区 | 100 | 马斯特模具（昆山）有限公司 | 昆　山 |

表4-19

# 全市工业利润总额百强企业（2012年）
# TOP 100 ENTERPRISES OF THE TOTAL PROFITS (2012)

| 序号 No. | 企业名称 Name of Enterprises | 所在地区 Location | 序号 No. | 企业名称 Name of Enterprises | 所在地区 Location |
|---|---|---|---|---|---|
| 1 | 仁宝信息技术（昆山）有限公司 | 昆　山 | 26 | 上海华电电力发展有限公司望亭发电厂 | 市　区 |
| 2 | 纬新资通（昆山）有限公司 | 昆　山 | 27 | 中利科技集团股份有限公司 | 常　熟 |
| 3 | 仁宝电子科技（昆山）有限公司 | 昆　山 | 28 | 常熟市龙腾特种钢有限公司 | 常　熟 |
| 4 | 纬创资通（昆山）有限公司 | 昆　山 | 29 | 可胜科技（苏州）有限公司 | 市　区 |
| 5 | 波司登股份有限公司 | 常　熟 | 30 | 道康宁（张家港）有限公司 | 张家港 |
| 6 | 仁宝资讯工业（昆山）有限公司 | 昆　山 | 31 | 三星电子（苏州）半导体有限公司 | 市　区 |
| 7 | 通力电梯有限公司 | 昆　山 | 32 | 苏州协鑫光伏科技有限公司 | 市　区 |
| 8 | 纬智资通（昆山）有限公司 | 昆　山 | 33 | 中达电子（江苏）有限公司 | 市　区 |
| 9 | 博世汽车部件（苏州）有限公司 | 市　区 | 34 | 亨通集团有限公司 | 市　区 |
| 10 | 江苏永钢集团有限公司 | 张家港 | 35 | 常熟开关制造有限公司 | 常　熟 |
| 11 | 三一重机有限公司 | 昆　山 | 36 | 克诺尔车辆设备（苏州）有限公司 | 市　区 |
| 12 | 南亚电子材料（昆山）有限公司 | 昆　山 | 37 | 雅鹿集团股份有限公司 | 太　仓 |
| 13 | 通鼎集团有限公司 | 市　区 | 38 | 华芳集团有限公司 | 张家港 |
| 14 | 华润电力（常熟）有限公司 | 常　熟 | 39 | 江苏旋力集团股份有限公司 | 常　熟 |
| 15 | 正新橡胶（中国）有限公司 | 昆　山 | 40 | 澳洋集团有限公司 | 张家港 |
| 16 | 苏州三星电子电脑有限公司 | 市　区 | 41 | 佳能（苏州）有限公司 | 市　区 |
| 17 | 牧田（昆山）有限公司 | 昆　山 | 42 | 住友橡胶（常熟）有限公司 | 常　熟 |
| 18 | 华能太仓发电有限责任公司 | 太　仓 | 43 | 德尔福电子（苏州）有限公司 | 市　区 |
| 19 | 瑞仪光电（苏州）有限公司 | 市　区 | 44 | 夏普办公设备（常熟）有限公司 | 常　熟 |
| 20 | 舍弗勒（中国）有限公司 | 太　仓 | 45 | 神华国华太仓发电有限公司 | 太　仓 |
| 21 | 太仓港协鑫发电有限公司 | 太　仓 | 46 | 中利腾晖光伏科技有限公司 | 常　熟 |
| 22 | 阿特斯光伏电子（常熟）有限公司 | 常　熟 | 47 | 张家港沙洲电力有限公司 | 张家港 |
| 23 | 芬欧汇川(中国)有限公司 | 常　熟 | 48 | 苏州三星电子有限公司 | 市　区 |
| 24 | 江苏沙钢集团有限公司 | 张家港 | 49 | 张家港保税区康得菲尔实业有限公司 | 张家港 |
| 25 | 卡特彼勒（苏州）有限公司 | 市　区 | 50 | 惠氏制药有限公司 | 市　区 |

表4-19 续表 Continued

| 序 号<br>No. | 企业名称<br>Name of Enterprises | 所在地区<br>Location | 序 号<br>No. | 企业名称<br>Name of Enterprises | 所在地区<br>Location |
|---|---|---|---|---|---|
| 51 | 特灵空调系统（中国）有限公司 | 太 仓 | 76 | 金华盛纸业（苏州）有限公司 | 市 区 |
| 52 | 可成科技（苏州）有限公司 | 市 区 | 77 | 常熟市汽车饰件有限公司 | 常 熟 |
| 53 | 江苏苏南特种装备集团有限责任公司 | 常 熟 | 78 | 金刚化工（昆山）有限公司 | 昆 山 |
| 54 | 艾默生环境优化技术（苏州）有限公司 | 市 区 | 79 | 苏州迅达电梯有限公司 | 市 区 |
| 55 | 康美包（苏州）有限公司 | 市 区 | 80 | 保利协鑫太阳能电力系统集成（太仓）有限公司 | 太 仓 |
| 56 | 万都底盘部件（苏州）有限公司 | 市 区 | 81 | 江苏理文造纸有限公司 | 常 熟 |
| 57 | SEW-传动设备（苏州）有限公司 | 市 区 | 82 | 苏州三星电子液晶显示器有限公司 | 市 区 |
| 58 | 罗地亚飞翔精细化工有限公司 | 张家港 | 83 | 安德鲁电信器材（苏州）有限公司 | 市 区 |
| 59 | 欧瑞康（中国）科技有限公司 | 市 区 | 84 | 碧辟（中国）工业油品有限公司 | 太 仓 |
| 60 | 江苏理文化工有限公司 | 常 熟 | 85 | 利乐包装（昆山）有限公司 | 昆 山 |
| 61 | NGK（苏州）环保陶瓷有限公司 | 市 区 | 86 | 昆山三一机械有限公司 | 昆 山 |
| 62 | 富士康（昆山）电脑接插件有限公司 | 昆 山 | 87 | 达富电脑（常熟）有限公司 | 常 熟 |
| 63 | 沪士电子股份有限公司 | 昆 山 | 88 | 昆山华冠商标印刷有限公司 | 昆 山 |
| 64 | 江苏恒力化纤股份有限公司 | 市 区 | 89 | 捷安特（中国）有限公司 | 昆 山 |
| 65 | 常熟三爱富中昊化工新材料有限公司 | 常 熟 | 90 | 鸿准精密模具（昆山）有限公司 | 昆 山 |
| 66 | 江苏隆力奇集团有限公司 | 常 熟 | 91 | 大金氟化工（中国）有限公司 | 常 熟 |
| 67 | 江苏梦兰集团有限公司 | 常 熟 | 92 | 久保田农业机械（苏州）有限公司 | 市 区 |
| 68 | 苏州纽威阀门股份有限公司 | 市 区 | 93 | 江苏宝洁有限公司 | 太 仓 |
| 69 | 江苏常熟发电有限公司 | 常 熟 | 94 | 中达光电工业（吴江）有限公司 | 市 区 |
| 70 | 国都化工（昆山）有限公司 | 昆 山 | 95 | 3M材料技术（苏州）有限公司 | 市 区 |
| 71 | 莱克电气股份有限公司 | 市 区 | 96 | 苏州市佳禾食品工业有限公司 | 市 区 |
| 72 | 可利科技苏州工业园区有限公司 | 市 区 | 97 | 希捷科技（苏州）有限公司 | 市 区 |
| 73 | 埃克森美孚（太仓）石油有限公司 | 太 仓 | 98 | 绿点（苏州）科技有限公司 | 市 区 |
| 74 | 苏州三星电子家电有限公司 | 市 区 | 99 | 瓦克化学（张家港）有限公司 | 张家港 |
| 75 | 昆山联滔电子有限公司 | 昆 山 | 100 | 马斯特模具（昆山）有限公司 | 昆 山 |

表4-20

# 全市工业资产总计百强企业（2012年）
# TOP 100 ENTERPRISES OF THE TOTAL ASSETS (2012)

| 序　号<br>No. | 企业名称<br>Name of Enterprises | 所在地区<br>Location | 序　号<br>No. | 企业名称<br>Name of Enterprises | 所在地区<br>Location |
|---|---|---|---|---|---|
| 1 | 江苏沙钢集团有限公司 | 张家港 | 26 | 江苏苏钢集团有限公司 | 市　区 |
| 2 | 江苏永钢集团有限公司 | 张家港 | 27 | 长春化工（江苏）有限公司 | 常　熟 |
| 3 | 波司登股份有限公司 | 常　熟 | 28 | 江苏苏南特种装备集团有限责任公司 | 常　熟 |
| 4 | 名硕电脑（苏州）有限公司 | 市　区 | 29 | 阿特斯光伏电子（常熟）有限公司 | 常　熟 |
| 5 | 亨通集团有限公司 | 市　区 | 30 | 常熟市龙腾特种钢有限公司 | 常　熟 |
| 6 | 南亚电子材料（昆山）有限公司 | 昆　山 | 31 | 江苏骏马集团有限责任公司 | 张家港 |
| 7 | 玖龙纸业（太仓）有限公司 | 太　仓 | 32 | 张家港沙洲电力有限公司 | 张家港 |
| 8 | 金红叶纸业集团有限公司 | 市　区 | 33 | 苏州三星电子电脑有限公司 | 市　区 |
| 9 | 东海粮油工业（张家港）有限公司 | 张家港 | 34 | 太仓港协鑫发电有限公司 | 太　仓 |
| 10 | 江苏盛虹化纤有限公司 | 市　区 | 35 | 纬新资通（昆山）有限公司 | 昆　山 |
| 11 | 江苏永恒钢铁实业有限公司 | 张家港 | 36 | 江苏华昌（集团）有限公司 | 张家港 |
| 12 | 江苏江南化纤集团有限公司 | 市　区 | 37 | 三一重机有限公司 | 昆　山 |
| 13 | 江苏恒力化纤有限公司 | 市　区 | 38 | 雅鹿集团股份有限公司 | 太　仓 |
| 14 | 澳洋集团有限公司 | 张家港 | 39 | 江苏腾晖电力科技有限公司 | 常　熟 |
| 15 | 昆山龙腾光电有限公司 | 昆　山 | 40 | 瑞仪光电（苏州）有限公司 | 市　区 |
| 16 | 上海华电电力发展有限公司望亭发电厂 | 市　区 | 41 | 纬创资通（昆山）有限公司 | 昆　山 |
| 17 | 金华盛纸业（苏州）有限公司 | 市　区 | 42 | 华芳集团有限公司 | 张家港 |
| 18 | 中利科技集团股份有限公司 | 常　熟 | 43 | 华润电力（常熟）有限公司 | 常　熟 |
| 19 | 江苏常熟发电有限公司 | 常　熟 | 44 | 博世汽车部件（苏州）有限公司 | 市　区 |
| 20 | 道康宁（张家港）有限公司 | 张家港 | 45 | 伟创力电子技术（苏州）有限公司 | 市　区 |
| 21 | 张家港浦项不锈钢有限公司 | 张家港 | 46 | 康准电子科技（昆山）有限公司 | 昆　山 |
| 22 | 江苏华尔润集团 | 张家港 | 47 | 正新橡胶（中国）有限公司 | 昆　山 |
| 23 | 通力电梯有限公司 | 昆　山 | 48 | 纬智资通（昆山）有限公司 | 昆　山 |
| 24 | 仁宝信息技术（昆山）有限公司 | 昆　山 | 49 | 舍弗勒（中国）有限公司 | 太　仓 |
| 25 | 芬欧汇川(中国)有限公司 | 常　熟 | 50 | 联建（苏州）科技有限公司 | 市　区 |

表4-20 续表 Continued

| 序 号<br>No. | 企业名称<br>Name of Enterprises | 所在地区<br>Location | 序 号<br>No. | 企业名称<br>Name of Enterprises | 所在地区<br>Location |
|---|---|---|---|---|---|
| 51 | 苏州阿特斯阳光电力科技有限公司 | 市 区 | 76 | 昆山市自来水集团有限公司 | 昆 山 |
| 52 | 通鼎集团有限公司 | 市 区 | 77 | 苏州长城开发科技有限公司 | 市 区 |
| 53 | 攀华集团有限公司 | 张家港 | 78 | 苏州天然气管网股份有限公司 | 市 区 |
| 54 | 张家港化工机械股份有限公司 | 张家港 | 79 | 神华国华太仓发电有限公司 | 太 仓 |
| 55 | 江苏国望高科纤维有限公司 | 市 区 | 80 | 佳能（苏州）有限公司 | 市 区 |
| 56 | 太仓市水处理有限责任公司 | 太 仓 | 81 | 苏州协鑫光伏科技有限公司 | 市 区 |
| 57 | 仁宝电子科技（昆山）有限公司 | 昆 山 | 82 | 盛虹集团有限公司 | 市 区 |
| 58 | 江苏隆力奇集团有限公司 | 常 熟 | 83 | 张家港华兴电力有限公司 | 张家港 |
| 59 | 上海绿地集团（昆山）商品混凝土有限公司 | 昆 山 | 84 | 苏州工业园区清源华衍水务有限公司 | 市 区 |
| 60 | 金龙联合汽车工业（苏州）有限公司 | 市 区 | 85 | 江苏苏南重工机械科技有限公司 | 常 熟 |
| 61 | 华能太仓发电有限责任公司 | 太 仓 | 86 | 富翔精密工业（昆山）有限公司 | 昆 山 |
| 62 | 江苏理文造纸有限公司 | 常 熟 | 87 | 国巨电子（中国）有限公司 | 市 区 |
| 63 | 三星电子（苏州）半导体有限公司 | 市 区 | 88 | 江苏新民纺织科技股份有限公司 | 市 区 |
| 64 | 沪士电子股份有限公司 | 昆 山 | 89 | 和舰科技（苏州）有限公司 | 市 区 |
| 65 | 达富电脑（常熟）有限公司 | 常 熟 | 90 | 苏州三星电子有限公司 | 市 区 |
| 66 | 富士康（昆山）电脑接插件有限公司 | 昆 山 | 91 | 友达光电（苏州）有限公司 | 市 区 |
| 67 | 永鼎集团有限公司 | 市 区 | 92 | 鸿准精密模具（昆山）有限公司 | 昆 山 |
| 68 | 苏州乐轩科技有限公司 | 市 区 | 93 | 亚旭电子科技（江苏）有限公司 | 市 区 |
| 69 | 苏州佳世达电通有限公司 | 市 区 | 94 | 江苏通润机电集团有限公司 | 常 熟 |
| 70 | 可利科技苏州工业园区有限公司 | 市 区 | 95 | 达研光电（常熟）有限公司 | 常 熟 |
| 71 | 牧田（昆山）有限公司 | 昆 山 | 96 | 南亚电路板（昆山）有限公司 | 昆 山 |
| 72 | 住友橡胶（常熟）有限公司 | 常 熟 | 97 | 常熟风范电力设备股份有限公司 | 常 熟 |
| 73 | 江苏鹰翔化纤股份有限公司 | 市 区 | 98 | 烨辉（中国）科技材料有限公司 | 常 熟 |
| 74 | 香塘集团有限公司 | 太 仓 | 99 | 苏州维信电子有限公司 | 市 区 |
| 75 | 江苏旋力集团股份有限公司 | 常 熟 | 100 | 常熟科弘材料科技有限公司 | 常 熟 |

表4-21

# 苏州的驰名商标(2012年末)
（行政认定）
# LIST OF RENOWNED AND DISTINGUISHED BRANDS IN SUZHOU (END OF 2012)
( ADMINISTRATIVE RECOGNITION )

| 商标名称 Brand Name | 主要产品 Main Product | 注册单位 Registered Units | 认定时间 Time of Recognition | 所在地区 Location |
|---|---|---|---|---|
| 春花 | 吸尘器 | 苏州春花国际贸易有限公司 | 2000年 | 市 区 |
| 亨通光电 | 通信电缆等 | 江苏亨通光电股份有限公司 | 2004年 | 市 区 |
| DER | 地板等 | 德尔国际家居股份有限公司 | 2005年 | 市 区 |
| BenQ | 液晶显示器、扫描仪 | 明基电通股份有限公司 | 2007年 | 市 区 |
| 羅普斯金LPSK | 金属建筑材料 | 苏州罗普斯金铝业股份有限公司 | 2007年 | 市 区 |
| 通鼎光电 | 电缆，光缆 | 江苏通鼎光电股份有限公司 | 2007年 | 市 区 |
| 罗技 | 计算机鼠标器、计算机周边设备 | 罗技科技(苏州)有限公司 | 2008年 | 市 区 |
| 洞庭山碧螺春及图 | 茶叶 | 苏州市吴中区洞庭（山）碧螺春茶业协会 | 2009年 | 市 区 |
| 七宝及图 | 电线、电缆 | 江苏七宝光电集团有限公司 | 2009年 | 市 区 |
| 盛虹及图SHENGHONG | 布、织物 | 盛虹集团有限公司 | 2009年 | 市 区 |
| SJEC | 升降机（电梯）、升降设备 | 苏州江南嘉捷电梯股份有限公司 | 2010年 | 市 区 |
| 科林kelin及图 | 除尘器 | 科林环保设备股份有限公司 | 2010年 | 市 区 |
| 桑罗 | 服装、领带、围巾 | 江苏华佳投资集团有限公司 | 2010年 | 市 区 |
| 雅士利 | 油漆、涂料（油漆） | 雅士利涂料（苏州）有限公司 | 2011年 | 市 区 |
| 苏净及图 | 空气净化装置和机器、水净化装置、洁净工作台(系列) | 江苏苏净集团有限公司 | 2011年 | 市 区 |
| 环球及图 | 套筒滚子链 | 苏州环球集团有限公司 | 2011年 | 市 区 |
| 牛头NIU TOU及图 | 纤维纺织原料、纺织品纤维 | 江苏江南高纤股份有限公司 | 2011年 | 市 区 |
| 二叶ERYE及图 | 西药 | 苏州二叶制药有限公司 | 2011年 | 市 区 |
| 恒远HENGYUAN及图 | 弹力丝(纺织用)；长丝 | 恒力集团有限公司 | 2011年 | 市 区 |
| 大卫及图 | 地板，木板材条 | 苏州大卫木业有限公司 | 2011年 | 市 区 |
| 第3394728号图形 | 物理学设备和仪器、材料检验仪器和机器 | 苏州东菱振动试验仪器有限公司 | 2012年 | 市 区 |
| 康力 | 电梯、自动梯、可移动楼梯 | 康力电梯股份有限公司 | 2012年 | 市 区 |
| 雷允上及图 | 中药成药 | 雷允上药业有限公司 | 2012年 | 市 区 |
| 丁家宜 | 洗面奶、化妆品 | 珈依生化科技（中国）有限公司 | 2012年 | 市 区 |

表4-21 续表 1　　Continued 1

| 商标名称<br>Brand Name | 主要产品<br>Main Product | 注册单位<br>Registered Units | 认定时间<br>Time of Recognition | 所在地区<br>Location |
|---|---|---|---|---|
| 吴通WUTONG及图 | 连接器(数据处理设备) | 江苏吴通通讯股份有限公司 | 2012年 | 市　区 |
| 波司登 | 服装、皮鞋 | 波司登股份有限公司 | 1999年 | 常　熟 |
| 梦兰 | 纺织品 | 江苏梦兰集团公司 | 2000年 | 常　熟 |
| 隆力奇 | 纯蛇粉 | 江苏隆力奇生物科技股份有限公司 | 2001年 | 常　熟 |
| 阪神 | 冷冻箱 | 江苏白雪电器股份有限公司 | 2004年 | 常　熟 |
| BaiXue | 冷冻设备等 | 江苏白雪电器股份有限公司 | 2004年 | 常　熟 |
| 龙达飞<br>LongDafei | 服装 | 江苏龙达飞投资实业有限公司 | 2006年 | 常　熟 |
| 隆力奇及图 | 化妆品等 | 江苏隆力奇生物科技股份有限公司 | 2007年 | 常　熟 |
| 雪中飞 | 羽绒服装 | 波司登股份有限公司 | 2007年 | 常　熟 |
| TORIN及图 | 第7类：千斤顶 | 江苏通润机电集团有限公司 | 2009年 | 常　熟 |
| 第1273835号图形 | 第9类：断路器 | 常熟开关制造有限公司 | 2009年 | 常　熟 |
| 洲艳ZhouYan图形 | 服装等 | 江苏洲艳服饰有限公司 | 2009年 | 常　熟 |
| 通润及图 | 千斤顶、货车用千斤顶 | 江苏通润机电集团有限公司 | 2010年 | 常　熟 |
| 千仞岗 | 服装、羽绒服装 | 常熟市千仞岗制衣有限公司 | 2010年 | 常　熟 |
| Enox | 化学试剂 | 江苏强盛化工有限公司 | 2011年 | 常　熟 |
| 阿里山 | 加工过的坚果、加工过的瓜子 | 江苏阿里山食品有限公司 | 2011年 | 常　熟 |
| 月龙YUELONG | 衣物、茄克、裤子、西服制服、 | 江苏月龙服饰有限公司 | 2011年 | 常　熟 |
| 扬帆SETSAIL | 针织服装 | 江苏扬帆服饰有限公司 | 2011年 | 常　熟 |
| 龙星LongXing及图 | 纺织机械、针织机械、手套机 | 常熟市金龙机械有限公司 | 2012年 | 常　熟 |
| 金丝狐Jinsihu及图 | 服装（休闲男装） | 江苏金丝狐服饰有限公司 | 2012年 | 常　熟 |
| 菊花 | 味精等 | 张家港市新菊味精有限公司 | 2002年 | 张家港 |
| 华芳 | 纺织纱等 | 华芳集团有限公司 | 2004年 | 张家港 |
| 沙洲SZ及图 | 黄酒 | 江苏张家港酿酒有限公司 | 2008年 | 张家港 |
| 沙钢及图 | 钢型材、金属建筑材料 | 江苏沙钢集团有限公司 | 2008年 | 张家港 |

表4-21 续表 2 Continued 2

| 商标名称<br>Brand Name | 主要产品<br>Main Product | 注册单位<br>Registered Units | 认定时间<br>Time of Recognition | 所在地区<br>Location |
|---|---|---|---|---|
| 港洋及图 | 精纺呢绒 | 江苏港洋实业股份有限公司 | 2009年 | 张家港 |
| AAA SANEIPAI及图 | 轴承 | 张家港市AAA轴承有限公司 | 2010年 | 张家港 |
| 沙洲优黄 | 黄酒 | 江苏张家港酿酒有限公司 | 2012年 | 张家港 |
| 捷星及图 | 电梯空心导轨 | 长江润发机械股份有限公司 | 2012年 | 张家港 |
| 浩波HOPE | 双乙烯酮 | 苏州浩波科技股份有限公司 | 2012年 | 张家港 |
| 港星 | 轻钢龙骨 | 张家港市新港星科技有限公司 | 2012年 | 张家港 |
| 联冠及图 | 塑料挤出机、塑料混合机、塑料切粒机 | 江苏联冠科技发展有限公司 | 2012年 | 张家港 |
| 好孩子 | 儿童车等 | 好孩子儿童用品有限公司 | 1999年 | 昆　山 |
| AB | 内衣裤等 | 江苏AB集团股份有限公司 | 2000年 | 昆　山 |
| 捷安特 | 自行车 | 巨大机械工业股份有限公司 | 2004年 | 昆　山 |
| 旗舰及图 | 办公用纸等 | 亚龙纸制品(昆山)有限公司 | 2006年 | 昆　山 |
| 哈森HARSONE及图 | 皮鞋 | 昆山珍兴鞋业有限公司 | 2006年 | 昆　山 |
| 并蒂莲 | 服装 | 昆山并蒂莲服装有限公司 | 2008年 | 昆　山 |
| 多威DOWIN | 运动鞋 | 昆山多威体育用品有限公司 | 2008年 | 昆　山 |
| 冠軍 | 瓷砖等 | 信益陶瓷(中国)有限公司 | 2010年 | 昆　山 |
| 櫻花SAKURA及图 | 排油烟机、电热水器、厨房炉灶 | 樱花卫厨（中国）股份有限公司 | 2011年 | 昆　山 |
| 南寳NANPAO | 油漆、涂料 | 南宝树脂化学工厂股份有限公司 | 2011年 | 昆　山 |
| MIYOU及图 | 粉碎机（机器）、机械密封件 | 密友集团有限公司 | 2012年 | 昆　山 |
| MAXXIS | 车轮胎；汽车轮胎；车辆轮胎 | 正新橡胶(中国)有限公司 | 2012年 | 昆　山 |
| 雅鹿 | 服装 | 苏州雅鹿控股股份有限公司 | 2001年 | 太　仓 |
| 太仓及图 | 肉松 | 太仓肉松食品有限公司 | 2008年 | 太　仓 |
| 第1080023号图形 | 聚氯乙烯树脂、合成树脂塑料 | 江苏德威新材料股份有限公司 | 2010年 | 太　仓 |
| 安佑 | 动物饲料；家畜饲料等 | 安佑（中国）动物营养研发有限公司 | 2012年 | 太　仓 |

# 主 要 统 计 指 标 解 释

**工业** 指从事自然资源的开采，对采掘品和农产品进行加工和再加工的物质生产部门。具体包括：(1)对自然资源的开采，如采矿、晒盐等(但不包括禽兽捕猎和水产捕捞)；(2)对农副产品的加工、再加工，如粮油加工、食品加工、缫丝、纺织、制革等；(3)对采掘品的加工、再加工，如炼铁、炼钢、化工生产、石油加工、机器制造、木材加工等，以及电力、自来水、煤气的生产和供应等；(4)对工业品的修理、翻新，如机器设备的修理、交通运输工具(如汽车)的修理等。

工业统计调查单位为独立核算法人工业企业。

独立核算法人工业企业指从事工业生产经营活动的单位。独立核算法人工业企业应同时具备以下条件：①依法成立，有自己的名称、组织机构和场所，能够承担民事责任；②独立拥有和使用资产，承担负债，有权与其他单位签订合同；③独立核算盈亏，并能够编制资产负债表。

本年鉴中涉及的企业登记注册类型：

**国有及国有控股企业** 指国有企业加上国有控股企业。国有企业(即原全民所有制工业或国营工业)指企业全部资产归国家所有，并按《中华人民共和国企业法人登记管理条例》规定登记注册的非公司制的经济组织。包括国有企业、国有独资公司和国有联营企业。1957年以前的公私合营和私营工业，后均改造为国营工业，1992年改为国有工业，这部分工业的资料不单独分列时，均包括在国有企业内。国有控股企业是对混合所有制经济的企业进行的“国有控股”分类。它是指这些企业的全部资产中国有资产(股份)相对其他所有者中的任何一个所有者占资(股)最多的企业。该分组反映了国有经济控股情况。

**集体企业** 指企业资产归集体所有，并按《中华人民共和国企业法人登记管理条例》规定登记注册的经济组织。是社会主义公有制经济的组成部分。包括城乡所有使用集体投资举办的企业，以及部分个人通过集资自愿放弃所有权并依法经工商行政管理机关认定为集体所有制的企业。

**股份合作企业** 指以合作制为基础，由企业职工共同出资入股，吸收一定比例的社会资产投资组建，实行自主经营，自负盈亏，共同劳动，民主管理，按劳分配与按股分红相结合的一种集体经济组织。

**联营企业** 指两个及两个以上相同或不同所有制性质的企业法人或事业单位法人，按自愿、平等、互利的原则，共同投资组成的经济组织。联营企业包括：

国有联营企业指国有企业与国有企业间的联营；

集体联营企业指集体企业与集体企业间的联营；

国有与集体联营企业指国有企业与集体企业间的联营。

**有限责任公司** 指根据《中华人民共和国公司登记管理条例》规定登记注册，由两个以上，五十个以下的股东共同出资，每个股东以其所认缴的出资额对公司承担有限责任，公司以其全部资产对其债务承担责任的经济组织。

有限责任公司包括国有独资公司以及其他有限责任公司。

**股份有限公司** 指根据《中华人民共和国企业法人登记管理条例》规定登记注册，其全部注册资本由等额股份构成并通过发行股票筹集资本，股东以其认购的股份对公司承担有限责任，公司以其全部资产对其债务承担责任的经济组织。

**私营企业** 指由自然人投资设立或由自然人控股，以雇佣劳动为基础的营利性经济组织。包括按照《公司法》、《合伙企业法》、《私营企业暂行条例》规定登记注册的私营有限责任公司、私营股份有限公司、私营合伙企业和私营独资企业。

**港、澳、台商投资企业** 指企业注册登记类型中的港、澳、台资合资、合作、独资经营企业和股份有限公司之和。

**外商投资企业** 指企业注册登记类型中的中外合资、合作经营企业、外资企业和外商投资股份有限公司之和。

**“三资”企业** 指港、澳、台商投资企业和外资企业的简称。

**轻工业** 指主要提供生活消费品和制作手工工具的工业。按其所使用的原料不同，可分为两大类：(1)以农产品为原料的轻工业，是指直接或间接以农产品为基本原料的轻工业。主要包括食品制造、饮料制造、烟草加工、纺织、缝纫、皮革和毛皮制作、造纸以及印刷等工业；(2)以非农产品为原料的轻工业，是指以工业品为原料的轻工业。主要包括文教体育用品、化学药品制造、合成纤维制造、日用化学制品、日用玻璃制品、日用金属制品、手工工具制造、医疗器械制造、文化和办公用机械制造等工业。

**重工业** 指为国民经济各部门提供物质技术基础的主要生产资料的工业。按其生产性质和产品用途，可以分为下列三类：(1)采掘(伐)工业，是指对自然资源的开采，包括石油开采、煤炭开采、金属矿开采、非金属矿开采等工业；(2)原材料工业，指向国民经济各部门提供基本材料、动力和燃料的工业。包括金属冶炼及加工、炼焦及焦炭、化学、化工原料、水泥、人造板以及电力、石油和煤炭加工等工业；(3)加工工业，是指对工业原材料进行再加工制造的工业。包括装备国民经济各部门的机械设备制造工业、金属结构、水泥制品等工业，以及为农业提供的生产资料如化肥、农药等工业。

根据上述划分原则，修理业中以重工业产品为修理作业对象的划为重工业，反之划为轻工业。

**工业总产值**

(1)定义：

工业总产值是以货币形式表现的，工业企业在一定时期内生产的工业最终产品或提供工业性劳务活动的总价值量。它反映一定时间内工业生产的总规模和总水平。

(2)计算原则：

工业生产的原则，即凡是企业在报告期生产的经检验合格的产品，不管是否在报告期销售，均包括在内。

最终产品的原则，即凡是计入工业总产值的产品，必须是本企业生产的经检验合格的，不需要再进行任何加工的最终产品。如果企业有中间产品(半成品)对外销售，则对外销售的中间产品应视为企业的最终产品。

工厂法原则，即工业总产值是以工业企业作为基本计算(核算)单位，即按企业的最终产品计算工业总产值。按这种方法计算的工业总产值，不允许同一产品价值在企业内部重复计算，不能把企业内部各个车间(分厂)生产的成果相加，但允许企业间的重复计算。

(3)内容及计算方法：

1995年全国工业普查对工业总产值(原规定)的内容及计算原则和方法做了某些修订，修订后的工业总产值(新规定)包括三项内容：即本期生产成品价值、对外加工费收入、在制品半成品期末期初差额价值三部分。

本期生产成品价值：指企业本期生产，并在报告期内不再进行加工，经检验、包装入库的全部工业成品(半成品)价值合计，包括企业生产的自制设备及提供给本企业在建工程、其他非工业部门和福利部门等单位使用的成品价值。本期生产成品价值为按自备原材料生产的产品的数量乘以本期不含增值税(销项税额)的产品实际销售平均单价计算；会计核算中按成本价格转帐的自制设备和自产自用的成品，按成本价格计算生产成品价值。生产成品价值中不包括用定货者来料加工的成品(半成品)价值。

对外加工费收入：指企业在报告期内完成的对外承接的工业品加工(包括用定货者来料加工产品)的加工费收入和对外工业修理作业所取得的加工费收入。对外加工费收入按不含增值税(销项税额)的价格计算，可根据会计“产品销售收入”科目的有关资料取得。

对于本企业对内非工业部门提供的加工修理、设备安装的劳务收入，如果企业会计核算基础较好，能取得这部分资料，而且这部分价值所占比重较大，应包括在对外加工费收入中。

自制半成品在制品期末期初差额价值：指企业报告期在制品期末减期初的差额价值，本指标一般可以从会计核算资料中取得。如果会计产品成本核算中不计算半成品、在制品的成本，则总产值中也不包括这部分价值，反之则包括。

(4)工业总产值统计范围变化和计算方法修订情况：

1984年以前工业总产值不包括村办工业，村办工业总产值划归农业。1984年以后工业总产值包括村办工业。

1995年工业普查对工业总产值计算方法做了修订，即从1995年始按新修订(新规定)方法计算工业总产值。新规定与原规定的区别如下：

全价与加工费的计算原则不同：新规定为凡自备原材料，不论其生产繁简程度如何，一律按全价计算工业总产值；凡来料加工，允许按加工费计算工业总产值。原规定则视生产加工的繁简程度不同，规定哪些行业按全价，哪些行业按加工费计算工业总产值。

自制半成品、在产品期末期初差额价值的计算原则不同：新规定要求，凡会计产品成本核算时计算了成本的差额价值，总产值中就应包括，否则可不包括；原规定则按生产周期六个月的界限区分，凡生产周期六个月以上的企业，总产值计算中应包括这部分差额价值，否则可不包括。

计算价格不同：新规定按不含增值税(销项税额)的价格计算；原规定则按含增值税(销项税额)的价格计算。

**资产总计**　指企业拥有或控制的能以货币计量的经济资源，包括各种财产、债权和其他权利。资产按流动性分为流动资产、长期投资、固定资产、无形资产、递延资产和其他资产。该指标根据企业会计“资产负债表”中“资产总计”项目的期末数增列。

**流动资产**　指企业可以在一年内或者超过一年的一个生产周期内变现或者耗用的资产，包括现金及各种存款、短期投资，应收及预付款项、存货等。

**流动资产平均余额**　指企业在报告期内全部流动资产的平均余额。

**固定资产原价**　指企业在建造、购置、安装、改建、扩建、技术改造某项固定资产时所支出的全部货币总额。它一般包括买价、包装费、运杂费和安装费等。

**固定资产净值年平均余额**　指固定资产净值在报告期内余额的平均数。计算公式为：

$$\text{固定资产净值年平均余额}=\frac{\text{1至12月各月月初、月末固定资产净值之和}}{24}$$

该指标根据“资产负债表”中“固定资产原价”、“累计折旧”指标的期初、期末数计算填列。

固定资产净值指固定资产原价减去历年已提折旧额后的净额。计算公式为：

固定资产净值=固定资产原价-累计折旧

**负债合计**　指企业所承担的能以货币计量，将以资产或劳务偿付的债务，偿还形式包括货币、资产或提供劳务。负债一般按偿还期长短分为流动负债和长期负债。根据会计“资产负债表”中“负债合计”的年末数填列。

**所有者权益**　指企业投资人对企业净资产的所有权。企业净资产等于企业全部资产减去全部负债后的余额，包括企业投资人对企业的最初投入的实际到位的资产及资本公积金、盈余公积金和未分配利润。所有者权益合计数小于零，表示企业资不抵债。

**主营业务收入**　指会计“利润表”中对应指标的本年累计数。未执行2001年《企业会计制度》的企业，用“产品销售收入”的本期累计数代替。

**主营业务成本**　指会计“利润表”中对应指标的本年累计数。未执行2001年《企业会计制度》的企业，用“产品销售成本”的本期累计数代替。

**主营业务税金及附加**　指会计“利润表”中对应指标的本年累计数。未执行2001年《企业会计制度》的企业，用“产品销售税金及附加” 的本期累计数代替。

**利润总额**　指企业生产经营活动的最终成果，是企业在一定时期内实现的盈亏相抵后的利润总额(亏损以“-”号表示)，它等于营业利润加上补贴收入加上投资收益加上营业外净收入再加上以前年度损益调整。

**本年应交增值税**　指企业在报告期内应交纳的增值税额。它等于本年销项税额加上出口退税加上进项税额转出数减去本年进项税额。小规模纳税企业直接按全年计税销售额乘以征收率计算取得。

**从业人员平均人数** 是指报告期内每天拥有的从业人员人数。其计算公式为：

$$季平均人数=\frac{季内各月平均人数之和}{3}$$

$$月平均人数=\frac{报告月内每天实有人数之和}{报告月日历日数}$$

$$年平均人数=\frac{年内各月平均人数之和}{12}$$

**总资产贡献率** 反映企业全部资产的获利能力，是企业经营业绩和管理水平的集中体现，是评价和考核企业盈利能力的核心指标。计算公式为：

$$总资产贡献率(\%)=\frac{利润总额+税金总额+利息支出}{平均资金总额}\times 100\%$$

公式中：税金总额为产品销售税金及附加与应交增值税之和；平均资产总额为期初期末资产之和的算术平均值。

**资产负债率** 该指标既反映企业经营风险的大小，也反映企业利用债权人提供的资金从事经营活动的能力。计算公式为：

$$资产负债率(\%)=\frac{负债总额}{资产总额}\times 100\%$$

资产与负债均为报告期期末数。

**流动资产周转次数** 指一定时期内流动资产完成的周转次数，反映投入工业企业流动资金的周转速度。计算公式为：

$$流动资产周转次数=\frac{产品销售收入}{全部流动资产平均余额}$$

公式中：全部流动资产平均余额为期初和期末的流动资产之和的算术平均值。

**成本费用利润率** 反映企业投入的生产成本及费用的经济效益，同时也反映企业降低成本所取得的经济效益。计算公式为：

$$成本费用利润率(\%)=\frac{利润总额}{成本费用总额}\times 100\%$$

公式中：成本费用总额为产品销售成本、销售费用、管理费用、财务费用之和。

**产品销售率** 该指标反映工业产品已实现销售的程度，是分析工业产销衔接情况，研究工业产品满足社会需求的指标。计算公式为：

$$产品销售率(\%)=\frac{工业销售产值}{工业总产值(现价)}\times 100\%$$

# EXPLANATORY NOTES ON MAIN STATISTICAL INDICATORS

**Industry** refers to the material production sector which is engaged in the extraction of natural resources and processing and reprocessing of minerals and agricultural products, including (1) extraction of natural resources, such as mining, salt production (but not including hunting and fishing); (2) processing and reprocessing of farm and sideline produces, such as rice husking, flour milling, wine making, oil pressing, silk reeling, spinning and weaving, and leather making; (3) manufacture of industrial products, such as steel making, iron smelting, chemicals manufacturing, petroleum processing, machine building, timber processing; water and gas production and electricity generation and supply; (4)repairing of industrial products such as the repairing of machinery and means of transport (including cars).

In industrial statistics surveys, the units of enquiry are corporate industrial enterprises with independent accounting systems.

Corporate industrial enterprises with independent accounting systems refer to enterprises engaging in industrial production activities, which meet the following requirements: (1) They are established legally, having their own names, organizations, location and able to take civil liability; (2) They possess and use their assets independently, assume liabilities and are entitled to sign contracts with other units; (3) They are financially independent and compile their own balance sheets.

Enterprises covered in the industrial statistics in the Yearbook include the following categories by their registration:

**State-owned and State-holding Enterprises** refer to state-owned enterprises plus State-holding enterprises. State-owned enterprises (originally known as State-run enterprises with ownership by the whole society) are non-corporate economic entities registered in accordance with the *Regulation of the People's Republic of China on the Management of Registration of Legal Enterprises*, where all assets are owned by the State. Included in this category are State-owned enterprises, State-funded corporations and State-owned joint-operation enterprises. Joint State-private industries and private industries, which existed before 1957, were transformed into state-run industries since 1957, and into State-owned industries after 1992. Statistics on those enterprises are included in the State-owned industries instead of being grouped them separately. State-holding enterprises are a sub-classification of enterprises with mixed ownership, referring to enterprises where the percentage of State assets (or shares by the State) is larger than any other single share holder of the same enterprise. This sub-classification illustrates the control of the State over a particular industry.

**Collective-owned Enterprises** refer to economic entities registered in accordance with the *Regulation of the People's Republic of China on the Management of Registration of Legal Enterprises*, where assets are owned collectively. Collective enterprises constitute an integral part of the socialist economy with public ownership. They include urban and rural enterprises invested collectively, and some enterprises registered in industrial and commercial administration agency as collective units where funds are pooled together by individuals who voluntarily give up their right of ownership.

**Share-holding Cooperative Enterprises** refer to economic units set up on a cooperative basis, with funding partly from employees of the enterprise and partly from outside investment, where the operation and management is decided by all the members who also participate in the production, and the distribution of income is based both on work (labour input) and on shares (capital input).

**Joint-operation Enterprises** refer to economic units that are established by joint investment by two or more corporate enterprises or institutions of the same or different types of ownership on voluntary, equal and mutual-beneficial basis. They include:

a) State-owned joint-operation enterprises (joint operation between State-owned enterprises);

b) Collective joint-operation enterprises (joint operation between collective enterprises; and

c) State-collective joint-operation enterprises (joint operation between state and collective enterprises).

**Limited Liability Corporations** refer to economic units registered in accordance with the *Regulation of the People's Republic of China on the Management of Registration of Corporations*, with capital from 2 to 49 investors, each investor bears limited liability to the corporation depending on his/her holding of shares, and the corporation bears liability to its debt to the maximum of its total assets.

**Share-holding Corporations Ltd.** refer to economic units registered in accordance with the *Regulation of the People's Republic of China on the Management of Registration of Corporate Enterprises*, with total registered capital divided into equal shares and raised through issuing stocks. Each investor bears limited liability to the corporation depending on the holding of shares, and the corporation bears liability to its debt to the maximum of its total assets.

**Private Enterprises** refer to economic units invested or controlled (by holding the majority of the shares) by natural persons who hire labours for profit-making activities. Included in this category are private limited liability corporations, private shareholding corporations Ltd., private partnership enterprises and private sole investment enterprises registered in accordance with the *Corporation Law, Partnership Enterprise Law and Tentative Regulation on Private Enterprises.*

**Enterprises with Funds from Hong Kong, Macao and Taiwan** refers to all industrial enterprises registered as the joint-venture, cooperative, sole (exclusive) investment industrial enterprises and limited liability corporations with funds from Hong Kong, Macao and Taiwan.

**Foreign Funded Enterprises** refer to all industrial enterprises registered as the joint-venture, cooperative, sole (exclusive) investment industrial enterprises and limited liability corporations with foreign funds.

**Enterprises with Hong Kong, Macao, Taiwan and Foreign Fund** refer to all the enterprises with funds from Hong Kong, Macao, Taiwan and foreign funded enterprises.

**Light Industry** refers to the industry that produces consumer goods and hand tools. It consists of two categories, depending on the materials used:

(1) Industries using farm products as raw materials. These are the branches of light industry which directly or indirectly use farm products as basic raw materials, including the manufacture of food and beverages, tobacco processing, textile, clothing, fur and leather manufacturing, paper making, printing, etc.

(2) Industries using non-farm products as raw materials. These are the branches of light industry which use manufactured goods as raw materials, including the manufacture of cultural, educational articles and sports goods, chemicals, synthetic fibre, chemical products for daily use, glass products for daily use, metal products for daily use, hand tools, medical apparatus and instruments, and the manufacture of cultural and office machinery.

**Heavy Industry** refers to the industry which produces capital goods, and provides various sectors of the national economy with necessary material and technical basis for production. It consists of the following three branches according to the purpose of production or the use of products:

(1) Mining, quarrying and logging industry, which refers to the industry that extracts natural resources, including extraction of petroleum, coal, metal and non-metal ores.

(2) Raw materials industry refers to the industry that provides various sectors of the national economy with raw materials, fuels and power. It includes smelting and processing of metals, coking and coke chemistry, chemical materials and building materials such as cement, plywood, and power, petroleum refining and coal dressing.

(3) Manufacturing industry which refers to the industry that processes raw materials. It includes machine-building industries which equip sectors of the national economy; industries producing metal structure and cement products; and industries producing means of agricultural production, such as chemical fertilizers and pesticides.

In accordance with the above principles of classification, the repairing trades, which are engaged primarily in repairing products of heavy industry, are classified as heavy industry while those which are engaged in repairing products of light industry are classified as light industry.

**Gross Industrial Output Value**

(1) Definition: Gross industrial output value is the total volume of final industrial products produced and industrial services provided during a given period. It reflects the total achievements and overall scale of industrial production during a given period.

(2) Principles for calculation:

Statistics on industrial production follow the principle that all products produced by the enterprises and accepted through quality check during the reference period are to be included no matter whether they are sold or not during the reference period.

Determination of final products follows the principle that all products that are included in the calculation of gross industrial output value are the final products of the enterprise which have been accepted through quality check and require no further processing. If an enterprise has intermediate (semi-finished) products to sell, these intermediate products are considered as the final products of the enterprise.

Gross industrial output value is calculated following the principle of factory approach, i.e. industrial enterprise is used as the basic accounting unit in calculating the gross industrial output value. By this approach, value of the same product is not to be double-counted, and the output value of different workshops (branch factories) within the enterprise should not be added. However, this approach allows the possibility of double counting between enterprises.

(3) Content and method of calculation: The old definition of gross industrial output value was modified during the 1995 National Industrial Census. The revised (new) definition of gross industrial output value consists of 3 components: value of the finished products during the reference period, income from processing for external parties, and value of change in semi-finished products between the end and the beginning of the reference period.

Value of finished products during the reference period: refers to the value of all finished (semi-finished) industrial products that are produced during the reference period without the need for further processing, checked for acceptance, packed and put into the warehouse of the enterprise, including the value of own-produced equipment and the value of products provided to the projects under construction of the enterprise, and to other non-industrial or welfare units. Value of finished products during the reference period is calculated by the quantity of products produced using own materials multiplied by the average unit prices at which products are sold (excluding value-added tax). Own-produced equipment and products produced for own use are valued at cost prices as in the case of enterprise accounting. Value of finished products does not include the value of finished products (semi-finished products) that are produced using the materials from the clients who place the orders.

Income from external processing: refers to income from contracted external processing of industrial products (including processing of industrial products using materials from the clients), and the income from industrial repairing work provided to other parties. Income from external processing is calculated using information from the item "products sales income" in the enterprise accounting at the prices with value-added tax excluded.

For income from services such as processing, repairing and installation of equipment provided to non-industrial units within the enterprise, if the accounting work of the enterprise is good enough to separate it from other records, and the share of such services is significant, it should also be included in the income from external processing.

Value of change in semi-finished products between the end and the beginning of the reference period: refers to the value of change in semi-finished products between the end and the beginning of the reference period, which generally can be obtained from accounting records of enterprises. If the enterprise accounting excludes the cost of semi-finished products, then it should not be included in the gross industrial output value, and the reverse if otherwise.

(4) Changes in the scope and method of calculation of the gross industrial output value

Prior to 1984, the value of rural industry run by villages was classified into agriculture instead of industry. Since 1984, it has been included in the gross industrial output value. Method of calculation for the gross industrial output value was modified in the industrial census in 1995. The difference in the new method as compared with the old one is outlined below:

Principle in using full value vs. processing fee: The new method stipulates that all products produced using own materials are to be calculated with full value in reporting the gross industrial output value irrespective of the complexity of production, and for external processing, it allows calculation using processing fee. In the old method, however, the use of full value or processing fee was determined by the degree of complexity of production in different branches of industries.

Principle in determining the value of change in semi-finished products: The new method requires that value of change in semi-finished products should be included in the gross industrial output value if it is included in the accounting record of the enterprise, otherwise it should not be included. In the old method, it is determined by the type of enterprises in terms of production cycle. If the production cycle is over 6 months, the value of change in semi-finished products is included in the gross industrial output value, otherwise it is not.

Difference in prices: The new method uses prices excluding value-added tax in the calculation of gross industrial output value, while the old method used prices including value-added tax.

**Total Assets** refer to all economic resources, in monetary term, these are owned or controlled by enterprises, including properties, creditor's equity and other economic rights of all forms. Classified by the degree of liquidity, total assets include working capitals, long-term investment, fixed assets, intangible assets, deferred assets and other assets. Data on this indicator can be obtained by the year-end figures of total assets in the *Assets and Liability Table* of accounting records of enterprises.

**Working Capital** refers to capital that an enterprise can cash or use during one year or one production cycle that may exceed one year, including cash and savings deposits of various forms, short-term investment, money receivable and prepaid money, inventories, etc.

**Annual Average Value of Working Capital** refers to the average value of all working capital of the enterprise during the reference period.

**Original Value of Fixed Assets** refers to the total value, in monetary terms, that an enterprise spent on fixed assets, through construction, purchase, installation, transformation, expansion or technical upgrading. Generally, it covers cost of purchase, packing, transportation and installation, etc.

**Annual Average of Net Value of Fixed Assets** refers to the average of the net value of fixed assets during the reference period, calculated with the following formula:

$$\text{Annual Average of Net Value of Fixed Assets} = \frac{\text{sum of net value of fixed assets at the beginning and at the end of each month from January to December}}{24}$$

Information on this indicator can be obtained from the beginning and ending figures of the original value of fixed assets and cumulative depreciation from the Assets and Liability Table of enterprises.

Net value of fixed assets refers to the original value of fixed assets minus depreciation over the years, i.e.:

Net value of fixed assets = original value of fixed assets - cumulative depreciation

**Total Liabilities** refer to payable liabilities of enterprises that have to be repaid in terms of money, assets or labour services. In terms of payment, it can be divided into liquid liabilities and long-term liabilities. Data on this item is obtained from the ending figures on total liabilities from the Assets and Liability Table from the enterprises.

**Owner's Equity** refers to the ownership of net assets of enterprise by its investors. Net assets equal total assets minus total liabilities of the enterprise, including the actual assets invested into the enterprise by investors, accumulation of capital and operating surplus and non-distributed profits. The enterprise's assets are less than its liabilities if the sum of owner's equity is smaller than zero.

**Revenue from Principal Business** refers to the annual accumulation of the corresponding item in the "profit table" of the accountant. For enterprises that do not follow the *2001 Enterprise Accounting Standards*, the year-end accumulation of revenue from the sales of products is used as a substitute.

**Cost of Principal Business** refers to the annual accumulation of the corresponding item in the "profit table" of the accountant. For enterprises that do not follow the *2001 Enterprise Accounting Standards*, the year-end accumulation of cost for the sales of products is used as a substitute.

**Tax and Extra Charges from Principal Business** refer to the annual accumulation of the corresponding item in the "profit table" of the accountant. For enterprises that do not follow the *2001 Enterprise Accounting Standards*, the year-end accumulation of tax and extra charges from the sales of products is used as a substitute.

**Total Profits** refer to the final achievement of production and operation activities of the enterprises, represented by total profits after deducting losses (loss is expressed by the negative figure). It is the sum of profits from operation, income from subsidies, investment earnings, net income from activities other than operation, and adjustment of profits and losses of previous years.

**Value-added Tax Payable in the Current Year** refers to the amount of the value-added tax which should be paid by the enterprises during the reference period. It is the sum of tax on sales, export rebate, and transferred tax on purchases of the current year, minus the tax on purchases of the current year. Value-added tax payable of small-size enterprises is determined by the taxable sales of the year multiplied by the tax rate.

**Average Annual Number of Employed Persons** Employed persons refer to all those who are employed in enterprises and receive remunerations there from, including currently working employees, retirees who are re-employed, teachers of local-run schools, as well as foreigners, staff from Hong Kong, Macao and Taiwan, part-time employees and persons with second job who are employed by the enterprise, and employees of other units temporarily working in the enterprises, but excluding former employees who left the enterprise with their employment records still being kept by the enterprises.

Average number of employed persons refers to the number of employee everyday during the reference period, calculated with the following formula:

$$\text{Monthly average number} = \frac{\text{sum of actual employees everyday in reference month}}{\text{number of calendar dates in reference month}}$$

$$\text{Quarterly average number} = \frac{\text{sum of monthly average number in reference quarter}}{3}$$

$$\text{Annual average number} = \frac{\text{sum of monthly average number in reference year}}{12}$$

**Ratio of Profits, Taxes and Interests to Average Assets** reflects the profit-making capability of all assets of the enterprise and is a key indicator manifesting the performance and management and evaluating the profit-making potential of the enterprise. It is calculated as follows:

$$\text{Ratio of Profits, Taxes and Interests to Average Assets (\%)} = \frac{\text{total profits + total taxes + interest payment}}{\text{average assets}} \times 100\%$$

In the above formula, total taxes is the sum of tax and extra charges on the sales of products and value-added tax payable; and average assets is the arithmetic mean of the sum of beginning assets and ending assets.

**Ratio of Debts to Assets** reflects both the operation risk and the capability of the enterprise in making use of the capital from the creditors. It is calculated as follows:

$$\text{Ratio of Debts to Assets (\%)} = \frac{\text{total debts}}{\text{total assets}} \times 100\%$$

Both assets and debts are figures at the end of the reference period.

**Turnover of Working Capital** refers to the number of times of turnover of working capital in a given period of time, which reflects the speed of the turnover of working capital of industrial enterprises, and is calculated as follows:

$$\text{Turnover of Working Capital} = \frac{\text{sales revenue of products}}{\text{average balance of total working capital}}$$

In the above formula, average balance of total working capital refers to the arithmetic mean of the sum of working capital at the beginning and at the end of the reference period.

**Ratio of Profits to Total Industrial Costs** refers to the ratio of profits realized in a given period to the total costs in the same period, which reflects the economic efficiency of input cost and is calculated as follows:

$$\text{Ratio of Profits to Total Industrial Cost (\%)} = \frac{\text{total profits}}{\text{total costs}} \times 100\%$$

Total costs in the above formula are the sum of cost of products sold, marketing cost, management cost and financial cost.

**Sales Ratio of Products** is an indicator reflecting the actual sale of industrial products, analyzing the production-selling and supply-demand relations. It is calculated as:

$$\text{Sales Ratio of Products (\%)} = \frac{\text{value of industrial sales}}{\text{gross industrial output value (current prices)}} \times 100\%$$

# 五、建筑业

# CHAPTER 5
# CONSTRUCTION

# 建 筑 业
# CONSTRUCTION

## 主 要 统 计 指 标
## MAJOR STATISTICAL INDICATORS

| | | | | |
|---|---|---|---|---|
| 2012年末建筑企业数 | Number of Construction Enterprise | 1 477 | 个 | unit |
| 2012年建筑业总产值 | Gross Output Value of Construction | 1 745.04 | 亿元 | 100 million yuan |
| 比上年增长 | Increase Over Last Year | 13.9 | % | |
| 2012年竣工产值 | Output Value of Buildings Completed | 1 386.01 | 亿元 | 100 million yuan |
| 比上年增长 | Increase Over Last Year | 23.0 | % | |
| 2012年房屋建筑施工面积 | Floor Space of Buildings Under Construction | 11 013.82 | 万平方米 | 10 000 sq.m. |
| 比上年增长 | Increase Over Last Year | 9.4 | % | |
| 2012年房屋建筑竣工面积 | Floor Space of Buildings Completed | 4 067.06 | 万平方米 | 10 000 sq.m. |
| 比上年增长 | Increase Over Last Year | 2.8 | % | |
| 2012年建筑业全员劳动生产率 | Overall Labor Productivity of Construction | 29.33 | 万元/人 | 10 000yuan/person |
| 比上年增长 | Increase Over Last Year | 14.3 | % | |

表5-1

# 分地区、分行业建筑业生产情况 (2012年)

| 指　　标 | | Item | | 全　市 Whole Municipality | 市　区 Urban Area |
|---|---|---|---|---|---|
| 企业数 | (个) | Number of Enterprises | (unit) | 1 477 | 902 |
| 签订的合同额 | (万元) | Contractual Value | (10 000yuan) | 28 613 500 | 17 948 508 |
| 建筑业总产值 | | Gross Output Value of Construction | | 17 450 359 | 11 132 246 |
| # 装饰装修产值 | | Decorate and Materials Construction | | 3 231 523 | 2 849 527 |
| # 在外省完成的产值 | | Output Value of Buildings Completed outside of Jiangsu province | | 3 001 487 | 2 564 312 |
| # 建筑工程 | | Construction | | 15 687 942 | 10 213 048 |
| 安装工程 | | Installation | | 1 584 841 | 836 338 |
| 其他产值 | | Others | | 177 577 | 82 860 |
| 竣工产值 | | Output Value of Buildings Completed | | 13 860 080 | 8 881 558 |
| 房屋建筑施工面积 | (万平方米) | Floor Space of Buildings Under Construction | (10 000sq.m) | 11 013.82 | 5 729.40 |
| # 本年新开工 | | Beginning Projects in this Year | | 4 574.28 | 2 393.67 |
| # 投标承包 | | Floor Space of Biding System | | 8 735.13 | 4 349.78 |
| # 本年新开工 | | Beginning Projects in this Year | | 3 533.01 | 1 777.52 |
| 房屋建筑竣工面积 | | Floor Space of Buildings Completed | | 4 067.06 | 2 178.87 |
| 自有施工机械设备年末总台数 | (台) | Number of Machinery and Equipment (year-end) | (unit) | 122 403 | 63 846 |
| 自有施工机械设备年末总功率 | (万千瓦) | Total Power of Machinery and Equipment | (10 000kw) | 262.26 | 131.03 |
| 自有施工机械设备年末净值 | (万元) | Net Value of Machinery and Equipment | (10 000yuan) | 446 605 | 241 571 |
| 平均从业人员 | (人) | Average Employed Persons | (person) | 595 063 | 359 731 |
| 全员劳动生产率 | (万元/人) | Overall Labor Productivity | (10 000yuan/person) | 29.33 | 30.95 |

## STATISTICS ON CONSTRUCTION BY REGION AND SECTOR (2012)

| 按地区分 Grouped by Region | | | | | 按行业分 Grouped by Sector | | | |
|---|---|---|---|---|---|---|---|---|
| # 吴江区 Wujiang District | 常熟 Changshu | 张家港 Zhangjiagang | 昆山 Kunshan | 太仓 Taicang | 房屋建筑业 Housing Construction | 土木工程建筑业 Civil Engineering Construction | 建筑安装业 Installation of Lines, Pipelines and Equipment | 建筑装饰和其他建筑业 Decoration and Other Construction |
| 111 | 163 | 132 | 199 | 81 | 374 | 325 | 301 | 477 |
| 1 862 841 | 2 256 926 | 2 862 840 | 4 773 205 | 772 021 | 15 169 806 | 7 231 748 | 1 554 372 | 4 657 574 |
| 1 245 207 | 1 591 631 | 1 588 537 | 2 562 507 | 575 438 | 8 290 731 | 3 941 798 | 1 267 259 | 3 950 571 |
| 34 502 | 176 376 | 33 174 | 112 928 | 59 518 | 89 447 | 8 382 | 22 306 | 3 111 388 |
| 15 542 | 90 109 | 97 487 | 225 494 | 24 085 | 350 592 | 1 012 193 | 205 156 | 1 433 546 |
| 1 177 415 | 1 516 579 | 1 436 685 | 2 018 985 | 502 645 | 8 186 311 | 3 711 300 | 321 907 | 3 468 424 |
| 44 203 | 67 436 | 120 626 | 517 512 | 42 929 | 61 946 | 137 345 | 934 521 | 451 030 |
| 23 590 | 7 616 | 31 225 | 26 011 | 29 864 | 42 474 | 93 154 | 10 831 | 31 118 |
| 1 071 650 | 1 307 754 | 1 228 615 | 1 935 408 | 506 745 | 6 700 882 | 2 621 158 | 1 418 280 | 3 119 759 |
| 1 202.63 | 1 383.21 | 1 541.76 | 1 950.99 | 408.45 | 10 632.04 | 252.65 | 101.57 | 27.55 |
| 360.00 | 602.49 | 643.69 | 762.54 | 171.90 | 4 423.36 | 111.03 | 31.76 | 8.12 |
| 747.23 | 1 227.52 | 1 377.46 | 1 568.70 | 211.67 | 8 482.43 | 175.67 | 55.25 | 21.79 |
| 220.43 | 508.85 | 561.16 | 606.97 | 78.51 | 3 456.35 | 61.70 | 10.13 | 4.83 |
| 477.38 | 571.00 | 564.96 | 565.80 | 186.42 | 3 889.73 | 110.36 | 47.51 | 19.46 |
| 7 871 | 18 667 | 19 736 | 15 794 | 4 360 | 56 778 | 20 794 | 26 984 | 17 847 |
| 18.42 | 33.36 | 20.35 | 69.38 | 8.13 | 141.72 | 81.16 | 13.53 | 25.84 |
| 30 420 | 48 179 | 55 987 | 80 082 | 20 786 | 179 325 | 188 232 | 20 797 | 58 251 |
| 53 629 | 58 922 | 60 828 | 83 459 | 32 123 | 359 570 | 91 680 | 37 498 | 106 315 |
| 23.22 | 27.01 | 26.12 | 30.70 | 17.91 | 23.06 | 43.00 | 33.80 | 37.16 |

表5-2

# 分登记注册类型建筑业生产情况 (2012年)

| 指　　标 | | Item | | 总　计 Total | 国有企业 State-owned Enterprises |
|---|---|---|---|---|---|
| 企业数 | (个) | Number of Enterprises | (unit) | 1 477 | 17 |
| 签订的合同额 | (万元) | Contractual Value | (10 000yuan ) | 28 613 500 | 3 502 023 |
| 建筑业总产值 | | Gross Output Value of Construction | | 17 450 359 | 1 242 888 |
| # 装饰装修产值 | | Decorate and Materials Construction | | 3 231 523 | 111 |
| # 在外省完成的产值 | | Output Value of Buildings Completed outside of Jiangsu province | | 3 001 487 | 859 582 |
| # 建筑工程 | | Construction | | 15 687 942 | 1 225 476 |
| 安装工程 | | Installation | | 1 584 841 | 17 413 |
| 其他产值 | | Others | | 177 577 | - |
| 竣工产值 | | Output Value of Buildings Completed | | 13 860 080 | 412 345 |
| 房屋建筑施工面积 | (万平方米) | Floor Space of Buildings Under Construction | (10 000sq.m) | 11 013.82 | 10.99 |
| # 本年新开工 | | Beginning Projects in this Year | | 4 574.28 | 6.84 |
| # 投标承包 | | Floor Space of Biding System | | 8 735.13 | 10.99 |
| # 本年新开工 | | Beginning Projects in this Year | | 3 533.01 | 6.84 |
| 房屋建筑竣工面积 | | Floor Space of Buildings Completed | | 4 067.06 | - |
| 自有施工机械设备年末总台数 | (台) | Number of Machinery and Equipment (year-end) | (unit) | 122 403 | 1 840 |
| 自有施工机械设备年末总功率 | (万千瓦) | Total Power of Machinery and Equipment | (10 000kw) | 262.26 | 12.63 |
| 自有施工机械设备年末净值 | (万元) | Net Value of Machinery and Equipment | (10 000yuan) | 446 605 | 24 942 |
| 平均从业人员 | (人) | Average Employed Persons | (person) | 595 063 | 15 327 |
| 全员劳动生产率 | (万元/人) | Overall Labor Productivity | (10 000yuan/person) | 29.33 | 81.09 |

# STATISTICS ON CONSTRUCTION BY TYPE OF REGISTRATION (2012)

| 集体企业 Collective-owned Enterprises | 股份合作制企业 Share-holding Cooperative Enterprises | 有限责任公司 Limited Liability Corporations | 股份有限公司 Share-holding Corporations Ltd. | 私营企业 Private Enterprises | 港澳台商投资企业 Enterprises With Investment From HongKong, Macao and Taiwan | 外商投资企业 Enterprises with Foreign Investment | 其它企业 Other Enterprises |
|---|---|---|---|---|---|---|---|
| 10 | 3 | 154 | 34 | 1 225 | 11 | 15 | 8 |
| 267 714 | 8 448 | 7 777 031 | 2 770 371 | 13 715 470 | 292 022 | 233 833 | 46 588 |
| 231 445 | 8 247 | 4 240 083 | 2 139 043 | 9 205 332 | 193 332 | 151 432 | 38 556 |
| 123 932 | – | 176 071 | 1 672 796 | 1 258 612 | – | – | – |
| 61 537 | – | 354 291 | 960 042 | 638 876 | 51 740 | 68 798 | 6 621 |
| 229 884 | 2 550 | 3 573 554 | 2 101 520 | 8 357 204 | 131 879 | 39 845 | 26 029 |
| 913 | 5 697 | 626 243 | 36 048 | 721 333 | 56 934 | 108 310 | 11 950 |
| 648 | – | 40 286 | 1 476 | 126 795 | 4 519 | 3 276 | 577 |
| 217 779 | 7 507 | 3 850 701 | 1 593 012 | 7 503 832 | 136 370 | 106 364 | 32 169 |
| 55.45 | 4.08 | 3 169.70 | 326.27 | 7 300.32 | 91.39 | 37.78 | 17.84 |
| 34.95 | 2.58 | 1 395.21 | 133.81 | 2 927.76 | 44.31 | 15.76 | 13.06 |
| 52.85 | – | 2 955.05 | 222.83 | 5 424.87 | 61.07 | – | 7.47 |
| 32.35 | – | 1 284.19 | 100.80 | 2 076.01 | 29.58 | – | 3.24 |
| 26.18 | 1.98 | 1 056.80 | 107.29 | 2 801.26 | 45.53 | 17.33 | 10.69 |
| 1 009 | 89 | 31 277 | 4 225 | 82 563 | 707 | 141 | 552 |
| 2.61 | 0.03 | 38.12 | 4.97 | 201.56 | 1.81 | 0.08 | 0.45 |
| 6 138 | 20 | 95 726 | 18 165 | 294 855 | 5 360 | 244 | 1 153 |
| 6 139 | 189 | 136 093 | 44 418 | 379 883 | 6 660 | 4 334 | 2 020 |
| 37.70 | 43.64 | 31.16 | 48.16 | 24.23 | 29.03 | 34.94 | 19.09 |

表5-3

# 分地区、分行业建筑业财务状况 (2012年)

单位：万元

| 指　　标 | Item | 全　市<br>Whole Municipality | 按 | |
|---|---|---|---|---|
| | | | 市　区<br>Urban Area | #吴江区<br>WujiangDistrict |
| **年末资产负债** | **Asset and Liabilities at Year-end** | | | |
| 流动资产 | Circulating Assets | 14 573 635 | 7 948 029 | 748 466 |
| # 存　货 | Stocks | 4 046 612 | 1 592 896 | 129 892 |
| 固定资产小计 | Fixed Assets | 1 075 050 | 664 476 | 66 229 |
| 固定资产原价 | Original Value of Fixed Assets | 1 520 686 | 912 585 | 92 142 |
| 累计折旧 | Accumulative Total Depreciation | 646 841 | 387 517 | 38 875 |
| # 本年折旧 | Depreciation Within the Year | 132 556 | 75 205 | 6 292 |
| 在建工程 | Project Under Construction | 159 078 | 113 916 | 9 296 |
| 资产总计 | Total Assets | 16 703 662 | 9 237 619 | 835 971 |
| 流动负债 | Liquid Liabilities | 11 079 749 | 5 668 446 | 441 440 |
| 非流动负债合计 | Total Non Liquid Liabilities | 288 436 | 235 137 | 13 118 |
| 负债合计 | Total Liabilities | 11 457 624 | 5 960 811 | 465 009 |
| 所有者权益 | Creditors' Equity | 5 245 693 | 3 276 808 | 370 962 |
| # 实收资本 | Actual Capital Hold | 4 084 725 | 1 743 233 | 216 382 |
| 国家资本 | State Capital | 111 284 | 76 463 | 3 414 |
| 集体资本 | Collective Capital | 61 147 | 37 779 | 4 977 |
| 法人资本 | Corporation Capital | 846 937 | 550 846 | 51 216 |
| 个人资本 | Individual Capital | 2 977 201 | 1 002 642 | 147 518 |
| 港、澳、台资本 | Capital from HongKong, Macao and Taiwan | 33 757 | 33 059 | 9 258 |
| 外商资本 | Foreign Capital | 54 400 | 42 445 | - |
| **损益及分配** | **Expenditure, Income and Distribution** | | | |
| 主营业务收入 | Main Business Income | 16 642 254 | 10 751 475 | 1 284 998 |
| 主营业务成本 | Main Business Cost | 14 641 689 | 9 466 034 | 1 144 852 |
| 主营业务税金及附加 | Main Business Taxes and Surcharges | 519 460 | 333 801 | 42 457 |
| 其他业务利润 | Profits of Other Business | 31 966 | 21 159 | 991 |
| 管理费用 | Management Fee | 599 418 | 376 176 | 35 323 |
| 财务费用 | Financial Expenses | 116 750 | 61 920 | 8 734 |
| 营业利润 | Operating Profit | 713 200 | 457 432 | 47 526 |
| 利润总额 | Total Profit | 731 311 | 465 273 | 54 838 |
| 应交所得税 | Income Tax Payable | 162 125 | 97 978 | 14 165 |
| **工资、福利费** | Wages and Welfare Expenscs | | | |
| 应付职工薪酬(本年贷方累计发生额) | Employee Compensation Payable ( the Cumulative Amount of Credits ) | 2 142 365 | 1 314 263 | 197 426 |

# FINANCIAL CONDITIONS OF CONSTRUCTION BY REGION AND SECTOR (2012)

(10 000yuan)

| 地区分 Grouped by Region | | | | 按行业分 Grouped by Sector | | | |
|---|---|---|---|---|---|---|---|
| 常熟 Changshu | 张家港 Zhangjiagang | 昆山 Kunshan | 太仓 Taicang | 房屋建筑业 Housing Construction | 土木工程建筑业 Civil Engineering Construction | 建筑安装业 Installation of Lines, Pipelines and Equipment | 建筑装饰和其他建筑业 Decoration and Other Construction |
| | | | | | | | |
| 1 684 931 | 1 680 518 | 2 586 424 | 673 733 | 5 892 169 | 4 172 142 | 1 625 765 | 2 883 559 |
| 630 291 | 746 635 | 876 470 | 200 321 | 1 981 465 | 1 133 257 | 603 403 | 328 488 |
| 76 965 | 118 982 | 160 324 | 54 303 | 342 988 | 348 812 | 180 377 | 202 872 |
| 134 089 | 165 546 | 243 623 | 64 843 | 454 023 | 618 723 | 174 941 | 272 998 |
| 60 398 | 70 818 | 102 400 | 25 707 | 178 534 | 311 060 | 58 193 | 99 053 |
| 9 489 | 20 166 | 21 882 | 5 814 | 36 487 | 62 544 | 13 985 | 19 540 |
| 1 388 | 16 945 | 13 238 | 13 591 | 50 740 | 31 168 | 59 529 | 17 641 |
| 1 835 539 | 1 839 300 | 2 992 919 | 798 284 | 6 631 608 | 4 883 856 | 1 938 971 | 3 249 227 |
| 1 346 648 | 1 401 442 | 2 131 224 | 531 988 | 4 658 277 | 3 140 963 | 1 259 079 | 2 021 430 |
| 10 889 | 17 133 | 10 043 | 15 233 | 50 578 | 90 386 | 23 365 | 124 107 |
| 1 372 219 | 1 425 404 | 2 148 108 | 551 082 | 4 738 844 | 3 250 307 | 1 299 715 | 2 168 758 |
| 463 320 | 413 551 | 844 811 | 247 203 | 1 892 764 | 1 633 549 | 639 256 | 1 080 124 |
| 289 665 | 258 541 | 533 883 | 1 259 402 | 1 264 051 | 886 077 | 378 588 | 1 556 009 |
| 20 689 | 10 832 | 3 300 | - | 3 110 | 91 676 | 10 904 | 5 595 |
| 8 768 | 5 700 | 8 451 | 450 | 14 851 | 35 645 | 176 | 10 475 |
| 83 593 | 55 302 | 121 547 | 35 649 | 325 010 | 272 141 | 114 833 | 134 953 |
| 176 615 | 186 707 | 390 160 | 1 221 076 | 910 242 | 471 269 | 211 575 | 1 384 114 |
| - | - | 698 | - | 3 138 | 7 720 | 22 166 | 733 |
| - | - | 9 727 | 2 228 | 7 700 | 7 626 | 18 935 | 20 139 |
| | | | | | | | |
| 1 374 801 | 1 336 728 | 2 560 483 | 618 768 | 7 625 836 | 3 986 665 | 1 359 871 | 3 669 882 |
| 1 209 197 | 1 174 676 | 2 263 149 | 528 634 | 6 924 911 | 3 500 137 | 1 126 390 | 3 090 251 |
| 46 861 | 41 191 | 77 707 | 19 900 | 252 128 | 116 816 | 39 218 | 111 298 |
| 4 217 | 1 630 | 4 395 | 565 | 10 670 | 8 887 | 6 821 | 5 588 |
| 46 972 | 56 577 | 93 897 | 25 796 | 194 934 | 160 201 | 104 880 | 139 403 |
| 11 347 | 12 129 | 26 004 | 5 350 | 62 680 | 38 789 | 7 078 | 8 202 |
| 63 254 | 52 037 | 104 676 | 35 802 | 204 368 | 171 757 | 79 971 | 257 104 |
| 72 151 | 52 551 | 105 716 | 35 620 | 208 326 | 181 983 | 81 636 | 259 367 |
| 18 593 | 12 107 | 25 682 | 7 765 | 47 405 | 41 879 | 18 325 | 54 516 |
| | | | | | | | |
| 221 055 | 219 917 | 302 380 | 84 751 | 1 327 894 | 266 134 | 116 389 | 431 947 |

表5-4

# 分登记注册类型建筑业财务状况（2012年）

单位：万元

| 指　　标 | Item | 总　计 Total | 国有企业 State-owned Enterprises |
|---|---|---|---|
| **年末资产负债** | **Asset and Liabilities at Year-end** | | |
| 流动资产 | Circulating Assets | 14 573 635 | 1 079 934 |
| # 存　货 | Stocks | 4 046 612 | 290 225 |
| 固定资产小计 | Fixed Assets | 1 075 050 | 65 099 |
| 固定资产原价 | Original Value of Fixed Assets | 1 520 686 | 139 470 |
| 累计折旧 | Accumulative Total Depreciation | 646 841 | 89 553 |
| # 本年折旧 | Depreciation Within the Year | 132 556 | 24 034 |
| 在建工程 | Project Under Construction | 159 078 | 12 792 |
| 资产总计 | Total Assets | 16 703 662 | 1 208 069 |
| 流动负债 | Liquid Liabilities | 11 079 749 | 790 311 |
| 非流动负债合计 | Total Non Liquid Liabilities | 288 436 | 52 431 |
| 负债合计 | Total Liabilities | 11 457 624 | 843 050 |
| 所有者权益 | Creditors' Equity | 5 245 693 | 365 020 |
| # 实收资本 | Actual Capital Hold | 4 084 725 | 103 817 |
| 国家资本 | State Capital | 111 284 | 58 817 |
| 集体资本 | Collective Capital | 61 147 | - |
| 法人资本 | Corporation Capital | 846 937 | 45 000 |
| 个人资本 | Individual Capital | 2 977 201 | - |
| 港、澳、台资本 | Capital from HongKong, Macao and Taiwan | 33 757 | - |
| 外商资本 | Foreign Capital | 54 400 | - |
| **损益及分配** | **Expenditure, Income and Distribution** | | |
| 主营业务收入 | Main Business Income | 16 642 254 | 1 321 298 |
| 主营业务成本 | Main Business Cost | 14 641 689 | 1 220 746 |
| 主营业务税金及附加 | Main Business Taxes and Surcharges | 519 460 | 32 548 |
| 其他业务利润 | Profits of Other Business | 31 966 | 565 |
| 管理费用 | Management Fee | 599 418 | 40 888 |
| 财务费用 | Financial Expenses | 116 750 | 4 417 |
| 营业利润 | Operating Profit | 713 200 | 22 757 |
| 利润总额 | Total Profit | 731 311 | 22 844 |
| 应交所得税 | Income Tax Payable | 162 125 | 4 207 |
| **工资、福利费** | Wages and Welfare Expenses | | |
| 应付职工薪酬(本年贷方累计发生额) | Employee Compensation Payable ( the Cumulative Amount of Credits ) | 2 142 365 | 55 137 |

# FINANCIAL CONDITIONS OF CONSTRUCTION BY TYPE OF REGISTRATION (2012)

(10 000yuan)

| 集体企业 Collective-owned Enterprises | 股份合作制企业 Share-holding Cooperative Enterprises | 有限责任公司 Limited Liability Corporations | 股份有限公司 Share-holding Corporations Ltd. | 私营企业 Private Enterprises | 港澳台商投资企业 Enterprises With Investment From HongKong, Macao and Taiwan | 外商投资企业 Enterprises with Foreign Investment | 其它企业 Other Enterprises |
|---|---|---|---|---|---|---|---|
| | | | | | | | |
| 236 364 | 4 026 | 3 598 185 | 1 795 549 | 7 468 074 | 195 011 | 144 524 | 51 968 |
| 110 077 | 599 | 1 365 689 | 137 599 | 2 104 679 | 20 139 | 13 172 | 4 434 |
| 6 656 | 396 | 205 586 | 101 683 | 664 586 | 17 478 | 9 777 | 3 789 |
| 22 715 | 723 | 315 319 | 120 441 | 884 840 | 21 494 | 12 359 | 3 326 |
| 16 304 | 326 | 150 330 | 40 851 | 334 205 | 9 295 | 4 708 | 1 268 |
| 1 481 | 44 | 26 496 | 7 485 | 70 408 | 1 433 | 668 | 505 |
| 246 | – | 34 599 | 21 053 | 81 256 | 5 279 | 2 123 | 1 731 |
| 278 326 | 4 582 | 4 009 696 | 2 074 084 | 8 680 879 | 232 767 | 158 182 | 57 076 |
| 223 750 | 160 | 3 072 287 | 1 300 697 | 5 480 957 | 114 412 | 81 863 | 15 312 |
| 800 | – | 44 024 | 121 104 | 41 828 | 13 608 | – | 14 640 |
| 224 550 | 1 510 | 3 128 925 | 1 421 801 | 5 586 022 | 133 021 | 84 245 | 34 501 |
| 53 776 | 3 073 | 880 425 | 652 283 | 3 094 857 | 99 746 | 73 937 | 22 576 |
| 22 339 | 1 800 | 470 555 | 178 086 | 3 197 274 | 57 594 | 33 453 | 19 808 |
| 500 | 4 | 41 033 | 6 862 | 4 068 | – | – | – |
| 14 111 | – | 37 077 | – | 9 959 | – | – | – |
| 7 402 | – | 175 126 | 47 988 | 557 443 | 4 777 | 523 | 8 677 |
| 325 | 1 797 | 216 958 | 103 097 | 2 625 804 | 17 272 | 817 | 11 131 |
| – | – | 360 | – | – | 31 899 | 1 497 | – |
| – | – | – | 20 139 | – | 3 646 | 30 615 | – |
| | | | | | | | |
| 212 018 | 8 247 | 3 851 620 | 2 036 027 | 8 785 713 | 217 851 | 172 013 | 37 467 |
| 187 932 | 6 932 | 3 427 380 | 1 693 353 | 7 737 453 | 190 641 | 145 133 | 32 119 |
| 3 179 | 293 | 118 786 | 66 249 | 288 415 | 4 706 | 4 049 | 1 236 |
| 1 | – | 7 230 | 3 858 | 17 264 | 78 | 2 970 | – |
| 5 396 | 418 | 146 298 | 45 934 | 337 416 | 9 629 | 12 119 | 1 319 |
| 2 863 | – | 23 076 | 2 506 | 79 175 | 3 603 | 720 | 390 |
| 12 723 | 599 | 147 413 | 181 236 | 325 892 | 6 532 | 14 375 | 1 673 |
| 12 308 | 597 | 157 096 | 182 257 | 327 962 | 12 464 | 14 108 | 1 675 |
| 3 238 | 116 | 38 023 | 31 919 | 79 662 | 1 645 | 2 755 | 561 |
| | | | | | | | |
| 17 828 | 485 | 588 066 | 258 717 | 1 190 732 | 12 072 | 12 846 | 6 482 |

表5-5

# 劳务分包建筑企业生产经营情况 (2012年) BUSINESS STATUS OF SUBCONTRACTING CONSTRUCTION ENTERPRISES (2012)

单位：万元 (10 000 yuan)

| 类别 | Type | 企业数（个） Number of Enterprises (unit) | 建筑业总产值 Gross Output Value of Construction | 营业收入合计 Total Business Revenue | #主营业务收入 Major Business Revenue | 资产合计 Total Assets | 负债合计 Total Liabilities |
|---|---|---|---|---|---|---|---|
| **全　市** | **Whole Municipality** | **93** | **200 405** | **176 524** | **176 475** | **90 375** | **73 838** |
| **按地区分** | **Grouped by Region** | | | | | | |
| 市　区 | Urban Area | 25 | 15 316 | 16 112 | 16 112 | 20 136 | 16 879 |
| # 吴江区 | Wujiang District | 1 | 150 | 135 | 135 | 72 | 20 |
| 常　熟 | Changshu | 15 | 5 003 | 5 141 | 5 093 | 10 259 | 4 187 |
| 张家港 | Zhangjiagang | 41 | 169 636 | 149 391 | 149 390 | 52 480 | 46 871 |
| 昆　山 | Kunshan | 8 | 6 396 | 1 825 | 1 825 | 5 270 | 4 978 |
| 太　仓 | Taicang | 4 | 4 055 | 4 055 | 4 055 | 2 230 | 924 |
| **按行业分** | **Grouped by Sector** | | | | | | |
| 房屋建筑业 | Housing Construction | 22 | 51 988 | 60 032 | 59 984 | 36 360 | 32 618 |
| 土木工程建筑业 | Civil Engineering Construction | 2 | 4 576 | 10 | 10 | 4 978 | 4 803 |
| 建筑安装业 | Construction Installation | 11 | 25 987 | 6 699 | 6 699 | 3 366 | 1 839 |
| 建筑装饰和其他建筑业 | Decoration and Other Construction | 58 | 117 855 | 109 783 | 109 782 | 45 671 | 34 578 |

表5-5续表 Continued

单位：万元 (10 000 yuan)

| 类别 | Type | 实收资本 Actual Capital Hold | 利润总额 Total Profits | 税金及附加 Taxes and Extra Charges Project Settlement Accounts | 从业人员(人) Number of Employed Persons (person) | 计算劳动生产率人数(人) Number of Persons Overall Labor Productivity (person) | 从业人员劳动报酬 Laborers' Remuneration of Employed Persons |
|---|---|---|---|---|---|---|---|
| **全　市** | **Whole Municipality** | **9 390** | **2 840** | **5 996** | **46 329** | **40 971** | **154 951** |
| **按地区分** | **Grouped by Region** | | | | | | |
| 市　区 | Urban Area | 2 548 | 259 | 582 | 1 574 | 1 495 | 5 175 |
| # 吴江区 | Wujiang District | 50 | 7 | 5 | 24 | 20 | 79 |
| 常　熟 | Changshu | 1 998 | 121 | 196 | 394 | 343 | 1 855 |
| 张家港 | Zhangjiagang | 3 908 | 2 262 | 4 991 | 41 940 | 37 196 | 141 447 |
| 昆　山 | Kunshan | 230 | 7 | 93 | 1 955 | 1 590 | 5 519 |
| 太　仓 | Taicang | 707 | 192 | 134 | 466 | 347 | 955 |
| **按行业分** | **Grouped by Sector** | | | | | | |
| 房屋建筑业 | Housing Construction | 2 704 | 605 | 2 029 | 12 144 | 11 380 | 47 225 |
| 土木工程建筑业 | Civil Engineering Construction | 150 | -15 | – | 1 465 | 1 241 | 4 576 |
| 建筑安装业 | Construction Installation | 1 100 | 1 151 | 231 | 1 217 | 1 167 | 4 194 |
| 建筑装饰和其他建筑业 | Decoration and Other Construction | 5 437 | 1 099 | 3 736 | 31 503 | 27 183 | 98 956 |

表5-6

# 建筑业总产值三十强企业（2012年）
# TOP 30 ENTERPRISES OF THE GROSS OUTPUT VALUE OF CONSTRUCTION (2012)

| 序　号<br>No. | 企业名称<br>Name of Enterprises | 所在地区<br>Location | 资质等级<br>Qualification Grade |
|---|---|---|---|
| 1 | 苏州金螳螂建筑装饰股份有限公司 | 工业园区 | 专业承包一级 |
| 2 | 苏州二建建筑集团有限公司 | 相城区 | 总承包特级 |
| 3 | 中铁四局集团第二工程有限公司 | 相城区 | 总承包一级 |
| 4 | 苏州第一建筑集团有限公司 | 姑苏区 | 总承包特级 |
| 5 | 中铁二十局集团第一工程有限公司 | 高新区、虎丘区 | 总承包一级 |
| 6 | 苏州中材建设有限公司 | 昆　山 | 总承包一级 |
| 7 | 江苏金土木建设集团有限公司 | 常　熟 | 总承包一级 |
| 8 | 中交一公局第二工程有限公司 | 高新区、虎丘区 | 总承包一级 |
| 9 | 苏州美瑞德建筑装饰有限公司 | 姑苏区 | 专业承包一级 |
| 10 | 苏州嘉盛建设工程有限公司 | 吴中区 | 总承包一级 |
| 11 | 苏州柯利达装饰股份有限公司 | 高新区、虎丘区 | 专业承包一级 |
| 12 | 江苏兴港建设集团有限公司 | 张家港 | 总承包一级 |
| 13 | 江苏金厦建设集团有限公司 | 张家港 | 总承包一级 |
| 14 | 苏州建鑫建设集团有限公司 | 高新区、虎丘区 | 总承包一级 |
| 15 | 苏州第五建筑集团有限公司 | 姑苏区 | 总承包一级 |
| 16 | 振华建设集团有限公司 | 昆　山 | 总承包一级 |
| 17 | 江苏德丰建设集团有限公司 | 张家港 | 总承包一级 |
| 18 | 吴江市建设工程（集团）有限公司 | 吴江区 | 总承包一级 |
| 19 | 江苏华新建设工程有限公司 | 吴中区 | 总承包一级 |
| 20 | 江苏苏鑫装饰（集团）公司 | 相城区 | 专业承包一级 |
| 21 | 苏州苏明装饰有限公司 | 相城区 | 专业承包一级 |
| 22 | 江苏城南建设集团有限公司 | 昆　山 | 总承包一级 |
| 23 | 江苏宏鑫路桥建设有限公司 | 昆　山 | 总承包一级 |
| 24 | 江苏五环建设有限公司 | 昆　山 | 总承包一级 |
| 25 | 张家港市市政工程有限公司 | 张家港 | 总承包一级 |
| 26 | 苏州建设（集团）有限责任公司 | 姑苏区 | 总承包一级 |
| 27 | 江苏永丰建设集团有限公司 | 常　熟 | 总承包一级 |
| 28 | 苏州金澄实业有限公司 | 高新区、虎丘区 | 总承包三级 |
| 29 | 江苏通力建设工程有限公司 | 太　仓 | 总承包一级 |
| 30 | 江苏汇丰建筑安装工程有限公司 | 常　熟 | 总承包一级 |

# 主 要 统 计 指 标 解 释

**建筑业统计单位** 指从事房屋、构筑物建造和设备安装活动的法人企业。建筑业法人企业应具有建筑业资质并能够独立核算，同时其应具备以下条件：①依法成立，有自己的名称、组织机构和场所，能够承担民事责任；②独立拥有和使用资产，承担负债，有权与其他单位签订合同；③独立核算盈亏，能够编制资产负债表。

**建筑业总产值** 是以货币形式表现的建筑业企业在一定时期内生产的建筑业产品和提供的服务的总和。建筑业总产值包括：

(1) 建筑工程产值：指列入建筑工程预算内的各种工程价值。

(2) 安装工程产值：指设备安装工程价值，不包括被安装设备本身的价值。

(3) 其他产值：建筑业总产值中除建筑工程、安装工程以外的产值。包括房屋构筑物修理产值、非标准设备制造产值、总包企业向分包企业收取的管理费以及不能明确划分的施工活动所完成的产值。

a.房屋构筑物修理产值：指房屋和构筑物修理所完成的产值，但不包括被修理房屋、构筑物本身价值和生产设备的修理产值。

b.非标准设备制造产值：指加工制造没有定型的非标准生产设备的加工费和原材料价值(如化工厂、炼油厂用的各种罐、槽，矿井生产统一使用的各种漏斗、三角槽、阀门等)以及附属加工厂为本企业承建工程制作的非标准设备的价值。

**房屋建筑施工面积** 指在报告期内施过工的全部房屋建筑面积，包括本期新开工的房屋面积、上期施工跨入本期继续施工的房屋面积、上期停缓建在本期恢复施工的房屋面积、本期竣工的房屋面积及本期施工后又停缓建的房屋面积。

**房屋建筑竣工面积** 指在报告期内房屋建筑按照设计要求全部完工，达到了使用条件，经验收鉴定合格，正式移交使用单位的房屋建筑面积。

**自有机械设备年末总台数** 指归本企业(或单位)所有，属于本企业（或单位）固定资产的生产性机械设备年末总台数。包括施工机械、生产设备、运输设备以及其他设备。

**自有机械设备年末总功率** 指本企业(或单位)自有施工机械、生产设备、运输设备以及其他设备等列为在册固定资产的生产性机械设备年末总功率，按设定能力或查定能力计算。包括机械本身的动力和为该机械服务的单独动力设备，如电动机等。计量单位用千瓦，动力换算可按 1 马力＝ 0.735 千瓦折合成千瓦数。电焊机、变压器、锅炉不计算动力。

**主营业务收入** 指企业(或单位)按承包工程实现的工程价款结算收入，以及向发包单位收取的除工程价款以外的按规定列作营业收入的各种款项，如临时设施费、劳动保险费、施工机械调迁费等以及向发包单位收取的各种索赔款。

# EXPLANATORY NOTES ON MAIN STATISTICAL INDICATORS

**Statistical Unit in the Construction Industry** refers to a corporate enterprise engaged in the construction of buildings and structures and in the installation of equipment. A corporate construction enterprise should have qualification certificates with independent accounting system, and should meet the following 3 requirements: a) being set up in line with relevant legal basis, having its full name, organization and location, and capable of taking civil liabilities; b) independently possessing and using its assets and assuming its liabilities, and entitled to sign contracts with other institutions; and c) making independent accounts of its profits and losses, and capable of compiling its own balance sheet.

**Gross Output Value of Construction** refers to total of construction products and services, expressed in money terms, produced or rendered by construction and installation enterprises during a given period of time. It includes:

(1) Output value of construction projects: the value of projects covered by the project budgets;

(2) Output value of installation projects: the value of the installation of equipment, (excluding the value of the equipment to be installed);

(3) Other output values: the output value of construction industry apart from that of construction projects and installation projects. It includes: output value of repair of buildings and structures; output value of non-standard equipment manufacturing; overhead expenses received by contracted enterprises from the sub-contracted enterprises and the completed output value of construction activities for which there is no clear definition.

a. Output value of repair of buildings and structures: the value created through the repairs of buildings or structures. It does not include the value of buildings or structures being repaired and the value of the repair of production equipment;

b. Output value of manufactured non-standard equipment: the value of non-standard production equipment, including raw materials and manufacturing cost, made for the construction project (i.e., chemical plant; kettles or tanks used by refineries; various fillers, triangle tanks, valves used by mines). It also includes the output value of equipment manufactured by subsidiary workshops.

**Floor Space of Buildings Under Construction** refers to floor space of buildings under construction during the reference period, including the floor space of buildings for which construction has newly started; buildings for which construction has started earlier and is continuing during the reference period; and buildings for which construction has been suspended earlier but has restarted during the reference period; buildings completed during the reference period; and buildings under construction but construction has subsequently been during the reference period.

**Floor Space of Buildings Completed** refers to the floor space of buildings that are completed in the reference period in accordance with the requirements of the design, up to the standard for being put into use, and having been checked and accepted by departments concerned as qualified ones.

**Total Number of Machinery and Equipment Owned by the End of Year** refers to the number of machines and equipment owned by the enterprises, and listed as the fixed assets of the enterprises by the end of the year, including machinery and equipment for construction, production and transportation.

**Total Power of Machinery and Equipment Owned by the End of Year** refers to the total power of machinery and equipment owned by the enterprises, and listed as the fixed assets of the enterprises by the end of the year, including machinery and equipment for construction, production and transportation. The power of the machinery is calculated on basis of the designed or verified capacity, covering the power of the machinery/equipment and the separate power equipment serving the machinery/equipment (such as electric motors), but excluding welders, transformers and boilers. The unit used for the calculation of power is kilowatt, with horsepower converted to kilowatt by 1 horsepower=0.735kilowatt.

**Main Business Income** refers to the income received by the construction enterprise from the contracted project through settlement procedures, and other charges to the contractor as operational costs in addition to the value of the project, such as temporary facility fee, labour insurance premium , moving cost of construction equipment, as well as various types of claims to the contractor.

# 六、运输邮电业

# CHAPTER 6 TRANSPORTATION, POST AND TELECOMMUNICATION

# 运　输　邮电业
# TRANSPORTATION, POST AND TELECOMMUNICATION

## 主要统计指标
## MAJOR STATISTICAL INDICATORS

| | | | | |
|---|---|---|---|---|
| 2012年全社会公路水运客运量 | Total Passenger Traffic of Highways and Waterways | 68 998 | 万人次 | 10 000 person-times |
| 比上年增长 | Increase Over Last Year | 8.2 | % | |
| 2012年全社会公路水运货运量 | Total Freight Traffic of Highways and Waterways | 17 325 | 万吨 | 10 000 tons |
| 比上年增长 | Increase Over Last Year | 11.0 | % | |
| 2012年苏州港货物吞吐量 | Cargo Handled at Suzhou Ports | 42 801 | 万吨 | 10 000 tons |
| 比上年增长 | Increase Over Last Year | 12.6 | % | |
| 2012年苏州港集装箱吞吐量 | Volume of Container Handled at Suzhou Ports | 586.35 | 万标箱 | 10 000 teu |
| 比上年增长 | Increase Over Last Year | 25.2 | % | |
| 2012年末私家车拥有量 | Number of Private Motor Vehicles | 144.54 | 万辆 | 10 000 coach |
| 比上年增长 | Increase Over Last Year | 20.6 | % | |
| 2012年邮电业务总收入 | Total Revenue of Postal and Telecommunication Services | 207.66 | 亿元 | 100 million yuan |
| 比上年增长 | Increase Over Last Year | 2.0 | % | |
| 2012年末移动电话用户 | Number of Mobile Telephone Subscribers | 1 554.52 | 万户 | 10 000 households |
| 比上年增长 | Increase Over Last Year | 6.5 | % | |
| 2012年末宽带接入用户 | Subscriber of Broad Band | 283.57 | 万户 | 10 000 households |
| 比上年增长 | Increase Over Last Year | 28.6 | % | |

表6-1

# 部分年份全社会交通运输量
# TOTAL TRAFFIC OF PARTIAL YEARS

| 项　　目 | | Item | | 1990年 | 2000年 | 2010年 | 2011年 | 2012年 |
|---|---|---|---|---|---|---|---|---|
| **铁　路** | | **Railway** | | | | | | |
| 旅客发送量 | (万人次) | Number of Passengers Dispatched | (10 000 person-times) | 755.78 | 940.23 | 2 044.68 | 2 274.68 | 2 627.98 |
| 市　区 | | Urban Area | | 673.20 | 726.78 | 1 445.61 | 1 604.59 | 1 868.00 |
| 昆　山 | | Kunshan | | 82.58 | 213.45 | 599.07 | 670.09 | 759.98 |
| 货物发送量 | (万吨) | Volume of Freight Dispatched | (10 000 tons) | 116.43 | 159.37 | 90.94 | 93.00 | 93.78 |
| 市　区 | | Urban Area | | 96.19 | 134.63 | 70.89 | 72.13 | 75.65 |
| 昆　山 | | Kunshan | | 20.24 | 24.74 | 20.05 | 20.87 | 18.13 |
| 货物到达量 | | Volume of Freight Arrived | | 557.97 | 391.51 | 400.06 | 406.34 | 311.43 |
| 市　区 | | Urban Area | | 455.37 | 332.13 | 353.76 | 355.13 | 272.94 |
| 昆　山 | | Kunshan | | 102.60 | 59.38 | 46.30 | 51.22 | 38.49 |
| **公　路** | | **Highways** | | | | | | |
| 客运量 | (万人次) | Passenger Traffic | (10 000 person-times) | 6 517 | 18 447 | 56 392 | 63 699 | 68 895 |
| 货运量 | (万吨) | Freight Traffic | (10 000 tons) | 746 | 4 567 | 12 768 | 14 798 | 16 441 |
| 旅客周转量 | (万人公里) | Passenger-kilometers | (10 000 person-km) | 218 521 | 1 009 983 | 2 411 917 | 2 745 297 | 3 076 263 |
| 货物周转量 | (万吨公里) | Freight Ton-kilometers | (10 000 ton-km) | 26 187 | 245 987 | 1 037 797 | 1 200 220 | 1 357 255 |
| **水　运** | | **Waterways** | | | | | | |
| 客运量 | (万人次) | Passenger Traffic | (10 000 person-times) | 247 | 112 | 83 | 94 | 103 |
| 货运量 | (万吨) | Freight Traffic | (10 000 tons) | 2 465 | 3 248 | 649 | 804 | 884 |
| 旅客周转量 | (万人公里) | Passenger-kilometers | (10 000 person-km) | 14 279 | 3 571 | 924 | 1 042 | 1 128 |
| 货物周转量 | (万吨公里) | Freight Ton-kilometers | (10 000 ton-km) | 182 386 | 212 929 | 199 590 | 298 155 | 347 829 |
| 地方港口吞吐量 | (万吨) | Cargo Handled at Local Ports | (10 000 tons) | | 8 028 | 37 382 | 42 859 | 48 302 |
| # 张家港港口吞吐量 | | Cargo Handled at Zhangjiagang Port | | 360 | 2 025 | 19 779 | 23 038 | 24 226 |

注：2009年起全社会公路水运运输量统计口径调整为营运性运输量。
Note:The 2009 statistics caliber of the volume of road and water transport of the whole society was adjusted to the trading volume of traffic.

表6-2

# 部分年份公路和航道通航里程
# LENGTH OF HIGHWAYS AND NAVIGABLE INLAND WATERWAYS OF PARTIAL YEARS

| 项　目 | Item | 1990年 | 2000年 | 2010年 | 2011年 | 2012年 |
|---|---|---|---|---|---|---|
| **一、公路总里程　(公里)** | **Total Length of Highways　(km)** | **1 532** | **1 925** | **12 754.2** | **13 047.4** | **13 089.5** |
| 1. 按技术等级分 | Rated by Technical Standards | | | | | |
| 高　速 | Express-way | – | 70 | 535.1 | 535.1 | 535.1 |
| 一　级 | A Qualification | – | 231 | 1 506.8 | 1 641.8 | 1 652.8 |
| 二　级 | B Qualification | 434 | 690 | 3 600.1 | 3 858.7 | 3 900.6 |
| 三　级 | C Qualification | 133 | 534 | 2 688.4 | 2 864.1 | 2 891.1 |
| 四　级 | D Qualification | 965 | 400 | 4 423.8 | 4 147.8 | 4 110.0 |
| 2.按行政等级分 | Grouped by Grade of Administration | | | | | |
| 国　道 | State Highway | 242 | 322 | 496.3 | 496.3 | 496.3 |
| 省　道 | Provincial Highway | 237 | 256 | 794.1 | 794.1 | 794.1 |
| 县　道 | County Highway | 213 | 916 | 1 687.5 | 1 744.3 | 1 751.6 |
| 乡　道 | Rural Highway | 840 | 431 | 4 004.4 | 4 048.0 | 4 060.0 |
| 村　道 | Village Highway | | | 5 732.2 | 5 925.4 | 5 947.8 |
| 专用公路 | Specialized Highway | | | 39.7 | 39.7 | 39.7 |
| 3. 按路面标准分 | Grouped by Standard of Road Surface | | | | | |
| 高　级 | High | 202 | 1 045 | 12 514.1 | 12 837.7 | 12 879.8 |
| 次高级 | Sub-high | 1 053 | 840 | 10.6 | – | – |
| 中级、低级 | Medium and Low | 278 | 40 | 229.5 | 209.7 | 209.7 |
| **二、公路桥梁　(座)** | **Highway Bridges　(unit)** | **1 458** | **4 603** | **9 128** | **9 646** | **9 690** |
| **(米)** | **(m)** | **33 105** | **123 587** | **458 640** | **489 448** | **490 011** |
| **三、内河航道通航里程　(公里)** | **Length of Navigable Inland Waterways　(km)** | **2 870.2** | **2 896.7** | **2 764.6** | **2 764.6** | **2 760.0** |
| # 水深1米以上里程 | Depths of One Meter and Over | 2 345.2 | 2 762.6 | 2 684.2 | 2 684.2 | 2 611.9 |
| **四、通航河流上建筑物　(座)** | **Construction in Navigable Waterways　(unit)** | **81** | **121** | **108** | **108** | **108** |
| 1.永久性闸坝 | Permanent Gate and Dam | 40 | 53 | 47 | 47 | 47 |
| 2.船　闸 | Lock Gate | 3 | 9 | 7 | 7 | 7 |
| 3.套　闸 | Gate Set | 38 | 59 | 54 | 54 | 54 |
| **五、内河航道上设立的航标** | **Navigation Mark in Inland Waterways** | **187** | **220** | **154** | **154** | **158** |
| # 发光的 | Luminary | 156 | 152 | 132 | 132 | 139 |

表6-3

# 部分年份全社会船舶数
# TOTAL NUMBER TRANSPORT VESSELS OF PARTIAL YEARS

| 指 标 | Item | | 1990年 | 2000年 | 2010年 | 2011年 | 2012年 |
|---|---|---|---|---|---|---|---|
| **客 船** (艘) | **Passenger Ship** | (unit) | **40** | **110** | **108** | **118** | **119** |
| (客位) | | (seat) | 4 634 | 4 994 | 4 203 | 4 804 | 4 937 |
| (千瓦) | | (kw) | | 11 569 | 8 477 | 9 630 | 10 676 |
| **货 船** (艘) | **Cargo Ship** | (unit) | **53** | **11 114** | **224** | **207** | **215** |
| (吨位) | | (ton) | 3 206 | 245 737 | 82 319 | 94 846 | 106 564 |
| (千瓦) | | (kw) | | 152 565 | 49 905 | 54 498 | 60 142 |
| **拖 船** (艘) | **Tug Boat** | (unit) | **453** | **255** | **8** | **6** | **5** |
| (千瓦) | | (kw) | | 21 033 | 1 254 | 1 135 | 967 |
| **驳 船** (艘) | **Barges** | (unit) | **3 685** | **1 291** | **73** | **45** | **42** |
| (吨位) | | (ton) | 173 719 | 79 522 | 6 046 | 4 946 | 4 748 |
| (客位) | | (seat) | 5 470 | 3 646 | 73 | - | - |

表6-4

# 分地区机动车拥有量 (2012年末)
# CIVIL MOTOR VEHICLES BY REGION (END OF 2012)

单位：辆 (coach)

| 地 区 Region | 机动车总计 Total Motor Vehicles | # 汽 车 Vehicles | # 私家客车 Personal Passenger Vehicles | # 私家货车 Personal Freight Trucks | 年内汽车上牌数 The number of Auto Registration in 2012 | 年末汽车驾驶员(人) The Number of Car Drivers (person) |
|---|---|---|---|---|---|---|
| **全 市 Whole Municipality** | **2 392 673** | **1 778 977** | **1 402 055** | **43 300** | **298 267** | **1 971 286** |
| 市 区 Urban Area | 1 192 890 | 950 847 | 749 876 | 19 288 | 158 440 | 1 053 049 |
| #吴江区 Wujiang District | 292 951 | 168 854 | 139 063 | 7 214 | 33 817 | 178 551 |
| 常 熟 Changshu | 372 358 | 238 304 | 193 072 | 4 927 | 37 094 | 346 431 |
| 张家港 Zhangjiagang | 299 328 | 203 643 | 160 689 | 9 378 | 34 374 | 215 002 |
| 昆 山 Kunshan | 328 680 | 267 095 | 206 322 | 4 107 | 48 449 | 223 145 |
| 太 仓 Taicang | 199 417 | 119 088 | 92 096 | 5 600 | 19 910 | 133 659 |

表6-5

# 历年全社会客运情况
# TOTAL PASSENGER TRAFFIC OVER THE YEARS

| 年份 Year | 客运量 (万人次) Passenger Traffic (10 000 person-times) | 公路 Highways | 水运 Waterways | 旅客周转量 (万人公里) Passenger-kilometers (10 000 person-km) | 公路 Highways | 水运 Waterways | 铁路旅客发送量 (万人次) Number of Passengers Dispatched on Railway (10 000 person-times) |
|---|---|---|---|---|---|---|---|
| 1949 | 56 | 45 | 11 | 1 486 | 1 299 | 187 | |
| 1952 | 383 | 167 | 216 | 8 651 | 3 232 | 5 419 | |
| 1957 | 2 270 | 1 887 | 383 | 26 754 | 18 024 | 8 730 | |
| 1962 | 1 486 | 845 | 641 | 39 595 | 23 076 | 16 519 | 366.45 |
| 1965 | 1 101 | 676 | 425 | 24 381 | 15 425 | 8 956 | 208.86 |
| 1970 | 1 724 | 1 054 | 670 | 33 280 | 21 241 | 12 039 | 226.06 |
| 1975 | 2 919 | 2 091 | 828 | 55 339 | 39 726 | 15 613 | 316.63 |
| 1978 | 3 296 | 2 477 | 819 | 64 766 | 48 775 | 15 991 | 356.44 |
| 1980 | 4 813 | 4 034 | 779 | 96 041 | 74 404 | 21 637 | 520.21 |
| 1985 | 6 757 | 6 340 | 417 | 188 795 | 165 851 | 22 944 | 745.40 |
| 1990 | 6 764 | 6 516 | 247 | 232 799 | 218 521 | 14 278 | 755.78 |
| 1991 | 7 276 | 7 024 | 252 | 254 165 | 239 681 | 14 484 | 806.28 |
| 1992 | 13 058 | 12 884 | 174 | 498 938 | 486 565 | 12 373 | 868.83 |
| 1993 | 10 844 | 10 703 | 141 | 682 940 | 672 495 | 10 445 | 966.49 |
| 1994 | 9 642 | 9 534 | 108 | 616 268 | 603 696 | 12 572 | 943.57 |
| 1995 | 18 945 | 18 840 | 104 | 628 147 | 620 152 | 7 995 | 917.64 |
| 1996 | 11 272 | 11 234 | 39 | 561 389 | 556 970 | 4 419 | 830.68 |
| 1997 | 15 672 | 15 639 | 32 | 581 201 | 577 878 | 3 323 | 800.61 |
| 1998 | 14 291 | 14 255 | 36 | 660 212 | 656 940 | 3 272 | 792.30 |
| 1999 | 16 845 | 16 752 | 93 | 820 104 | 816 339 | 3 765 | 883.25 |
| 2000 | 18 559 | 18 447 | 112 | 1 013 554 | 1 009 983 | 3 571 | 940.23 |
| 2001 | 19 508 | 19 394 | 114 | 1 064 044 | 1 060 708 | 3 336 | 1 043.47 |
| 2002 | 21 031 | 20 935 | 96 | 1 199 190 | 1 196 358 | 2 832 | 1 161.83 |
| 2003 | 22 921 | 22 835 | 86 | 1 518 126 | 1 515 701 | 2 425 | 1 211.27 |
| 2004 | 25 292 | 25 265 | 27 | 1 792 342 | 1 791 228 | 1 114 | 1 481.92 |
| 2005 | 30 707 | 30 703 | 4 | 1 919 138 | 1 918 713 | 425 | 1 663.78 |
| 2006 | 35 186 | 35 182 | 4 | 2 149 435 | 2 149 035 | 400 | 1 707.07 |
| 2007 | 40 163 | 40 163 | - | 2 498 592 | 2 498 592 | - | 1 625.41 |
| 2008 | 45 386 | 45 386 | - | 2 855 005 | 2 855 005 | - | 1 893.33 |
| 2009 | 39 338 | 39 263 | 75 | 1 679 103 | 1 678 269 | 834 | 1 939.87 |
| 2010 | 56 475 | 56 392 | 83 | 2 412 841 | 2 411 917 | 924 | 2 044.68 |
| 2011 | 63 793 | 63 699 | 94 | 2 746 339 | 2 745 297 | 1 042 | 2 274.68 |
| 2012 | 68 998 | 68 895 | 103 | 3 077 391 | 3 076 263 | 1 128 | 2 627.98 |

表6-6

# 历年全社会货运情况
# TOTAL FREIGHT TRAFFIC OVER THE YEARS

单位：万吨 (10 000 tons)

| 年份 Year | 货运量 Freight Traffic | 公路 Highways | 水运 Waterways | 货物周转量（万吨公里）Freight Ton-kilometers (10 000 ton-km) | 公路 Highways | 水运 Waterways | 铁路货物发送量 Volume of Freight Dispatched on Railway | 铁路货物到达量 Volume of Freight Arrived on Railway |
|---|---|---|---|---|---|---|---|---|
| 1949 | 55 | 1 | 54 | 2 419 | 26 | 2 393 | | |
| 1952 | 209 | 34 | 175 | 8 995 | 257 | 8 738 | | |
| 1957 | 365 | 21 | 344 | 19 991 | 287 | 19 704 | | |
| 1962 | 501 | 78 | 422 | 19 753 | 883 | 18 870 | 35.03 | 141.85 |
| 1965 | 777 | 108 | 668 | 35 314 | 1 128 | 34 186 | 41.61 | 222.96 |
| 1970 | 926 | 122 | 805 | 56 138 | 1 432 | 54 706 | 52.33 | 250.44 |
| 1975 | 1 645 | 226 | 1 419 | 92 848 | 3 392 | 89 456 | 79.54 | 317.52 |
| 1978 | 2 195 | 329 | 1 866 | 115 434 | 6 086 | 109 348 | 87.28 | 465.79 |
| 1980 | 2 712 | 399 | 2 313 | 138 610 | 8 663 | 129 947 | 92.93 | 541.90 |
| 1985 | 6 041 | 871 | 5 170 | 258 795 | 24 060 | 234 735 | 124.05 | 630.52 |
| 1990 | 3 211 | 746 | 2 465 | 208 573 | 26 187 | 182 386 | 116.43 | 557.97 |
| 1991 | 3 707 | 1 046 | 2 662 | 221 670 | 30 558 | 191 112 | 114.34 | 705.18 |
| 1992 | 7 680 | 3 657 | 4 023 | 420 397 | 137 386 | 283 011 | 137.34 | 765.74 |
| 1993 | 7 229 | 3 338 | 3 890 | 489 826 | 222 277 | 267 549 | 123.98 | 751.14 |
| 1994 | 6 898 | 3 385 | 3 513 | 445 496 | 181 119 | 264 377 | 124.50 | 759.55 |
| 1995 | 8 561 | 4 746 | 3 815 | 496 290 | 190 242 | 306 048 | 164.13 | 740.91 |
| 1996 | 8 296 | 4 810 | 3 486 | 508 238 | 216 659 | 291 579 | 158.88 | 704.22 |
| 1997 | 7 237 | 4 373 | 2 864 | 449 609 | 231 801 | 217 808 | 157.91 | 661.83 |
| 1998 | 6 201 | 3 060 | 3 142 | 386 075 | 151 758 | 234 317 | 134.70 | 608.19 |
| 1999 | 6 870 | 3 738 | 3 132 | 500 869 | 218 030 | 282 839 | 154.98 | 561.22 |
| 2000 | 7 816 | 4 567 | 3 248 | 458 916 | 245 987 | 212 929 | 159.37 | 391.51 |
| 2001 | 7 988 | 4 738 | 3 250 | 464 030 | 254 699 | 209 331 | 174.53 | 564.09 |
| 2002 | 8 350 | 5 010 | 3 340 | 478 850 | 275 550 | 203 300 | 164.44 | 703.81 |
| 2003 | 7 354 | 5 389 | 1 965 | 454 889 | 334 060 | 120 829 | 165.94 | 838.26 |
| 2004 | 8 833 | 6 941 | 1 892 | 522 670 | 397 170 | 125 500 | 167.72 | 800.78 |
| 2005 | 10 393 | 7 762 | 2 631 | 684 229 | 515 208 | 169 021 | 145.92 | 741.27 |
| 2006 | 11 099 | 8 891 | 2 208 | 746 045 | 590 016 | 156 029 | 147.15 | 644.36 |
| 2007 | 11 834 | 9 958 | 1 876 | 820 219 | 656 395 | 163 824 | 131.30 | 632.35 |
| 2008 | 12 631 | 10 863 | 1 768 | 902 918 | 733 993 | 168 925 | 127.61 | 494.50 |
| 2009 | 11 370 | 10 820 | 550 | 1 032 213 | 887 006 | 145 207 | 118.40 | 452.66 |
| 2010 | 13 417 | 12 768 | 649 | 1 237 387 | 1 037 797 | 199 590 | 90.94 | 400.06 |
| 2011 | 15 602 | 14 798 | 804 | 1 498 375 | 1 200 220 | 298 155 | 93.00 | 406.34 |
| 2012 | 17 325 | 16 441 | 884 | 1 705 084 | 1 357 255 | 347 829 | 93.78 | 311.43 |

表6-7

# 分地区客运量(2012年)
# PASSENGER TRAFFIC BY REGION (2012)

| 地 区 | Region | 客运量 (万人次) Passenger Traffic (10 000 person-times) | 公 路 Highways | 水 运 Waterways | 旅客周转量 (万人公里) Passenger-kilometers (10 000 person-km) | 公 路 Highways | 水 运 Waterways |
|---|---|---|---|---|---|---|---|
| **全 市** | **Whole Municipality** | **68 998** | **68 895** | **103** | **3 077 391** | **3 076 263** | **1 128** |
| 市 区 | Urban Area | 40 228 | 40 188 | 40 | 1 796 550 | 1 796 114 | 436 |
| # 吴江区 | Wujiang District | 5 274 | 5 271 | 2 | 233 321 | 233 295 | 26 |
| 常 熟 | Changshu | 8 724 | 8 707 | 16 | 391 924 | 391 746 | 178 |
| 张家港 | Zhangjiagang | 8 007 | 7 982 | 25 | 356 857 | 356 586 | 272 |
| 昆 山 | Kunshan | 8 673 | 8 669 | 4 | 382 281 | 382 234 | 48 |
| 太 仓 | Taicang | 3 367 | 3 349 | 18 | 149 779 | 149 584 | 195 |

表6-8

# 分地区货运量(2012年)
# FREIGHT TRAFFIC BY REGION (2012)

| 地 区 | Region | 货运量 (万吨) Freight Traffic (10 000 tons) | 公 路 Highways | 水 运 Waterways | 货物周转量 (万吨公里) Freight-kilometers (10 000 ton-km) | 公 路 Highways | 水 运 Waterways |
|---|---|---|---|---|---|---|---|
| **全 市** | **Whole Municipality** | **17 325** | **16 441** | **884** | **1 705 084** | **1 357 255** | **347 829** |
| 市 区 | Urban Area | 7 704 | 7 520 | 184 | 692 946 | 620 779 | 72 167 |
| # 吴江区 | Wujiang District | 1 104 | 1 097 | 7 | 93 308 | 90 570 | 2 738 |
| 常 熟 | Changshu | 2 296 | 1 983 | 313 | 286 975 | 163 733 | 123 243 |
| 张家港 | Zhangjiagang | 3 109 | 2 943 | 166 | 308 321 | 242 938 | 65 383 |
| 昆 山 | Kunshan | 2 008 | 1 962 | 46 | 180 113 | 161 990 | 18 122 |
| 太 仓 | Taicang | 2 208 | 2 033 | 175 | 236 730 | 167 815 | 68 915 |

表6-9

# 苏州港码头泊位和吞吐量 (2012年) NUMBER OF BERTHS AND THROUGHPUT OF SUHZOU PORT (2012 )

| 项　　目 | Item | 合　计 Total | 常熟港区 Changshu Port | 张家港港区 Zhangjiagang Port | 太仓港区 Taicang Port |
|---|---|---|---|---|---|
| **码头泊位个数　(个)** | **Number of Berths　(unit)** | **240** | **30** | **150** | **60** |
| # 万吨级以上 | 10 000 Ton Class | 116 | 17 | 67 | 32 |
| # 公用码头 | Public Berths | 113 | 11 | 56 | 46 |
| # 集装箱码头 | Containen Berths | 19 | 3 | 4 | 12 |
| **货物吞吐量　(万吨)** | **Cargo at Ports Throughput (10 000 tons)** | **42 801** | **6 312** | **24 226** | **12 262** |
| # 外　贸 | Freight Trade | 10 463 | 1 082 | 5 037 | 4 344 |
| **集装箱吞吐量(万标箱)** | **International Containes (10 000TEU)** | **586.35** | **34.65** | **150.24** | **401.46** |
| 重　量　(万吨) | Weight　(10 000 tons) | 7 218.31 | 390.92 | 1 638.25 | 5 189.14 |
| # 货　物 | Freight | 6 033.32 | 321.62 | 1 343.89 | 4 367.80 |

注:标箱指折合20英尺标准箱，英文缩写TEU。　Note:TEU is the abbreviation, Which refers to 20-foot equivalent unit.

表6-10

# 苏州港集装箱吞吐量 (2012年) VOLUME OF CONTAINER HANDLED OF SUZHOU PORT (2012)

| 项　　目 | Item | 合　计 Total | 其中 of which 进　港 In-Port | 其中 of which 出　港 Out-Port | 按航线分 Grouped by Routes 国际航线 International Routes | 按航线分 Grouped by Routes 内支线 Ports of Inland Rivers | 按航线分 Grouped by Routes 国内航线 Domestic Routes |
|---|---|---|---|---|---|---|---|
| **箱量合计　(标箱)** | **Total Containers (TEU)** | **5 863 479** | **2 924 892** | **2 938 587** | **235 039** | **1 811 039** | **3 817 401** |
| 空箱小计 | Light Case Subtotal | 1 752 351 | 813 975 | 938 377 | 61 393 | 455 103 | 1 235 856 |
| # 45英尺箱 (箱) | 45-foot equivalent unit (unit) | 1 133 | 359 | 774 | – | 107 | 1 026 |
| 40英尺箱 | 40-foot equivalent unit | 549 456 | 231 391 | 318 065 | 14 399 | 129 714 | 405 343 |
| 20英尺箱 | 20-foot equivalent unit | 650 890 | 350 385 | 300 505 | 32 595 | 195 434 | 422 861 |
| 重箱小计　(标箱) | Heavy Case Subtotal (TEU) | 4 111 128 | 2 110 917 | 2 000 210 | 173 646 | 1 355 936 | 2 581 546 |
| # 45英尺箱 (箱) | 45-foot equivalent unit (unit) | 802 | 433 | 369 | 1 | 411 | 390 |
| 40英尺箱 | 40-foot equivalent unit | 1 139 254 | 622 993 | 516 261 | 57 520 | 494 255 | 587 479 |
| 20英尺箱 | 20-foot equivalent unit | 1 830 815 | 863 957 | 966 858 | 58 604 | 366 501 | 1 405 710 |
| **重量合计　(吨)** | **Total Weight　(ton)** | **72 183 080** | **36 949 633** | **35 233 447** | **2 133 940** | **1 9247 571** | **50 801 569** |
| # 货　重 | Freight Weight | 60 333 189 | 30 986 048 | 29 347 141 | 1 652 070 | 1 5591 158 | 43 089 961 |

表6-11

# 苏州港进出港口货物分类流向一览 (2012年)
# FREIGHT HANDLED AT SUZHOU PORT BY DIRECTION (2012)

单位：万吨　(10 000 tons)

| 类　别 | Type | 总　计 Total | 总计中 In Total | | 总计中 In Total | |
|---|---|---|---|---|---|---|
| | | | 进　港 Arrival | 出　港 Departure | 外　贸 Foreign Trade | 内　贸 Domestic Trade |
| **总　计** | **Total** | **42 800.71** | **26 639.92** | **16 160.79** | **10 462.95** | **32 337.76** |
| 1.煤炭及其制品 | Coal and Its Products | 10 352.14 | 8 315.34 | 2 036.80 | 218.47 | 10 133.67 |
| 2.石油、天然气及制品 | Petroleum, Natural Gas and Related Products | 384.45 | 220.93 | 163.52 | 91.57 | 292.88 |
| #成品油 | Product Oil | 13.87 | 9.83 | 4.04 | 1.49 | 12.38 |
| 3.金属矿石 | Metal Ores | 9 784.64 | 6 983.21 | 2 801.43 | 3 160.28 | 6 624.36 |
| #铁矿石 | Iron Ore | 9 048.40 | 6 365.39 | 2 683.01 | 3 058.56 | 5 989.84 |
| 4.钢　铁 | Iron and Steel | 4 852.72 | 1 085.11 | 3 767.61 | 1 151.29 | 3 701.43 |
| #钢　材 | Rolled Steel | 3 727.11 | 243.02 | 3 484.09 | 557.13 | 3 169.98 |
| 5.矿物性建筑材料 | Mineral Building Materials | 4 052.27 | 2 292.98 | 1 759.29 | 11.66 | 4 040.62 |
| 6.水　泥 | Cement | 309.79 | 121.53 | 188.26 | 178.07 | 131.72 |
| 7.木　材 | Timber | 1 052.63 | 890.59 | 162.04 | 883.88 | 168.76 |
| #原　木 | Log | 746.18 | 637.44 | 108.74 | 632.90 | 113.28 |
| 8.非金属矿石 | Nonmetal Ores | 101.77 | 82.62 | 19.14 | 15.04 | 86.73 |
| 9.化学肥料及农药 | Chemical Fertilizers and Pesticides | 79.30 | 39.55 | 39.75 | 36.83 | 42.47 |
| 10.盐 | Salt | 22.33 | 22.13 | 0.20 | 11.26 | 11.07 |
| 11.粮　食 | Grain | 419.09 | 356.90 | 62.20 | 268.69 | 150.40 |
| #黄　豆 | Bean | 283.41 | 282.25 | 1.16 | 236.76 | 46.66 |
| 12.机械、设备、电器 | Machine, Equipment and Wiring | 65.14 | 8.30 | 56.84 | 55.28 | 9.86 |
| 13.化工原料及制品 | Chemical Industry Materials and Products | 1 991.59 | 1 439.11 | 552.47 | 1 317.88 | 673.71 |
| 14.有色金属 | Nonferrous Metals | 29.04 | 19.56 | 9.48 | 12.49 | 16.55 |
| 15.轻工、医药产品 | Products of Light Industry and Medicine & Pharmacy | 392.89 | 236.86 | 156.03 | 228.61 | 164.28 |
| 16.农林牧渔业产品 | The Output of Agricultural Products | 178.29 | 113.47 | 64.82 | 99.03 | 79.26 |
| 17.其　他 | Others | 8 732.64 | 4 411.72 | 4 320.92 | 2 722.62 | 6 010.01 |

表6-12

# 邮政电信基本情况 (2012年)

| 项　目 | | Item | | 全　市 Whole Municipality |
|---|---|---|---|---|
| 一、邮电局 | (所) | Number of Post & Telecommunications Offices | (unit) | 645 |
| # 邮政局 | | Post Offices | | 246 |
| 二、城市投递段道长度（单程） | (公里) | The Route Length Of Urban Delivery (One Way) | (km) | 10 485 |
| 农村投递路线长度（单程） | | The Route Length Of Rural Delivery (One Way) | | 31 028 |
| 三、城乡电话交换机总容量 | (门) | Total Capacity of Urban and Rural Telephone Exchanges | (line) | 5 462 572 |
| 1. 市话交换机总容量 | | Total Capacity of Urban Telephone Exchanges | | 3 836 701 |
| 2. 农话交换机总容量 | | Total Capacity of Rural Telephone Exchanges | | 1 625 871 |
| 四、邮电业务总收入 | (万元) | Business Volume of Post & Telecommunications | (10 000 yuan) | 2 076 637 |
| 1. 函　件 | (万件) | Number of Letters | (10 000 pcs) | 29 167 |
| 2. 汇　票 | (万张) | Number of Bill of Exchange | ( 10 000 pcs) | 295 |
| 3. 报刊杂志累计数 | (万份) | Number of Newspapers and Magazines Circulation | (10 000 copies) | 32 157 |
| 4. 邮政储蓄余额 | (万元) | Savings Balance | (10 000 yuan) | 4 338 302 |
| 5. 集　邮 | (万枚) | Philately | (10 000 pcs) | 1 425 |
| 6. 特快专递 | (万件) | Express | (10 000 pcs) | 2 313 |
| 五、固定电话用户 | (户) | Fixed Telephone Subscribers | (household) | 3 303 670 |
| 1. 普通电话 | | Telephones | | 2 981 479 |
| 城市住宅 | | Urban Housing | | 1 072 158 |
| 城市政企 | | Urban Enterprises | | 551 222 |
| 乡村住宅 | | Rural Housing | | 1 020 815 |
| 乡村政企 | | Rural Enterprises | | 337 283 |
| 2. 小灵通 | | (Xiaolingtong) Hand Phone | | 104 109 |
| 3. 公用电话 | | Public Telephone | | 218 082 |
| 六、移动电话用户 | (户) | Number of Mobile Telephone Subscribers | ( household) | 15 545 197 |
| # 3G用户 | | 3G userS | | 4 645 532 |
| 七、互联网用户 | (户) | International Exchange Network Users | (household) | 6 927 493 |
| # 宽带用户 | | Subscriber of Broad Band | | 2 835 654 |
| # 用3G业务的互联网用户数 | | 3G service users | | 3 918 471 |
| # 用上网卡的互联网用户数 | | Spending NIC users | | 170 276 |

注:2012年起,互联网用户中包含用3G业务的互联网用户数和用上网卡的互联网用户数。

# POSTS AND TELECOMMUNICATIONS (2012)

| 市 区<br>Urban Area | # 吴江区<br>Wujiang District | 常 熟<br>Changshu | 张家港<br>Zhangjiagang | 昆 山<br>Kunshan | 太 仓<br>Taicang |
|---|---|---|---|---|---|
| 280 | 66 | 111 | 76 | 91 | 87 |
| 103 | 27 | 48 | 35 | 34 | 26 |
| 4 724 | 1 096 | 2 228 | 915 | 2 029 | 589 |
| 13 100 | 4 478 | 6 117 | 5 931 | 2 964 | 2 916 |
| 3 240 939 | 558 568 | 530 091 | 562 853 | 835 760 | 292 929 |
| 2 817 245 | 134 874 | 198 449 | 186 173 | 444 682 | 190 152 |
| 423 694 | 423 694 | 331 642 | 376 680 | 391 078 | 102 777 |
| 1 127 907 | 238 277 | 243 678 | 204 281 | 379 584 | 121 187 |
| 23 062 | 1 172 | 1 968 | 1 539 | 2 067 | 530 |
| 136 | 52 | 26 | 33 | 75 | 25 |
| 17 232 | 2 572 | 5 641 | 3 492 | 3 657 | 2 135 |
| 2 018 321 | 655 176 | 850 391 | 544 575 | 584 328 | 340 687 |
| 850 | 43 | 164 | 133 | 180 | 99 |
| 997 | 190 | 308 | 197 | 517 | 294 |
| 1 775 229 | 362 171 | 427 553 | 367 859 | 527 229 | 205 801 |
| 1 605 394 | 325 578 | 380 628 | 327 462 | 480 916 | 187 079 |
| 629 594 | 59 676 | 112 360 | 121 075 | 160 635 | 48 493 |
| 300 899 | 29 052 | 61 473 | 68 351 | 94 875 | 25 624 |
| 507 557 | 181 849 | 163 660 | 115 912 | 145 229 | 88 457 |
| 167 344 | 55 001 | 43 134 | 22 124 | 80 177 | 24 504 |
| 49 737 | 14 082 | 16 137 | 13 474 | 19 123 | 5 639 |
| 120 099 | 22 511 | 30 787 | 26 922 | 27 191 | 13 083 |
| 8 298 199 | 1 874 327 | 1 920 783 | 1 622 977 | 2 797 504 | 905 734 |
| 2 468 076 | 565 360 | 557 452 | 508 873 | 822 783 | 288 349 |
| 3 727 477 | 757 235 | 845 705 | 749 605 | 1 179 760 | 424 946 |
| 1 545 921 | 302 910 | 339 554 | 319 854 | 457 064 | 173 261 |
| 2 082 821 | 437 044 | 485 245 | 412 305 | 696 596 | 241 505 |
| 97 101 | 16 933 | 20 477 | 17 102 | 25 607 | 9 989 |

Note: Since 2012 Internet users have included those using 3G services and those spending NIC.

# 主 要 统 计 指 标 解 释

**公路里程** 指在一定时期内实际达到《公路工程[WTBZ]技术标准JTJ01-88》规定的等级公路，并经公路主管部门正式验收交付使用的公路里程数。包括大中城市的郊区公路以及通过小城镇街道部分的公路里程和桥梁、渡口的长度，不包括大中城市的街道、厂矿、林区生产用道和农业生产用道的里程。两条或多条公路共同经由同一路段，只计算一次，不得重复计算里程长度。该指标可以反映公路建设的发展规模，也是计算运输网密度等指标的基础资料。

**内河航道里程** 也称内河通航里程，指在一定时期内，能通航运输船舶及排筏的天然河流、湖泊水库、运河及通航渠道的长度。包括全年季节性通航累计三个月以上的航道，不包括仅供零散流放竹、木排的河道。该指标可以反映内河水运网的规模、水平和发展情况。

**货(客)运量** 指在一定时期内，各种运输工具实际运送的货物(旅客)数量。该指标是反映运输业为国民经济和人民生活服务的数量指标，也是制定和检查运输生产计划、研究运输发展规模和速度的重要指标。货运按吨计算，客运按人计算。货物不论运输距离长短、货物类别，均按实际重量统计。旅客不论行程远近或票价多少，均按一人一次客运量统计；半价票、小孩票也按一人统计。

**货物(旅客)周转量** 指在一定时期内，由各种运输工具运送的货物(旅客)数量与其相应运输距离的乘积之总和。该指标可以反映运输业生产的总成果，也是编制和检查运输生产计划，计算运输效率、劳动生产率以及核算运输单位成本的主要基础资料。计算货物周转量通常按发出站与到达站之间的最短距离，也就是计费距离计算。计算公式为：

货物（旅客）周转量=Σ（货物（旅客）运输量×运输距离）

**民用汽车拥有量** 指报告期末，在公安交通管理部门按照《机动车注册登记工作规范》，已注册登记领有民用车辆牌照的全部汽车数量。汽车拥有量统计的主要分类：根据汽车结构分为载客汽车、载货汽车及其他汽车；根据汽车所有者不同分为个人(私人)汽车、单位汽车；根据汽车的使用性质分为营运汽车、非营运汽车；根据汽车大小规格不同载客汽车分为大型、中型、小型和微型，载货汽车分为重型、中型、轻型和微型。

**邮电业务总量** 指以价值量形式表现的邮电通信企业为社会提供各类邮电通信服务的总数量。邮电业务量按专业分类包括函件、包件、汇票、报刊发行、邮政快件、特快专递、邮政储蓄、集邮、传真、长途电话、出租电路、移动电话、分组交换数据通信、出租代维等。计算方法为各类产品乘以相应的平均单价(不变价)之和，再加上出租电路和设备、代用户维护电话交换机和线路等的服务收入。该指标综合反映了一定时期邮电业务发展的总成果，是研究邮电业务量构成和发展趋势的重要指标。计算公式为：

邮电业务总量=Σ（各类邮电业务量×不变单价）+出租代维及其他业务收入

=邮政业务总量+电信业务总量

**移动电话用户** 指在电信运营企业营业网点办理开户登记手续，通过移动电话交换机进入移动电话网，占用移动电话号码的各类电话用户。包括GSM数字移动电话用户、CDMA数字移动电话用户和电信运营企业发行的报告期末已激活充值的能异地漫游的各种智能卡用户。

# EXPLANATORY NOTES ON MAIN STATISTICAL INDICATORS

**Length of Highways** refers to the length of highways which are built in conformity with the grades specified by the highway engineering standard [Highways WTBZ-Technical Standard JTJ01-88]formulated by the Ministry of Communications, and have been formally checked and accepted by the departments of highways and put into use. The length of highways includes that of the suburb highways at large and medium-sized cities, highways passing through streets at small cities and towns, and also the length of bridges and ferry piers. It does not include the length of streets in big and medium-sized cities and highways built for the production purpose at factories, mines, forest areas and agricultural areas. If two or more highways go the same section of the way, the length of the section is only calculated for once and no duplication is allowed. The length of highways is an indicator to show the development of the scale of highway construction and to provide essential information to calculate the transport network density.

**Length of Navigable Inland Waterways** is an indicator reflecting the size and development of inland water network. It refers to the length of the natural rivers, lakes, reservoirs, canals, and ditches open to navigation during a given period, which enables transportation by ships and rafts. It includes the channels open to navigation for over an accumulated period of 3 months in a year, yet this does not include the river courses which are only used to float odd logs and bamboo rafts. This indicator can reflect the scale, level and development situation of the inland waterway network.

**Freight (Passenger) Traffic** refers to the volume of freight (passenger) transported with various means within a specific period of time. This indicator reflects the service of the transport industry towards the national economy and people's living conditions, as well as an important indicator used in formulating and monitoring transport production plans and research into the scale and pace of transport development. Freight transport is calculated in tons and passenger traffic is calculated in terms of number of persons. Freight transport is calculated in terms of the actual weight of the goods and takes no account of the type of freight and distance of travel. Passenger traffic is calculated by the principle that one person can be counted only once in one trip and takes no account of the travelling distance and ticket price. The passengers who travel with a half price ticket or a child's ticket is also calculated as one person.

**Freight Ton-kilometres (Passenger-kilometres)** refers to the sum of the product of the volume of transported cargo (passengers) multiplied by the transport distance. It is an important indicator to reflect the achievement of the transportation industry. This is an important indicator to show the total results of the transport industry; to prepare and examine the transport plan; and to serve as the main basic data for calculating the efficiency, labour productivity and unit cost of transport. Normally, the shortest distance between the departure station and the destination station (i.e., the payable distance) is the basis in calculating the freight ton-kilometres. The formula is as follows:

$$\begin{matrix}\text{Freight ton - kilometres}\\ \text{(passenger - kilometres)}\end{matrix} = \sum \begin{matrix}\text{freight}\\ \text{(passenger)traffic}\end{matrix} \times \begin{matrix}\text{distance of}\\ \text{transportation}\end{matrix}$$

**Possession of Civil Motor Vehicles** refer to the total numbers of vehicles that are registered and received vehicles license tags according to the *Work Standard for Motor Vehicles Registration* formulated by the Transport Management Office under the department of public security at the end of the reference period. They are divided into categories. According to the structure of motor vehicles, they are divided into passenger vehicles, trucks and others; according to ownership into private vehicles and vehicles for the unit's use; according to kind of usage into working vehicles and non-working vehicles; and according to size of vehicles into large passenger vehicles, medium-sized passenger vehicles, small passenger vehicles and mini passenger vehicles, heavy trucks, light-heavy trucks, light trucks and mini-trucks.

**Business Volume of Post and Telecommunications** refers to the total amount of postal and telecommunication services, expressed in value terms, provided by the post and telecommunications departments for society. Postal and telecommunication services can be classified as letters, parcels, remittance, issue of newspapers and magazines, fast mail service, express mail service, savings deposits, stamps for collection, facsimiles, long-distance telephone service, leasing of telephone lines, mobile telephone service, data transmission, income from leasing, maintenance, etc. The accounting approach is to multiply the service products of all types with their average unit price (constant price) to get the total business value, and to add to it income from other services such as leasing of telephone lines and equipment and maintenance of telephone switchboards and lines on behalf of customers. This indicator reflects the overall results of postal and telecommunication services during a given period, and is important for studying the composition of business service and the trend of development of postal and telecommunication services. The formula is as follows:

Business volume of post and telecommunications
=∑(Transaction of post and telecommunication services
×price[constant price] )
+Income from leasing, maintenance and other services
= business volume of postal service
+ business volume of telecommunications service

**Mobile Telephone Subscribers** refer to persons who have gone through registration procedures in the operation points of enterprises engaged in telecommunications and are hence connected with the mobile telephone communication network through the mobile telephone switchboards and occupy mobile phone numbers. Included are GSM digital mobile phone subscribers, CDMA digital mobile phone subscribers and subscribers to intelligent phone cards with roaming facility issued by telecommunications enterprises and which have been subscribed to and activated at the end of the reference period.

# 七、贸易餐饮业

# CHAPTER 7
# TRADE AND CATERING BUSINESS

# 贸易餐饮业 TRADE AND CATERING BUSINESS

## 主 要 统 计 指 标 MAJOR STATISTICAL INDICATORS

| | | | | |
|---|---|---|---|---|
| 2012年社会消费品零售总额 | Total Retail Sales of Consumer Goods | 3 240.97 | 亿元 | 100 million yuan |
| 比上年增长 | Increase Over Last Year | 14.5 | % | |
| 2012年批发和零售业零售额 | Wholesale and Retail Sale Trades | 2 830.37 | 亿元 | 100 million yuan |
| 比上年增长 | Increase Over Last Year | 14.3 | % | |
| 2012年住宿和餐饮业零售额 | Accommodation and Catering Trade | 382.73 | 亿元 | 100 million yuan |
| 比上年增长 | Increase Over Last Year | 19.1 | % | |
| 2012年限额以上批发和零售业 | Enterprises Above Designated Size in Wholesale and Retail Trades | | | |
| 商品购进总额 | Total Purchases | 8 826.97 | 亿元 | 100 million yuan |
| 商品销售总额 | Total Sales | 9 613.78 | 亿元 | 100 million yuan |
| 商品年末库存总额 | Inventory (year-end) | 449.94 | 亿元 | 100 million yuan |
| 2012年限额以上住宿业营业总额 | Total Business Turnover of Hotel Accommodation Above Designated Size | 70.07 | 亿元 | 100 million yuan |
| 2012年限额以上餐饮业营业总额 | Total Business Turnover of Catering Trade Above Designated Size | 66.96 | 亿元 | 100 million yuan |
| 2012年亿元以上商品交易市场商品成交总额 | Total Business Turnover of Transaction Markets Over 100 Million Yuan | 4 855.09 | 亿元 | 100 million yuan |
| 比上年增长 | Increase Over Last Year | 38.2 | % | |

表7-1

# 历年分地区社会消费品零售总额
# TOTAL RETAIL SALES OF CONSUMER GOODS OVER THE YEARS BY REGION

单位：万元 (10 000 yuan)

| 年 份 Year | 全 市 Whole Municipality | 市 区 Urban Area | # 吴江区 Wujiang District | 常 熟 Changshu | 张家港 Zhangjiagang | 昆 山 Kunshan | 太 仓 Taicang |
|---|---|---|---|---|---|---|---|
| 1949 | 23 818 | 15 576 | 3 604 | 2 867 | 1 562 | 2 067 | 1 746 |
| 1952 | 31 193 | 18 652 | 4 125 | 5 004 | 2 319 | 2 663 | 2 555 |
| 1957 | 35 788 | 22 027 | 3 615 | 5 863 | 2 533 | 2 627 | 2 738 |
| 1962 | 42 967 | 26 191 | 5 011 | 7 294 | 3 187 | 3 383 | 2 912 |
| 1965 | 48 564 | 27 345 | 5 103 | 8 510 | 4 977 | 3 912 | 3 820 |
| 1970 | 51 397 | 28 185 | 5 397 | 8 636 | 5 299 | 4 922 | 4 355 |
| 1975 | 77 612 | 44 546 | 8 102 | 12 415 | 8 418 | 6 140 | 6 093 |
| 1978 | 94 747 | 51 986 | 10 208 | 15 313 | 13 233 | 6 924 | 7 291 |
| 1980 | 156 707 | 84 305 | 17 124 | 26 894 | 20 571 | 11 114 | 13 823 |
| 1985 | 370 485 | 194 924 | 42 027 | 69 891 | 44 214 | 30 366 | 31 090 |
| 1990 | 721 514 | 375 196 | 72 891 | 147 881 | 75 660 | 65 017 | 57 760 |
| 1995 | 2 423 094 | 1 217 029 | 207 724 | 507 723 | 285 642 | 247 284 | 165 416 |
| 1996 | 2 750 057 | 1 345 191 | 238 811 | 604 680 | 321 754 | 289 704 | 188 728 |
| 1997 | 3 056 010 | 1 526 465 | 270 537 | 635 027 | 360 472 | 329 069 | 204 977 |
| 1998 | 3 358 952 | 1 736 292 | 290 077 | 650 138 | 371 298 | 385 066 | 216 158 |
| 1999 | 3 716 368 | 1 961 917 | 305 090 | 687 124 | 393 140 | 443 114 | 231 073 |
| 2000 | 4 281 714 | 2 293 890 | 345 989 | 756 715 | 458 523 | 516 558 | 256 028 |
| 2001 | 4 914 382 | 2 652 807 | 393 390 | 847 521 | 522 342 | 609 046 | 282 666 |
| 2002 | 5 713 157 | 3 113 126 | 456 687 | 975 385 | 600 748 | 703 170 | 320 728 |
| 2003 | 6 640 502 | 3 633 803 | 526 263 | 1 108 282 | 705 690 | 831 572 | 361 155 |
| 2004 | 7 768 800 | 4 255 432 | 613 551 | 1 296 788 | 820 809 | 980 079 | 415 692 |
| 2005 | 9 343 000 | 5 103 568 | 762 873 | 1 509 313 | 996 237 | 1 226 497 | 507 385 |
| 2006 | 11 236 000 | 6 099 528 | 952 656 | 1 764 594 | 1 211 273 | 1 536 685 | 623 920 |
| 2007 | 13 706 000 | 7 378 277 | 1 207 675 | 2 099 770 | 1 494 469 | 1 955 155 | 778 329 |
| 2008 | 17 488 000 | 9 318 800 | 1 620 000 | 2 629 000 | 1 949 000 | 2 557 000 | 1 034 200 |
| 2009 | 20 268 405 | 10 774 312 | 1 874 029 | 3 045 857 | 2 261 813 | 2 980 480 | 1 205 943 |
| 2010 | 24 020 199 | 12 759 030 | 2 229 679 | 3 601 883 | 2 678 564 | 3 566 414 | 1 414 308 |
| 2011 | 28 295 794 | 14 987 098 | 2 636 452 | 4 262 612 | 3 164 556 | 4 209 816 | 1 671 712 |
| 2012 | 32 409 679 | 16 820 177 | 3 080 430 | 4 995 373 | 3 707 280 | 4 936 190 | 1 950 659 |

注：2005年开始数据根据经济普查已作调整，下同。
Note: From 2005, the statistics data has been adjusted in accord with the economic general investigation, same as the following.

表7-2

# 部分年份分行业社会消费品零售总额
# TOTAL RETAIL SALES OF CONSUMER GOODS OF PARTIAL YEARS BY SECTOR

单位：万元 (10 000 yuan)

| 年 份<br>Year | 社会消费品<br>零售总额<br>Total Retail Sales of<br>Consumer Goods | # 批发和零售业<br>Wholesale and<br>Retail Sale Trades | # 住宿和餐饮业<br>Accommodation and<br>Catering Trade |
|---|---|---|---|
| 1990 | 721 514 | 654 249 | 39 794 |
| 1995 | 2 423 094 | 2 177 435 | 207 724 |
| 2000 | 4 281 714 | 3 760 650 | 488 204 |
| 2001 | 4 914 382 | 4 290 204 | 590 511 |
| 2002 | 5 713 157 | 4 959 154 | 721 325 |
| 2003 | 6 640 502 | 5 753 184 | 852 147 |
| 2004 | 7 768 800 | 6 720 264 | 1 010 942 |
| 2005 | 9 343 000 | 8 119 628 | 1 179 960 |
| 2006 | 11 236 000 | 9 774 077 | 1 424 519 |
| 2007 | 13 706 000 | 11 924 334 | 1 749 650 |
| 2008 | 17 488 000 | 15 021 411 | 2 459 714 |
| 2009 | 20 268 405 | 17 792 291 | 2 256 499 |
| 2010 | 24 020 199 | 21 075 139 | 2 725 445 |
| 2011 | 28 295 794 | 24 764 557 | 3 213 714 |
| 2012 | 32 409 679 | 28 303 744 | 3 827 257 |

表7-3

# 分地区社会消费品零售总额（2012年）
# TOTAL RETAIL SALES OF CONSUMER GOODS BY REGION (2012)

单位：万元 (10 000 yuan)

| 地 区 Region | 社会消费品零售总额<br>Total Retail Sales of<br>Consumer Goods | # 个 体<br>Individual | 按行业分 Grouped by Sector<br>#批发和零售业<br>Wholesale and<br>Retail Sale Trades | #住宿和餐饮业<br>Accommodation and<br>Catering Trade |
|---|---|---|---|---|
| **全 市 Whole Municipality** | **32 409 679** | **12 547 796** | **28 303 744** | **3 827 257** |
| 市 区 Urban Area | 16 820 177 | 5 432 673 | 14 983 584 | 1 672 934 |
| # 吴江区 Wujiang District | 3 080 430 | 1 311 459 | 2 615 864 | 438 766 |
| 常 熟 Changshu | 4 995 373 | 2 364 931 | 4 522 363 | 451 071 |
| 张家港 Zhangjiagang | 3 707 280 | 1 788 406 | 3 207 513 | 476 414 |
| 昆 山 Kunshan | 4 936 190 | 2 156 996 | 3 901 425 | 965 039 |
| 太 仓 Taicang | 1 950 659 | 804 790 | 1 688 859 | 261 800 |

表7-4

# 分月社会消费品零售总额（2012年）
# RETAIL SALES OF CONSUMER GOODS BY MONTH (2012)

单位：万元 (10 000 yuan)

| 月　份 | Month | 全　市 Whole Municipality | 市　区 Urban Area | #吴江区 Wujiang District | 常　熟 Changshu | 张家港 Zhangjiagang | 昆　山 Kunshan | 太　仓 Taicang |
|---|---|---|---|---|---|---|---|---|
| **总　计** | **Total** | **32 409 679** | **16 820 177** | **3 080 430** | **4 995 373** | **3 707 280** | **4 936 190** | **1 950 659** |
| **一季度** | **1st Quarter** | **8 288 030** | **4 347 611** | **828 383** | **1 268 163** | **945 224** | **1 220 411** | **506 621** |
| 1月 | Jan. | 2 713 941 | 1 420 607 | 277 758 | 427 733 | 305 754 | 389 073 | 170 774 |
| 2月 | Feb. | 2 889 961 | 1 552 306 | 280 862 | 431 470 | 312 451 | 417 546 | 176 188 |
| 3月 | Mar. | 2 684 128 | 1 374 698 | 269 763 | 408 960 | 327 019 | 413 792 | 159 659 |
| **二季度** | **2nd Quarter** | **7 581 279** | **3 941 158** | **734 937** | **1 215 733** | **836 043** | **1 124 127** | **464 218** |
| 4月 | Apr. | 2 498 158 | 1 294 469 | 251 543 | 412 778 | 279 826 | 356 682 | 154 403 |
| 5月 | May. | 2 616 625 | 1 375 434 | 235 800 | 412 433 | 293 102 | 381 589 | 154 067 |
| 6月 | June | 2 466 496 | 1 271 255 | 247 594 | 390 522 | 263 115 | 385 856 | 155 748 |
| **三季度** | **3rd Quarter** | **7 877 605** | **4 101 673** | **755 643** | **1 206 214** | **890 753** | **1 199 672** | **479 293** |
| 7月 | July | 2 518 498 | 1 311 538 | 243 057 | 389 587 | 278 632 | 379 102 | 159 639 |
| 8月 | Aug. | 2 566 004 | 1 328 618 | 239 524 | 396 663 | 284 473 | 402 391 | 153 859 |
| 9月 | Sept. | 2 793 103 | 1 461 517 | 273 062 | 419 964 | 327 648 | 418 179 | 165 795 |
| **四季度** | **4th Quarter** | **8 662 765** | **4 429 735** | **761 467** | **1 305 263** | **1 035 260** | **1 391 980** | **500 527** |
| 10月 | Oct. | 2 814 156 | 1 444 071 | 248 859 | 432 295 | 333 849 | 438 717 | 165 224 |
| 11月 | Nov. | 2 800 408 | 1 453 813 | 246 866 | 411 467 | 329 796 | 443 998 | 161 334 |
| 12月 | Dec. | 3 048 201 | 1 531 851 | 265 742 | 461 501 | 371 615 | 509 265 | 173 969 |

表7-5 限额以上批发和零售、住宿和餐饮法人企业基本情况（2012年）

BASIC CONDITION OF WHOLESALE AND RETAIL, ACCOMMODATION AND CATERING CORPORATE ENTERPRISES ABOVE THE DESIGNATED SIZE (2012)

| 项 目 | Item | 法人企业数(个) Number of Corporation (unit) | 经营网点数(个) Number of Operation Network (unit) | 零售或餐饮营业面积(平方米) Floor Space of Retail or Catering Business (sq.m) | 年末从业人员(人) Year-end Employees (person) |
|---|---|---|---|---|---|
| **总 计** | **Total** | **3 670** | **9 662** | **5 685 184** | **258 510** |
| 市 区 | Urban Area | 1 839 | 5 083 | 3 312 842 | 135 747 |
| # 吴江区 | Wujiang District | 623 | 854 | 405 350 | 19 192 |
| 常 熟 | Changshu | 542 | 1 527 | 688 997 | 25 068 |
| 张家港 | Zhangjiagang | 587 | 1 214 | 500 313 | 28 447 |
| 昆 山 | Kunshan | 528 | 1 178 | 900 818 | 60 172 |
| 太 仓 | Taicang | 174 | 660 | 282 214 | 9 076 |
| **一、批发和零售业小计** | **Wholesale Trades and Retail Sales** | **3 204** | **8 484** | **4 387 707** | **181 862** |
| **按行业分** | **Grouped by Sector** | | | | |
| 批发业 | Wholesale Trades | 2 331 | 4 581 | 291 413 | 83 653 |
| 零售业 | Retail Sales | 873 | 3 903 | 4 096 294 | 98 209 |
| **按地区分** | **Grouped by Region** | | | | |
| 市 区 | Urban Area | 1 559 | 4 211 | 2 446 707 | 81 188 |
| # 吴江区 | Wujiang District | 579 | 789 | 267 130 | 13 204 |
| 常 熟 | Changshu | 494 | 1 463 | 573 266 | 19 772 |
| 张家港 | Zhangjiagang | 549 | 1 158 | 385 640 | 22 837 |
| 昆 山 | Kunshan | 446 | 1 028 | 754 842 | 51 639 |
| 太 仓 | Taicang | 156 | 624 | 227 252 | 6 426 |
| **二、住宿和餐饮业小计** | **Accommodation and Catering Trade** | **466** | **1 178** | **1 297 477** | **76 648** |
| **按行业分** | **Grouped by Sector** | | | | |
| 住宿业 | Accommodation | 211 | 341 | 509 095 | 35 643 |
| 餐饮业 | Catering Trade | 255 | 837 | 788 382 | 41 005 |
| **按地区分** | **Grouped by Region** | | | | |
| 市 区 | Urban Area | 280 | 872 | 866 135 | 54 559 |
| # 吴江区 | Wujiang District | 44 | 65 | 138 220 | 5 988 |
| 常 熟 | Changshu | 48 | 64 | 115 731 | 5 296 |
| 张家港 | Zhangjiagang | 38 | 56 | 114 673 | 5 610 |
| 昆 山 | Kunshan | 82 | 150 | 145 976 | 8 533 |
| 太 仓 | Taicang | 18 | 36 | 54 962 | 2 650 |

表7-6　限额以上批发和零售业商品购进、销售、库存总额 (2012年)

单位：万元

| 项　　目 | Item | 购进总额 Total Purchases |
|---|---|---|
| **总　　计** | **Total** | **88 269 679** |
| **一、批发业** | **Wholesale Trades** | **74 047 523** |
| # 国有及国有控股 | State-owned and State Holding Majority Shares | 3 582 532 |
| **1. 按地区分** | **Grouped by Region** | |
| 市　区 | Urban Area | 21 255 797 |
| # 吴江区 | Wujiang District | 5 217 817 |
| 常　熟 | Changshu | 6 233 601 |
| 张家港 | Zhangjiagang | 37 863 917 |
| 昆　山 | Kunshan | 4 491 894 |
| 太　仓 | Taicang | 4 202 315 |
| **2. 按登记注册类型分** | **Grouped by Registration Status** | |
| 国有企业 | State-owned Enterprises | 1 995 358 |
| 集体企业 | Collective-owned Enterprises | 142 128 |
| 股份合作企业 | Share-holding Cooperative Enterprises | 64 489 |
| 联营企业 | Joint Ownership Enterprises | 56 683 |
| 有限责任公司 | Limited Liability Corporations | 24 896 254 |
| 股份有限公司 | Share-holding Cooperative Ltd. | 2 148 878 |
| 私营企业 | Private Enterprises | 29 543 999 |
| 其他企业 | Other Enterprises | 886 206 |
| 港澳台商投资企业 | Enterprises with Investment from HongKong, Macao and Taiwan | 2 121 205 |
| 外商投资企业 | Enterprises with Foreign Investment | 12 192 324 |
| **3. 按主要行业分** | **Grouped by Sector** | |
| 农畜产品批发 | Wholesale of Farm and Animal Products | 903 645 |
| 食品、饮料及烟草制品批发 | Wholesale of Food, Beverages and Tobaccos | 2 173 168 |
| 纺织、服装及日用品批发 | Wholesale of Textiles, Garments and Daily Articles | 12 304 496 |
| # 服装批发 | Wholesale of Garments | 3 899 619 |
| 文化、体育用品及器材批发 | Wholesale of Cultural, Sports and Appliances Goods | 703 354 |

# TOTAL PURCHASES, SALES AND INVENTORY OF WHOLESALE AND RETAIL TRADE ABOVE DESIGNATED SIZE (2012)

(10 000 yuan)

| #进口 Imports | 销售总额 Total Sales | 批发 Wholesale | #出口 Exports | 零售 Retail Sale | 年末库存总额 Inventory (year-end) |
|---|---|---|---|---|---|
| **7 648 496** | **96 137 798** | **80 322 353** | **6 973 544** | **15 815 445** | **4 499 390** |
| **7 231 693** | **80 231 435** | **79 157 169** | **6 971 366** | **1 074 266** | **3 234 858** |
| 742 947 | 5 171 340 | 5 049 581 | 1 459 066 | 121 760 | 317 207 |
| | | | | | |
| 1 382 604 | 23 219 974 | 22 863 477 | 2 550 702 | 356 497 | 1 083 155 |
| 118 519 | 5 625 086 | 5 596 489 | 766 429 | 28 597 | 119 232 |
| 139 305 | 6 556 791 | 6 380 754 | 667 138 | 176 037 | 463 103 |
| 4 997 587 | 40 014 894 | 39 782 045 | 3 166 725 | 232 849 | 1 004 230 |
| 268 486 | 4 884 466 | 4 831 142 | 344 194 | 53 324 | 398 180 |
| 443 711 | 5 555 311 | 5 299 752 | 242 607 | 255 559 | 286 191 |
| | | | | | |
| 662 407 | 3 607 895 | 3 552 267 | 1 228 927 | 55 628 | 165 879 |
| - | 147 179 | 146 999 | 9 495 | 180 | 7 243 |
| 2 154 | 71 389 | 70 916 | 8 444 | 473 | 5 004 |
| - | 57 725 | 57 725 | 268 | - | 216 |
| 4 198 201 | 25 224 797 | 24 888 603 | 2 764 758 | 336 193 | 815 087 |
| 55 584 | 2 280 742 | 2 219 352 | 201 050 | 61 390 | 91 684 |
| 1 004 350 | 31 117 952 | 30 828 751 | 2 222 662 | 289 200 | 1 281 115 |
| 6 429 | 908 293 | 906 260 | 47 784 | 2 034 | 54 891 |
| 724 804 | 3 577 014 | 3 357 871 | 297 164 | 219 143 | 421 747 |
| 577 765 | 13 238 451 | 13 128 426 | 190 813 | 110 025 | 391 993 |
| | | | | | |
| 168 457 | 879 611 | 874 209 | 1 182 | 5 402 | 45 936 |
| 105 893 | 2 563 787 | 2 484 710 | 12 527 | 79 076 | 169 504 |
| 1 715 789 | 16 087 184 | 15 685 381 | 4 201 077 | 401 803 | 814 661 |
| 1 045 373 | 5 407 762 | 5 263 376 | 2 281 925 | 144 386 | 311 547 |
| 16 587 | 807 270 | 786 425 | 42 904 | 20 844 | 264 938 |

表7-6 续表 1

单位：万元

| 项　　目 | Item | 购进总额 Total Purchases |
|---|---|---|
| 医药及医疗器材批发 | Wholesale of Medicines and Medical Appliances | 752 786 |
| 矿产品、建材及化工产品批发 | Wholesale of Mineral Products, Building Materials and Chemical Products | 50 402 353 |
| 机械设备、五金交电及电子产品批发 | Wholesale of Machinery, Hardware, Transport, Electric and Electronic Equipment | 4 523 110 |
| # 农业机械批发 | Wholesale Agricultural Machinery | 15 453 |
| 汽车、摩托车及零配件批发 | Wholesale of Motor Vehicles, Motorcycles and Parts | 342 821 |
| 五金、交电批发 | Wholesale of Hardware, Transport and Electric | 684 711 |
| 家用电器批发 | Wholesale Household Appliances | 787 814 |
| 计算机、软件及辅助设备批发 | Wholesale of Computers, Software and Appliances | 505 033 |
| 贸易经纪与代理 | Trade Management and Agency | 757 137 |
| 其他批发 | Other Wholesale | 1 527 473 |
| **二、零售业** | **Retail Trades** | **14 222 156** |
| # 国有及国有控股 | State-owned and State Holding Majority Shares | 1 768 408 |
| **1. 按地区分** | **Grouped by Region** | |
| 市　区 | Urban Area | 8 370 671 |
| # 吴江区 | Wujiang District | 939 892 |
| 常　熟 | Changshu | 1 592 417 |
| 张家港 | Zhangjiagang | 1 038 013 |
| 昆　山 | Kunshan | 2 881 728 |
| 太　仓 | Taicang | 339 328 |
| **2. 按登记注册类型分** | **Grouped by Registration Status** | |
| 国有企业 | State-owned Enterprises | 95 595 |
| 集体企业 | Collective-owned Enterprises | 70 211 |
| 股份合作企业 | Share-holding Cooperative Enterprises | 34 399 |
| 联营企业 | Joint Ownership Enterprises | 69 703 |
| 有限责任公司 | Limited Liability Corporations | 3 236 232 |
| 股份有限公司 | Share-holding Cooperative Ltd. | 702 067 |
| 私营企业 | Private Enterprises | 5 717 274 |

Continued 1

(10 000 yuan)

| # 进口 Imports | 销售总额 Total Sales | 批发 Wholesale | # 出口 Exports | 零售 Retail Sale | 年末库存总额 Inventory (year-end) |
|---|---|---|---|---|---|
| 3 730 | 803 841 | 702 534 | 28 675 | 101 307 | 64 385 |
| 4 351 521 | 51 787 347 | 51 564 854 | 1 792 092 | 222 493 | 1 368 104 |
| 618 056 | 4 887 899 | 4 649 711 | 477 440 | 238 188 | 459 236 |
| – | 17 465 | 17 465 | – | – | 1 630 |
| 25 589 | 358 731 | 341 686 | 39 028 | 17 045 | 20 589 |
| 35 708 | 789 803 | 780 230 | 74 773 | 9 573 | 28 852 |
| – | 820 290 | 650 497 | 8 542 | 169 793 | 132 783 |
| 14 390 | 573 674 | 557 644 | 2 975 | 16 030 | 43 887 |
| 87 679 | 799 406 | 799 115 | 238 925 | 290 | 9 277 |
| 163 981 | 1 615 092 | 1 610 230 | 176 545 | 4 862 | 38 818 |
| **416 803** | **15 906 362** | **1 165 184** | **2 179** | **14 741 179** | **1 264 532** |
| – | 1 880 113 | 527 464 | – | 1 352 649 | 56 113 |
| | | | | | |
| 315 109 | 9 155 756 | 860 462 | – | 8 295 295 | 596 616 |
| 132 461 | 973 868 | 17 725 | – | 956 143 | 69 023 |
| 32 820 | 1 758 316 | 161 041 | 675 | 1 597 275 | 143 245 |
| 26 712 | 1 232 615 | 46 227 | 1 504 | 1 186 388 | 133 791 |
| 17 640 | 3 401 285 | 85 764 | – | 3 315 521 | 350 820 |
| 24 522 | 358 390 | 11 691 | – | 346 699 | 40 060 |
| | | | | | |
| – | 116 544 | 1 111 | – | 115 433 | 8 787 |
| – | 84 202 | 5 881 | – | 78 320 | 2 902 |
| – | 41 660 | 9 718 | – | 31 942 | 2 760 |
| – | 74 185 | 6 663 | – | 67 522 | 5 285 |
| 203 213 | 3 824 251 | 368 610 | – | 3 455 641 | 325 215 |
| – | 900 169 | 57 715 | – | 842 454 | 62 402 |
| 213 052 | 5 877 923 | 218 511 | 2 179 | 5 659 412 | 503 808 |

表7-6 续表 2

单位：万元

| 项　　目 | Item | 购进总额 Total Purchases |
|---|---|---|
| 其他企业 | Other Enterprises | 138 350 |
| 港澳台商投资企业 | Enterprises with Investment from HongKong, Macao and Taiwan | 2 023 559 |
| 外商投资企业 | Enterprises with Foreign Investment | 2 134 766 |
| **3.按主要行业分** | **Grouped by Sector** | |
| 综合零售 | Retail of Integrated | 3 999 434 |
| 百货零售 | Retail of Consumer Goods | 1 184 578 |
| 超级市场零售 | Retail of Supermarket | 2 775 167 |
| 其他综合零售 | Others Retail of Integrated | 39 689 |
| 食品、饮料及烟草制品专门零售 | Retail of Food, Beverages and Tobaccos | 184 231 |
| 纺织、服装及日用品专门零售 | Retail of Textiles, Garments and Daily Articles | 312 726 |
| 文化、体育用品及器材专门零售 | Retail of Culture, Sports Articles and Equipment | 535 532 |
| 医药及医疗器材专门零售 | Retail of Medicines and Medical Appliances | 1 096 844 |
| 汽车、摩托车、燃料及零配件专门零售 | Retail of Motor Vehicles, Motorcycles, Fuels and Parts | 6 983 408 |
| # 汽车零售 | Retail of Motor Vehicles | 5 247 311 |
| 家用电器及电子产品专门零售 | Retail of Household Appliances and Electronic Products | 798 462 |
| # 家用电器零售 | Retail of Household Appliances | 632 272 |
| 计算机、软件及辅助设备零售 | Retail of Computers, Software and Appliances | 48 913 |
| 五金、家具及室内装修材料专门零售 | Retail of Hardware Furniture and Materials for Ornament | 94 000 |
| 无店铺及其他零售 | Retail of Non-shop and Others | 217 519 |
| **4.按经营方式分** | **Grouped by Means of Operation** | |
| 独立商店 | Independent Shop | 8 102 507 |
| 连锁商店总店 | Central Shop of Chain Shops | 3 509 796 |
| 连锁门店 | Outlets of Chain Shops | 903 486 |
| 其　他 | Others | 1 706 367 |
| **5.按零售业态分** | **Grouped by Retail Size** | |
| 百货商店 | Department Store | 1 288 795 |
| 超级市场 | Supermarket | 2 847 065 |
| 专业店 | Special Store | 5 999 087 |
| 专卖店 | Monopoly Store | 3 548 730 |
| 其　他 | Others | 538 479 |

Continued 2

(10 000 yuan)

| # 进 口 Imports | 销售总额 Total Sales | 批 发 Wholesale | # 出 口 Exports | 零 售 Retail Sale | 年末库存总额 Inventory (year-end) |
|---|---|---|---|---|---|
| – | 173 407 | 17 285 | – | 156 122 | 22 790 |
| – | 2 554 511 | 3 400 | – | 2 551 111 | 221 030 |
| 538 | 2 259 510 | 476 289 | – | 1 783 221 | 109 552 |
| | | | | | |
| 2 087 | 5 077 591 | 125 848 | – | 4 951 742 | 393 377 |
| 1 550 | 1 630 724 | 60 523 | – | 1 570 201 | 101 783 |
| 538 | 3 404 425 | 65 326 | – | 3 339 099 | 289 362 |
| – | 42 442 | – | – | 42 442 | 2 232 |
| – | 223 979 | 16 478 | – | 207 501 | 22 371 |
| 6 | 414 137 | 50 555 | 675 | 363 582 | 72 420 |
| 4 191 | 651 178 | 33 373 | – | 617 806 | 108 671 |
| 6 | 1 157 062 | 248 346 | – | 908 716 | 86 706 |
| 410 307 | 7 353 345 | 627 600 | – | 6 725 746 | 519 426 |
| 408 165 | 5 540 193 | 114 882 | – | 5 425 311 | 473 677 |
| – | 668 398 | 47 511 | – | 620 886 | 46 238 |
| – | 494 745 | 26 258 | – | 468 487 | 29 224 |
| – | 41 915 | 3 312 | – | 38 603 | 7 912 |
| 207 | 107 470 | 5 403 | 1 504 | 102 067 | 10 674 |
| – | 253 202 | 10 070 | – | 243 132 | 4 648 |
| | | | | | |
| 411 144 | 9 259 939 | 390 529 | 1 791 | 8 869 411 | 785 696 |
| 538 | 4 115 421 | 490 124 | – | 3 625 298 | 297 603 |
| – | 726 851 | 1 254 | – | 725 597 | 74 222 |
| 5 121 | 1 804 151 | 283 278 | 388 | 1 520 873 | 107 011 |
| | | | | | |
| 1 550 | 1 842 948 | 60 523 | – | 1 782 426 | 123 711 |
| 538 | 3 478 050 | 65 376 | – | 3 412 673 | 298 365 |
| 197 774 | 6 156 784 | 849 665 | 675 | 5 307 119 | 474 661 |
| 216 734 | 3 801 605 | 128 872 | – | 3 672 733 | 345 876 |
| 207 | 626 976 | 60 748 | 1 504 | 566 228 | 21 918 |

表7-7 限额以上住宿和餐饮业经营情况 (2012年)

| 项　目 | Item | 营业总额 (万元) Total Business Turnover (10 000 yuan) |
|---|---|---|
| **总　计** | **Total** | **1 370 308** |
| **一、住宿业** | **Accommodation** | **700 691** |
| # 国有及国有控股 | State-owned and State Holding Majority Shares | 213 507 |
| **1. 按地区分** | **Grouped by Region** | |
| 市　区 | Urban Area | 478 160 |
| # 吴江区 | Wujiang District | 73 069 |
| 常　熟 | Changshu | 58 219 |
| 张家港 | Zhangjiagang | 63 146 |
| 昆　山 | Kunshan | 66 996 |
| 太　仓 | Taicang | 34 170 |
| **2. 按登记注册类型分** | **Grouped by Registration Status** | |
| 国有企业 | State-owned Enterprises | 122 232 |
| 集体企业 | Collective-owned Enterprises | 23 478 |
| 股份合作企业 | Share-holding Cooperative Enterprises | 886 |
| 联营企业 | Joint Ownership Enterprises | 8 396 |
| 有限责任公司 | Limited Liability Corporations | 174 713 |
| 股份有限公司 | Share-holding Cooperative Ltd. | 11 866 |
| 私营企业 | Private Enterprises | 204 671 |
| 其他企业 | Other Enterprises | 14 099 |
| 港澳台商投资企业 | Enterprises with Investment from HongKong, Macao and Taiwan | 62 682 |
| 外商投资企业 | Enterprises with Foreign Investment | 77 669 |
| **3. 按主要行业分** | **Grouped by Sector** | |
| 旅游饭店 | Tourist Hotel | 652 357 |
| 一般旅馆 | Regular Hotel | 41 782 |
| 其他住宿服务 | Other Accommodation Service | 6 552 |
| **4. 按星级等级分** | **Grouped by Star Rated** | |
| 五　星 | Five Star | 273 307 |
| 四　星 | Four Star | 197 948 |
| 三　星 | Three Star | 47 278 |
| 二　星 | Two Star | 4 078 |
| 一　星 | One Star | - |
| 其　他 | Other | 178 080 |

# BUSINESS CONDITION OF ACCOMMODATION AND CATERING ENTERPRISES ABOVE DESIGNATED SIZE(2012)

| 客房收入 Room Rate Revenues | 餐费收入 Catering Revenues | 商品销售收入 Commodity Sales Revenues | 其他收入 Others Revenues | 年末拥有床位数(个) Year-end Guest Beds (unit) | 年末拥有餐位数(个) Dining Seats by the Year end (unit) |
|---|---|---|---|---|---|
| **341 548** | **950 725** | **11 769** | **66 266** | **76 607** | **295 858** |
| **300 361** | **337 982** | **8 998** | **53 349** | **66 590** | **126 678** |
| 80 750 | 113 381 | 790 | 18 586 | 16 783 | 39 841 |
| | | | | | |
| 209 753 | 220 733 | 7 201 | 40 473 | 43 702 | 76 518 |
| 19 701 | 46 803 | 1 118 | 5 446 | 5 882 | 17 874 |
| 22 141 | 32 715 | 908 | 2 455 | 5 964 | 14 068 |
| 23 390 | 35 469 | 439 | 3 848 | 4 649 | 13 732 |
| 32 168 | 30 747 | 353 | 3 728 | 9 562 | 16 848 |
| 12 909 | 18 318 | 98 | 2 845 | 2 713 | 5 512 |
| | | | | | |
| 41 935 | 68 625 | 548 | 11 124 | 9 922 | 25 047 |
| 8 605 | 12 387 | 498 | 1 988 | 2 123 | 4 790 |
| 529 | 357 | – | – | 204 | 200 |
| 1 396 | 4 080 | 2 360 | 560 | 284 | 680 |
| 78 314 | 79 576 | 940 | 15 882 | 14 783 | 28 996 |
| 7 427 | 3 767 | 24 | 648 | 1 070 | 980 |
| 88 906 | 99 859 | 3 328 | 12 579 | 24 842 | 45 947 |
| 6 153 | 7 312 | 41 | 594 | 2 195 | 3 250 |
| 25 894 | 32 918 | 336 | 3 534 | 5 412 | 10 416 |
| 41 204 | 29 101 | 924 | 6 440 | 5 755 | 6 372 |
| | | | | | |
| 270 166 | 325 474 | 8 621 | 48 096 | 58 315 | 119 249 |
| 24 876 | 12 161 | 377 | 4 368 | 7 690 | 7 129 |
| 5 320 | 347 | – | 885 | 585 | 300 |
| | | | | | |
| 110 489 | 142 578 | 2 412 | 17 828 | 13 556 | 39 838 |
| 68 544 | 109 643 | 4 551 | 15 211 | 18 575 | 39 648 |
| 20 777 | 20 060 | 669 | 5 773 | 8 308 | 14 880 |
| 1 842 | 1 931 | 40 | 265 | 1 070 | 2 267 |
| – | – | – | – | – | – |
| 98 709 | 63 771 | 1 327 | 14 273 | 25 081 | 30 045 |

表7-7 续表

| 项　　目 | Item | 营业总额 (万元) Total Business Turnover (10 000 yuan) |
|---|---|---|
| **二、餐饮业** | **Catering Services** | **669 617** |
| #国有及国有控股 | State-owned and State Holding Majority Shares | 18 872 |
| **1. 按地区分** | **Grouped by Region** | |
| 市　区 | Urban Area | 516 719 |
| # 吴江区 | Wujiang District | 25 577 |
| 常　熟 | Changshu | 35 071 |
| 张家港 | Zhangjiagang | 32 557 |
| 昆　山 | Kunshan | 74 439 |
| 太　仓 | Taicang | 10 832 |
| **2. 按登记注册类型分** | **Grouped by Registration Status** | |
| 国有企业 | State-owned Enterprises | 8 050 |
| 集体企业 | Collective-owned Enterprises | 10 831 |
| 股份合作企业 | Share-holding Cooperative Enterprises | – |
| 联营企业 | Joint Ownership Enterprises | – |
| 有限责任公司 | Limited Liability Corporations | 69 014 |
| 股份有限公司 | Share-holding Cooperative Ltd. | 24 950 |
| 私营企业 | Private Enterprises | 254 975 |
| 其他企业 | Other Enterprises | 12 671 |
| 港澳台商投资企业 | Enterprises with Investment from HongKong, Macao and Taiwan | 42 631 |
| 外商投资企业 | Enterprises with Foreign Investment | 246 494 |
| **3. 按主要行业分** | **Grouped by Sector** | |
| 正餐服务 | Dinner | 370 552 |
| 快餐服务 | Fast Food | 218 085 |
| 饮料及冷饮服务 | Beverage and Cold Drink Services | 34 746 |
| 其他餐饮服务 | Other | 46 234 |
| **4. 按经营方式分** | **Grouped by Management Forms** | |
| 独立经营 | Independent-stores | 346 231 |
| 连锁经营总店 | Chain-stores-General | 220 982 |
| 连锁经营分店 | Chain-stores-Branch | 66 502 |
| 其　他 | Other | 35 903 |

Continued

| 客房收入 Room Rate Revenues | 餐费收入 Catering Revenues | 商品销售收入 Commodity Sales Revenues | 其他收入 Others Revenues | 年末拥有床位数(个) Year-end Guest Beds (unit) | 年末拥有餐位数(个) Dining Seats by the Year end (unit) |
|---|---|---|---|---|---|
| **41 187** | **612 742** | **2 771** | **12 917** | **10 017** | **169 180** |
| 4 869 | 13 734 | 74 | 196 | 1 068 | 5 060 |
| | | | | | |
| 14 482 | 492 162 | 428 | 9 648 | 3 352 | 119 980 |
| 4 106 | 20 291 | 110 | 1 070 | 1 181 | 10 158 |
| 4 610 | 29 904 | 177 | 380 | 1 084 | 11 730 |
| 3 747 | 27 558 | 384 | 867 | 1 046 | 8 900 |
| 17 492 | 53 548 | 1 717 | 1 682 | 4 097 | 24 320 |
| 856 | 9 570 | 65 | 340 | 438 | 4 250 |
| | | | | | |
| 1 622 | 6 277 | 74 | 77 | 611 | 2 310 |
| 750 | 9 778 | – | 303 | 463 | 3 440 |
| – | – | – | – | – | – |
| – | – | – | – | – | – |
| 14 767 | 50 690 | 2 | 3 556 | 2 155 | 14 771 |
| 181 | 24 465 | 304 | – | 71 | 12 324 |
| 12 785 | 237 896 | 2 171 | 2 124 | 4 310 | 92 326 |
| 1 325 | 10 672 | 29 | 645 | 603 | 5 032 |
| 9 757 | 30 622 | 122 | 2 130 | 1 804 | 9 634 |
| – | 242 342 | 69 | 4 083 | – | 29 343 |
| | | | | | |
| 39 167 | 321 237 | 1 453 | 8 695 | 9 711 | 125 948 |
| – | 218 085 | – | – | – | 27 948 |
| – | 30 486 | 177 | 4 083 | – | 4 652 |
| 2 021 | 42 934 | 1 141 | 139 | 306 | 10 632 |
| | | | | | |
| 37 594 | 298 477 | 1 481 | 8 679 | 8 836 | 109 997 |
| – | 216 899 | – | 4 083 | – | 27 945 |
| 764 | 65 572 | 149 | 16 | 542 | 19 203 |
| 2 830 | 31 794 | 1 141 | 139 | 639 | 12 035 |

表7-8 限额以上批发和零售法人企业主要财务指标 (2012年)

单位：万元

| 项　　目 | Item | 流动资产合计 Total Circulating Funds | 固定资产合计 Total Fixed Assets |
|---|---|---|---|
| **总　　计** | **Total** | **27 241 678** | **2 107 234** |
| **一、批发业** | **Wholesale Trades** | **23 148 950** | **1 176 250** |
| # 国有及国有控股 | State-owned and State Holding Majority Shares | 2 318 951 | 247 162 |
| **1. 按地区分** | **Grouped by Region** | | |
| 市　区 | Urban Area | 7 682 252 | 347 055 |
| # 吴江区 | Wujiang District | 1 656 837 | 83 986 |
| 常　熟 | Changshu | 2 739 163 | 205 512 |
| 张家港 | Zhangjiagang | 8 288 576 | 297 617 |
| 昆　山 | Kunshan | 1 987 988 | 126 960 |
| 太　仓 | Taicang | 2 450 972 | 199 107 |
| **2. 按登记注册类型分** | **Grouped by Registration Status** | | |
| 国有企业 | State-owned Enterprises | 1 419 138 | 206 949 |
| 集体企业 | Collective-owned Enterprises | 55 983 | 1 346 |
| 股份合作企业 | Share-holding Cooperative Enterprises | 22 534 | 1 378 |
| 联营企业 | Joint Ownership Enterprises | 21 094 | 104 |
| 有限责任公司 | Limited Liability Corporations | 5 840 983 | 230 437 |
| 股份有限公司 | Share-holding Cooperative Ltd. | 655 036 | 79 568 |
| 私营企业 | Private Enterprises | 11 204 432 | 393 793 |
| 其他企业 | Other Enterprises | 192 600 | 9 736 |
| 港澳台商投资企业 | Enterprises with Investment from HongKong, Macao and Taiwan | 1 620 888 | 176 251 |
| 外商投资企业 | Enterprises with Foreign Investment | 2 116 264 | 76 690 |
| **3. 按主要行业分** | **Grouped by Sector** | | |
| 农畜产品批发 | Wholesale of Agriculture and Livestock Products | 213 149 | 9 279 |
| 食品、饮料及烟草制品批发 | Wholesale of Food, Beverages and Tobaccos | 1 132 174 | 118 042 |
| 纺织、服装及日用品批发 | Wholesale of Textiles, Garments and Daily Articles | 5 450 024 | 414 375 |
| # 服装批发 | Wholesale of Garments | 2 195 250 | 196 359 |
| 文化、体育用品及器材批发 | Wholesale of Cultural, Sports Equipments and Appliances | 352 989 | 14 116 |

# MAIN FINANCIAL INDICATORS OF WHOLESALE AND RETAIL CORPORATION ABOVE DESIGNATED SIZE (2012)

(10 000 yuan)

| 固定资产原价 Original Value of Fixed Assets | 累计折旧 Accumulative Total Depreciation | 资产总计 Total Assets | 负债总计 Total Liabilities | 营业收入 Business Revenue | # 主营业务收入 Major Business Revenue | 营业成本 Business Cost | # 主营业务成本 Major Business Cost |
|---|---|---|---|---|---|---|---|
| **2 921 895** | **971 588** | **33 451 618** | **26 622 823** | **82 127 606** | **81 657 153** | **76 564 777** | **76 265 143** |
| **1 623 551** | **529 976** | **27 506 354** | **21 933 194** | **68 761 157** | **68 412 128** | **64 863 228** | **64 593 898** |
| 355 423 | 108 955 | 3 051 110 | 1 826 176 | 4 727 342 | 4 619 166 | 4 146 353 | 4 093 968 |
| | | | | | | | |
| 533 890 | 204 233 | 8 840 077 | 6 367 304 | 19 519 782 | 19 354 337 | 17 985 679 | 17 834 102 |
| 99 910 | 22 929 | 2 158 371 | 1 610 211 | 5 149 256 | 5 144 558 | 4 972 784 | 4 968 303 |
| 236 768 | 61 616 | 3 094 087 | 2 560 009 | 5 880 315 | 5 867 165 | 5 580 266 | 5 576 663 |
| 422 479 | 125 055 | 10 326 299 | 8 961 342 | 34 441 591 | 34 292 216 | 33 745 675 | 33 638 197 |
| 189 942 | 69 269 | 2 240 327 | 1 645 723 | 4 119 624 | 4 106 548 | 3 703 249 | 3 697 277 |
| 240 472 | 69 804 | 3 005 564 | 2 398 817 | 4 799 845 | 4 791 861 | 3 848 359 | 3 847 659 |
| | | | | | | | |
| 300 020 | 93 335 | 1 880 840 | 895 940 | 3 388 107 | 3 290 223 | 2 875 954 | 2 825 863 |
| 2 867 | 1 521 | 57 467 | 47 537 | 136 242 | 136 242 | 131 070 | 131 070 |
| 1 913 | 535 | 26 274 | 15 998 | 62 323 | 62 307 | 59 371 | 59 370 |
| 129 | 25 | 25 157 | 19 433 | 49 476 | 49 388 | 48 494 | 48 489 |
| 280 177 | 80 405 | 7 044 716 | 6 113 414 | 22 064 195 | 21 858 101 | 21 570 054 | 21 380 667 |
| 76 594 | 22 380 | 857 933 | 698 909 | 1 855 388 | 1 853 427 | 1 771 894 | 1 771 216 |
| 566 804 | 191 121 | 12 811 065 | 10 660 557 | 27 232 456 | 27 200 660 | 26 364 989 | 26 339 884 |
| 16 615 | 6 914 | 213 581 | 150 931 | 790 518 | 790 249 | 753 271 | 753 258 |
| 220 552 | 52 060 | 1 845 102 | 1 365 578 | 2 984 883 | 2 981 519 | 1 969 845 | 1 967 195 |
| 157 879 | 81 680 | 2 744 218 | 1 964 897 | 10 197 570 | 10 190 011 | 9 318 287 | 9 316 887 |
| | | | | | | | |
| 11 983 | 2 767 | 224 878 | 213 744 | 799 737 | 799 657 | 789 337 | 789 335 |
| 159 437 | 46 628 | 1 301 368 | 566 021 | 2 237 625 | 2 235 644 | 1 903 923 | 1 903 501 |
| 617 059 | 216 737 | 6 828 199 | 5 008 660 | 13 834 986 | 13 676 840 | 11 665 003 | 11 565 405 |
| 316 543 | 123 930 | 2 719 040 | 1 917 890 | 5 094 819 | 4 991 947 | 4 144 027 | 4 093 739 |
| 22 819 | 8 704 | 373 596 | 286 658 | 684 385 | 683 623 | 595 073 | 594 730 |

表7-8 续表 1

单位：万元

| 项 目 | Item | 流动资产合计 Total Circulating Funds | 固定资产合计 Total Fixed Assets |
|---|---|---|---|
| 医药及医疗器材批发 | Wholesale of Medicines and Medical Appliances | 273 102 | 13 236 |
| 矿产品、建材及化工产品批发 | Wholesale of Mineral Products, Building Materials and Chemical Products | 12 936 078 | 463 818 |
| 机械设备、五金交电及电子产品批发 | Wholesale of Machinery, Hardware, Transport, Electric and Electronic Equipment | 1 942 019 | 105 699 |
| #农业机械批发 | Wholesale Agricultural Machinery | 10 849 | 2 163 |
| 汽车、摩托车及零配件批发 | Wholesale of Motor Vehicles, Motorcycles and Parts | 185 171 | 6 996 |
| 五金、交电批发 | Wholesale of Hardware, Transport and Electric | 243 898 | 13 456 |
| 家用电器批发 | Wholesale Household Appliances | 393 546 | 42 281 |
| 计算机、软件及辅助设备批发 | Wholesale of Computer, Software and Assistant Equipments | 194 915 | 2 900 |
| 贸易经纪与代理 | Trade Management and Agency | 379 392 | 2 518 |
| 其他批发 | Other Wholesale | 470 023 | 35 167 |
| **二、零售业** | **Retail Trades** | **4 092 728** | **930 984** |
| # 国有及国有控股 | State-owned and State Holding Majority Shares | 250 928 | 91 950 |
| **1. 按地区分** | **Grouped by Region** | | |
| 市 区 | Urban Area | 2 321 323 | 529 167 |
| # 吴江区 | Wujiang District | 271 571 | 46 411 |
| 常 熟 | Changshu | 431 402 | 84 442 |
| 张家港 | Zhangjiagang | 371 720 | 91 701 |
| 昆 山 | Kunshan | 876 719 | 206 286 |
| 太 仓 | Taicang | 91 564 | 19 387 |
| **2. 按登记注册类型分** | **Grouped by Registration Status** | | |
| 国有企业 | State-owned Enterprises | 64 299 | 14 725 |
| 集体企业 | Collective-owned Enterprises | 10 677 | 3 364 |
| 股份合作企业 | Share-holding Cooperative Enterprises | 10 645 | 1 558 |
| 联营企业 | Joint Ownership Enterprises | 7 877 | 2 261 |
| 有限责任公司 | Limited Liability Corporations | 1 080 104 | 221 383 |
| 股份有限公司 | Share-holding Cooperative Ltd. | 149 169 | 91 247 |
| 私营企业 | Private Enterprises | 1 790 322 | 275 600 |

Continued 1

(10 000 yuan)

| 固定资产原价 Original Value of Fixed Assets | 累计折旧 Accumulative Total Depreciation | 资产总计 Total Assets | 负债总计 Total Liabilities | 营业收入 Business Revenue | #主营业务收入 Major Business Revenue | 营业成本 Business Cost | #主营业务成本 Major Business Cost |
|---|---|---|---|---|---|---|---|
| 19 616 | 7 300 | 312 148 | 251 033 | 700 444 | 698 325 | 655 281 | 654 629 |
| 607 454 | 174 216 | 15 357 102 | 13 290 574 | 44 212 217 | 44 048 985 | 43 305 934 | 43 148 415 |
| 129 989 | 48 240 | 2 158 655 | 1 547 116 | 4 117 261 | 4 096 658 | 3 821 870 | 3 812 391 |
| 2 699 | 536 | 13 277 | 6 830 | 17 167 | 16 615 | 15 442 | 15 286 |
| 8 394 | 1 970 | 210 075 | 165 354 | 300 744 | 297 982 | 284 290 | 283 452 |
| 20 724 | 7 715 | 266 616 | 192 248 | 677 835 | 674 846 | 633 249 | 631 016 |
| 29 635 | 10 282 | 456 858 | 374 747 | 709 599 | 705 145 | 650 263 | 648 797 |
| 4 768 | 1 869 | 207 697 | 147 691 | 501 409 | 497 918 | 478 872 | 475 557 |
| 6 055 | 3 536 | 393 673 | 378 421 | 763 502 | 762 074 | 748 449 | 747 372 |
| 49 138 | 21 849 | 556 734 | 390 966 | 1 410 999 | 1 410 324 | 1 378 357 | 1 378 121 |
| **1 298 344** | **441 611** | **5 945 264** | **4 689 629** | **13 366 449** | **13 245 025** | **11 701 550** | **11 671 244** |
| 137 382 | 45 498 | 528 929 | 358 424 | 1 607 930 | 1 595 516 | 1 487 859 | 1 481 249 |
| | | | | | | | |
| 792 043 | 276 987 | 3 475 720 | 2 712 458 | 7 875 771 | 7 786 188 | 6 974 601 | 6 952 015 |
| 65 469 | 19 420 | 335 381 | 273 871 | 829 616 | 824 230 | 762 637 | 761 895 |
| 120 171 | 46 976 | 585 157 | 447 476 | 1 442 460 | 1 437 392 | 1 303 330 | 1 301 851 |
| 137 933 | 46 527 | 620 721 | 505 764 | 1 003 169 | 992 696 | 907 596 | 907 059 |
| 217 743 | 59 886 | 1 139 601 | 924 533 | 2 732 057 | 2 721 108 | 2 232 416 | 2 227 927 |
| 30 455 | 11 235 | 124 066 | 99 398 | 312 992 | 307 641 | 283 608 | 282 391 |
| | | | | | | | |
| 22 754 | 8 029 | 89 888 | 59 012 | 103 256 | 96 809 | 83 644 | 81 119 |
| 6 249 | 2 884 | 15 429 | 7 041 | 73 487 | 73 398 | 68 288 | 68 247 |
| 4 595 | 3 038 | 12 844 | 11 798 | 30 934 | 30 934 | 28 065 | 28 065 |
| 3 941 | 1 681 | 12 724 | 5 408 | 63 406 | 63 406 | 58 983 | 58 983 |
| 326 178 | 115 069 | 1 596 993 | 1 380 139 | 3 167 533 | 3 136 481 | 2 817 127 | 2 810 394 |
| 73 726 | 39 415 | 290 748 | 186 579 | 769 050 | 765 527 | 575 616 | 574 453 |
| 423 834 | 155 226 | 2 389 227 | 1 900 901 | 5 029 281 | 4 976 834 | 4 570 184 | 4 554 588 |

表7-8 续表 2

单位：万元

| 项　目 | Item | 流动资产合计 Total Circulating Funds | 固定资产合计 Total Fixed Assets |
|---|---|---|---|
| 其他企业 | Other Enterprises | 59 752 | 16 496 |
| 港澳台商投资企业 | Enterprises with Investment from HongKong, Macao and Taiwan | 713 229 | 177 421 |
| 外商投资企业 | Enterprises with Foreign Investment | 206 654 | 126 929 |
| **3. 按主要行业分** | **Grouped by Sector** | | |
| 综合零售 | Retail of Integrated | 1 302 222 | 473 422 |
| 百货零售 | Retail of Consumer Goods | 481 436 | 230 836 |
| 超级市场零售 | Retail of Supermarket | 813 360 | 240 615 |
| 其他综合零售 | Others  Retail of Integrated | 7 426 | 1 971 |
| 食品、饮料及烟草制品专门零售 | Wholesale of Foodstuff, Drink and Tobacco | 68 401 | 17 643 |
| 纺织、服装及日用品专门零售 | Wholesale of Textiles, Garments, Shoes and Hats | 166 985 | 15 135 |
| 文化、体育用品及器材专门零售 | Wholesale of Cultural, Sports Equipments and Appliances | 194 074 | 25 710 |
| 医药及医疗器材专门零售 | Wholesale of Medicines and Medical Appliances | 348 502 | 26 422 |
| 汽车、摩托车、燃料及零配件专门零售 | Wholesale of Timber | 1 565 415 | 335 366 |
| # 汽车零售 | Wholesale of Timber | 1 417 636 | 258 977 |
| 家用电器及电子产品专门零售 | Retail of Textiles, Garments, Shoes and Hats | 284 707 | 10 772 |
| # 家用电器零售 | Retail of Daily Sundry Articles | 233 902 | 7 246 |
| 计算机、软件及辅助设备零售 | Retail of Computer, Software and Assistant Equipments | 18 666 | 2 443 |
| 五金、家具及室内装修材料专门零售 | Retail of Hardware Furniture and Materials for Ornament | 37 623 | 4 577 |
| 无店铺及其他零售 | Retail of Non-shop and Others | 124 798 | 21 936 |
| **4. 按经营方式分** | **Grouped by Means of Operation** | | |
| 独立商店 | Independent shop | 2 564 196 | 605 748 |
| 连锁商店总店 | Central shop of chain shops | 918 088 | 231 586 |
| 连锁门店 | Chain Shop Outlets | 112 700 | 29 909 |
| 其　他 | Others | 497 744 | 63 740 |
| **5. 按零售业态分** | **Grouped by Retail Size** | | |
| 百货商店 | Department Store | 547 640 | 242 654 |
| 超级市场 | Supermarket | 831 215 | 244 792 |
| 专业店 | Special Store | 1 544 212 | 258 495 |
| 专卖店 | Monopoly Store | 971 757 | 166 351 |
| 其　他 | Others | 197 904 | 18 691 |

Continued 2

(10 000 yuan)

| 固定资产原价 Original Value of Fixed Assets | 累计折旧 Accumulative Total Depreciation | 资产总计 Total Assets | 负债总计 Total Liabilities | 营业收入 Business Revenue | # 主营业务收入 Major Business Revenue | 营业成本 Business Cost | # 主营业务成本 Major Business Cost |
|---|---|---|---|---|---|---|---|
| 24 488 | 7 993 | 86 348 | 75 815 | 149 069 | 148 622 | 128 866 | 128 686 |
| 232 946 | 55 572 | 1 012 485 | 832 528 | 2 191 226 | 2 181 113 | 1 705 058 | 1 704 054 |
| 179 633 | 52 704 | 438 580 | 230 408 | 1 789 207 | 1 771 901 | 1 665 719 | 1 662 656 |
| | | | | | | | |
| 615 620 | 207 106 | 2 030 371 | 1 749 956 | 4 233 311 | 4 177 788 | 3 313 545 | 3 306 170 |
| 280 366 | 106 405 | 884 686 | 691 597 | 1 405 996 | 1 372 455 | 1 068 236 | 1 064 857 |
| 331 314 | 98 665 | 1 135 320 | 1 045 945 | 2 789 476 | 2 767 612 | 2 215 205 | 2 211 210 |
| 3 941 | 2 036 | 10 365 | 12 414 | 37 839 | 37 721 | 30 103 | 30 103 |
| 27 102 | 9 801 | 97 656 | 52 501 | 171 531 | 168 924 | 136 315 | 135 860 |
| 25 195 | 10 222 | 255 360 | 211 915 | 299 638 | 296 944 | 234 996 | 232 188 |
| 59 907 | 34 205 | 290 049 | 198 224 | 407 952 | 402 959 | 335 687 | 335 653 |
| 39 961 | 13 541 | 389 117 | 322 071 | 994 646 | 993 405 | 906 039 | 905 967 |
| 471 978 | 144 137 | 2 359 194 | 1 762 135 | 6 386 619 | 6 345 806 | 6 007 033 | 5 991 241 |
| 358 376 | 106 413 | 1 988 403 | 1 551 905 | 4 847 863 | 4 812 234 | 4 540 591 | 4 527 289 |
| 18 168 | 7 419 | 319 244 | 240 840 | 559 233 | 552 439 | 494 853 | 494 036 |
| 12 457 | 5 235 | 262 543 | 207 551 | 418 320 | 415 148 | 367 175 | 367 166 |
| 3 205 | 762 | 21 165 | 13 449 | 36 409 | 36 409 | 32 899 | 32 899 |
| 9 397 | 5 126 | 44 414 | 27 873 | 87 330 | 87 319 | 76 175 | 75 817 |
| 31 017 | 10 054 | 159 860 | 124 115 | 226 188 | 219 440 | 196 908 | 194 314 |
| | | | | | | | |
| 831 422 | 299 673 | 3 807 743 | 3 005 805 | 8 035 705 | 7 948 715 | 7 150 484 | 7 129 146 |
| 332 084 | 100 638 | 1 297 079 | 1 058 375 | 3 521 544 | 3 502 876 | 2 923 494 | 2 918 116 |
| 38 563 | 8 699 | 168 039 | 128 602 | 414 582 | 408 326 | 348 208 | 347 212 |
| 96 275 | 32 602 | 672 403 | 496 847 | 1 394 617 | 1 385 109 | 1 279 364 | 1 276 770 |
| | | | | | | | |
| 309 552 | 123 772 | 1 019 740 | 787 502 | 1 573 680 | 1 537 981 | 1 214 929 | 1 211 550 |
| 339 625 | 102 865 | 1 160 959 | 1 076 625 | 2 852 290 | 2 829 754 | 2 265 047 | 2 261 052 |
| 388 252 | 132 846 | 2 215 488 | 1 585 877 | 5 304 494 | 5 272 268 | 4 884 586 | 4 876 382 |
| 231 561 | 71 200 | 1 258 270 | 996 298 | 3 246 238 | 3 219 634 | 2 987 090 | 2 975 031 |
| 29 355 | 10 927 | 290 806 | 243 327 | 389 746 | 385 389 | 349 898 | 347 230 |

表7-8 续表 3

单位：万元

| 项目 | Item | 所有者权益合计 Total Creditors Equity | 营业税金及附加 Taxes and Extra Charges from Business | #主营业务税金及附加 Taxes and Extra Charges from Major Business |
|---|---|---|---|---|
| **总计** | **Total** | **6 828 795** | **237 571** | **235 621** |
| **一、批发业** | **Wholesale Trades** | **5 573 160** | **129 503** | **128 451** |
| # 国有及国有控股 | State-owned and State Holding Majority Shares | 1 224 934 | 70 506 | 70 420 |
| **1. 按地区分** | **Grouped by Region** | | | |
| 市区 | Urban Area | 2 472 773 | 79 220 | 79 057 |
| # 吴江区 | Wujiang District | 548 160 | 2 709 | 2 702 |
| 常熟 | Changshu | 534 078 | 6 635 | 6 576 |
| 张家港 | Zhangjiagang | 1 364 957 | 17 137 | 17 132 |
| 昆山 | Kunshan | 594 604 | 8 101 | 7 294 |
| 太仓 | Taicang | 606 748 | 18 410 | 18 392 |
| **2. 按登记注册类型分** | **Grouped by Registration Status** | | | |
| 国有企业 | State-owned Enterprises | 984 899 | 66 473 | 66 404 |
| 集体企业 | Collective-owned Enterprises | 9 930 | 107 | 107 |
| 股份合作企业 | Share-holding Cooperative Enterprises | 10 277 | 147 | 147 |
| 联营企业 | Joint Ownership Enterprises | 5 724 | 15 | 15 |
| 有限责任公司 | Limited Liability Corporations | 931 302 | 10 450 | 10 424 |
| 股份有限公司 | Share-holding Cooperative Ltd. | 159 024 | 1 290 | 1 289 |
| 私营企业 | Private Enterprises | 2 150 508 | 16 267 | 15 312 |
| 其他企业 | Other Enterprises | 62 650 | 550 | 550 |
| 港澳台商投资企业 | Enterprises with Investment from HongKong, Macao and Taiwan | 479 525 | 18 903 | 18 903 |
| 外商投资企业 | Enterprises with Foreign Investment | 779 321 | 15 301 | 15 300 |
| **3. 按主要行业分** | **Grouped by Sector** | | | |
| 农畜产品批发 | Wholesale of Agriculture and Livestock Products | 11 135 | 278 | 278 |
| 食品、饮料及烟草制品批发 | Wholesale of Food, Beverages and Tobaccos | 735 348 | 57 112 | 57 112 |
| 纺织、服装及日用品批发 | Wholesale of Textiles, Garments and Daily Articles | 1 819 539 | 44 164 | 44 138 |
| # 服装批发 | Wholesale of Garments | 801 150 | 22 565 | 22 565 |
| 文化、体育用品及器材批发 | Wholesale of Cultural, Sports Equipments and ppliances | 86 938 | 1 297 | 1 297 |

Continued 3

(10 000 yuan)

| 其他业务利润 Other Business Profits | 销售费用 Cost Related With Sale | 管理费用 Managerial Cost | 财务费用 Financing Activities Cost | 营业利润 Business Profits | 利润总额 Total Profits | 应交增值税 Value Added Tax Payable |
|---|---|---|---|---|---|---|
| **211 224** | **1 910 660** | **1 718 347** | **507 458** | **1 240 748** | **1 010 380** | **898 345** |
| **70 504** | **1 285 584** | **1 140 353** | **404 354** | **1 056 485** | **887 099** | **717 434** |
| 17 361 | 105 677 | 97 763 | 17 659 | 312 718 | 285 389 | 320 144 |
| | | | | | | |
| 38 460 | 510 096 | 404 745 | 93 225 | 466 270 | 486 408 | 414 921 |
| 3 683 | 57 270 | 43 789 | 44 882 | 29 112 | 28 045 | 24 481 |
| 13 753 | 105 637 | 78 582 | 65 637 | 38 504 | 47 737 | 24 295 |
| 4 035 | 237 879 | 141 211 | 159 170 | 231 236 | -5 322 | 92 845 |
| 9 639 | 191 922 | 86 486 | 32 406 | 103 154 | 108 760 | 55 458 |
| 4 618 | 240 051 | 429 329 | 53 917 | 217 322 | 249 516 | 129 914 |
| | | | | | | |
| 3 942 | 85 652 | 76 850 | 1 897 | 304 408 | 270 423 | 314 467 |
| 20 | 925 | 2 395 | 598 | 1 167 | 1 153 | 556 |
| 192 | 1 338 | 1 170 | 302 | 171 | 872 | 1 100 |
| 83 | 117 | 293 | 94 | 335 | 1 465 | 121 |
| 22 344 | 155 657 | 97 877 | 106 606 | 136 937 | 38 763 | 71 690 |
| 1 995 | 36 371 | 16 866 | 18 304 | 10 748 | 15 242 | 10 427 |
| 32 234 | 384 765 | 268 758 | 250 849 | 4 827 | 8 074 | 131 771 |
| 40 | 20 639 | 4 828 | 3 099 | 8 999 | 9 261 | 4 142 |
| 2 701 | 330 063 | 428 541 | 19 435 | 218 340 | 251 630 | 139 336 |
| 6 954 | 270 057 | 242 774 | 3 171 | 370 553 | 290 218 | 43 824 |
| | | | | | | |
| 33 | 4 691 | 2 397 | 4 230 | -1 196 | 1 342 | 2 654 |
| 2 104 | 68 218 | 42 869 | -7 749 | 173 587 | 178 489 | 318 517 |
| 18 503 | 720 478 | 775 450 | 81 410 | 582 999 | 604 566 | 181 493 |
| 9 177 | 315 423 | 277 377 | 13 028 | 348 740 | 321 028 | 24 195 |
| 303 | 58 204 | 12 135 | 2 973 | 15 317 | 16 204 | 6 319 |

表7-8 续表 4

单位：万元

| 项　　目 | Item | 所有者权益合　计 Total Creditors Equity | 营业税金及附加 Taxes and Extra Charges from Business | #主营业务税金及附加 Taxes and Extra Charges from Major Business |
|---|---|---|---|---|
| 医药及医疗器材批发 | Wholesale of Medicines and Medical Appliances | 61 115 | 630 | 630 |
| 矿产品、建材及化工产品批发 | Wholesale of Mineral Products, Building Materials and Chemical Products | 2 066 528 | 17 559 | 16 635 |
| 机械设备、五金交电及电子产品批发 | Wholesale of Machinery, Hardware, Transport, Electric and Electronic Equipment | 611 539 | 6 250 | 6 150 |
| # 农业机械批发 | Wholesale Agricultural Machinery | 6 447 | 84 | 15 |
| 汽车、摩托车及零配件批发 | Wholesale of Motor Vehicles, Motorcycles and Parts | 44 721 | 146 | 146 |
| 五金、交电批发 | Wholesale of Hardware, Transport and Electric | 74 368 | 873 | 873 |
| 家用电器批发 | Wholesale Household Appliances | 82 111 | 1 074 | 1 074 |
| 计算机、软件及辅助设备批发 | Wholesale of Computer, Software and Assistant Equipments | 60 006 | 729 | 729 |
| 贸易经纪与代理 | Trade Management and Agency | 15 252 | 237 | 237 |
| 其他批发 | Other Wholesale | 165 768 | 1 976 | 1 976 |
| **二、零售业** | **Retail Trades** | **1 255 635** | **108 068** | **107 170** |
| # 国有及国有控股 | State-owned and State Holding Majority Shares | 170 504 | 3 001 | 2 559 |
| **1. 按地区分** | **Grouped by Region** | | | |
| 市　区 | Urban Area | 763 262 | 24 500 | 23 638 |
| # 吴江区 | Wujiang District | 61 510 | 1 576 | 1 573 |
| 常　熟 | Changshu | 137 681 | 4 110 | 4 107 |
| 张家港 | Zhangjiagang | 114 957 | 2 667 | 2 654 |
| 昆　山 | Kunshan | 215 068 | 75 900 | 75 881 |
| 太　仓 | Taicang | 24 668 | 891 | 891 |
| **2. 按登记注册类型分** | **Grouped by Registration Status** | | | |
| 国有企业 | State-owned Enterprises | 30 876 | 467 | 256 |
| 集体企业 | Collective-owned Enterprises | 8 388 | 119 | 119 |
| 股份合作企业 | Share-holding Cooperative Enterprises | 1 046 | 205 | 205 |
| 联营企业 | Joint Ownership Enterprises | 7 316 | 95 | 95 |
| 有限责任公司 | Limited Liability Corporations | 216 854 | 10 953 | 10 737 |
| 股份有限公司 | Share-holding Cooperative Ltd. | 104 168 | 2 580 | 2 580 |
| 私营企业 | Private Enterprises | 488 326 | 14 657 | 14 417 |

Continued 4

(10 000 yuan)

| 其他业务利润 Other Business Profits | 销售费用 Cost Related With Sale | 管理费用 Managerial Cost | 财务费用 Financing Activities Cost | 营业利润 Business Profits | 利润总额 Total Profits | 应交增值税 Value Added Tax Payable |
|---|---|---|---|---|---|---|
| 10 057 | 19 020 | 11 924 | 5 399 | 8 842 | 6 873 | 5 717 |
| 23 602 | 291 385 | 189 406 | 281 701 | 202 077 | -6 528 | 134 662 |
| 13 802 | 105 723 | 86 968 | 19 515 | 79 415 | 87 405 | 51 054 |
| 327 | 323 | 867 | -153 | 604 | 776 | 124 |
| 2 920 | 6 473 | 6 934 | 2 320 | 1 410 | 2 747 | 696 |
| 1 064 | 15 133 | 13 898 | 3 051 | 11 868 | 17 120 | 6 974 |
| 1 664 | 30 712 | 13 048 | 3 800 | 9 657 | 9 730 | 13 529 |
| 342 | 5 320 | 7 321 | 219 | 9 050 | 8 691 | 5 138 |
| 1 390 | 7 788 | 5 364 | 6 892 | -3 724 | -3 822 | 1 286 |
| 710 | 10 077 | 13 840 | 9 982 | -833 | 2 569 | 15 733 |
| **140 719** | **625 077** | **577 994** | **103 104** | **184 263** | **123 281** | **180 911** |
| 17 561 | 77 601 | 22 038 | 3 713 | 21 584 | 23 522 | 14 188 |
| | | | | | | |
| 101 092 | 434 770 | 242 233 | 69 892 | 39 779 | 39 031 | 99 856 |
| 6 929 | 41 004 | 16 696 | 12 423 | -2 211 | -2 035 | 7 688 |
| 16 442 | 65 995 | 50 595 | 10 494 | 20 348 | 22 768 | 18 976 |
| 8 743 | 43 818 | 39 783 | 9 890 | 2 544 | 3 398 | 10 528 |
| 11 289 | 67 022 | 232 628 | 9 982 | 122 098 | 56 621 | 48 653 |
| 3 154 | 13 471 | 12 756 | 2 847 | -506 | 1 463 | 2 898 |
| | | | | | | |
| 4 306 | 8 076 | 4 078 | 188 | 7 253 | 8 079 | 1 753 |
| 374 | 2 163 | 1 938 | 81 | 1 241 | 1 306 | 906 |
| 604 | 1 384 | 1 065 | 483 | 335 | 292 | 382 |
| 292 | 2 084 | 1 470 | 78 | 989 | 1 009 | 678 |
| 44 597 | 214 800 | 103 766 | 28 842 | 23 145 | 26 003 | 40 086 |
| 10 479 | 19 404 | 27 414 | 4 786 | 14 777 | 15 428 | 7 681 |
| 43 915 | 219 906 | 173 771 | 56 801 | 13 443 | 6 813 | 58 130 |

表7-8 续表 5

单位：万元

| 项 目 | Item | 所有者权益合计 Total Creditors Equity | 营业税金及附加 Taxes and Extra Charges from Business | #主营业务税金及附加 Taxes and Extra Charges from Major Business |
|---|---|---|---|---|
| 其他企业 | Other Enterprises | 10 533 | 986 | 909 |
| 港澳台商投资企业 | Enterprises with Investment from HongKong, Macao and Taiwan | 179 957 | 75 516 | 75 516 |
| 外商投资企业 | Enterprises with Foreign Investment | 208 172 | 2 491 | 2 337 |
| **3. 按主要行业分** | **Grouped by Sector** | | | |
| 综合零售 | Retail of Integrated | 280 415 | 88 207 | 87 914 |
| 百货零售 | Retail of Consumer Goods | 193 089 | 10 508 | 10 307 |
| 超级市场零售 | Retail of Supermarket | 89 375 | 77 584 | 77 570 |
| 其他综合零售 | Others Retail of Integrated | -2 049 | 114 | 37 |
| 食品、饮料及烟草制品专门零售 | Wholesale of Foodstuff, Drink and Tobacco | 45 155 | 678 | 678 |
| 纺织、服装及日用品专门零售 | Wholesale of Textiles, Garments, Shoes and Hats | 43 445 | 1 363 | 1 331 |
| 文化、体育用品及器材专门零售 | Wholesale of Cultural, Sports Equipments and Appliances | 91 825 | 6 792 | 6 712 |
| 医药及医疗器材专门零售 | Wholesale of Medicines and Medical Appliances | 67 046 | 1 474 | 1 473 |
| 汽车、摩托车、燃料及零配件专门零售 | Wholesale of Timber | 597 059 | 7 214 | 6 934 |
| # 汽车零售 | Wholesale of Timber | 436 499 | 5 667 | 5 540 |
| 家用电器及电子产品专门零售 | Retail of Textiles, Garments, Shoes and Hats | 78 404 | 1 510 | 1 508 |
| # 家用电器零售 | Retail of Daily Sundry Articles | 54 992 | 1 035 | 1 035 |
| 计算机、软件及辅助设备零售 | Retail of Computer, Software and Assistant Equipments | 7 716 | 68 | 68 |
| 五金、家具及室内装修材料专门零售 | Retail of Hardware Furniture and Materials for Ornament | 16 542 | 231 | 231 |
| 无店铺及其他零售 | Retail of Non-shop and Others | 35 745 | 601 | 390 |
| **4. 按经营方式分** | **Grouped by Means of Operation** | | | |
| 独立商店 | Independent shop | 801 938 | 26 036 | 25 678 |
| 连锁商店总店 | Central shop of chain shops | 238 703 | 77 291 | 76 988 |
| 连锁门店 | Chain Shop Outlets | 39 437 | 1 220 | 1 199 |
| 其 他 | Others | 175 557 | 3 522 | 3 305 |
| **5. 按零售业态分** | **Grouped by Retail Size** | | | |
| 百货商店 | Department Store | 232 239 | 11 715 | 11 505 |
| 超级市场 | Supermarket | 84 334 | 77 795 | 77 704 |
| 专业店 | Special Store | 629 611 | 10 600 | 10 029 |
| 专卖店 | Monopoly Storo | 261 973 | 6 817 | 6 795 |
| 其 他 | Others | 47 479 | 1 142 | 1 138 |

Continued 5

(10 000 yuan)

| 其他业务利润<br>Other Business Profits | 销售费用<br>Cost Related With Sale | 管理费用<br>Managerial Cost | 财务费用<br>Financing Activities Cost | 营业利润<br>Business Profits | 利润总额<br>Total Profits | 应交增值税<br>Value Added Tax Payable |
|---|---|---|---|---|---|---|
| 970 | 10 607 | 10 640 | 2 020 | -3 755 | -2 839 | 3 226 |
| 7 691 | 50 881 | 226 128 | 6 471 | 127 188 | 62 940 | 52 800 |
| 27 491 | 95 771 | 27 726 | 3 356 | -353 | 4 251 | 15 268 |
| | | | | | | |
| 77 554 | 254 087 | 347 455 | 21 745 | 110 714 | 54 840 | 86 966 |
| 43 944 | 93 119 | 101 011 | 17 031 | 4 145 | 11 226 | 24 987 |
| 32 815 | 150 985 | 245 004 | 4 712 | 109 696 | 46 792 | 61 081 |
| 795 | 9 983 | 1 439 | 2 | -3 126 | -3 178 | 898 |
| 3 997 | 17 618 | 9 959 | 851 | 9 023 | 8 550 | 4 809 |
| 1 901 | 40 712 | 20 599 | 5 667 | 4 706 | 4 713 | 8 435 |
| 4 384 | 30 530 | 23 688 | 3 254 | 9 599 | 13 010 | 8 354 |
| 2 666 | 39 097 | 18 768 | 3 997 | 28 141 | 26 360 | 12 313 |
| 35 691 | 180 661 | 130 543 | 65 123 | 6 856 | 9 022 | 47 019 |
| 25 020 | 144 931 | 107 540 | 60 310 | -1 237 | 755 | 35 959 |
| 9 109 | 42 822 | 14 838 | 1 590 | 6 496 | -2 468 | 6 889 |
| 3 205 | 34 932 | 9 111 | 748 | 5 427 | -3 801 | 5 745 |
| 239 | 1 286 | 1 482 | 372 | 439 | 413 | 377 |
| 1 275 | 6 947 | 3 002 | 407 | 2 146 | 2 549 | 1 330 |
| 4 143 | 12 603 | 9 142 | 470 | 6 583 | 6 706 | 4 796 |
| | | | | | | |
| 96 714 | 376 401 | 285 845 | 89 718 | 28 735 | 34 718 | 95 276 |
| 30 685 | 151 607 | 253 081 | 4 144 | 119 595 | 56 365 | 56 773 |
| 3 990 | 44 419 | 6 916 | 2 499 | 11 924 | 2 790 | 14 313 |
| 9 330 | 52 649 | 32 151 | 6 743 | 24 010 | 29 409 | 14 549 |
| | | | | | | |
| 44 915 | 100 167 | 108 948 | 18 150 | 9 047 | 16 508 | 28 498 |
| 34 217 | 167 303 | 248 238 | 4 729 | 103 618 | 40 788 | 62 543 |
| 39 755 | 191 414 | 129 691 | 41 427 | 57 579 | 62 288 | 51 505 |
| 16 208 | 139 822 | 73 725 | 35 017 | 11 537 | 987 | 33 737 |
| 5 625 | 26 371 | 17 391 | 3 782 | 2 483 | 2 710 | 4 627 |

表7-9

# 限额以上住宿和餐饮法人企业主要财务指标 (2012年)

单位：万元

| 项　目 | Item | 流动资产合计 Total Circulating Funds | 固定资产合计 Total Fixed Assets |
|---|---|---|---|
| **总　计** | **Total** | **1 112 641** | **1 156 248** |
| **一、住宿业** | **Accommodation** | **769 128** | **921 973** |
| **1. 按地区分** | **Grouped by Region** | | |
| 市　区 | Urban Area | 555 937 | 660 435 |
| # 吴江区 | Wujiang District | 129 677 | 50 572 |
| 常　熟 | Changshu | 40 570 | 82 640 |
| 张家港 | Zhangjiagang | 69 791 | 58 401 |
| 昆　山 | Kunshan | 81 413 | 83 226 |
| 太　仓 | Taicang | 21 419 | 37 272 |
| **2. 按登记注册类型分** | **Grouped by Registration Status** | | |
| 国有企业 | State-owned Enterprises | 90 868 | 293 343 |
| 集体企业 | Collective-owned Enterprises | 42 492 | 19 273 |
| 股份合作企业 | Share-holding Cooperative Enterprises | – | – |
| 联营企业 | Joint Ownership Enterprises | 2 326 | 3 644 |
| 有限责任公司 | Limited Liability Corporations | 338 272 | 257 612 |
| 股份有限公司 | Share-holding Cooperative Ltd. | 1 604 | 3 425 |
| 私营企业 | Private Enterprises | 188 010 | 176 158 |
| 其他企业 | Other Enterprises | 8 309 | 24 435 |
| 港澳台商投资企业 | Enterprises with Investment from HongKong, Macao and Taiwan | 17 982 | 57 766 |
| 外商投资企业 | Enterprises with Foreign Investment | 79 265 | 86 317 |
| **3. 按星级分组** | **Grouped by Sear Rated** | | |
| # 五　星 | Five Star | 277 358 | 496 482 |
| 四　星 | Four Star | 197 498 | 182 279 |
| 三　星 | Three Star | 38 962 | 37 599 |
| 二　星 | Two Star | 2 274 | 2 197 |

# MAIN FINANCIAL INDICATORS OF ACCOMMODATION AND CATERING CORPORATION ABOVE DESIGNATED SIZE (2012)

(10 000 yuan)

| 固定资产原价 Original Value of Fixed Assets | 累计折旧 Accumulative Total Depreciation | 资产总计 Total Assets | 负债总计 Total Liabilities | 营业收入 Business Revenue | #主营业务收入 Major Business Revenue | 营业成本 Business Cost | #主营业务成本 Major Business Cost |
|---|---|---|---|---|---|---|---|
| **1 640 913** | **555 765** | **3 123 738** | **2 266 015** | **1 181 745** | **1 172 309** | **477 185** | **472 444** |
| **1 371 467** | **477 427** | **2 379 974** | **1 630 936** | **575 814** | **567 238** | **177 542** | **175 045** |
| | | | | | | | |
| 979 317 | 326 288 | 1 725 447 | 1 103 562 | 388 389 | 383 823 | 115 986 | 113 650 |
| 76 411 | 29 671 | 210 216 | 162 869 | 62 206 | 62 083 | 22 325 | 22 325 |
| 95 228 | 26 898 | 197 654 | 178 669 | 48 019 | 48 017 | 15 672 | 15 672 |
| 107 709 | 49 666 | 196 903 | 133 702 | 48 161 | 47 005 | 17 037 | 16 984 |
| 136 712 | 58 453 | 192 149 | 155 867 | 57 075 | 54 787 | 19 681 | 19 647 |
| 52 502 | 16 123 | 67 821 | 59 136 | 34 170 | 33 606 | 9 167 | 9 093 |
| | | | | | | | |
| 394 927 | 106 701 | 614 158 | 254 132 | 106 212 | 103 426 | 31 071 | 30 950 |
| 33 829 | 14 556 | 75 293 | 68 500 | 21 167 | 20 673 | 8 436 | 8 436 |
| – | – | – | – | – | – | – | – |
| 6 702 | 3 058 | 7 980 | 8 124 | 8 434 | 8 396 | 4 793 | 4 793 |
| 361 744 | 105 065 | 812 428 | 594 827 | 150 387 | 148 255 | 44 910 | 44 257 |
| 6 578 | 3 359 | 6 003 | 4 225 | 3 493 | 3 468 | 215 | 211 |
| 256 429 | 98 216 | 528 601 | 469 379 | 184 663 | 182 961 | 63 143 | 61 424 |
| 34 036 | 11 140 | 40 707 | 27 949 | 13 452 | 13 452 | 4 077 | 4 077 |
| 106 485 | 48 719 | 109 604 | 47 026 | 37 497 | 37 382 | 8 739 | 8 739 |
| 170 736 | 86 613 | 185 201 | 156 775 | 50 508 | 49 225 | 12 159 | 12 159 |
| | | | | | | | |
| 682 533 | 202 487 | 1 146 382 | 795 441 | 191 577 | 190 715 | 48 405 | 48 332 |
| 336 320 | 159 448 | 517 206 | 326 977 | 191 064 | 188 024 | 68 369 | 67 927 |
| 74 677 | 37 160 | 129 863 | 87 601 | 44 650 | 42 553 | 14 002 | 13 941 |
| 4 268 | 2 072 | 6 926 | 4 173 | 4 069 | 4 050 | 1 224 | 1 222 |

表7-9 续表 1

单位：万元

| 项　目 | Item | 流动资产合计 Total Circulating Funds | 固定资产合计 Total Fixed Assets | 固定资产原价 Original Value of Fixed Assets |
|---|---|---|---|---|
| **二、餐饮业** | **Catering Services** | **343 512** | **234 275** | **269 446** |
| **1. 按地区分** | **Grouped by Region** | | | |
| 市　区 | Urban Area | 236 940 | 147 927 | 157 996 |
| # 吴江区 | Wujiang District | 10 224 | 37 602 | 38 225 |
| 常　熟 | Changshu | 20 362 | 40 529 | 43 734 |
| 张家港 | Zhangjiagang | 19 351 | 21 048 | 26 433 |
| 昆　山 | Kunshan | 59 865 | 23 520 | 39 304 |
| 太　仓 | Taicang | 6 995 | 1 252 | 1 980 |
| **2. 按登记注册类型分** | **Grouped by Registration Status** | | | |
| 国有企业 | State-owned Enterprises | 2 947 | 781 | 1 341 |
| 集体企业 | Collective-owned Enterprises | 5 318 | 665 | 1 030 |
| 股份合作企业 | Share-holding Cooperative Enterprises | – | – | – |
| 联营企业 | Joint Ownership Enterprises | – | – | – |
| 有限责任公司 | Limited Liability Corporations | 33 573 | 41 509 | 46 557 |
| 股份有限公司 | Share-holding Cooperative Ltd. | 59 663 | 420 | 1 366 |
| 私营企业 | Private Enterprises | 148 035 | 111 017 | 107 167 |
| 其他企业 | Other Enterprises | 45 893 | 593 | 1 329 |
| 港澳台商投资企业 | Enterprises with Investment from HongKong, Macao and Taiwan | 17 303 | 54 637 | 69 739 |
| 外商投资企业 | Enterprises with Foreign Investment | 30 781 | 24 653 | 40 918 |
| **3. 按主要行业分** | **Grouped by Sector** | | | |
| 正　餐 | Dinner | 294 076 | 208 788 | 225 109 |
| 快　餐 | Fast Food | 19 756 | 13 542 | 26 120 |
| 饮料及冷饮服务 | Beverage and Cold Drink Services | 13 947 | 10 613 | 14 437 |
| 其他餐饮业 | Other | 15 733 | 1 332 | 3 780 |

Continued 1

(10 000 yuan)

| 累计折旧 Accumulative Total Depreciation | 资产总计 Total Assets | 负债总计 Total Liabilities | 营业收入 Business Revenue | #主营业务收入 Major Business Revenue | 营业成本 Business Cost | #主营业务成本 Major Business Cost |
|---|---|---|---|---|---|---|
| **78 338** | **743 764** | **635 079** | **605 932** | **605 071** | **299 642** | **297 398** |
| | | | | | | |
| 43 663 | 494 827 | 410 459 | 483 042 | 482 504 | 241 248 | 239 706 |
| 4 615 | 55 572 | 40 240 | 23 437 | 23 407 | 10 631 | 9 963 |
| 12 293 | 71 753 | 65 378 | 33 779 | 33 735 | 17 334 | 17 311 |
| 5 610 | 63 418 | 52 631 | 23 831 | 23 810 | 11 402 | 11 400 |
| 16 044 | 102 536 | 97 490 | 54 894 | 54 688 | 23 800 | 23 126 |
| 729 | 11 230 | 9 121 | 10 386 | 10 335 | 5 858 | 5 856 |
| | | | | | | |
| 561 | 4 145 | 7 234 | 6 237 | 6 237 | 2 979 | 2 979 |
| 507 | 11 963 | 12 140 | 10 831 | 10 821 | 6 012 | 6 012 |
| – | – | – | – | – | – | – |
| – | – | – | – | – | – | – |
| 9 410 | 107 030 | 103 554 | 62 687 | 62 661 | 26 014 | 26 011 |
| 1 004 | 71 987 | 70 758 | 24 416 | 24 416 | 10 601 | 10 601 |
| 34 755 | 306 046 | 275 390 | 233 183 | 232 799 | 129 558 | 128 149 |
| 736 | 46 506 | 43 138 | 11 809 | 11 809 | 6 289 | 6 289 |
| 15 102 | 93 068 | 63 504 | 30 922 | 30 913 | 9 457 | 9 457 |
| 16 264 | 103 020 | 59 361 | 225 847 | 225 415 | 108 733 | 107 900 |
| | | | | | | |
| 59 453 | 616 686 | 561 157 | 323 669 | 323 377 | 154 103 | 152 789 |
| 12 613 | 66 051 | 44 290 | 210 655 | 210 223 | 112 434 | 111 602 |
| 3 825 | 40 745 | 18 394 | 27 533 | 27 533 | 6 517 | 6 517 |
| 2 448 | 20 281 | 11 238 | 44 075 | 43 939 | 26 587 | 26 491 |

表7-9 续表 2

单位：万元

| 项 目 | Item | 所有者权益合计 Total Creditors Equity | 营业税金及附加 Taxes and Extra Charges from Business | #主营业务税金及附加 Taxes and Extra Charges from Major Business |
|---|---|---|---|---|
| **总 计** | **Total** | **857 723** | **64 956** | **64 640** |
| **一、住宿业** | **Accommodation** | **749 038** | **31 536** | **31 275** |
| **1. 按地区分** | **Grouped by Region** | | | |
| 市 区 | Urban Area | 621 885 | 21 389 | 21 165 |
| # 吴江区 | Wujiang District | 47 347 | 3 429 | 3 429 |
| 常 熟 | Changshu | 18 985 | 2 649 | 2 649 |
| 张家港 | Zhangjiagang | 63 201 | 2 607 | 2 605 |
| 昆 山 | Kunshan | 36 282 | 3 023 | 2 989 |
| 太 仓 | Taicang | 8 685 | 1 868 | 1 868 |
| **2. 按登记注册类型分** | **Grouped by Registration Status** | | | |
| 国有企业 | State-owned Enterprises | 360 026 | 5 749 | 5 749 |
| 集体企业 | Collective-owned Enterprises | 6 794 | 1 128 | 1 120 |
| 股份合作企业 | Share-holding Cooperative Enterprises | – | – | – |
| 联营企业 | Joint Ownership Enterprises | -145 | 470 | 470 |
| 有限责任公司 | Limited Liability Corporations | 217 601 | 8 456 | 8 454 |
| 股份有限公司 | Share-holding Cooperative Ltd. | 1 778 | 196 | 195 |
| 私营企业 | Private Enterprises | 59 222 | 10 217 | 10 216 |
| 其他企业 | Other Enterprises | 12 759 | 797 | 764 |
| 港澳台商投资企业 | Enterprises with Investment from HongKong Macao and Taiwan | 62 578 | 2 051 | 2 051 |
| 外商投资企业 | Enterprises with Foreign Investment | 28 426 | 2 472 | 2 256 |
| **3. 按星级分组** | **Grouped by Sear Rated** | | | |
| # 五 星 | Five Star | 350 941 | 10 135 | 10 135 |
| 四 星 | Four Star | 190 229 | 10 602 | 10 601 |
| 三 星 | Three Star | 42 262 | 2 381 | 2 380 |
| 二 星 | Two Star | 2 753 | 206 | 206 |

Continued 2

(10 000 yuan)

| 其他业务利润<br>Other Business Profits | 销售费用<br>Cost Related With Sale | 管理费用<br>Managerial Cost | 财务费用<br>Financing Activities Cost | 营业利润<br>Business Profits | 利润总额<br>Total Profits |
|---|---|---|---|---|---|
| **3 222** | **358 549** | **278 683** | **67 088** | **-61 775** | **-47 552** |
| **2 226** | **182 070** | **202 473** | **48 252** | **-64 143** | **-51 980** |
| | | | | | |
| 69 | 130 180 | 139 632 | 29 882 | -47 388 | -33 248 |
| 144 | 25 567 | 11 569 | 4 070 | -4 731 | -778 |
| 662 | 13 302 | 17 806 | 7 412 | -8 161 | -8 819 |
| 283 | 14 566 | 11 838 | 2 821 | -707 | -1 808 |
| 703 | 16 209 | 17 767 | 3 797 | -3 491 | -3 832 |
| 511 | 7 813 | 15 431 | 4 340 | -4 396 | -4 272 |
| | | | | | |
| 1 298 | 33 698 | 40 962 | 4 546 | -9 859 | -2 727 |
| -147 | 7 233 | 3 696 | 696 | -22 | -703 |
| – | – | – | – | – | – |
| – | 907 | 2 245 | 26 | -7 | 49 |
| 766 | 45 841 | 57 407 | 19 574 | -24 884 | -17 840 |
| – | 2 353 | 616 | 32 | 82 | 98 |
| -509 | 58 281 | 54 807 | 16 124 | -17 875 | -18 661 |
| 703 | 5 060 | 4 607 | 640 | -758 | -769 |
| 115 | 13 018 | 16 956 | 3 418 | -6 678 | -7 343 |
| – | 15 679 | 21 178 | 3 196 | -4 144 | -4 084 |
| | | | | | |
| 396 | 58 198 | 79 074 | 26 285 | -30 079 | -28 119 |
| 1 930 | 56 126 | 58 720 | 6 635 | -8 332 | 2 172 |
| 671 | 15 096 | 12 014 | 2 419 | -1 267 | -2 083 |
| – | 1 342 | 660 | 194 | 443 | 438 |

表7-9 续表 3

单位：万元

| 项 目 | Item | 所有者权益合计 Total Creditors Equity | 营业税金及附加 Taxes and Extra Charges from Business | #主营业务税金及附加 Taxes and Extra Charges from Major Business |
|---|---|---|---|---|
| **二、餐饮业** | **Catering Services** | **108 686** | **33 420** | **33 365** |
| **1. 按地区分** | **Grouped by Region** | | | |
| 市 区 | Urban Area | 84 368 | 26 491 | 26 443 |
| # 吴江区 | Wujiang District | 15 332 | 1 362 | 1 326 |
| 常 熟 | Changshu | 6 376 | 2 030 | 2 023 |
| 张家港 | Zhangjiagang | 10 788 | 1 316 | 1 316 |
| 昆 山 | Kunshan | 5 046 | 3 031 | 3 031 |
| 太 仓 | Taicang | 2 109 | 552 | 552 |
| **2. 按登记注册类型分** | **Grouped by Registration Status** | | | |
| 国有企业 | State-owned Enterprises | -3 090 | 391 | 391 |
| 集体企业 | Collective-owned Enterprises | -177 | 686 | 686 |
| 股份合作企业 | Share-holding Cooperative Enterprises | - | - | - |
| 联营企业 | Joint Ownership Enterprises | - | - | - |
| 有限责任公司 | Limited Liability Corporations | 3 476 | 3 422 | 3 422 |
| 股份有限公司 | Share-holding Cooperative Ltd. | 1 229 | 1 366 | 1 366 |
| 私营企业 | Private Enterprises | 30 656 | 12 409 | 12 354 |
| 其他企业 | Other Enterprises | 3 368 | 629 | 629 |
| 港澳台商投资企业 | Enterprises with Investment from HongKong Macao and Taiwan | 29 564 | 1 733 | 1 733 |
| 外商投资企业 | Enterprises with Foreign Investment | 43 660 | 12 784 | 12 784 |
| **3. 按主要行业分** | **Grouped by Sector** | | | |
| 正 餐 | Dinner | 55 529 | 18 248 | 18 200 |
| 快 餐 | Fast Food | 21 762 | 11 653 | 11 653 |
| 饮料及冷饮服务 | Beverage and Cold Drink Services | 22 351 | 1 537 | 1 537 |
| 其他餐饮业 | Other | 9 044 | 1 982 | 1 975 |

Continued 3

(10 000 yuan)

| 其他业务利润 Other Business Profits | 销售费用 Cost Related With Sale | 管理费用 Managerial Cost | 财务费用 Financing Activities Cost | 营业利润 Business Profits | 利润总额 Total Profits |
|---|---|---|---|---|---|
| **995** | **176 479** | **76 210** | **18 836** | **2 369** | **4 428** |
| 139 | 140 829 | 49 404 | 11 746 | 14 148 | 16 109 |
| 33 | 7 566 | 5 157 | 2 057 | -2 624 | -2 542 |
| 491 | 8 568 | 7 081 | 3 632 | -4 390 | -4 845 |
|  | 8 507 | 4 085 | 1 969 | -3 448 | -3 236 |
| 318 | 16 111 | 13 504 | 1 432 | -3 260 | -2 939 |
| 48 | 2 463 | 2 137 | 57 | -681 | -661 |
|  |  |  |  |  |  |
| 9 | 1 994 | 1 963 | 27 | -1 109 | -1 109 |
| 5 | 3 655 | 1 402 | 52 | -982 | -424 |
| – | – | – | – | – | – |
| – | – | – | – | – | – |
| 8 | 24 577 | 9 986 | 3 187 | -4 499 | -4 410 |
| 27 | 7 637 | 4 394 | 902 | -457 | -416 |
| 1 120 | 61 772 | 27 845 | 9 345 | -6 983 | -7 312 |
| – | 2 680 | 2 291 | 24 | -104 | -316 |
| 228 | 11 797 | 7 614 | 4 014 | -3 465 | -3 344 |
| -401 | 62 368 | 20 714 | 1 285 | 19 966 | 21 759 |
|  |  |  |  |  |  |
| 1 377 | 104 624 | 51 328 | 17 299 | -20 937 | -20 422 |
| -401 | 47 595 | 17 817 | 824 | 20 334 | 20 609 |
| – | 14 679 | 4 042 | 486 | 271 | 1 515 |
| 19 | 9 580 | 3 023 | 228 | 2 700 | 2 726 |

表7-10

# 连锁总店经营情况 (2012年末)

| 项　　目 | Item | 连锁总店数(个) Number of Chain Shops (unit) |
|---|---|---|
| **总　　计** | **Total** | **56** |
| **一、零售业** | **Retail Trades** | **51** |
| **（一）按登记注册类型分** | **Grouped by Registration Status** | |
| 内资企业 | Domestic Funded Enterprises | 44 |
| # 有限责任公司 | Limited Liability Corporations | 18 |
| 私营企业 | Private Enterprises | 21 |
| 港澳台商投资企业 | Enterprises with Investment from HongKong, Macao and Taiwan | 3 |
| 外商投资企业 | Enterprises with Foreign Investment | 4 |
| **（二）按连锁经营业务分** | **Grouped by Scope of Business** | |
| # 综合零售 | Retail of Integrated | 22 |
| 食品、饮料及烟草制品专门零售 | Retail of Food, Beverages and Tobaccos | 6 |
| 医疗及医疗器材专门零售 | Retail of Medicines and Medical Appliances | 12 |
| 家用电器及电子产品专门零售 | Retail of Household Appliances and Electronic Products | 4 |
| **（三）按零售业态分** | **Grouped by Retail Size** | |
| # 便利店 | Convenience Store | 7 |
| 超　市 | Supermarket | 14 |
| 专业店 | Special Store | 20 |
| 专卖店 | Monopoly Store | 7 |
| **二、住宿业** | **Accommodation** | **1** |
| **三、餐饮业** | **Catering Services** | **4** |
| 正　餐 | Dinner | - |
| 快　餐 | Fast Food | 1 |
| 饮料及冷饮服务 | Beverage and Cold Drink Services | 1 |
| 其　他 | Other | 2 |
| **附：外省在苏连锁门店** | **Number of Chain Shops in Suzhou of Other Provinces** | **-** |

# BASIC STATISTICS OF CENTRAL SHOPS OF CHAIN STORES (END OF 2012)

| 连锁门店数(个) Number of Chain Shop Outlets (unit) | 直营店 Factory Outlet | 加盟店 Join-in Outlet | 营业面积(平方米) Floor Space for Business (sq.m) | 从业人员(人) Total Employment | 销售总额(营业额)(万元) Total Sales Business Income (10 000 yuan) | # 商品零售额 Retail Sale Trade |
|---|---|---|---|---|---|---|
| **3 411** | **2 269** | **1 142** | **1 731 105** | **59 958** | **4 546 549** | **4 471 187** |
| **3 152** | **2 010** | **1 142** | **1 627 259** | **44 636** | **4 321 979** | **4 250 103** |
| 2 896 | 1 754 | 1 142 | 647 281 | 22 464 | 1 019 554 | 947 940 |
| 1 998 | 1 271 | 727 | 526 066 | 16 226 | 661 866 | 616 763 |
| 736 | 321 | 415 | 102 590 | 5 008 | 297 876 | 282 382 |
| 35 | 35 | – | 348 055 | 16 861 | 1 851 585 | 1 851 585 |
| 221 | 221 | – | 631 923 | 5 311 | 1 450 841 | 1 450 578 |
| 1 639 | 853 | 786 | 933 776 | 34 026 | 2 616 485 | 2 567 800 |
| 214 | 209 | 5 | 7 528 | 1 241 | 47 130 | 45 215 |
| 639 | 635 | 4 | 68 123 | 3 455 | 116 780 | 109 190 |
| 26 | 26 | – | 23 509 | 981 | 197 250 | 184 577 |
| 281 | 250 | 31 | 24 216 | 1 990 | 56 212 | 56 212 |
| 1 354 | 599 | 755 | 897 560 | 31 702 | 2 552 393 | 2 503 708 |
| 740 | 717 | 23 | 91 105 | 4 761 | 286 327 | 266 064 |
| 589 | 256 | 333 | 47 528 | 3 003 | 109 522 | 106 856 |
| **5** | **5** | **–** | **150** | **141** | **3 588** | **102** |
| **254** | **254** | **–** | **103 696** | **15 181** | **220 982** | **220 982** |
| – | – | – | – | – | – | – |
| 178 | 178 | – | 67 873 | 11 480 | 191 453 | 191 453 |
| 70 | 70 | – | 32 200 | 3 528 | 26 093 | 26 093 |
| 6 | 6 | – | 3 623 | 173 | 3 437 | 3 437 |
| **53** | **52** | **1** | **107 678** | **4 134** | **535 683** | **249 396** |

表7-11

# 市场建设情况（2012年末）
# CONSTRUCTION OF MARKETS (END OF 2012)

单位：个 (unit)

| 项目 | Item | 全市总计 Total | # 城市 City |
|---|---|---|---|
| **总计** | **Total** | **635** | **339** |
| **一、商品交易市场** | **Transaction Markets** | **625** | **330** |
| （一）消费品市场 | Consumer Goods Markets | 542 | 296 |
| 1. 消费品综合市场 | General Consumer Goods Markets | 26 | 18 |
| 2. 农副产品市场 | Market of Agricultural Products and By-products | 445 | 228 |
| （1）农副产品综合市场 | General Market | 331 | 171 |
| （2）农副产品专业市场 | Specialized Market | 114 | 57 |
| 3. 工业消费品市场 | Industrial Consumer Goods Market | 68 | 49 |
| （1）工业消费品综合市场 | General Market | 34 | 18 |
| （2）工业消费品专业市场 | Specialized Market | 34 | 31 |
| 4. 其他 | Others | 3 | 1 |
| （二）生产资料市场 | Means of Production Market | 83 | 34 |
| 1. 生产资料综合市场 | General Market | 13 | 4 |
| 2. 工业生产资料市场 | Market of Means of Industrial Production | 59 | 27 |
| 3. 农业生产资料市场 | Market of Means of Agriculture Production | 1 | - |
| 4. 其他 | Others | 10 | 3 |
| **二、要素市场** | **Elements Market** | **10** | **9** |
| （一）房地产市场 | Real Estate Market | 2 | 2 |
| （二）金融市场 | Financial Market | - | - |
| （三）劳动力市场 | Labor Force Market | 4 | 4 |
| （四）技术市场 | Technology Market | 2 | 2 |
| （五）信息市场 | Information Market | - | - |
| （六）产权市场 | Property Right Market | - | - |
| （七）其他要素市场 | Others | 2 | 1 |

表7-12

# 亿元以上商品交易市场基本情况（2012年）
# GENERAL INFORMATION OF COMMODITY EXCHANGE MARKET WITH TOTAL SALE OVER 100 MILLION YUAN (2012)

| 项　　目 | Item | 市场数(个) Number of Markets (unit) | 年末已出租摊位数(个) Year-end Number of Hired Booths (unit) | 商品成交额(万元) Transaction Value (10 000 yuan) | # 商品零售额 Consumer Goods Retail Sale |
|---|---|---|---|---|---|
| **总　　计** | **Total** | **90** | **72 224** | **48 550 858** | **6 313 443** |
| **一、按经营环境分** | **Grouped by Form of Operation Environment** | | | | |
| 露天式 | Open Air | 6 | 1 489 | 362 487 | 15 601 |
| 封闭式 | Seal Off | 67 | 63 507 | 30 946 339 | 5 758 661 |
| 其　他 | Others | 17 | 7 228 | 17 242 032 | 539 181 |
| **二、按经营方式分** | **Grouped by Form of Operation** | | | | |
| 批　发 | Whole sale | 54 | 60 858 | 46 250 865 | 5 101 832 |
| 零　售 | Retail Sale | 36 | 11 366 | 2 299 993 | 1 211 611 |
| **三、按市场类别分** | **Grouped by Category of Market** | | | | |
| 综合市场 | Integrated Market | 25 | 12 478 | 3 494 548 | 1 050 462 |
| 生产资料综合市场 | General Market | – | – | – | – |
| 工业品综合市场 | Industrial Products | 3 | 1 665 | 174 919 | 74 721 |
| 农产品综合市场 | Farm and Side-line Products | 21 | 9 778 | 2 915 712 | 571 824 |
| 其他综合市场 | Others | 1 | 1 035 | 403 917 | 403 917 |
| 专业市场 | Special Market | 65 | 59 746 | 45 056 310 | 5 262 981 |
| # 建材市场 | Building Materials | 6 | 2 465 | 380 575 | 61 880 |
| 金属材料市场 | Metal Material | 11 | 2 609 | 11 557 210 | 13 249 |
| 粮油市场 | Grain and Oil | 2 | 197 | 131 393 | 3 746 |
| 肉食禽蛋市场 | Meat, Poultry and Eggs | 4 | 1 184 | 729 699 | 19 243 |
| 水产品市场 | Aquatic Products | 5 | 1 370 | 397 024 | 364 067 |
| 蔬菜市场 | Vegetables | 2 | 455 | 47 818 | 12 000 |
| 食品饮料烟酒市场 | Food, Beverage and Tobacco | 2 | 570 | 612 120 | 6 972 |
| 纺织品服装鞋帽市场 | Textile Products, Garments, Shoes and Hats | 3 | 31 729 | 22 199 425 | 3 258 948 |
| 小商品市场 | Small Commodities | 1 | 2 332 | 55 000 | 16 500 |
| 家具市场 | Furniture | 3 | 4 302 | 962 000 | 497 100 |
| 汽车市场 | Vehicles | 3 | 427 | 765 896 | 415 202 |

# 主要统计指标解释

**社会消费品零售总额** 指批发和零售业、餐饮业、新闻出版业、邮政业和其他服务业等，售予城乡居民用于生活消费的商品和社会集团用于公共消费的商品之总量。社会消费品零售总额包括：

一、批发和零售业企业（单位）售予城乡居民用于生活消费和社会集团用于公共消费的商品。包括：

1.售予城乡居民的各种生活消费品；

2.售予入境旅游的外国人、华侨、港澳台同胞的各类商品；

3.售予行政事业单位、社会团体、军队和武警等机构的商品，以及以零售方式售予各类企业的商品。具体包括：用于非生产和社会交往的办公用品，如通讯设备、计算器具和设备、电讯网络设备、文印设备、音像视听器材和设备、纸张、本册、文具及装订文印材料、家具、日用电器、针纺织品、清洁卫生用品、文体用品、奖品、纪念品、礼品等；供内部人员乘坐的交通工具和燃料；用于办公设施修缮的各类配件、材料、工具等；用于取暖和防暑降温的设备、燃料、材料及食品等；专用于教学的用品和设备；非营利医疗机构的中、西药品、中药材和医疗设备器材；非专用的劳动保护用品；不对外营业的内部食堂用的餐具、炊具、设备、清洁卫生工具和食品、燃料等；军队、武警用于其人员生活的衣着品和个人用品；其他各类非生产性设备和用品。

二、餐饮业出售的主食、菜肴、烟酒饮料和其他商品。

三、新闻出版业、邮政业售予城乡居民、企事业单位、军队和武警等机构的书报杂志、音像制品、邮品等。

四、其他服务业出售的食品、烟酒饮料、服装鞋帽、日常生活用品、医药保健用品、艺术品、工艺美术品、玩具、殡葬用品以及其他消费品。

**批发和零售业商品购进、销售、库存总额** 指各种登记注册类型的批发和零售业企业(单位)以本企业(单位)为总体的，从国内、国外市场购进的商品总量，销售和出口的商品总量、库存的商品总量等情况。该指标可以反映商品流转过程中商品的购进、销售、库存之间的比例关系和存在的问题。

**商品购进总额** 指从本企业(单位)以外的单位和个人购进(包括从境外直接进口)作为转卖或加工后转卖的商品总额。它反映批发和零售业从国内、国外市场上购进商品的总量。商品购进总额包括：(1)从工农业生产者购进的商品；(2)从出版社、报社的出版发行部门购进的图书、杂志和报纸；(3)从各种登记注册类型的批发和零售业企业(单位)购进的商品；(4)从其他单位购进的商品，如从机关、团体、企业等单位购进的剩余物资，从住宿和餐饮业、其他服务业购进的商品，从海关、市场管理部门购进的缉私和没收的商品，从居民手中收购的废旧商品等；(5)从国(境)外直接进口的商品。不包括企业(单位)为自身经营用和未通过买卖行为而收入的商品以及销售退回、商品升溢等。

**销售总额** 指对本企业(单位)以外的单位和个人出售(包括对境外直接出口)的商品总额。它反映批发和零售业在国内市场上销售商品以及出口商品的总量。商品销售总额包括：(1)售给城乡居民和社会集团消费用的商品；(2)售给工业、农业、建筑业、运输邮电业、批发和零售业、住宿和餐饮业、其他服务业等作为生产、经营使用的商品；(3)售给批发和零售业作为转卖或加工后转卖的商品；(4)对国(境)外直接出口的商品。不包括出售本企业(单位)自用的废旧包装用品，未通过买卖行为付出的商品，经本单位介绍、由买卖双方直接结算、本单位只收取手续费的业务，购货退出的商品以及商品损耗和损失等。

**库存总额** 指报告期末各种登记注册类型的批发和零售业企业(单位)已取得所有权的商品。它反映批发和零售业企业(单位)的商品库存情况和对市场商品供应的保证程度。商品库存总额包括：(1)存放在批发和零售业经营单位(如门市部、批发站、经营处)仓库、货场、货柜和货架中的商品；(2)挑选、整理、包装中的商品；(3)已记入购进而尚未运到本单位的商品，即发货单或银行承兑凭证已到而货未到的商品；(4)寄放他处的商品，如因购货方拒绝承付而暂时存放在购货方的商品和已办完加工成品收回手续而未提回的商品；(5)委托其他单位代销(未作销售或调出)尚未售出的商品；(6)代其他单位购进尚未交付的商品。不包括所有权不属于本单位的商品、委托外单位加工生产尚未收回成品的商品、外贸企业代理其他单位从国外进口尚未付给订货单位的商品、代国家物资储备部门保管的商品等。

**住宿和餐饮业营业额** 指住宿和餐饮业法人企业（单位）在经营活动中因提供服务或销售商品等取得的收入。包括：客房收入、餐费收入、商品销售收入和其他收入。客房收入指住宿和餐饮业法人企业（单位）在经营活动中因提供住宿服务取得的收入。餐费收入指住宿和餐饮业法人企业、（单位）因为顾客提供就餐服务取得的收入，包括经烹饪、调制加工后出售的各种食品，如主食、炒菜、凉拌菜等的收入。商品销售收入指住宿和餐饮业法人企业（单位）伴随服务而出售商品所取得的收入。其他收入指营业收入中除客房收入、餐费收入、商品销售收入以外的其他收入，包括娱乐、健身和商务服务等。

**亿元商品交易市场成交额** 指经工商部门批准、专门从事商品批发、零售业务活动年成交额在亿元以上的市场的所有摊位商品交易额之和。

**连锁企业（或称连锁店、连锁公司）** 指在核心企业或总店的领导下，由分散的、经营同类商品或服务的企业或活动单位，采取共同方针，实行集中采购和分散销售的有机结合，通过规范化经营，实现规模效益的经济联合组织形式。一般连锁店应由若干个分店组成。其经营特征：(1)经营同类商品；(2)使用统一商号；(3)统一采购配送，采购与销售相分离（部分商品可根据物流合理和保质保鲜原则，由供应商直接送货到门店，其余均由总部统一配送）。

连锁门店的形式分为直营连锁和加盟连锁。

直营连锁也叫正规连锁。指连锁门店均由总部独资或控股开设，在总部的直接领导下统一经营。总部采取纵深似的管理方式，直接下令掌管所有的零售门店，零售门店也必须完全接受总部指挥。这是大型垄断商业资本通过吞并、兼并或独资、控股等途径，发展壮大自身实力和规模的一种形式。

加盟连锁包括特许连锁和自由连锁两种形式。

特许连锁指各连锁门店（被特许人）通过合同形式，取得使用总部（特许人）商标、商号、经营技术和销售总部开发的商品的特许权，各加盟连锁门店为独立法人，在总部指导下统一经营。

自由连锁也称自愿连锁。指连锁公司的门店均为独立法人，各自的资产所有权关系不变，在公司总部的指导下共同经营。各成员店使用共同的店名，与总部订阅有关购、销、宣传等方面的合同，并按合同开展经营活动。在合同规定的范围之外，各成员店可以自由活动。根据自愿原则，各成员店可自由加入连锁体系，也可自由退出。

# EXPLANATORY NOTES ON MAIN STATISTICAL INDICATORS

**Total Retail Sales of Consumer Goods** refer to the sum of retail sales of commodities sold by wholesale and retail trades, catering services, publishing, post and telecommunications and other service industries to urban and rural households for household consumption and to social institutions for public consumption. Retail sales of consumer goods include:

1) Sales sold by wholesale and retail trades to urban and rural households for household consumption and to social institutions for public consumption.

a) of commodities to urban and rural households;

b) of commodities to foreigners, overseas Chinese and Chinese compatriots from Hong Kong, Macao and Taiwan visiting China;

c) of commodities to government agencies, institutions, social organizations, military and armed police units, and commodities to enterprises in the form of retail sales. More specifically, they include: office facilities and articles for non-production purposes such as communications equipment, computing equipment and instruments, TV and network equipment, printing and copying equipment, audio-visual equipment and instruments, paper, notebooks, stationeries, furniture, electric appliances, knitwear, sanitation and cleaning articles, cultural and sport articles, articles for prizes, souvenirs, etc.; transport vehicles and fuels for employees; materials, spare parts and tools for the maintenance of office facilities; equipment, fuels, materials and food for winter heating or summer cooling purposes; articles and equipment for teaching purpose; Chinese and western medicines and medical equipment and facilities purchased by non profit-making medical institutes; non-specialized work safety articles; cooking utensils, tableware, equipment, cleaning articles, food and fuels purchased by in-house cafeterias; clothes and personal articles purchased by military or armed police units for their officials and soldiers; and other equipment and articles for non-production purposes.

2) Sales of stable food, cooked dishes, beverages, tobaccos and other articles by catering units.

3) Sales of books, newspapers, magazines, audio-visual products and post products by publishing, post and telecommunications departments to urban and rural households and to enterprises, institutions, military and armed police units.

4) Sales of food, beverages, tobaccos, clothing, hats, footwear, articles for daily use, medicines, medical and health articles, work of art, handicrafts, toys, funeral articles and other articles by other service industries.

**Purchase, Sales and Stock of Commodities by Wholesale and Retail Trades** refer to the total volume of commodities purchased, total volume of sales and exports, and the stock of commodities by wholesale and retail enterprises (establishments) of different status of registration from domestic and overseas markets. This indicator reflects the relationship among purchase, sales and stock of commodities in the circulation of goods and reveals the existing problems.

**Total Purchases of Commodities** refer to the total value of purchases of commodities by enterprises (establishments) from other establishments or individuals (including direct import from abroad) for the purpose of re-selling, either with or without further processing of the commodities purchased. This indicator is used to show the total value of purchases of commodities by wholesale and retail establishments from domestic and overseas markets. The total purchases include: (1) agricultural and industrial products purchased from producers; (2) books, magazines and newspapers purchased from distribution departments of the publishers; (3) commodities purchased from wholesale and retail establishments of different status of registration; (4) commodities purchased from other units, such as surplus materials purchased from government agencies, enterprises or institutions, commodities purchased from catering and service establishments, confiscated goods purchased from customs authorities or market management agencies, second-hand goods and wastes purchased from residents; and (5) commodities directly imported from abroad. Excluded are commodities purchased by enterprises (establishments) for use in their own business operation, commodities obtained without buying or selling procedures, rejected commodities, etc.

**Total Sales of Commodities** refer to value of commodities sold by the establishments to other establishments and individuals (including direct export). This indicator is used to show the total value of sales of commodities at domestic markets and export. The total sales include: (1) commodities sold to urban and rural residents and social groups for their consumption; (2) commodities sold to establishments in industry, agriculture, construction, transportation, post and telecommunications, wholesale and retail trades, hotels and catering services, and public utility for their production and operation; (3) commodities sold to wholesale and retail establishments for re-selling, with or without further processing; and (4)commodities for direct export to other countries.

Excluded are selling of waste packaging materials used by the establishments (units) themselves, commodities transferred without buying or selling procedures, commission income from brokerage in transactions for which settlement is directly handled by buyers and sellers, rejected commodities in the purchase, loss in commodities, etc.

**Commodity Stock of Wholesale and Retail Enterprises** refers to total commodities possessed by wholesale and retail enterprises (units) of various types of registration status at the end of the reference period, reflecting the commodity stock level of various wholesale and retail enterprises and the potential for market supply. It includes: (1) commodities located in storage, garages, counters, and shelves of operating units (such as sale stores, wholesale centres, and operating offices) of wholesale and retail enterprises; (2) commodities in the process of being selected, sorted, and packed; (3) commodities not arrived but recorded as purchase in the account, i.e. commodities not arrived but payment receipts for the commodities from the sellers or the banks arrived; (4) commodities deposited in other places rather than places mentioned above, for instance: commodities in the hold of purchasers temporarily due to the refusal of payment and commodities not taken back after going through the formalities; (5) commodities entrusted to other units to sell but not sold yet; (6) commodities purchased for other units but not delivered yet. Commodities not included as stock are those not owned by the enterprises (units), commodities on commission for processing but not yet delivered, imported commodities of agency of foreign trade enterprise but not yet delivered to ordering units and finally those put in stock on behalf of the state material reserves units.

**Business Revenue of Hotels and Catering Services** refers to revenue received from providing services or selling commodities by corporate enterprises and establishments engaged in hotels and catering services, including income from hotel rooms, from meals, from selling of commodities and from other services. Income from hotel rooms refers to income of corporate enterprises and establishments by providing lodging services. Income from catering services refers to income of corporate enterprises and establishments by providing catering services, including selling of cooked or prepared foods such as staple food, cooked dishes or cold dishes. Income from selling of commodities refers to income of corporate enterprises and establishments by selling commodities that accompany the services they provide. Income from other activities refers to income received other than income from hotel rooms, catering services or selling of commodities, such as income from providing recreation, fitness or business services.

**Volume of Transaction at Large Commodity Markets with Transaction Value over 100 Million Yuan** refers to markets approved by the industrial and commercial administration departments, which specialize in wholesale and retail trades of commodities with an annual transaction of over 100 million yuan. The sum of sales of all sellers in the market makes up the transaction value of the market.

**Chain Enterprises (also called chain stores or chain corporations)** refers to a form of joint economic entities under which scattered enterprises or establishments engaged in providing homogeneous commodities or services, with the central leadership of core enterprise or headquarters and guided by common policies, conduct centralized purchase and distributed selling of commodities, in order to gain better efficiency through standardized operation. Consisting of a number of branch stores, the chain stores have in general the following features: 1) homogeneous commodities, 2) unique name of stores, 3) centralized purchase and delivery which is separated from distributed selling operation (most commodities are delivered from the headquarters except some items which, for logistics, quality or freshness considerations, might be delivered by suppliers directly).

The modes of chain operation include Regular Chain and Franchise Operation.

Regular Chain: refers to chain that are invested or controlled by the headquarters. They operate under direct and unified management from the headquarters. Adopting a direct management approach, the headquarters gives orders and controls all retail stores, which follow completely the directives from the headquarters. Large monopolized commercial companies develop and expand their business through purchasing, merging, direct investment and controlling of shares.

Franchise Operation includes Franchise Chain and Voluntary Chain.

Franchise Chain: Through contracts, chain stores (or their owners) obtain licenses from the headquarters (franchisee) to use designated trade marks, names, operation know-how, and to sell commodities developed by the headquarters. Under this arrangement, each store in the chain is an independent legal entity and operates under the guidance from the headquarters.

Voluntary Chain: Under this arrangement, all stores operate together under the guidance of the headquarters, while maintaining their status of independent legal entities with full ownership of their assets. They use the same store name and sign contracts with the headquarters concerning purchase, sale, and promotion. They will operate under the contracts. They are free to engage in other activities which are not bounded in the contract. They are free to join in or leave the chain.

# 八、对外经济 国际旅游

# CHAPTER 8
# FOREIGN TRADE ECONOMY
# AND
# INTERNATIONAL TOURISM

# 对外经济 国际旅游
# FOREIGN TRADE ECONOMY AND INTERNATIONAL TOURISM

## 主要统计指标
## MAJOR STATISTICAL INDICATORS

| | | | | |
|---|---|---|---|---|
| 2012年进出口总额 | Total Imports and Exports | 3 056.92 | 亿美元 | USD 100 million |
| 比上年增长 | Increase Over Last Year | 1.6 | % | |
| 2012年出口总额 | Total Exports | 1 746.89 | 亿美元 | USD100 million |
| 比上年增长 | Increase Over Last Year | 4.5 | % | |
| 2012年新签外资合同数 | Nember of Projects Of Signed Contracts | 1 189 | 个 | unit |
| 比上年增长 | Increase Over Last Year | -21.6 | % | |
| 2012年合同外资金额 | Value of Foreign Capital Signed | 151.68 | 亿美元 | USD100 million |
| 比上年增长 | Increase Over Last Year | -10.9 | % | |
| 2012年实际利用外资金额 | Value of Foreign Capital Actually Used | 91.65 | 亿美元 | USD 100 million |
| 比上年增长 | Increase Over Last Year | 2.8 | % | |
| 2012年接待境外旅游者人数 | Number of Received Foreign Tourister | 321.87 | 万人次 | 10 000 persons |
| 比上年增长 | Increase Over Last Year | 8.1 | % | |

表8-1

# 部分年份对外经济主要指标

| 指　　标 | | Item | | 1990年 | 2000年 |
|---|---|---|---|---|---|
| **外　贸** | | **Foreign Trade** | | | |
| 进出口总额 | (万美元) | Total Imports and Exports | (USD 10 000) | 18 816 | 2 007 036 |
| 出　口 | | Exports | | 15 524 | 1 048 095 |
| 进　口 | | Imports | | 3 292 | 958 941 |
| **外　资** | | **Foreign Capital** | | | |
| **新签合同数** | (个) | **Number of Projects of Signed Contracts** | (unit) | **164** | **943** |
| 1.对外借款 | | Foreign Loans | | 10 | – |
| 2.外商直接投资 | | Foreign Direct Investments | | 130 | 943 |
| 独资经营 | | Solely Owned Enterprises | | 10 | 683 |
| 合资经营 | | Joint Venture Enterprises | | 116 | 227 |
| 合作经营 | | Cooperative Operation Enterprises | | 4 | 33 |
| 股份制经营 | | Share-holding Corporations Enterprises | | – | – |
| 3.商品信贷及其他 | | Commodity Credit Loans and Others | | 24 | – |
| **合同外资金额** | (万美元) | **Value of Foreign Capital Signed** | (USD 10 000) | **14 361** | **467 787** |
| 1.对外借款 | | Foreign Loans | | 1 779 | – |
| 2.外商直接投资 | | Foreign Direct Investments | | 11 000 | 467 787 |
| 独资经营 | | Solely Owned Enterprises | | 1 315 | 401 738 |
| 合资经营 | | Joint Venture Enterprises | | 7 175 | 54 583 |
| 合作经营 | | Cooperative Operation Enterprises | | 2 510 | 11 466 |
| 股份制经营 | | Share-holding Corporations Enterprises | | – | – |
| 3.商品信贷及其他 | | Commodity Credit Loans and Others | | 1 582 | – |
| **实际利用外资金额** | | **Value of Foreign Capital Actually Used** | | **6 954** | **288 338** |
| 1.对外借款 | | Foreign Loans | | 2 409 | – |
| 2.外商直接投资 | | Foreign Direct Investments | | 3 371 | 288 338 |
| 独资经营 | | Solely Owned Enterprises | | 17 | 226 093 |
| 合资经营 | | Joint Venture Enterprises | | 3 287 | 53 607 |
| 合作经营 | | Cooperative Operation Enterprises | | 67 | 8 638 |
| 股份制经营 | | Share-holding Corporations Enterprises | | – | – |
| 3.商品信贷及其他 | | Commodity Credit Loans and Others | | 1 174 | – |
| **外　经** | | **Foreign Economy** | | | |
| 对外承包工程及劳务合作合同金额 | | Contractual Value of Contracted Projects and Cooperation with Foreign Countries or Regions | | 2 249 | 12 199 |
| 实际营业额 | | Value of Business Fulfilled | | 1 100 | 12 122 |
| 当年外派劳务人员 | (人) | Persons Abroad in Labour Cooperation | (person) | 399 | 3 625 |

# MAJOR STATISTICAL INDICATORS OF FOREIGN TRADE ECONOMIC OF PARTIAL YEARS

| 2005年 | 2006年 | 2007年 | 2008年 | 2009年 | 2010年 | 2011年 | 2012年 |
|---|---|---|---|---|---|---|---|
| | | | | | | | |
| 14 058 895 | 17 426 360 | 21 179 567 | 22 852 565 | 20 144 633 | 27 407 639 | 30 086 256 | 30 569 196 |
| 7 277 472 | 9 468 488 | 11 888 422 | 13 172 260 | 11 408 529 | 15 310 849 | 16 723 345 | 17 468 868 |
| 6 781 423 | 7 957 872 | 9 291 145 | 9 680 305 | 8 736 104 | 12 096 790 | 13 362 911 | 13 100 328 |
| **2 181** | **2 281** | **2 022** | **1 462** | **1 426** | **1 537** | **1 516** | **1 189** |
| – | – | – | – | – | – | – | – |
| 2 181 | 2 281 | 2 022 | 1 462 | 1 426 | 1 537 | 1 516 | 1 189 |
| 1 834 | 1 867 | 1 743 | 1 257 | 1 174 | 1 275 | 1 232 | 1 007 |
| 335 | 401 | 270 | 197 | 240 | 258 | 277 | 181 |
| 11 | 12 | 9 | 8 | 12 | 4 | 7 | 1 |
| 1 | 1 | – | – | – | – | – | – |
| – | – | – | – | – | – | – | – |
| **1 533 971** | **1 592 383** | **1 836 349** | **1 638 953** | **1 583 786** | **1 691 980** | **1 702 391** | **1 516 828** |
| – | – | – | – | – | – | – | – |
| 1 533 971 | 1 592 383 | 1 836 349 | 1 638 953 | 1 583 786 | 1 691 980 | 1 702 391 | 1 516 828 |
| 1 413 181 | 1 462 037 | 1 613 826 | 1 462 543 | 1 347 474 | 1 523 008 | 1 378 781 | 1 330 245 |
| 118 367 | 121 654 | 212 117 | 161 717 | 198 554 | 156 391 | 310 234 | 174 502 |
| 2 139 | 8 375 | 8 845 | 8 601 | 33 444 | 6 489 | 2 782 | 1 940 |
| 284 | 317 | 1 561 | 6 092 | 4 314 | 6 092 | 10 594 | 10 141 |
| – | – | – | – | – | – | – | – |
| **511 607** | **610 462** | **716 471** | **813 262** | **822 653** | **853 511** | **891 222** | **916 490** |
| – | – | – | – | – | – | – | – |
| 511 607 | 610 462 | 716 471 | 813 262 | 822 653 | 853 511 | 891 222 | 916 490 |
| 468 129 | 503 248 | 620 962 | 695 431 | 703 469 | 753 770 | 758 234 | 748 489 |
| 40 034 | 104 778 | 85 539 | 112 869 | 89 512 | 87 135 | 125 108 | 145 181 |
| 3 444 | 2 408 | 8 534 | 1 758 | 25 711 | 5 642 | 2 360 | 2 432 |
| – | 27 | 1 436 | 3 204 | 3 961 | 6 964 | 5 520 | 20 389 |
| – | – | – | – | – | – | – | – |
| | | | | | | | |
| 41 379 | 49 278 | 34 526 | 38 930 | 55 579 | 91 294 | 95 097 | 102 574 |
| 39 811 | 42 668 | 30 757 | 37 033 | 43 968 | 57 046 | 76 850 | 83 716 |
| 2 595 | 2 691 | 2 148 | 2 368 | 1 955 | 1 599 | 1 361 | 2 776 |

表8-2

# 分地区进出口总额(2012年)
# TOTAL IMPORT AND EXPORT VALUE BY REGION (2012)

单位：万美元 (USD 10 000)

| 类别和地区 | Type and Region | 进出口总额 Total Imports and Exports | 出口 Exports | 进口 Imports |
|---|---|---|---|---|
| **全 市** | **Whole Municipality** | **30 569 196** | **17 468 868** | **13 100 328** |
| 市 区 | Urban Area | 15 479 114 | 8 777 866 | 6 701 248 |
| 姑苏区 | Gusu District | 276 424 | 226 220 | 50 204 |
| 吴中区 | Wuzhong District | 1 033 132 | 610 746 | 422 387 |
| 相城区 | Xiangcheng District | 412 563 | 263 819 | 148 744 |
| 高新区、虎丘区 | New & Hi-tech Zone, Huqiu District | 3 533 910 | 2 201 870 | 1 332 040 |
| 工业园区 | Industrial Park | 7 951 855 | 4 226 832 | 3 725 023 |
| 吴江区 | Wujiang District | 2 271 229 | 1 248 379 | 1 022 850 |
| 常 熟 | Changshu | 1 974 928 | 1 292 108 | 682 819 |
| 张家港 | Zhangjiagang | 3 196 195 | 1 281 147 | 1 915 048 |
| 昆 山 | Kunshan | 8 656 828 | 5 551 707 | 3 105 121 |
| 太 仓 | Taicang | 1 262 132 | 566 040 | 696 092 |
| **一、国有企业** | **State-owed Enterprises** | **1 391 005** | **1 021 273** | **369 731** |
| 市 区 | Urban Area | 1 028 691 | 753 362 | 275 329 |
| 姑苏区 | Gusu District | 89 496 | 82 362 | 7 133 |
| 吴中区 | Wuzhong District | 2 384 | 1 536 | 848 |
| 相城区 | Xiangcheng District | – | – | – |
| 高新区、虎丘区 | New & Hi-tech Zone, Huqiu District | 20 264 | 16 350 | 3 914 |
| 工业园区 | Industrial Park | 916 548 | 653 114 | 263 434 |
| 吴江区 | Wujiang District | – | – | – |
| 常 熟 | Changshu | 7 877 | 5 990 | 1 887 |
| 张家港 | Zhangjiagang | 316 261 | 238 859 | 77 402 |
| 昆 山 | Kunshan | 22 597 | 15 079 | 7 518 |
| 太 仓 | Taicang | 15 577 | 7 983 | 7 594 |
| **二、外商及港澳台投资企业** | **Enterprises with Investment from Foreign ,Hong Kong, Macao and Taiwan** | **22 735 119** | **12 871 770** | **9 863 349** |
| 市 区 | Urban Area | 12 169 009 | 6 635 466 | 5 533 543 |
| 姑苏区 | Gusu District | 34 167 | 26 107 | 8 060 |
| 吴中区 | Wuzhong District | 527 063 | 317 967 | 209 095 |
| 相城区 | Xiangcheng District | 278 803 | 170 980 | 107 823 |
| 高新区、虎丘区 | New & Hi-tech Zone, Huqiu District | 3 101 557 | 1 995 087 | 1 106 471 |
| 工业园区 | Industrial Park | 6 465 132 | 3 219 912 | 3 245 220 |
| 吴江区 | Wujiang District | 1 762 288 | 905 414 | 856 874 |
| 常 熟 | Changshu | 1 468 255 | 900 478 | 567 777 |
| 张家港 | Zhangjiagang | 1 225 958 | 392 059 | 833 899 |
| 昆 山 | Kunshan | 6 978 585 | 4 533 688 | 2 444 897 |
| 太 仓 | Taicang | 893 311 | 410 079 | 483 232 |

表8-2 续表 Continued

单位：万美元 (USD 10 000)

| 类别和地区 | Type and Region | 进出口总额 Total Imports and Exports | 出口 Exports | 进口 Imports |
|---|---|---|---|---|
| **三、集体企业** | **Collective-owned Enterprises** | **1 006 522** | **488 634** | **517 888** |
| 市 区 | Urban Area | 76 726 | 69 279 | 7 447 |
| 姑苏区 | Gusu District | 53 261 | 47 746 | 5 515 |
| 吴中区 | Wuzhong District | 14 219 | 13 540 | 678 |
| 相城区 | Xiangcheng District | 3 579 | 3 578 | 1 |
| 高新区、虎丘区 | New & Hi-tech Zone, Huqiu District | 1 580 | 1 504 | 76 |
| 工业园区 | Industrial Park | 3 304 | 2 191 | 1 113 |
| 吴江区 | Wujiang District | 784 | 719 | 65 |
| 常 熟 | Changshu | 58 655 | 30 330 | 28 324 |
| 张家港 | Zhangjiagang | 710 096 | 287 788 | 422 308 |
| 昆 山 | Kunshan | 70 674 | 64 548 | 6 125 |
| 太 仓 | Taicang | 90 372 | 36 688 | 53 683 |
| **四、私营企业** | **Private Enterprises** | **5 419 819** | **3 075 379** | **2 344 440** |
| 市 区 | Urban Area | 2 196 286 | 1 315 107 | 881 180 |
| 姑苏区 | Gusu District | 99 475 | 69 980 | 29 495 |
| 吴中区 | Wuzhong District | 484 467 | 273 793 | 210 673 |
| 相城区 | Xiangcheng District | 130 111 | 89 245 | 40 866 |
| 高新区、虎丘区 | New & Hi-tech Zone, Huqiu District | 410 482 | 188 914 | 221 568 |
| 工业园区 | Industrial Park | 563 651 | 350 929 | 212 722 |
| 吴江区 | Wujiang District | 508 101 | 342 246 | 165 856 |
| 常 熟 | Changshu | 439 935 | 355 276 | 84 659 |
| 张家港 | Zhangjiagang | 943 880 | 362 441 | 581 439 |
| 昆 山 | Kunshan | 1 576 869 | 931 266 | 645 604 |
| 太 仓 | Taicang | 262 848 | 111 289 | 151 559 |
| **五、其 他** | **Others** | **16 731** | **11 811** | **4 920** |
| 市 区 | Urban Area | 8 401 | 4 651 | 3 750 |
| 姑苏区 | Gusu District | 26 | 26 | – |
| 吴中区 | Wuzhong District | 5 001 | 3 908 | 1 092 |
| 相城区 | Xiangcheng District | 71 | 16 | 54 |
| 高新区、虎丘区 | New & Hi-tech Zone, Huqiu District | 26 | 14 | 12 |
| 工业园区 | Industrial Park | 3 221 | 687 | 2 534 |
| 吴江区 | Wujiang District | 56 | – | 56 |
| 常 熟 | Changshu | 206 | 34 | 171 |
| 张家港 | Zhangjiagang | – | – | – |
| 昆 山 | Kunshan | 8 102 | 7 126 | 976 |
| 太 仓 | Taicang | 23 | – | 23 |
| **总计中：一般贸易** | **In Total: Ordinary Trade** | **7 760 316** | **4 417 056** | **3 343 260** |
| **加工贸易** | **Processing Trade** | **16 312 279** | **10 602 922** | **5 709 357** |

表8-3

# 分国别（地区）进出口总额（2012年）
# TOTAL IMPORT AND EXPORT VALUE BY COUNTRY AND REGION (2012)

单位：万美元 (USD 10 000)

| 国别和地区 | Country and Region | 进出口总额 Total Imports and Exports | 出口 Exports | 进口 Imports |
|---|---|---|---|---|
| **总计** | **Total** | **30 569 196** | **17 468 868** | **13 100 328** |
| **亚洲** | **Asia** | **18 131 649** | **7 968 229** | **10 163 420** |
| # 中国香港 | HongKong, China | 2 408 697 | 2 365 873 | 42 824 |
| 印度 | India | 447 377 | 346 332 | 101 045 |
| 日本 | Japan | 3 238 775 | 1 597 331 | 1 641 443 |
| 马来西亚 | Malaysia | 908 190 | 247 632 | 660 557 |
| 新加坡 | Singapore | 594 737 | 315 794 | 278 943 |
| 韩国 | Republic of Korea | 2 979 694 | 757 958 | 2 221 737 |
| 泰国 | Thailand | 637 108 | 281 262 | 355 846 |
| 阿拉伯联合酋长国 | United Arab Emirates | 226 336 | 212 768 | 13 568 |
| 中国台湾 | Taiwan, China | 3 259 691 | 802 066 | 2 457 625 |
| **非洲** | **Africa** | **314 306** | **267 780** | **46 526** |
| **欧洲** | **Europe** | **4 879 403** | **3 757 032** | **1 122 371** |
| # 比利时 | Belgium | 143 253 | 112 275 | 30 978 |
| 英国 | United Kingdom | 443 268 | 385 693 | 57 575 |
| 德国 | Federal Republic of Germany | 1 145 147 | 684 215 | 460 932 |
| 法国 | France | 334 886 | 237 250 | 97 636 |
| 意大利 | Italy | 276 596 | 167 560 | 109 036 |
| 荷兰 | Netherlands | 953 863 | 921 606 | 32 257 |
| 西班牙 | Spain | 132 531 | 101 488 | 31 044 |
| 芬兰 | Finland | 144 736 | 117 427 | 27 309 |
| 瑞士 | Switzerland | 89 056 | 32 461 | 56 595 |
| **南美洲** | **South America** | **1 330 752** | **897 875** | **432 877** |
| # 巴西 | Brazil | 573 397 | 323 513 | 249 885 |
| **北美洲** | **North America** | **5 107 175** | **4 234 234** | **872 941** |
| # 加拿大 | Canada | 385 011 | 257 703 | 127 308 |
| 美国 | United States | 4 722 132 | 3 976 499 | 745 634 |
| **大洋洲** | **Oceania** | **805 247** | **343 719** | **461 528** |
| # 澳大利亚 | Australia | 744 412 | 302 811 | 441 601 |
| **总计中：东盟组织** | **In Total: Association of Southeast Asian Nations** | **3 113 747** | **1 338 636** | **1 775 111** |
| **欧盟组织** | **European Union** | **4 363 280** | **3 362 944** | **1 000 335** |

表8-4

# 分商品类章进出口总额（2012年）
# TOTAL IMPORTS AND EXPORTS OF GOODS OF SUB-CATEGORY CHAPTERS (2012)

单位：万美元 (USD 10 000)

| 商品名称 | Item | 进出口总额 Total Imports and Exports | 出口 Exports | 进口 Imports |
|---|---|---|---|---|
| **总　计** | **Total** | **30 569 196** | **17 468 868** | **13 100 328** |
| 活动物，动物产品 | Live Animals, Animal Products | 32 941 | 3 680 | 29 261 |
| 植物产品 | Vegetable Products | 196 167 | 8 185 | 187 983 |
| 动，植物油，脂，蜡及其分解产品 | Animal or Vegetable Fats and Oils and their Cleavage Products | 87 689 | 4 961 | 82 728 |
| 食品，饮料，酒及醋，烟草及制品 | Prepared Foodstuffs, Beverages, Spirits And Vinegar, Tobacco and Manufactured Tobacco Substitutes | 35 528 | 25 103 | 10 425 |
| 矿产品 | Mineral Products | 749 128 | 49 271 | 699 858 |
| 化学工业及其相关工业的产品 | Products of The Chemical or Industries Allied | 1 578 542 | 427 127 | 1 151 415 |
| 塑料及其制品，橡胶及其制品 | Plastics and Articles Thereof Rubber and Articles Thereof | 1 157 427 | 428 651 | 728 776 |
| 生皮，皮革，毛皮及其制品 | Raw Hides and Skins, Leather, Fur Skins and Articles Thereof | 90 675 | 70 354 | 20 321 |
| 木及木制品，其他编结材料制品 | Wood and Articles of Wood, Other Plaiting Materials | 54 271 | 23 742 | 30 529 |
| 纸浆，纸，纸板及其制品 | Pulp of Paper，Paper and Paperboard and Articles Thereof | 441 532 | 140 420 | 301 112 |
| 纺织原料及纺织制品 | Textiles and Textile Articles | 1 814 812 | 1 484 874 | 329 938 |
| 鞋帽伞杖鞭，羽毛制品，人造花 | Footwear, Headgear, Umbrellas, Sun Umbrellas, Walking-Sticks, Seat-Sticks, Feathers and Articles Made , Artificial Flowers | 116 749 | 75 531 | 41 218 |
| 石料及其制品，陶瓷玻璃及制品 | Articles of Stone, Ceramic Products, Glass and Glassware | 219 349 | 114 831 | 104 518 |
| 珍珠，宝石，贵金属，仿首饰，硬币 | Pearls, Precious , Precious Metals, Imitation Jewellery , Coin | 53 284 | 19 244 | 34 040 |
| 贱金属及其制品 | Base Metals and Articles of Base Metal | 1 551 574 | 880 089 | 671 486 |
| 机器，电子产品，电气设备及零件 | Machinery, electronic products, electrical equipment and parts | 18 745 096 | 11 606 651 | 7 138 445 |
| 车辆，航空器，船舶及运输设备 | Vehicles, Aircraft, Vessels And Associated Transport Equipment | 524 435 | 441 447 | 82 989 |
| 光学，检测，医疗设备，钟表，乐器 | Optical, detection, medical equipment, clocks and watches, and musical instruments | 2 685 343 | 1 253 726 | 1 431 617 |
| 武器，弹药及其零件，附件 | Arms and Ammunition, Parts and Accessories Thereof | 230 | 229 | … |
| 杂项制品 | Miscellaneous Manufactured Articles | 431 342 | 410 483 | 20 860 |
| 艺术品，收藏品及古物 | Works of Art, Collectors' Pieces and Antiques | 186 | 171 | 15 |
| 特殊交易品及未分类商品 | Commodities and Transactions not Classified According to Kind | 2 893 | 100 | 2 794 |
| **总计中：机电产品** | **In Total: Mechanical and electrical products** | **22 639 216** | **13 822 542** | **8 816 675** |
| **高新技术产品** | **High-tech products** | **16 814 466** | **9 963 130** | **6 851 336** |

表8-5

# 外商直接投资 (2012年)

| 指　　标 | Item | 全　市 Whole Municipality |
|---|---|---|
| **批准外商投资企业合同数**　(个) | **Number of Foreign Invested Enterprises Contracts Approved** (unit) | |
| 本年批准企业数 | Number of Foreign Invested Enterprises Contracts Approved in 2012 | 1 189 |
| 独资经营 | Solely Owned Enterprises | 1 007 |
| 合资经营 | Joint Venture Enterprises | 181 |
| 合作经营 | Cooperative Operation Enterprises | 1 |
| 股份有限公司 | Share-holding Corporations Ltd. | – |
| 历年累计批准企业数 | Accumulative Total of Approved Enterprises The Years | 28 054 |
| **批准外商投资合同金额**　(万美元) | **Amount of Foreign Investment Contracts** (USD 10 000) | |
| 本年批准合同外资金额 | Amount of Foreign Investment Contracts Approved in 2012 | 1 516 828 |
| 独资经营 | Solely Owned Enterprises | 1 330 245 |
| 合资经营 | Joint Venture Enterprises | 174 502 |
| 合作经营 | Cooperative Operation Enterprises | 1 940 |
| 股份有限公司 | Share-holding Corporations Ltd. | 10 141 |
| 历年累计合同外资金额　(万美元) | Accumulative Foreign Contracts Investment The Years (USD 10 000) | 18 641 279 |
| **实际利用外资金额**　(万美元) | **Foreign Capital Actually Used** (USD 10 000) | |
| 本年实际利用外资 | Foreign Capital Actually Used in 2012 | 916 490 |
| 独资经营 | Solely Owned Enterprises | 755 354 |
| 合资经营 | Joint Venture Enterprises | 138 315 |
| 合作经营 | Cooperative Operation Enterprises | 2 432 |
| 股份有限公司 | Share-holding Corporations Ltd. | 20 389 |
| 历年累计实际利用外资　(万美元) | Total Amount of Foreign Capital Actually Used The Years (USD 10 000) | 10 111 000 |
| **历年累计已开业投产的外商投资企业数** (个) | **Accumulative Total of Enterprises with Foreign Investment that Have Entered Production or Operation The Years** (unit) | **15 138** |

# FOREIGN DIRECT INVESTMENT (2012)

| 市 区<br>Urban Area | # 吴江区<br>Wujiang District | 常 熟<br>Changshu | 张家港<br>Zhangjiagang | 昆 山<br>Kunshan | 太 仓<br>Taicang |
|---|---|---|---|---|---|
| | | | | | |
| 554 | 102 | 87 | 118 | 314 | 116 |
| 464 | 88 | 76 | 92 | 272 | 103 |
| 89 | 14 | 11 | 26 | 42 | 13 |
| 1 | – | – | – | – | – |
| – | – | – | – | – | – |
| 14 066 | 2 784 | 2 143 | 2 847 | 6 334 | 2 664 |
| | | | | | |
| 662 706 | 227 849 | 211 933 | 161 015 | 320 593 | 160 581 |
| 576 801 | 202 870 | 174 607 | 153 485 | 293 009 | 132 343 |
| 79 187 | 19 731 | 37 227 | 7 549 | 22 414 | 28 125 |
| 1 104 | – | – | – | 723 | 113 |
| 5 614 | 5 248 | 99 | -19 | 4 447 | – |
| 7 813 429 | 1 942 937 | 1 953 334 | 1 869 614 | 3 502 451 | 3 502 451 |
| | | | | | |
| 469 260 | 95 155 | 95 619 | 95 155 | 175 356 | 81 100 |
| 385 755 | 85 376 | 79 262 | 65 655 | 158 772 | 65 910 |
| 79 303 | 7 456 | 16 072 | 13 398 | 15 671 | 13 871 |
| 392 | 160 | – | 15 | 706 | 1 319 |
| 3 810 | 2 163 | 285 | 16 087 | 207 | – |
| 5 127 326 | 484 955 | 1 063 995 | 1 070 663 | 2 074 647 | 774 369 |
| **6 485** | **1 463** | **1 363** | **1 678** | **3 858** | **1 754** |

表8-6

# 外商及港澳台商投资企业国别(地区)分组(2012年)
# ENTERPRISES WITH INVESTMENT FROM FOREIGN , HONG KONG, MACAO AND TAIWAN BY COUNTRY (REGION)(2012)

单位：万美元 (USD 10 000)

| 地　区 | Region | 新签合同数(个) Number of Projects of Signed Contracts (unit) | 合同外资金额 Value of Foreign Capital Signed | 实际利用外资金额 Value of Foreign Capital Actually Used |
|---|---|---|---|---|
| **总　计** | **Total** | **1 189** | **1 516 828** | **916 490** |
| 中国香港 | HongKong,China | 224 | 456 677 | 280 742 |
| 中国澳门 | Macao,China | 3 | 1 845 | 1 205 |
| 中国台湾 | Taiwan,China | 226 | 211 783 | 39 100 |
| 新加坡 | Singapore | 60 | 74 169 | 93 680 |
| 马来西亚 | Malaysia | 10 | 20 504 | 11 818 |
| 日　本 | Japan | 156 | 197 779 | 139 507 |
| 韩　国 | Republic of Korea | 95 | 93 304 | 39 854 |
| 泰　国 | Thailand | 1 | -687 | 2 150 |
| 澳大利亚 | Australia | 10 | 5 529 | 802 |
| 法　国 | France | 9 | 11 265 | 5 188 |
| 意大利 | Italy | 20 | 15 113 | 3 398 |
| 德　国 | Germany | 45 | 26 031 | 18 976 |
| 英　国 | United Kingdom | 24 | 44 374 | 2 675 |
| 丹　麦 | Denmark | 9 | 3 843 | 693 |
| 瑞　士 | Switzerland | 6 | 15 073 | 7 200 |
| 荷　兰 | Netherlands | 6 | 11 661 | 7 073 |
| 西班牙 | Spain | 5 | 3 709 | 5 867 |
| 美　国 | The United States | 91 | 50 454 | 35 719 |
| 加拿大 | Canada | 14 | 16 424 | 4 978 |
| 维尔京群岛 | Virgin Islands | 13 | 33 118 | 59 529 |
| 开曼群岛 | Cayman Islands | 7 | 18 535 | 11 314 |
| 萨摩亚 | Samoan | 77 | 61 421 | 33 618 |
| 毛里求斯 | Mauritius | 5 | -20 750 | 15 141 |
| 文　莱 | Brunei | 11 | 16 691 | 3 852 |
| 其　他 | Others | 62 | 148 963 | 92 411 |
| **总计中：东盟组织** | **In Total: Association of Southeast Asian Nations** | **85** | **110 858** | **111 874** |
| **欧盟组织** | **European Union** | **143** | **134 833** | **59 692** |

表8-7

# 外商及港澳台商投资企业行业分组（2012年）
# ENTERPRISES WITH INVESTMENT FROM FOREIGN, HONG KONG, MACAO AND TAIWAN BY SECTOR (2012)

单位：万美元 (USD 10 000)

| 行业 | Sector | 新签合同数(个) Number of Projects of Signed Contracts (unit) | 合同外资金额 Value of Foreign Capital Signed | 实际利用外资金额 Value of Foreign Capital Actually Used |
|---|---|---|---|---|
| **总计** | **Total** | **1 189** | **1 516 828** | **916 490** |
| **第一产业** | **Primary Industry** | **13** | **13 214** | **1 070** |
| **第二产业** | **Secondary Industry** | **620** | **1 083 418** | **612 982** |
| 工业 | Industry | 612 | 1 075 976 | 612 275 |
| # 机械 | Machinery | 307 | 499 924 | 171 014 |
| 仪器、办公用品 | Equipment and office supplies | 14 | 20 779 | 6 991 |
| 电子通讯 | Electronic communications | 76 | 119 176 | 108 564 |
| 电气器材 | Electronic Equipment | 67 | 127 794 | 49 989 |
| 化工 | Chemical | 29 | 89 275 | 101 851 |
| 建材 | Building Materials | 9 | 35 549 | 37 057 |
| 冶金 | Metallurgy | 8 | 14 779 | 31 406 |
| 塑料制品 | Plastic Products | 25 | 26 601 | 19 350 |
| 纺织服装 | Textile and Apparel | 19 | 20 786 | 18 724 |
| 食品加工 | Food processing | 11 | 20 088 | 26 099 |
| 建筑业 | Construction | 8 | 7 442 | 707 |
| **第三产业** | **Tertiary Industry** | **556** | **420 196** | **302 438** |
| 交通运输业 | Transportation | 17 | 57 861 | 13 943 |
| # 仓储业 | Logistics | 11 | 50 477 | 10 510 |
| 房地产业 | Real Estate | 15 | 102 081 | 160 128 |
| 传输、计算机服务业 | Information Transmission, Computer Services | 7 | 5 443 | 2 701 |
| 软件业 | Software | 31 | 6 560 | 5 643 |
| 批发和零售业 | Wholesale and Retail Trades | 284 | 81 240 | 29 307 |
| 住宿和餐饮业 | Hotels and Catering Services | 17 | 6 961 | 3 492 |
| 文化、体育、娱乐业 | Culture, Sports and Entertainment | - | - | 433 |
| 租赁和商品服务业 | Leasing and Business Services | 112 | 108 346 | 47 442 |
| 科技和技术服务 | Scientific Research, Technical Service | 42 | 11 578 | 14 480 |
| 卫生、教育 | Health and Education | 2 | 12 003 | 120 |
| 其他 | Others | 29 | 28 123 | 24 749 |

表8-8

## 国家级、省级开发区建设发展情况 (2012年)

| 开发区名称 | Development Zones | 新批外商投资企业数(个) Number of Foreign Invested Enterprises Contracts Approved (unit) | 合同外资(万美元) Contractual Foreign Investment (USD 10 000) |
|---|---|---|---|
| **总　计** | **Total** | **816** | **1 165 973** |
| **一、国家级开发区** | **State Development Zones** | **709** | **986 406** |
| 苏州工业园区 | Suzhou Industrial Park | 241 | 145 152 |
| 苏州高新技术产业开发区 | Suzhou New and Hi-tech Development Zone | 103 | 157 985 |
| 昆山经济技术开发区 | Kunshan Economic and Technological Development Zone | 83 | 83 891 |
| 张家港保税区 | Zhangjiagang Bonded Area | 25 | 64 128 |
| 苏州太湖旅游度假区 | Suzhou Taihu National Tourism and Vacation Zone | 7 | 10 823 |
| 昆山高新技术产业开发区 | Kunshan New and Hi-tech industrial Development Zone | 26 | 52 100 |
| 常熟经济技术开发区 | Changshu Economic and Technological Development Zone | 31 | 117 483 |
| 吴江经济技术开发区 | Wujiang Economic and Technological Development Zone | 47 | 99 467 |
| 太仓港经济技术开发区 | Taicang Economic and Technological Development Zone | 62 | 103 854 |
| 张家港经济技术开发区 | Zhangjiagang Economicand Technological Development Zone | 49 | 64 476 |
| 吴中经济技术开发区 | Wuzhong Economic Technological Development Zone | 35 | 87 047 |
| **二、省级开发区** | **Provincial Development Zones** | **112** | **193 785** |
| 相城经济开发区 | Xiangcheng Economic Development Zone | 7 | 6 568 |
| 浒墅关经济开发区 | Xushuguan Economic Development Zone | 5 | 14 218 |
| 昆山旅游度假区 | Kunshan Tourism and Holiday Zone | 9 | 10 104 |
| 吴江汾湖经济开发区 | Wujiang Fenhu Economic Development Zone | 12 | 40 515 |
| 常熟高新技术产业开发区 | Changshu New and Hi-tech Development Zone | 43 | 70 066 |
| 昆山花桥经济开发区 | Kunshan Huaqiao Economic Development Zone | 36 | 52 314 |

注:苏州高新技术产业开发区中包含浒墅关经济开发区数据，下同。

# CONSTRUCTION OF STATE AND PROVINCIAL DEVELOPMENT ZONES (2012)

| 实际利用外资 (万美元) Foreign Capital Actually Used (USD 10 000) | 业务总收入 (万元) Total Business Revenue (10 000 yuan) | 财政收入 (万元) Financial Revenue (10 000 yuan) | #地方公共财政预算收入 General Budgetary Revenue | 出口额 (万美元) Total Exports (USD 10 000) | 进口额 (万美元) Total Imports (USD 10 000) |
|---|---|---|---|---|---|
| **760 886** | **366 485 116** | **16 295 087** | **6 888 676** | **15 106 781** | **11 487 489** |
| **683 797** | **336 637 239** | **14 574 355** | **6 138 828** | **14 512 015** | **11 146 790** |
| 196 060 | 64 161 000 | 4 164 247 | 1 850 006 | 4 205 021 | 3 693 421 |
| 90 020 | 31 670 000 | 2 384 664 | 820 365 | 2 021 990 | 1 129 678 |
| 73 268 | 64 418 026 | 1 818 757 | 676 902 | 4 590 520 | 2 444 992 |
| 30 187 | 50 203 414 | 713 881 | 320 174 | 274 719 | 1 111 065 |
| 1 033 | 1 345 614 | 88 552 | 64 580 | 5 592 | 6 611 |
| 41 500 | 27 035 000 | 1 120 797 | 470 117 | 479 161 | 358 357 |
| 70 523 | 24 470 310 | 874 849 | 368 238 | 678 358 | 488 954 |
| 50 305 | 15 103 312 | 695 342 | 299 976 | 889 786 | 802 076 |
| 53 493 | 17 744 913 | 1 043 545 | 469 249 | 436 593 | 591 946 |
| 41 472 | 21 591 384 | 964 225 | 476 279 | 519 608 | 168 633 |
| 35 936 | 18 894 266 | 705 496 | 322 942 | 410 667 | 351 057 |
| **100 283** | **37 890 707** | **2 046 182** | **909 319** | **789 919** | **512 438** |
| 3 702 | 7 302 699 | 276 827 | 136 020 | 153 088 | 108 002 |
| 23 194 | 8 042 830 | 325 450 | 159 471 | 195 153 | 171 739 |
| 1 893 | 501 447 | 24 544 | 13 596 | 1 239 | 66 |
| 22 028 | 6 505 005 | 333 497 | 153 700 | 108 402 | 39 706 |
| 29 670 | 7 443 989 | 457 328 | 172 832 | 237 448 | 107 930 |
| 19 796 | 8 094 737 | 628 536 | 273 700 | 94 589 | 84 995 |

Note:The data of Suzhou New and Hi-tech Development Zone includes the data of Xushuguan Economic Development Zone, same as the following.

表8-9 国家级、省级开发区建设发展情况 (至2012年累计)

| 开发区名称 | Development Zones | 已开发面积 (平方公里) Area of Development (sq.km) | 全社会固定资产投资 (亿元) Total Value of Investment in Fixed Assets (100 million yuan) |
|---|---|---|---|
| **总　计** | **Total** | **562.93** | **18 772.85** |
| **一、国家级开发区** | **State Development Zones** | **446.03** | **16 262.85** |
| 苏州工业园区 | Suzhou Industrial Park | 80.00 | 4 723.09 |
| 苏州高新技术产业开发区 | Suzhou New and Hi-tech Development Zone | 36.00 | 2 203.63 |
| 昆山经济技术开发区 | Kunshan Economic and Technological Development Zone | 50.00 | 1 673.04 |
| 张家港保税区 | Zhangjiagang Bonded Area | 10.60 | 745.00 |
| 苏州太湖旅游度假区 | Suzhou Taihu National Tourism and Vacation Zone | 20.00 | 253.99 |
| 昆山高新技术产业开发区 | Kunshan New and Hi-tech industrial Development Zone | 14.05 | 633.68 |
| 常熟经济技术开发区 | Changshu Economic and Technological Development Zone | 45.00 | 1 531.87 |
| 吴江经济技术开发区 | Wujiang Economic and Technological Development Zone | 47.90 | 1 020.68 |
| 太仓港经济技术开发区 | Taicang Economic and Technological Development Zone | 71.46 | 1 585.69 |
| 张家港经济技术开发区 | Zhangjiagang Economic and Technological Development Zone | 34.45 | 867.54 |
| 吴中经济技术开发区 | Wuzhong Economic and Technological Development Zone | 36.57 | 1 024.63 |
| **二、省级开发区** | **Provincial Development Zones** | **131.03** | **2 944.28** |
| 相城经济开发区 | Xiangcheng Economic Development Zone | 20.00 | 468.20 |
| 浒墅关经济开发区 | Xushuguan Economic Development Zone | 14.13 | 434.28 |
| 昆山旅游度假区 | Kunshan Tourism and Holiday Zone | 22.50 | 134.34 |
| 吴江汾湖经济开发区 | Wujiang Fenhu Economic Development Zone | 18.60 | 727.24 |
| 常熟高新技术产业开发区 | Changshu New and Hi-tech Development Zone | 29.12 | 643.26 |
| 昆山花桥经济开发区 | Kunshan Huaqiao Economic Development Zone | 26.68 | 536.96 |

# CONSTRUCTION OF STATE AND PROVINCIAL DEVELOPMENT ZONES (BY 2012)

| 基础设施投入(亿元) Investment In Infrastructure (100 million yuan) | 期末内资企业数(个) Number of Domestic Enterprise by Year End (unit) | 内资企业注册资本额(亿元) Registered Capital of Domestic Enterprise (100 million yuan) | 期末注册外商企业数(个) Number of Enterprises with Foreign Investment that Have Registered by Year End (unit) | 实际到帐外资额(亿美元) Foreign Capital Actually Used (USD 100 million) | 期末从业人数(万人) Number of Employee Persons by Year End (10 000 persons) |
|---|---|---|---|---|---|
| **3 198.58** | **92 051** | **8 277.62** | **15 141** | **780.03** | **316.27** |
| **2 739.67** | **83 836** | **7 263.90** | **13 499** | **702.43** | **276.78** |
| 688.26 | 20 591 | 2 868.05 | 4 818 | 179.85 | 68.34 |
| 401.29 | 12 857 | 1 179.52 | 1 124 | 98.56 | 30.56 |
| 270.06 | 11 879 | 408.86 | 1 941 | 80.99 | 50.37 |
| 154.95 | 5 188 | 364.48 | 558 | 35.32 | 5.84 |
| 49.82 | 1 374 | 111.51 | 108 | 4.05 | 9.00 |
| 80.77 | 6 050 | 180.55 | 714 | 47.35 | 16.20 |
| 209.56 | 4 704 | 473.52 | 519 | 64.18 | 29.41 |
| 194.42 | 3 554 | 181.61 | 930 | 61.41 | 17.69 |
| 225.94 | 5 502 | 630.97 | 1 015 | 55.59 | 20.66 |
| 236.46 | 4 133 | 169.43 | 507 | 32.00 | 9.06 |
| 228.15 | 8 004 | 695.40 | 1 265 | 43.14 | 19.66 |
| **639.41** | **9 058** | **1 227.43** | **1 892** | **87.88** | **46.58** |
| 79.51 | 2 936 | 360.98 | 415 | 9.05 | 5.93 |
| 180.50 | 843 | 213.71 | 250 | 10.26 | 7.09 |
| 35.43 | 131 | 24.80 | 55 | 4.55 | 1.56 |
| 89.53 | 1 463 | 247.20 | 448 | 21.02 | 10.09 |
| 85.28 | 1 444 | 226.30 | 441 | 27.88 | 11.73 |
| 169.16 | 2 241 | 154.44 | 283 | 15.12 | 10.17 |

表8-10

# 对外承包工程劳务合作及服务外包情况（2012年）
# CONTRACTED PROJECTS AND LABOR COOPERATION WITH FOREIGN COUNTRIES OR REGIONS (2012)

| 地区 | Region | 签订合同金额（万美元）Contractual Value (USD 10 000) | 实际营业额（万美元）Value of Business Fulfilled (USD 10 000) | 当年外派人员（人）Persons Sent Abroad in the Year (person) | 接包合同额（万美元）Outsourcing Contract Value (USD 10 000) | 离岸接包执行额（万美元）Offshore Outsourcing Execution Value (USD 10 000) |
|---|---|---|---|---|---|---|
| **全市** | **Whole Municipality** | **102 574** | **83 716** | **2 776** | **559 619** | **305 409** |
| 市区 | Urban Area | 31 019 | 24 406 | 606 | 415 838 | 245 486 |
| # 吴江区 | Wujiang District | 14 351 | 7 467 | 73 | 10 863 | 6 044 |
| 常熟 | Changshu | 13 176 | 11 985 | 275 | 20 143 | 10 360 |
| 张家港 | Zhangjiagang | 18 445 | 24 198 | 211 | 20 231 | 10 458 |
| 昆山 | Kunshan | 37 780 | 21 028 | 1 669 | 63 149 | 20 596 |
| 太仓 | Taicang | 2 154 | 2 099 | 15 | 40 258 | 18 509 |

表8-11

# 海外企业（2012年）
# INVESTMENT ABROAD (2012)

| 地区 | Region | 新批境外企业数（个）Number of Newly Approved Foreign Enterprises (unit) | | 开业境外企业数（个）Number of Foreign Enterprises Opening to Business (unit) | | 新批中方境外投资额（万美元）New Registered Oversea Investment from China (USD 10 000) |
|---|---|---|---|---|---|---|
| | | 新增 Newly Added | 累计 Total | 新增 Newly Added | 累计 Total | |
| **全市** | **Whole Municipality** | **187** | **744** | **102** | **300** | **122 163** |
| 市区 | Urban Area | 92 | 375 | 44 | 124 | 60 414 |
| # 吴江区 | Wujiang District | 17 | 74 | 9 | 29 | 36 532 |
| 常熟 | Changshu | 42 | 105 | 23 | 34 | 12 856 |
| 张家港 | Zhangjiagang | 28 | 131 | 15 | 45 | 27 787 |
| 昆山 | Kunshan | 19 | 83 | 16 | 67 | 10 392 |
| 太仓 | Taicang | 6 | 50 | 4 | 30 | 10 714 |

表8-12

# 部分年份国际旅游情况
# INTERNATIONAL TOURISM OF PARTIAL YEARS

| 项　　目 | Item | 1990年 | 2000年 | 2010年 | 2011年 | 2012年 |
|---|---|---|---|---|---|---|
| **一、旅游外汇收入** (万美元) | **Foreign Exchange Earnings of Tourism** (USD 10 000) | **1 581** | **20 135** | **125 059** | **146 998** | **164 723** |
| **二、接待境外旅游者** (万人次) | **Number of Foreign Tourists** (10 000 person-times) | **27.84** | **71.41** | **265.15** | **297.75** | **321.87** |
| **三、接待过夜境外旅游者** | **Number of Foreign Tourists Staying Overnight** | **26.16** | **55.73** | **207.53** | **232.63** | **249.22** |
| # 外国人 | Foreigners | 8.07 | 37.58 | 147.23 | 167.03 | 179.54 |
| 港澳台同胞 | Compatriots from HongKong, Macao and Taiwan | 17.34 | 18.15 | 60.30 | 65.60 | 69.68 |
| **四、境外旅游者过夜人天数** (万人天) | **Person-days of Foreign Tourists Staying Overnight** (10 000 person-days) | **31.93** | **88.32** | **668.01** | **749.36** | **827.97** |
| # 外国人 | Foreigners | 11.38 | 62.67 | 453.03 | 502.27 | 556.73 |
| 港澳台同胞 | Compatriots from HongKong, Macao and Taiwan | 19.75 | 25.65 | 214.98 | 247.09 | 271.24 |
| **五、接待外国人分国别** (人次) | **Foreign Tourists by Country** (person-time) | | | | | |
| # 日　本 | Japan | 31 321 | 114 870 | 426 352 | 473 156 | 465 723 |
| 新加坡 | Singapore | 2 494 | 19 217 | 57 832 | 71 202 | 85 797 |
| 泰　国 | Thailand | | 7 595 | 24 363 | 26 347 | 30 524 |
| 印度尼西亚 | Indonesia | | 4 688 | 21 808 | 24 277 | 32 217 |
| 马来西亚 | Malaysia | | 36 570 | 59 078 | 64 418 | 74 408 |
| 美　国 | United States | 5 864 | 36 027 | 192 581 | 222 804 | 244 889 |
| 加拿大 | Canada | | 4 312 | 43 358 | 47 745 | 65 485 |
| 英　国 | United Kingdom | 2 314 | 10 823 | 44 071 | 48 115 | 56 541 |
| 法　国 | France | 3 606 | 20 920 | 38 428 | 41 012 | 44 846 |
| 德　国 | Germany | 2 367 | 10 604 | 68 084 | 92 981 | 110 010 |
| 意大利 | Italy | | 7 555 | 20 422 | 29 076 | 33 796 |
| 瑞　士 | Switzerland | | 1 926 | 5 808 | 9 006 | 8 509 |
| 澳大利亚 | Australia | | 5 779 | 33 131 | 39 894 | 42 449 |
| **六、接待能力** | **Reception Capacity** | | | | | |
| 星级宾馆 (家) | Star-rated Hotels (unit) | 12 | 67 | 159 | 150 | 144 |
| 星级宾馆床位 (张) | Number of Beds Star-rated Hotels (unit) | 3 212 | 14 816 | 41 183 | 40 256 | 36 657 |
| **七、接待国内旅游人数** (万人次) | **Number of Received Domestic Tourists (10 000 person-times)** | | **1 496.05** | **7 004.88** | **7 775.38** | **8 624.43** |
| 国内旅游收入 (亿元) | Earnings form Domestic Tourism (100 million yuan) | | 125.22 | 917.76 | 1 084.82 | 1 254.38 |

表8-13

# 人民币对主要外币年平均汇价（中间价）
# AVERAGE EXCHANGE RATE OF RMB YUAN AGAINST MAIN CONVERTIBLE CURRENCIES (MIDDLE PRICE)

| 年 份<br>Year | 100美元<br>100 US Dollars | 100日元<br>100 Japanese yen | 100港元<br>100 Hong Kong Dollars | 100欧元<br>100 Euro |
|---|---|---|---|---|
| 1985 | 293.66 | 1.2457 | 37.57 | |
| 1986 | 345.28 | 2.0694 | 44.22 | |
| 1987 | 372.21 | 2.5799 | 47.74 | |
| 1988 | 372.21 | 2.9082 | 47.70 | |
| 1989 | 376.51 | 2.7360 | 48.28 | |
| 1990 | 478.32 | 3.3233 | 61.39 | |
| 1991 | 532.33 | 3.9602 | 68.45 | |
| 1992 | 551.46 | 4.3608 | 71.24 | |
| 1993 | 576.20 | 5.2020 | 74.41 | |
| 1994 | 861.87 | 8.4370 | 111.53 | |
| 1995 | 835.10 | 8.9225 | 107.96 | |
| 1996 | 831.42 | 7.6352 | 107.51 | |
| 1997 | 828.98 | 6.8600 | 107.09 | |
| 1998 | 827.91 | 6.3488 | 106.88 | |
| 1999 | 827.83 | 7.2932 | 106.66 | |
| 2000 | 827.84 | 7.6864 | 106.18 | |
| 2001 | 827.70 | 6.8075 | 106.08 | |
| 2002 | 827.70 | 6.6237 | 106.07 | 800.58 |
| 2003 | 827.70 | 7.1466 | 106.24 | 936.13 |
| 2004 | 827.68 | 7.6552 | 106.23 | 1 029.00 |
| 2005 | 819.17 | 7.4484 | 105.30 | 1 019.53 |
| 2006 | 797.18 | 6.8570 | 102.62 | 1 001.90 |
| 2007 | 760.40 | 6.4632 | 97.46 | 1 041.75 |
| 2008 | 694.51 | 6.7427 | 89.19 | 1 022.27 |
| 2009 | 683.10 | 7.2986 | 88.12 | 952.70 |
| 2010 | 676.95 | 7.7279 | 87.13 | 897.25 |
| 2011 | 645.88 | 8.1050 | 82.97 | 900.11 |
| 2012 | 631.25 | 7.9037 | 81.38 | 810.67 |

表8-14

# 四星级及以上饭店、宾馆一览(2012年末)
# LIST OF HOTELS ABOVE 4-STAR STANDARD (END OF 2012)

| 单位<br>Hotels and Restaurants | 地址<br>Address | 电话<br>Telephone Number | 星级标准<br>Standard | 客房数(间)<br>Number of Guest Rooms (room) |
|---|---|---|---|---|
| 苏州吴宫泛太平洋酒店 | 苏州市新市路259号 | 65103388 | 5 | 385 |
| 苏州中茵皇冠假日酒店 | 苏州市工业园区星港街168号 | 67616688 | 5 | 344 |
| 苏州雅都大酒店 | 苏州市三香路488号 | 68291888 | 5 | 361 |
| 苏州新城花园酒店 | 苏州市高新区狮山路1号 | 68250228 | 5 | 457 |
| 江苏国泰南园宾馆 | 苏州市十全街655号 | 67786778 | 5 | 236 |
| 苏州工业园区金鸡湖大酒店 | 苏州市工业园区国宾路168号 | 62887878 | 5 | 62 |
| 苏州工业园区阳澄湖澜廷度假酒店 | 苏州工业园区阳澄湖半岛 | 62988888 | 5 | 187 |
| 苏州金鸡湖凯宾斯基酒店 | 苏州工业园区国宾路168号 | 62897888 | 5 | 458 |
| 苏州香格里拉大酒店 | 苏州市高新区塔园路168号 | 68080168 | 5 | 390 |
| 苏州宝岛花园酒店 | 苏州市太湖国家旅游度假区长沙岛18号 | 82276999 | 5 | 130 |
| 苏州怡景太湖高尔夫酒店 | 苏州市太湖国家旅游度假区墅里路2号 | 66217777 | 5 | 118 |
| 吴江同里湖大饭店 | 苏州市吴江区九里湖路8号 | 63337888 | 5 | 244 |
| 吴江东恒盛国际大酒店 | 苏州市吴江区文苑路88号 | 63928888 | 5 | 424 |
| 常熟虞山锦江饭店 | 常熟市北门大街8号 | 52118888 | 5 | 78 |
| 常熟国际饭店 | 常熟市黄河路288号 | 52101888 | 5 | 332 |
| 常熟天铭国际大酒店 | 常熟市海虞北路12号 | 52877777 | 5 | 270 |
| 常熟中江广场皇冠假日酒店 | 常熟市开元大道6号 | 52729999 | 5 | 269 |
| 常熟裕坤国贸酒店 | 常熟市珠江路176号 | 52988888 | 5 | 286 |
| 常熟市金海华丽嘉酒店 | 常熟市西门大街73号 | 52188888 | 5 | 192 |
| 张家港国贸酒店 | 张家港市人民中路42号 | 58687788 | 5 | 519 |
| 张家港市馨苑度假村 | 张家港市长安南路279号 | 58818888 | 5 | 250 |
| 张家港市华芳金陵国际酒店 | 张家港市长安中路388号 | 58811999 | 5 | 368 |
| 昆山马穆拉卡酒店有限公司 | 昆山市前进中路387号 | 57885788 | 5 | 387 |
| 昆山开发区一醉皇冠酒店 | 昆山市前进中路216号 | 57338888 | 5 | 239 |
| 太仓金陵花园酒店 | 太仓市人民北路11号 | 53531888 | 5 | 251 |

表8-14 续表 1 Continued 1

| 单 位<br>Hotels and Restaurants | 地 址<br>Address | 电 话<br>Telephone Number | 星级标准<br>Standard | 客房数(间)<br>Number of Guest Rooms (room) |
|---|---|---|---|---|
| 太仓锦江国际大酒店 | 太仓市上海东路89号 | 53580000 | 5 | 316 |
| 苏州竹辉饭店 | 苏州市竹辉路168号 | 65205601 | 4 | 356 |
| 苏州胥城大厦 | 苏州市三香路333号 | 68286688 | 4 | 395 |
| 苏州凯莱大酒店 | 苏州市干将东路535号 | 65218855 | 4 | 294 |
| 苏州乐乡饭店 | 苏州市大井巷18号区 | 65228888 | 4 | 195 |
| 苏州雅戈尔富宫大酒店 | 苏州市宫巷63号 | 65159998 | 4 | 201 |
| 苏州冠云大酒店 | 苏州市桐泾北路538号 | 68018118 | 4 | 169 |
| 苏州新世纪大酒店 | 苏州市广济路23号 | 68015555 | 4 | 192 |
| 苏州会议中心 | 苏州市道前街100号 | 65226691 | 4 | 373 |
| 苏州园外楼饭店 | 苏州市留园路477号 | 85888588 | 4 | 155 |
| 苏州三元宾馆 | 苏州市人民路887号 | 65113608 | 4 | 96 |
| 苏州桃园度假村 | 苏州市高新区金山东路68号 | 68018888 | 4 | 210 |
| 苏州金龙大酒店 | 苏州市高新区玉山路28号 | 68253538 | 4 | 139 |
| 苏州建屋国际酒店 | 苏州市工业园区星湖街金鸡湖商业广场 | 62966666 | 4 | 177 |
| 苏州商旅美居酒店 | 苏州市苏州工业园区凤里街336号 | 62967888 | 4 | 193 |
| 独墅湖书香世家会所酒店 | 苏州市吴中区通达路2699号 | 62795888 | 4 | 184 |
| 苏州天平大酒店 | 苏州市吴中区金山南路168号 | 66268888 | 4 | 277 |
| 苏州中华园大饭店 | 苏州市吴中区金山南路198号 | 66256666 | 4 | 196 |
| 苏州西山宾馆 | 苏州市吴中区石公山风景区 | 66278888 | 4 | 182 |
| 苏州阳明山花园酒店 | 苏州市吴中区苏沪机场路角直段38号 | 66011111 | 4 | 200 |
| 苏州山水度假村 | 苏州市吴中区东山镇西泾山 | 66399888 | 4 | 130 |
| 苏州苏苑饭店 | 苏州市吴中区东吴北路130号 | 66018888 | 4 | 271 |
| 苏州南亚宾馆 | 苏州市相城区阳澄湖东路1号 | 65761688 | 4 | 276 |
| 苏州金澄锦江国际酒店 | 苏州市相城区兴太路260号 | 65431888 | 4 | 185 |

表8-14 续表 2 Continued 2

| 单 位<br>Hotels and Restaurants | 地 址<br>Address | 电 话<br>Telephone Number | 星级标准<br>Standard | 客房数(间)<br>Number of Guest Rooms (room) |
|---|---|---|---|---|
| 吴江宾馆 | 苏州市吴江区鲈乡南路2155号 | 63420888 | 4 | 176 |
| 吴江盛虹国际酒店 | 苏州市吴江区舜新南路2008号 | 63477777 | 4 | 126 |
| 吴江新世纪国际酒店 | 苏州市吴江区平望镇平波台3号 | 65059888 | 4 | 66 |
| 吴江汇丰国际花园酒店 | 苏州市吴江区震泽镇南699路 | 63779888 | 4 | 74 |
| 吴江同里湖度假村 | 苏州市吴江区同里镇和尚圩 | 63330888 | 4 | 111 |
| 吴江盛世锦江国际大酒店 | 苏州市吴江区盛泽镇盛泽大道88号 | 63139999 | 4 | 176 |
| 吴江汉唐国际酒店 | 苏州市吴江区鲈乡南路1433号 | 63115555 | 4 | 93 |
| 吴江鲈乡山庄 | 苏州市吴江区笠泽路607号 | 63470000 | 4 | 137 |
| 吴江松陵饭店 | 苏州市吴江区中山北路51号 | 63472888 | 4 | 359 |
| 常熟虞城大酒店 | 常熟市海虞南路64号 | 52777777 | 4 | 281 |
| 常熟森林大酒店 | 常熟市虞山北路79号 | 52102888 | 4 | 155 |
| 常熟时风国际假日酒店 | 常熟市海虞南路62号 | 52228888 | 4 | 322 |
| 常熟凯悦国际酒店 | 常熟市东南开发区新都路1号 | 52111805 | 4 | 139 |
| 常熟恒隆东航国际酒店 | 常熟市方塔街106号 | 52989999 | 4 | 248 |
| 张家港沙洲宾馆 | 张家港市暨阳中路170号 | 58810888 | 4 | 242 |
| 张家港江南宾馆 | 张家港市港区长江中路132号 | 58812568 | 4 | 146 |
| 张家港长江大酒店 | 张家港市港区镇长江村 | 58318518 | 4 | 150 |
| 昆山宾馆 | 昆山市人民北路99号 | 57888000 | 4 | 196 |
| 昆山嘉顿国际饭店 | 昆山市马鞍山东路18号 | 57558888 | 4 | 214 |
| 昆山富贵大酒店 | 昆山市朝阳中路459号 | 57166888 | 4 | 168 |
| 昆山威尼斯假日酒店 | 昆山市民权路18号 | 57016888 | 4 | 211 |
| 昆山上湖龙乐·宝曼酒店 | 昆山市巴城镇迎宾路3555号 | 57650222 | 4 | 446 |
| 太仓陆渡宾馆 | 太仓市陆渡镇北康富路8号 | 53459890 | 4 | 208 |
| 太仓娄东宾馆 | 太仓市县府街6号 | 53712222 | 4 | 282 |
| 太仓世代大酒店 | 太仓市县府东街30号 | 53587778 | 4 | 112 |

表8-15

# 国际友好城市一览 (2012年末)
# LIST OF INTERNATIONAL SISTER CITIES OF SUZHOU (END OF 2012)

| 友好城市 | Sister Cities | 缔结时间 Time of Establishment of Relationship |
|---|---|---|
| **苏州市** | **Suzhou** | |
| 意大利威尼斯市 | Venice, Italy | 1980年03月24日 |
| 加拿大维多利亚市 | Victoria, Canada | 1980年10月20日 |
| 日本池田市 | Ikeda, Japan | 1981年06月06日 |
| 日本金泽市 | Kanazawa, Japan | 1981年06月13日 |
| 美国波特兰市 | Portland, USA | 1988年06月07日 |
| 罗马尼亚图尔恰县 | Tulcea, Romania | 1995年09月20日 |
| 韩国全州市 | Chonju, Republic of Korea | 1996年03月21日 |
| 拉脱维亚里加市 | Riga, Latvia | 1997年09月22日 |
| 埃及伊斯梅利亚市 | Ismailia, Egypt | 1998年03月03日 |
| 法国格勒诺布尔市 | Grenoble, France | 1998年09月20日 |
| 荷兰奈梅亨市 | Nijmegen, The Netherlands | 1999年09月23日 |
| 丹麦埃斯比约市 | Esbjerg, Denmark | 2002年08月20日 |
| 巴西阿雷格里港市 | Porto Alegre, Brazil | 2004年06月22日 |
| 马达加斯加塔那那利佛市 | Antananarivo, Madagascar | 2005年11月29日 |
| 德国康斯坦茨市 | Konstanz, Germany | 2007年10月18日 |
| 新西兰陶波市 | Taupo, New Zealand | 2008年02月07日 |
| 澳大利亚洛根市 | Logan, Australia | 2009年11月09日 |
| 瑞典南斯莫兰地区 | Southern Smaland Region, Sweden | 2012年08月22日 |
| **姑苏区** | **Gusu** | |
| 马耳他桑塔露西亚市 | Santa Lucija, Malta | 2001年11月09日 |
| **吴中区** | **Wuzhong** | |
| 德国里萨市 | Riesa, Germany | 1999年08月16日 |
| 新西兰罗托鲁瓦市 | Rotorua, New Zealand | 2000年02月18日 |
| **相城区** | **Xiangcheng** | |
| 韩国荣州市 | Yongju, Republic of Korea | 1998年04月23日 |

表8-15 续表 Continued

| 友好城市 | Sister Cities | 缔结时间 Time of Establishment of Relationship |
|---|---|---|
| **吴江区** | **Wujiang** | |
| 法国布尔昆-雅里昂市 | Bourgoin - Jallieu, France | 1993年10月07日 |
| 澳大利亚达博市 | Dubbo, Australia | 1995年06月07日 |
| 日本千叶市 | Chiba, Japan | 1996年10月10日 |
| 韩国华城市 | Hwa Sung County, Republic of Korea | 2000年09月27日 |
| 日本内滩町市 | Uchinada, Japan | 2006年10月08日 |
| 南非莫哈林市 | Mogale, South Africa | 2006年11月14日 |
| 美国马伯洛市 | Marlboro Township,USA | 2011年12月09日 |
| **常熟市** | **Changshu** | |
| 日本绫部市 | Ayabe, Japan | 1989年05月12日 |
| 日本萨摩川内市 | Satsuma Sendai, Japan | 1991年07月26日 |
| 澳大利亚汤斯维尔市 | Townsville, Australia | 1995年04月30日 |
| 美国惠蒂尔市 | Whitter, USA | 1995年05月12日 |
| 法国布莱斯特市 | Brest, France | 1996年07月16日 |
| 加拿大本拿比市 | Burnaby, Canada | 2009年07月20日 |
| **张家港市** | **Zhangjiagang** | |
| 澳大利亚波特兰市 | Portland, Australia | 1995年08月08日 |
| 日本丸龟市 | Marugame, Japan | 1999年05月28日 |
| 俄罗斯维亚基马市 | Vyazama, Russia | 2004年10月11日 |
| 美国丽浪多市 | Redondo Beach, USA | 2007年05月21日 |
| **昆山市** | **Kunshan** | |
| 美国南艾尔蒙地市 | South Elmonte, USA | 1993年06月07日 |
| 纳米比亚赫鲁特方丹市 | Grootfontein, Namibia | 2003年07月21日 |
| 日本馆林市 | Tatebayashi, Japan | 2006年05月16日 |
| **太仓市** | **Taicang** | |
| 意大利罗索里纳市 | Rosolina, Italy | 2000年02月23日 |

# 主要统计指标解释

**进出口总额** 指实际进出我国国境的货物总金额。包括对外贸易实际进出口货物，来料加工装配进出口货物，国家间、联合国及国际组织无偿援助物资和赠送品，华侨、港澳台同胞和外籍华人捐赠品，租赁期满归承租人所有的租赁货物，进料加工进出口货物，边境地方贸易及边境地区小额贸易进出口货物(边民互市贸易除外)，中外合资企业、中外合作经营企业、外商独资经营企业进出口货物和公用物品，到、离岸价格在规定限额以上的进出口货样和广告品(无商业价值、无使用价值和免费提供出口的除外)，从保税仓库提取在中国境内销售的进口货物，以及其他进出口货物。该指标可以观察一个国家在对外贸易方面的总规模。我国规定出口货物按离岸价格统计，进口货物按到岸价格统计。

**利用外资** 指我国各级政府、部门、企业和其他经济组织通过对外借款、吸收外商直接投资以及用其他方式筹措的境外现汇、设备、技术等。

**对外借款** 指通过对外正式签订借款协议，从境外筹措的资金，包括外国政府贷款、国际金融组织贷款、外国银行商业贷款、出口信贷以及对外发行债券等。1996年及以前还包括对外发行股票。该指标是我国利用外资的重要部分。

**外商直接投资** 指外国企业和经济组织或个人(包括华侨、港澳台胞以及我国在境外注册的企业)按我国有关政策、法规，用现汇、实物、技术等在我国境内开办外商独资企业、与我国境内的企业或经济组织共同举办中外合资经营企业、合作经营企业或合作开发资源的投资(包括外商投资收益的再投资)，以及经政府有关部门批准的项目投资总额内企业从境外借入的资金。

**外商其他投资** 指除对外借款和外商直接投资以外的各种利用外资的形式。包括企业在境内外股票市场公开发行的以外币计价的股票（目前主要是在香港证券市场发行的H股和在境内证券市场发行的B股）发行价总额，国际租赁进口设备的应付款，补偿贸易中外商提供的进口设备、技术、物料的价款，加工装配贸易中外商提供的进口设备、物料的价款。

**对外直接投资** 指我国国内投资者以现金、实物、无形资产等方式在国外及港澳台地区设立、购买国（境）外企业，并以控制该企业的经营管理权为核心的经济活动。

**对外承包工程** 指各对外承包公司以招标议标承包方式承揽的下列业务：(1)承包国外工程建设项目；(2)承包我国对外经援项目；(3)承包我国驻外机构的工程建设项目；(4)承包我国境内利用外资进行建设的工程项目；(5)与外国承包公司合营或联合承包工程项目时我国公司分包部分；(6)对外承包兼营的房屋开发业务。对外承包工程的营业额是以货币表现的本期内完成的对外承包工程的工作量，包括以前年度签订的合同和本年度新签订的合同在报告期内完成的工作量。

**对外劳务合作** 指以收取工资的形式向业主或承包商提供技术和劳动服务的活动。我国对外承包公司在境外开办的合营企业，中国公司同时又提供劳务的，其劳务部分也纳入劳务合作统计。劳务合作营业额按报告期内向雇主提交的结算数(包括工资、加班费和奖金等)统计。

**旅游人数**

(1)入境旅游人数：指报告期内来我国观光、度假、探亲访友、就医疗养、购物、参加会议或从事经济、文化、体育、宗教活动的外国人、港澳台同胞等入境游客。统计时，外国人、港澳台同胞每入境一次统计1人次。

(2)出境人数：指中国（大陆）居民因公或因私出境前往其他国家、中国香港特别行政区、澳门特别行政区和台湾省观光、度假、探亲访友、就医疗养、购物、参加会议或从事经济、文化、体育、宗教活动的人数，即出境游客。统计时，按每出境一次统计1人次。

(3)国内旅游人数：指在报告期内在中国（大陆）观光游览、度假、探亲访友、就医疗养、购物、参加会议或从事经济、文化、体育、宗教活动的中国（大陆）居民人数，其出游的目的不是通过所从事的活动谋取报酬。统计时，国内游客按每出游一次统计1人次。

**国际旅游(外汇)收入** 指入境游客在中国（大陆）境内旅行、游览过程中用于交通、参观游览、住宿、餐饮、购物、娱乐等全部花费。

**国内旅游收入** 指国内游客在国内旅行、游览过程中用于交通、参观游览、住宿、餐饮、购物、娱乐等全部花费。

**星级饭店** 指设备、设施、服务符合《旅游饭店星级的划分与评定》（GB/T14308-2003），通过相关旅游管理部门评定，并取得星级饭店称号的饭店（含预备星级饭店）。

# EXPLANATORY NOTES ON MAIN STATISTICAL INDICATORS

**Total Imports and Exports at Customs** refer to the real value of commodities imported and exported across the border of China. They include the actual imports and exports through foreign trade, imported and exported goods under the processing and assembling trades and materials, supplies and gifts as aid given gratis between governments and by the United Nations and other international organizations, and contributions donated by overseas Chinese, compatriots in Hong Kong and Macao and Chinese with foreign citizenship, leasing commodities owned by tenant at the expiration of leasing period, the imported and exported commodities processed with imported materials, commodities trading in border areas (excluding mutual exchange goods), the imported and exported commodities and articles for public use of the Sino-foreign joint ventures, cooperative enterprises and ventures with sole foreign investment. Also included is import or export of samples and advertising goods for which CIF or FOB value are beyond the permitted ceiling (excluding goods of no trading or use value and free commodities for export), imported goods sold in China from bonded warehouses and other imported or exported goods. The indicator of the total imports and exports at customs can be used to observe the total size of external trade in a country. In accordance with the stipulation of the Chinese government, imports are calculated at CIF, while exports are calculated at FOB.

**Utilization of Foreign Capitals** refers to remittance, equipment and technology financed from abroad, by loans, foreign direct investment and other forms undertaken by the Chinese governments at all levels, by various departments, enterprises and other economic units.

**Foreign Borrowings** refer to funds borrowed from abroad through formal signing of borrowing agreements with foreign institutions, including loans of foreign governments, loans of international financial institutions, commercial loans of foreign banks, export credit, and funds raised by Chinese bonds (and shares before 1996) issued abroad. It is an important part of China's utilization of foreign capitals.

**Foreign Direct Investment** refers to the investments inside China by foreign enterprises and economic organizations or individuals (including overseas Chinese, compatriots from Hong Kong, Macao and Taiwan, and Chinese enterprises registered abroad), following the relevant policies and laws of China, for the establishment of ventures exclusively with foreign own investment, Sino-foreign joint ventures and cooperative enterprises or for co-operative exploration of resources with enterprises or economic organizations in China. It includes the re- investment of the foreign entrepreneurs with the profits gained from the investment and the funds that enterprises borrow from abroad in the total investment of projects which are approved by the relevant department of the government.

**Other Foreign Investment** refers to all forms of utilization of foreign capitals other than foreign borrowings and foreign direct investment. It includes the total value of stock shares in foreign currencies issued by enterprises at domestic or foreign stock exchanges (now mainly consisting of H shares issued at Hong Kong Security Market and B shares issued at domestic security markets), rent payable for the imported equipment through international leasing arrangement, cost of imported equipment, technology and materials provided by foreign counterparts in compensation trade and processing and assembly trade.

**Overseas Direct Investment** refers to enterprises set up or bought by domestic investors in foreign countries and in Hong Kong, Macao and Taiwan, and the economic activities centring on operation and management of those enterprises are under the control of domestic investors.

**Overseas Contracted Project** refers to projects undertaken by Chinese contractors (project contracting companies) through bidding process. They include: (1) overseas civil engineering construction projects financed by foreign investors; (2) overseas projects financed by the Chinese government through its foreign aid programs; (3) construction projects of Chinese diplomatic missions, trade offices and other institutions stationed abroad; (4) construction projects in China financed by foreign investment; (5) sub-contracted projects to be taken by Chinese contractors through a joint umbrella project with foreign contractor(s); (6) housing development projects. The business income from international contracted projects is the work volume of contracted projects completed during the reference period, expressed in monetary terms, including completed work on projects signed in previous years.

**Overseas Labour Services** refer to the activities of providing technology and labour services to employers or contractors in the forms of receiving salaries and wages. Labour services providing by contractual joint ventures of Chinese international contracting corporations should be included in the statistics of service co-operation with foreign countries. The business income of labour service cooperation is the income in the form of wages and salaries, overtime pay, bonuses and other remuneration received from the employers during the reference period.

**Number of Tourists**

(1) Visitor arrivals refer to the number of foreigners, Chinese compatriots from Hong Kong, Macao and Taiwan Chinese (mainland) who come to China (mainland) for sight-seeing, vacation, visiting relatives, medical treatment, shopping, attending conference, or to engage in economic, cultural, sports and religious activities. In compiling statistics, each time of entering China is counted as one person-time.

(2) Number of Chinese residents going abroad refer to the number of Chinese (mainland) residents going to other countries, Hong Kong Special Administrative region, Macao Special Administrative region and Taiwan for on official or private purposes, for sight-seeing, vacation, visiting relatives, medical treatment, shopping, attending conference, or to engage in economic, cultural, sports and religious activities. In compiling statistics, each time of leaving is counted as one person-time.

(3) Number of domestic tourists refers to the number Of Chinese (mainland) residents who travel within China (mainland) for sight-seeing, vacation, visiting relatives, medical treatment, shopping, attending conference, or to engage in economic, cultural, sports and religious activities. In compiling statistics, each time of travelling is counted as one person-time.

**Foreign Exchange Earnings from International Tourism** refer to the total expenditure of foreigners, overseas Chinese, Chinese compatriots from Hong Kong, Macao and Taiwan during their stay in the mainland of China on transportation,sighting, accommodation, food, shopping and entertainment.

**Income from Domestic Tourism** refer to expenditure of domestic tourists on transportation, sighting, accommodation, food, shopping and entertainment while they travel.

**Star-rated Hotels** refer to hotels rated with stars as assessed by the relevant tourism authorities according to GB/T14308-2003 standard with reference to their infrastructure, facilities and service levels.

# 九、能源消费

## CHAPTER 9
## CONSUMPTION OF ENERGY

# 能源消费
# CONSUMPTION OF ENERGY

## 主 要 统 计 指 标
## MAJOR STATISTICAL INDICATORS

| | | | | |
|---|---|---|---|---|
| 2012年规模以上工业企业能源消费总量 | Total Energy Consumption of Industry Above Designated Size | 7 712.09 | 万吨标准煤 | 10 000 tons of SCE |
| # 原　煤 | Raw Coal | 5 005.21 | 万吨 | 10 000 tons |
| 焦　炭 | Coke | 1 066.60 | 万吨 | 10 000 tons |
| 汽　油 | Gasoline | 7.16 | 万吨 | 10 000 tons |
| 柴　油 | Diesel Oil | 21.62 | 万吨 | 10 000 tons |
| 燃料油 | Fuel Oil | 47.37 | 万吨 | 10 000 tons |
| 热　力 | Heat | 87 726 811 | 百万千焦 | 1 million kilo-joule |
| 电　力 | Electricity | 807.36 | 亿千瓦时 | 100 million kwh |
| 2012年全社会用电量 | Total Consumption of Electricity | 1 189.93 | 亿千瓦时 | 100 million kwh |
| 比上年增长 | Increase Over Last Year | 5.2 | % | |
| 2012年工业用电量 | Industrial Consumption of Electricity | 982.66 | 亿千瓦时 | 100 million kwh |
| 比上年增长 | Increase Over Last Year | 3.9 | % | |
| 2012年第三产业用电量 | Tertiary Industry Consumption of Electricity | 106.69 | 亿千瓦时 | 100 million kwh |
| 比上年增长 | Increase Over Last Year | 11.5 | % | |
| 2012年城乡居民生活用电量 | Consumption of Electricity for Non-production Purposes | 86.49 | 亿千瓦时 | 100 million kwh |
| 比上年增长 | Increase Over Last Year | 12.1 | % | |

表9-1 全市规模以上工业企业能源购进、消费及库存量（2012年）

ENERGY PURCHASES, CONSUMPTION AND STOCK OF INDUSTRIAL ENTERPRISES OF WHOLE MUNICIPALITY ABOVE DESIGNATED SIZE(2012)

| 能源品种 | Type of Energy | 购进量 Purchases | 消费量 Consumption | # 工业生产 Industrial Production | # 原材料 Raw Materials | 年末库存量 Stock (year-end) |
|---|---|---|---|---|---|---|
| **能源合计 （吨标准煤）** | **Total Energy (ton of SCE)** | **64 171 999** | **77 120 918** | **76 623 082** | **331 150** | **2 377 917** |
| 原　煤 （吨） | Raw Coal (ton) | 49 871 293 | 50 052 064 | 49 988 463 | – | 2 434 663 |
| 洗精煤 | Washing Coal | 9 375 534 | 9 582 168 | 9 582 064 | – | 479 362 |
| 其他洗煤 | Other Washed Coals | 4 700 | 4 898 | 4 888 | – | 154 |
| 煤制品 | Coal Products | 91 947 | 92 271 | 92 216 | – | 131 |
| 焦　炭 | Coke | 4 941 576 | 10 665 980 | 10 665 712 | – | 203 003 |
| 其他焦化产品 | Other Coking Products | 303 787 | 299 387 | 299 377 | 275 427 | 26 608 |
| 焦炉煤气 （万立方米） | Coke Oven Gas (10 000cu.m) | 3 090 | 181 347 | 181 246 | – | – |
| 高炉煤气 | Blast-furnace Gas | – | 2 408 166 | 2 406 518 | – | – |
| 转炉煤气 | Converter Gas | – | 148 442 | 148 442 | – | – |
| 发生炉煤气 | Furnace Gas | – | – | – | – | – |
| 天然气 | Natural Gas | 369 937 | 369 932 | 368 208 | – | – |
| 液化天然气 （吨） | LNG (ton) | 7 853 | 7 864 | 7 523 | – | – |
| 汽　油 | Gasoline | 71 285 | 71 619 | 14 188 | 169 | 377 |
| 煤　油 | Kerosene | 2 238 | 2 294 | 2 272 | 42 | 157 |
| 柴　油 | Diesel Oil | 215 476 | 216 182 | 135 309 | – | 7 452 |
| 燃料油 | Fuel Oil | 478 858 | 473 680 | 473 318 | – | 26 313 |
| 液化石油气 | LPG | 20 362 | 20 447 | 19 877 | – | 305 |
| 润滑油 | Lubricating Oil | 686 | 691 | 680 | – | 2 |
| 溶剂油 | Solvent Oil | 720 | 720 | 720 | – | – |
| 石油沥青 | Petroleum Asphalt | – | – | – | – | – |
| 其他石油制品 | Other Petroleum Products | 7 635 | 8 180 | 8 147 | – | 382 |
| 热　力 （百万千焦） | Heat (1 million kilo-joule) | 59 302 370 | 87 726 811 | 86 563 009 | – | – |
| 电　力 （万千瓦时） | Electricity ( 10 000 kwh) | 6 997 973 | 8 073 615 | 7 922 832 | – | – |
| 城市垃圾用于燃料 （吨） | City Waste For Fuel (Ton) | 1 105 737 | 1 113 489 | 1 113 489 | – | – |
| 生物质废料用于燃料 | Biomass Waste For Fuel | 53 385 | 53 159 | 53 159 | – | – |
| 余热余压 （百万千焦） | Heat and Pressure (1 million kilo-joule) | – | 8 957 331 | 8 957 331 | – | – |
| 其他工业废料用于燃料 （吨） | Other Industrial Waste For Fuel (Ton) | 5 524 | 5 524 | 5 524 | – | – |
| 其他燃料 （吨标准煤） | Other Fuels (ton of SCE) | 7 117 | 7 097 | 7 097 | – | 20 |

表9-2

# 市区规模以上工业企业能源购进、消费及库存量 (2012年)

# ENERGY PURCHASES，CONSUMPTION AND STOCK OF INDUSTRIAL ENTERPRISES OF URBAN AREA ABOVE DESIGNATED SIZE(2012)

| 能源品种 | Type of Energy | 购进量 Purchases | 消费量 Consumption | # 工业生产 Industrial Production | # 原材料 Raw Materials | 年末库存量 Stock (year-end) |
|---|---|---|---|---|---|---|
| **能源合计 (吨标准煤)** | **Total Energy (ton of SCE)** | **16 157 898** | **16 894 139** | **16 701 602** | **330 822** | **323 756** |
| 原　煤 (吨) | Raw Coal (ton) | 12 872 547 | 12 810 187 | 12 797 459 | – | 419 807 |
| 洗精煤 | Washing Coal | 482 617 | 505 654 | 505 616 | – | 4 956 |
| 其他洗煤 | Other Washed Coals | 2 580 | 2 717 | 2 707 | – | 145 |
| 煤制品 | Coal Products | 77 739 | 78 063 | 78 044 | – | 38 |
| 焦　炭 | Coke | 8 493 | 309 813 | 309 813 | – | 1 365 |
| 其他焦化产品 | Other Coking Products | 303 787 | 299 387 | 299 377 | 275 427 | 26 608 |
| 焦炉煤气 (万立方米) | Coke Oven Gas (10 000cu.m) | 3 090 | 5 699 | 5 598 | – | – |
| 高炉煤气 | Blast-furnace Gas | – | 41 428 | 39 780 | – | – |
| 转炉煤气 | Converter Gas | – | | – | – | – |
| 发生炉煤气 | Furnace Gas | – | – | – | – | – |
| 天然气 | Natural Gas | 175 952 | 175 946 | 174 750 | – | – |
| 液化天然气 (吨) | LNG (ton) | 1 615 | 1 619 | 1 507 | – | – |
| 汽　油 | Gasoline | 27 132 | 27 343 | 6 872 | 169 | 156 |
| 煤　油 | Kerosene | 370 | 371 | 365 | 42 | 9 |
| 柴　油 | Diesel Oil | 76 454 | 76 742 | 42 095 | – | 1 316 |
| 燃料油 | Fuel Oil | 43 810 | 43 843 | 43 793 | – | 6 069 |
| 液化石油气 | LPG | 5 363 | 5 393 | 5 274 | – | 5 |
| 润滑油 | Lubricating Oil | 506 | 512 | 501 | – | 2 |
| 溶剂油 | Solvent Oil | – | – | – | – | – |
| 石油沥青 | Petroleum Asphalt | – | – | – | – | – |
| 其他石油制品 | Other Petroleum Products | 3 251 | 4 060 | 4 060 | – | 5 |
| 热　力 (百万千焦) | Heat (1 million kilo-joule) | 28 305 444 | 34 684 460 | 34 361 956 | – | – |
| 电　力 (万千瓦时) | Electricity ( 10 000 kwh) | 2 725 848 | 2 875 069 | 2 814 859 | – | – |
| 城市垃圾用于燃料 (吨) | City Waste For Fuel (Ton) | 721 372 | 721 372 | 721 372 | – | – |
| 生物质废料用于燃料 | Biomass Waste For Fuel | 15 194 | 15 194 | 15 194 | – | – |
| 余热余压 (百万千焦) | Heat and Pressure (1 million kilo-joule) | – | 851 369 | 851 369 | – | – |
| 其他工业废料用于燃料(吨) | Other Industrial Waste For Fuel (Ton) | – | – | – | – | – |
| 其他燃料 (吨标准煤) | Other Fuels (ton of SCE) | 7 069 | 7 069 | 7 069 | – | – |

表9-3

# 分地区规模以上工业企业能源消费量 (2012年)

| 能源品种 | | Type of Energy | | 全 市 Whole Municipality | 市 区 Urban Area |
|---|---|---|---|---|---|
| **能源合计** | (吨标准煤) | **Total Energy** | (ton of SCE) | **77 120 918** | **16 894 139** |
| 原 煤 | (吨) | Raw Coal | (ton) | 50 052 064 | 12 810 187 |
| 洗精煤 | | Washing Coal | | 9 582 168 | 505 654 |
| 其他洗煤 | | Other Washed Coals | | 4 898 | 2 717 |
| 煤制品 | | Coal Products | | 92 271 | 78 063 |
| 焦 炭 | | Coke | | 10 665 980 | 309 813 |
| 其他焦化产品 | | Other Coking Products | | 299 387 | 299 387 |
| 焦炉煤气 | (万立方米) | Coke Oven Gas | (10 000cu.m) | 181 347 | 5 699 |
| 高炉煤气 | | Blast-furnace Gas | | 2 408 166 | 41 428 |
| 转炉煤气 | | Converter Gas | | 148 442 | - |
| 发生炉煤气 | | Furnace Gas | | - | - |
| 天然气 | | Natural Gas | | 369 932 | 175 946 |
| 液化天然气 | (吨) | LNG | (ton) | 7 864 | 1 619 |
| 汽 油 | | Gasoline | | 71 619 | 27 343 |
| 煤 油 | | Kerosene | | 2 294 | 371 |
| 柴 油 | | Diesel Oil | | 216 182 | 76 742 |
| 燃料油 | | Fuel Oil | | 473 680 | 43 843 |
| 液化石油气 | | LPG | | 20 447 | 5 393 |
| 润滑油 | | Lubricating Oil | | 691 | 512 |
| 溶剂油 | | Solvent Oil | | 720 | - |
| 石油沥青 | | Petroleum Asphalt | | - | - |
| 其他石油制品 | | Other Petroleum Products | | 8 180 | 4 060 |
| 热 力 | (百万千焦) | Heat | (1 million kilo-joule) | 87 726 811 | 34 684 460 |
| 电 力 | (万千瓦时) | Electricity | ( 10 000 kwh) | 8 073 615 | 2 875 069 |
| 城市垃圾用于燃料 | (吨) | City Waste For Fuel | (Ton) | 1 113 489 | 721 372 |
| 生物质废料用于燃料 | | Biomass Waste For Fuel | | 53 159 | 15 194 |
| 余热余压 | (百万千焦) | Heat and Pressure | (1 million kilo-joule) | 8 957 331 | 851 369 |
| 其他工业废料用于燃料 | (吨) | Other Industrial Waste For Fuel | (Tons) | 5 524 | - |
| 其他燃料 | (吨标准煤) | Other Fuels | (ton of SCE) | 7 097 | 7 069 |

# ENERGY CONSUMPTION OF INDUSTRIAL ENTERPRISES ABOVE DESIGNATED SIZE BY REGION (2012)

| # 吴江区 Wujiang District | 常熟 Changshu | 张家港 Zhangjiagang | 昆山 Kunshan | 太仓 Taicang |
|---|---|---|---|---|
| **5 156 661** | **11 033 851** | **33 354 625** | **3 878 223** | **11 960 079** |
| 4 233 050 | 11 431 718 | 8 994 909 | 1 651 160 | 15 164 089 |
| 6 371 | 530 039 | 8 546 474 | – | – |
| 610 | 1 966 | 215 | – | – |
| 67 130 | 2 417 | 5 511 | 6 280 | – |
| 7 430 | 590 604 | 9 764 015 | 577 | 971 |
| – | – | – | – | – |
| – | – | 175 648 | – | – |
| – | – | 2 366 738 | – | – |
|  | – | 148 442 | – | – |
| – | – | – | – | – |
| 5 157 | 32 739 | 107 384 | 42 185 | 11 679 |
| 8 | 445 | 1 907 | 3 893 | – |
| 4 346 | 12 674 | 5 347 | 19 742 | 6 513 |
| 164 | 795 | 334 | 647 | 146 |
| 12 633 | 32 012 | 43 472 | 44 651 | 19 305 |
| 7 501 | 29 435 | 274 290 | 122 909 | 3 202 |
| 427 | 461 | 4 885 | 7 868 | 1 841 |
| – | 68 | 26 | 68 | 16 |
| – | 129 | – | 591 | – |
| – | – | – | – | – |
| – | 1 805 | 1 503 | 2 | 810 |
| 19 700 643 | 6 925 489 | 21 323 637 | 6 834 427 | 17 958 798 |
| 1 176 751 | 996 238 | 2 184 635 | 1 220 782 | 796 890 |
| – | – | – | 384 365 | 7 752 |
| 2 323 | – | 3 060 | 17 727 | 17 178 |
| – | – | 8 105 962 | – | – |
| – | – | – | 5 524 | – |
| – | – | – | – | 28 |

表9-4

# 全市规模以上工业企业分行业能源消费量 (2012年)

| 行业 | Sector | 综合能源消费量 (吨标准煤) Overall Consumption Volume of Energy (ton of SCE) | 原煤 (吨) Raw Coal (ton) |
|---|---|---|---|
| **总计** | **Total** | **50 147 184** | **50 052 064** |
| 有色金属矿采选业 | Nonferrous Metals Mining and Dressing | 956 | - |
| 非金属矿采选业 | Nonmetal Minerals Mining and Dressing | 3 092 | - |
| 农副食品加工业 | Farming and Side-line Food Processing Trade | 177 383 | 30 778 |
| 食品制造业 | Food Production | 110 544 | 9 490 |
| 酒、饮料和精制茶制造业 | Wine, Beverage and Refined tea manufacturing | 53 074 | 16 525 |
| 烟草制品业 | Manufacture of Tobacco | 6 285 | - |
| 纺织业 | Textile Industry | 3 473 122 | 2 462 794 |
| 纺织服装、服饰业 | Garments and Apparel Industry | 237 848 | 197 111 |
| 皮革、毛皮、羽绒及其制品业 | Leather, Furs, Down and Related Products | 37 832 | 10 263 |
| 木材加工及竹、藤、棕、草制品业 | Timber Processing, Bamboo, Cane, Palm Fiber &Straw Products | 76 135 | 46 831 |
| 家具制造业 | Furniture Manufacturing | 20 096 | 114 |
| 造纸及纸制品业 | Papermaking and Paper Products | 2 495 890 | 3 520 028 |
| 印刷和记录媒介复制业 | Printing and Record Medium Reproduction | 39 617 | 9 264 |
| 文教工美体育和娱乐用品制造业 | Stationary,Educational,Industrial arts, Sports and Entertainment products | 46 816 | 5 697 |
| 石油加工、炼焦和核燃料加工业 | Petroleum Processing, Coking and Nuclear Fuel Processing | 16 957 | 6 535 |
| 化学原料及化学制品制造业 | Raw Chemical Materials and Chemical Products | 3 178 329 | 2 157 263 |
| 医药制造业 | Medical and Pharmaceutical Products | 210 362 | 190 542 |
| 化学纤维制造业 | Chemical Fiber | 1 902 472 | 1 186 137 |
| 橡胶和塑料制品业 | Rubber and Plastic Products | 656 856 | 238 201 |
| 非金属矿物制品业 | Nonmetal Mineral Products | 1 517 121 | 335 293 |
| 黑色金属冶炼及压延加工业 | Smelting and Pressing of Ferrous Metals | 16 075 646 | 2 069 311 |
| 有色金属冶炼及压延加工业 | Smelting and Pressing of Nonferrous Metals | 362 880 | 34 411 |
| 金属制品业 | Metal Products | 466 755 | 85 980 |
| 通用设备制造业 | Ordinary Machinery | 317 331 | 26 949 |
| 专用设备制造业 | Equipment for Special Purposes | 220 265 | 1 974 |
| 汽车制造业 | Automobile Manufacturing | 368 884 | 597 |
| 铁路船舶航空航天和其他运输设备制造业 | Railway, Ship, Aerospace and other transportation equipment manufacturing | 75 979 | 5 070 |
| 电气机械及器材制造业 | Electric Equipment and Machinery | 483 525 | 22 430 |
| 计算机通信和其他电子设备制造业 | Computer Telecommunications and Other Electronic Equipment Manufacture | 2 088 198 | 573 566 |
| 仪器仪表制造业 | Instruments, Meters Machinery | 161 470 | 86 075 |
| 其他制造业 | Others Industry | 9 102 | 3 449 |
| 废弃资源综合利用业 | Comprehensive Utilization of Waste Resources | 37 644 | 8 238 |
| 金属制品、机械和设备修理业 | Metal Products, Machinery and Equipment Repair | 73 | - |
| 电力、热力生产和供应业 | Production and Supply of Electric Power and Heat Energy | 15 145 616 | 36 708 575 |
| 燃气生产和供应业 | Production and Supply of Gas | 7 785 | 2 572 |
| 水的生产和供应业 | Production and Supply of Water | 65 243 | - |

注:综合能源消费量=各种能源工业生产消费量合计-能源加工厂转换-能源回收利用。

# TOTAL ENERGY CONSUMPTION OF INDUSTRIAL ENTERPRISES ABOVE DESIGNATED SIZE BY SECTOR (2012)

| 洗精煤 (吨) Washing Coal (ton) | 焦炭 (吨) Coke (ton) | 汽油 (吨) Gasoline (ton) | 柴油 (吨) Diesel Oil (ton) | 燃料油 (吨) Fuel Oil (ton) | 液化石油气 (吨) Liquefied Petroleum Gas (ton) | 热力 (百万千焦) Heat (1 million kilo-joule) | 电力 (万千瓦时) Electricity (10 000 kwh) |
|---:|---:|---:|---:|---:|---:|---:|---:|
| **9 582 168** | **10 665 980** | **71 619** | **216 182** | **473 680** | **20 447** | **87 726 811** | **8 073 615** |
| – | – | – | – | – | – | – | 809 |
| 925 | – | 60 | 203 | – | – | – | 1 674 |
| – | – | 90 | 1 750 | 392 | 20 | 2 949 486 | 38 141 |
| – | – | 272 | 972 | 349 | 245 | 1 316 041 | 22 245 |
| – | – | 122 | 951 | – | – | 159 366 | 13 772 |
| – | – | – | – | – | – | 134 822 | 1 396 |
| 12 127 | 437 | 4 886 | 8 639 | 7 851 | 1 244 | 28 264 994 | 918 414 |
| 386 | 99 | 4 375 | 5 013 | 35 | 65 | 727 438 | 53 289 |
| – | – | 826 | 1 220 | 2 409 | 28 | 301 058 | 13 112 |
| – | – | 272 | 1 014 | – | – | 84 953 | 31 342 |
| – | – | 407 | 1 555 | 62 | 697 | 2 427 | 12 567 |
| – | – | 1 676 | 8 434 | 956 | 1 457 | 19 810 632 | 346 802 |
| – | – | 1 733 | 910 | 62 | 312 | 7 096 | 23 933 |
| – | – | 716 | 1 076 | 117 | 938 | 158 107 | 22 269 |
| – | – | 113 | 171 | 3 894 | – | 100 438 | 1 665 |
| 13 981 | 214 | 6 724 | 17 307 | 4 756 | 489 | 12 838 542 | 681 842 |
| – | – | 489 | 587 | – | – | 2 025 026 | 53 909 |
| – | – | 604 | 1 338 | 10 872 | – | 8 053 508 | 781 114 |
| – | – | 3 504 | 5 494 | 996 | 127 | 3 154 887 | 262 620 |
| 2 927 | – | 1 579 | 70 507 | 400 778 | 994 | 409 651 | 233 888 |
| 9 548 790 | 10 650 351 | 2 295 | 20 854 | 265 | 1 660 | 995 773 | 1 389 764 |
| – | 1 359 | 1 308 | 4 987 | 22 427 | 145 | 153 363 | 131 237 |
| 2 918 | 1 695 | 4 763 | 10 708 | 5 189 | 1 271 | 257 044 | 209 855 |
| – | 3 581 | 6 148 | 7 964 | 1 156 | 2 154 | 194 024 | 195 124 |
| – | 382 | 5 838 | 4 593 | 74 | 1 450 | 168 620 | 151 415 |
| – | – | 2 879 | 5 245 | 215 | 1 440 | 397 265 | 173 703 |
| 63 | 734 | 969 | 834 | 121 | 616 | 6 670 | 35 455 |
| 52 | 206 | 6 046 | 8 353 | 7 516 | 1 030 | 153 174 | 315 690 |
| – | – | 10 467 | 17 002 | 2 224 | 3 046 | 3 276 272 | 1 346 304 |
| – | – | 1 210 | 976 | 18 | 842 | 1 385 940 | 72 976 |
| – | – | 247 | 118 | 870 | 15 | 2 524 | 3 596 |
| – | 6 922 | 130 | 2 384 | – | 162 | – | 17 082 |
| – | – | – | – | – | – | – | 66 |
| – | – | 449 | 4 382 | 73 | – | 237 669 | 457 457 |
| – | – | 239 | 477 | – | – | – | 5 655 |
| – | – | 183 | 165 | – | – | – | 53 434 |

Note: Comprehensive energy consumption= All kinds of energy consumption of industrial production–energy conversion by energy plants-Energy recycling

表9-5 市区规模以上工业企业分行业能源消费量 (2012年)

| 行 业 | Sector | 综合能源消费量 (吨标准煤) Overall Consumption Volume of Energy (ton of SCE) | 原 煤 (吨) Raw Coal (ton) |
|---|---|---|---|
| **总 计** | **Total** | **11 324 499** | **12 810 187** |
| 有色金属矿采选业 | Nonferrous Metals Mining and Dressing | 956 | - |
| 非金属矿采选业 | Nonmetal Minerals Mining and Dressing | 3 092 | - |
| 农副食品加工业 | Farming and Side-line Food Processing Trade | 30 855 | 18 176 |
| 食品制造业 | Food Production | 66 338 | 7 616 |
| 酒、饮料和精制茶制造业 | Wine, Beverage and Refined tea manufacturing | 31 162 | 6 558 |
| 烟草制品业 | Manufacture of Tobacco | - | - |
| 纺织业 | Textile Industry | 1 854 909 | 1 140 277 |
| 纺织服装、服饰业 | Garments and Apparel Industry | 43 667 | 19 294 |
| 皮革、毛皮、羽绒及其制品业 | Leather, Furs, Down and Related Products | 9 088 | 1 730 |
| 木材加工及竹、藤、棕、草制品业 | Timber Processing, Bamboo, Cane, Palm Fiber &Straw Products | 18 291 | 13 726 |
| 家具制造业 | Furniture Manufacturing | 5 097 | - |
| 造纸及纸制品业 | Papermaking and Paper Products | 551 784 | 847 566 |
| 印刷和记录媒介复制业 | Printing and Record Medium Reproduction | 10 832 | - |
| 文教工美体育和娱乐用品制造业 | Stationary,Educational,Industrial arts, Sports and Entertainment products | 12 062 | 4 832 |
| 石油加工、炼焦和核燃料加工业 | Petroleum Processing, Coking and Nucleus Fuel Machining Trade | 5 288 | 6 139 |
| 化学原料及化学制品制造业 | Raw Chemical Materials and Chemical Products | 596 517 | 72 163 |
| 医药制造业 | Medical and Pharmaceutical Products | 82 641 | 15 178 |
| 化学纤维制造业 | Chemical Fiber | 1 134 432 | 805 362 |
| 橡胶和塑料制品业 | Rubber and Plastic Products | 149 025 | 20 220 |
| 非金属矿物制品业 | Nonmetal Mineral Products | 390 792 | 160 162 |
| 黑色金属冶炼及压延加工业 | Smelting and Pressing of Ferrous Metals | 529 520 | 119 096 |
| 有色金属冶炼及压延加工业 | Smelting and Pressing of Nonferrous Metals | 119 544 | 6 957 |
| 金属制品业 | Metal Products | 132 330 | 28 754 |
| 通用设备制造业 | Ordinary Machinery | 128 426 | 1 722 |
| 专用设备制造业 | Equipment for Special Purposes | 88 644 | - |
| 汽车制造业 | Automobile Manufacturing | 82 629 | 137 |
| 铁路船舶航空航天和其他运输设备制造业 | Railway, Ship, Aerospace and other transportation equipment manufacturing | 13 024 | 465 |
| 电气机械及器材制造业 | Electric Equipment and Machinery | 245 424 | 11 489 |
| 计算机通信和其他电子设备制造业 | Computer Telecommunications and Other Electronic Equipment Manufacture | 995 933 | - |
| 仪器仪表制造业 | Instruments, Meters Machinery | 34 348 | - |
| 其他制造业 | Others Industry | 1 021 | 90 |
| 废弃资源综合利用业 | Comprehensive Utilization of Waste Resources | 12 100 | 8 238 |
| 金属制品、机械和设备修理业 | Metal Products, Machinery and Equipment Repair | - | - |
| 电力、热力生产和供应业 | Production and Supply of Electric Power and Heat Energy | 3 902 916 | 9 491 669 |
| 燃气生产和供应业 | Production and Supply of Gas | 1 863 | 2 572 |
| 水的生产和供应业 | Production and Supply of Water | 39 947 | - |

# ENERGY CONSUMPTION OF INDUSTRIAL ENTERPRISES ABOVE DESIGNATED SIZE BY SECTOR IN URBAN AREA (2012)

| 洗精煤 (吨) Washing Coal (ton) | 焦炭 (吨) Coke (ton) | 汽油 (吨) Gasoline (ton) | 柴油 (吨) Diesel Oil (ton) | 燃料油 (吨) Fuel Oil (ton) | 液化石油气 (吨) Liquefied Petroleum Gas (ton) | 热力 (百万千焦) Heat (1 million kilo-joule) | 电力 (万千瓦时) Electricity (10 000 kwh) |
|---|---|---|---|---|---|---|---|
| **505 654** | **309 813** | **27 343** | **76 742** | **43 843** | **5 393** | **34 684 460** | **2 875 069** |
| – | – | – | – | – | – | – | 809 |
| 925 | – | 60 | 203 | – | – | – | 1 674 |
| – | – | 22 | 332 | 392 | – | 117 052 | 8 145 |
| – | – | 212 | 249 | 349 | 170 | 548 825 | 11 881 |
| – | – | 47 | 150 | – | – | 27 720 | 10 711 |
| – | – | – | – | – | – | – | – |
| 3 444 | 437 | 994 | 835 | 229 | 245 | 18 815 260 | 484 445 |
| – | 99 | 1 273 | 1 373 | – | 24 | 247 889 | 14 916 |
| – | – | 404 | 581 | – | – | 45 852 | 3 765 |
| – | – | 144 | 443 | – | – | 82 492 | 4 322 |
| – | – | 108 | 1 071 | 41 | 124 | – | 2 433 |
| – | – | 451 | 2 930 | – | 882 | 4 153 840 | 98 776 |
| – | – | 851 | 263 | – | – | 5 746 | 8 354 |
| – | – | 234 | 138 | – | – | – | 3 721 |
| – | – | – | – | – | – | – | 508 |
| – | 214 | 3 043 | 5 402 | 660 | 4 | 1 412 480 | 94 385 |
| – | – | 184 | 356 | – | – | 894 775 | 27 075 |
| – | – | 77 | 356 | 5 452 | – | 5 776 384 | 410 286 |
| – | – | 1 470 | 1 398 | 48 | 45 | 414 200 | 93 538 |
| 2 927 | – | 545 | 36 112 | 33 787 | 151 | 11 278 | 78 121 |
| 498 359 | 305 434 | 369 | 682 | – | – | 298 478 | 94 621 |
| – | 516 | 333 | 1 434 | 1 216 | 57 | 136 869 | 55 327 |
| – | 1 658 | 1 845 | 3 222 | 139 | 469 | 78 824 | 58 279 |
| – | 1 335 | 2 971 | 3 385 | 16 | 1 287 | 87 564 | 81 803 |
| – | – | 2 184 | 1 182 | 16 | 71 | 49 433 | 63 957 |
| – | – | 969 | 1 846 | 18 | 19 | 260 410 | 38 501 |
| – | – | 165 | 134 | – | – | – | 8 312 |
| – | 120 | 2 987 | 2 373 | 812 | 160 | 139 538 | 180 506 |
| – | – | 4 752 | 7 678 | 257 | 1 685 | 828 205 | 738 587 |
| – | – | 470 | 9 | – | – | 13 031 | 26 979 |
| – | – | 15 | 30 | 339 | – | 2 524 | 324 |
| – | – | 34 | 1 588 | – | – | – | 3 195 |
| – | – | – | – | – | – | – | – |
| – | – | 19 | 745 | 73 | – | 235 791 | 133 150 |
| – | – | 97 | 245 | – | – | – | 872 |
| – | – | 14 | – | – | – | – | 32 792 |

表9-6

# 全市规模以上工业企业用水情况 (2012年)
# WATER CONSUMPTION OF INDUSTRIAL ENTERPRISES ABOVE DESIGNATED SIZE (2012)

| 行　　业 | Sector | 工业取水总量 (万立方米) Total industrial water (10000 $M^3$) | 重复用水量 (万立方米) Repetitive water consumption (10000 $M^3$) |
|---|---|---|---|
| **总　　计** | **Total** | **246 080** | **596 017** |
| 有色金属矿采选业 | Nonferrous Metals Mining and Dressing | 11 | 28 |
| 非金属矿采选业 | Nonmetal Minerals Mining and Dressing | 20 | 14 |
| 农副食品加工业 | Farming and Side-line Food Processing Trade | 471 | 130 |
| 食品制造业 | Food Production | 402 | 120 |
| 酒、饮料和精制茶制造业 | Wine, Beverage and Refined tea manufacturing | 520 | 87 |
| 烟草制品业 | Manufacture of Tobacco | 49 | – |
| 纺织业 | Textile Industry | 19 325 | 3 010 |
| 纺织服装、服饰业 | Garments and Apparel Industry | 3 732 | 403 |
| 皮革、毛皮、羽绒及其制品业 | Leather, Furs, Down and Related Products | 444 | 17 |
| 木材加工及竹、藤、棕、草制品业 | Timber Processing, Bamboo, Cane, Palm Fiber &Straw Products | 101 | 1 |
| 家具制造业 | Furniture Manufacturing | 236 | 2 |
| 造纸及纸制品业 | Papermaking and Paper Products | 5 805 | 50 844 |
| 印刷和记录媒介复制业 | Printing and Record Medium Reproduction | 218 | – |
| 文教工美体育和娱乐用品制造业 | Stationary,Educational,Industrial arts, Sports and Entertainment products | 350 | 15 |
| 石油加工、炼焦和核燃料加工业 | Petroleum Processing, Coking and Nuclear Fuel Processing | 15 | 1 |
| 化学原料及化学制品制造业 | Raw Chemical Materials and Chemical Products | 6 382 | 63 999 |
| 医药制造业 | Medical and Pharmaceutical Products | 1 040 | 4 186 |
| 化学纤维制造业 | Chemical Fiber | 2 504 | 13 048 |
| 橡胶和塑料制品业 | Rubber and Plastic Products | 1 602 | 342 |
| 非金属矿物制品业 | Nonmetal Mineral Products | 2 558 | 228 |
| 黑色金属冶炼及压延加工业 | Smelting and Pressing of Ferrous Metals | 13 355 | 328 773 |
| 有色金属冶炼及压延加工业 | Smelting and Pressing of Nonferrous Metals | 839 | 572 |
| 金属制品业 | Metal Products | 2 111 | 130 |
| 通用设备制造业 | Ordinary Machinery | 1 644 | 277 |
| 专用设备制造业 | Equipment for Special Purposes | 1 295 | 87 |
| 汽车制造业 | Automobile Manufacturing | 891 | 490 |
| 铁路船舶航空航天和其他运输设备制造业 | Railway, Ship, Aerospace and other transportation equipment manufacturing | 540 | 15 |
| 电气机械及器材制造业 | Electric Equipment and Machinery | 2 820 | 2 487 |
| 计算机通信和其他电子设备制造业 | Telecommunications Equipment, Computer and Other Electronic Equipment Manufacture | 14 681 | 16 924 |
| 仪器仪表制造业 | Instruments, Meters Machinery | 464 | 414 |
| 其他制造业 | Others Industry | 88 | – |
| 废弃资源综合利用业 | Comprehensive Utilization of Waste Resources | 86 | 192 |
| 金属制品、机械和设备修理业 | Metal Products, Machinery and Equipment Repair | 1 | – |
| 电力、热力生产和供应业 | Production and Supply of Electric Power and Heat Energy | 12 650 | 108 956 |
| 燃气生产和供应业 | Production and Supply of Gas | 27 | 9 |
| 水的生产和供应业 | Production and Supply of Water | 148 800 | 214 |

表9-7

# 主要工业产品单位产量能耗（2012年）
# THE ENERGY CONSUMPTION OF MAJOR INDUSTRIAL PRODUCTS (2012)

| 项目 | | Item | | 数值 Numerical Value |
|---|---|---|---|---|
| 每吨纱(线)混合数全厂生产用电量 | (千瓦时) | Electricity Consumption Per Ton on the Factory's Production of Yarn | (kwh) | 1 802 |
| 每百米布混合数全厂生产用电量 | | Electricity Consumption Per 100 Meters Cloth of the Factory | | 49 |
| 每百米印染布用标准煤量 | (千克标准煤) | Coal Consumption Per 100 Meter Dyed Fabric | (kg of SCE) | 22 |
| 每百米丝织品用电量 | (千瓦时) | Electricity Consumption Per 100 Meter Silk Fabric | (kwh) | 46 |
| 每百米丝织品用标准煤量 | (千克标准煤) | Coal Consumption Per 100 Meter Silk Fabric | (kg of SCE) | 7 |
| 每吨机制纸及纸板耗电 | (千瓦时) | Electricity Consumption Per Ton of Machine Finish Paper and Paper Board | (kwh) | 631 |
| 每吨机制纸及纸板综合能耗 | (千克标准煤) | Comprehensive Unit Energy Consumption Per Ton of Machine Finish Paper and Paper Board | (kg of SCE) | 306 |
| 每吨纯碱生产综合能耗 | | Comprehensive Unit Energy Consumption Per Ton on Soda Ash Production | | 176 |
| 每吨合成氨生产综合能耗 | | Comprehensive Unit Energy Consumption Per Ton on Synthetic Ammonia Production | | 1 239 |
| 每吨涤纶用电量(长丝) | (千瓦时) | Electricity Consumption Per Ton Terylene Production (Long Fibre) | (kwh) | 888 |
| 每吨涤纶用标准煤量(长丝) | (千克标准煤) | Standard Coal Consumption Per Ton Terylene Production (Long Fibre) | (kg of SCE) | 214 |
| 每吨水泥综合能耗 | | Comprehensive Energy Consumption Per Ton Cement Production | | 4 |
| 每重量箱平板玻璃综合能耗 | | Comprehensive Energy Consumption Per One Weighing Tank of Sheet Glass Production | | 13 |
| 吨钢综合能耗 | | Comprehensive Energy Consumption Per Ton Steel Production | | 548 |
| 吨钢耗电 | (千瓦时) | Electricity Consumption Per Ton Steel Production | (kwh) | 399 |
| 吨钢可比能耗 | (千克标准煤) | Comparable Energy Consumption Per Ton Steel Production | (kg of SCE) | 527 |
| 火力发电标准煤耗 | (克标准煤/千瓦时) | Standard Coal Consumption of Thermal Power Generation | (g of SCE/kwh) | 287 |
| 火力发电供电标准煤耗 | | Standard Coal Consumption of Thermal Power Generation and Power Supply | | 301 |
| 发电厂用电率 | (%) | Electricity Consumption of Power Plants | (%) | 5 |

表9-8

# 部分年份分行业用电情况
# ENERGY CONSUMPTION BY SECTOR OF PARTIAL YEARS

单位：万千瓦时 (10 000 kwh)

| 年份 Year | 全社会用电量 Electricity Consumption | 全行业用电量 Electricity by Sector | 第一产业 Primary Industry | 第二产业 Secondary Industry | # 工业 Industry | 第三产业 Tertiary Industry | 城乡居民生活用电 Electricity Consumption by Urban and Rural Residents |
|---|---|---|---|---|---|---|---|
| 1986 | 348 398 | 335 660 | 47 455 | 278 290 | 276 982 | 9 915 | 12 738 |
| 1987 | 414 500 | 398 870 | 61 251 | 324 947 | 323 435 | 12 672 | 15 630 |
| 1988 | 465 355 | 447 053 | 69 520 | 356 585 | 354 553 | 20 948 | 18 302 |
| 1989 | 473 882 | 450 438 | 68 532 | 361 120 | 359 404 | 20 786 | 23 444 |
| 1990 | 507 687 | 479 512 | 70 821 | 383 297 | 381 394 | 25 394 | 28 175 |
| 1991 | 576 975 | 543 672 | 78 876 | 438 278 | 436 385 | 26 518 | 33 303 |
| 1992 | 680 698 | 639 687 | 91 190 | 516 370 | 513 597 | 32 127 | 41 011 |
| 1993 | 781 374 | 730 783 | 101 470 | 588 418 | 581 777 | 40 895 | 50 591 |
| 1994 | 892 271 | 819 691 | 116 611 | 649 052 | 639 885 | 54 028 | 72 580 |
| 1995 | 998 485 | 907 323 | 131 909 | 716 671 | 707 424 | 58 743 | 91 162 |
| 1996 | 1 126 972 | 1 023 750 | 131 616 | 825 147 | 815 410 | 66 987 | 103 222 |
| 1997 | 1 233 419 | 1 119 353 | 136 434 | 894 080 | 884 124 | 88 839 | 114 066 |
| 1998 | 1 327 589 | 1 204 818 | 132 671 | 973 282 | 960 857 | 98 865 | 122 771 |
| 1999 | 1 538 193 | 1 409 790 | 114 363 | 1 198 521 | 1 186 270 | 96 906 | 128 403 |
| 2000 | 1 900 439 | 1 730 448 | 69 778 | 1 547 146 | 1 531 665 | 113 524 | 169 991 |
| 2001 | 2 259 217 | 2 072 342 | 63 833 | 1 878 092 | 1 861 413 | 130 417 | 186 875 |
| 2002 | 2 735 800 | 2 555 864 | 37 781 | 2 361 451 | 2 339 938 | 156 632 | 179 936 |
| 2003 | 3 576 083 | 3 333 262 | 38 653 | 3 084 335 | 3 041 342 | 210 274 | 242 821 |
| 2004 | 4 544 696 | 4 261 961 | 37 838 | 3 944 098 | 3 868 402 | 280 025 | 282 735 |
| 2005 | 5 660 372 | 5 314 255 | 29 646 | 4 908 405 | 4 835 611 | 376 204 | 346 117 |
| 2006 | 6 864 926 | 6 436 636 | 29 352 | 5 949 106 | 5 884 112 | 458 178 | 428 290 |
| 2007 | 8 072 735 | 7 587 350 | 30 980 | 7 020 584 | 6 957 336 | 535 786 | 485 385 |
| 2008 | 8 484 230 | 7 917 897 | 30 956 | 7 255 717 | 7 183 172 | 631 224 | 566 333 |
| 2009 | 8 799 436 | 8 198 015 | 30 730 | 7 457 042 | 7 385 410 | 710 243 | 601 421 |
| 2010 | 10 241 031 | 9 514 098 | 30 044 | 8 630 199 | 8 552 481 | 853 855 | 726 933 |
| 2011 | 11 316 316 | 10 544 566 | 31 281 | 9 556 668 | 9 461 876 | 956 617 | 771 750 |
| 2012 | 11 899 281 | 11 034 355 | 34 268 | 9 933 221 | 9 826 579 | 1 066 866 | 864 926 |

表9-9

# 部分年份分地区全社会用电情况
# TOTAL ELECTRICITY CONSUMPTION BY REGION OF PARTIAL YEARS

单位：万千瓦时 (10 000 kwh)

| 年 份 Year | 全 市 Whole Municipality | 市 区 Urban Area | # 吴江区 Wujiang District | 常 熟 Changshu | 张家港 Zhangjiagang | 昆 山 Kunshan | 太 仓 Taicang |
|---|---|---|---|---|---|---|---|
| 1978 | 138 808 | 91 452 | 12 024 | 15 924 | 10 263 | 11 097 | 10 072 |
| 1979 | 165 231 | 108 676 | 14 743 | 18 882 | 12 099 | 13 169 | 12 405 |
| 1980 | 205 298 | 133 206 | 18 852 | 24 936 | 16 812 | 14 943 | 15 401 |
| 1985 | 311 110 | 172 271 | 29 680 | 45 483 | 42 084 | 24 123 | 27 149 |
| 1986 | 348 398 | 189 125 | 33 246 | 52 006 | 50 851 | 27 392 | 29 024 |
| 1987 | 414 500 | 219 416 | 41 139 | 63 993 | 61 649 | 34 773 | 34 669 |
| 1988 | 465 355 | 241 398 | 46 794 | 70 985 | 71 934 | 40 868 | 40 170 |
| 1989 | 473 882 | 245 460 | 48 363 | 72 402 | 71 737 | 43 131 | 41 152 |
| 1990 | 507 687 | 261 706 | 51 440 | 77 178 | 79 486 | 47 193 | 42 124 |
| 1991 | 576 975 | 290 322 | 59 824 | 86 428 | 95 583 | 55 643 | 48 999 |
| 1992 | 680 698 | 332 054 | 72 093 | 98 870 | 127 698 | 61 764 | 57 312 |
| 1993 | 781 374 | 377 816 | 88 287 | 114 514 | 153 527 | 71 894 | 63 623 |
| 1994 | 892 271 | 439 174 | 111 226 | 126 616 | 174 599 | 81 084 | 70 798 |
| 1995 | 998 485 | 495 962 | 124 318 | 140 406 | 192 717 | 92 293 | 77 107 |
| 1996 | 1 126 972 | 547 926 | 138 220 | 153 003 | 239 546 | 104 768 | 81 729 |
| 1997 | 1 233 419 | 591 387 | 153 872 | 166 149 | 263 076 | 123 566 | 89 241 |
| 1998 | 1 327 589 | 639 045 | 164 801 | 169 582 | 284 233 | 143 046 | 91 683 |
| 1999 | 1 538 193 | 728 939 | 177 281 | 215 680 | 320 260 | 170 913 | 102 401 |
| 2000 | 1 900 439 | 901 274 | 236 722 | 265 272 | 387 696 | 219 556 | 126 641 |
| 2001 | 2 259 217 | 1 037 898 | 302 808 | 314 308 | 493 471 | 263 767 | 149 773 |
| 2002 | 2 735 800 | 1 240 050 | 394 185 | 356 277 | 614 238 | 347 936 | 177 299 |
| 2003 | 3 576 083 | 1 611 285 | 544 873 | 431 064 | 826 736 | 477 193 | 229 805 |
| 2004 | 4 544 696 | 2 007 707 | 741 799 | 538 955 | 1 060 249 | 618 148 | 317 295 |
| 2005 | 5 660 372 | 2 415 752 | 894 024 | 665 584 | 1 388 054 | 798 771 | 389 621 |
| 2006 | 6 864 926 | 2 868 272 | 1 057 185 | 784 605 | 1 712 749 | 1 021 111 | 475 222 |
| 2007 | 8 072 735 | 3 369 140 | 1 254 637 | 922 355 | 1 967 880 | 1 231 591 | 576 003 |
| 2008 | 8 484 230 | 3 563 320 | 1 295 607 | 980 504 | 2 018 468 | 1 319 483 | 602 455 |
| 2009 | 8 799 436 | 3 647 936 | 1 351 511 | 1 064 578 | 2 143 411 | 1 322 036 | 621 475 |
| 2010 | 10 241 031 | 4 283 235 | 1 590 285 | 1 246 016 | 2 384 474 | 1 619 135 | 708 171 |
| 2011 | 11 316 316 | 4 780 971 | 1 881 632 | 1 413 760 | 2 595 963 | 1 746 314 | 779 308 |
| 2012 | 11 899 281 | 5 140 791 | 2 103 025 | 1 473 379 | 2 655 946 | 1 819 148 | 810 017 |

表9-10

# 全社会用电情况 (2012年)

单位：万千瓦时

| 行　　业 | Sector | 全　市<br>Whole Municipality |
|---|---|---|
| **全社会用电量总计** | **Total Electricity Consumption** | **11 899 281** |
| **一、全行业用电合计** | **Total Electricity by Sector** | **11 034 355** |
| **按产业分** | **Grouped by Industry** | |
| 第一产业 | Primary Industry | 34 268 |
| 第二产业 | Secondary Industry | 9 933 221 |
| 第三产业 | Tertiary Industry | 1 066 866 |
| **按行业分** | **Grouped by Sector** | |
| （一）农、林、牧、渔业 | Farming, Forestry, Animal Husbandry and Fishery | 34 268 |
| （二）工　业 | Industry | 9 826 579 |
| 采矿业 | Mining and Quarrying | 3 558 |
| 制造业 | Manufacturing | 8 807 024 |
| 1.食品、饮料和烟草制造业 | Food ,Beverage and Tobacco Manufacturing | 102 569 |
| 2.纺织业 | Textile Industry | 2 028 871 |
| 3.服装鞋帽、皮革羽绒及其制品业 | Garments, Shoes, Leather and Feather Products | 148 660 |
| 4.木材加工及制品和家具制品业 | Wood Processing and Related Products and Furniture Manufacture | 60 818 |
| 5.造纸及纸制品业 | Papermaking and Paper Products | 192 628 |
| 6.印刷业和记录媒介的复制 | Printing and Record Duplicating | 42 119 |
| 7.文体用品制造业 | Stationary, Educational and Sports Goods | 17 210 |
| 8.石油加工、炼焦及核燃料加工业 | Oil Processing, Coking and Nuclear Fuel Processing | 8 500 |
| 9.化学原料及化学制品制造业 | Raw Chemical Materials and Chemical Products | 643 249 |
| 10.医药制造业 | Medical and Pharmaceutical Products | 64 873 |
| 11.化学纤维制造业 | Chemical Fiber Manufacturing | 287 867 |
| 12.橡胶和塑料制品业 | Rubber and Plastic Products | 496 055 |
| 13.非金属矿物制品业 | Nonmetal Mineral Products | 240 961 |
| 14.黑色金属冶炼及压延加工业 | Smelting and Pressing of Ferrous Metals | 1 197 853 |
| 15.有色金属冶炼及压延加工业 | Smelting and Pressing of Nonferrous Metals | 64 291 |
| 16.金属制品业 | Metal Products | 582 304 |

# TOTAL ELECTRICITY CONSUMPTION (2012)

(10 000 kwh)

| 市 区<br>Urban Area | # 吴江区<br>Wujiang District | 常 熟<br>Changshu | 张家港<br>Zhangjiagang | 昆 山<br>Kunshan | 太 仓<br>Taicang |
|---|---|---|---|---|---|
| **5 140 791** | **2 103 025** | **1 473 379** | **2 655 946** | **1 819 148** | **810 017** |
| **4 684 577** | **2 004 850** | **1 357 698** | **2 565 159** | **1 665 867** | **761 054** |
| 16 693 | 12 296 | 5 249 | 2 713 | 5 103 | 4 510 |
| 4 032 464 | 1 900 745 | 1 242 102 | 2 477 739 | 1 484 318 | 696 598 |
| 635 420 | 91 809 | 110 347 | 84 707 | 176 446 | 59 946 |
| 16 693 | 12 296 | 5 249 | 2 713 | 5 103 | 4 510 |
| 3 969 926 | 1 885 617 | 1 236 513 | 2 467 475 | 1 464 730 | 687 935 |
| 3 099 | 3 | – | 283 | 154 | 22 |
| 3 525 703 | 1 733 950 | 989 403 | 2 311 769 | 1 353 594 | 626 555 |
| 45 940 | 14 293 | 5 436 | 27 649 | 15 075 | 8 469 |
| 1 179 819 | 1 080 033 | 221 624 | 338 689 | 34 910 | 253 829 |
| 67 084 | 37 646 | 36 326 | 11 062 | 17 766 | 16 422 |
| 27 222 | 10 665 | 8 877 | 4 629 | 14 496 | 5 594 |
| 34 750 | 4 694 | 67 436 | 20 286 | 20 370 | 49 786 |
| 18 686 | 1 582 | 2 141 | 2 188 | 16 975 | 2 129 |
| 5 668 | 1 876 | 1 871 | 2 639 | 5 851 | 1 181 |
| 161 | 157 | 55 | 379 | 64 | 7 841 |
| 52 528 | 22 297 | 63 675 | 370 025 | 141 067 | 15 954 |
| 40 985 | 3 906 | 6 325 | 8 763 | 5 067 | 3 733 |
| 159 108 | 119 001 | 59 060 | 55 814 | 1 149 | 12 736 |
| 213 783 | 53 654 | 49 812 | 57 144 | 134 460 | 40 856 |
| 80 761 | 31 965 | 19 044 | 54 083 | 65 682 | 21 391 |
| 53 288 | 419 | 19 417 | 1 099 276 | 344 | 25 528 |
| 17 556 | 5 506 | 1 151 | 30 166 | 3 000 | 12 418 |
| 210 378 | 52 723 | 205 228 | 101 227 | 44 458 | 21 013 |

表9-10 续表

单位：万千瓦时

| 行　　业 | Sector | 全　市 Whole Municipality |
|---|---|---|
| 17.通用及专用设备制造业 | General and Special Equipment Manufacture | 527 736 |
| 18.交通运输、电气、电子设备制造业 | Transportation, Electrical, Electronic Equipment Manufacturing | 1 954 781 |
| 19.工艺品及其他制造业 | Artworks and Other Products Manufacture | 124 905 |
| 20.废弃资源和废旧材料回收加工业 | Waste Resources and Materials Recycling and Processing | 20 774 |
| 电力、燃气及水的生产和供应业 | Power, Gas and Water Production and Supply | 1 015 997 |
| 1.电力、热力的生产和供应业 | Production and Supply of Electricity and Thermal Power | 928 885 |
| 2.燃气生产和供应业 | Production and Supply of Gas | 6 649 |
| 3.水的生产和供应业 | Production and Supply of Water | 80 463 |
| 工业总计中：轻工业 | In Total: Light Industry | 3 522 943 |
| 重工业 | Heavy Industry | 6 303 636 |
| （三）建筑业 | Construction | 106 642 |
| （四）交通运输、仓储和邮政业 | Transportation, Warehousing and Post | 86 056 |
| # 交通运输业 | Transportation | 61 495 |
| 仓储业 | Warehousing | 22 076 |
| （五）信息传输、计算机服务和软件业 | Information Transmission, Computer Services and Software Industries | 58 378 |
| （六）商业、住宿和餐饮业 | Wholesale, Retail Trade Services, Accommodation and Catering Services | 334 910 |
| 批发和零售业 | Wholesale and Retail Trade Services | 231 826 |
| 住宿和餐饮业 | Accommodation and Catering Services | 103 084 |
| （七） 金融、房地产、商务及居民服务业 | Banking, Real Estate, Business and Community Service | 294 366 |
| # 金融业 | Financial Industries | 20 433 |
| 房地产业 | Real Estate | 197 794 |
| （八）公共事业及管理组织 | Public Administration and Social Organizations | 293 156 |
| # 教育、文化、体育和娱乐业 | Education, Culture, Sports and Entertainment | 87 225 |
| 卫生、社会保障和社会福利业 | Health Care, Social Security and Social Welfare | 43 757 |
| **二、城乡居民生活用电合计** | **Total Electricity Consumption by Urban and Rural Residents** | **864 926** |
| 城镇居民 | Urban Residents | 474 641 |
| 乡村居民 | Rural Residents | 390 285 |

Continued

(10 000 kwh)

| 市　区 Urban Area | # 吴江区 Wujiang District | 常　熟 Changshu | 张家港 Zhangjiagang | 昆　山 Kunshan | 太　仓 Taicang |
|---|---|---|---|---|---|
| 199 626 | 48 747 | 72 341 | 57 323 | 145 078 | 53 368 |
| 1 027 793 | 236 720 | 134 690 | 60 498 | 665 999 | 65 801 |
| 85 763 | 6 847 | 14 043 | 940 | 20 338 | 3 821 |
| 4 804 | 1 219 | 851 | 8 989 | 1 445 | 4 685 |
| 441 124 | 151 664 | 247 110 | 155 423 | 110 982 | 61 358 |
| 395 036 | 134 859 | 234 279 | 146 124 | 97 488 | 55 958 |
| 2 600 | 128 | 447 | 1 972 | 622 | 1 008 |
| 43 488 | 16 677 | 12 384 | 7 327 | 12 872 | 4 392 |
| 1 877 935 | 1 312 109 | 476 739 | 517 917 | 239 687 | 410 665 |
| 2 091 991 | 573 508 | 759 774 | 1 949 558 | 1 225 043 | 277 270 |
| 62 538 | 15 128 | 5 589 | 10 264 | 19 588 | 8 663 |
| 34 298 | 3 381 | 5 056 | 7 849 | 29 283 | 9 570 |
| 21 985 | 2 342 | 2 537 | 5 002 | 25 218 | 6 753 |
| 10 710 | 858 | 2 303 | 2 646 | 3 731 | 2 686 |
| 30 643 | 3 974 | 4 824 | 4 377 | 15 304 | 3 230 |
| 184 306 | 41 094 | 43 149 | 32 195 | 56 320 | 18 940 |
| 122 288 | 29 208 | 32 587 | 22 198 | 41 735 | 13 018 |
| 62 018 | 11 886 | 10 562 | 9 997 | 14 585 | 5 922 |
| 207 540 | 11 972 | 24 349 | 14 596 | 37 907 | 9 974 |
| 12 872 | 2 036 | 2 390 | 2 075 | 1 777 | 1 319 |
| 154 546 | 5 281 | 16 052 | 5 886 | 17 300 | 4 010 |
| 178 633 | 31 388 | 32 969 | 25 690 | 37 632 | 18 232 |
| 59 371 | 5 869 | 7 666 | 6 728 | 9 310 | 4 150 |
| 24 321 | 4 419 | 5 444 | 5 506 | 5 873 | 2 613 |
| **456 214** | **98 175** | **115 681** | **90 787** | **153 281** | **48 963** |
| 303 469 | 39 276 | 44 630 | 27 884 | 80 185 | 18 473 |
| 152 745 | 58 899 | 71 051 | 62 903 | 73 096 | 30 490 |

# 主 要 统 计 指 标 解 释

**工业企业能源消费量** 是指工业企业在生产过程中作为燃料、原材料、动力、辅助材料使用的能源、工艺用能及非生产用能，具体指：

1. 用于生产本企业的产品、工业性作业和其它生产性活动所消费的能源。
2. 用于技术更新改造措施、新技术研究和新产品试制以及科学试验等方面消费的能源。
3. 用于经营维修及本单位机电设备、交通运输工具、建筑物等大修理消费的能源。

不包括以下各项：

1. 由仓库发到车间，但报告期最后一天并未消费，这部分能源不应计入消费量，应办理假退手续，计入库存量，不能以拨代消。
2. 拨到外单位委托加工的能源。
3. 调出本单位或借出的能源。

**工业生产消费** 是指工业企业为进行工业生产活动所使用的能源。主要包括：

1. 产品生产过程中作为原材料使用，直接构成产品实体的能源消费。
2. 产品生产过程中作为辅助材料使用的能源。
3. 生产工艺过程所消费的工艺用能。
4. 生产过程中作为燃料、动力使用的能源。
5. 新技术研究、新产品试制、科学试验等方面使用的能源。
6. 为工业生产活动而进行的各项修理所使用的能源。

**非工业生产消费** 是指工业企业内不从事工业生产活动的非独立核算的单位所消费使用的能源产品，如本企业附属的科学研究单位、农场、车队、学校、医院、食堂、托儿所等单位所消费的能源；本企业附属的自营施工单位所使用的能源；本企业从事运输邮电活动所使用的能源。

**库存量** 是指工业企业在报告期初(年初)期末(年末)结存的能源数量，仅统计本单位使用的能源库存，不包括本企业产品库存，对于一次能源生产企业只填留作自用的(即本企业消费)的那一部分能源库存，对于能源加工转换企业因消费与生产同时存在，投入能源品种无疑是企业的消费，但产出的能源品种有可能一部分外销，甚至全部外销，对于这种用作对外销售的那部分能源不应填报在所有的能源报表中，因为对外销售的能源其性质属于企业生产的产品，它的库存变化属于产、销、存变化的范畴。

# EXPLANATORY NOTES ON MAIN STATISTICAL INDICATORS

**Volume of Energy Consumption of Industrial Enterprises** refers to the energies, technical energies and non-production cost energies that are used as fuels, raw materials, power, accessory materials in production in industrial enterprises. They include:

1. energy cost for products, industrial operation and other production activities;

2. energy cost for technical innovation, new-tech research, trial of new products and scientific experiments;

3. energy cost in maintenance business and the large-scale maintenance of the units' own electromechanical equipment, communication and transportation tools, building and the like.

They exclude:

1. energy that was allocated from the warehouse to the workshops but was not used within the reported deadline. This part of the energy should not be included into the consumption volume but be counted into the stock volume;

2. energy allocated for outside processing;

3. energy transferred or borrowed to other units.

**Consumption of Industrial Production** refers to the energy cost for industrial production, including:

1. energy consumed as part of the raw materials and constitutes directly as part of the products;

2. energy used as accessory materials in production;

3. technical energy consumed in production technological process;

4. energy consumed as fuel and power in production;

5. energy consumed in new-tech, research, new product trial, scientific research, and the like.

6. energy consumed for various maintenance for industrial production.

**Consumption in Non-industrial Production** refers to the energy products consumed by units that do not engage into industrial production and have no independent business accounting in industrial enterprises. They include energy consumed by the attached scientific research institutes of the enterprises, farms, motorcade, schools, hospitals, dining-halls, kindergartens and the like; energy consumed by the attached construction units of the enterprises; energy consumed for the communication and transportation of the enterprises.

**Storage** refers to the energy storage at the beginning and the end of the year reports of the industrial enterprises. This only includes the energy storage, not the product storage of the enterprise. For the one-time energy production enterprises, they just register the part of energy used for their own consumption as storage. For the enterprises of energy processing or transferring that have both consumption and production, the total input energy is their consumption but part or even all the output energy is for sale. So the part that is used for sale cannot be counted into the energy report, since this part belongs to products, the storage change of which belongs to the change of product production, sale and storage.

# 十、固定资产投资

## CHAPTER 10
## INVESTMENT IN FIXED ASSETS

# 固定资产投资 INVESTMENT IN FIXED ASSETS

## 主要统计指标 MAJOR STATISTICAL INDICATORS

| | | | | |
|---|---|---|---|---|
| 2012年全社会固定资产投资额 | Total Value of Investment in Fixed Assets | 5 266.49 | 亿元 | 100 million yuan |
| 比上年增长 | Increase Over Last Year | 17.0 | % | |
| 2012年城镇固定资产投资额 | Investment in Fixed Assets Collective Units | 2 649.90 | 亿元 | 100 million yuan |
| 比上年增长 | Increase Over Last Year | 21.5 | % | |
| 2012年房地产开发投资额 | Value of Investment in Real Estate Development | 1 263.36 | 亿元 | 100 million yuan |
| 比上年增长 | Increase Over Last Year | 5.4 | % | |
| 2012年农村固定资产投资额 | Investment in Fixed Assets by Rural Units | 1 353.23 | 亿元 | 100 million yuan |
| 比上年增长 | Increase Over Last Year | 20.6 | % | |
| 2012年三资企业投资额 | Enterprises with Foreign Investment | 1 087.64 | 亿元 | 100 million yuan |
| 比上年增长 | Increase Over Last Year | 12.5 | % | |
| 2012年私营个体经济投资额 | Value of Investment in Fixed Assets Private and Individuals | 1 586.95 | 亿元 | 100 million yuan |
| 比上年增长 | Increase Over Last Year | 14.2 | % | |

表10-1

# 历年全社会固定资产投资完成额
# TOTAL FIXED ASSETS INVESTMENT OVER THE YEARS

单位：万元 (10 000 yuan)

| 年 份<br>Year | 总 计<br>Total | 城镇投资<br>City &Town Collective Units | 房地产开发<br>Real Estate Development | 农村投资<br>Investment in Rural Area | 城镇和工矿区私人建房<br>Building Construction by Privates in Industrial and Mining Regions of Cities and Towns | 农村私人建房<br>Building Construction by Privates in Countryside |
|---|---|---|---|---|---|---|
| 1980 | | 28 734 | | | | |
| 1981 | 91 574 | 33 820 | | 27 504 | 600 | 29 650 |
| 1982 | 97 528 | 47 561 | | 24 383 | 662 | 24 922 |
| 1983 | 116 452 | 46 198 | | 23 393 | 405 | 46 456 |
| 1984 | 168 333 | 58 161 | | 48 598 | 792 | 60 782 |
| 1985 | 297 042 | 105 289 | | 111 856 | 1 940 | 77 957 |
| 1986 | 345 930 | 134 743 | | 95 987 | 4 800 | 110 400 |
| 1987 | 465 014 | 159 333 | | 129 908 | 8 525 | 167 248 |
| 1988 | 675 192 | 208 554 | | 191 101 | 40 732 | 234 805 |
| 1989 | 548 573 | 169 215 | | 129 988 | 28 938 | 220 432 |
| 1990 | 553 691 | 168 478 | 16 516 | 133 604 | 22 740 | 212 353 |
| 1991 | 762 972 | 254 472 | 22 578 | 252 177 | 27 237 | 206 508 |
| 1992 | 1 543 906 | 489 408 | 61 858 | 728 503 | 83 954 | 180 183 |
| 1993 | 2 718 565 | 937 402 | 336 437 | 1 195 929 | 33 953 | 214 844 |
| 1994 | 3 076 978 | 1 155 910 | 400 268 | 1 218 258 | 31 304 | 271 238 |
| 1995 | 3 340 991 | 1 376 431 | 586 461 | 1 058 640 | 27 437 | 292 022 |
| 1996 | 3 805 873 | 1 928 167 | 501 411 | 1 061 991 | 42 993 | 271 311 |
| 1997 | 4 051 760 | 2 241 943 | 512 313 | 1 025 717 | 24 092 | 247 695 |
| 1998 | 4 501 061 | 2 796 693 | 585 447 | 862 366 | 14 326 | 242 229 |
| 1999 | 4 751 365 | 2 802 355 | 601 124 | 1 076 565 | 17 550 | 253 771 |
| 2000 | 5 164 346 | 2 663 738 | 611 792 | 1 620 871 | 29 405 | 238 540 |
| 2001 | 5 648 539 | 2 552 976 | 686 178 | 2 188 554 | 13 757 | 207 074 |
| 2002 | 8 128 145 | 3 382 839 | 1 073 363 | 3 434 968 | 10 021 | 226 954 |
| 2003 | 14 089 329 | 6 771 660 | 1 779 403 | 5 358 733 | 8 173 | 171 360 |
| 2004 | 15 547 986 | 6 818 852 | 3 343 245 | 5 315 751 | 5 034 | 65 104 |
| 2005 | 18 701 431 | 8 194 266 | 4 143 333 | 6 291 928 | 2 578 | 69 326 |
| 2006 | 21 069 898 | 9 984 723 | 4 707 472 | 6 350 903 | - | 26 800 |
| 2007 | 23 663 595 | 10 709 659 | 6 019 565 | 6 934 371 | - | - |
| 2008 | 26 111 595 | 11 568 544 | 7 180 805 | 7 362 246 | - | - |
| 2009 | 29 673 482 | 13 404 912 | 7 243 408 | 9 025 162 | - | - |
| 2010 | 36 178 211 | 16 575 403 | 9 358 018 | 10 244 790 | - | - |
| 2011 | 45 020 211 | 21 805 957 | 11 991 278 | 11 222 976 | - | - |
| 2012 | 52 664 852 | 26 498 973 | 12 633 597 | 13 532 282 | - | - |

表10-2

# 历年城镇固定资产投资情况

# TOWNSHIP INVESTMENT IN FIXED ASSETS OVER THE YEARS

| 年 份<br>Year | 投资额（万元）<br>Investment<br>(10 000 yuan) | 新增固定资产(万元)<br>Newly Increased Fixed Assets<br>(10 000 yuan) | 竣工房屋面积(万平方米)<br>Floor Space of Buildings Completed<br>(10 000 sq.m) | # 住 宅(万平方米)<br>Residential Housing<br>(10 000 sq.m) |
|---|---|---|---|---|
| 1949 | 16 | 13 | | |
| 1952 | 699 | 608 | | |
| 1957 | 1 487 | 1 398 | | |
| 1962 | 999 | 928 | | |
| 1965 | 2 289 | 2 207 | | |
| 1970 | 3 566 | 2 687 | | |
| 1975 | 6 004 | 4 528 | | |
| 1978 | 14 035 | 11 166 | 64.27 | 21.27 |
| 1980 | 28 734 | 25 113 | 124.29 | 57.28 |
| 1985 | 105 289 | 92 130 | 213.67 | 80.22 |
| 1990 | 168 478 | 132 367 | 150.66 | 55.57 |
| 1991 | 254 472 | 199 078 | 163.89 | 46.17 |
| 1992 | 489 408 | 314 408 | 222.17 | 63.38 |
| 1993 | 937 402 | 823 221 | 301.75 | 70.63 |
| 1994 | 1 155 910 | 942 099 | 272.06 | 68.45 |
| 1995 | 1 376 431 | 1 154 609 | 291.12 | 51.73 |
| 1996 | 1 928 167 | 1 339 111 | 240.60 | 49.28 |
| 1997 | 2 241 943 | 1 612 033 | 295.95 | 46.17 |
| 1998 | 2 796 693 | 2 218 385 | 269.09 | 29.44 |
| 1999 | 2 802 355 | 2 133 715 | 214.62 | 37.32 |
| 2000 | 2 663 738 | 3 065 624 | 315.46 | 29.71 |
| 2001 | 2 552 976 | 3 051 174 | 354.38 | 12.12 |
| 2002 | 3 382 839 | 2 708 203 | 354.51 | 14.45 |
| 2003 | 6 771 660 | 3 020 313 | 513.05 | 73.02 |
| 2004 | 6 818 852 | 6 393 977 | 760.95 | 10.25 |
| 2005 | 8 194 266 | 8 867 554 | 753.99 | 51.88 |
| 2006 | 9 984 723 | 10 789 085 | 1 215.40 | 20.60 |
| 2007 | 10 709 659 | 7 974 567 | 1 193.37 | 43.69 |
| 2008 | 11 568 544 | 8 080 053 | 1 153.78 | 97.63 |
| 2009 | 13 404 912 | 10 850 924 | 1 504.40 | 99.55 |
| 2010 | 16 575 403 | 14 126 653 | 1 309.81 | 102.64 |
| 2011 | 21 805 957 | 17 751 318 | 2 128.85 | 169.83 |
| 2012 | 26 498 973 | 19 764 979 | 2 369.84 | 179.52 |

表10-3 分地区全社会固定资产投资完成额 (2012年)

单位：万元

| 项　目 | Item | 全　市 Whole Municipality |
|---|---|---|
| **全　市** | **Whole Municipality** | **52 664 852** |
| **按建设性质分** | **Grouped by Type of Construction** | |
| 新　建 | New Construction | 19 578 559 |
| 扩　建 | Expansion | 12 419 619 |
| 改　建 | Reconstruction | 2 621 647 |
| 其　他 | Others | 18 045 027 |
| **按构成分** | **Grouped by Use of Funds** | |
| 建筑工程 | Construction | 28 827 571 |
| 安装工程 | Installation | 1 222 408 |
| 设备工器具购置 | Purchase of Equipment and Instruments | 14 647 988 |
| 其他费用 | Others | 7 966 885 |
| **按登记注册类型分** | **Grouped by Registration Status** | |
| 国有企业 | State-owed Enterprises | 8 646 608 |
| 集体企业 | Collective-owned Enterprises | 3 999 866 |
| 股份合作企业 | Share-holding Cooperative Enterprises | 146 226 |
| 联营企业 | Joint Ownership Enterprises | 121 260 |
| 有限责任公司 | Limited Liability Corporations | 8 786 859 |
| 股份有限公司 | Share-holding Corporations Ltd. | 2 747 806 |
| 私营个体经济 | Individuals | 15 869 453 |
| 其　他 | Others | 886 830 |
| 港澳台商投资企业 | Enterprises with Investment from HongKong, Macao and Taiwan | 3 646 414 |
| 外商投资企业 | Enterprises with Foreign Investment | 7 813 530 |
| **按产业分** | **Grouped by Industry** | |
| 第一产业 | Primary Industry | 100 052 |
| 第二产业 | Secondary Industry | 21 848 885 |
| #工　业 | Industry | 21 764 295 |
| 第三产业 | Tertiary Industry | 30 715 915 |

# TOTAL FIXED ASSETS INVESTMENT BY REGION (2012)

(10 000 yuan)

| 市 区<br>Urban Area | # 吴江区<br>Wujiang District | 常 熟<br>Changshu | 张家港<br>Zhangjiagang | 昆 山<br>Kunshan | 太 仓<br>Taicang |
|---|---|---|---|---|---|
| **26 859 457** | **6 300 746** | **6 354 752** | **7 029 782** | **7 700 434** | **4 720 427** |
| | | | | | |
| 10 034 319 | 1 899 670 | 2 365 584 | 2 379 780 | 2 828 127 | 1 970 749 |
| 5 675 379 | 2 186 278 | 1 679 501 | 2 959 733 | 1 035 263 | 1 069 743 |
| 914 901 | 310 664 | 508 729 | 796 856 | 353 905 | 47 256 |
| 10 234 858 | 1 904 134 | 1 800 938 | 893 413 | 3 483 139 | 1 632 679 |
| | | | | | |
| 14 529 025 | 3 242 665 | 3 281 070 | 3 614 028 | 4 917 884 | 2 485 564 |
| 641 657 | 44 331 | 87 725 | 162 437 | 161 432 | 169 157 |
| 6 399 860 | 2 275 458 | 2 266 026 | 2 437 850 | 1 802 645 | 1 741 607 |
| 5 288 915 | 738 292 | 719 931 | 815 467 | 818 473 | 324 099 |
| | | | | | |
| 3 869 267 | 1 181 838 | 1 207 662 | 1 143 584 | 1 289 385 | 1 136 710 |
| 2 429 051 | 434 256 | 614 135 | 198 224 | 415 252 | 343 204 |
| 50 722 | 34 669 | 4 500 | 76 474 | 5 830 | 8 700 |
| 10 751 | 1 751 | 580 | – | 91 794 | 18 135 |
| 6 034 299 | 329 657 | 535 338 | 1 238 018 | 904 112 | 75 092 |
| 720 734 | 190 643 | 91 340 | 1 328 151 | 176 824 | 430 757 |
| 7 446 772 | 3 040 497 | 1 938 754 | 2 388 712 | 2 362 775 | 1 732 440 |
| 694 428 | 18 357 | 65 908 | 1 000 | 90 881 | 34 613 |
| 1 882 201 | 559 406 | 670 439 | 173 775 | 738 507 | 181 492 |
| 3 721 232 | 509 672 | 1 226 096 | 481 844 | 1 625 074 | 759 284 |
| | | | | | |
| 61 065 | 32 079 | 29 497 | 7 490 | 2 000 | – |
| 9 029 468 | 3 252 305 | 3 321 084 | 4 126 483 | 3 002 271 | 2 369 579 |
| 8 948 598 | 3 234 025 | 3 320 164 | 4 124 683 | 3 001 271 | 2 369 579 |
| 17 768 924 | 3 016 362 | 3 004 171 | 2 895 809 | 4 696 163 | 2 350 848 |

表10-3 续表 1

单位：万元

| 项　目 | Item | 全　市 Whole Municipality |
|---|---|---|
| **按行业分** | **Grouped by Sector** | |
| 农林牧渔业 | Farming, Forestry, Animal Husbandry and Fishery | 100 052 |
| 采矿业 | Mining and Quarrying | 200 |
| 制造业 | Manufacturing | 20 475 692 |
| 农副食品加工业 | Farm and Sideline Products | 116 197 |
| 食品制造业 | Food Production | 112 142 |
| 酒、饮料和精制茶制造业 | Wine, Beverage and Refined tea manufacturing | 39 766 |
| 烟草制品业 | Tobacco Production | 10 432 |
| 纺织业 | Textile Industry | 1 777 288 |
| 纺织服装和服饰业 | Garments and Apparel Industry | 265 759 |
| 皮革毛皮羽毛及其制品和制鞋业 | Leather, Fur, Wool and shoes Products | 39 888 |
| 木材加工及木、竹、藤、棕、草制品业 | Wood Processing, Wood, Bamboo, Rattan and Coir Products Straw Products | 73 647 |
| 家具制造业 | Furniture Manufacturing | 87 630 |
| 造纸及纸制品业 | Papermaking and Paper Products | 219 985 |
| 印刷业和记录媒介的复制 | Printing and Record Duplicating | 122 377 |
| 文教体育用品制造业 | Stationary, Educational and Sports Goods | 99 068 |
| 石油加工、炼焦及核燃料加工 | Petroleum Processing, Coking and Nuclear Fuel Processing | 35 182 |
| 化学原料及化学制品制造业 | Raw Chemical Materials and Chemical Products | 1 610 241 |
| 医药制造业 | Medical and Pharmaceutical Products | 231 235 |
| 化学纤维制造业 | Chemical Fiber Manufacturing | 964 198 |
| 橡胶和塑料制品业 | Rubber and Plastic Products | 812 528 |
| 非金属矿物制品业 | Nonmetal Mineral Products | 767 335 |
| 黑色金属冶炼及压延加工业 | Smelting and Pressing of Ferrous Metals | 1 070 525 |
| 有色金属冶炼及压延加工业 | Smelting and Pressing of Nonferrous Metals | 361 091 |
| 金属制品业 | Metal Products | 1 037 954 |
| 通用设备制造业 | General Equipment Manufacture | 2 052 919 |
| 专用设备制造业 | Special Purposes Equipment Manufacturing | 1 747 653 |
| 汽车制造业 | Automobile Manufacturing | 1 526 849 |
| 铁路船舶航空航天和其他运输设备制造业 | Railway, Ship, Aerospace and Other Transportation Equipment Manufacturing | 114 647 |
| 电气机械及器材制造业 | Electric Equipment and Machinery Manufacturing | 1 693 486 |
| 计算机、通信和其他电子设备制造业 | Computer Telecommunications and Other Electronic Equipment Manufacture | 2 871 153 |
| 仪器仪表制造业 | Instruments, Meters Machinery | 287 546 |
| 其他制造业 | Other Products Manufacture | 260 229 |

Continued 1

(10 000 yuan)

| 市 区 Urban Area | # 吴江区 Wujiang District | 常 熟 Changshu | 张家港 Zhangjiagang | 昆 山 Kunshan | 太 仓 Taicang |
|---|---|---|---|---|---|
| 61 065 | 32 079 | 29 497 | 7 490 | 2 000 | – |
| 200 | – | – | – | – | – |
| 8 507 446 | 3 030 360 | 2 937 711 | 3 912 546 | 2 945 840 | 2 172 149 |
| 65 429 | 37 456 | 485 | 16 566 | 14 005 | 19 712 |
| 71 912 | 17 947 | 1 858 | 3 100 | 24 682 | 10 590 |
| 30 254 | 28 854 | 1 861 | 6 300 | 1 351 | – |
| – | – | – | – | – | 10 432 |
| 1 109 578 | 1 021 759 | 292 765 | 295 564 | 34 235 | 45 146 |
| 99 837 | 36 388 | 80 646 | 33 683 | 36 228 | 15 365 |
| 14 383 | 6 871 | 2 685 | 1 000 | 7 000 | 14 820 |
| 54 778 | 40 649 | 3 760 | 1 220 | 13 279 | 610 |
| 37 730 | 6 310 | 11 294 | 3 950 | 22 364 | 12 292 |
| 107 461 | 11 926 | 31 803 | 25 110 | 17 936 | 37 675 |
| 83 679 | 24 913 | 8 865 | 10 650 | 17 292 | 1 891 |
| 38 879 | 14 769 | 4 292 | 16 356 | 29 279 | 10 262 |
| 1 523 | – | 14 941 | – | – | 18 718 |
| 272 297 | 47 276 | 463 955 | 485 085 | 85 662 | 303 242 |
| 106 331 | 17 069 | 23 834 | 43 091 | 22 323 | 35 656 |
| 519 206 | 414 301 | 62 598 | 67 010 | 7 300 | 308 084 |
| 271 581 | 60 410 | 50 107 | 138 173 | 222 295 | 130 372 |
| 312 279 | 160 909 | 93 265 | 109 630 | 133 951 | 118 210 |
| 53 601 | 20 222 | 111 220 | 856 240 | 23 150 | 26 314 |
| 165 617 | 41 639 | 83 245 | 42 660 | 28 644 | 40 925 |
| 426 055 | 68 377 | 138 984 | 295 438 | 82 421 | 95 056 |
| 816 477 | 134 654 | 202 463 | 322 961 | 330 310 | 380 708 |
| 802 852 | 153 779 | 144 747 | 421 145 | 295 282 | 83 627 |
| 444 220 | 76 764 | 588 214 | 123 602 | 274 459 | 96 354 |
| 40 455 | 3 166 | 3 661 | 27 365 | 30 059 | 13 107 |
| 716 902 | 316 864 | 251 439 | 287 472 | 228 347 | 209 326 |
| 1 580 476 | 258 102 | 173 214 | 167 599 | 885 471 | 64 393 |
| 123 883 | 8 986 | 42 090 | 34 980 | 40 531 | 46 062 |
| 97 808 | – | 46 051 | 76 026 | 22 394 | 17 950 |

表10-3 续表 2

单位：万元

| 项　　目 | Item | 全　市 Whole Municipality |
|---|---|---|
| 废弃资源综合利用业 | Comprehensive Utilization of Waste Resources | 44 234 |
| 金属制品、机械和设备修理业 | Metal Products, Machinery and Equipment Repair | 22 508 |
| 电力、煤气及水的生产和供应业 | Power, Gas and Water Production and Supply | 1 288 403 |
| 建筑业 | Construction | 84 590 |
| 交通运输、仓储和邮政业 | Transportation, Logistics and Postal | 2 277 097 |
| 信息传输、软件和信息技术服务业 | Information Transmission, Computer Services and Software Industries | 372 577 |
| 批发和零售业 | Wholesale and Retail Trade Services | 716 357 |
| 住宿和餐饮业 | Accommodation and Catering Services | 642 636 |
| 金融业 | Financial Industries | 312 821 |
| 房地产业 | Real Estate | 16 051 008 |
| 租赁和商务服务业 | Leasing and Business Services | 2 693 187 |
| 科学研究和技术服务业 | Scientific Research and Technical Services | 1 183 382 |
| 水利、环境和公共设施管理业 | Water Conservancy, Environment and Public Facilities Management | 4 483 463 |
| 居民服务和其他服务业 | Community Service and Other Services | 137 880 |
| 教　育 | Education | 498 024 |
| 卫生和社会工作 | Health Care and Social Work | 251 840 |
| 文化、体育和娱乐业 | Culture, Sports and Entertainment | 583 548 |
| 公共管理和社会组织 | Public Administration and Social Organizations | 512 095 |
| **本年资金来源合计** | **Total** | **76 877 511** |
| 1.上年末结余资金 | Balance of Last Year | 9 527 614 |
| 2.本年资金来源小计 | Total Fund for This Year | 67 349 897 |
| (1) 国家预算内资金 | State Budgetary Appropriation | 660 491 |
| (2) 国内贷款 | Domestic Loans | 8 787 488 |
| (3) 债　券 | Bonds | - |
| (4) 利用外资 | Foreign Investment | 4 423 797 |
| (5) 自筹资金 | Fundraising | 39 905 158 |
| (6) 其他资金来源 | Others | 13 572 963 |
| **本年新增固定资产** | **Newly Increased Fixed Assets this year** | **40 357 569** |
| **房屋建筑面积**　（万平方米） | **Floor Space of Buildings**　(10 000 sq. m) | |
| 施工房屋建筑面积 | Floor space of Buildings under Construction | 18 543.29 |
| # 住　宅 | Residential Buildings | 7 209.88 |
| 竣工房屋建筑面积 | Floor Space of Buildings Completed | 6 252.25 |
| # 住　宅 | Residential Building | 1 783.73 |

Continued 2

(10 000 yuan)

| 市　区<br>Urban Area | # 吴江区<br>Wujiang District | 常　熟<br>Changshu | 张家港<br>Zhangjiagang | 昆　山<br>Kunshan | 太　仓<br>Taicang |
|---|---|---|---|---|---|
| 36 155 | – | 3 369 | 570 | 3 490 | 650 |
| 5 808 | – | – | – | 12 100 | 4 600 |
| 440 952 | 203 665 | 382 453 | 212 137 | 55 431 | 197 430 |
| 80 870 | 18 280 | 920 | 1 800 | 1 000 | – |
| 955 412 | 109 164 | 449 357 | 348 140 | 155 275 | 368 913 |
| 282 018 | 2 900 | 4 600 | – | 82 909 | 3 050 |
| 375 539 | 21 174 | 76 969 | 178 712 | 70 577 | 14 560 |
| 415 506 | 37 710 | 110 234 | 37 100 | 60 141 | 19 655 |
| 213 113 | – | 8 148 | 3 420 | 78 028 | 10 112 |
| 9 253 719 | 1 822 133 | 1 401 231 | 1 650 909 | 2 609 646 | 1 135 503 |
| 1 855 992 | 120 579 | 24 755 | 44 487 | 478 839 | 289 114 |
| 905 660 | 69 443 | 147 984 | 8 349 | 71 265 | 50 124 |
| 2 285 562 | 640 232 | 584 535 | 465 327 | 852 267 | 295 772 |
| 109 822 | 18 946 | 3 700 | 19 636 | 4 722 | – |
| 262 263 | 31 786 | 43 851 | 51 862 | 87 291 | 52 757 |
| 166 990 | 31 446 | 23 874 | 17 475 | 23 351 | 20 150 |
| 362 907 | 93 783 | 65 052 | 19 757 | 102 932 | 32 900 |
| 324 421 | 17 066 | 59 881 | 50 635 | 18 920 | 58 238 |
| **41 537 141** | **7 854 073** | **8 014 397** | **9 153 674** | **11 536 298** | **6 636 001** |
| 6 181 773 | 567 370 | 877 965 | 511 853 | 1 333 217 | 622 806 |
| 35 355 368 | 7 286 703 | 7 136 432 | 8 641 821 | 10 203 081 | 6 013 195 |
| 622 721 | 416 699 | 36 319 | – | 1 251 | 200 |
| 5 972 080 | 795 719 | 655 282 | 602 134 | 887 551 | 670 441 |
| – | – | – | – | – | – |
| 1 298 113 | 616 386 | 1 141 344 | 232 968 | 1 499 998 | 251 374 |
| 19 533 757 | 4 555 959 | 4 008 768 | 6 786 091 | 5 050 245 | 4 526 297 |
| 7 928 697 | 901 940 | 1 294 719 | 1 020 628 | 2 764 036 | 564 883 |
| **19 523 166** | **4 689 140** | **5 573 572** | **5 497 682** | **5 937 295** | **3 825 854** |
| 9 310.82 | 2 054.26 | 1 643.52 | 2 232.03 | 4 061.73 | 1 295.19 |
| 3 468.45 | 785.45 | 634.27 | 869.65 | 1 775.04 | 462.48 |
| 3 178.12 | 843.93 | 584.35 | 894.34 | 1 171.03 | 424.42 |
| 927.01 | 152.94 | 125.73 | 253.34 | 326.40 | 151.26 |

表10-4

# 城镇固定资产投资完成额 (2012年)

单位：万元

| 项　目 | Item | 全　市 Whole Municipality |
|---|---|---|
| **投资额** | **Investment** | **26 498 973** |
| **一、按建设性质分** | **Grouped by Type of Construction** | |
| 新　建 | New Construction | 13 516 348 |
| 扩　建 | Expansion | 6 401 166 |
| 改　建 | Reconstruction | 2 661 121 |
| 其　他 | Others | 3 920 338 |
| **二、按工程构成分** | **Grouped by Use of Funds** | |
| 建筑工程 | Construction | 14 276 155 |
| 安装工程 | Installation | 529 593 |
| 设备工器具购置 | Purchase of Equipment and Instruments | 8 588 995 |
| 其他费用 | Others | 3 104 230 |
| **三、按登记注册类型分** | **Grouped by Registration Status** | |
| 国有企业 | State-owed Enterprises | 6 957 861 |
| 集体企业 | Collective-owned Enterprises | 1 410 184 |
| 股份合作企业 | Share-holding Cooperative Enterprises | 83 635 |
| 联营企业 | Joint Ownership Enterprises | 51 135 |
| 有限责任公司 | Limited Liability Corporations | 3 511 941 |
| # 国有独资 | State-owned Sole Investment | 1 630 270 |
| 股份有限公司 | Share-holding Corporations Ltd. | 2 330 121 |
| 私营个体经济 | Individuals | 3 997 234 |
| 其　他 | Others | 116 545 |
| 港澳台商投资企业 | Enterprises with Investment from HongKong, Macao and Taiwan | 2 220 264 |
| 外商投资企业 | Enterprises with Foreign Investment | 5 820 053 |
| **四、按行业分** | **Grouped by Sector** | |
| 农林牧渔业 | Farming, Forestry, Animal Husbandry and Fishery | 31 314 |
| 采矿业 | Mining and Quarrying | - |
| 制造业 | Manufacturing | 11 900 554 |
| 电力、煤气及水的生产和供应业 | Power, Gas and Water Production and Supply | 1 008 760 |
| 建筑业 | Construction | 54 421 |
| 交通运输、仓储和邮政业 | Transportation, Logistics and Postal | 1 864 251 |
| 信息传输、软件和信息技术服务业 | Information Transmission, Software and Information Technology Services | 313 719 |

# AMOUNT OF COMPLETED FIXED ASSETS INVESTMENT IN REAL ESTATE OF TOWNSHIPS (2012)

(10 000 yuan)

| 市区 Urban Area | # 吴江区 Wujiang District | 常熟 Changshu | 张家港 Zhangjiagang | 昆山 Kunshan | 太仓 Taicang |
|---|---|---|---|---|---|
| **13 743 131** | **2 807 472** | **3 170 934** | **3 731 374** | **3 239 532** | **2 614 002** |
| | | | | | |
| 7 473 217 | 1 167 456 | 1 521 113 | 1 485 697 | 1 814 412 | 1 221 909 |
| 3 095 332 | 1 035 973 | 790 835 | 1 720 873 | 156 091 | 638 035 |
| 1 069 284 | 248 702 | 485 089 | 522 836 | 472 768 | 111 144 |
| 2 105 298 | 355 341 | 373 897 | 1 968 | 796 261 | 642 914 |
| | | | | | |
| 7 405 903 | 1 477 117 | 1 654 306 | 1 915 593 | 1 944 078 | 1 356 275 |
| 334 889 | 28 941 | 53 028 | 70 876 | 11 775 | 59 025 |
| 4 023 312 | 1 158 263 | 1 142 694 | 1 358 032 | 1 064 429 | 1 000 528 |
| 1 979 027 | 143 151 | 320 906 | 386 873 | 219 250 | 198 174 |
| | | | | | |
| 3 124 855 | 815 829 | 1 052 553 | 753 894 | 936 159 | 1 090 400 |
| 1 176 059 | 262 214 | 46 363 | – | 114 272 | 73 490 |
| 16 185 | 240 | – | 67 450 | – | – |
| – | – | – | – | 33 000 | 18 135 |
| 2 751 581 | 72 658 | 100 627 | 537 632 | 103 733 | 18 368 |
| 1 621 635 | 1 273 | – | – | – | 8 635 |
| 550 352 | 109 012 | 37 890 | 1 311 151 | 67 251 | 363 477 |
| 2 146 869 | 864 529 | 324 404 | 511 258 | 670 638 | 344 065 |
| 48 105 | 4 568 | 63 828 | – | 4 612 | – |
| 954 718 | 357 518 | 563 047 | 170 225 | 422 826 | 109 448 |
| 2 974 407 | 320 904 | 982 222 | 379 764 | 887 041 | 596 619 |
| | | | | | |
| 27 714 | 11 729 | 2 000 | – | 1 600 | – |
| – | – | – | – | – | – |
| 5 224 114 | 1 491 254 | 1 473 565 | 2 389 615 | 1 615 182 | 1 198 078 |
| 280 397 | 126 115 | 349 892 | 155 639 | 34 359 | 188 473 |
| 54 421 | 18 280 | – | – | – | – |
| 745 802 | 76 830 | 441 657 | 232 390 | 114 986 | 329 416 |
| 247 960 | 2 500 | 4 600 | – | 61 159 | – |

表10-4 续表

单位：万元

| 项　目 | Item | 全　市 Whole Municipality |
|---|---|---|
| 批发和零售业 | Wholesale and Retail Trade Services | 490 416 |
| 住宿和餐饮业 | Accommodation and Catering Services | 414 745 |
| 金融业 | Financial Industries | 260 423 |
| 房地产业 | Real Estate | 1 826 711 |
| 租赁和商务服务业 | Leasing and Business Services | 2 446 073 |
| 科学研究和技术服务业 | Scientific Research and Technical Services | 1 024 601 |
| 水利、环境和公共设施管理业 | Water Conservancy, Environment and Public Facilities Management | 3 458 712 |
| 居民服务和其他服务业 | Community Service and Other Services | 89 169 |
| 教　育 | Education | 358 366 |
| 卫生和社会工作 | Health Care and Social Work | 156 598 |
| 文化、体育和娱乐业 | Culture, Sports and Entertainment | 461 756 |
| 公共管理和社会组织 | Public Administration and Social Organizations | 338 384 |
| **本年资金来源合计** | **Total** | **29 869 424** |
| 1.上年末结余资金 | Balance of Last Year | 873 503 |
| 2.本年资金来源小计 | Total Fund for This Year | 28 995 921 |
| (1) 国家预算内资金 | State Budgetary Appropriation | 596 389 |
| (2) 国内贷款 | Domestic Loans | 2 793 197 |
| (3) 债　券 | Bonds | - |
| (4) 利用外资 | Foreign Investment | 3 042 890 |
| (5) 自筹资金 | Fundraising | 22 404 760 |
| (6) 其他资金来源 | Others | 158 685 |
| **本年新增固定资产** | **Newly Increased Fixed Assets this year** | **19 764 979** |
| **房屋建筑面积** (万平方米) | **Floor Space of Buildings** (10 000 sq.m) | |
| 施工房屋建筑面积 | Floor space of Buildings under Construction | 6 194.56 |
| # 住　宅 | Residential Buildings | 471.47 |
| 竣工房屋建筑面积 | Floor Space of Buildings Completed | 2 369.84 |
| # 住　宅 | Residential Building | 179.52 |

Continued

(10 000 yuan)

| 市 区<br>Urban Area | # 吴江区<br>Wujiang District | 常 熟<br>Changshu | 张家港<br>Zhangjiagang | 昆 山<br>Kunshan | 太 仓<br>Taicang |
|---|---|---|---|---|---|
| 300 991 | 4 724 | 51 344 | 86 650 | 38 741 | 12 690 |
| 340 501 | 24 350 | 50 034 | 600 | 21 830 | 1 780 |
| 171 113 | – | – | 2 000 | 77 198 | 10 112 |
| 992 194 | 262 894 | 109 563 | 458 304 | 14 900 | 251 750 |
| 1 693 662 | 78 361 | 21 900 | 15 137 | 450 572 | 264 802 |
| 875 083 | 47 906 | 87 769 | 6 349 | 54 700 | 700 |
| 1 860 495 | 526 069 | 438 052 | 286 697 | 603 916 | 269 552 |
| 69 903 | 5 440 | 210 | 19 056 | – | – |
| 208 259 | 16 821 | 30 054 | 20 702 | 63 981 | 35 370 |
| 115 854 | 9 160 | 6 704 | 15 175 | 8 865 | 10 000 |
| 286 309 | 88 673 | 63 102 | 11 757 | 67 688 | 32 900 |
| 248 359 | 16 366 | 40 488 | 31 303 | 9 855 | 8 379 |
| **15 723 639** | **3 026 716** | **3 097 444** | **4 154 973** | **3 562 321** | **3 331 047** |
| 789 194 | 152 059 | 46 528 | 30 581 | – | 7 200 |
| 14 934 445 | 2 874 657 | 3 050 916 | 4 124 392 | 3 562 321 | 3 323 847 |
| 584 171 | 416 699 | 12 218 | – | – | – |
| 2 100 871 | 204 682 | 297 716 | 164 947 | 70 500 | 159 163 |
| – | – | – | – | – | – |
| 885 331 | 406 289 | 1 051 856 | 140 838 | 803 228 | 161 637 |
| 11 215 729 | 1 833 979 | 1 683 030 | 3 815 441 | 2 688 593 | 3 001 967 |
| 148 343 | 13 008 | 6 096 | 3 166 | – | 1 080 |
| **10 109 511** | **2 402 566** | **2 505 698** | **2 656 518** | **2 704 842** | **1 788 410** |
| 3 494.87 | 582.02 | 371.62 | 957.72 | 985.07 | 385.28 |
| 161.07 | 13.14 | 6.11 | 193.12 | 25.46 | 85.70 |
| 1 231.40 | 322.22 | 146.12 | 353.51 | 422.82 | 215.98 |
| 62.40 | 13.14 | 0.30 | 31.38 | 3.78 | 81.66 |

表10-5

# 项目投资新增固定资产 (2012年)

单位：万元

| 项　目 | Item | 全　市 Whole Municipality |
| --- | --- | --- |
| **全　市** | **Whole Municipality** | **31 403 344** |
| **按建设性质分** | **Grouped by Type of Construction** | |
| 新　建 | New Construction | 12 163 944 |
| 扩　建 | Expansion | 12 100 059 |
| 改　建 | Reconstruction | 2 292 268 |
| 其　他 | Others | 4 847 073 |
| **按登记注册类型分** | **Grouped by Registration Status** | |
| 国有企业 | State-owed Enterprises | 5 802 963 |
| 集体企业 | Collective-owned Enterprises | 2 907 358 |
| 股份合作企业 | Share-holding Cooperative Enterprises | 56 094 |
| 联营企业 | Joint Ownership Enterprises | 35 559 |
| 有限责任公司 | Limited Liability Corporations | 2 209 465 |
| 股份有限公司 | Share-holding Corporations Ltd. | 2 172 434 |
| 私营个体经济 | Individuals | 10 498 982 |
| 其　他 | Others | 127 572 |
| 港澳台商投资企业 | Enterprises with Investment from HongKong, Macao and Taiwan | 2 068 364 |
| 外商投资企业 | Enterprises with Foreign Investment | 5 524 553 |
| **按产业分** | **Grouped by Industry** | |
| 第一产业 | Primary Industry | 87 794 |
| 第二产业 | Secondary Industry | 18 761 487 |
| # 工　业 | Industry | 18 640 432 |
| 第三产业 | Tertiary Industry | 12 554 063 |

# THE NEW FIXED ASSETS OF PROJECT INVESTMENT (2012)

(10 000 yuan)

| 市 区<br>Urban Area | # 吴江区<br>Wujiang District | 常 熟<br>Changshu | 张家港<br>Zhangjiagang | 昆 山<br>Kunshan | 太 仓<br>Taicang |
|---|---|---|---|---|---|
| **14 527 709** | **3 992 063** | **4 697 692** | **4 834 759** | **4 279 802** | **3 063 382** |
| | | | | | |
| 5 581 883 | 1 159 332 | 1 851 652 | 1 350 226 | 2 112 431 | 1 267 752 |
| 5 650 990 | 2 097 054 | 1 692 835 | 2 690 782 | 994 725 | 1 070 727 |
| 856 355 | 284 019 | 340 631 | 736 483 | 302 043 | 56 756 |
| 2 438 481 | 451 658 | 812 574 | 57 268 | 870 603 | 668 147 |
| | | | | | |
| 2 468 046 | 923 428 | 1 179 462 | 683 719 | 798 568 | 673 168 |
| 1 689 841 | 336 423 | 426 660 | 193 992 | 301 865 | 295 000 |
| 19 194 | 1 396 | 17 200 | 9 000 | 2 000 | 8 700 |
| 1 000 | – | 580 | – | 15 844 | 18 135 |
| 1 562 189 | 108 972 | 225 833 | 308 961 | 93 026 | 19 456 |
| 597 716 | 171 512 | 123 823 | 1 114 143 | 79 436 | 257 316 |
| 4 561 926 | 1 761 824 | 1 591 298 | 2 032 367 | 1 100 558 | 1 212 833 |
| 63 166 | 3 103 | 37 042 | 1 000 | 18 364 | 8 000 |
| 853 895 | 326 990 | 537 948 | 78 702 | 494 631 | 103 188 |
| 2 710 736 | 358 415 | 557 846 | 412 875 | 1 375 510 | 467 586 |
| | | | | | |
| 53 177 | 30 009 | 29 697 | 3 720 | 1 200 | – |
| 7 710 525 | 2 504 311 | 2 865 284 | 3 634 690 | 2 678 782 | 1 872 206 |
| 7 594 190 | 2 486 031 | 2 864 364 | 3 631 890 | 2 677 782 | 1 872 206 |
| 6 764 007 | 1 457 743 | 1 802 711 | 1 196 349 | 1 599 820 | 1 191 176 |

表10-5 续表

单位：万元

| 项　目 | Item | 全　市 Whole Municipality |
|---|---|---|
| **按行业分** | **Grouped by Sector** | |
| 农林牧渔业 | Farming, Forestry, Animal Husbandry and Fishery | 87 794 |
| 采矿业 | Mining and Quarrying | 200 |
| 制造业 | Manufacturing | 17 975 709 |
| 电力、煤气及水的生产和供应业 | Power, Gas and Water Production and Supply | 664 523 |
| 建筑业 | Construction | 121 055 |
| 交通运输、仓储和邮政业 | Transportation, Logistics and Postal | 1 088 909 |
| 信息传输、软件和信息技术服务业 | Information Transmission, Software and Information Technology Services | 216 008 |
| 批发和零售业 | Wholesale and Retail Trade Services | 479 345 |
| 住宿和餐饮业 | Hoteling and Catering Services | 392 930 |
| 金融业 | Financial Industries | 140 275 |
| 房地产业 | Real Estate | 2 229 716 |
| 租赁和商务服务业 | Leasing and Business Services | 1 553 846 |
| 科学研究和技术服务业 | Scientific Research and Technical Services | 763 614 |
| 水利、环境和公共设施管理业 | Water Conservancy, Environment and Public Facilities Management | 4 051 735 |
| 居民服务和其他服务业 | Community Service and Other Services | 97 705 |
| 教　育 | Education | 480 320 |
| 卫生和社会工作 | Health Care and Social Work | 252 549 |
| 文化、体育和娱乐业 | Culture, Sports and Entertainment | 377 586 |
| 公共管理和社会组织 | Public Administration and Social Organizations | 429 525 |

Continued

(10 000 yuan)

| 市 区<br>Urban Area | # 吴江区<br>Wujiang District | 常 熟<br>Changshu | 张家港<br>Zhangjiagang | 昆 山<br>Kunshan | 太 仓<br>Taicang |
|---|---|---|---|---|---|
| 53 177 | 30 009 | 29 697 | 3 720 | 1 200 | – |
| 200 | – | – | – | – | – |
| 7 507 743 | 2 451 933 | 2 740 335 | 3 383 947 | 2 590 519 | 1 753 165 |
| 86 247 | 34 098 | 124 029 | 247 943 | 87 263 | 119 041 |
| 116 335 | 18 280 | 920 | 2 800 | 1 000 | – |
| 255 645 | 70 601 | 314 489 | 102 408 | 216 132 | 200 235 |
| 170 458 | 2 500 | 4 600 | – | 37 900 | 3 050 |
| 192 205 | 36 944 | 65 009 | 94 900 | 110 071 | 17 160 |
| 179 803 | 15 860 | 104 458 | 50 400 | 40 394 | 17 875 |
| 106 875 | – | 3 030 | 3 200 | 27 170 | – |
| 1 173 041 | 337 364 | 286 122 | 550 247 | 103 962 | 116 344 |
| 868 316 | 61 835 | 2 855 | 30 350 | 352 396 | 299 929 |
| 597 303 | 43 447 | 42 139 | 7 200 | 67 522 | 49 450 |
| 2 270 659 | 754 312 | 671 381 | 236 988 | 512 809 | 359 898 |
| 74 644 | 17 495 | 3 700 | 18 161 | 1 200 | – |
| 274 641 | 18 106 | 25 244 | 53 000 | 73 959 | 53 476 |
| 189 239 | 70 715 | 36 110 | 2 300 | 15 250 | 9 650 |
| 146 575 | 5 110 | 170 452 | 28 530 | 32 029 | – |
| 264 603 | 23 454 | 73 122 | 18 665 | 9 026 | 64 109 |

表10-6

# 城镇项目投资新增固定资产 (2012年)

单位：万元

| 项　目 | Item | 全　市 Whole Municipality |
|---|---|---|
| **全　市** | **Whole Municipality** | **19 764 979** |
| **按建设性质分** | **Grouped by Type of Construction** | |
| 新　建 | New Construction | 7 754 098 |
| 扩　建 | Expansion | 7 087 225 |
| 改　建 | Reconstruction | 1 413 864 |
| 其　他 | Others | 3 509 792 |
| **按登记注册类型分** | **Grouped by Registration Status** | |
| 国有企业 | State-owed Enterprises | 5 043 241 |
| 集体企业 | Collective-owned Enterprises | 1 018 108 |
| 股份合作企业 | Share-holding Cooperative Enterprises | 25 038 |
| 联营企业 | Joint Ownership Enterprises | 18 135 |
| 有限责任公司 | Limited Liability Corporations | 2 128 557 |
| 股份有限公司 | Share-holding Corporations Ltd. | 2 050 408 |
| 私营个体经济 | Individuals | 3 332 698 |
| 其　他 | Others | 101 392 |
| 港澳台商投资企业 | Enterprises with Investment from HongKong, Macao and Taiwan | 1 608 304 |
| 外商投资企业 | Enterprises with Foreign Investment | 4 439 098 |
| **按产业分** | **Grouped by Industry** | |
| 第一产业 | Primary Industry | 28 114 |
| 第二产业 | Secondary Industry | 10 732 391 |
| #工　业 | Industry | 10 676 736 |
| 第三产业 | Tertiary Industry | 9 004 474 |

# THE NEW FIXED ASSETS OF PROJECT INVESTMENT IN TOWNSHIPS (2012)

(10 000 yuan)

| 市　区 Urban Area | # 吴江区 Wujiang District | 常　熟 Changshu | 张家港 Zhangjiagang | 昆　山 Kunshan | 太　仓 Taicang |
|---|---|---|---|---|---|
| **10 109 511** | **2 402 566** | **2 505 698** | **2 656 518** | **2 704 842** | **1 788 410** |
| 3 981 372 | 690 263 | 1 101 195 | 611 835 | 1 401 982 | 657 714 |
| 3 640 138 | 1 220 672 | 898 297 | 1 458 045 | 357 928 | 732 817 |
| 381 206 | 137 780 | 220 383 | 584 670 | 207 516 | 20 089 |
| 2 106 795 | 353 851 | 285 823 | 1 968 | 737 416 | 377 790 |
| | | | | | |
| 2 303 576 | 805 812 | 1 058 162 | 336 279 | 681 013 | 664 211 |
| 838 491 | 166 103 | 41 562 | – | 116 505 | 21 550 |
| 18 038 | 240 | – | 7 000 | – | – |
| – | – | – | – | – | 18 135 |
| 1 527 391 | 108 972 | 216 123 | 284 561 | 85 026 | 15 456 |
| 524 906 | 153 432 | 97 773 | 1 114 143 | 56 270 | 257 316 |
| 1 743 673 | 689 212 | 251 309 | 504 788 | 501 477 | 331 451 |
| 53 266 | 3 103 | 34 962 | – | 13 164 | |
| 692 703 | 252 686 | 455 238 | 75 152 | 323 264 | 61 947 |
| 2 407 467 | 223 006 | 350 569 | 334 595 | 928 123 | 418 344 |
| | | | | | |
| 24 914 | 10 729 | 2 000 | – | 1 200 | – |
| 4 666 145 | 1 353 151 | 1 272 320 | 2 277 573 | 1 553 394 | 962 959 |
| 4 610 490 | 1 334 871 | 1 272 320 | 2 277 573 | 1 553 394 | 962 959 |
| 5 418 452 | 1 038 686 | 1 231 378 | 378 945 | 1 150 248 | 825 451 |

表10-6 续表

单位：万元

| 项　目 | Item | 全　市 Whole Municipality |
| --- | --- | --- |
| **按行业分** | **Grouped by Sector** | |
| 农林牧渔业 | Farming, Forestry, Animal Husbandry and Fishery | 28 114 |
| 采矿业 | Mining and Quarrying | - |
| 制造业 | Manufacturing | 10 195 691 |
| 电力、煤气及水的生产和供应业 | Power, Gas and Water Production and Supply | 481 045 |
| 建筑业 | Construction | 55 655 |
| 交通运输、仓储和邮政业 | Transportation, Logistics and Postal | 880 273 |
| 信息传输、软件和信息技术服务业 | Information Transmission, Software and Information Technology Services | 194 400 |
| 批发和零售业 | Wholesale and Retail Trade Services | 289 078 |
| 住宿和餐饮业 | Hoteling and Catering Services | 191 461 |
| 金融业 | Financial Industries | 119 315 |
| 房地产业 | Real Estate | 1 022 939 |
| 租赁和商务服务业 | Leasing and Business Services | 1 413 885 |
| 科学研究和技术服务业 | Scientific Research and Technical Services | 634 038 |
| 水利、环境和公共设施管理业 | Water Conservancy, Environment and Public Facilities Management | 3 095 823 |
| 居民服务和其他服务业 | Community Service and Other Services | 55 798 |
| 教　育 | Education | 360 715 |
| 卫生和社会工作 | Health Care and Social Work | 153 243 |
| 文化、体育和娱乐业 | Culture, Sports and Entertainment | 309 551 |
| 公共管理和社会组织 | Public Administration and Social Organizations | 283 955 |

Continued

(10 000 yuan)

| 市 区<br>Urban Area | # 吴江区<br>Wujiang District | 常 熟<br>Changshu | 张家港<br>Zhangjiagang | 昆 山<br>Kunshan | 太 仓<br>Taicang |
|---|---|---|---|---|---|
| 24 914 | 10 729 | 2 000 | – | 1 200 | – |
| – | – | – | – | – | – |
| 4 565 193 | 1 304 423 | 1 178 962 | 2 104 128 | 1 494 533 | 852 875 |
| 45 297 | 30 448 | 93 358 | 173 445 | 58 861 | 110 084 |
| 55 655 | 18 280 | – | – | – | – |
| 134 581 | 44 195 | 307 589 | 86 958 | 190 407 | 160 738 |
| 166 800 | 2 500 | 4 600 | – | 23 000 | – |
| 119 591 | 4 494 | 53 494 | 14 000 | 86 703 | 15 290 |
| 122 873 | 1 400 | 59 158 | 600 | 8 830 | – |
| 92 025 | – | – | 2 000 | 25 290 | – |
| 728 406 | 221 972 | 52 437 | 144 827 | 18 400 | 78 869 |
| 799 961 | 36 370 | – | 1 000 | 336 007 | 276 917 |
| 566 976 | 22 160 | 4 824 | 5 200 | 56 338 | 700 |
| 1 946 959 | 630 296 | 505 948 | 75 724 | 336 264 | 230 928 |
| 37 427 | 5 440 | 210 | 18 161 | – | – |
| 213 560 | 1 326 | 21 947 | 17 540 | 60 559 | 47 109 |
| 135 753 | 45 779 | 11 240 | – | 6 250 | – |
| 128 149 | – | 168 502 | 11 700 | 1 200 | – |
| 225 391 | 22 754 | 41 429 | 1 235 | 1 000 | 14 900 |

表10-7

# 固定资产投资效果情况（2012年）
# EFFECT OF INVESTMENT IN FIXED ASSETS (2012)

单位：% (%)

| 项　目 | Item | 项目建成投产率 Rate of Projects Completed and Put into Use | 建设周期（年）Construction Cycle (year) | 固定资产交付使用率 Rate of Fixed Assets Put into Use | 房屋竣工率 Rate of Buildings Completed | #住宅 Residential Buildings |
|---|---|---|---|---|---|---|
| **一、按种类分** | **Grouped by Type** | | | | | |
| **总　计** | **Total** | **79.3** | **3.1** | **76.6** | **33.7** | **24.7** |
| 城镇投资 | City &Town Collective Units | 72.3 | 2.5 | 74.6 | 38.3 | 38.1 |
| 房地产开发 | Real Estate Development | – | 5.6 | 70.9 | 21.7 | 22.9 |
| 农村投资 | Investment in Rural Area | 84.9 | 1.9 | 86.0 | 52.1 | 31.6 |
| **二、按地区分** | **Grouped by Region** | | | | | |
| **全　市** | **Whole Municipality** | **79.3** | **3.1** | **76.6** | **33.7** | **24.7** |
| 市　区 | Urban Area | 81.9 | 3.3 | 72.7 | 34.1 | 26.7 |
| #吴江区 | Wujiang District | 75.8 | 2.7 | 74.4 | 41.1 | 19.5 |
| 常　熟 | Changshu | 80.5 | 2.5 | 87.7 | 35.6 | 19.8 |
| 张家港 | Zhangjiagang | 84.9 | 2.3 | 78.2 | 40.1 | 29.1 |
| 昆　山 | Kunshan | 63.0 | 4.1 | 77.1 | 28.8 | 18.4 |
| 太　仓 | Taicang | 75.9 | 2.4 | 81.0 | 32.8 | 32.7 |

表10-8

# 历年房地产投资情况
# REAL ESTATE DEVELOPMENT OVER THE YEARS

| 年　份<br>Year | 投资额(万元)<br>Investment<br>(10 000yuan) | 新增固定资产(万元)<br>Newly Increased<br>Fixed Assets<br>(10 000yuan) | 竣工房屋面积(万平方米)<br>Floor Space of<br>Buildings Completed<br>(10 000sq.m) | #住　宅(万平方米)<br>Residential　Housing<br>(10 000sq.m) |
|---|---|---|---|---|
| 1990 | 16 516 | 16 049 | 46.95 | 40.21 |
| 1991 | 22 578 | 18 015 | 44.42 | 39.15 |
| 1992 | 61 858 | 32 111 | 89.12 | 65.36 |
| 1993 | 336 437 | 150 033 | 337.47 | 282.81 |
| 1994 | 400 268 | 218 471 | 378.39 | 299.81 |
| 1995 | 586 461 | 364 429 | 398.24 | 301.47 |
| 1996 | 501 411 | 430 700 | 334.16 | 250.45 |
| 1997 | 512 313 | 440 908 | 354.96 | 277.46 |
| 1998 | 585 447 | 541 232 | 403.23 | 313.12 |
| 1999 | 601 124 | 515 846 | 425.72 | 349.99 |
| 2000 | 611 792 | 611 091 | 444.49 | 376.30 |
| 2001 | 686 178 | 701 954 | 467.24 | 386.26 |
| 2002 | 1 073 363 | 829 151 | 558.05 | 464.94 |
| 2003 | 1 779 403 | 1 218 305 | 825.89 | 709.15 |
| 2004 | 3 343 245 | 2 024 119 | 1 462.78 | 1 269.29 |
| 2005 | 4 143 333 | 3 439 283 | 1 677.29 | 1 380.58 |
| 2006 | 4 707 472 | 4 070 670 | 1 823.12 | 1 484.16 |
| 2007 | 6 019 565 | 4 794 361 | 1 873.29 | 1 481.42 |
| 2008 | 7 180 805 | 4 023 663 | 1 481.24 | 1 131.91 |
| 2009 | 7 243 408 | 6 488 907 | 1 878.68 | 1 409.81 |
| 2010 | 9 358 018 | 7 054 660 | 1 761.08 | 1 221.53 |
| 2011 | 11 991 278 | 6 361 455 | 1 514.52 | 1 102.41 |
| 2012 | 12 633 597 | 8 954 225 | 1 827.56 | 1 386.17 |

表10-9

# 房地产投资完成额(2012年)

单位：万元

| 项　目 | Item | 全　市<br>Whole Municipality |
|---|---|---|
| **投资额** | **Investment** | **12 633 597** |
| # 住宅投资完成额 | Completed Investment Value of Residential Housing | 8 516 517 |
| **一、按工程构成分** | **Grouped by Use of Funds** | |
| 建筑工程 | Construction | 7 938 118 |
| 安装工程 | Installation | 466 277 |
| 设备、工器具购置 | Purchase of Equipment and Instruments | 215 964 |
| 其他费用 | Others | 4 013 238 |
| **二、按登记注册类型分** | **Grouped by Registration Status** | |
| 国有企业 | State-owed Enterprises | 799 263 |
| 集体企业 | Collective-owned Enterprises | 208 244 |
| 股份合作企业 | Share-holding Cooperative Enterprises | 44 235 |
| 联营经济 | Joint Ventures of State-owned and Collective Enterprises | - |
| 国有独资 | State-owned Enterprises | 109 421 |
| 其他有限责任公司 | Limited Liability Corporations | 4 656 432 |
| 股份有限公司 | Share-holding Corporations Ltd. | 266 650 |
| 私营个体企业 | Private and Individuals Enterprises | 4 264 183 |
| 港澳台商投资企业 | Enterprises with Investment from HongKong, Macao and Taiwan | 790 531 |
| 外商投资企业 | Enterprises with Foreign Investment | 746 802 |
| 其　他 | Others | 747 836 |
| **本年资金来源合计** | **Total** | **33 266 419** |
| 1.上年末结余资金 | Balance of Last Year | 8 615 405 |
| 2.本年资金来源小计 | Total Fund for This Year | 24 651 014 |
| (1) 国家预算内资金 | State Budgetary Appropriation | - |
| (2) 国内贷款 | Domestic Loans | 5 607 537 |
| (3) 债　券 | Bonds | - |
| (4) 利用外资 | Foreign Investment | 137 010 |
| (5) 自筹资金 | Fundraising | 5 807 687 |
| (6) 其他资金来源 | Others | 13 098 780 |
| **本年新增固定资产** | **Newly Increased Fixed Assets this year** | **8 954 225** |
| **房屋建筑面积** (万平方米) | **Floor Space of Buildings** (10 000 sq.m) | |
| 施工房屋建筑面积 | Floor space of Buildings under Construction | 8 403.89 |
| # 住　宅 | Residential Buildings | 6 049.39 |
| 竣工房屋建筑面积 | Floor Space of Buildings Completed | 1 827.56 |
| # 住　宅 | Residential Building | 1 386.17 |

# INVESTMENT IN REAL ESTATE DEVELOPMENT (2012)

(10 000 yuan)

| 市 区<br>Urban Area | # 吴江区<br>Wujiang District | 常 熟<br>Changshu | 张家港<br>Zhangjiagang | 昆 山<br>Kunshan | 太 仓<br>Taicang |
|---|---|---|---|---|---|
| **7 786 934** | **1 450 986** | **864 089** | **837 645** | **2 450 221** | **694 708** |
| 5 403 430 | 1 060 355 | 575 216 | 536 195 | 1 626 874 | 374 802 |
| | | | | | |
| 4 463 729 | 995 974 | 554 820 | 510 698 | 1 926 558 | 482 313 |
| 210 377 | 8 939 | 14 337 | 46 984 | 109 125 | 85 454 |
| 116 730 | 26 443 | 15 329 | 8 924 | 48 213 | 26 768 |
| 2 996 098 | 419 630 | 279 603 | 271 039 | 366 325 | 100 173 |
| | | | | | |
| 461 239 | 192 598 | 23 949 | 120 860 | 160 612 | 32 603 |
| 138 464 | 14 152 | – | – | 69 780 | – |
| 33 381 | 33 273 | – | 7 024 | 3 830 | – |
| – | – | – | – | – | – |
| 13 410 | – | 51 811 | – | 44 200 | – |
| 3 130 504 | 254 393 | 373 190 | 373 286 | 726 728 | 52 724 |
| 125 705 | 54 433 | – | – | 90 125 | 50 820 |
| 2 206 024 | 839 367 | 357 334 | 336 475 | 903 454 | 460 896 |
| 634 429 | 33 193 | 43 982 | – | 98 017 | 14 103 |
| 401 355 | 15 788 | 13 823 | – | 273 475 | 58 149 |
| 642 423 | 13 789 | | – | 80 000 | 25 413 |
| **20 394 010** | **2 753 484** | **2 894 398** | **2 266 041** | **5 820 583** | **1 891 387** |
| 5 359 455 | 415 311 | 831 437 | 481 272 | 1 327 835 | 615 406 |
| 15 034 555 | 2 338 173 | 2 062 961 | 1 784 769 | 4 492 748 | 1 275 981 |
| – | – | – | – | – | – |
| 3 644 417 | 473 985 | 273 866 | 437 187 | 776 419 | 475 648 |
| – | – | – | – | – | – |
| – | – | – | – | 137 010 | – |
| 3 737 634 | 986 018 | 500 472 | 330 120 | 993 331 | 246 130 |
| 7 652 504 | 878 170 | 1 288 623 | 1 017 462 | 2 585 988 | 554 203 |
| **4 995 457** | **697 077** | **875 880** | **662 923** | **1 657 493** | **762 472** |
| | | | | | |
| 4 351.07 | 989.05 | 705.33 | 494.85 | 2 277.00 | 575.63 |
| 3 217.50 | 772.31 | 462.87 | 333.23 | 1 659.02 | 376.78 |
| 1 015.92 | 178.80 | 160.57 | 156.10 | 398.79 | 96.19 |
| 821.63 | 139.79 | 102.92 | 107.11 | 284.92 | 69.60 |

表10-10 房地产开发基本情况 (2012年)

| 项　目 | | Item | | 全　市 Whole Municipality |
|---|---|---|---|---|
| **开发企业数** | (个) | **Number of Development Enterprises** | (unit) | **1 311** |
| **按资质等级分** | | **Classified by Qualification** | | |
| 一　级 | | A Qualification | | 14 |
| 二　级 | | B Qualification | | 370 |
| 三　级 | | C Qualification | | 300 |
| 四　级 | | D Qualification | | 17 |
| 暂　定 | | Provisional | | 546 |
| 其　他 | | Others | | 64 |
| **平均从业人员** | (人) | **Number of Employed Persons** | ( person) | **27 939** |
| **土地开发及购置** | (平方米) | **Land Development and Acquisition** | (sq.m) | |
| 待开发土地面积 | | Area of Land to be Developed | | 9 113 238 |
| 本年土地购置面积 | | Acreage of Land Acquired Within the Year | | 3 524 350 |
| 本年土地成交价款 | (万元) | Actual Land Price of the Year | (10 000 yuan) | 1 559 716 |
| **资产及损益情况** | | **Assets and Expenditure** | | |
| 资产总计 | | Total Assets | | 81 372 543 |
| 负债总计 | | Total Liabilities | | 57 586 164 |
| 所有者权益 | | Creditors Equity | | 23 786 379 |
| 实收资本合计 | | Total Capital Hold | | 18 357 974 |
| 主营业务收入总计 | | Total from Business Revenue | | 13 522 920 |
| 土地转让收入 | | Revenue from Land Transfer | | 488 820 |
| 商品房销售收入 | | Revenue  Sale of Housing | | 12 437 376 |
| 房屋出租收入 | | Income for House Lease | | 186 607 |
| 其他收入 | | Other Revenue | | 410 118 |
| 主营业务成本 | | Cost from Major Business | | 9 473 507 |
| 销售费用 | | Cost Related With Sale | | 472 896 |
| 主营业务税金及附加 | | Taxes and Extra Charges from Major Business | | 1 295 810 |
| 其他业务利润 | | Other Business Profits | | 40 348 |
| 管理费用及财务费用 | | Cost of Management and Financing Activities | | 8 724 710 |
| 投资收益及营业外收入 | | Benefits of Investment and Non-Business Income | | 195 871 |
| 营业外支出 | | Non-Business Expenditure | | 54 553 |
| 利润总额 | | Total Profits | | 1 538 353 |

# BASIC CONDITION OF REAL ESTATE DEVELOPMENT (2012)

| 市　区<br>Urban Area | # 吴江区<br>Wujiang District | 常　熟<br>Changshu | 张家港<br>Zhangjiagang | 昆　山<br>Kunshan | 太　仓<br>Taicang |
|---|---|---|---|---|---|
| **625** | **146** | **130** | **100** | **307** | **149** |
| 12 | 3 | – | 1 | 1 | – |
| 229 | 70 | 21 | 25 | 65 | 30 |
| 155 | 59 | 14 | 32 | 55 | 44 |
| 3 | 2 | 5 | 2 | 1 | 6 |
| 198 | 6 | 77 | 34 | 175 | 62 |
| 28 | 6 | 13 | 6 | 10 | 7 |
| **14 729** | **2 899** | **2 406** | **1 876** | **6 617** | **2 311** |
| 3 472 516 | 829 109 | 1 131 144 | 357 777 | 3 822 558 | 329 243 |
| 1 955 849 | 899 950 | 283 387 | 841 619 | 231 399 | 212 096 |
| 796 792 | 231 610 | 181 622 | 455 369 | 58 280 | 67 653 |
| | | | | | |
| 51 418 284 | 6 339 426 | 5 858 227 | 4 637 767 | 15 474 723 | 3 983 543 |
| 35 439 045 | 5 239 818 | 4 179 959 | 3 633 997 | 11 449 526 | 2 883 636 |
| 15 979 238 | 1 099 609 | 1 678 268 | 1 003 769 | 4 025 197 | 1 099 908 |
| 12 614 103 | 984 247 | 1 136 454 | 464 638 | 3 100 855 | 1 041 925 |
| 7 188 450 | 881 153 | 1 316 156 | 901 862 | 3 193 591 | 922 860 |
| 449 335 | – | – | 39 484 | – | – |
| 6 334 353 | 869 226 | 1 309 782 | 855 619 | 3 027 558 | 910 063 |
| 147 443 | 3 551 | 5 158 | 1 354 | 25 799 | 6 851 |
| 257 319 | 8 376 | 1 216 | 5 404 | 140 234 | 5 946 |
| 5 022 309 | 716 314 | 849 477 | 647 296 | 2 206 168 | 748 258 |
| 238 607 | 30 875 | 55 389 | 16 553 | 121 610 | 40 737 |
| 688 068 | 74 861 | 154 641 | 100 459 | 287 866 | 64 776 |
| 17 624 | 4 435 | 4 905 | 4 046 | 12 955 | 818 |
| 5 209 719 | 666 044 | 701 197 | 553 984 | 1 642 497 | 617 313 |
| 159 092 | 14 416 | 1 306 | 15 556 | 10 081 | 9 836 |
| 20 255 | 8 473 | 6 199 | 5 680 | 15 620 | 6 799 |
| 856 257 | -2 578 | 185 728 | 93 220 | 392 423 | 10 724 |

表10-10 续表

| 项　目 | Item | 全　市 Whole Municipality |
|---|---|---|
| **房屋施工面积** (平方米) | **Floor Space of Buildings under Construction** (sq. m) | **84 038 894** |
| 1. 住　宅 | Residential Buildings | 60 493 933 |
| 2. 办公楼 | Office Buildings | 2 953 150 |
| 3. 商业营业用房 | Commercial Business Premises | 11 628 380 |
| 4. 其　他 | Others | 8 963 431 |
| **新开工面积** | **Floor Space of Starting This Year** | **20 605 080** |
| 1. 住　宅 | Residential Buildings | 13 968 427 |
| 2. 办公楼 | Office Buildings | 484 767 |
| 3. 商业营业用房 | Commercial Business Premises | 3 716 347 |
| 4. 其　他 | Others | 2 435 539 |
| **房屋竣工面积** | **Floor Space of Buildings Completed** | **18 275 640** |
| 1. 住　宅 | Residential Buildings | 13 861 747 |
| 2. 办公楼 | Office Buildings | 408 203 |
| 3. 商业营业用房 | Commercial Business Premises | 2 215 595 |
| 4. 其　他 | Others | 1 790 095 |
| **商品房销售面积** | **Floor Space of Housing Sold** | **14 662 867** |
| 1. 住　宅 | Residential Buildings | 12 631 096 |
| 2. 办公楼 | Office Buildings | 343 482 |
| 3. 商业营业用房 | Commercial Business Premises | 1 499 013 |
| 4. 其　他 | Others | 189 276 |
| **待售面积** | **Area Of Land For Sale** | **6 855 182** |
| 1. 住　宅 | Residential Buildings | 3 546 245 |
| 2. 办公楼 | Office Buildings | 619 453 |
| 3. 商业营业用房 | Commercial Business Premises | 2 183 856 |
| 4. 其　他 | Others | 505 628 |
| **商品房销售额** (万元) | **Sales of housing** (10 000 yuan) | **13 364 267** |
| 1. 住　宅 | Residential Buildings | 11 342 783 |
| 2. 办公楼 | Office Buildings | 279 027 |
| 3. 商业营业用房 | Commercial Business Premises | 1 663 937 |
| 4. 其　他 | Others | 78 520 |

Continued

| 市 区<br>Urban Area | # 吴江区<br>Wujiang District | 常 熟<br>Changshu | 张家港<br>Zhangjiagang | 昆 山<br>Kunshan | 太 仓<br>Taicang |
|---|---|---|---|---|---|
| **43 510 718** | **9 890 504** | **7 053 326** | **4 948 526** | **22 770 027** | **5 756 297** |
| 32 174 955 | 7 723 122 | 4 628 681 | 3 332 331 | 16 590 155 | 3 767 811 |
| 1 253 608 | 4 798 | 378 699 | 97 396 | 1 013 524 | 209 923 |
| 5 403 147 | 961 134 | 1 452 151 | 881 981 | 2 882 122 | 1 008 979 |
| 4 679 008 | 1 201 450 | 593 795 | 636 818 | 2 284 226 | 769 584 |
| **11 550 695** | **2 883 225** | **1 164 775** | **1 074 837** | **5 847 944** | **966 829** |
| 7 665 007 | 2 215 060 | 817 883 | 670 063 | 4 159 759 | 655 715 |
| 259 608 | – | 41 235 | 19 508 | 121 647 | 42 769 |
| 2 159 126 | 315 091 | 189 376 | 224 446 | 965 372 | 178 027 |
| 1 466 954 | 353 074 | 116 281 | 160 820 | 601 166 | 90 318 |
| **10 159 208** | **1 787 995** | **1 605 654** | **1 561 011** | **3 987 904** | **961 863** |
| 8 216 293 | 1 397 936 | 1 029 158 | 1 071 138 | 2 849 195 | 695 963 |
| 102 880 | – | – | 16 644 | 276 328 | 12 351 |
| 896 905 | 180 320 | 450 577 | 265 922 | 463 520 | 138 671 |
| 943 130 | 209 739 | 125 919 | 207 307 | 398 861 | 114 878 |
| **8 155 855** | **1 586 242** | **1 557 938** | **894 364** | **3 215 947** | **838 763** |
| 7 375 167 | 1 374 994 | 1 213 698 | 723 620 | 2 691 023 | 627 588 |
| 84 221 | 6 364 | 40 870 | 13 035 | 189 183 | 16 173 |
| 656 160 | 193 651 | 296 856 | 109 559 | 288 553 | 147 885 |
| 40 307 | 11 233 | 6 514 | 48 150 | 47 188 | 47 117 |
| **3 343 024** | **935 816** | **827 679** | **680 797** | **1 429 286** | **574 396** |
| 1 907 148 | 447 686 | 348 152 | 353 364 | 654 916 | 282 665 |
| 155 795 | 14 267 | 28 964 | 125 829 | 247 203 | 61 662 |
| 1 026 209 | 451 018 | 411 218 | 119 707 | 428 083 | 198 639 |
| 253 872 | 22 845 | 39 345 | 81 897 | 99 084 | 31 430 |
| **7 953 013** | **1 158 203** | **1 397 539** | **843 259** | **2 539 337** | **631 119** |
| 7 095 511 | 967 033 | 1 085 178 | 688 592 | 2 029 315 | 444 187 |
| 98 018 | 4 807 | 22 651 | 14 511 | 135 282 | 8 565 |
| 739 742 | 182 478 | 288 997 | 124 016 | 347 384 | 163 798 |
| 19 742 | 3 885 | 713 | 16 140 | 27 356 | 14 569 |

表10-11 房地产开发四大指标前十位企业（2012年）

| 序 号<br>No. | 开发企业名称<br>Name of Development Enterprises | 资质等级<br>Grouped by Grade | 地 区<br>Region | 经济类型<br>Ownership |
|---|---|---|---|---|
| **一、完成投资额 Investment** | | | | |
| 1 | 苏州绿城玫瑰园房地产开发有限公司 | 暂定二级 | 工业园区 | 有限责任公司 |
| 2 | 吴江城市房地产开发有限公司 | 二 级 | 吴江区 | 国 有 |
| 3 | 太仓万达广场投资有限公司 | 二 级 | 太 仓 | 有限责任公司 |
| 4 | 苏州市相城区城市建设有限责任公司 | 二 级 | 相城区 | 有限责任公司 |
| 5 | 苏州乾宁置业有限公司 | 二 级 | 工业园区 | 有限责任公司 |
| 6 | 苏州金梁置业有限公司 | 二 级 | 姑苏区 | 有限责任公司 |
| 7 | 苏州工业园区娄葑建发房地产有限公司 | 二 级 | 工业园区 | 有限责任公司 |
| 8 | 苏州高龙房产发展有限公司 | 暂定二级 | 工业园区 | 中外合资经营 |
| 9 | 金科集团苏州房地产开发有限公司 | 暂定二级 | 高新区、虎丘区 | 有限责任公司 |
| 10 | 苏州市方圆房地产发展有限公司 | 二 级 | 吴中区 | 有限责任公司 |
| **二、施工房屋面积 Floor Space of Building under Construction** | | | | |
| 1 | 昆山市阳澄湖房产有限责任公司 | 二 级 | 昆 山 | 有限责任公司 |
| 2 | 吴江城市房地产开发有限公司 | 二 级 | 吴江区 | 国 有 |
| 3 | 苏州市相城区城市建设有限责任公司 | 二 级 | 相城区 | 有限责任公司 |
| 4 | 昆山市临丰房产开发有限公司 | 三 级 | 昆 山 | 有限责任公司 |
| 5 | 苏州工业园区地产经营管理公司 | 暂定二级 | 工业园区 | 国 有 |
| 6 | 常熟市世茂新发展置业有限公司 | 二 级 | 常 熟 | 有限责任公司 |
| 7 | 中海发展（苏州）有限公司 | 一 级 | 工业园区 | 港澳台商独资 |
| 8 | 昆山花桥国际商务城置业有限公司 | 暂定二级 | 昆 山 | 国有独资公司 |
| 9 | 苏州工业园区建屋发展集团有限公司 | 一 级 | 工业园区 | 有限责任公司 |
| 10 | 苏州市合景房地产开发有限公司 | 二 级 | 相城区 | 有限责任公司 |

# TOP 10 OF REAL ESTATE DEVELOPMENT ENTERPRISES THAT BEST COMPLETED THE FOUR MAJOR INDICATORS (2012)

| 序　号<br>No. | 开发企业名称<br>Name of Development Enterprises | 资质等级<br>Grouped by Grade | 地　区<br>Region | 经济类型<br>Ownership |
|---|---|---|---|---|
| **三、竣工房屋面积** | **Floor Space of Building Completed** | | | |
| 1 | 苏州工业园区地产经营管理公司 | 暂定二级 | 工业园区 | 国　有 |
| 2 | 昆山市阳澄湖房产有限责任公司 | 二　级 | 昆　山 | 有限责任公司 |
| 3 | 苏州市相城区城市建设有限责任公司 | 二　级 | 相城区 | 有限责任公司 |
| 4 | 苏州工业园区唯亭镇房地产开发公司 | 二　级 | 工业园区 | 集　体 |
| 5 | 苏州工业园区建屋发展集团有限公司 | 一　级 | 工业园区 | 有限责任公司 |
| 6 | 苏州市惠民置业投资有限公司 | 暂定二级 | 吴中区 | 有限责任公司 |
| 7 | 中海发展（苏州）有限公司 | 一　级 | 工业园区 | 港澳台商独资 |
| 8 | 中新苏州工业园区置地有限公司 | 一　级 | 工业园区 | 有限责任公司 |
| 9 | 吴江区联发置业有限公司 | 二　级 | 吴江区 | 有限责任公司 |
| 10 | 张家港市城市投资发展有限公司 | 二　级 | 张家港 | 国　有 |
| **四、销售房屋面积** | **Floor Space of Building Sale** | | | |
| 1 | 中海发展（苏州）有限公司 | 一　级 | 工业园区 | 港澳台商独资 |
| 2 | 苏州高龙房产发展有限公司 | 暂定二级 | 工业园区 | 中外合资经营 |
| 3 | 苏州招商南山地产有限公司 | 二　级 | 吴中区 | 有限责任公司 |
| 4 | 苏州雅戈尔置业有限公司 | 二　级 | 工业园区 | 有限责任公司 |
| 5 | 苏州隽御地产有限公司 | 二　级 | 工业园区 | 中外合资经营 |
| 6 | 常熟市中南世纪城房地产开发有限公司 | 二　级 | 常　熟 | 有限责任公司 |
| 7 | 苏州鼎基房地产开发有限公司 | 二　级 | 吴江区 | 有限责任公司 |
| 8 | 苏州新城创佳置业有限公司 | 暂定二级 | 姑苏区 | 有限责任公司 |
| 9 | 苏州协信圆融房地产开发有限公司 | 暂定二级 | 工业园区 | 有限责任公司 |
| 10 | 苏州保利隆胜置业有限公司 | 暂定二级 | 吴中区 | 有限责任公司 |

表10-12

# 农村固定资产投资 (2012年)

| 项　　目 | Item | 全　市 Whole Municipality |
|---|---|---|
| **一、施工项目　　（个）** | **Projects under Construction　　(unit)** | **5 095** |
| **投产项目** | **Projects Put into Use** | **4 326** |
| **二、计划总投资　　（万元）** | **Plan of General Investment　　(10 000 yuan)** | **26 129 723** |
| **三、本年完成额** | **Investments Completed in This year** | **13 532 282** |
| **（一）按行业分** | **Grouped by Sector** | |
| 农林牧渔业 | Farming, Forestry, Animal Husbandry and Fishery | 68 738 |
| 采矿业 | Mining and Quarrying | 200 |
| 制造业 | Manufacturing | 8 575 138 |
| 电力、煤气及水的生产和供应业 | Production and Supply of Electric Power, Gas and Water | 279 643 |
| 建筑业 | Construction | 30 169 |
| 交通运输、仓储和邮政业 | Transportation, Logistics and Postal | 412 846 |
| 信息传输、软件和信息技术服务业 | Information Transmission, Software and Information Technology Services | 58 858 |
| 批发和零售业 | Wholesale and Retail Trade Services | 225 941 |
| 住宿和餐饮业 | Hoteling and Catering Services | 227 891 |
| 金融业 | Financial Industries | 52 398 |
| 房地产业 | Real Estate | 1 590 700 |
| 租赁和商务服务业 | Leasing and Business Services | 247 114 |
| 科学研究和技术服务业 | Scientific Research and Technical Services | 158 781 |
| 水利、环境和公共设施管理业 | Water Conservancy, Environment and Public Facilities Management | 1 024 751 |
| 居民服务和其他服务业 | Community Service and Other Services | 48 711 |
| 教　育 | Education | 139 658 |
| 卫生和社会工作 | Health Care and Social Work | 95 242 |
| 文化、体育和娱乐业 | Culture, Sports and Entertainment | 121 792 |
| 公共管理和社会组织 | Public Administration and Social Organizations | 173 711 |

# INVESTMENT IN FIXED ASSETS BY RURAL UNITS (2012)

| 市 区<br>Urban Area | # 吴江区<br>Wujiang District | 常 熟<br>Changshu | 张家港<br>Zhangjiagang | 昆 山<br>Kunshan | 太 仓<br>Taicang |
|---|---|---|---|---|---|
| **2 644** | **597** | **695** | **680** | **696** | **380** |
| **2 393** | **493** | **587** | **609** | **444** | **293** |
| **10 187 630** | **4 380 196** | **3 514 985** | **4 648 469** | **5 050 403** | **2 728 236** |
| **5 329 392** | **2 042 288** | **2 319 729** | **2 460 763** | **2 010 681** | **1 411 717** |
| 33 351 | 20 350 | 27 497 | 7 490 | 400 | – |
| 200 | – | – | – | – | – |
| 3 283 332 | 1 539 106 | 1 464 146 | 1 522 931 | 1 330 658 | 974 071 |
| 160 555 | 77 550 | 32 561 | 56 498 | 21 072 | 8 957 |
| 26 449 | – | 920 | 1 800 | 1 000 | – |
| 209 610 | 32 334 | 7 700 | 115 750 | 40 289 | 39 497 |
| 34 058 | 400 | – | – | 21 750 | 3 050 |
| 74 548 | 16 450 | 25 625 | 92 062 | 31 836 | 1 870 |
| 75 005 | 13 360 | 60 200 | 36 500 | 38 311 | 17 875 |
| 42 000 | – | 8 148 | 1 420 | 830 | – |
| 474 591 | 108 253 | 427 579 | 354 960 | 144 525 | 189 045 |
| 162 330 | 42 218 | 2 855 | 29 350 | 28 267 | 24 312 |
| 30 577 | 21 537 | 60 215 | 2 000 | 16 565 | 49 424 |
| 425 067 | 114 163 | 146 483 | 178 630 | 248 351 | 26 220 |
| 39 919 | 13 506 | 3 490 | 580 | 4 722 | – |
| 54 004 | 14 965 | 13 797 | 31 160 | 23 310 | 17 387 |
| 51 136 | 22 286 | 17 170 | 2 300 | 14 486 | 10 150 |
| 76 598 | 5 110 | 1 950 | 8 000 | 35 244 | – |
| 76 062 | 700 | 19 393 | 19 332 | 9 065 | 49 859 |

表10-12 续表

| 项 目 | Item | 全 市 Whole Municipality |
|---|---|---|
| **（二）按登记注册类型分** | **Grouped by Registration Status** | |
| 国 有 | State-owned | 889 484 |
| 农村集体经济 | Rural Collective Units | 2 381 438 |
| 股份合作 | Share-holding Cooperative Enterprises | 18 356 |
| 联营企业 | Joint Ownership Enterprises | 70 125 |
| 有限责任公司 | Responsibility Co.Ltd. | 509 065 |
| 股份有限公司 | Share-holding Corporations Ltd. | 151 035 |
| 私营个体 | Individuals | 7 608 036 |
| 其 他 | Others | 22 449 |
| 港澳台投资经济 | HongKong, Macao and Taiwan Funded | 635 619 |
| 外商投资经济 | Enterprises with Foreign Investment | 1 246 675 |
| **四、本年资金来源** | **Fund for This Year** | **13 741 668** |
| # 国内贷款 | Domestic Loans | 386 754 |
| 引进外资 | Foreign Investment | 1 243 897 |
| 自筹资金 | Fundraising | 11 692 711 |
| **五、本年新增固定资产** | **Newly Increased Fixed Assets this year** | **11 638 365** |
| **六、房屋建筑面积** (万平方米) | **Floor Space of Buildings** (10 000 sq.m) | |
| 施工房屋建筑面积 | Floor space of Buildings under Construction | 3 944.84 |
| # 住 宅 | Residential Buildings | 689.03 |
| 竣工房屋建筑面积 | Floor Space of Buildings Completed | 2 054.85 |
| # 住 宅 | Residential Building | 218.03 |

Continued

| 市 区<br>Urban Area | # 吴江区<br>Wujiang District | 常 熟<br>Changshu | 张家港<br>Zhangjiagang | 昆 山<br>Kunshan | 太 仓<br>Taicang |
|---|---|---|---|---|---|
| | | | | | |
| 283 173 | 173 411 | 131 160 | 268 830 | 192 614 | 13 707 |
| 1 114 528 | 157 890 | 567 772 | 198 224 | 231 200 | 269 714 |
| 1 156 | 1 156 | 4 500 | 2 000 | 2 000 | 8 700 |
| 10 751 | 1 751 | 580 | – | 58 794 | – |
| 138 804 | 2 606 | 9 710 | 327 100 | 29 451 | 4 000 |
| 44 677 | 27 198 | 53 450 | 17 000 | 19 448 | 16 460 |
| 3 093 879 | 1 336 601 | 1 257 016 | 1 540 979 | 788 683 | 927 479 |
| 3 900 | – | 2 080 | 1 000 | 6 269 | 9 200 |
| 293 054 | 168 695 | 63 410 | 3 550 | 217 664 | 57 941 |
| 345 470 | 172 980 | 230 051 | 102 080 | 464 558 | 104 516 |
| **5 419 492** | **2 073 873** | **2 022 555** | **2 732 660** | **2 153 394** | **1 413 567** |
| 226 792 | 117 052 | 83 700 | – | 40 632 | 35 630 |
| 412 782 | 210 097 | 89 488 | 92 130 | 559 760 | 89 737 |
| 4 580 394 | 1 735 962 | 1 825 266 | 2 640 530 | 1 368 321 | 1 278 200 |
| **4 418 198** | **1 589 497** | **2 191 994** | **2 178 241** | **1 574 960** | **1 274 972** |
| | | | | | |
| 1 464.88 | 483.19 | 566.57 | 779.46 | 799.66 | 334.28 |
| 89.88 | – | 165.29 | 343.29 | 90.56 | – |
| 930.80 | 342.91 | 277.67 | 384.72 | 349.41 | 112.25 |
| 42.98 | – | 22.51 | 114.84 | 37.70 | – |

表10-13

# 建成投产的主要建设项目一览（2012年）
# KEY CONSTRUCTION PROJECTS COMPLETED (2012)

| 项目名称<br>Name of Projects | 开工年月<br>Start of Construction | 全部建成投产年月<br>Date of Projects Completed and Put into Use | 新增生产能力或效益<br>Newly Increased Production Capacity and Benefit | 累计投资总额(万元)<br>Total Increased (10 000 yuan) |
|---|---|---|---|---|
| 苏州轨道交通1号线工程 | 2007.12 | 2012.04 | 新建轨道交通25.739公里 | 1 266 398 |
| 园区屹立工程塑料苏州公司厂房扩建项目 | 2012.01 | 2012.12 | 塑料树脂及共聚物6000吨/年 | 22 164 |
| 苏州供电公司公园输变电工程 | 2012.01 | 2012.12 | 输电线路长度(110KV及以上)3.2公里 | 4 000 |
| 高新区圣晖工程新建生产厂房 | 2011.11 | 2012.12 | 塑料树脂及共聚物1000吨/年 | 2 260 |
| 吴中区太湖路（含夏连路南段）综合改造 | 2011.10 | 2012.12 | 改建二级公路3公里 | 10 000 |
| 苏州市新华化纤有限公司购置设备 | 2012.01 | 2012.02 | 化学纤维30000吨/年 | 4 000 |
| 江苏银奕达铝业有限公司新建厂房和设备 | 2012.05 | 2012.12 | 铝加工10000吨/年 | 4 900 |
| 常熟市支梅线改建工程 | 2009.05 | 2012.11 | 改建二级公路18公里 | 84 652 |
| 常熟市自来水公司滨江自来水厂扩建工程 | 2008.08 | 2012.11 | 城市自来水供水能力20万吨/日 | 42 534 |
| 常熟市恒意化纤有限公司新建厂房 | 2010.03 | 2012.12 | 化学纤维160000吨/年 | 73 700 |
| 中电投常熟光伏发电有限公司太阳能发电站 | 2012.01 | 2012.06 | 太阳能发电0.98万千瓦 | 26 461 |
| 江苏克罗德科技有限公司高精度板材 | 2010.07 | 2012.11 | 钢材10万吨/年 | 39 500 |
| 常熟涤纶有限公司扩建厂房及设备 | 2011.01 | 2012.12 | 化学纤维9000吨/年 | 9 460 |
| 常熟长江港务有限公司新建码头 | 2010.10 | 2012.11 | 新(扩)建港口码头8个、574万吨、72标 | 37 800 |
| 常熟宝进钢材加工有限公司二期 | 2010.12 | 2012.11 | 钢材22.5万吨/年 | 25 446 |
| 常熟亨通港务有限公司新建码头 | 2011.01 | 2012.12 | 新(扩)建港口码头3个、105万吨、12标 | 25 917 |
| 江苏宏宝光电科技有限公司太阳能屋顶并网发电项目 | 2011.08 | 2012.07 | 其他发电0.15万千瓦 | 2 500 |
| 张家港市新乐天元毛业有限公司生产线 | 2011.07 | 2012.05 | 毛纺锭20000锭 | 9 500 |
| 江苏富淼科技股份有限公司聚丙烯酰胺(一期) | 2012.01 | 2012.06 | 塑料树脂及共聚物60000吨/年 | 9 800 |
| 张家港市金浩淳铝业有限公司铝型材项目 | 2012.05 | 2012.09 | 铝加工7000吨/年 | 4 000 |
| 张家港沃斯汀新材料新建车间项目 | 2012.04 | 2012.11 | 塑料树脂及共聚物10000吨/年 | 8 300 |
| 张家港长源热电有限公司五期工程 | 2009.08 | 2012.04 | 火力发电8.4万千瓦 | 42 612 |
| 东洋轮胎张家港有限公司年产子午线 | 2010.11 | 2012.03 | 轮胎外胎200万条/年 | 57 726 |
| 张家港保税区万纤制条有限公司腈纶条 | 2012.01 | 2012.10 | 化学纤维20000吨/年 | 6 000 |
| 江苏启蓝新材料有限公司高端塑料合金 | 2012.01 | 2012.10 | 塑料树脂及共聚物30000吨/年 | 4 760 |

表10-13 续表 Continued

| 项目名称<br>Name of Projects | 开工年月<br>Start of Construction | 全部建成投产年月<br>Date of Projects Completed and Put into Use | 新增生产能力或效益<br>Newly Increased Production Capacity and Benefit | 累计投资总额(万元)<br>Total Increased (10 000 yuan) |
|---|---|---|---|---|
| 张家港市给排水公司生活污水处理扩建一期工程 | 2011.01 | 2012.09 | 城市污水处理能力9.2万吨/日 | 144 853 |
| 国都化工（昆山）有限公司厂房设备 | 2012.01 | 2012.12 | 塑料树脂及共聚物500吨/年 | 4 400 |
| 昆山市伏曦园输变电工程 | 2008.07 | 2012.11 | 输电线路长度(110KV及以上)10.5公里 | 7 550 |
| 昆山市交通局江浦路南延伸工程 | 2008.12 | 2012.12 | 新建一级公路10.8公里 | 17 029 |
| 昆山鹿城垃圾发电有限公司扩建项目 | 2008.09 | 2012.12 | 其他发电1.18万千瓦 | 22 100 |
| 昆山市源丰铝业有限公司1#厂房 | 2012.03 | 2012.10 | 铝加工8000吨/年 | 3 000 |
| 昆山市泗桥输变电工程 | 2009.10 | 2012.11 | 输电线路长度(110KV及以上)10公里 | 6 600 |
| 昆山市交通局古城路南延工程 | 2009.03 | 2012.12 | 新建一级公路8.2公里 | 22 773 |
| 昆山市交通局东城大道快速化工程 | 2009.12 | 2012.12 | 新建一级公路11公里 | 44 383 |
| 昆山市交通局城北大道改建 | 2010.09 | 2012.12 | 改建一级公路6.6公里 | 42 040 |
| 正新橡胶（中国）全钢丝载重子午轮胎项目 | 2011.05 | 2012.12 | 轮胎外胎180万条/年 | 58 391 |
| 昆山张浦污水厂污水工程 | 2008.07 | 2012.12 | 城市污水处理能力1.35万吨/日 | 10 200 |
| 建大橡胶（中国）PCR成品仓库项目及设备 | 2012.01 | 2012.10 | 轮胎外胎17万条/年 | 11 027 |
| 吴江区交通局连接线改建工程 | 2011.05 | 2012.03 | 改建二级公路7.5公里 | 15 100 |
| 吴江区沪苏浙高速公路平望互通连接线工程 | 2011.02 | 2012.12 | 新建一级公路3.5公里 | 16 090 |
| 吴江区科欧污水处理有限公司新建 | 2012.01 | 2012.08 | 城市污水处理能力5万吨/日 | 2 500 |
| 苏州顶智特种纤维科技有限公司设备 | 2012.05 | 2012.12 | 化学纤维350吨/年 | 7 833 |
| 太仓市水利局荡茜河河道桥梁工程 | 2010.01 | 2012.01 | 新建独立公路桥梁1座、1000延长米 | 16 700 |
| 太仓市交通局协星公路 | 2010.03 | 2012.01 | 新建公路14.1公里 | 31 050 |
| 江苏明辉化纤科技股份有限公司新建 | 2010.11 | 2012.11 | 化学纤维160000吨/年 | 120 000 |
| 太仓市振辉化纤有限公司二期扩建 | 2010.11 | 2012.09 | 化学纤维210000吨/年 | 68 300 |
| 江苏中润化纤3万吨多孔超细旦涤纶纤维丝项目 | 2012.01 | 2012.08 | 化学纤维9900吨/年 | 10 500 |
| 江苏长乐纤维科技有限公司POY纺丝生产线 | 2012.10 | 2012.11 | 化学纤维9900吨/年 | 20 400 |
| 上海佳方钢管集团太仓有限公司扩建合资工程 | 2012.02 | 2012.08 | 钢材2万吨/年 | 9 391 |
| 苏州华苏塑料有限公司生产线及电机技改工程 | 2012.07 | 2012.12 | 塑料树脂及共聚物5000吨/年 | 3 503 |

# 主 要 统 计 指 标 解 释

**全社会固定资产投资** 是以货币形式表现的在一定时期内全社会建造和购置固定资产的工作量以及与此有关的费用的总称。该指标是反映固定资产投资规模、结构和发展速度的综合性指标,又是观察工程进度和考核投资效果的重要依据。全社会固定资产投资按登记注册类型可分为国有、集体、个体、联营、股份制、外商、港澳台商、其他等。

**城镇固定资产投资** 指城镇各种登记注册类型的企业、事业、行政单位及个体户进行的计划总投资(或实际需要总投资)50万元及50万元以上的建设项目投资、房地产开发投资、城镇和工矿区私人建房投资。县城及以上区域内发生的投资，县及县以上各级政府及主管部门直接领导、管理的建设项目和企业事业单位的投资均为城镇固定资产投资。

**房地产开发投资** 指各种登记注册类型的房地产开发公司、商品房建设公司及其他房地产开发法人单位和附属于其他法人单位实际从事房地产开发或经营活动的单位统一开发的包括统代建、拆迁还建的住宅、厂房、仓库、饭店、宾馆、度假村、写字楼、办公楼等房屋建筑物和配套的服务设施，土地开发工程（如道路、给水、排水、供电、供热、通讯、平整场地等基础设施工程）的投资；不包括单纯的土地交易活动。

**农村投资** 包括在农村区域范围内进行固定资产投资活动的企业、事业、行政单位及农村个人投资。

**固定资产投资的资金来源** 根据固定资产投资的资金来源不同，分为国家预算内资金、国内贷款、利用外资、自筹资金和其他资金。

(1)国家预算内资金：分为财政拨款和财政安排的贷款两部分。包括中央财政的基本建设基金(分经营性基金和非经营性基金两部分)、专项支出(如煤代油专项等)、收回再贷、贴息资金，财政安排的挖潜改造和新产品试制支出、城建支出、商业部门简易建筑支出、不发达地区发展基金等资金中用于固定资产投资的资金；地方财政中由国家统筹安排的资金等。

(2)国内贷款：指报告期固定资产投资单位向银行及非银行金融机构借入的用于固定资产投资的各种国内借款，包括银行利用自有资金及吸收的存款发放的贷款、上级主管部门拨入的国内贷款、国家专项贷款、地方财政专项资金安排的贷款、国内储备贷款、周转贷款等。

(3)利用外资：指报告期收到的用于固定资产建造和购置的国外资金(包括设备、材料、技术在内)。包括对外借款(外国政府、国际金融组织贷款、出口信贷、外国银行商业贷款、对外发行债券和股票)、外商直接投资及外商其他投资。不包括我国自有外汇资金(国家外汇、地方外汇、留成外汇、调剂外汇和中国银行自有资金发行的外汇贷款等)。计算利用外资时，需要折算成人民币，折算中所使用的外汇汇率按现汇计算，即按使用外汇时的汇率计算。

(4)自筹资金：指固定资产投资单位报告期收到的，由各地区、各部门及企、事业单位筹集用于固定资产投资的预算外资金，包括中央各部门、各级地方和企、事业单位的自筹资金。

(5)其他资金：指在报告期收到的除以上各种资金之外其他用于固定资产投资的资金，包括企业或金融机构通过发行各种债券筹集到的资金、群众集资、个人资金、无偿捐赠的资金及其他单位拨入的资金等。

**固定资产投资按国民经济行业分** 根据建设项目建成投产后的主要产品或主要用途及社会经济活动性质来确定国民经济行业。一般情况下，一个建设项目或一个企业、事业单位只能属于一种国民经济行业。

**固定资产投资按隶属关系分** 是按建设单位或企业、事业、行政单位的主管上级机关确定的。

（1）中央：是指中共中央、人大常委会和国务院各部、委、局、总公司以及直属机构直接领导的建设项目和企业、事业、行政单位。这些单位的固定资产投资计划由国务院各部门直接编制和下达，建设中所需物资、主要设备以及建设中的问题都由中央有关部门安排和解决。

（2）地方：是由省（自治区、直辖市）、地区（州、盟、省辖市）、县（旗、县级市）三级政府及业务主管部门直接领导和管理的建设项目、企业、事业、行政单位。地方项目还包括不隶属以上各级政府及主管部门的建设项目和企业、事业单位，如外商投资企业和无主管部门的企业等。

**固定资产投资按建设性质分** 根据整个建设项目情况来确定。建设项目的性质一般分为新建、扩建、改建和技术改造、迁建、恢复。房地产开发单位、农村投资、城镇工矿区私人建房投资不划分建设性质。

(1)新建：一般指从无到有开始建设的企业、事业和行政单位或建设项目。现有企业、事业、行政单位一般不属于新建。但如有的单位原有基础很小，经过建设后新增的固定资产价值超过该企、事业、行政单位原有固定资产价值(原值)三倍以上的也应作为新建。

(2)扩建：指在厂内或其他地点，为扩大原有产品的生产能力(或效益)或增加新的产品生产能力，而增建主要的生产车间(或主要工程)、分厂、独立的生产线。行政、事业单位在原单位增建业务用房(如学校增建教学用房、医院增建门诊部、病房等)也作为扩建。

现有企、事业单位为扩大原有主要产品生产能力或增加新的产品生产能力，增建一个或几个主要生产车间(或主要工程)、分厂，同时进行一些更新改造工程的，也应作为扩建。

(3)改建和技术改造：指现有企业、事业单位，对原有设施进行技术改造或更新(包括相应配套的辅助性生产、生活福利设施) 的建设项目。现有企业、事业单位为适应市场变化的需要，而改变企业的主要产品种类(如军工企业转产民用品等) 的建设项目，应作为改建。原有产品生产作业线由于各工序(车间)之间能力不平衡，为填平补齐充分发挥原有生产能力而增建不增加本企业主要产品设计能力的车间，也应作为改建。技术改造是指企业、事业单位在现有基础上，用先进的技术代替落后的技术，用先进的工艺和装备代替落后的工艺和装备，以改变企业落后的技术经济面貌，实现以内涵为主的扩大再生产，达到提高产品质量、促进产品更新换代、节约能源、降低消耗、扩大生产规模、全面提高社会经济效益的目的。技术改造具体包括以下内容：机器设备和工具的更新改造；生产工艺改革、节约能源和原材料的改造；厂房建筑和公共设施的改造；劳动条件和生产环境的改造等。

**固定资产投资按构成分** 固定资产投资活动按其工作内容和实现方式分为建筑安装工程，设备、工具、器具购置，其他费用三个部分。

(1)建筑安装工程(建筑安装工作量)：指各种房屋、建筑物的建造工程和各种设备、装置的安装工程。包括各种房屋建造工程；各种用途设备基础和各种工业窑炉的砌筑工程及金属结构工程；为施工而进行的各种准备工作和临时工程以及完工后的清理工作等；铁路、道路的铺设，矿井的开凿及石油管道的架设等；水利工程；防空地下建筑等特殊工程；列入房屋工程预算内的暖气、卫生、通风、照明、煤气等设备的价值及装设油饰工程；列入建筑工程预算内的各种管道(蒸汽、压缩空气、石油、给排水等管道)、电力、电讯电缆导线等的敷设工程；以及各种机械设备的安装工程；为测定安装工程质量，对设备进行的试运工作；房地产开发单位进行的商品房屋开发建设工程、土地开发工程。

在安装工程中，不包括被安装设备本身的价值。

(2)设备、工具、器具购置：指建设单位或企、事业单位购置或自制的，达到固定资产标准的设备、工具、器具的价值。新建单位及扩建单位的新建车间，按照设计或计划要求购置或自制的全部设备、工具、器具，不论是否达到固定资产标准均计入“设备、工具、器具购置”中。

(3)其他费用：指在固定资产建造和购置过程中发生的，除上述几项内容以外的各种应分摊计入固定资产的费用。

**施工项目** 指报告期内进行过建筑或安装施工活动的项目。凡是报告期内施过工的建设项目，不论施工时间长短，均作为施工项目统计。施工项目个数可以反映一定时期固定资产投资的实际规模，与同期全部建成投产项目个数相比，可以从建设速度的角度反映固定资产投资的效果。根据建设项目施工活动的不同性质，施工项目又分为：本年正式施工项目、本年收尾项目和以前年度全部停缓建项目。

**全部建成投产项目** 工业项目指设计文件规定形成生产能力的主体工程及其相应配套的辅助设施全部建成，经负荷试运转，证明具备生产设计规定合格产品的条件，并经过验收鉴定合格或达到竣工验收标准，与生产性工程配套的生活福利设施可以满足近期正常生产的需要，正式移交生产的建设项目。非工业项目指设计文件规定的主体工程和相应的配套工程全部建成，能够发挥设计规定的全部效益，经验收鉴定合格或达到竣工验收标准，正式移交使用的建设项目。

**新增生产能力(或工程效益)** 指通过固定资产投资活动而增加的设计能力(或工程效益)，该指标是以实物形态表现的反映固定资产投资成果的指标，也是考核投资经济效果的重要依据之一。

新增生产能力(或工程效益)一般有以下几种表现形式：

(1)用产品数量表示，以工程在单位时间内(一般是一年)所能生产的产品数量(即年产量)表示。如原煤开采用万吨／年表示，化学农药用吨／年表示，拖拉机制造用台／年表示等。某些化工产品由于含量差别较大，按其设计含量计算折合量表示，如硫酸、纯碱、烧碱等。

(2)用单位时间内所能处理的原料数量表示，以工程每天(或小时)所能处理原料的数量表示。如机制糖工程日处理原料吨，食用植物油日处理原料吨，城市污水处理能力用万吨／日表示等。

(3)用新增加的主要设备的数量或容量表示，如新增棉布织机、丝织机等台数，毛纺锭等锭数，发电厂新增发电机组容量用千瓦表示等。

(4)用建筑物容积、容量、面积、长度表示，是非工业项目或工程新增效益的一种表现形式。如铁路投产里程、新建公路、水库容量、粮食仓库、学校学生席位、医院病床、有效灌溉面积等。

根据工程的特点，有时需要用两种或两种以上的复合计量单位表示新增生产能力(或工程效益)，如新增内燃机生产能力同时用年产台数、千瓦数表示等。

为了规范新增生产能力(或工程效益)的名称和计算单位，国家统计局制订了《新增生产能力(或工程效益)目录及代码》。各固定资产投资单位在统计新增生产能力(或工程效益)时，必须按目录中规定的名称、计量单位和代码填报。

**房屋建筑面积** 指房屋建筑物勒脚以上外墙外围的水平截面面积，包括房屋建筑物的有效面积和结构面积。该指标是从实物形态上反映建设规模和建设成果的重要指标之一，也是检查工程形象进度、计算工程造价、分析投资效果、研究施工任务和建筑材料之间平衡情况的重要依据。

**住宅建筑面积** 指施工和竣工房屋建筑面积中供居住用的房屋建筑面积。

**施工面积** 指报告期内施工的全部房屋建筑面积。包括本期新开工的面积和上期开工跨入本期继续施工的房屋面积，以及上期已停建在本期恢复施工的房屋面积。本期竣工和本期施工后又停缓建的房屋，其建筑面积仍计入本期房屋施工面积中。

**竣工面积** 指在报告期内房屋建筑按照设计要求已经全部完工，达到住人和使用条件，经验收鉴定合格(或达到竣工验收标准)，正式移交使用单位的各栋房屋建筑面积的总和。

**房屋建筑面积竣工率** 指一定时期内房屋竣工面积占同期房屋施工面积的比率。

**新增固定资产** 指报告期内已经完成建造和购置过程，并已交付生产或使用单位的固定资产价值。该指标是表示固定资产投资成果的价值指标，也是反映建设进度，计算固定资产投资效果的重要指标。

**项目建成投产率** 指一定时期内全部建成投产项目个数与同期施工项目个数的比率。该指标是从建设单位建设速度的角度反映投资效果的指标。

**固定资产交付使用率** 指一定时期新增固定资产与同期完成投资额的比率。该指标是反映固定资产动用速度，衡量建设过程中宏观投资效果的综合指标。由于新增固定资产是较长时期内形成的结果，而投资额则是当年完成的，因此，该指标一般适宜于反映较长时期内固定资产的动用情况。

**商品房销售面积** 指报告期内出售商品房屋的合同总面积(即双方签署的正式买卖合同中所确定的建筑面积)。由现房销售建筑面积和期房销售建筑面积两部分组成。

**商品房销售额** 指报告期内出售商品房屋的合同总价款(即双方签署的正式买卖合同中所确定的合同总价)。该指标与商品房销售面积同口径，由现房销售额和期房销售额两部分组成。

# EXPLANATORY NOTES ON MAIN STATISTICAL INDICATORS

**Total Investment in Fixed Assets in the Whole Country** refers to the volume of activities in construction and purchases of fixed assets of the whole country and related fees, expressed in monetary terms during the reference period. It is a comprehensive indicator which shows the size, structure and growth of the investment in fixed assets, providing a basis for observing the progress of construction projects and evaluating results of investment. Total investment in fixed assets in the whole country includes, by type of ownership, the investment by State-owned units, collective-owned units, individuals, joint ownership units, share-holding units, as well as investments by entrepreneurs from foreign countries and from Hong Kong, Macao and Taiwan, and by other units.

**Urban Investment in Fixed Assets** refers to construction projects involving a total planned (or required) investment of 500,000 yuan and over by enterprises of various types of ownership, institutions, administrative units and individuals in urban areas, investment in real estate development, and private investment in housing construction in urban areas and industrial and mining areas. In other words, all investments that take place in county towns and urban areas, investment in construction projects under the direct leadership and management of government agencies at and above county levels and investments by enterprises and institutions at and above county levels are covered in urban investment in fixed assets.

**Investment in Real Estate Development** refers to investment by real estate development companies, commercialized buildings construction companies and other real estate development units of various types of ownership in the construction of buildings, such as residential buildings, factory buildings, warehouses, hotels, guesthouses, holiday villages, office buildings, and the complementary service facilities and land development projects, such as roads, water supply, water drainage, power supply, heating supply, telecommunications, land leveling and other infrastructural projects. It does not include activities in pure land transactions.

**Investment in Rural Areas** refers to investment in fixed assets by enterprises, institutions, administrative units and individuals in rural areas.

**Sources of Funds for Investment in Fixed Assets** are categorized as funds from the State budget, domestic loans, foreign investment, self-raised funds, and others, depending on the sources of investment.

(1) Fund from the State budget consists of budgetary appropriation and loans from the State budget. More specifically, it includes, from the budget of the central government, capital construction fund (operation fund and non-operational fund), special expenses (e.g. expenses on substituting petroleum with coal), loans from repayment, discount fund, expenses on innovation and trial production of new products, expenses on urban construction, expenses on temporary construction from business departments, development fund for less developed areas, as well as local budgetary fund transferred from the central budget.

(2) Domestic loans refer to loans of various forms borrowed by investing units from banks and non-bank financial institutions during the reference period for the purpose of investment in fixed assets, including loans issued by banks from their self-owned funds and deposit, loans appropriated by higher authorities, special loans by government, loans arranged by local government from special funds, domestic reserve loan, and working loan.

(3) Foreign investment refers to foreign funds received during the reference period for the construction and purchase of investment in fixed assets (covering equipment, materials and technology), including foreign borrowings (loans from foreign governments and international financial institutions, export credit, commercial loans from foreign banks, issue of bonds and stocks overseas), foreign direct investment and other foreign investments. Excluded from this category is capital in foreign exchanges owned by China (foreign exchanges owned by the central and local governments, foreign exchanges retained by enterprises, foreign exchanges by enterprises through the regulating mechanism, loans in foreign exchanges issued by the Bank of China with its own fund, etc.). In calculating the utilization of foreign capital, foreign currencies are converted into Chinese Renminbi applying the current exchange rate when the foreign capitals are actually used.

(4) Self-raised funds refer to extra-budgetary funds for investment in fixed assets received during the reference period by investing units from central government ministries, local governments, enterprises and institutions, including their self-raised funds.

(5) Others refer to funds for investment in fixed assets received from sources other than those listed above, including capital raised through issuing bonds by enterprises or financial institutions, funds raised from individuals and through donations, and funds transferred from other units.

**Investment in Fixed Assets by Sector** The classification of construction projects by sector is determined by the major products or the purpose of the projects when they are put into production or use, and by the nature of their social economic activities. In general, one project or one enterprise or institution can only be classified into one sector.

**Investment in Fixed Assets by Jurisdiction of Management** refers to the classification of investment by the competent authorities under which investment is made by construction units, enterprises, institutions or administrative units.

(1) Central investment refers to the investment in projects or by enterprises, institutions or administrative units which are under the direct leadership and management of the State Council and of the national commissions, ministries, agencies and State-owned large corporations. Various ministries and departments of the State Council prepare and implement plans for investment in fixed assets by those departments, and arrange and ensure the supply of materials and key equipment required for the projects.

(2) Local investment refers to the investment in projects or by enterprises, institutions or administrative units which are under the direct leadership and management of departments under the provincial, prefecture and county governments. Also included are projects by foreign-invested enterprises and enterprises without competent managing authorities.

**Investment in Fixed Assets by Type of Construction** Construction projects in general can be classified, by the type of construction, into new construction, expansion, reconstruction and technical transformation, moving and restoration. However, investment by type of construction is not applied to investment by real-estate development units, investment in rural areas and private investment in housing construction in urban areas and in industrial and mining areas.

(1) New construction in general refers to construction projects, which start from scratch, of enterprises, institutions, administrative agencies. Construction in existing enterprises, institutions or agencies is generally not considered as new construction. In case the size of the existing unit is quite small, and the value of newly added fixed assets is more than three times of the original value, the expansion will be considered as new construction.

(2) Expansion refers to construction of new major production workshop, branch factory or independent production line within a factory or in other locations, for the purpose of increasing the production capacity (or improving efficiency) or adding new production capacity. Newly constructed accommodation for the operation of institutions and administrative organizations (such as newly constructed buildings for teaching in schools, buildings for clinics or wards in hospitals, etc.) are also classified as expansion.

Also included in expansion are investments by existing enterprises or institutions in building major production line(s) or branch factory(ies) along with some work on innovation, for the purpose of expanding the production capacity of original products or producing new products.

(3) Reconstruction and technical transformation refers to construction projects by existing enterprises or institutions in innovation or technical transformation of the old facilities (including auxiliary production equipment and welfare facilities). Also considered as reconstruction is the construction of new workshops by the existing enterprises or institutions to change the variety of products to meet the market demand (such as the production of civil products by defence industries), or to bring the designed production capacity into full play through a more balanced production process on production lines. Technical transformation refers to replacement of old technology or equipment by new technology or equipment, in order to expand the reproduction through improvement of technology contents in production, to improve product quality, to promote new products, to save energy, to reduce consumption, to expand the production scale and to improve overall social-economic efficiency. Contents of technical transformation include: updating of machinery, equipment and tools; reforming production process by using energy or materials saving technology; construction of factory workshops and transformation of public facilities; improvement of working conditions and environment, etc.

**Investment in Fixed Assets by Structure** By their contents and the mode of implementation, investment activities are classified into 3 categories, i.e. construction and installation, purchase of equipment and instrument, and other expenses.

(1) Construction and installation (work volume of construction and installation) refers to the construction of houses and buildings and the installation of various kinds of equipment and instruments. They include construction of houses; equipment foundations, industrial kilns and stoves, and metal structure work; preparation works and temporary works for project construction, and clearing up works post project construction; pavement of railways and roads, drilling of mines and putting up of oil pipes; construction of water conservancy; construction of underground air-raid shelters and construction of other special projects; value of equipment for heating, sanitation, ventilation, lighting, gas, painting, etc. that are covered by the budget of housing projects; laying out of various pipelines (for steam, compressed air, petroleum, tap water and sewage) and wiring and cabling for electric power and for communications; installation of various machinery and equipment; testing operation for pre-testing the quality of installation projects, and land and other development work conducted by real estate developers for commercialized housing. The value of equipment installed is itself not included in the value of installation projects.

(2) Purchase of equipment and instruments refers to the total value of equipment, tools, and instruments purchased or self-

produced which come up to the cut-off point for fixed assets by the construction units or investing enterprises or institutions. Equipment, tools and instruments purchased or self-produced for new workshops by newly established or expanded units are categorized as "purchase of equipment and instruments" no matter whether they come up to the cut-off point for fixed assets.

(3) Other expenses refer to expenses arising during the construction or purchase of fixed assets other than those mentioned above.

**Projects under Construction** refer to projects with construction and installation activities undertaken in the reference period. All projects that have construction activities undertaken during the reference period are reported as projects under construction irrespective of the length of construction work. The number of projects under construction can reflect the actual size of investment in fixed assets during a given period, and when compared with the number of projects completed and put into use during the same period, it demonstrates the results of investment in fixed assets from the angle of the speed of the construction. Depending on the nature of construction activities, projects under construction can also be classified into projects beginning construction in current year, winding-up projects in current year and stopped or suspended projects in previous years (with resumption of work in current year).

**Projects Completed and Put into Use** Industrial projects refer to the major projects and anxilliary facilities having been completed in accordance with the design documents, resulting in forming production capacity and having checked and accepted after relevant tests, while the living and welfare facilities having been completed and being capable of ensuring normal production. Non-industrial projects refer to the major projects and anxilliary facilities which have been completed in accordance with the design documents ; have been checked, accepted after relevant examination; and have been formally delivered for use.

**Newly Increased Production Capacity (or Project Efficiency)** refers to the increase in design capacity (or project efficiency) through investment in fixed assets, which reflects the accomplishment of investment in fixed assets in physical form and serves as an important basis for evaluating the economic efficiency of investment.

The newly increased production capacity (project efficiency) are usually expressed in one of the following forms:

(1) volume of output of products, i.e. the volume of output that the project can produce during a given period (usually a year). For instance, the capacity in coal mining is expressed in 10,000 tons/year, the capacity in producing chemical pesticides expressed in ton/year, the capacity in producing tractors in tractor/year, etc. For some chemical products where the effective contents differ significantly, the production capacity is expressed as the designed effective content equivalent, such as in the case of sulphuric acid, soda ash, caustic soda, etc;

(2) volume of raw materials processed per unit of time, i.e. the volume of raw materials that could be processed by the project per day (or per hour), such as tons of materials processed per day by a sugar refining project or edible vegetable oil project, or tons of urban sewage processed per day;

(3) number or capacity of major equipment increased, such as number of cotton or silk looms increased, wool spindles increased, or capacity (in kilowatts) of power generators increased; and

(4) physical measures (volume, capacity, area, and length) of construction, which is typical for non-industrial projects, for instance, the length of railways put into operation, the length of highways, the capacity of reservoirs, the capacity of warehouses, the floor space of housing projects, capacity for new students in schools or beds in hospitals, areas under new irrigation project, etc.

The special features of projects may sometimes call for the combined use of two or more measurements to reflect the increase in production capacity (or project efficiency); for instance, the new capacity for the production of internal combustion engines is expressed in sets per year and kilowatts per year simultaneously.

To standardize the nomenclature and unit of measurement for newly increased production capacity (or project efficiency), the National Bureau of Statistics has developed the *Nomenclature and Codes for New Production Capacity (Project Efficiency)*. All reporting units with investment activities are required to follow these two nomenclatures in reporting statistics on new production capacity (project efficiency).

**Floor Space of Buildings under Construction** refers to the total floor space of the horizontal section of outer walls above the plinth of the building, including the effective area and the area occupied by the structure. This indicator is one of the important indicators in physical terms to reflect the scale and accomplishment of the construction industry and also an important basis for monitoring the progress, calculating the cost, analyzing the efficiency and studying the supply of building materials in relation to the construction projects.

**Floor Space of Residential Buildings** refers to the floor space of the residential buildings among the total space of buildings under construction or completed.

**Floor Space under Construction** refers to total floor space of all buildings under construction during the reference period, including floor space of newly started buildings during the reference period, floor space of construction extended from the previous period to the current period, and floor space of construction suspended during the previous period and resumed in the current period. Floor space of construction completed in the current period, and floor space of construction started and then suspended in the current period are also included in the floor space under construction of the current year.

**Floor Space Completed** refers to the floor space of all buildings completed in the reference period, which have been appraised and accepted (or come up to the designed standards) and have been transferred to owner units.

**Completion Rate of Floor Space of Buildings** refers to the ratio of the floor space of buildings completed in a certain period of time to the floor space of buildings under construction in the same period.

**Newly Increased Fixed Assets** refer to the newly increased value of fixed assets, constructed or purchased, that have been transferred to the investors. This is an indicator that demonstrates the results of investment in fixed assets in monetary terms, and an important indicator to reflect the speed of construction and to calculate the efficiency of investment.

**Rate of Construction Projects Completed and Put into Use** refers to the ratio of the number of construction projects completed and put into use in a certain period of time to the number of projects under construction in the same period. This reflects the investment efficiency from the perspective of the speed of projects construction.

**Rate of Projects of Fixed Assets Completed and Put into Operation** refers to the ratio of the newly increased fixed assets to the total investment made in the same period. This is a comprehensive indicator reflecting the speed of the employment of fixed assets and the investment efficiency at the macro-level. As the newly increase fixed assets is the result of a long period while the investment is completed in the current year, this indicator is expected to be used to reflect the employment of fixed assets over a long period of time.

**Area of Commercialized Housing Sold** refers to total contracted area of commercialized housing (i.e. area of floor space as designated in the formal contracts signed by both sides) during the reference time. It constitutes floor space of completed housing and floor space of future housing.

**Value of Commercialized Housing Sold** refers to the total contracted value (i.e. value of sales/purchase for selling/purchase of commercialized housing as designated in the contract signed by both sides) during the reference time. This indicator has the same coverage as the area of commercialized housing sold, which constitutes floor space of completed housing and floor space of housing yet to be completed.

# 十一、企业调查

# CHAPTER 11
# ENTERPRISES SURVEY

# 企业调查
# ENTERPRISES SURVEY

## 主要统计指标
## MAJOR STATISTICAL INDICATORS

| | | | | |
|---|---|---|---|---|
| 2012年苏州市重点企业（集团）个数 | Number of Key Enterprises Groups | 85 | 个 | unit |
| 2012年苏州市重点企业（集团）营业收入 | Revenue of Key Enterprises Groups | 7 240.79 | 亿元 | 100 million yuan |
| 2012年苏州市重点企业（集团）利润总额 | Total Profits of Key Enterprises Groups | 220.05 | 亿元 | 100 million yuan |
| 2012年苏州上市公司个数 | The Number of Suzhou Listing Corporation | 82 | 个 | unit |
| 2012年苏州上市公司营业收入 | Business Income of Suzhou Listing Corporation | 1 562.57 | 亿元 | 100 million yuan |
| 2012年苏州上市公司利润总额 | Total Profits of Suzhou Listing Corporation | 111.56 | 亿元 | 100 million yuan |
| 2012年苏州总部企业个数 | The Number of Suzhou Corporate Headquarters | 45 | 个 | unit |
| 2012年苏州总部企业营业收入 | The Business Income of Suzhou Corporate Headquarters | 5 089.81 | 亿元 | 100 million yuan |
| 2012年苏州总部企业利润总额 | Total Profits of Suzhou Corporate Headquarters | 197.67 | 亿元 | 100 million yuan |

表11-1

# 重点企业（集团）主要经济指标 (2012年)

单位：万元

| 项　目 | Item | 单位数(个) Number of Units (unit) | 从业人员(人) Number of Employed Persons (person) |
|---|---|---|---|
| **企业集团** | **Enterprises Groups** | **85** | **430 502** |
| **按母公司控股情况分** | **Classified by Number Shares Held by Parent Companies** | | |
| 国有控股 | Stately Majority Share Holding | 16 | 58 521 |
| 集体控股 | Collectively Majority Share Holding | 8 | 21 077 |
| 私人控股 | Privately Majority Share Holding | 60 | 350 010 |
| 港澳台商控股 | Majority Share Holding by Investors from Hong Kong, Macau and Taiwan | 1 | 894 |
| 外商控股 | Majority Share Holding by Foreign Investors | – | – |
| **按企业集团主营行业分** | **Classified by Main Field of Operation** | | |
| 工　业 | Industry | 56 | 287 599 |
| 建筑业 | Construction | 5 | 91 996 |
| 交通运输、仓储和邮政业 | Transportation,Logistics and Postal | 2 | 12 505 |
| 批发零售贸易业 | Wholesale and Retail Sale Trades | 11 | 20 018 |
| 房地产业 | Real Estate | 7 | 16 358 |
| 其　他 | Others | 4 | 2 026 |
| **附：上市公司** | **Public Enlisted Company** | **82** | **173 196** |
| **总部企业** | **Corporate Headquarters** | **45** | **246 694** |

注：上市公司数据中不包含停牌公司数据。

# MAIN ECONOMIC INDICATORS ON KEY ENTERPRISES GROUPS (2012)

(10 000 yuan)

| 研发人员(人) Research and Development Personnel (person) | 从业人员劳动报酬 Labor Reward of Employed Persons | 研发人员劳动报酬 Labor Reward of Research and Development Personnel | 固定资产投资完成额 Actually Completed Investment in Fixed Assets | 年末资产总计 Total Assets at the End of Year | 固定资产净值 Net Value of Fixed Assets |
|---|---|---|---|---|---|
| **19 670** | **2 226 698** | **152 454** | **2 595 470** | **68 226 446** | **14 568 414** |
| | | | | | |
| 2 552 | 364 297 | 22 010 | 633 428 | 17 471 621 | 1 833 924 |
| 386 | 111 544 | 2 453 | 88 762 | 2 027 713 | 386 510 |
| 16 732 | 1 747 594 | 127 991 | 1 873 280 | 48 652 240 | 12 338 843 |
| – | 3 263 | – | – | 74 872 | 9 137 |
| – | – | – | – | – | – |
| | | | | | |
| 17 680 | 1 323 663 | 131 342 | 1 881 568 | 46 132 569 | 12 406 611 |
| 1 858 | 570 838 | 20 091 | 59 360 | 2 691 436 | 176 271 |
| – | 88 800 | – | 50 671 | 834 355 | 281 621 |
| 65 | 124 990 | 624 | 21 552 | 7 663 640 | 659 498 |
| 62 | 101 953 | 372 | 570 505 | 9 389 725 | 804 882 |
| 5 | 16 454 | 25 | 11 814 | 1 514 721 | 239 531 |
| **17 229** | **983 340** | **91 400** | **848 530** | **22 434 575** | **4 114 173** |
| **16 262** | **1 472 658** | **104 943** | **1 587 682** | **64 327 270** | **10 377 782** |

Note: The date of public enlisted company does not include companies of which trading has been suspended.

表11-1 续表 1

单位：万元

| 项　　目 | Item | 累计折旧 Accumulated Depreciation | 本年折旧 Depreciation Charge of the Year |
|---|---|---|---|
| **企业集团** | **Enterprises Groups** | **8 600 278** | **1 364 848** |
| **按母公司控股情况分** | **Classified by Number Shares Held by Parent Companies** | | |
| 国有控股 | Stately Majority Share Holding | 985 200 | 124 845 |
| 集体控股 | Collectively Majority Share Holding | 306 937 | 40 280 |
| 私人控股 | Privately Majority Share Holding | 7 299 424 | 1 197 969 |
| 港澳台商控股 | Majority Share Holding by Investors from Hong Kong, Macau and Taiwan | 8 717 | 1 754 |
| 外商控股 | Majority Share Holding by Foreign Investors | – | – |
| **按企业集团主营行业分** | **Classified by Main Field of Operation** | | |
| 工　业 | Industry | 7 691 502 | 1 228 325 |
| 建筑业 | Construction | 79 696 | 12 610 |
| 交通运输、仓储和邮政业 | Transportation, Logistics and Postal | 194 806 | 20 842 |
| 批发零售贸易业 | Wholesale and Retail Sale Trades | 230 706 | 44 113 |
| 房地产业 | Real Estate | 266 389 | 47 880 |
| 其　他 | Others | 137 179 | 11 078 |
| **附：上市公司** | **Public Enlisted Company** | **1 989 844** | **382 174** |
| **总部企业** | **Corporate Headquarters** | **5 863 982** | **1 020 337** |

Continued 1

(10 000 yuan)

| 累计对外投资 Accumulated Value of Investing Abroad | # 本年对外投资 Value of Investing Abroad of the Year | 存货 Inventory | 流动资产年平均余额 Annual Average Balance of Circulation Funds | 年末负债合计 Total Liabilities at the End of Year | 流动负债 Liquid Liabilities | 年末股东(所有者)权益合计 Total Creditors Equity |
|---|---|---|---|---|---|---|
| **5 160 399** | **1 113 994** | **11 887 240** | **39 331 790** | **45 828 987** | **36 193 087** | **22 397 459** |
| 1 150 212 | 137 900 | 4 050 235 | 10 921 168 | 12 371 108 | 8 105 004 | 5 100 513 |
| 203 400 | 79 542 | 288 236 | 1 094 489 | 1 334 375 | 1 229 812 | 693 338 |
| 3 789 631 | 896 552 | 7 534 703 | 27 254 949 | 32 063 889 | 26 798 656 | 16 588 351 |
| 17 156 | – | 14 066 | 61 184 | 59 615 | 59 615 | 15 257 |
| – | – | – | – | – | – | – |
| | | | | | | |
| 3 700 296 | 911 237 | 6 972 141 | 25 121 376 | 29 996 670 | 25 263 525 | 16 135 899 |
| 41 743 | 8 800 | 192 958 | 2 046 945 | 1 887 055 | 1 664 292 | 804 381 |
| 209 230 | 51 754 | 3 482 | 49 791 | 397 536 | 292 248 | 436 819 |
| 342 402 | 62 248 | 1 133 668 | 5 415 041 | 5 875 413 | 5 343 265 | 1 788 227 |
| 807 796 | 65 879 | 3 469 564 | 5 940 636 | 6 886 903 | 2 945 055 | 2 502 822 |
| 58 932 | 14 076 | 115 427 | 758 001 | 785 410 | 684 702 | 729 311 |
| **1 054 262** | **414 633** | **3 953 077** | **13 423 834** | **11 722 407** | **10 257 805** | **10 712 168** |
| **3 131 745** | **852 359** | **5 931 281** | **33 463 518** | **47 379 575** | **33 969 777** | **16 947 695** |

表11-1 续表 2

单位：万元

| 项 目 | Item | 营业收入 Business Revenue | # 营业成本 Business costs |
|---|---|---|---|
| **企业集团** | **Enterprises Groups** | **72 407 890** | **66 626 162** |
| **按母公司控股情况分** | **Classified by Number Shares Held by Parent Company** | | |
| 国有控股 | Stately Majority Share Holding | 10 038 416 | 8 668 297 |
| 集体控股 | Collectively Majority Share Holding | 1 882 363 | 1 678 953 |
| 私人控股 | Privately Majority Share Holding | 60 254 898 | 56 060 729 |
| 港澳台商控股 | Majority Share Holding by Investors from Hong Kong, Macau and Taiwan | 232 213 | 218 183 |
| 外商控股 | Majority Share Holding by Foreign Investors | – | – |
| **按企业集团主营行业分** | **Classified by Main Field of Operation** | | |
| 工 业 | Industry | 57 329 173 | 53 190 313 |
| 建筑业 | Construction | 3 481 828 | 2 990 214 |
| 交通运输、仓储和邮政业 | Transportation, Logistics and Postal | 422 798 | 317 642 |
| 批发零售贸易业 | Wholesale and Retail Sale Trades | 8 274 582 | 7 945 170 |
| 房地产业 | Real Estate | 2 303 724 | 1 695 129 |
| 其 他 | Others | 595 785 | 487 694 |
| **附：上市公司** | **Public Enlisted Company** | **15 625 693** | **12 966 422** |
| **总部企业** | **Corporate Headquarters** | **50 898 099** | **46 490 753** |

Continued 2

(10 000 yuan)

| # 营业税金及附加 Business tax and surcharges | 出口额 Value of Exports | 利润总额 Total Profits | 应交所得税 Income Taxes Payable | 应交增值税 Added Value Tax Payable | 研究开发费用 Expenditure for Research and Development |
|---|---|---|---|---|---|
| **529 510** | **6 874 103** | **2 200 510** | **512 381** | **931 623** | **976 202** |
| | | | | | |
| 223 763 | 2 773 886 | 501 839 | 124 736 | 98 642 | 77 813 |
| 34 907 | 119 754 | 82 277 | 17 617 | 10 917 | 15 506 |
| 270 639 | 3 980 463 | 1 613 503 | 369 863 | 820 874 | 882 883 |
| 201 | – | 2 891 | 165 | 1 190 | |
| – | – | – | – | – | – |
| | | | | | |
| 158 448 | 4 578 111 | 1 390 665 | 326 431 | 837 085 | 923 445 |
| 113 496 | 7 539 | 202 116 | 37 343 | 5 515 | 50 132 |
| 10 021 | – | 70 640 | 15 643 | 3 206 | – |
| 72 927 | 2 285 253 | 209 378 | 51 674 | 74 271 | 2 200 |
| 166 488 | 3 200 | 253 782 | 70 612 | 4 984 | 125 |
| 8 130 | – | 73 929 | 10 678 | 6 562 | 300 |
| **136 858** | **3 381 366** | **1 115 624** | **176 012** | **222 126** | **377 326** |
| **313 730** | **4 367 285** | **1 976 702** | **343 669** | **568 461** | **766 910** |

表11-2

# 部分重点企业(集团)名单 (2012年)
# THE LIST OF KEY ENTERPRISES GROUPS OF PARTIAL (2012)

| 企业名称<br>Name of Enterprises | 所在地区<br>Location | 企业名称<br>Name of Enterprises | 所在地区<br>Location |
|---|---|---|---|
| 江苏沙钢集团有限公司* | 张家港 | 长江润发集团有限公司 | 张家港 |
| 盛虹控股集团有限公司 | 市　区 | 雅鹿集团股份有限公司 | 太　仓 |
| 恒力集团有限公司 | 市　区 | 江苏通润机电集团有限公司 | 常　熟 |
| 江苏国泰国际集团有限公司 | 张家港 | 江苏新民纺织科技股份有限公司 | 市　区 |
| 亨通集团有限公司 | 市　区 | 苏州高新区经济发展集团总公司 | 市　区 |
| 华芳集团有限公司 | 张家港 | 苏州汽车客运集团有限公司 | 市　区 |
| 波司登股份有限公司 | 常　熟 | 苏州市苏创集团有限公司 | 太　仓 |
| 苏州创元投资发展（集团）有限公司 | 市　区 | 吴江赴东纺织集团有限公司 | 市　区 |
| 江苏丰立集团有限公司 | 张家港 | 江苏苏净集团有限公司 | 市　区 |
| 澳洋集团有限公司 | 张家港 | 苏州华成集团有限公司 | 市　区 |
| 通鼎集团有限公司 | 市　区 | 苏州工业园区建屋发展集团有限公司 | 市　区 |
| 苏州金螳螂企业（集团）有限公司 | 市　区 | 震雄铜业集团有限公司 | 昆　山 |
| 永鼎集团有限公司 | 市　区 | 江苏沙印集团有限公司 | 张家港 |
| 苏州市相城区江南化纤集团有限公司 | 市　区 | 苏州函数集团有限责任公司 | 市　区 |
| 苏州二建建筑集团有限公司 | 市　区 | 江苏东渡纺织集团有限公司 | 张家港 |
| 苏州进出口（集团）有限公司 | 市　区 | 江苏白雪电器股份有限公司 | 常　熟 |
| 江苏吴中集团有限公司 | 市　区 | 江苏万宝铜业集团有限公司 | 市　区 |
| 江苏华尔润集团有限公司 | 张家港 | 江苏江南商贸集团有限责任公司 | 常　熟 |
| 江苏骏马集团有限责任公司 | 张家港 | 江苏鹿港科技股份有限公司 | 张家港 |
| 江苏天铭集团有限公司 | 常　熟 | 苏州市宏达集团有限公司 | 太　仓 |
| 江苏隆力奇集团有限公司 | 常　熟 | 苏州燃气集团有限责任公司 | 市　区 |
| 江苏华昌（集团）有限公司 | 张家港 | 江苏AB集团股份有限公司 | 昆　山 |
| 中利科技集团股份有限公司 | 常　熟 | 苏州宝利来粮油集团有限公司 | 太　仓 |
| 江苏苏钢集团有限公司 | 市　区 | 江苏盛氏国际投资集团有限公司 | 市　区 |
| 江苏梦兰集团有限公司 | 常　熟 | 中新苏州工业园区市政公用发展集团有限公司 | 市　区 |
| 中新苏州工业园区开发集团股份有限公司 | 市　区 | 宏宝集团有限公司 | 张家港 |
| 香塘集团有限公司 | 太　仓 | 江苏梁丰食品集团有限公司 | 张家港 |
| 苏州第一建筑集团有限公司 | 市　区 | 江苏华机集团（江苏华机环保设备有限责任公司） | 张家港 |
| 苏州国信集团有限公司 | 太　仓 | 江苏东盾木业集团有限公司 | 常　熟 |
| 江苏苏化集团有限公司 | 市　区 | 江苏常盛集团有限公司 | 常　熟 |
| 江苏金土木建设集团 | 常　熟 | 张家港港务集团有限公司 | 张家港 |
| 攀华集团有限公司 | 张家港 | 江苏长顺集团有限公司 | 张家港 |
| 鹰翔集团公司 | 市　区 | 江苏新芳科技集团股份有限公司 | 张家港 |
| 江苏旋力集团股份有限公司 | 常　熟 | 江苏五洋集团有限公司 | 太　仓 |

注：带“*”为国家重点企业(集团)。 Note:“*” is the key state enterprise (group).

表11-3

# 制造业采购经理指数（2012年）
# THE MANUFACTURING PURCHASING MANAGERS INDEX (2012)

| 月 份 | 制造业采购经理指数 The Manufacturing Purchasing Managers Index | 分项指数 Partial Index | | | | |
|---|---|---|---|---|---|---|
| | | 生产指数 The Production Index | 新订单指数 The New Orders Index | 原材料库存指数 Raw Materials Inventory Index | 从业人员指数 Practitioners Index | 供应商配送时间指数 The Supplier Delivery Time Index |
| 3 | 55.98 | 60.26 | 60.46 | 50.54 | 53.08 | 47.37 |
| 4 | 52.41 | 55.02 | 53.09 | 48.96 | 51.99 | 49.56 |
| 5 | 50.03 | 54.34 | 49.50 | 46.76 | 49.85 | 46.25 |
| 6 | 45.36 | 44.26 | 42.58 | 41.51 | 50.47 | 48.50 |
| 7 | 47.55 | 48.96 | 46.16 | 44.84 | 48.25 | 48.85 |
| 8 | 49.70 | 52.95 | 49.84 | 45.56 | 48.63 | 48.11 |
| 9 | 50.82 | 54.85 | 50.40 | 47.81 | 49.80 | 48.29 |
| 10 | 49.74 | 51.21 | 48.96 | 48.40 | 49.86 | 50.28 |
| 11 | 48.83 | 49.44 | 48.21 | 46.01 | 48.96 | 50.80 |
| 12 | 50.52 | 51.47 | 52.26 | 46.30 | 48.25 | 51.34 |

表11-4

# 非制造业采购经理指数（2012年）
# NON THE MANUFACTURING PURCHASING MANAGERS INDEX (2012)

| 月 份 | 非制造业采购经理指数 Non Manufacturing Purchasing Managers Index | 分项指数 Partial Index | | | |
|---|---|---|---|---|---|
| | | 业务总量指数 The Total Business Index | 新订单指数 The New Orders Index | 从业人员指数 Practitioners Index | 供应商配送时间指数 The Supplier Delivery Time Index |
| 3 | 51.77 | 53.51 | 51.61 | 50.48 | 50.39 |
| 4 | 52.55 | 55.96 | 52.11 | 50.57 | 49.39 |
| 5 | 50.20 | 52.67 | 48.72 | 52.12 | 46.19 |
| 6 | 49.69 | 51.29 | 46.65 | 53.78 | 48.16 |
| 7 | 48.03 | 47.20 | 46.64 | 51.92 | 47.77 |
| 8 | 48.18 | 49.50 | 45.00 | 50.60 | 49.70 |
| 9 | 52.28 | 54.49 | 51.88 | 51.86 | 49.30 |
| 10 | 52.89 | 56.07 | 52.57 | 52.67 | 47.55 |
| 11 | 50.73 | 52.85 | 49.35 | 52.87 | 46.89 |
| 12 | 52.08 | 51.19 | 51.61 | 52.53 | 46.64 |

注：采购经理指数从2012年3月起编制。
Note: The Purchasing Managers Index formulated from 2012 March.

# 主 要 统 计 指 标 解 释

**企业集团** 是指以母子公司为主体，通过投资及生产经营协作等多种方式，与众多的企事业单位共同组成的经济联合体。企业集团的统计范围包括：一是由国务院批准的国家试点企业集团；二是国家重点企业 (包括 520 户国家重点企业、重组为集团公司的原 512 户国家重点企业和国务院确定的建立现代企业制度原百户试点企业)；三是由国务院及国务院主管部门批准的企业集团；四是由省政府及省级主管部门批准的企业集团；五是列入全省产业经济结构调整规划的市重点企业集团；六是年营业收入和资产总计均在 5 亿元以上的其他各类企业 (集团)。上述企业集团中交叉重复的只报一套报表。企业集团内部的统计范围包括：企业集团的母公司、在中国境内和境外的全资子公司 (单位)、绝对控股子公司 (单位) 和相对控股子公司 (单位)。

**上市公司** 其统计范围是在境内外证券交易所上市的，在苏州注册的上市企业。

**总部企业** 其统计范围是苏府[2013]8号文件认定的总部企业。

**采购经理指数**（简称PMI） 是宏观经济先行监测指标，是经济景气监测的重要指标和反映经济增长和衰退的晴雨表。PMI指数体系无论对于政府部门、金融机构、投资公司，还是企业来说，在经济预测和商业分析方面都有重要的意义。是政府部门调控、金融机构与投资公司决策的重要依据。也是企业及时判断行业供应及整体走势，更好地进行决策的依据。PMI是一个综合指数，由5个扩散指数（分类指数）加权计算而成。5个分类指数及其权数是依据其对经济的先行影响程度确定的。具体包括：（1）新订单指数；（2）生产量指数；（3）从业人员指数；（4）供应商配送时间指数；（5）原材料库存指数。PMI是国际上通行的宏观经济监测指标体系之一，通常以50%作为经济强弱的分界点，PMI高于50%时，反映经济扩张；低于50%，则反映经济衰退。

# EXPLANATORY NOTES ON MAIN STATISTICAL INDICATORS

**Enterprise Group** refers to the economic entities joined together with the parent company and its branch companies as the main body, incorporating various economic entities through investment, joint production. The group enterprises can be categorized into following: first is the enterprise groups designated as country's experimental units approved by the State Council; Second is the country's key enterprises (including the 520 key enterprises, the 512 key enterprises and enterprises designated by the State Council as modern management experiment units which now have been transformed into enterprise groups); The third is the enterprise groups approved by the State Council or relevant ministries of the State Council; the forth is the enterprise groups approved by the provincial government or relevant ministries of the provincial government; The fifth is the key enterprises groups which have been included in the provincial economic restructuring plan ; the sixty is the enterprises with annual sales exceeding 500 million yuan. The classification of the enterprise groups can also be set in the following method: the headquarters, wholly owned branch companies both in and outside China, wholly controlled companies and partly owned companies, no including the companies of business partners and share holding companies.

**Public Enlisted Company** the statistics include those enterprises registered in Suzhou and enlisted in domestic and overseas.

**Corporate headquarters** Its statistical range is the corporate headquarters recognized by Suzhou Government [2013] Document No. 8.

**Purchasing Managers Index** (PMI for short) is the first monitoring indicators of the macro-economy, an important indicator of economic monitoring and a barometer reflecting economic growth and decline. The PMI index system is of important significance both for government departments, financial institutions, investment companies, and for enterprises, in terms of economic forecasts and business analysis. It is an important basis for the regulation of government departments, and for the decision-making of financial institutions and investment companies. It is also a basis for enterprises to make timely judgment of the industry supply and the overall trend, and to make better decisions. PMI is a composite index comprised of five diffusion indices (sub-indices) weighted together. The five sub-indices and their weights are based on their first identified impact on the economy. These include: (1) the new orders index; (2) production index; (3) employment index; (4) supplier delivery time index; (5) raw materials inventory index. PMI is one of the systems of macro-economic monitoring indicators internationally accepted, usually with 50% as the cut-off point of an economic strength, PMI above 50%, reflecting the economic expansion; less than 50%, reflecting the recession.

# 十二、财政 金融 保险

# CHAPTER 12
# FINANCE, BANKING AND INSURANCE

# 财政 金融 保险
# FINANCE，BANKING AND INSURANCE

## 主 要 统 计 指 标
## MAJOR STATISTICAL INDICATORS

| | | | | |
|---|---|---|---|---|
| 2012年地方公共财政预算收入 | General Budgetary Revenue | 1 204.33 | 亿元 | 100 million yuan |
| 比上年增长 | Increase Over Last Year | 9.4 | % | |
| 2012年地方公共财政预算支出 | General Budgetary Expenditure | 1 113.47 | 亿元 | 100 million yuan |
| 比上年增长 | Increase Over Last Year | 11.1 | % | |
| 2012年末金融机构人民币存款余额 | Deposits of National Banking System at Year-end | 17 663.50 | 亿元 | 100 million yuan |
| 比上年末增长 | Increase Over Last Year | 16.4 | % | |
| # 城乡居民储蓄存款余额 | Urban and Rural Savings Balance at Year-end | 5 787.75 | 亿元 | 100 million yuan |
| 比上年末增长 | Increase Over Last Year | 14.0 | % | |
| 2012年末金融机构人民币贷款余额 | Balance of Loans of National Banking System at year-end | 13 626.86 | 亿元 | 100 million yuan |
| 比上年末增长 | Increase Over Last Year | 14.8 | % | |

表12-1

# 历年财政收入
# FINANCIAL REVENUE OVER THE YEARS

单位：万元 (10 000 yuan)

| 年份<br>Year | 全市<br>Whole Municipality | 市区<br>Urban Area | #吴江区<br>Wujiang District | 常熟<br>Changshu | 张家港<br>Zhangjiagang | 昆山<br>Kunshan | 太仓<br>Taicang |
|---|---|---|---|---|---|---|---|
| 1952 | 11 251 | 6 106 | 1 421 | 1 930 | 765 | 1 209 | 1 241 |
| 1957 | 17 138 | 9 966 | 1 636 | 3 104 | 1 027 | 1 367 | 1 674 |
| 1962 | 16 563 | 11 668 | 1 670 | 1 959 | 729 | 1 034 | 1 173 |
| 1965 | 27 813 | 19 879 | 1 854 | 3 399 | 1 404 | 1 636 | 1 495 |
| 1970 | 41 165 | 31 014 | 2 269 | 4 325 | 1 628 | 2 149 | 2 049 |
| 1975 | 65 520 | 49 938 | 3 824 | 6 687 | 3 258 | 2 654 | 2 983 |
| 1978 | 82 766 | 62 001 | 5 111 | 9 194 | 4 450 | 3 460 | 3 661 |
| 1980 | 94 589 | 67 815 | 6 442 | 11 557 | 5 789 | 3 556 | 5 872 |
| 1985 | 159 096 | 97 221 | 13 584 | 25 537 | 16 713 | 8 384 | 11 241 |
| 1990 | 214 680 | 126 502 | 18 986 | 36 318 | 24 951 | 13 203 | 13 706 |
| 1995 | 538 593 | 279 951 | 49 787 | 98 009 | 73 734 | 51 115 | 35 784 |
| 1996 | 640 757 | 326 326 | 57 334 | 115 312 | 95 003 | 60 160 | 43 956 |
| 1997 | 765 384 | 387 414 | 68 093 | 138 426 | 115 227 | 73 734 | 50 583 |
| 1998 | 876 327 | 440 359 | 73 743 | 159 545 | 130 249 | 86 128 | 60 046 |
| 1999 | 1 093 804 | 557 107 | 81 264 | 186 523 | 150 258 | 127 172 | 72 744 |
| 2000 | 1 582 711 | 833 883 | 106 646 | 243 622 | 205 188 | 201 301 | 98 717 |
| 2001 | 2 089 492 | 1 069 290 | 152 901 | 304 622 | 320 800 | 273 562 | 121 218 |
| 2002 | 2 908 234 | 1 490 171 | 223 888 | 410 202 | 430 845 | 415 188 | 161 828 |
| 2003 | 4 099 267 | 2 055 731 | 328 818 | 556 785 | 627 867 | 642 696 | 216 188 |
| 2004 | 5 851 358 | 2 982 783 | 511 746 | 800 228 | 892 464 | 858 288 | 317 595 |
| 2005 | 7 181 043 | 3 594 932 | 585 761 | 882 272 | 1 083 838 | 1 168 196 | 451 805 |
| 2006 | 9 180 988 | 4 671 269 | 827 594 | 1 017 168 | 1 368 866 | 1 513 797 | 609 888 |
| 2007 | 12 177 211 | 6 152 990 | 1 105 026 | 1 259 335 | 1 945 775 | 2 018 523 | 800 588 |
| 2008 | 14 575 825 | 7 290 004 | 1 360 000 | 1 449 914 | 2 334 586 | 2 472 075 | 1 029 246 |
| 2009 | 15 933 881 | 7 999 765 | 1 680 152 | 1 611 302 | 2 336 753 | 2 821 062 | 1 164 999 |
| 2010 | 19 506 250 | 9 564 134 | 1 988 296 | 2 076 075 | 2 665 601 | 3 806 191 | 1 394 249 |
| 2011 | 23 116 177 | 11 445 413 | 2 372 558 | 2 503 456 | 3 173 383 | 4 244 896 | 1 749 029 |
| 2012 | 25 616 731 | 13 130 082 | 2 698 828 | 2 651 427 | 3 241 958 | 4 636 206 | 1 957 058 |

注：财政收入中不含土地类基金。 Note: Financial revenue excluding land class funds.

表12-2

# 历年财政支出
# FINANCIAL EXPENDITURE OVER THE YEARS

单位：万元 (10 000 yuan)

| 年 份<br>Year | 全 市<br>Whole Municipality | 市 区<br>Urban Area | # 吴江区<br>Wujiang District | 常 熟<br>Changshu | 张家港<br>Zhangjiagang | 昆 山<br>Kunshan | 太 仓<br>Taicang |
|---|---|---|---|---|---|---|---|
| 1952 | 1 046 | 551 | 110 | 241 | 85 | 84 | 85 |
| 1957 | 3 716 | 2 436 | 268 | 597 | 240 | 206 | 237 |
| 1962 | 3 114 | 1 857 | 344 | 472 | 298 | 248 | 239 |
| 1965 | 4 217 | 2 713 | 337 | 546 | 349 | 327 | 282 |
| 1970 | 5 652 | 3 494 | 499 | 686 | 575 | 497 | 400 |
| 1975 | 9 145 | 5 609 | 932 | 1 216 | 817 | 840 | 663 |
| 1978 | 13 547 | 8 737 | 1 290 | 1 573 | 1 197 | 1 072 | 968 |
| 1980 | 16 735 | 10 819 | 1 353 | 2 107 | 1 384 | 1 178 | 1 247 |
| 1985 | 40 495 | 23 874 | 3 941 | 5 984 | 4 697 | 2 895 | 3 045 |
| 1990 | 79 935 | 46 049 | 6 965 | 13 612 | 7 450 | 7 465 | 5 359 |
| 1995 | 247 333 | 129 417 | 21 096 | 42 195 | 35 238 | 26 941 | 13 542 |
| 1996 | 315 448 | 162 435 | 24 415 | 53 210 | 47 272 | 32 506 | 20 025 |
| 1997 | 393 869 | 209 549 | 28 111 | 64 492 | 57 210 | 40 036 | 22 582 |
| 1998 | 463 983 | 250 919 | 34 555 | 75 710 | 63 863 | 44 949 | 28 542 |
| 1999 | 571 415 | 309 081 | 41 040 | 88 058 | 75 918 | 61 232 | 37 126 |
| 2000 | 799 092 | 445 210 | 53 973 | 112 178 | 101 957 | 92 028 | 47 719 |
| 2001 | 1 137 936 | 617 789 | 75 501 | 158 178 | 178 492 | 125 668 | 57 809 |
| 2002 | 1 585 494 | 858 574 | 119 282 | 222 005 | 224 959 | 196 736 | 83 220 |
| 2003 | 2 321 003 | 1 236 312 | 170 532 | 284 839 | 342 600 | 342 366 | 114 886 |
| 2004 | 2 948 045 | 1 518 476 | 232 270 | 463 078 | 417 782 | 386 915 | 161 794 |
| 2005 | 4 098 596 | 2 179 226 | 300 925 | 559 251 | 545 977 | 567 256 | 246 886 |
| 2006 | 4 868 722 | 2 599 693 | 392 220 | 562 639 | 650 922 | 747 909 | 307 559 |
| 2007 | 6 106 391 | 3 153 268 | 523 669 | 650 083 | 962 482 | 958 123 | 382 435 |
| 2008 | 7 732 756 | 4 017 169 | 670 001 | 814 542 | 1 088 361 | 1 215 399 | 597 286 |
| 2009 | 8 570 438 | 4 502 427 | 959 441 | 833 603 | 1 280 797 | 1 361 232 | 592 379 |
| 2010 | 10 957 462 | 5 306 909 | 1 142 832 | 1 246 422 | 1 569 294 | 2 113 446 | 721 391 |
| 2011 | 12 848 077 | 6 370 115 | 1 400 303 | 1 502 618 | 1 685 041 | 2 311 790 | 978 513 |
| 2012 | 14 795 934 | 7 560 218 | 1 614 201 | 1 695 190 | 1 841 592 | 2 571 453 | 1 127 481 |

注：财政支出中不含土地类基金。 Note: Financial expenditure excluding land class funds.

表12-3

# 历年地方公共财政预算收入
# PUBLIC FINANCE BUDGETARY REVENUE OVER THE YEARS

单位：万元 (10 000 yuan)

| 年 份 Year | 全 市 Whole Municipality | 市 区 Urban Area | # 吴江区 Wujiang District | 常 熟 Changshu | 张家港 Zhangjiagang | 昆 山 Kunshan | 太 仓 Taicang |
|---|---|---|---|---|---|---|---|
| 1998 | 450 672 | 235 316 | 34 966 | 77 365 | 64 941 | 43 437 | 29 613 |
| 1999 | 549 832 | 291 332 | 42 259 | 94 065 | 76 646 | 53 144 | 34 645 |
| 2000 | 803 864 | 445 455 | 56 143 | 118 919 | 100 605 | 90 389 | 48 496 |
| 2001 | 1 088 083 | 578 465 | 84 198 | 144 216 | 179 545 | 125 967 | 59 890 |
| 2002 | 1 237 382 | 661 452 | 98 906 | 163 360 | 180 060 | 164 104 | 68 406 |
| 2003 | 1 704 977 | 904 360 | 148 022 | 223 860 | 246 102 | 241 717 | 88 938 |
| 2004 | 2 195 667 | 1 142 030 | 182 188 | 300 598 | 316 380 | 315 368 | 121 291 |
| 2005 | 3 167 841 | 1 607 909 | 249 298 | 370 725 | 483 838 | 516 168 | 189 201 |
| 2006 | 4 002 284 | 2 030 997 | 350 788 | 430 845 | 610 858 | 653 718 | 275 866 |
| 2007 | 5 418 177 | 2 739 597 | 480 957 | 600 630 | 839 800 | 865 562 | 372 588 |
| 2008 | 6 689 063 | 3 289 067 | 601 600 | 701 528 | 1 039 800 | 1 156 868 | 501 800 |
| 2009 | 7 451 800 | 3 701 670 | 702 000 | 780 778 | 1 050 018 | 1 331 331 | 588 003 |
| 2010 | 9 005 527 | 4 512 708 | 902 828 | 1 000 864 | 1 160 618 | 1 631 331 | 700 006 |
| 2011 | 11 008 808 | 5 504 360 | 1 128 772 | 1 225 011 | 1 423 188 | 2 002 188 | 854 061 |
| 2012 | 12 043 336 | 6 161 435 | 1 193 202 | 1 281 504 | 1 496 131 | 2 202 750 | 901 516 |

注:2012年起地方一般预算收入更名为地方公共财政预算收入。
Note:Local General Budget Revenue Changes Its Name to Public Finance Budgetary Revenue since 2012.

表12-4

# 历年地方公共财政预算支出
# PUBLIC FINANCE BUDGETARY EXPENDITURE OVER THE YEARS

单位：万元 (10 000 yuan)

| 年 份<br>Year | 全 市<br>Whole Municipality | 市 区<br>Urban Area | # 吴江区<br>Wujiang District | 常 熟<br>Changshu | 张家港<br>Zhangjiagang | 昆 山<br>Kunshan | 太 仓<br>Taicang |
|---|---|---|---|---|---|---|---|
| 1998 | 459 927 | 247 165 | 34 257 | 75 706 | 63 863 | 44 667 | 28 526 |
| 1999 | 565 065 | 304 851 | 40 565 | 87 996 | 75 883 | 59 954 | 36 381 |
| 2000 | 781 116 | 438 872 | 53 291 | 102 686 | 101 276 | 91 126 | 47 156 |
| 2001 | 1 103 617 | 604 354 | 74 599 | 139 945 | 177 519 | 124 218 | 57 581 |
| 2002 | 1 363 942 | 747 019 | 106 271 | 171 273 | 196 867 | 171 093 | 77 690 |
| 2003 | 1 835 976 | 1 027 454 | 154 202 | 204 747 | 264 175 | 235 768 | 103 832 |
| 2004 | 2 331 312 | 1 252 319 | 191 322 | 272 511 | 337 245 | 329 541 | 139 696 |
| 2005 | 3 352 789 | 1 823 140 | 254 902 | 408 625 | 476 269 | 442 380 | 202 375 |
| 2006 | 3 861 990 | 2 064 381 | 308 308 | 420 980 | 556 075 | 562 293 | 258 261 |
| 2007 | 4 969 424 | 2 576 611 | 420 502 | 537 613 | 787 004 | 718 040 | 350 156 |
| 2008 | 6 223 668 | 3 197 262 | 530 858 | 643 676 | 942 317 | 968 965 | 471 448 |
| 2009 | 6 867 778 | 3 510 161 | 638 326 | 678 286 | 988 444 | 1 143 625 | 547 262 |
| 2010 | 8 256 650 | 4 116 504 | 840 293 | 953 904 | 1 140 706 | 1 387 647 | 657 889 |
| 2011 | 10 026 263 | 4 997 507 | 1 080 593 | 1 150 183 | 1 327 723 | 1 745 761 | 805 089 |
| 2012 | 11 134 678 | 5 609 766 | 1 088 494 | 1 282 681 | 1 429 162 | 1 951 473 | 861 596 |

注:2012年起地方一般预算支出更名为地方公共财政预算支出。
Note:Local General Budget Expenditure Changes Its Name to Public Finance Budgetary Expenditure since 2012.

表12-5

# 财 政 收 入 (2012年)

单位：万元

| 指　　标 | Item | 全　市 Whole Municipality |
|---|---|---|
| **财政收入合计** | **Total of Financial Revenue** | **25 616 731** |
| **一、上划中央收入** | **Revenue of Central Government** | **9 928 654** |
| 增值税 (75%) | Value-added Tax (75%) | 6 128 154 |
| 消费税 | Consumption Tax | 100 578 |
| 企业所得税 (60%) | Enterprise's Income Tax (60%) | 2 850 251 |
| 个人所得税 (60%) | Individual Income Tax (60%) | 849 671 |
| **二、地方财政收入** | **Local Financial Revenue** | **15 688 077** |
| **(一)地方公共财政预算收入** | **Public Finance Budgetary Revenue** | **12 043 336** |
| # 税收收入 | Tax Revenue | 10 238 763 |
| 1. 增值税 (25%) | Value-added Tax (25%) | 2 089 236 |
| 2. 营业税 | Business Tax | 2 561 008 |
| 3. 企业所得税 (40%) | Enterprise's Income Tax (40%) | 1 900 166 |
| 4. 个人所得税 (40%) | Individual Income Tax (40%) | 566 447 |
| 5. 资源税 | Resources Tax | 32 |
| 6. 城市维护建设税 | Tax on Urban Construction and Maintenance | 707 139 |
| 7. 房产税 | Tax on Real Estates | 480 390 |
| 8. 印花税 | Stamp Tax | 163 186 |
| 9. 城镇土地使用税 | Tax on Use of Urban Land | 321 527 |
| 10.土地增值税 | Land Value Added Tax | 604 770 |
| 11.车船使用税和牌照税 | Tax on the Use of Vehicles and Ships | 61 321 |
| 12.耕地占用税 | Tax on the Occupancy of Cultivated Land | 87 505 |
| 13.契　税 | Contract Tax | 696 034 |
| 14.专项收入 | Expert Project Income | 405 055 |
| 15.行政性收费收入 | Income From Administrative Fees | 377 262 |
| 16.罚没收入 | Penalty and Confiscatory Income | 128 632 |
| 17.国有资本经营收入 | State-downed Assets Profit | 447 123 |
| 18.国有资源(资产)有偿使用收入 | The revenues of the compensation for the use of state-owned resources (assets) | 294 031 |
| 19.其他收入 | Other Income | 152 470 |
| **(二)基金收入** | **Fund Revenue** | **3 644 741** |
| 政府性基金收入 | Government Fund's Income | 575 866 |
| 社保基金收入 | Social Security Fund's Income | 3 068 875 |
| **增值税出口退税** | **VAT Export Tax Drawback** | **7 035 135** |
| **土地基金收入** | **Land Fund Income** | **6 162 905** |

# FINANCIAL REVENUE (2012)

(10 000 yuan)

| 市 区 Urban Area | # 吴江区 Wujiang District | 常 熟 Changshu | 张家港 Zhangjiagang | 昆 山 Kunshan | 太 仓 Taicang |
|---|---|---|---|---|---|
| **13 130 082** | **2 698 828** | **2 651 427** | **3 241 958** | **4 636 206** | **1 957 058** |
| **5 017 945** | **988 397** | **963 616** | **1 319 055** | **1 832 358** | **795 680** |
| 2 926 659 | 624 623 | 594 820 | 886 081 | 1 198 496 | 522 098 |
| 74 790 | 6 378 | 3 810 | 3 025 | 11 926 | 7 027 |
| 1 543 017 | 279 978 | 280 880 | 298 696 | 505 992 | 221 666 |
| 473 479 | 77 418 | 84 106 | 131 253 | 115 944 | 44 889 |
| **8 112 137** | **1 710 431** | **1 687 811** | **1 922 903** | **2 803 848** | **1 161 378** |
| **6 161 435** | **1 193 202** | **1 281 504** | **1 496 131** | **2 202 750** | **901 516** |
| 5 351 659 | 961 202 | 1 040 675 | 1 221 995 | 1 898 152 | 726 282 |
| 1 000 559 | 209 877 | 201 305 | 302 181 | 406 441 | 178 750 |
| 1 381 879 | 215 557 | 238 036 | 257 049 | 502 043 | 182 001 |
| 1 028 677 | 186 652 | 187 253 | 199 130 | 337 328 | 147 778 |
| 315 652 | 51 612 | 56 071 | 87 502 | 77 297 | 29 925 |
| 32 | – | – | – | – | – |
| 370 549 | 67 274 | 66 681 | 80 682 | 134 317 | 54 910 |
| 259 238 | 45 186 | 57 325 | 45 072 | 88 763 | 29 992 |
| 74 770 | 15 591 | 16 511 | 30 417 | 30 600 | 10 888 |
| 139 204 | 40 959 | 40 195 | 41 827 | 66 561 | 33 740 |
| 330 530 | 40 065 | 78 271 | 61 883 | 110 055 | 24 031 |
| 35 429 | 5 995 | 7 614 | 6 588 | 8 186 | 3 504 |
| 35 098 | 2 896 | 17 889 | 24 051 | 5 143 | 5 324 |
| 380 040 | 79 536 | 73 524 | 85 613 | 131 418 | 25 439 |
| 197 814 | 36 999 | 43 449 | 62 440 | 69 525 | 31 827 |
| 175 706 | 31 524 | 35 964 | 43 719 | 84 663 | 37 210 |
| 75 156 | 15 234 | 20 001 | 15 778 | 11 133 | 6 564 |
| 252 919 | 144 780 | 849 | 128 250 | 65 105 | – |
| 64 933 | 3 463 | 91 926 | 23 474 | 31 228 | 82 470 |
| 43 248 | – | 48 640 | 475 | 42 944 | 17 163 |
| **1 950 702** | **517 229** | **406 307** | **426 772** | **601 098** | **259 862** |
| 299 162 | 34 146 | 106 307 | 58 710 | 64 825 | 46 862 |
| 1 651 540 | 483 083 | 300 000 | 368 062 | 536 273 | 213 000 |
| **3 579 470** | **715 885** | **726 944** | **825 353** | **1 514 803** | **388 565** |
| **3 018 097** | **859 266** | **814 585** | **894 713** | **1 090 831** | **344 679** |

表12-6

# 财 政 支 出 (2012年)

单位：万元

| 指　　标 | Item | 全　市 Whole Municipality |
|---|---|---|
| **财政支出** | **Financial Expenditure** | **14 795 934** |
| **一、地方公共财政预算支出** | **Public Finance Budgetary Expenditure** | **11 134 678** |
| 1. 一般公共服务支出 | General Public Services Spending | 1 384 281 |
| 2. 国防支出 | Expenditure on National Defense | 41 641 |
| 3. 公共安全支出 | Public Safety Spending | 754 863 |
| 4. 教育支出 | Expenditure for Operating Expenses of Education | 1 806 986 |
| 5. 科学技术支出 | Science and Technology Spending | 665 898 |
| 6. 文化体育与传媒 | Culture, Sports and the Media | 249 369 |
| 7. 社会保障与就业 | Social Security and Employment | 1 016 052 |
| 8. 医疗卫生支出 | Expenditure for Medicine and Public Health | 552 918 |
| 9. 节能环保支出 | Energy Saving and Environmental Protection Spending | 418 018 |
| 10. 城乡社区事务支出 | Urban and Rural Community Affairs Spending | 1 829 997 |
| 11. 农林水事务支出 | Agricultural, Forestry and Water Affairs Spending | 865 643 |
| 12. 交通运输支出 | Transportation Spending | 478 658 |
| 13. 资源勘探电力信息等事务 | Resource Exploring, Mining, Power, Information and Other Matters | 365 031 |
| 14. 粮油物资储备等管理事务 | Grain, Oil and Materials Reserves, and Other Management Services | 256 746 |
| 15. 金融监管支出 | Financial Supervision Expenditures | 26 523 |
| 16. 住房保障支出 | Housing Security Expenditure | 212 121 |
| 17. 其他支出 | Other Expenditure | 209 933 |
| **二、基金支出** | **Fund Expenditure** | **3 661 256** |
| 1.政府性基金支出 | Government Funds Spending | 592 381 |
| 2.社会保险基金支出 | Social Insurance Funds Spending | 3 068 875 |
| **土地基金支出** | **Land Fund Expenditures** | **6 383 816** |

# FINANCIAL EXPENDITURE (2012)

(10 000 yuan)

| 市 区 Urban Area | # 吴江区 Wujiang District | 常 熟 Changshu | 张家港 Zhangjiagang | 昆 山 Kunshan | 太 仓 Taicang |
|---|---|---|---|---|---|
| **7 560 218** | **1 614 201** | **1 695 190** | **1 841 592** | **2 571 453** | **1 127 481** |
| **5 609 766** | **1 088 494** | **1 282 681** | **1 429 162** | **1 951 473** | **861 596** |
| 716 512 | 137 250 | 158 161 | 163 049 | 218 554 | 128 005 |
| 31 167 | 5 | 14 | – | 10 281 | 179 |
| 440 575 | 80 251 | 80 210 | 74 185 | 107 938 | 51 955 |
| 924 014 | 209 441 | 236 263 | 223 602 | 270 570 | 152 537 |
| 338 076 | 76 183 | 87 435 | 71 800 | 124 742 | 43 845 |
| 120 067 | 10 848 | 34 420 | 24 324 | 52 594 | 17 964 |
| 522 694 | 114 118 | 67 987 | 113 457 | 254 710 | 57 204 |
| 309 904 | 60 410 | 70 387 | 71 093 | 65 601 | 35 933 |
| 182 851 | 45 129 | 42 800 | 55 267 | 109 633 | 27 467 |
| 774 411 | 108 219 | 249 390 | 318 320 | 332 394 | 155 482 |
| 328 288 | 112 511 | 110 213 | 146 683 | 185 940 | 94 519 |
| 305 991 | 28 657 | 42 652 | 46 316 | 59 290 | 24 409 |
| 253 639 | 16 781 | 31 253 | 20 583 | 36 076 | 23 480 |
| 124 945 | 15 836 | 17 323 | 28 388 | 69 879 | 16 211 |
| 14 175 | 3 259 | 2 556 | 4 166 | 3 632 | 1 994 |
| 120 992 | 29 380 | 15 605 | 44 136 | 19 399 | 11 989 |
| 101 465 | 40 216 | 36 012 | 23 793 | 30 240 | 18 423 |
| **1 950 452** | **525 707** | **412 509** | **412 430** | **619 980** | **265 885** |
| 298 912 | 42 624 | 112 509 | 44 368 | 83 707 | 52 885 |
| 1 651 540 | 483 083 | 300 000 | 368 062 | 536 273 | 213 000 |
| **3 261 352** | **860 290** | **790 585** | **896 081** | **1 094 196** | **341 602** |

表12-7

# 历年金融机构人民币存贷款余额
# RMB SAVINGS DEPOSITS AND LOANS BALANCES OF BANK OVER THE YEARS

单位：万元 (10 000 yuan)

| 年 份 Year | 存款余额 Deposits Balance | # 单位存款 Deposits of Enterprises | # 个人存款 Personal Deposits | 贷款余额 Loans Balance | # 短期贷款 Short-term Loans | # 中长期贷款 Medium-term & Long-term Loans |
|---|---|---|---|---|---|---|
| 1949 | 156 | | | 42 | | |
| 1952 | 2 628 | | | 1 129 | | |
| 1957 | 10 086 | | | 14 829 | | |
| 1962 | 15 282 | | | 43 349 | | |
| 1970 | 46 648 | | | 55 652 | | |
| 1975 | 58 822 | | | 107 202 | | |
| 1978 | 73 712 | | | 154 512 | | |
| 1980 | 156 817 | | | 211 885 | | |
| 1985 | 375 702 | | | 530 070 | | |
| 1990 | 1 321 970 | | | 1 340 967 | | |
| 1995 | 5 666 541 | | | 4 240 689 | | |
| 1996 | 7 447 982 | | | 5 370 165 | | |
| 1997 | 9 115 624 | 3 777 846 | 5 337 778 | 6 109 437 | 5 222 982 | 704 285 |
| 1998 | 11 124 378 | 4 633 989 | 6 490 389 | 7 242 834 | 6 012 839 | 738 929 |
| 1999 | 12 938 251 | 5 425 457 | 7 512 794 | 8 116 631 | 6 622 337 | 870 493 |
| 2000 | 14 770 111 | 6 733 142 | 8 036 969 | 9 705 954 | 7 932 854 | 1 083 065 |
| 2001 | 17 316 246 | 7 946 830 | 9 369 416 | 10 598 232 | 7 180 674 | 2 092 396 |
| 2002 | 22 320 343 | 10 677 086 | 11 643 257 | 14 909 634 | 9 628 354 | 3 566 462 |
| 2003 | 31 497 894 | 16 792 849 | 14 705 045 | 23 592 819 | 13 182 488 | 7 852 521 |
| 2004 | 38 145 281 | 21 022 535 | 17 122 746 | 29 157 370 | 13 238 438 | 12 332 891 |
| 2005 | 47 300 532 | 26 705 335 | 20 595 197 | 34 783 428 | 14 500 920 | 16 102 524 |
| 2006 | 57 979 732 | 33 705 530 | 24 274 202 | 44 297 084 | 19 137 227 | 20 910 608 |
| 2007 | 70 688 313 | 44 754 186 | 25 934 127 | 53 438 723 | 23 500 261 | 27 119 966 |
| 2008 | 83 407 921 | 50 034 758 | 33 373 163 | 63 018 052 | 25 972 919 | 32 042 110 |
| 2009 | 109 502 460 | 69 961 663 | 39 540 797 | 85 053 331 | 29 919 426 | 49 617 005 |
| 2010 | 135 703 495 | 89 147 878 | 46 555 617 | 101 331 459 | 36 213 284 | 62 210 323 |
| 2011 | 151 807 837 | 93 011 695 | 51 819 980 | 118 738 914 | 46 491 697 | 68 747 120 |
| 2012 | 176 634 972 | 107 584 791 | 59 720 133 | 136 268 590 | 57 167 975 | 75 039 745 |

表12-8

# 历年分地区城乡居民人民币储蓄存款余额
# RMB SAVINGS DEPOSITS OF URBAN AND RURAL RESIDENTS OVER THE YEARS BY REGION

单位：万元 (10 000 yuan)

| 年 份<br>Year | 全 市<br>Whole Municipality | 市 区<br>Urban Area | # 吴江区<br>Wujiang District | 常 熟<br>Changshu | 张家港<br>Zhangjiagang | 昆 山<br>Kunshan | 太 仓<br>Taicang |
|---|---|---|---|---|---|---|---|
| 1952 | | | | 146 | | 73 | 77 |
| 1957 | | 346 | 346 | 237 | | 243 | 125 |
| 1962 | | 206 | 206 | 479 | | 272 | 343 |
| 1965 | 6 474 | 3 430 | 253 | 1 393 | 389 | 517 | 745 |
| 1970 | 6 594 | 3 248 | 366 | 1 372 | 628 | 401 | 945 |
| 1975 | 12 166 | 6 483 | 734 | 2 510 | 1 290 | 594 | 1 289 |
| 1978 | 17 650 | 9 195 | 966 | 3 502 | 1 927 | 1 151 | 1 875 |
| 1980 | 36 420 | 18 145 | 2 394 | 7 302 | 3 859 | 3 238 | 3 876 |
| 1985 | 148 233 | 70 885 | 12 565 | 28 046 | 21 082 | 11 861 | 16 359 |
| 1990 | 733 332 | 347 646 | 59 407 | 145 781 | 105 913 | 63 927 | 70 065 |
| 1995 | 2 964 938 | 1 321 069 | 240 825 | 575 609 | 511 887 | 301 570 | 254 803 |
| 1996 | 4 082 649 | 1 814 960 | 370 600 | 837 401 | 693 996 | 398 843 | 337 449 |
| 1997 | 5 337 778 | 2 396 520 | 476 463 | 1 167 116 | 836 985 | 493 287 | 443 870 |
| 1998 | 6 490 389 | 2 943 064 | 614 061 | 1 412 262 | 1 018 310 | 581 477 | 535 276 |
| 1999 | 7 512 794 | 3 423 525 | 731 059 | 1 637 148 | 1 177 583 | 673 184 | 601 354 |
| 2000 | 8 036 969 | 3 679 369 | 779 731 | 1 688 509 | 1 280 208 | 764 219 | 624 664 |
| 2001 | 9 369 416 | 4 377 810 | 915 158 | 1 920 292 | 1 447 239 | 923 303 | 700 772 |
| 2002 | 11 643 257 | 5 636 011 | 1 131 190 | 2 342 284 | 1 719 504 | 1 138 562 | 806 896 |
| 2003 | 14 705 045 | 7 461 035 | 1 497 336 | 2 791 462 | 1 989 168 | 1 488 977 | 974 403 |
| 2004 | 17 122 746 | 8 672 455 | 1 747 441 | 3 187 039 | 2 285 995 | 1 827 811 | 1 149 446 |
| 2005 | 20 595 197 | 10 582 414 | 2 231 149 | 3 790 046 | 2 668 182 | 2 229 722 | 1 324 832 |
| 2006 | 24 274 202 | 12 646 581 | 2 715 870 | 4 207 394 | 3 162 974 | 2 740 382 | 1 516 871 |
| 2007 | 25 934 127 | 13 413 765 | 2 861 672 | 4 404 905 | 3 385 526 | 3 126 929 | 1 603 002 |
| 2008 | 33 373 163 | 17 243 013 | 3 648 183 | 5 545 651 | 4 393 591 | 4 148 668 | 2 042 241 |
| 2009 | 39 540 797 | 20 485 695 | 4 414 443 | 6 522 628 | 5 208 800 | 4 921 289 | 2 402 385 |
| 2010 | 46 555 617 | 23 992 753 | 5 155 580 | 7 563 039 | 5 970 374 | 6 092 794 | 2 936 656 |
| 2011 | 50 785 927 | 25 914 766 | 5 556 569 | 8 120 828 | 6 656 161 | 6 840 035 | 3 254 137 |
| 2012 | 57 877 466 | 29 695 083 | 6 349 442 | 9 071 807 | 7 467 598 | 7 871 313 | 3 771 664 |

表12-9

# 金融机构人民币信贷收支情况（2012年）

单位：万元

| 指　标 | Item | 全　市 Whole Municipality |
|---|---|---|
| **年末金融机构人民币存款余额** | **Deposits Balance of National Banking System by Year End** | **176 634 972** |
| # 单位存款 | Deposits of Enterprises | 107 584 791 |
| # 活　期 | Current Deposit | 30 396 353 |
| 定　期 | Dated Deposit | 31 584 168 |
| 个人存款 | Personal Deposit | 59 720 133 |
| # 储蓄存款 | Savings Deposit | 57 877 466 |
| 财政性存款 | Fiscal Deposit | 1 972 453 |
| **年末金融机构人民币贷款余额** | **Loans Balance of National Banking System by Year End** | **136 268 590** |
| 境内贷款 | Domestic Loans | 135 859 044 |
| # 短期贷款 | Short-term Loans | 57 167 975 |
| # 个人贷款及透支 | Personal Loans and Overdrafts | 7 542 081 |
| 单位普通贷款及透支 | Unit General Loans and Overdrafts | 45 094 944 |
| 中长期贷款 | Medium-term & Long-term Loans | 75 039 745 |
| # 个人贷款 | Personal Loans | 26 891 172 |
| 单位普通贷款 | Unit General Loans | 41 193 788 |
| 票据融资 | Bill Financing | 3 397 568 |
| # 贴现 | Discount | 3 397 568 |
| 境外贷款 | External Loans | 409 546 |

注：人民银行统计制度自2011年起新增“个人存款”，其中包括“储蓄存款”“保证金存款”和“结构性存款”。

# RMB CREDIT FUNDS BALANCE OF FINANCIAL INSTITUTIONS (2012)

(10 000 yuan)

| 市 区<br>Urban Area | # 吴江区<br>Wujiang District | 常 熟<br>Changshu | 张家港<br>Zhangjiagang | 昆 山<br>Kunshan | 太 仓<br>Taicang |
|---|---|---|---|---|---|
| **101 846 342** | **18 248 337** | **20 311 857** | **20 646 780** | **23 641 194** | **10 188 800** |
| 63 700 935 | 11 286 918 | 10 533 404 | 12 021 633 | 15 148 367 | 6 180 452 |
| 19 204 353 | 3 066 733 | 2 704 753 | 2 868 078 | 4 088 374 | 1 530 794 |
| 17 686 854 | 3 254 509 | 2 892 014 | 3 064 237 | 6 243 038 | 1 698 023 |
| 30 876 215 | 6 571 502 | 9 287 489 | 7 593 036 | 8 118 188 | 3 845 205 |
| 29 695 083 | 6 349 442 | 9 071 807 | 7 467 598 | 7 871 313 | 3 771 664 |
| 1 566 121 | 27 369 | 137 469 | 84 905 | 170 081 | 13 877 |
| **81 615 655** | **15 050 925** | **15 097 397** | **14 907 524** | **16 013 914** | **8 634 100** |
| 81 348 628 | 15 043 468 | 15 092 892 | 14 905 522 | 15 883 904 | 8 628 098 |
| 31 007 630 | 9 251 001 | 8 764 090 | 8 632 894 | 4 973 228 | 3 790 133 |
| 4 010 261 | 1 185 643 | 1 709 984 | 655 812 | 697 479 | 468 545 |
| 24 928 398 | 7 560 237 | 6 471 005 | 6 916 996 | 3 876 468 | 2 902 076 |
| 48 675 128 | 5 682 371 | 5 947 687 | 5 374 678 | 10 456 953 | 4 585 298 |
| 16 832 784 | 2 022 903 | 2 100 326 | 1 425 700 | 5 405 974 | 1 126 389 |
| 26 162 853 | 3 505 098 | 3 328 538 | 3 487 215 | 4 882 269 | 3 332 914 |
| 1 550 226 | 76 250 | 314 315 | 844 670 | 438 769 | 249 589 |
| 1 550 226 | 76 250 | 314 315 | 844 670 | 438 769 | 249 589 |
| 267 027 | 7 457 | 4 505 | 2 003 | 130 009 | 6 002 |

Notes:According to Statistical System of People's Bank of China, from 2011,"Personal Deposit" which includes "Savings Deposit", "Margin Deposit" and "Structured deposit" is newly increased.

表12-10

# 金融机构本外币信贷收支情况 (2012年)

单位：万元

| 指 标 | Item | 全 市 Whole Municipality |
|---|---|---|
| **年末金融机构本外币存款余额** | **Deposits Balance of National Banking System by Year End** | **187 960 574** |
| # 单位存款 | Deposits of Enterprises | 118 245 551 |
| # 活 期 | Current Deposit | 34 525 166 |
| 定 期 | Dated Deposit | 33 938 489 |
| 个人存款 | Personal Deposit | 60 340 707 |
| # 储蓄存款 | Savings Deposit | 58 459 118 |
| 财政性存款 | Fiscal Deposit | 1 972 453 |
| **年末金融机构本外币贷款余额** | **Loans Balance of National Banking System by Year End** | **148 778 436** |
| 境内贷款 | Domestic Loans | 148 052 466 |
| # 短期贷款 | Short-term Loans | 68 432 819 |
| # 个人贷款及透支 | Personal Loans and Overdrafts | 7 543 479 |
| 单位普通贷款及透支 | Unit General Loans and Overdrafts | 47 242 335 |
| 中长期贷款 | Medium-term & Long-term Loans | 75 966 408 |
| # 个人贷款 | Personal Loans | 26 892 927 |
| 单位普通贷款 | Unit General Loans | 41 946 209 |
| 票据融资 | Bill Financing | 3 398 056 |
| # 贴现 | Discount | 3 398 031 |
| 境外贷款 | External Loans | 725 970 |

# RMB AND FOREIGN CURRENCY CREDIT FUNDS BALANCE OF FINANCIAL INSTITUTIONS (2012)

(10 000 yuan)

| 市 区<br>Urban Area | # 吴江区<br>Wujiang District | 常 熟<br>Changshu | 张家港<br>Zhangjiagang | 昆 山<br>Kunshan | 太 仓<br>Taicang |
|---|---|---|---|---|---|
| **108 140 584** | **19 295 260** | **21 237 111** | **21 604 665** | **26 393 421** | **10 584 793** |
| 69 523 755 | 12 299 831 | 11 403 532 | 12 932 420 | 17 839 714 | 6 546 131 |
| 21 837 456 | 3 410 023 | 2 928 978 | 3 176 871 | 4 834 122 | 1 747 739 |
| 19 088 281 | 3 371 581 | 3 130 217 | 3 313 832 | 6 593 472 | 1 812 687 |
| 31 312 921 | 6 604 640 | 9 342 073 | 7 637 287 | 8 173 333 | 3 875 093 |
| 30 103 702 | 6 381 755 | 9 122 679 | 7 509 550 | 7 922 958 | 3 800 230 |
| 1 566 121 | 27 369 | 137 469 | 84 905 | 170 081 | 13 877 |
| **87 003 027** | **16 280 467** | **16 064 658** | **17 786 829** | **18 638 653** | **9 285 268** |
| 86 419 576 | 16 273 010 | 16 060 154 | 17 784 826 | 18 508 644 | 9 279 266 |
| 35 288 294 | 10 381 325 | 9 726 311 | 11 495 337 | 7 538 440 | 4 384 437 |
| 4 011 659 | 1 185 643 | 1 709 984 | 655 812 | 697 479 | 468 545 |
| 25 902 719 | 7 662 752 | 6 491 200 | 7 644 504 | 4 172 260 | 3 031 651 |
| 49 464 698 | 5 781 589 | 5 952 672 | 5 390 414 | 10 516 480 | 4 642 143 |
| 16 834 539 | 2 022 903 | 2 100 326 | 1 425 700 | 5 405 974 | 1 126 389 |
| 26 812 848 | 3 604 316 | 3 332 044 | 3 502 950 | 4 919 168 | 3 379 200 |
| 1 550 291 | 76 250 | 314 371 | 845 017 | 438 769 | 249 608 |
| 1 550 266 | 76 250 | 314 371 | 845 017 | 438 769 | 249 608 |
| 583 451 | 7 457 | 4 505 | 2 003 | 130 009 | 6 002 |

表12-11

# 保险业务情况 (2012年)

单位：万元

| 指　　标 | Item | 全　市 Whole Municipality |
|---|---|---|
| **一、承保额(财产险)** | **Insurance Value ( Property Insurance )** | **521 174 781** |
| # 企业财产险 | Enterprise Property Insurance | 198 522 061 |
| 机动车辆险 | Motor Vehicle Insurance | 126 611 960 |
| 货物运输险 | Freight Transport Insurance | 93 700 779 |
| 家庭财产险 | Family Property Insurance | 16 930 081 |
| **二、保费收入** | **Premiums** | **2 374 157** |
| 1.财产险 | Property Insurance | 1 047 741 |
| # 企业财产险 | Enterprise Property Insurance | 123 757 |
| 机动车辆险 | Motor Vehicle Insurance | 760 434 |
| 货物运输险 | Freight Transport Insurance | 26 667 |
| 家庭财产险 | Family Property Insurance | 6 997 |
| 2.人身险 | Life Insurance | 1 326 416 |
| # 寿　险 | Life Insurance | 1 118 412 |
| **三、当年赔款和给付** | **Indemnity Expenditure and Payment of the Year** | **716 395** |
| 1.财产险 | Property Insurance | 551 201 |
| # 企业财产险 | Enterprise Property Insurance | 57 142 |
| 机动车辆险 | Motor Vehicle Insurance | 450 465 |
| 货物运输险 | Freight Transport Insurance | 11 478 |
| 家庭财产险 | Family Property Insurance | 1 760 |
| 2.人身险 | Life Insurance | 165 194 |
| # 寿　险 | Life Insurance | 112 404 |

# CONDITIONS OF INSURANCE BUSINESS (2012)

(10 000 yuan)

| 市 区<br>Urban Area | # 吴江区<br>Wujiang District | 常 熟<br>Changshu | 张家港<br>Zhangjiagang | 昆 山<br>Kunshan | 太 仓<br>Taicang |
|---|---|---|---|---|---|
| **362 178 336** | **32 895 825** | **42 130 571** | **41 904 751** | **55 058 515** | **19 902 608** |
| 130 386 708 | 11 934 360 | 18 225 202 | 19 630 676 | 22 100 555 | 8 178 920 |
| 88 020 383 | 9 616 617 | 11 893 045 | 9 014 774 | 12 363 956 | 5 319 801 |
| 74 372 694 | 4 410 027 | 3 984 913 | 8 690 859 | 3 849 841 | 2 802 472 |
| 7 120 556 | 857 836 | 3 151 954 | 875 279 | 4 568 963 | 1 213 329 |
| **1 433 948** | **229 382** | **293 835** | **259 806** | **250 003** | **136 565** |
| 632 817 | 93 220 | 119 369 | 106 269 | 133 181 | 56 104 |
| 72 877 | 10 321 | 17 212 | 13 421 | 13 132 | 7 116 |
| 438 879 | 75 955 | 91 851 | 80 147 | 107 064 | 42 494 |
| 19 897 | 1 386 | 1 155 | 2 880 | 1 685 | 1 050 |
| 3 630 | 1 091 | 1 144 | 896 | 599 | 727 |
| 801 131 | 136 161 | 174 466 | 153 538 | 116 821 | 80 461 |
| 657 235 | 123 341 | 158 225 | 137 226 | 93 337 | 72 390 |
| **436 528** | **65 037** | **88 524** | **70 799** | **83 579** | **36 964** |
| 327 685 | 51 804 | 67 115 | 56 969 | 70 392 | 29 039 |
| 26 831 | 4 843 | 14 919 | 6 381 | 4 617 | 4 393 |
| 273 663 | 44 797 | 49 390 | 46 525 | 58 693 | 22 195 |
| 8 233 | 363 | 279 | 487 | 2 238 | 241 |
| 692 | 369 | 586 | 99 | 75 | 308 |
| 108 843 | 13 234 | 21 409 | 13 830 | 13 187 | 7 925 |
| 75 993 | 9 288 | 16 737 | 8 479 | 5 733 | 5 461 |

表12-12

# 外资金融机构及代表处一览表

# LIST OF FOREIGN FINANCIAL LNSTITUTIONS AND REPRESENTATIVE OFFICES

| 机构(代表处)名称及所属国家(地区) Name of Institutions (Representative Offices) | 所在地区 Location | 批准日期 Date of Approval |
|---|---|---|
| 三井住友银行（中国）有限公司苏州分行(日本) | 高新区、虎丘区 | 1997年11月11日 |
| 汇丰银行（中国）有限公司苏州分行(中国香港) | 工业园区 | 2004年10月15日 |
| 渣打银行（中国）有限公司苏州分行(英国) | 工业园区 | 2005年11月08日 |
| 星展银行（中国）有限公司苏州分行(新加坡) | 工业园区 | 2006年03月16日 |
| 友利银行（中国）有限公司苏州分行（韩国） | 工业园区 | 2007年07月19日 |
| 企业银行（中国）有限公司苏州分行（韩国） | 工业园区 | 2007年11月05日 |
| 东亚银行（中国）有限公司苏州分行（中国香港） | 工业园区 | 2010年3月08日 |
| 国民银行（中国）有限公司苏州分行（韩国） | 工业园区 | 2010年6月07日 |
| 瑞穗实业银行（中国）有限公司苏州分行(日本) | 工业园区 | 2010年08月24日 |
| 合作金库商业银行股份有限公司苏州分行（中国台湾） | 工业园区 | 2010年12月17日 |
| 彰化商业银行股份有限公司昆山分行（中国台湾） | 昆山市 | 2010年12月17日 |
| 华一银行(中国）苏州分行（合资银行） | 工业园区 | 2011年06月22日 |
| 摩根大通银行（中国）有限公司苏州分行(美国) | 工业园区 | 2012年05月08日 |
| 兆丰国际商业银行股份有限公司苏州分行（中国台湾） | 工业园区 | 2012年06月13日 |
| 日本池田泉州银行股份有限公司苏州代表处(日本) | 吴中区 | 2006年07月17日 |
| 台北富邦商业银行股份有限公司苏州代表处（中国台湾） | 工业园区 | 2011年10月14日 |

表12-13

# 外资保险公司及代表处一览表

# LIST OF FOREIGN INSURANCE COMPANIES AND REPRESENTATIVE OFFICES

| 机构(代表处)名称及所属国家(地区) Name of Institutions (Representative Offices) | 所在地区 Location | 批准日期 Date of Approval |
|---|---|---|
| 信诚人寿苏州营销服务部（英国） | 吴中区 | 2005年04月21日 |
| 北大方正人寿苏州营销服务部（日本） | 姑苏区 | 2006年12月19日 |
| 国泰人寿江苏分公司苏州营销服务部（ 中国台湾） | 姑苏区 | 2007年11月9日 |
| 中德安联人寿江苏分公司苏州营销服务部（德国） | 工业园区 | 2007年12月26日 |
| 华泰人寿苏州中心支公司（美国） | 工业园区 | 2008年03月28日 |
| 恒安标准人寿江苏分公司苏州中心支公司（英国） | 姑苏区 | 2008年05月26日 |
| 友邦保险苏州中心支公司（美国） | 姑苏区 | 2008年05月29日 |
| 三星财产（中国）苏州分公司（韩国） | 工业园区 | 2008年07月10日 |
| 工银金盛人寿苏州营销服务部（法国） | 姑苏区 | 2008年12月02日 |
| 中美联泰大都会人寿保险有限公司苏州支公司（美国） | 高新区、虎丘区 | 2010年03月05日 |
| 日本财险（中国）江苏分公司（日本） | 工业园区 | 2010年06月10日 |
| 长生人寿江苏分公司苏州营销服务部（日本） | 高新区、虎丘区 | 2010年07月21日 |
| 乐爱金苏州营销服务部（韩国） | 工业园区 | 2011年01月04日 |
| 三井住友海上火灾保险（中国）江苏分公司苏州营销服务部（日本） | 工业园区 | 2011年05月20日 |
| 东京海上日动（中国）江苏分公司（日本） | 工业园区 | 2011年07月19日 |
| 国泰产险江苏分公司苏州营销服务部（中国台湾） | 工业园区 | 2011年07月21日 |
| 中意人寿江苏省分公司苏州中心支公司（意大利） | 工业园区 | 2011年08月02日 |
| 中宏保险江苏分公司苏州中心支公司（中国香港） | 姑苏区 | 2011年08月03日 |
| 交银康联苏州市中心支公司（澳大利亚） | 工业园区 | 2012年04月10日 |

表12-14 分地区养老、医疗、失业、工伤、生育及农村保险人数（2012年末）

# ENDOWMENT, MEDICAL, UNEMPLOYMENT , LABOR INJURY, CHILDBIRTH AND RURAL INSURANCE BY REGION (END OF 2012)

单位：人 (person)

| 地区 | Region | 养老保险参保人数 Number of People Covered by Endowment Insurance | 医疗保险参保人数 Number of People Covered by Medical Insurance | | |
|---|---|---|---|---|---|
| | | | | 在职职工参保人数 Fully Employed Staff and Workers | 离退休人员参保人数 Number of Retired People |
| **全　市** | **Whole Municipality** | **4 728 756** | **5 415 597** | **4 498 192** | **917 405** |
| **市　区** | **Urban Area** | **2 376 557** | **2 749 661** | **2 320 914** | **428 747** |
| 本　级 | The Level | 709 180 | 957 437 | 694 812 | 262 625 |
| 吴中区 | Wuzhong District | 307 922 | 346 633 | 304 321 | 42 312 |
| 相城区 | Xiangcheng District | 144 668 | 174 170 | 158 690 | 15 480 |
| 工业园区 | Industrial Park | 692 319 | 706 762 | 692 333 | 14 429 |
| 吴江区 | Wujiang District | 522 468 | 564 659 | 470 758 | 93 901 |
| **县级市** | **Cities at County Level** | | | | |
| 常　熟 | Changshu | 597 566 | 681 554 | 542 986 | 138 568 |
| 张家港 | Zhangjiagang | 470 791 | 597 550 | 474 854 | 122 696 |
| 昆　山 | Kunshan | 1 001 825 | 1 007 342 | 884 482 | 122 860 |
| 太　仓 | Taicang | 282 017 | 379 490 | 274 956 | 104 534 |

表12-14 续表 Continued

单位：人 (person)

| 地区 | Region | 失业保险参保人数 Number of People Covered by Unemployment Insurance | 工伤保险参保人数 Number of People Covered by Work Injury Insurance | 生育保险参保人数 Number of People Covered by Childbirth Insurance | 农村养老保险参保人数 Rural Number of People Covered by Endowment Insurance |
|---|---|---|---|---|---|
| **全　市** | **Whole Municipality** | **3 757 367** | **4 040 742** | **4 039 722** | **83 927** |
| **市　区** | **Urban Area** | **2 120 890** | **2 125 144** | **2 210 443** | **55 690** |
| 本　级 | The Level | 639 742 | 635 414 | 688 337 | 12 444 |
| 吴中区 | Wuzhong District | 265 733 | 264 201 | 298 806 | 7 117 |
| 相城区 | Xiangcheng District | 110 703 | 137 238 | 129 204 | 478 |
| 工业园区 | Industrial Park | 679 291 | 679 291 | 692 333 | - |
| 吴江区 | Wujiang District | 425 421 | 409 000 | 401 763 | 35 651 |
| **县级市** | **Cities at County Level** | | | | |
| 常　熟 | Changshu | 406 084 | 516 300 | 377 967 | 8 657 |
| 张家港 | Zhangjiagang | 377 006 | 374 289 | 446 683 | 1 717 |
| 昆　山 | Kunshan | 616 377 | 785 479 | 770 427 | 12 882 |
| 太　仓 | Taicang | 237 010 | 239 530 | 234 202 | 4 981 |

注：本级数据为姑苏区和新区、虎丘区的合计数。
Note: The level data is the totals of Gusu District, Suzhou New District and Huqiu (Tiger Hill) District.

# 主 要 统 计 指 标 解 释

**财政收入** 指国家财政参与社会产品分配所取得的收入，是实现国家职能的财力保证。财政收入所包括的内容几经变化，目前主要包括：

(1)各项税收：包括增值税、营业税、消费税、土地增值税、城市维护建设税、资源税、城市土地使用税、企业所得税、个人所得税、关税、证券交易印花税、车辆购置税、农牧业税和耕地占用税等。

(2)专项收入：包括排污费收入、城市水资源费收入、矿产资源补偿费收入、教育费附加收入等。

(3)其他收入：包括利息收入、基本建设贷款归还收入、基本建设收入、捐赠收入等。

(4)国有企业亏损补贴：此项为负收入，冲减财政收入。主要包括对工业企业、商业企业、粮食企业的补贴。

**财政支出** 国家财政将筹集起来的资金进行分配使用，以满足经济建设和各项事业的需要，主要包括：

**中央财政收入和地方财政收入** 指按现行分税制财政体制划分的中央本级收入和地方本级收入。1994年实行分税制财政体制以后，属于中央财政的收入包括关税、海关代征消费税和增值税，消费税，中央企业所得税，地方银行和外资银行及非银行金融企业所得税，铁道部门、各银行总行、各保险总公司等集中缴纳的营业税、利润和城市维护建设税，车辆购置税，船舶吨税，增值税的75%部分，证券交易税(印花税)94%部分，个人所得税中的利息所得税，利息所得税之外的个人所得税中央分享的部分，海洋石油资源税。属于地方财政的收入包括营业税，地方企业所得税，利息所得税之外的个人所得税地方分享的部分，城镇土地使用税，固定资产投资方向调节税，城镇维护建设税，房产税，车船使用税，印花税，屠宰税，农牧业税，农业特产税，耕地占用税，契税，土地增值税、国有土地有偿使用收入，增值税25%部分，证券交易税(印花税)6%部分和除海洋石油资源税以外的其他资源税。

**中央财政支出和地方财政支出** 指根据政府在经济和社会活动中的不同职责，划分中央和地方政府的责权，按照政府的责权划分确定的支出。中央财政支出包括国防支出，武装警察部队支出，中央级行政管理费和各项事业费，重点建设支出以及中央政府调整国民经济结构、协调地区发展、实施宏观调控的支出。地方财政支出主要包括地方行政管理和各项事业费，地方统筹的基本建设、技术改造支出，支援农村生产支出，城市维护和建设经费，价格补贴支出等。

**存款** 指企业、机关、团体或居民根据资金必须收回的原则，把货币资金存入银行或其他信贷机构保管并取得一定利息的一种信用活动形式。根据存款对象或性质的不同可划分为企业存款、财政存款、机关团体存款、城乡储蓄存款、农业存款、信托及委托类存款、其他存款等科目。它是银行信贷资金的主要来源。

**贷款** 指银行或其他信贷机构根据资金必须归还的原则，按一定利率，为企业、个人等提供资金的一种信用活动形式。我国银行贷款分为短期贷款、委托及信托类贷款、其他类贷款等。

**保险公司** 在中国境内的、经过保险监督管理部门批准设立，并依法登记注册的各类商业保险公司。

**保险金额** 指保险人承担赔偿或者给付保险金责任的最高限额。

**保费** 指投保人为取得保险人在约定范围内所承担赔偿责任而支付给保险人的费用。

**赔款** 指保险人根据保险合同的规定，向被保险人支付的赔偿保险责任损失的金额。

**给付** 包括死伤医疗给付和满期给付。死伤医疗给付是指保险人根据人寿保险及长期健康保险合同的规定，因被保险人在保险期内发生保险责任范围内的保险事故支付给被保险人(或受益人)的金额。满期给付是指被保险人生存期满，保险人按人寿保险合同规定支付给被保险人的满期保险金额。

**基本养老保险（参保）职工人数** 指报告期末按照国家法律、法规和有关政策规定参加基本养老保险并在社保经办机构已建立缴费记录档案的职工人数，包括中断缴费但未终止养老保险关系的职工人数，不包括只登记未建立缴费记录档案的人数。

**基本医疗保险参保人数** 指报告期末按国家有关规定参加基本医疗保险的人数。包括参加保险的职工人数和退休人员人数。

**失业保险参保人数** 指报告期末按照国家法律、法规和有关政策规定参加了失业保险的城镇企业事业单位的职工及地方政府规定参加失业保险的其他人员的人数。

**工伤保险参加保险人数** 指报告期末依据国家有关规定参加工伤保险的职工人数。

**生育保险参保人数** 指报告期末依据有关规定参加生育保险的职工人数。

# EXPLANATORY NOTES ON MAIN STATISTICAL INDICATORS

**Government Revenue** refers to income for the government finance through participating in the distribution of social products. It is the financial guarantee to ensure government functioning. The contents of government revenue have changed several times. Now it includes the following main items:

(1) Various tax revenues, including value added tax, business tax, consumption tax, land value added tax, tax on city maintenance and construction, resources tax, tax on use of urban land, enterprise income tax, personal income tax, tariff, stamp tax on security transactions, tax on purchase of motor vehicles, tax on agriculture and animal husbandry and tax on occupancy of cultivated land, etc.

(2) Special revenues, including revenues from the fee on sewage treatment, fee on urban water resources, fee for the compensation of mineral resources and extra-charges for education, etc.

(3) Other revenues, including revenue from interest, revenue from the repayment of capital construction loan, revenue from capital construction projects, and donations and grants.

(4) Subsidies for the losses of State-owned enterprises. This is an item of negative revenue, counteracting revenues and consisting of subsidies to industrial, commercial and grain purchasing and supply enterprises.

**Government Expenditure** refers to the distribution and use of the funds which the government finance has raised, so as to meet the needs of economic construction and various causes. It includes the following main items:

**Revenue of the Central Government and Revenue of the Local Governments** refer to the revenue of the Central Government and that of the local governments as defined by the decentralized taxation system starting from 1994. In accordance with this system, the revenue of the Central Government includes tariff, consumption tax and value added tax levied by the Customs, consumption tax, income tax of the enterprises subordinate to the Central Government, income taxes of local banks, foreign-funded banks and non-bank financial institutions, business tax and profits of railways, head offices of banks, head office of insurance company, which are handed over to the government in a centralized way, tax on city maintenance and construction, tax on purchasing motor vehicles, tonnage tax of ships, 75% of the value added tax, 94% of the tax on stock dealing (stamp tax), interest income tax in the personal income tax, that proportion of the personal income tax (other that interest income tax) to be shared by the Central Government, and tax on ocean petroleum resources. The revenue of the local governments includes business tax, income tax of the enterprises subordinate to the local government, that proportion of the personal income tax (other that interest income tax) to be shared by the Central Government, tax on the use of urban land, tax on the adjustment of investment in fixed assets, tax on town maintenance and construction, tax on real estates, tax on the use of vehicles and ships, stamp tax, slaughter tax, tax on agriculture and animal husbandry, tax on special agricultural products, tax on the occupancy of cultivated land, contract tax, value-added tax on land, income from charges on use of State-owned land, 25% of the value added tax, 6% of the tax on stock dealing (stamp tax) and tax on resources other than the tax on ocean petroleum resources.

**Expenditure of the Central Government and Expenditure of the Local Governments** according to the different functions of the Central Government and local governments in economic and social activities, the rights of affairs administration are demarcated between those of the Central Government and those of local governments; and the classification of the expenditure between the Central Government and local governments are made on the basis of the classification of the rights of affairs administration between them. The expenditure of the Central Government includes the expenditure for national defence, expenditure for armed police forces, the administrative expenses and various operating expenses at the level of Central Government, expenditure for key projects and the expenditure of the Central Government for adjusting the national economic structure; coordinating the development among different regions; and exercising macro-economic regulation and control. The expenditure of the local governments includes mainly the administrative expenses and various operating expenses at the level of local governments, the expenditure for capital construction and technological innovation with the funds raised by the local government, expenditure for supporting rural production, expenditure for city maintenance and construction and expenditure for price subsidies, etc.

**Deposit** is a form of credit by which enterprises, institutions, organizations or households can put money into banks and other credit institutions for safekeeping and interest earning under the principle of free withdrawal. According to different depositors, deposits are divided into enterprise deposits, fiscal deposits, deposits of government agencies and organizations, savings deposits of rural and urban households, agricultural savings deposits, entrusted deposits and other deposits. Deposits are major sources of the credit funds of banks.

**Loan** is a form of credit by which banks and other credit institutions provide funds at certain interest rate to enterprises and individuals in the light of the principle of unconditional repayment. Loans from Chinese banks include short-term loan, medium-term and long-term loans, entrusted loans, and other loans.

**Insurance Companies** refer to commercial insurance companies of various forms registered by law and established in China with the approval of insurance regulatory agencies.

**Amount Insured** refers to the maximum that the insurant will get for the claim of the case insured.

**Premium** is the fee paid by the insurant to the insurer to obtain the obligation of compensation from the insurance within the agreed terms.

**Settled Claim** is the compensation paid by the insurer to the insurant in accordance with the insurance contract.

**Payment** includes payment for death, injury or medical treatment and payment at maturity. Payment for death, injury or medical treatment refers to the money paid to the insurant (or the beneficiary) in accordance with the life or health insurance contract when the insurant encounters accidents within the insured period covered in the contract. Payment at maturity refers to the payment to the insurant in accordance with the life insurance contract at the end of the insured period.

**Number of People Covered by Endowment Insurance** refers to staff and workers participating in the basic pension insurance programme according to national laws, regulations and related policies at the end of the reference period, who have already had payment records in social security management agencies, including those who have interrupt payment without terminating the insurance programme. Those who have registered in the programme but with no payment records are not included.

**Number of People Covered by Medical Insurance** refers to people participating in the basic medical care insurance programme according to related regulations as at the end of reference period, including number of staff and workers and retirees participating in this insurance programme.

**Number of People Covered by Unemployment Insurance** refers to staff and workers in urban enterprises or institutions who have participated in the unemployment insurance programme according to relevant policies and regulations, and other people who have participated according to local government regulations, as at the end of reference period.

**Number of People Covered by Labor Injury Work Injury Insurance** refers to staff and workers who have participated in the work injury insurance programme according to relevant national regulations.

**Number of People Covered by Insurance** refers to staff and workers who have participated in the maternity insurance programme according to relevant regulation at the end of the reporting period.

# 十三、物价指数

## CHAPTER 13
## PRICE INDICES

# 物价指数
# PRICE INDICES

## 主 要 统 计 指 标
## MAJOR STATISTICAL INDICATORS

(以上年价格为100 The Price of Preceding Year is Taken as 100 )

| | | |
|---|---|---|
| 2012年市区居民消费价格总指数 | General Consumer Price Index of Urban Residents | 102.7 |
| 食品类价格指数 | General Price Index of Food in Urban Area | 105.1 |
| 烟酒品类价格指数 | General Price Index of Tobacco and Alcohol Products in Urban Area | 101.7 |
| 衣着类价格指数 | General Price Index of Clothing in Urban Area | 104.4 |
| 家庭设备用品及维修服务类价格指数 | General Price Index of Household Appliance and Maintenance in Urban Area | 105.3 |
| 医疗保健和个人用品类价格指数 | General Price Index of Medical Service and Personal Articles in Urban Area | 102.1 |
| 交通和通信类价格指数 | General Price Index of Transportation and Communication Tools in Urban Area | 98.5 |
| 娱乐教育文化用品及服务类价格指数 | General Price Index of Recreation ,Education and Cultural Goods and Service in Urban Area | 99.8 |
| 居住类价格指数 | General Price Index of Residence in Urban Area | 102.7 |
| 2012年市区商品零售价格总指数 | General Retail Price Index in Urban Area | 101.9 |

表13-1

# 市区居民消费价格指数及商品零售价格指数
# RESIDENTS CONSUMER PRICE INDICES AND RETAIL PRICE INDICES OF COMMODITIES

(2012年以下列各年价格为100 The Price of Following Years is Taken as 100 in 2012)

| 年 份 Year | 居民消费价格总指数 General Residents Consumer Price Index | # 食品类 Food | # 衣着类 Clothing | # 居住类 Inhabitation | # 服务项目 Services | 商品零售价格总指数 General Retail Price Index |
|---|---|---|---|---|---|---|
| 1978 | – | – | – | – | – | 507.1 |
| 1979 | – | – | – | – | – | 496.8 |
| 1980 | – | – | – | – | – | 476.7 |
| 1981 | – | – | – | – | – | 471.6 |
| 1982 | – | – | – | – | – | 466.9 |
| 1983 | – | – | – | – | – | 458.7 |
| 1984 | 621.8 | 1 091.3 | 445.0 | – | 1 144.5 | 442.7 |
| 1985 | 555.7 | 929.6 | 436.7 | – | 1 042.4 | 394.9 |
| 1986 | 521.7 | 855.2 | 422.4 | – | 969.7 | 371.1 |
| 1987 | 469.2 | 735.9 | 386.5 | – | 938.7 | 331.9 |
| 1988 | 382.4 | 578.6 | 301.4 | – | 869.9 | 268.0 |
| 1989 | 327.4 | 514.8 | 248.4 | – | 693.7 | 230.8 |
| 1990 | 315.1 | 497.9 | 232.5 | – | 618.9 | 223.6 |
| 1991 | 290.7 | 440.6 | 215.6 | – | 586.6 | 205.7 |
| 1992 | 263.7 | 395.0 | 204.0 | – | 451.6 | 190.1 |
| 1993 | 214.5 | 319.1 | 177.6 | 381.1 | 323.0 | 156.6 |
| 1994 | 173.8 | 242.5 | 141.3 | 347.7 | 271.0 | 127.8 |
| 1995 | 147.3 | 198.4 | 117.5 | 276.6 | 228.5 | 112.8 |
| 1996 | 132.7 | 181.2 | 109.6 | 198.9 | 200.8 | 106.1 |
| 1997 | 131.9 | 184.9 | 107.9 | 178.5 | 171.8 | 107.9 |
| 1998 | 133.2 | 191.2 | 115.3 | 161.1 | 161.5 | 111.3 |
| 1999 | 134.3 | 200.5 | 117.6 | 150.8 | 143.4 | 115.3 |
| 2000 | 134.4 | 203.7 | 118.1 | 142.4 | 136.0 | 117.2 |
| 2001 | 135.2 | 209.8 | 121.1 | 137.9 | 125.2 | 119.4 |
| 2002 | 134.6 | 206.7 | 124.3 | 138.4 | 120.6 | 120.0 |
| 2003 | 133.5 | 200.3 | 122.3 | 137.1 | 117.5 | 120.6 |
| 2004 | 127.1 | 179.6 | 119.3 | 129.2 | 111.4 | 118.6 |
| 2005 | 124.2 | 171.8 | 117.9 | 121.9 | 107.6 | 117.3 |
| 2006 | 122.2 | 166.1 | 116.4 | 116.0 | 106.4 | 116.3 |
| 2007 | 117.3 | 150.1 | 113.6 | 109.6 | 105.4 | 113.3 |
| 2008 | 111.4 | 130.6 | 111.4 | 106.9 | 104.6 | 108.1 |
| 2009 | 111.6 | 127.7 | 106.5 | 109.8 | 105.3 | 110.0 |
| 2010 | 108.0 | 120.4 | 108.5 | 105.8 | 102.1 | 106.7 |
| 2011 | 102.7 | 105.1 | 104.4 | 102.7 | 101.6 | 101.9 |

注:本章市区数据不包含吴江区。
Note: The data of urban area in this chapter does not include Wujiang District.

表13-2

# 市区居民消费价格指数及商品零售价格指数
# RESIDENTS CONSUMER PRICE INDICES AND RETAIL PRICE INDICES OF COMMODITIES

(各年以上年价格为100 The Price of Preceding Year is Taken as 100)

| 年 份<br>Year | 居民消费价格总指数<br>General Residents Consumer Price Index | # 食品类<br>Food | # 衣着类<br>Clothing | # 居住类<br>Inhabitation | # 服务项目<br>Services | 商品零售价格总指数<br>General Retail Price Index |
|---|---|---|---|---|---|---|
| 1979 | - | - | - | - | - | 102.1 |
| 1980 | - | - | - | - | - | 104.2 |
| 1981 | - | - | - | - | - | 101.1 |
| 1982 | - | - | - | - | - | 101.0 |
| 1983 | - | - | - | - | - | 101.8 |
| 1984 | - | - | - | - | - | 103.6 |
| 1985 | 111.9 | 117.4 | 101.9 | - | 109.8 | 112.1 |
| 1986 | 106.5 | 108.7 | 103.4 | - | 107.5 | 106.4 |
| 1987 | 111.2 | 116.2 | 109.3 | - | 103.3 | 111.8 |
| 1988 | 122.7 | 127.2 | 128.2 | - | 107.9 | 123.9 |
| 1989 | 116.8 | 112.4 | 121.3 | - | 125.4 | 116.1 |
| 1990 | 103.9 | 103.4 | 106.9 | - | 112.1 | 103.2 |
| 1991 | 108.4 | 113.0 | 107.8 | - | 105.5 | 108.7 |
| 1992 | 110.2 | 111.5 | 105.7 | - | 129.9 | 108.2 |
| 1993 | 123.0 | 123.8 | 114.9 | - | 139.8 | 121.4 |
| 1994 | 123.4 | 131.6 | 125.7 | 109.6 | 119.2 | 122.6 |
| 1995 | 118.0 | 122.3 | 120.2 | 125.7 | 118.6 | 113.3 |
| 1996 | 111.0 | 109.4 | 107.2 | 139.1 | 113.8 | 106.2 |
| 1997 | 100.6 | 98.0 | 101.6 | 111.4 | 116.9 | 98.4 |
| 1998 | 99.0 | 96.7 | 93.6 | 110.8 | 106.4 | 97.0 |
| 1999 | 99.2 | 95.4 | 97.8 | 106.9 | 112.6 | 96.4 |
| 2000 | 99.9 | 98.4 | 99.8 | 105.8 | 105.4 | 98.5 |
| 2001 | 99.5 | 97.1 | 97.5 | 103.3 | 108.7 | 98.1 |
| 2002 | 100.4 | 101.5 | 97.5 | 99.7 | 103.8 | 99.5 |
| 2003 | 100.8 | 103.2 | 101.6 | 100.9 | 102.6 | 99.5 |
| 2004 | 105.0 | 111.6 | 102.5 | 106.1 | 105.4 | 101.7 |
| 2005 | 102.4 | 104.5 | 101.2 | 106.0 | 103.6 | 101.1 |
| 2006 | 101.6 | 103.4 | 101.3 | 105.1 | 101.1 | 100.9 |
| 2007 | 104.2 | 110.7 | 102.4 | 105.8 | 101.0 | 102.6 |
| 2008 | 105.3 | 114.9 | 102.0 | 102.5 | 100.7 | 104.8 |
| 2009 | 99.8 | 102.3 | 104.6 | 97.4 | 99.4 | 98.3 |
| 2010 | 103.4 | 106.0 | 98.1 | 103.7 | 103.1 | 103.1 |
| 2011 | 105.1 | 114.6 | 104.0 | 103.1 | 100.5 | 104.7 |
| 2012 | 102.7 | 105.1 | 104.4 | 102.7 | 101.6 | 101.9 |

表13-3

# 居民消费价格指数
# RESIDENTS CONSUMER PRICE INDICES

(2012年以上年价格为100　The Price of 2012 Takes the Price of Preceding Year as 100)

| 项　　目 | Item | 城　市<br>Urban Indices | 农　村<br>Rural Indices |
|---|---|---|---|
| **居民消费价格总指数** | **General Residents Consumer Price Index** | **102.7** | **102.0** |
| **服务项目价格指数** | **Price Index of Service** | **101.6** | **100.7** |
| **消费品价格指数** | **Price Index of Consumer Goods** | **103.2** | **102.6** |
| **一、食　品** | **Food** | **105.1** | **103.7** |
| 1.粮　食 | Grain | 101.7 | 103.6 |
| 2.淀　粉 | Starches | 107.3 | 105.3 |
| 3.干豆类及豆制品 | Bean and Its Products | 102.8 | 96.4 |
| 4.油　脂 | Oil or Fat | 102.9 | 103.2 |
| 5.肉禽及其制品 | Meat, Poultry and Their Products | 103.7 | 100.0 |
| 6.蛋 | Eggs | 100.3 | 99.3 |
| 7.水产品 | Aquatic Products | 107.3 | 108.7 |
| 8.菜 | Vegetables | 111.7 | 106.6 |
| #鲜　菜 | Fresh Vegetables | 112.6 | 104.9 |
| 9.调味品 | Flavoring | 107.9 | 111.6 |
| 10.糖 | Carbohydrate | 104.4 | 105.2 |
| #食　糖 | Sugar | 105.2 | 106.1 |
| 11.茶及饮料 | Tea and Beverage | 106.5 | 104.9 |
| 12.干鲜瓜果 | Dried and Fresh Melons and Fruits | 97.3 | 91.1 |
| #鲜瓜果 | Fresh Fruits | 97.2 | 88.2 |
| 13.糕点饼干面包 | Cake, Biscuit and Bread | 102.5 | 102.0 |
| 14.液体乳及乳制品 | Milk and Its Products | 106.5 | 102.8 |
| 15.在外用膳食品 | Foods Consumed not at Home | 106.6 | 108.9 |
| 16.其他食品 | Other Food and Foods Processing | 104.3 | 101.9 |
| **二、烟　酒** | **Cigarette and Wine** | **101.7** | **103.3** |
| 1.烟　草 | Cigarette | 99.7 | 101.3 |
| 2.酒 | Wine | 107.8 | 110.4 |
| **三、衣　着** | **Clothing** | **104.4** | **102.4** |

表13-3 续表 Continued

| 项　　目 | Item | 城　市<br>Urban Indices | 农　村<br>Rural Indices |
|---|---|---|---|
| 1.服　装 | Garments | 103.2 | 100.3 |
| #男式服装 | Man's Garments | 100.9 | 100.5 |
| 女式服装 | Women's Garments | 105.6 | 100.6 |
| 儿童服装 | Children's Garments | 101.7 | 97.5 |
| 2.衣着材料 | Clothing Material | 108.0 | 105.5 |
| 3.鞋袜帽 | Footwear and Hats | 107.1 | 108.0 |
| 4.衣着加工服务 | Tailoring Service | 118.2 | 104.9 |
| **四、家庭设备用品及维修服务** | **Household Appliance and Maintenance** | **105.3** | **104.2** |
| 1.耐用消费品 | Durable Consumer Goods | 103.6 | 103.4 |
| （1）家　具 | Furniture | 107.6 | 98.5 |
| （2）家庭设备 | Household Facilities | 101.2 | 105.7 |
| 2.室内装饰品 | Interior Decorations | 99.9 | 100.3 |
| 3.床上用品 | Bed Articles | 104.5 | 110.2 |
| 4.家庭日用杂品 | Daily Use Household Articles | 107.3 | 103.7 |
| 5.家庭服务及加工维修服务 | Household Service and Maintenance | 109.3 | 107.1 |
| **五、医疗保健和个人用品** | **Medical Service and Personal Articles** | **102.1** | **100.3** |
| 1.医疗保健 | Medical and Health Service | 100.8 | 100.6 |
| 2.个人用品及服务 | Traditional Chinese Medicine | 104.2 | 99.8 |
| **六、交通和通信** | **Transportation and Communication** | **98.5** | **100.5** |
| 1.交　通 | Transportation | 98.6 | 100.7 |
| 2.通　信 | Communication | 98.1 | 99.8 |
| **七、娱乐教育文化用品及服务** | **Recreation ,Education and Cultural Goods and Service** | **99.8** | **99.6** |
| 1.文娱用耐用消费品及服务 | Durable Consumer Goods and Service on Cultural Recreation | 93.8 | 94.2 |
| 2.教　育 | Education | 100.3 | 97.4 |
| 3.文化娱乐类 | Cultural and Recreational Articles | 100.8 | 101.5 |
| 4.旅　游 | Tourism and Travel | 101.9 | 105.9 |
| **八、居　住** | **Residence** | **102.7** | **101.6** |
| 1.建房及装修材料 | Household Construction and Upholstering | 103.5 | 102.1 |
| 2.租　房 | House Rent | 104.0 | 101.6 |
| 3.自有住房 | Own Residence | 101.7 | 101.3 |
| 4.水、电、燃料 | Water, Electricity and Fuels | 102.1 | 101.8 |

表13-4

# 商品零售价格指数

# RETAIL PRICE INDICES OF COMMODITIES

(2012年以上年价格为100 The Price of 2012 Takes the Price of Preceding Year as 100)

| 项 目 | Item | 城 市 Urban Indices | 农 村 Rural Indices |
|---|---|---|---|
| **商品零售价格总指数** | **General Retail Price Index** | **101.9** | **102.4** |
| **一、食品类** | **Food** | **105.3** | **104.1** |
| 1.粮 食 | Grain | 101.7 | 103.6 |
| 2.淀 粉 | Starches | 107.3 | 105.3 |
| 3.干豆类及豆制品 | Bean and Its Products | 102.8 | 96.4 |
| 4.油 脂 | Oil or Fat | 102.9 | 103.2 |
| 5.肉禽及其制品 | Meat, Poultry and Related Products | 103.8 | 99.9 |
| 6.蛋 | Eggs | 100.3 | 99.9 |
| 7.水产品 | Aquatic Products | 107.3 | 108.7 |
| 8.菜 | Vegetables | 111.7 | 106.6 |
| 9.调味品 | Condiments | 107.9 | 111.6 |
| 10.糖 | Sugar | 104.4 | 105.2 |
| 11.干鲜瓜果 | Dried and Fresh Melons & Fruits | 97.3 | 91.1 |
| 12.糕点饼干面包 | Cake, Biscuits and Bread | 102.5 | 102.0 |
| 13.液体乳及乳制品 | Milk and Its Products | 106.5 | 102.8 |
| 14.在外用膳食品 | Foods Consumed not at Home | 106.6 | 108.9 |
| 15.其他食品 | Other Food | 104.3 | 101.9 |
| **二、饮料、烟酒** | **Beverage, Tobacco and Liquor** | **103.2** | **104.1** |
| 1.茶及饮料 | Tea and Beverage | 106.5 | 104.9 |
| 2.烟 草 | Cigarette | 99.7 | 101.3 |
| 3.酒 | Wine | 107.8 | 110.4 |
| **三、服装、鞋帽** | **Garments, Shoes and Hats** | **104.2** | **101.8** |
| 1.服 装 | Garments | 103.2 | 100.3 |
| 2.鞋袜帽 | Footwear and Hats | 107.1 | 108.0 |
| 3.其 他 | Other Clothing | 102.1 | 94.6 |
| **四、纺织品类** | **Textiles** | **105.5** | **107.9** |
| 1.衣着材料 | Clothing Material | 108.0 | 105.5 |
| 2.床上用品 | Bed Articles | 104.7 | 109.7 |
| **五、家用电器及音像器材** | **Household Electric Appliances and Sound-video Equipments** | **98.0** | **100.8** |
| 1.家庭设备 | Household Facilities and Articles | 101.2 | 105.7 |
| 2.文娱用耐用消费品 | Durable Consumer Goods for Recreational Use | 90.3 | 88.2 |

表13-4 续表　Continued

| 项　　目 | Item | 城　市<br>Urban Indices | 农　村<br>Rural Indices |
|---|---|---|---|
| 3.音像器材类 | Sound-video Equipments | 98.1 | 101.6 |
| **六、文化办公用品** | **Culture and Office Articles** | **97.9** | **99.4** |
| **七、日用品** | **Articles for Daily Use** | **106.0** | **103.2** |
| 1.日用百货 | Daily Consumer Goods | 104.2 | 98.6 |
| 2.日用杂品 | Daily Sundry Articles | 107.0 | 97.8 |
| 3.洗涤用品 | Washing Articles | 111.8 | 108.9 |
| 4.其他日用品 | Others Articles for Daily Use | 102.9 | 107.5 |
| **八、体育娱乐用品** | **Sports and Recreational Goods** | **99.5** | **103.0** |
| 1. 体育用品 | Sports Goods | 99.0 | 99.3 |
| 2. 娱乐用品 | Recreational Goods | 99.8 | 103.9 |
| **九、交通、通信用品** | **Transportation and Communication** | **94.7** | **100.3** |
| 1. 交通运输机械 | Transportation Machines | 96.8 | 100.4 |
| 2. 通讯器材 | Communication Apparatus | 88.7 | 99.3 |
| **十、家　具** | **Furniture** | **107.6** | **98.5** |
| **十一、化妆品类** | **Cosmetics** | **102.8** | **100.0** |
| **十二、金银珠宝类** | **Jewelry** | **102.5** | **101.2** |
| **十三、中西药品及医疗保健用品类** | **Chinese and Western Medicines and Medical Care Articles** | **101.3** | **99.3** |
| 1.医疗器具及用品 | Medical Appliances and Articles | 101.0 | 100.2 |
| 2.中药材及中成药 | Traditional Chinese Medicine | 107.1 | 107.4 |
| 3.西　药 | Western Medicine | 97.7 | 96.4 |
| 4.保健器具及用品 | Health Articles | 100.8 | 100.4 |
| **十四、书报杂志及电子出版物类** | **Newspapers, Magazines and Electronic Publication** | **106.4** | **100.8** |
| 1.教材及参考书 | Teaching Materials and Reference Books | 107.3 | 97.8 |
| 2.书报杂志 | Newspapers and Magazines | 106.9 | 101.1 |
| 3.电子音像制品 | Electric and Sound-video Materials | 100.0 | 105.2 |
| **十五、燃料类** | **Fuels** | **102.0** | **103.0** |
| 1. 煤炭及制品类 | Coal and Coal Products | 97.4 | 99.3 |
| 2. 石油及制品类 | Petroleum and Petroleum Products | 102.2 | 103.1 |
| **十六、建筑材料及五金电料类** | **Building Materials and Metal Hardware** | **101.0** | **102.5** |
| 1. 建筑装璜材料 | Building Decoration Materials | 100.3 | 101.0 |
| 2. 五金电料类 | Hardware and Electrical Appliances | 102.3 | 106.8 |

表13-5

# 分月居民消费价格指数及商品零售价格指数

(2012年以上年价格为100)

| 项　目 | Item | 全　年 Annual Total | 1月 Jan. | 2月 Feb. | 3月 Mar. |
|---|---|---|---|---|---|
| **城市居民消费价格总指数** | **Urban General Consumer Price Index** | **102.7** | **103.7** | **103.3** | **103.4** |
| 1.食　品 | Food | 105.1 | 111.0 | 107.2 | 107.9 |
| 2.烟　酒 | Tobacco and Alcohol | 101.7 | 103.0 | 103.3 | 103.7 |
| 3.衣　着 | Clothing | 104.4 | 100.6 | 110.6 | 108.1 |
| 4.家庭设备用品及维修服务 | Household Facilities Articles and Service | 105.3 | 109.6 | 109.7 | 109.1 |
| 5.医疗保健和个人用品 | Medicines and Medical Services, Personal Related Articles | 102.1 | 103.0 | 103.3 | 102.9 |
| 6.交通和通信 | Transport, Post and Communication Service | 98.5 | 99.2 | 99.4 | 98.4 |
| 7.娱乐教育文化用品及服务 | Recreation, Education and Cultural Services | 99.8 | 98.3 | 98.1 | 98.0 |
| 8.居　住 | Residence | 102.7 | 100.0 | 100.0 | 101.0 |
| **农村居民消费价格总指数** | **Rural General Consumer Price Index** | **102.0** | **104.5** | **103.8** | **102.8** |
| **城市商品零售价格总指数** | **Urban General Retail Price Index** | **101.9** | **102.5** | **102.9** | **103.1** |
| 1.食　品 | Food | 105.3 | 110.8 | 107.0 | 108.0 |
| 2.饮料、烟酒类 | Beverages, Tobacco and Liquor | 103.2 | 104.6 | 104.0 | 103.8 |
| 3.服装、鞋帽类 | Garments , Shoes and Hats | 104.2 | 100.9 | 110.9 | 108.3 |
| 4.纺织品类 | Textiles | 105.5 | 97.3 | 137.7 | 118.6 |
| 5.家用电器及音像器材 | Household Electric Appliances and Sound-video Equipments | 98.0 | 96.4 | 97.2 | 95.9 |
| 6.文化办公用品 | Culture and Office Articles | 97.9 | 95.6 | 95.8 | 96.8 |
| 7.日用品 | Articles for Daily Use | 106.0 | 108.9 | 108.3 | 108.0 |
| 8.体育娱乐用品 | Sports and Recreational Goods | 99.5 | 98.1 | 100.1 | 99.0 |
| 9.交通、通信用品 | Transportation and Communication | 94.7 | 91.7 | 92.1 | 92.8 |
| 10.家　具 | Furniture | 107.6 | 127.3 | 125.7 | 124.2 |
| 11.化妆品类 | Cosmetics | 102.8 | 99.8 | 99.1 | 101.0 |
| 12.金银珠宝类 | Jewelry | 102.5 | 107.0 | 112.3 | 106.5 |
| 13.中西药品及医疗保健用品类 | Chinese and Western Medicines and Medical Care Articles | 101.3 | 100.4 | 100.2 | 100.5 |
| 14.书报杂志及电子出版物类 | Newspapers, Magazines and Electronic Publication | 106.4 | 106.6 | 106.6 | 106.4 |
| 15.燃料类 | Fuels | 102.0 | 103.1 | 104.2 | 105.0 |
| 16.建筑材料及五金电料类 | Building Materials and Metal Hardware | 101.0 | 100.7 | 99.9 | 101.2 |
| **农村商品零售价格总指数** | **Rural General Retail Price Index** | **102.4** | **105.4** | **105.2** | **104.9** |

# CONSUMER PRICE INDICES AND RETAIL PRICE INDICES OF COMMODITIES BY MONTH

( The Price of 2012 Takes the Price of Preceding Year as 100)

| 4月 Apr. | 5月 May | 6月 Jun. | 7月 Jul. | 8月 Aug. | 9月 Sept. | 10月 Oct. | 11月 Nov. | 12月 Dec. |
|---|---|---|---|---|---|---|---|---|
| **103.4** | **103.1** | **101.8** | **102.4** | **102.5** | **102.1** | **101.9** | **102.1** | **102.6** |
| 107.4 | 106.2 | 102.4 | 103.0 | 103.7 | 102.7 | 101.9 | 103.4 | 105.1 |
| 103.7 | 103.0 | 102.3 | 101.7 | 101.7 | 100.4 | 99.6 | 99.4 | 98.8 |
| 105.2 | 103.2 | 101.9 | 100.8 | 104.2 | 109.2 | 107.0 | 102.9 | 100.3 |
| 108.9 | 107.5 | 105.1 | 105.5 | 103.0 | 100.9 | 103.2 | 101.5 | 100.5 |
| 102.9 | 102.5 | 101.7 | 101.7 | 100.7 | 100.6 | 102.1 | 101.6 | 102.0 |
| 97.2 | 97.3 | 97.1 | 97.3 | 98.5 | 98.8 | 98.8 | 99.8 | 100.1 |
| 99.6 | 99.0 | 98.9 | 100.8 | 100.7 | 100.6 | 100.9 | 101.1 | 101.8 |
| 102.1 | 104.0 | 104.7 | 105.8 | 104.3 | 103.0 | 102.5 | 102.4 | 102.8 |
| **102.1** | **101.4** | **100.0** | **99.8** | **100.4** | **101.4** | **102.3** | **102.7** | **103.0** |
| **102.7** | **101.9** | **100.3** | **100.6** | **101.2** | **101.4** | **101.8** | **102.0** | **102.5** |
| 107.5 | 106.2 | 102.5 | 103.4 | 104.2 | 103.0 | 102.1 | 103.6 | 105.3 |
| 104.1 | 105.0 | 102.5 | 102.3 | 102.9 | 102.0 | 102.4 | 102.7 | 102.4 |
| 105.3 | 103.0 | 101.4 | 100.3 | 103.5 | 108.8 | 106.4 | 102.2 | 100.3 |
| 114.5 | 110.0 | 104.3 | 99.9 | 99.8 | 94.5 | 102.4 | 103.3 | 97.1 |
| 97.7 | 98.0 | 97.2 | 97.2 | 98.4 | 96.9 | 101.3 | 100.5 | 100.0 |
| 97.5 | 97.7 | 98.3 | 99.5 | 99.1 | 96.4 | 99.2 | 99.4 | 99.4 |
| 107.2 | 107.0 | 107.3 | 107.2 | 105.8 | 104.4 | 104.2 | 102.4 | 102.5 |
| 98.9 | 99.3 | 99.3 | 99.1 | 99.4 | 100.1 | 100.2 | 100.2 | 100.4 |
| 90.8 | 90.8 | 92.6 | 94.2 | 96.3 | 98.4 | 98.1 | 99.5 | 100.7 |
| 121.4 | 112.7 | 105.5 | 110.4 | 98.6 | 96.0 | 95.8 | 94.0 | 93.7 |
| 101.7 | 104.1 | 103.7 | 103.8 | 102.8 | 102.2 | 105.2 | 104.4 | 105.7 |
| 104.1 | 101.2 | 98.5 | 101.7 | 96.4 | 97.8 | 101.2 | 100.6 | 104.2 |
| 102.0 | 102.5 | 102.4 | 101.6 | 101.0 | 100.4 | 101.2 | 101.4 | 101.4 |
| 106.4 | 106.4 | 106.4 | 106.4 | 106.4 | 106.4 | 106.4 | 106.4 | 106.4 |
| 106.5 | 103.8 | 98.7 | 97.5 | 98.2 | 100.4 | 101.7 | 102.4 | 103.4 |
| 101.4 | 101.5 | 101.3 | 101.5 | 100.2 | 99.7 | 101.0 | 101.6 | 101.6 |
| **103.6** | **101.8** | **100.2** | **100.9** | **100.7** | **101.1** | **101.6** | **101.8** | **101.9** |

# 主 要 统 计 指 标 解 释

**居民消费价格指数** 是反映一定时期内城乡居民所购买的生活消费品价格和服务项目价格变动趋势和程度的相对数，是对城市居民消费价格指数和农村居民消费价格指数进行综合汇总计算的结果。该指数可以观察和分析消费品的零售价格和服务项目价格变动对城乡居民实际生活费支出的影响程度。

**城市居民消费价格指数** 是反映一定时期内城市居民家庭所购买的生活消费品价格和服务项目价格变动趋势和程度的相对数。该指数可以观察和分析消费品的零售价格和服务项目价格变动对城镇职工货币工资的影响，作为研究职工生活和确定工资政策的依据。

**农村居民消费价格指数** 是反映一定时期内农村居民家庭所购买的生活消费品价格和服务项目价格变动趋势和程度的相对数。该指数可以观察农村消费品的零售价格和服务项目价格变动对农村居民生活消费支出的影响，直接反映农民生活水平的实际变化情况，为分析和研究农村居民生活问题提供依据。

**商品零售价格指数** 是反映一定时期内城乡商品零售价格变动趋势和程度的相对数。商品零售价格的变动直接影响到城乡居民的生活支出和国家的财政收入，影响居民购买力和市场供需的平衡，影响到消费与积累的比例关系。因此，该指数可以从一个侧面对上述经济活动进行观察和分析。

# EXPLANATORY NOTES ON MAIN STATISTICAL INDICATORS

**Consumer Price Indices** reflect the trend and degree of changes in prices of consumer goods and services purchased by urban and rural households during a given period. They are obtained by combining the Urban Consumer Price Indices and the Rural Consumer Price Indices. The Indices enable the observation and analysis of the degree of impact of the changes in the prices of retailed goods and services on the actual living expenses of urban and rural residents.

**Urban Consumer Price Indices** reflect the trend and degree of changes in prices of consumer goods and services purchased by urban households during a given period. It can be used to observe and analyze the impact of price changes in consumer goods and services on wages (in monetary terms) of urban staff and workers, and provide a basis for research on the livelihood of staff and workers and policy-making concerning wages.

**Rural Consumer Price Indices** reflect the trend and degree of changes in prices of consumer goods and services purchased by rural households during a given period. It can be used to observe the impact of change in retail prices of consumer goods and service prices in rural areas on living expenditure of rural households, and to show the changes in the living standard of peasants. It provides a basis for analysis and research on the condition of life in rural areas.

**Retail Price Indices** reflect the trend and degree of change in retail prices of commodities during a given period. The change in retail prices of commodities directly affect the living expenses of urban and rural residents, government revenue, purchasing power of residents and the equilibrium of market supply and demand, and the ratio of consumption to accumulation. Therefore, the retail price indices are useful from an oblique perspective for observing and analyzing the changes of the above economic activities.

# 十四、人民生活

## CHAPTER 14
## PEOPLE'S LIVELIHOOD

# 人民生活
# PEOPLE'S LIVELIHOOD

## 主要统计指标
## MAJOR STATISTICAL INDICATORS

| | | | | |
|---|---|---|---|---|
| 2012年市区居民人均可支配收入 | Per Capita Disposable Income of Urban Residents | 37 531 | 元 | yuan |
| 比上年增长 | Increase Over Last Year | 12.9 | % | |
| 2012年市区居民人均消费性支出 | Per Capita Living Expenditure of Urban Residents | 23 092 | 元 | yuan |
| 比上年增长 | Increase Over Last Year | 9.7 | % | |
| 2012年每百户市区居民家庭拥有 | Number of Major Durable Consumer Goods Owned of Urban Households at Year-end Per 100 Households | | | |
| 洗衣机 | Washing Machines | 106.4 | 台 | unit |
| 电冰箱 | Refrigerators | 110.1 | 台 | unit |
| 彩色电视机 | Color TV Sets | 199.1 | 台 | unit |
| 家用电脑 | Computer | 125.4 | 台 | unit |
| 2012年农民人均纯收入 | Per Capita Net Income of Rural Residents | 19 396 | 元 | yuan |
| 比上年增长 | Increase Over Last Year | 12.6 | % | |
| 2012年农民人均消费性支出 | Per Capita Living Expenditure of Rural Residents | 14 381 | 元 | yuan |
| 比上年增长 | Increase Over Last Year | 15.2 | % | |
| 2012年每百户农村居民家庭拥有 | Number of Major Durable Consumer Goods Owned of Rural Households at Year-end Per 100 Households | | | |
| 洗衣机 | Washing Machines | 100.3 | 台 | unit |
| 电冰箱 | Refrigerators | 103.5 | 台 | unit |
| 彩色电视机 | Color TV Sets | 197.5 | 台 | unit |
| 空调器 | Air Conditioners | 193.7 | 台 | unit |

表14-1

# 城乡居民家庭人均收入和消费支出 (1985-2012年)
# PER CAPITA ANNUAL INCOME AND LIVING EXPENDITURE OF URBAN HOUSEHOLDS (1985-2012)

单位：元 (yuan)

| 年 份 Year | 农村居民家庭人均纯收入 Per Capital Annual Net Income of Rural Households | 农村居民家庭人均生活消费支出 Per Capital Living Expenditure of Rural Households | 市区居民家庭人均可支配收入 Per Capital Annual Disposable Income of Urban Households | 市区居民家庭人均消费性支出 Per Capita Living Expenditure for Consumption of Urban Households | 农村居民家庭恩格尔系数(%) Engle Coefficient of Rural Households (%) | 市区居民家庭恩格尔系数(%) Engle Coefficient of City Households (%) |
|---|---|---|---|---|---|---|
| 1985 | 739 | 661 | 918 | 787 | | 52.8 |
| 1989 | 1 470 | 1 281 | 1 865 | 1 619 | | 53.6 |
| 1990 | 1 664 | 1 415 | 2 150 | 1 805 | 48.3 | 53.5 |
| 1991 | 1 731 | 1 527 | 2 427 | 2 187 | 46.4 | 51.2 |
| 1992 | 2 001 | 1 722 | 2 788 | 2 199 | 44.2 | 54.8 |
| 1993 | 2 558 | 1 893 | 3 695 | 3 416 | 42.5 | 48.6 |
| 1994 | 3 457 | 2 676 | 4 885 | 4 027 | 46.6 | 50.1 |
| 1995 | 4 444 | 3 414 | 5 790 | 4 877 | 48.1 | 49.6 |
| 1996 | 5 088 | 3 804 | 6 591 | 5 264 | 46.0 | 50.8 |
| 1997 | 5 219 | 4 014 | 7 479 | 5 955 | 43.2 | 47.7 |
| 1998 | 5 347 | 3 958 | 7 812 | 6 289 | 41.2 | 44.8 |
| 1999 | 5 308 | 3 785 | 8 406 | 6 545 | 40.7 | 43.6 |
| 2000 | 5 462 | 4 073 | 9 274 | 7 027 | 40.1 | 42.7 |
| 2001 | 5 796 | 4 127 | 10 515 | 7 270 | 43.5 | 42.0 |
| 2002 | 6 140 | 4 229 | 10 617 | 7 682 | 40.6 | 42.1 |
| 2003 | 6 681 | 4 641 | 12 361 | 9 272 | 37.6 | 37.8 |
| 2004 | 7 503 | 5 436 | 14 451 | 9 783 | 36.8 | 40.1 |
| 2005 | 8 393 | 6 143 | 16 276 | 11 163 | 37.7 | 37.4 |
| 2006 | 9 278 | 6 811 | 18 532 | 12 472 | 36.3 | 36.1 |
| 2007 | 10 475 | 7 623 | 21 260 | 13 959 | 35.7 | 37.9 |
| 2008 | 11 785 | 8 443 | 23 867 | 15 183 | 35.4 | 39.3 |
| 2009 | 12 969 | 9 354 | 26 320 | 16 402 | 34.5 | 37.6 |
| 2010 | 14 657 | 10 397 | 29 219 | 17 879 | 33.9 | 38.8 |
| 2011 | 17 226 | 12 485 | 33 243 | 21 046 | 33.8 | 37.3 |
| 2012 | 19 396 | 14 381 | 37 531 | 23 092 | 33.9 | 36.8 |

注:本章城市居民家庭调查中市区数据不包含吴江区。
Note: The data of urban area by investigation of urban households in this chapter does not include Wujiang District.

表14-2

# 部分年份市区居民家庭基本情况
# BASIC INDICATORS OF URBAN HOUSEHOLDS OF PARTIAL YEARS

| 指　　标 | Item | 2000年 | 2010年 | 2011年 | 2012年 |
|---|---|---|---|---|---|
| 调查户数 (户) | Number of Households Surveyed (household) | 200 | 300 | 300 | 300 |
| 户均家庭人口 (人) | Average Household Size (person) | 2.87 | 2.77 | 2.84 | 2.82 |
| 户均就业人口数 | Average Number of Employed Persons Per Household | 1.43 | 1.34 | 1.36 | 1.36 |
| 就业人口人均负担人数 | Number of Persons Supported by Each Employee | 2.01 | 2.07 | 2.09 | 2.07 |
| 人均住房建筑面积 (平方米) | Per Capita Floor Space of Residential Buildings (sq.m) | | 33.10 | 34.07 | 34.10 |
| 人均住房使用面积 | Per Capita Gross Living Space of Residential Buildings | 16.29 | 24.83 | 25.55 | 25.58 |
| 人均家庭总收入 (元) | Per Capita Total income of household (yuan) | 9 336.12 | 32 549.08 | 37 452.56 | 41 822.19 |
| # 可支配收入 | Disposable Income | 9 274.24 | 29 219.08 | 33 243.27 | 37 531.12 |
| 工薪收入 | Salary Income | 5 780.87 | 19 011.95 | 21 995.86 | 24 417.82 |
| 财产性收入 | Income from Property | 99.62 | 1 014.27 | 1 397.74 | 1 625.72 |
| 转移性收入 | Income from Transfer | 3 347.89 | 11 064.77 | 11 638.86 | 12 646.32 |
| 人均出售财物收入 | Per Capita Income by Selling Properties | 185.21 | 10.11 | 16.32 | 977.31 |
| 人均借贷收入 | Per Capita Income from Debit and Credit | 2 722.57 | 4 184.87 | 5 048.61 | 7 157.79 |
| # 提取储蓄存款 | Pick up Bank Savings | 2 282.12 | 3 945.50 | 4 906.53 | 7 000.40 |
| 人均家庭总支出 | Per Capita Total Expenditure of Household | 9 392.76 | 24 363.00 | 29 137.25 | 32 633.99 |
| 消费支出 | Living Expenditures | 7 027.49 | 17 878.80 | 21 046.17 | 23 092.33 |
| # 服务性消费支出 | Living Expenditures Services | | 4 590.40 | 5 597.14 | 6 551.19 |
| 购房与建房支出 | Expenditure of Purchasing or Building Houses | 1 456.97 | 177.50 | – | 1 170.61 |
| 转移性支出 | Transfer Expenditure | 898.77 | 3 230.60 | 3 989.41 | 3 987.36 |
| 财产性支出 | Expenditure on Properties | | 344.13 | 581.62 | 682.22 |
| 社保支出 | Expenditure on Insurance | | 2 731.96 | 3 520.04 | 3 701.47 |
| 人均储蓄借贷支出 | Per Capita Expending on Debit and Credit | 2 169.87 | 11 776.15 | 11 887.84 | 17 280.97 |
| 人均年末手存现金 | Per Capita Cash in Hand at Year-end | 700.43 | 2 950.51 | 2 159.00 | 2 043.63 |

表14-3

# 市区居民家庭基本情况

(按收入等级分, 2012年)

| 项　　目 | | Item | 总平均 Average | 10% 最低收入户 Lowest Income House-holds (first decile) |
|---|---|---|---|---|
| 调查户数 | (户) | Number of Households Surveyed (household) | 300 | 30 |
| 平均每户家庭人口 | (人) | Average Household Size (person) | 2.82 | 3.32 |
| 平均每户就业人口 | | Average Number of Employees per Household | 1.36 | 1.65 |
| 平均每户就业面 | (%) | Percentage of Employed Persons per Household (%) | 48.23 | 49.70 |
| 平均每一就业者负担人数(包括就业者本人) | (人) | Number of Persons Supported by Each Employee (including the employee himself or herself) (person) | 2.07 | 2.01 |
| 平均每人家庭总收入 | (元) | Per Capita Annual Income (yuan) | 41 822.19 | 17 393.83 |
| 平均每人可支配收入 | | Per Capita Disposable Income | 37 531.12 | 14 618.58 |
| **平均每人消费性支出** | | **Per Capita Annual Living Expenditure** | **23 092.33** | **15 061.73** |
| 食　品 | | Food | 8 503.39 | 6 989.11 |
| 衣　着 | | Clothing | 1 883.42 | 1 018.32 |
| 居　住 | | Residence | 1 456.30 | 1 060.00 |
| 家庭设备用品及服务 | | Household Facilities, Articles and Services | 1 607.59 | 681.86 |
| 医疗保健 | | Medicine and Medical Services | 1 161.35 | 551.04 |
| 交通通信 | | Transport, Post and Communication Services | 3 690.41 | 2 270.84 |
| 教育文化娱乐服务 | | Education，Cultural and Recreation Services | 3 914.69 | 1 982.90 |
| 杂项商品与服务 | | Miscellaneous Commodities and Services | 875.17 | 507.65 |
| **消费性支出构成** | (%) | **Total Living Expenditures** (%) | **100.00** | **100.00** |
| 食　品 | | Food | 36.82 | 46.40 |
| 衣　着 | | Clothing | 8.16 | 6.76 |
| 居　住 | | Residence | 6.31 | 7.04 |
| 家庭设备用品及服务 | | Household Facilities, Articles and Services | 6.96 | 4.53 |
| 医疗保健 | | Medicine and Medical Services | 5.03 | 3.66 |
| 交通通信 | | Transport, Post and Communication Services | 15.98 | 15.08 |
| 教育文化娱乐服务 | | Education，Cultural and Recreation Services | 16.95 | 13.17 |
| 杂项商品与服务 | | Miscellaneous Commodities and Services | 3.79 | 3.36 |

# BASIC CONDITION OF URBAN HOUSEHOLDS

(Grouped by Percentile of Households, 2012)

| 10% | 20% | 20% | 20% | 10% | 10% |
|---|---|---|---|---|---|
| 低收入户 Low Income House-holds (second decile) | 中等偏下户 Lower Middle In-come House-holds (second quintile) | 中等收入户 Middle Income House-holds (third quintile) | 中等偏上户 Upper Middle Income House-holds (fourth quintile) | 高收入户 High Income House-holds (ninth decile) | 最高收入户 Highest Income House-holds (tenth decile) |
| 30 | 60 | 60 | 60 | 30 | 30 |
| 3.15 | 2.65 | 2.84 | 2.80 | 2.52 | 2.66 |
| 1.43 | 0.92 | 1.38 | 1.50 | 1.20 | 1.68 |
| 45.40 | 34.72 | 48.59 | 53.57 | 47.62 | 63.16 |
| 2.20 | 2.88 | 2.06 | 1.87 | 2.10 | 1.58 |
| 22 974.24 | 28 259.39 | 36 606.82 | 49 607.14 | 62 669.19 | 98 052.78 |
| 20 151.22 | 25 322.82 | 32 790.53 | 45 207.55 | 57 628.67 | 87 267.27 |
| **15 200.85** | **16 855.55** | **20 739.44** | **26 369.45** | **33 787.32** | **43 461.53** |
| 7 648.57 | 7 685.75 | 8 210.48 | 8 896.95 | 10 187.71 | 11 334.87 |
| 1 245.91 | 1 174.02 | 1 619.79 | 2 330.22 | 2 650.06 | 4 082.26 |
| 1 014.17 | 912.74 | 1 256.08 | 1 373.78 | 3 860.74 | 1 965.33 |
| 959.38 | 960.66 | 1 445.22 | 1 864.54 | 3 208.93 | 3 183.21 |
| 1 015.57 | 1 521.55 | 1 164.44 | 1 058.87 | 1 804.41 | 1 006.98 |
| 1 229.13 | 2 134.13 | 3 047.52 | 4 628.61 | 5 462.01 | 9 298.27 |
| 1 661.14 | 2 067.88 | 3 240.87 | 5 384.39 | 5 310.04 | 9 804.89 |
| 426.99 | 398.84 | 755.05 | 832.08 | 1 303.41 | 2 785.73 |
| **100.00** | **100.00** | **100.00** | **100.00** | **100.00** | **100.00** |
| 50.32 | 45.60 | 39.59 | 33.74 | 30.15 | 26.08 |
| 8.20 | 6.97 | 7.81 | 8.84 | 7.84 | 9.39 |
| 6.67 | 5.42 | 6.06 | 5.21 | 11.43 | 4.52 |
| 6.31 | 5.70 | 6.97 | 7.07 | 9.50 | 7.32 |
| 6.68 | 9.03 | 5.61 | 4.02 | 5.34 | 2.32 |
| 8.09 | 12.66 | 14.69 | 17.55 | 16.17 | 21.39 |
| 10.93 | 12.27 | 15.63 | 20.42 | 15.72 | 22.56 |
| 2.80 | 2.35 | 3.64 | 3.15 | 3.85 | 6.42 |

表14-4

# 部分年份市区居民家庭居住情况
# HOUSING CONDITIONS OF URBAN HOUSEHOLDS OF PARTIAL YEARS

单位：户 (household)

| 项　目 | Item | 2000年 | 2010年 | 2011年 | 2012年 |
|---|---|---|---|---|---|
| **总　计** | **Total** | **200** | **300** | **300** | **300** |
| **一、按人均现住房面积分** | **Grouped by Residential Space** | | | | |
| 无房户 | No housing | – | – | – | – |
| 8平方米以下 | Below 8 sq.m | 1 | – | – | – |
| 8-12平方米 | 8-12 sq.m | 10 | 4 | 5 | 5 |
| 12-16平方米 | 12-16 sq.m | 43 | 22 | 13 | 13 |
| 16-20平方米 | 16-20 sq.m | 46 | 36 | 31 | 32 |
| 20-24平方米 | 20-24 sq.m | 30 | 35 | 43 | 43 |
| 24-28平方米 | 24-28 sq.m | 25 | 41 | 37 | 41 |
| 28-30平方米 | 28-30 sq.m | 5 | 30 | 15 | 15 |
| 30-35平方米 | 30-35 sq.m | 22 | 28 | 42 | 39 |
| 35-40平方米 | 35-40 sq.m | 3 | 32 | 25 | 23 |
| 40平方米以上 | Above 40 sq.m | 15 | 72 | 89 | 89 |
| **二、按卫生设备拥有情况分** | **Grouped by Possession of Sanitary Equipment** | | | | |
| 无卫生设备 | No Sanitary Equipment | 64 | 16 | 3 | 3 |
| 有浴室厕所 | Provided with Bathroom and Toilet | 118 | 277 | 294 | 293 |
| 有厕所无浴室 | With Toilet But No Bathroom | 18 | 6 | 3 | 4 |
| 公　用 | For Public Use | – | 1 | – | - |
| **三、按燃料使用情况分** | **Grouped by Usage of Fuel** | | | | |
| 管道煤气 | Piping Gas | 95 | 211 | 249 | 248 |
| 液化石油气 | Liquefied Petroleum Gas | 105 | 89 | 51 | 52 |
| 煤 | Coal | – | – | – | – |
| 其　他 | Others | – | – | – | – |
| **四、按取暖设备分** | **Classified by Heating Apparatus** | | | | |
| 无取暖设备 | Without Heating Facilities | 104 | 6 | 6 | 5 |
| 空调设备 | Air-Conditioning Equipment | 96 | 294 | 294 | 295 |
| 其　他 | Others | – | – | – | – |
| **五、按房屋产权分** | **Grouped by Ownership of Housing** | | | | |
| 租赁公房 | Public Leasing House | 71 | 37 | 26 | 28 |
| 租赁私房 | Rent Private Owned Residence | – | 2 | – | 1 |
| 原有私房 | Originally Private Owned house | – | 42 | 29 | 30 |
| 房改私房 | House Privatized Through Housing Reform | – | 123 | 73 | 74 |
| 商品房 | Commercial Buildings | – | 96 | 172 | 167 |
| 其　他 | Others | – | – | – | – |

表14-5

# 部分年份市区居民家庭人均消费支出情况
# PER CAPITA LIVING EXPENDITURE OF URBAN HOUSEHOLDS OF PARTIAL YEARS

单位：元 (yuan)

| 项 目 | Item | 2000年 | 2010年 | 2011年 | 2012年 |
|---|---|---|---|---|---|
| **总 计** | **Total** | **7 027.49** | **17 878.80** | **21 046.17** | **23 092.33** |
| **1. 食 品** | **Food** | **2 998.61** | **6 935.83** | **7 849.68** | **8 503.39** |
| # 粮 食 | Grain | 191.91 | 546.13 | 619.59 | 611.69 |
| 油脂类 | Oil and Fats | 78.84 | 125.09 | 141.37 | 146.63 |
| 肉禽蛋及制品 | Meat, Poultry, Eggs and Related Products | 772.64 | 1 406.69 | 1 567.69 | 1 721.97 |
| 水产品 | Aquatic Products | 388.33 | 692.58 | 756.47 | 856.69 |
| 鲜 菜 | Fresh Vegetables | 225.70 | 605.24 | 608.97 | 711.19 |
| **2. 衣着支出** | **Clothing** | **488.97** | **1 310.22** | **1 911.33** | **1 883.42** |
| # 服 装 | Garments | 341.93 | 950.14 | 1 400.43 | 1 354.47 |
| 衣着材料 | Clothing Materials | 14.24 | 16.97 | 21.67 | 14.60 |
| 衣着加工费 | Tailoring and Laundering Service Fees | 8.33 | 9.55 | 13.05 | 12.07 |
| **3. 居 住** | **Residence** | **512.12** | **1 567.72** | **1 333.57** | **1 456.30** |
| # 住 房 | Housing | 80.33 | 664.28 | 461.54 | 433.23 |
| 水电燃料及其他 | Water, Electricity, Fuels and Others | 431.79 | 791.08 | 732.37 | 793.18 |
| **4. 家庭设备用品及服务** | **Facilities, Articles and Service** | **940.14** | **1 200.76** | **1 457.01** | **1 607.59** |
| # 耐用消费品 | Durable Consumer Goods | 656.36 | 572.93 | 583.03 | 550.77 |
| 室内装饰品 | Room Decorations | 15.10 | 17.69 | 19.82 | 26.94 |
| 床上用品 | Bed Articles | 23.73 | 93.31 | 148.89 | 165.36 |
| 家庭日用杂品 | Household Articles for Daily Use | 154.86 | 411.12 | 563.68 | 657.16 |
| **5. 医疗保健** | **Medicine and Medical Service** | **392.86** | **918.60** | **1 249.98** | **1 161.35** |
| # 医疗费 | Medical Expenses | 271.57 | 156.67 | 307.14 | 309.59 |
| 滋补保健品 | Nutriment Products | 66.53 | 303.49 | 401.92 | 362.29 |
| **6. 交通和通信** | **Transportation and Communications** | **441.29** | **2 951.67** | **3 321.69** | **3 690.41** |
| 交 通 | Transportation | 170.32 | 2 056.17 | 2 438.97 | 2 603.58 |
| 通 信 | Communications | 270.97 | 895.50 | 882.72 | 1 086.83 |
| **7. 教育文化娱乐服务** | **Service of Education, Culture and Entertainment** | **911.25** | **2 459.46** | **3 048.85** | **3 914.69** |
| # 教 育 | Education | 431.15 | 890.78 | 1 123.21 | 1 153.59 |
| **8. 杂项商品和服务** | **Miscellaneous Commodities and Services** | **342.25** | **534.55** | **874.07** | **875.17** |

表14-6

# 部分年份市区居民家庭主要食品人均消费量
# PER CAPITA CONSUMPTION OF MAJOR FOOD OF URBAN RESIDENTS OF PARTIAL YEARS

单位：公斤 (kg)

| 项　　目 | Item | 1990年 | 2000年 | 2010年 | 2011年 | 2012年 |
|---|---|---|---|---|---|---|
| 大　米 | Rice | 87.37 | 67.48 | 53.39 | 47.22 | 43.67 |
| 面　粉 | Flour | 1.11 | 0.87 | 1.78 | 2.74 | 2.68 |
| 食用植物油 | Edible Vegetable Oil | 7.89 | 9.96 | 8.80 | 8.23 | 8.18 |
| 猪　肉 | Pork | 20.25 | 21.08 | 25.49 | 22.49 | 22.67 |
| 牛　肉 | Beef | 0.29 | 0.90 | 2.06 | 2.08 | 1.93 |
| 羊　肉 | Mutton | 0.21 | 0.25 | 0.55 | 0.61 | 0.72 |
| 家　禽 | Poultry | 3.42 | 8.80 | 11.75 | 16.47 | 16.79 |
| 蛋 | Eggs | 8.04 | 12.81 | 9.77 | 11.20 | 11.62 |
| 鱼 | Fish | 10.23 | 14.18 | 15.15 | 14.38 | 14.82 |
| 虾 | Shrimp | 1.25 | 4.61 | 4.64 | 4.41 | 4.47 |
| 鲜　菜 | Fresh Vegetables | 111.28 | 107.76 | 128.26 | 119.46 | 125.08 |
| 白　酒 | Liquor | 0.92 | 1.14 | 1.14 | 1.14 | 1.32 |
| 啤　酒 | Beer | 3.66 | 4.20 | 3.33 | 1.96 | 2.23 |
| 茶　叶 | Tea | 0.33 | 0.35 | 0.45 | 0.36 | 0.36 |
| 汽水、可乐 | Soft Drink, Cola | 1.13 | 4.19 | 2.07 | 1.82 | 1.67 |
| 干鲜瓜果 | Dried and Fresh Melons & Fruits | 63.48 | 72.46 | 64.59 | 55.81 | 59.73 |
| 鲜　果 | Fresh Fruits | | | 36.51 | 37.25 | 39.05 |
| 鲜　瓜 | Fresh Melons | | | 28.08 | 18.56 | 20.68 |
| 糕　点 | Cake | 4.75 | 2.95 | 5.27 | 5.41 | 4.95 |
| 鲜乳品 | Fresh Dairy Products | 14.39 | 22.87 | 21.52 | 22.56 | 23.34 |

表14-7

# 部分年份市区每百户居民家庭购买商品量
# PURCHASES OF COMMODITIES PER 100 URBAN HOUSEHOLDS OF PARTIAL YEARS

| 商品名称 | | Commodities | | 1990年 | 2000年 | 2010年 | 2011年 | 2012年 |
|---|---|---|---|---|---|---|---|---|
| 各类服装 | (件) | Garments | (piece) | 1 960.0 | 1 971.0 | 2 354.5 | 2 760.5 | 2 642.3 |
| 各类鞋 | (双) | Shoes | (pair) | 739.2 | 692.5 | 778.4 | 908.8 | 840.4 |
| 洗衣机 | (台) | Washing Machine | (unit) | 4.2 | 2.0 | 8.3 | 6.3 | 5.4 |
| 电冰箱 | | Refrigerator | | 4.2 | 6.0 | 13.1 | 7.0 | 7.0 |
| 微波炉 | | Microwave Oven | | | 10.5 | 3.3 | 5.7 | 6.4 |
| 空调器 | | Air Conditioner | | | 4.0 | 13.3 | 8.7 | 9.4 |
| 淋浴热水器 | | Shower | | | 6.5 | 10.0 | 9.7 | 6.7 |
| 助力车 | | Motor Bicycle | | | | 13.7 | 9.0 | 10.4 |
| 家用汽车 | | Cars for Household Use | | | | 3.0 | 2.3 | 2.7 |
| 电话机 | (部) | Telephone Sets | (unit) | | 10.5 | 32.3 | 9.3 | 9.0 |
| 移动电话 | | Mobile Telephone | | | | 25.3 | 35.3 | 41.8 |
| 彩色电视机 | (台) | Color TV Set | (unit) | 7.5 | 10.0 | 13.7 | 11.1 | 11.0 |
| 家用电脑 | | Computer | | | 5.5 | 10.3 | 11.1 | 11.4 |
| 组合音响 | (套) | Hi-Fi Stereo Component System | (set) | | 1.5 | 0.3 | 2.7 | 0.3 |
| 摄像机 | (架) | Video Camera | (unit) | | | 0.3 | 0.3 | 0.7 |
| 照相机 | | Camera | | 1.7 | 0.5 | 3.7 | 6.3 | 4.0 |
| 中高档乐器 | (件) | Medium and High Grade Musical Instrument | (unit) | 0.8 | 1.0 | 2.2 | 3.6 | 4.6 |
| 健身器材 | (套) | Healthy Equipment | (unit) | | | 0.7 | 3.0 | 3.0 |
| 电子辞典 | (部) | Electronic Dictionaries | (unit) | | | 2.0 | 0.7 | 1.7 |

表14-8

# 市区每百户居民家庭耐用消费品拥有量

(按收入等级分, 2012年末)

| 项目 | | Item | | 总平均 Average | 10% 最低收入户 Lowest Income House-holds (first decile) |
|---|---|---|---|---|---|
| 摩托车 | (辆) | Motorcycle | (unit) | 1.0 | 3.2 |
| 助力车 | | Helping Hand Car | | 122.0 | 154.8 |
| 家用汽车 | | Cars for Household Use | | 42.7 | 19.4 |
| 洗衣机 | (台) | Washing Machine | (set) | 106.3 | 103.2 |
| 电冰箱 | | Refrigerator | | 110.0 | 103.2 |
| 彩色电视机 | | Color Television Set | | 199.1 | 193.6 |
| 家用电脑 | | Computer | | 125.3 | 109.7 |
| 组合音响 | (套) | Hi-Fi Stereo Component System | (set) | 30.7 | 22.6 |
| 摄像机 | (架) | Video Camera | (set) | 14.7 | 6.5 |
| 照相机 | | Camera | | 77.0 | 51.6 |
| 钢　琴 | | Piano | | 4.3 | – |
| 其他中高档乐器 | (件) | Other Medium and High Grade Musical Instrument | (unit) | 6.3 | 3.2 |
| 微波炉 | (台) | Microwave Oven | (unit) | 99.7 | 96.8 |
| 空调器 | | Air Conditioner | | 254.3 | 212.9 |
| 淋浴热水器 | | Shower | | 108.3 | 103.2 |
| 消毒碗柜 | | Disinfection Cupboard | | 12.3 | 3.2 |
| 洗碗机 | | Dishwasher | | 0.7 | – |
| 健身器材 | (套) | Healthy Equipment | (unit) | 7.3 | 3.2 |
| 普通电话 | (部) | Telephone | (unit) | 104.3 | 100.0 |
| 移动电话 | | Mobile Telephone | | 230.7 | 241.9 |

注：普通电话包括小灵通，移动电话不包括。

# NUMBER OF DURABLE CONSUMER GOODS OWNED PER 100 URBAN HOUSEHOLDS

(Grouped by Percentile of Households, End of 2012)

| 10% 低收入户 Low Income House-holds (second decile) | 20% 中等偏下户 Lower Middle Income House-holds (second quintile) | 20% 中等收入户 Middle Income House-holds (third quintile) | 20% 中等偏上户 Upper Middle Income House-holds (fourth quintile) | 10% 高收入户 High Income House-holds (ninth decile) | 10% 最高收入户 Highest Income House-holds (tenth decile) |
|---|---|---|---|---|---|
| 3.3 | – | 1.6 | – | – | – |
| 143.3 | 115.0 | 114.8 | 131.7 | 117.2 | 79.7 |
| 16.6 | 18.3 | 44.3 | 53.3 | 69.1 | 93.1 |
| 100.0 | 103.3 | 108.2 | 105.0 | 110.7 | 117.2 |
| 100.0 | 103.3 | 111.5 | 106.7 | 124.4 | 131.3 |
| 183.3 | 195.0 | 200.0 | 200.0 | 211.0 | 214.1 |
| 126.7 | 108.3 | 131.2 | 128.3 | 128.2 | 155.3 |
| 16.7 | 28.3 | 37.7 | 31.7 | 30.9 | 41.6 |
| 3.3 | 15.0 | 13.1 | 18.3 | 30.9 | 13.8 |
| 53.3 | 55.0 | 85.3 | 90.0 | 86.3 | 121.0 |
| 3.3 | 3.3 | 4.9 | 6.7 | 3.4 | 6.9 |
| 10.0 | 1.7 | 9.8 | 5.0 | 10.3 | 6.9 |
| 100.0 | 100.0 | 101.6 | 100.0 | 96.9 | 100.0 |
| 196.7 | 230.0 | 254.1 | 283.3 | 275.6 | 328.2 |
| 100.0 | 103.3 | 113.1 | 106.7 | 113.8 | 121.0 |
| 3.3 | 3.3 | 18.0 | 16.7 | 20.6 | 21.0 |
| – | – | 1.6 | 1.7 | – | – |
| – | 3.3 | 9.8 | 8.3 | 14.1 | 13.8 |
| 116.7 | 105.0 | 96.7 | 101.7 | 110.3 | 110.3 |
| 243.3 | 193.3 | 229.5 | 250.0 | 207.9 | 269.4 |

Note:Xiaolingtong (Hand Phone) was included in the category of telephone, not in the category of mobile phone.

表14-9 市区不同收入水平居民家庭综合调查情况 (2012年)

| 指 标 | Item | 总 计 Total | 按平均每人 | |
|---|---|---|---|---|
| | | | 800元以下 Under 800 Yuan | 800-1000 |
| 一、调查户数 (户) | Number of Households Surveyed (household) | 300 | 2 | 6 |
| 各组户数占总户数比重 (%) | Proportion (%) | 100.00 | 0.67 | 2.00 |
| 二、户均家庭人口 (人) | Average Household Size (person) | 2.82 | 3.10 | 3.47 |
| 户均就业人口数 | Average Number of Employed Persons Per Household | 1.36 | 1.06 | 1.65 |
| 就业人口人均负担人数 | Number of Persons Supported by Each Employee | 2.07 | 2.92 | 2.10 |
| 三、人均家庭总收入 (元) | Per Capita Total Income of Household (yuan) | 41 822.19 | 9 729.19 | 14 319.06 |
| # 可支配收入 | Per Capita Disposable Income | 37 531.12 | 6 578.74 | 11 264.99 |
| 四、人均储蓄借贷收入 | Per Capita Income of Savings and Credit | 7 157.79 | 6 188.39 | 6 303.50 |
| 五、人均家庭总支出 | Per Capita Total Expenditure of Household | 32 633.99 | 14 743.34 | 19 730.17 |
| # 消费性支出 | Per Capita Expenditure for Consumption | 23 092.33 | 10 266.25 | 16 162.72 |
| (一) 食 品 | Food | 8 503.39 | 5 057.59 | 5 453.32 |
| # 粮 食 | Grain | 611.69 | 468.39 | 353.96 |
| 肉禽及其制品 | Meat, Poultry and Related Products | 1 581.98 | 1 106.98 | 1 069.29 |
| 蛋 类 | Eggs | 139.99 | 56.50 | 84.51 |
| 水产品 | Aquatic Products | 856.69 | 336.24 | 528.68 |
| 菜 类 | Vegetables | 807.16 | 489.18 | 518.77 |
| 干鲜瓜果 | Dried and Fresh Melons and Fruits | 752.76 | 441.40 | 400.91 |
| (二) 衣 着 | Clothing | 1 883.42 | 860.21 | 990.79 |
| (三) 居 住 | Residence | 1 456.30 | 671.58 | 810.18 |
| (四) 设备用品及服务 | Facilities, Articles and Services | 1 607.59 | 582.29 | 539.29 |
| (五) 医疗保健 | Medicine and Medical Services | 1 161.35 | 146.70 | 502.42 |
| (六) 交通与通信 | Transportation and Communications | 3 690.41 | 858.28 | 5 724.44 |
| (七) 教育文化娱乐服务 | Education and Cultural, Recreation Services | 3 914.69 | 1 859.21 | 1 945.65 |
| (八) 杂项商品与服务 | Miscellaneous Commodities and Services | 875.17 | 230.40 | 196.62 |
| 六、人均储蓄借贷支出 | Per Capita Expenditure for Savings And Credit | 17 280.97 | 2 677.11 | 1 881.25 |
| 七、人均期末手存现金 | Per Capita Cash in Hand Household at Year-end | 2 043.63 | 500.79 | 754.44 |

# GENERAL SURVEY OF DIFFERENT INCOME LEVELS OF URBAN HOUSEHOLDS (2012)

| 每月可支配收入分组（元） Per Capita Monthly Disposable Income Grouping (yuan) | | | | | | |
|---|---|---|---|---|---|---|
| 1000-1500 | 1500-2000 | 2000-2500 | 2500-3000 | 3000-4000 | 4000-5000 | 5000元以上 Above 5000 Yuan |
| 34 | 51 | 55 | 37 | 48 | 26 | 41 |
| 11.33 | 17.00 | 18.33 | 12.33 | 16.00 | 8.67 | 13.67 |
| 3.20 | 2.97 | 2.77 | 2.73 | 2.68 | 2.60 | 2.67 |
| 1.62 | 1.33 | 1.17 | 1.36 | 1.23 | 1.28 | 1.60 |
| 1.98 | 2.23 | 2.37 | 2.01 | 2.18 | 2.03 | 1.67 |
| 18 470.41 | 24 236.34 | 30 009.37 | 36 581.96 | 44 877.34 | 58 403.25 | 106 441.86 |
| 15 221.47 | 21 198.03 | 26 590.91 | 32 802.29 | 40 767.01 | 53 050.89 | 97 675.71 |
| 3 391.74 | 4 069.50 | 6 685.11 | 6 392.52 | 5 326.15 | 10 844.70 | 16 948.43 |
| 19 974.28 | 21 557.87 | 27 116.38 | 31 175.57 | 33 430.27 | 41 999.06 | 67 740.86 |
| 15 263.98 | 16 461.58 | 19 827.57 | 22 298.54 | 25 075.69 | 31 405.16 | 40 676.88 |
| 7 396.82 | 7 395.68 | 7 716.61 | 8 576.66 | 9 203.88 | 9 500.15 | 11 670.27 |
| 532.51 | 575.37 | 637.34 | 630.13 | 687.17 | 638.14 | 644.24 |
| 1 666.82 | 1 518.82 | 1 549.47 | 1 585.56 | 1 603.46 | 1 667.33 | 1 688.68 |
| 125.64 | 133.03 | 164.45 | 153.84 | 148.48 | 121.10 | 135.50 |
| 851.75 | 845.37 | 863.80 | 795.37 | 930.18 | 949.24 | 882.76 |
| 834.78 | 798.53 | 836.52 | 785.89 | 832.34 | 805.60 | 821.91 |
| 560.62 | 593.89 | 697.57 | 758.61 | 923.03 | 1 000.25 | 979.91 |
| 1 271.88 | 1 240.90 | 1 450.39 | 1 854.30 | 2 354.33 | 2 496.84 | 3 371.93 |
| 1 471.31 | 1 022.43 | 1 696.64 | 1 449.66 | 1 372.04 | 2 026.76 | 1 653.64 |
| 898.97 | 980.69 | 1 122.13 | 1 707.65 | 2 632.05 | 1 990.02 | 2 635.36 |
| 489.58 | 1 262.49 | 1 321.74 | 1 406.05 | 1 199.86 | 1 559.20 | 1 147.39 |
| 1 321.01 | 1 574.79 | 3 204.25 | 2 823.46 | 2 814.02 | 7 404.84 | 9 157.81 |
| 1 848.84 | 2 471.79 | 2 863.00 | 3 642.25 | 4 520.74 | 4 814.48 | 9 098.36 |
| 565.58 | 512.82 | 452.81 | 838.50 | 978.78 | 1 612.88 | 1 942.12 |
| 2 784.98 | 7 308.29 | 9 947.62 | 11 340.22 | 16 754.78 | 25 857.01 | 61 874.75 |
| 1 114.81 | 1 744.65 | 2 491.36 | 1 719.21 | 1 833.05 | 2 017.40 | 3 083.19 |

表14-10

# 部分年份市区每百户居民家庭耐用消费品拥有量
# NUMBER OF DURABLE CONSUMER GOODS OWNED PER 100 URBAN HOUSEHOLDS OF PARTIAL YEARS

| 耐用消费品 | | Durable Consumer Goods | | 1990年 | 2000年 | 2010年 | 2011年 | 2012年 |
|---|---|---|---|---|---|---|---|---|
| 摩托车 | (辆) | Motorcycle | (coach) | 0.8 | 11.0 | 2.7 | 0.7 | 1.0 |
| 助力车 | | Motor Bicycle | | | | 117.3 | 120.4 | 122.0 |
| 家用汽车 | | Cars for Household Use | | | | 20.3 | 41.5 | 42.7 |
| 洗衣机 | (台) | Washing Machine | (unit) | 92.5 | 98.5 | 106.3 | 106.3 | 106.4 |
| 电冰箱 | | Refrigerator | | 82.5 | 99.5 | 108.3 | 108.6 | 110.1 |
| 彩色电视机 | | Color TV Set | | 66.7 | 149.0 | 193.7 | 198.4 | 199.1 |
| 家用电脑 | | Computer | | | 19.5 | 96.7 | 122.4 | 125.4 |
| 组合音响 | (套) | Hi-Fi Stereo Component System | (set) | 2.5 | 26.0 | 29.9 | 31.9 | 30.7 |
| 摄像机 | (架) | Video Cameras | (unit) | | 2.0 | 8.3 | 14.5 | 14.7 |
| 照相机 | | Camera | | 38.3 | 58.0 | 53.5 | 76.3 | 77.1 |
| 钢　琴 | | piano | | | 1.0 | 2.7 | 3.6 | 4.3 |
| 其他中高档乐器 | (件) | Other Medium and High Grade Musical Instrument | (unit) | 4.2 | 3.5 | 3.7 | 5.6 | 6.3 |
| 微波炉 | (台) | Microwave Oven | (unit) | | 61.0 | 94.0 | 100.0 | 99.7 |
| 空调器 | | Air Conditioner | | 0.8 | 71.0 | 210.0 | 254.6 | 254.4 |
| 淋浴热水器 | | Shower | | | 58.5 | 99.0 | 108.6 | 108.4 |
| 消毒碗柜及洗碗机 | (台) | Sterilizing Cupboard and Dish Washing Machine | (unit) | | | 8.6 | 14.2 | 13.0 |
| 健身器材 | (套) | Exercise Apparatus | (set) | | | 3.7 | 5.6 | 7.4 |
| 普通电话 | (部) | Phone | (set) | | | 138.2 | 105.9 | 104.3 |
| 移动电话 | | Mobile Telephones | | | | 170.8 | 224.3 | 230.8 |

注：普通电话包括小灵通，移动电话不包括。
Note:Xiaolingtong (Hand Phone) was included in the category of telephone, not in the category of mobile phone.

表14-11

# 部分年份农民家庭基本情况
# BASIC CONDITION OF RURAL HOUSEHOLDS OF PARTIAL YEARS

| 指标 | Item | 2000年 | 2010年 | 2011年 | 2012年 |
|---|---|---|---|---|---|
| **一、调查户数** (户) | **Number of Households Surveyed** (household) | **600** | **750** | **890** | **890** |
| **二、调查人口** | **Number of Residents Surveyed** | | | | |
| 常住人口 (人) | Number of Permanent Residents in the Households Surveyed (person) | 2 185 | 2 802 | 3 153 | 3165 |
| 户均常住人口 | Average Number of Permanent Residents Per household | 3.64 | 3.74 | 3.54 | 3.56 |
| 户均整、半劳动力 | Average Number of Able-bodied and Semi-able-bodied Laborers Per Household | 2.67 | 2.76 | 2.57 | 2.58 |
| 平均每一劳动力负担人数 | Average Number of Persons Supported by a Laborer | 1.36 | 1.36 | 1.38 | 1.38 |
| **三、人均年收入** | **Per Capita Annual Income** | | | | |
| 总收入 (元) | Total Revenue (yuan) | 6 456.09 | 16 093.10 | 20 413.62 | 23 542.30 |
| 纯收入 | Net Income | 5 462.45 | 14 656.75 | 17 225.78 | 19 396.24 |
| 现金收入 | Cash Income | 5 790.98 | 15 829.24 | 20 282.91 | 23 341.52 |
| **四、各组纯收入的比重** (%) | **Percentage of Households Grouped by Per Capita Annual Net Income** (%) | | **100.0** | **100.0** | **100.0** |
| 5000元以下 | Under 5000 Yuan | | 2.3 | 2.1 | 1.3 |
| 5000-8000元 | 5000-8000 Yuan | | 10.9 | 6.8 | 5.1 |
| 8000-11000元 | 8000-11000 Yuan | | 20.0 | 12.6 | 9.3 |
| 11000-14000元 | 11000-14000 Yuan | | 22.4 | 18.2 | 14.5 |
| 14000-17000元 | 14000-17000 Yuan | | 15.7 | 18.2 | 18.2 |
| 17000-20000元 | 17000-20000 Yuan | | 10.7 | 15.2 | 15.0 |
| 20000元以上 | 20000 Yuan and Over | | 18.0 | 26.9 | 36.6 |
| **五、农民家庭住房情况** | **Housing Conditions of Rural Residential Buildings** | | | | |
| 户均住房面积 (平方米) | Average Floor Space of Residential Buildings Per Household (sq.m) | 217.52 | 251.85 | 240.07 | 239.38 |
| 户均住房价值 (元) | Average Value of Residential Buildings (yuan) | 63 373 | 230 239 | 321 656 | 321 136 |
| 人均住房面积 (平方米) | Per Capita Floor Space of Residential Buildings (sq.m) | 59.73 | 68.42 | 69.00 | 68.35 |
| 户均年内新建(购)房屋面积 | Average Floor Space of Rooms Newly Built Per Household Within the Year | 3.34 | 0.47 | 1.40 | 1.20 |
| 新建(购)房屋每平方米造价 (元) | Value Per Square Meter of Rooms Newly Built (yuan) | 837 | 1 682 | 3 083 | 1 342 |

注:2011年起住房面积统计口径调整为建筑面积,不包含出租的部分。
Note: Since 2011, statistic caliber of floor space was adjusted for construction area, not contain rental part.

表14-12

# 农民家庭基本情况

(按收入等级分, 2012年)

| 项　　目 | | Item | | 总平均 Average | 10% 最低收入户 Lowest Income House-holds (first decile) |
|---|---|---|---|---|---|
| 平均每户常住人口 | (人) | Average Number of Permanent Residents per Household | (person) | 3.56 | 3.02 |
| 平均每户整半劳动力 | | Average Number of Able-bodied and Semi-able-bodied Laborers per Household | | 2.58 | 2.00 |
| 平均每个劳动力负担人口 | | Average Number of Persons Supported by a Laborer | | 1.38 | 1.51 |
| 平均每人总收入 | (元) | Per Capita Annual Income | (yuan) | 23 542.30 | 1 0291.79 |
| # 现金收入 | | Cash Income | | 23 341.52 | 9 873.07 |
| 平均每人总支出 | | Per Capita Annual Expenditures | | 20 216.37 | 11 973.72 |
| # 现金支出 | | Cash Expenditures | | 20 047.66 | 11 724.20 |
| 平均每人纯收入 | | Per Capita Annual Net Income | | 19 396.24 | 8 961.17 |
| 工资性收入 | | Wages Income | | 12 564.49 | 5 544.47 |
| 家庭经营纯收入 | | Household Business Income | | 4 105.21 | 1 074.26 |
| 财产性收入 | | Property Income | | 1 389.01 | 452.24 |
| 转移性收入 | | Transfer Income | | 1 337.54 | 1 890.20 |
| **人均生活消费总支出** | | **Per Capita Living Expenditure** | | **14 381.27** | **8 765.23** |
| 食　品 | | Food | | 4 875.20 | 3 714.84 |
| 衣　着 | | Clothing | | 995.68 | 423.89 |
| 居　住 | | Residence | | 1 599.47 | 1 052.69 |
| 家庭设备用品及服务 | | Household Facilities, Articles and Services | | 771.17 | 409.65 |
| 医疗保健 | | Medicines and Medical Services | | 761.54 | 1 094.99 |
| 交通通讯 | | Transport, Post and Telecommunications | | 2 438.70 | 922.14 |
| 文教娱乐用品及服务 | | Cultural, Educational and Recreational Articles and Services | | 2 643.39 | 1 011.44 |
| 其他商品及服务 | | Other Commodities and Services | | 296.13 | 135.60 |
| **人均生活消费现金支出** | | **Per Capita Consumption Paid in Cash** | | **14 250.86** | **8 585.04** |
| 食　品 | | Food | | 4 744.80 | 3 534.64 |
| 衣　着 | | Clothing | | 995.68 | 423.89 |
| 居　住 | | Residence | | 1 599.45 | 1 052.69 |
| 家庭设备用品及服务 | | Household Facilities, Articles and Services | | 771.17 | 409.65 |
| 医疗保健 | | Medicines and Medical Services | | 761.54 | 1 094.99 |
| 交通通讯 | | Transport, Post and Telecommunications | | 2 438.70 | 922.14 |
| 文教娱乐用品及服务 | | Cultural, Educational and Recreational Articles and Services | | 2 643.39 | 1 011.44 |
| 其他商品及服务 | | Other Commodities and Services | | 296.13 | 135.60 |

# BASIC CONDITION OF RURAL HOUSEHOLDS

(Grouped by Percentile of Households, 2012)

| 10% | 20% | 20% | 20% | 10% | 10% |
|---|---|---|---|---|---|
| 低收入户 Low Income House-holds (second decile) | 中等偏下户 Lower Middle In-come House-holds (second quintile) | 中等收入户 Middle Income House-holds (third quintile) | 中等偏上户 Upper Middle In-come House-holds (fourth quintile) | 高收入户 High Income House-holds (ninth decile) | 最高收入户 Highest Income House-holds (tenth decile) |
| 3.55 | 3.87 | 3.86 | 3.33 | 3.10 | 3.20 |
| 2.47 | 2.61 | 2.87 | 2.58 | 2.62 | 2.54 |
| 1.44 | 1.48 | 1.34 | 1.29 | 1.18 | 1.26 |
| 12 027.04 | 16 574.73 | 19 353.61 | 24 653.08 | 31 237.38 | 68 458.89 |
| 12 060.84 | 16 472.87 | 19 143.87 | 24 456.05 | 30 804.26 | 68 167.07 |
| 12 673.43 | 15 996.93 | 15 392.02 | 19 810.19 | 22 202.97 | 57 556.41 |
| 12 464.90 | 15 847.59 | 15 229.52 | 19 672.14 | 22 044.20 | 57 338.93 |
| 10 552.38 | 13 897.67 | 17 322.23 | 21 748.54 | 27 896.77 | 46 123.20 |
| 7 712.28 | 10 053.54 | 13 012.19 | 14 322.71 | 18 325.05 | 21 347.78 |
| 977.91 | 1 672.91 | 2 208.57 | 4 852.35 | 6 233.03 | 18 173.25 |
| 459.44 | 678.10 | 905.53 | 1 439.65 | 2 107.55 | 5 428.72 |
| 1 402.75 | 1 493.13 | 1 195.93 | 1 133.82 | 1 231.14 | 1 173.45 |
| **9 251.89** | **12 064.40** | **12 688.77** | **15 516.68** | **16 791.95** | **30 154.57** |
| 3 857.25 | 4 460.75 | 4 559.60 | 5 356.66 | 5 471.01 | 7 137.19 |
| 493.45 | 755.51 | 886.47 | 1 185.94 | 1 221.24 | 2 215.45 |
| 920.67 | 1 130.16 | 1 711.10 | 1 721.78 | 2 140.15 | 2 988.17 |
| 379.73 | 459.06 | 675.52 | 904.98 | 939.64 | 2 057.76 |
| 710.28 | 874.58 | 638.32 | 653.48 | 680.97 | 775.64 |
| 1 289.11 | 2 447.86 | 1 628.41 | 2 522.99 | 2 532.56 | 6 937.75 |
| 1 417.46 | 1 750.13 | 2 364.00 | 2 880.89 | 3 321.80 | 7 229.70 |
| 183.94 | 186.35 | 225.37 | 289.97 | 484.58 | 812.92 |
| **9 087.62** | **11 938.39** | **12 559.28** | **15 396.44** | **16 656.85** | **30 061.18** |
| 3 692.98 | 4 334.81 | 4 430.11 | 5 236.42 | 5 335.91 | 7 043.80 |
| 493.45 | 755.51 | 886.47 | 1 185.94 | 1 221.24 | 2 215.45 |
| 920.67 | 1 130.10 | 1 711.10 | 1 721.78 | 2 140.15 | 2 988.17 |
| 379.73 | 459.06 | 675.52 | 904.98 | 939.64 | 2 057.76 |
| 710.28 | 874.58 | 638.32 | 653.48 | 680.97 | 775.64 |
| 1 289.11 | 2 447.86 | 1 628.41 | 2 522.99 | 2 532.56 | 6 937.75 |
| 1 417.46 | 1 750.13 | 2 364.00 | 2 880.89 | 3 321.80 | 7 229.70 |
| 183.94 | 186.35 | 225.37 | 289.97 | 484.58 | 812.92 |

表14-13

# 分地区农民家庭基本情况 (2012年)

| 指　　标 | | Item | | 全　市 Whole Municipality |
|---|---|---|---|---|
| **一、调查户数** | (户) | **Number of Households Surveyed** | (household) | **890** |
| **二、调查人口** | | **Number of Residents Surveyed** | | |
| 常住人口 | (人) | Number of Permanent Residents in the Households Surveyed | (person) | 3 165 |
| 户均常住人口 | | Average Number of Permanent Residents Per household | | 3.56 |
| 户均整、半劳动力 | | Average Number of Able-bodied and Semi-able-bodied Laborers Per Household | | 2.58 |
| 平均每一劳动力负担人数 | | Average Number of Persons Supported by a laborer | | 1.38 |
| **三、人均收入** | | **Per Capita Annual Income** | | |
| 总收入 | (元) | Total Revenue | (yuan) | 23 542.30 |
| 纯收入 | | Net Income | | 19 396.24 |
| 现金收入 | | Cash Income | | 23 341.52 |
| **四、各组纯收入水平户数的比重** | (%) | **Percentage of households Grouped by Per Capita Annual Net Income** | (%) | **100.0** |
| 5000元以下 | | Under 5000 Yuan | | 1.3 |
| 5000-8000元 | | 5000-8000 Yuan | | 5.1 |
| 8000-11000元 | | 8000-11000 Yuan | | 9.3 |
| 11000-14000元 | | 11000-14000 Yuan | | 14.5 |
| 14000-17000元 | | 14000-17000 Yuan | | 18.2 |
| 17000-20000元 | | 17000-20000 Yuan | | 15.0 |
| 20000元以上 | | 20000 Yuan and Over | | 36.6 |
| **五、农民家庭住房情况** | | **Housing Conditions of Rural Residential Buildings** | | |
| 户均住房面积 | (平方米) | Average Housing Area of Residential Buildings Per Household | (sq.m) | 239.38 |
| 户均住房价值 | (元) | Average Value of Residential Buildings | (yuan) | 321 136 |
| 人均住房面积 | (平方米) | Per Capita Housing Area of Residential Buildings | (sq.m) | 68.35 |
| 户均年内新建(购)房屋面积 | | Average Floor Space of Rooms Newly Built Per Household Within the Year | | 1.20 |

# BASIC CONDITION OF RURAL HOUSEHOLDS BY REGION (2012)

| 市区 Urban Area | # 吴江区 Wujiang District | 常熟 Changshu | 张家港 Zhangjiagang | 昆山 Kunshan | 太仓 Taicang |
|---|---|---|---|---|---|
| **370** | **150** | **150** | **150** | **120** | **100** |
| 1 384 | 574 | 480 | 487 | 432 | 382 |
| 3.74 | 3.83 | 3.20 | 3.25 | 3.60 | 3.82 |
| 2.71 | 2.77 | 2.50 | 2.38 | 2.47 | 2.88 |
| 1.38 | 1.38 | 1.28 | 1.36 | 1.46 | 1.33 |
| | | | | | |
| 21 652.21 | 22 598.78 | 22 502.78 | 26 936.75 | 26 501.69 | 21 976.96 |
| 19 255.26 | 19 277.14 | 19 467.11 | 19 459.99 | 19 563.13 | 19 410.96 |
| 21 550.90 | 22 515.05 | 22 126.90 | 26 457.89 | 26 695.35 | 2 188.88 |
| **100.0** | **100.0** | **100.0** | **100.0** | **100.0** | **100.0** |
| 0.3 | – | 0.7 | 6.6 | – | – |
| 1.9 | 2.0 | 5.3 | 12.7 | 7.5 | 2.0 |
| 6.2 | 4.0 | 4.7 | 15.3 | 14.2 | 13.0 |
| 13.2 | 11.3 | 14.7 | 12.0 | 13.3 | 24.0 |
| 24.3 | 22.7 | 19.3 | 10.7 | 12.5 | 12.0 |
| 18.7 | 25.3 | 16.7 | 10.7 | 11.7 | 9.0 |
| 35.4 | 34.7 | 38.6 | 32.0 | 40.8 | 40.0 |
| | | | | | |
| 237.13 | 217.91 | 263.47 | 218.58 | 211.44 | 280.50 |
| 335 423 | 247 367 | 290 973 | 214 090 | 466 885 | 409 920 |
| 63.26 | 56.92 | 82.42 | 67.39 | 58.73 | 73.48 |
| 3.10 | 2.67 | – | – | – | 1.30 |

表14-14

# 部分年份农民家庭人均生活消费支出情况
# PER CAPITA LIVING EXPENDITURE OF RURAL HOUSEHOLDS OF PARTIAL YEARS

单位：元 (yuan)

| 指标 | Item | 2000年 | 2010年 | 2011年 | 2012年 |
|---|---|---|---|---|---|
| **生活消费支出** | **Living Expenditure** | **4 073.00** | **10 396.53** | **12 485.16** | **14 381.27** |
| **一、食　品** | **Food** | **1 631.40** | **3 526.57** | **4 221.20** | **4 875.20** |
| # 主　食 | Staple Food | 221.35 | 333.22 | 360.25 | 377.83 |
| **二、衣　着** | **Clothing** | **203.97** | **694.22** | **865.74** | **995.68** |
| **三、居　住** | **Residence** | **699.05** | **1 356.20** | **1 477.96** | **1 599.47** |
| # 住　房 | Housing | 520.93 | 137.17 | 104.25 | 23.41 |
| 建筑材料 | Building Materials | 103.50 | 502.15 | 537.93 | 646.96 |
| 电　费 | Electricity | 59.26 | 341.74 | 343.68 | 398.89 |
| 燃　料 | Fuels | 52.73 | 136.91 | 164.51 | 175.97 |
| **四、家庭设备用品及服务** | **Household Facilities, Articles and Services** | **391.82** | **526.28** | **652.10** | **771.17** |
| # 耐用消费品 | Durable Consumer Goods | 121.93 | 293.90 | 326.95 | 394.96 |
| 床上用品 | Bed Articles | 11.19 | 35.46 | 63.69 | 65.25 |
| 家庭日用杂品 | Household Articles for Daily Use | 192.63 | 153.65 | 217.00 | 247.47 |
| **五、医疗保健** | **Medicine and Medicinal Services** | **341.21** | **518.60** | **664.08** | **761.54** |
| **六、交通和通信** | **Transportation and Communications** | **315.22** | **1 639.49** | **1 994.22** | **2 438.70** |
| **七、文教娱乐用品及服务** | **Cultural, Education and Recreation Articles and Services** | **335.32** | **1 889.65** | **2 293.51** | **2 643.39** |
| 文教娱乐用品 | Cultural, Education & Recreation Articles | 79.88 | 288.41 | 487.63 | 551.84 |
| 文教娱乐服务 | Cultural, Education & Recreation Services | 255.44 | 1 601.24 | 1 805.88 | 2 091.55 |
| **八、其他商品和服务** | **Other Commodities and Services** | **155.01** | **245.52** | **316.35** | **296.13** |
| 商品性支出 | Expenditure for Commodities | 45.11 | 172.60 | 228.24 | 214.18 |
| # 金银珠宝饰品 | Jewelry | 14.56 | 70.59 | 89.15 | 56.64 |
| 服务性支出 | Expenditure for Services | 109.90 | 72.92 | 88.11 | 81.95 |

表14-15

# 分地区农民家庭人均生活消费支出情况 (2012年) PER CAPITA LIVING EXPENDITURE OF RURAL HOUSEHOLDS BY REGION (2012)

单位：元 (yuan)

| 地区 | Region | 生活消费支出 Living Expenditure | 食品 Food | 衣着 Clothing | 居住 Residence | 家庭设备用品及服务 Hosehold Facilities, Aricles and Service |
|---|---|---|---|---|---|---|
| **全　市** | **Whole Municipality** | **14 381.27** | **4 875.20** | **995.68** | **1 599.47** | **771.17** |
| 市　区 | Urban Area | 13 539.37 | 5 021.16 | 936.22 | 1 353.21 | 635.53 |
| # 吴江区 | Wujiang District | 13 362.60 | 4 844.45 | 866.07 | 1 321.47 | 558.93 |
| 常　熟 | Changshu | 14 684.84 | 4 745.18 | 1 041.43 | 1 721.11 | 799.63 |
| 张家港 | Zhangjiagang | 15 128.51 | 4 599.22 | 995.96 | 1 799.59 | 993.09 |
| 昆　山 | Kunshan | 16 121.77 | 5 393.72 | 1 046.49 | 1 901.85 | 894.09 |
| 太　仓 | Taicang | 13 090.82 | 4 447.15 | 1 074.86 | 1 485.48 | 598.44 |

表14-15 续表　Continued

单位：元 (yuan)

| 地区 | Region | 医疗保健 Medicine and Medicinal Services | 交通和通信 Transportation and Communications | 文教娱乐用品及服务 Cultural, Education and Recreation Articles and Service | 其他商品和服务 Other Commodities and Service |
|---|---|---|---|---|---|
| **全　市** | **Whole Municipality** | **761.54** | **2 438.70** | **2 643.39** | **296.13** |
| 市　区 | Urban Area | 719.55 | 2 256.09 | 2 373.20 | 244.41 |
| # 吴江区 | Wujiang District | 679.60 | 2 438.86 | 2 421.50 | 231.71 |
| 常　熟 | Changshu | 853.61 | 2 366.71 | 2 736.16 | 421.01 |
| 张家港 | Zhangjiagang | 706.40 | 3 027.29 | 2 794.47 | 212.48 |
| 昆　山 | Kunshan | 860.57 | 2 396.27 | 3 265.27 | 363.50 |
| 太　仓 | Taicang | 715.97 | 2 081.39 | 2 358.80 | 328.73 |

表14-16

# 每百户农民家庭耐用消费品拥有量

(按收入等级分, 2012年末)

| 项　目 | | Item | | 总平均 Average | 10% 最低收入户 Lowest Income House-holds (first decile) |
|---|---|---|---|---|---|
| 洗衣机 | (台) | Washing Machine | (unit) | 100.3 | 92.5 |
| 电冰箱 | | Refrigerator | | 103.5 | 86.9 |
| 空调器 | | Air Conditioner | | 193.7 | 154.3 |
| 抽油烟机 | | Smoke Absorber | | 73.1 | 48.9 |
| 吸尘器 | | Dust Catcher | | 21.7 | 13.3 |
| 微波炉 | | Microwave Oven | | 79.9 | 60.3 |
| 热水器 | | Water Heater | | 100.8 | 83.4 |
| 自行车 | (辆) | Bicycle | (coach) | 165.2 | 135.8 |
| 摩托车 | | Motorcycle | | 56.2 | 47.9 |
| 汽　车 (生活用) | | Vehicles (For Living) | | 28.5 | 8.3 |
| 电话机 | (部) | Telephone | (unit) | 98.1 | 89.2 |
| 移动电话 | | Mobile Telephone | | 253.3 | 172.8 |
| 彩色电视机 | (台) | Color TV Set | (unit) | 197.5 | 157.2 |
| 黑白电视机 | | Black and White TV Set | | 1.2 | 4.6 |
| 摄像机 | | Video Camera | | 6.4 | 2.0 |
| 影碟机 | | Video Disc Player | | 37.2 | 25.4 |
| 照相机 | | Camera | | 35.3 | 13.3 |
| 家用计算机 | | Computer | | 86.0 | 39.2 |

注:移动电话包括小灵通，普通电话不包括；自行车包括电动自行车。

# NUMBER OF DURABLE CONSUMER GOODS OWNED PER 100 RURAL HOUSEHOLDS

(Grouped by Percentile of Households, End of 2012)

| 10%<br>低收入户<br>Low Income House-holds (second decile) | 20%<br>中等偏下户<br>Lower Middle Income House-holds (second quintile) | 20%<br>中等收入户<br>Middle Income House-holds (third quintile) | 20%<br>中等偏上户<br>Upper Middle Income House-holds (fourth quintile) | 10%<br>高收入户<br>High Income House-holds (ninth decile) | 10%<br>最高收入户<br>Highest Income House-holds (tenth decile) |
|---|---|---|---|---|---|
| 87.8 | 102.8 | 104.1 | 102.6 | 99.6 | 106.3 |
| 96.5 | 104.4 | 105.5 | 104.5 | 109.1 | 114.3 |
| 160.5 | 190.4 | 191.6 | 193.8 | 203.7 | 266.2 |
| 54.9 | 75.0 | 74.5 | 75.4 | 86.3 | 88.6 |
| 14.3 | 23.0 | 13.6 | 26.4 | 18.9 | 39.9 |
| 69.9 | 81.0 | 84.6 | 79.8 | 83.5 | 90.2 |
| 95.3 | 97.1 | 99.7 | 106.5 | 105.9 | 113.6 |
| 169.9 | 167.4 | 176.6 | 172.4 | 167.7 | 140.8 |
| 36.4 | 51.2 | 72.8 | 59.2 | 66.1 | 50.4 |
| 15.8 | 27.2 | 26.3 | 25.7 | 31.1 | 71.2 |
| 91.1 | 99.9 | 101.2 | 99.7 | 95.5 | 101.9 |
| 224.4 | 248.8 | 271.3 | 263.3 | 269.1 | 291.7 |
| 176.7 | 190.2 | 201.9 | 208.6 | 201.7 | 236.5 |
| 1.6 | 0.4 | 1.2 | 0.4 | 1.7 | - |
| 2.9 | 6.0 | 3.2 | 9.8 | 5.6 | 17.1 |
| 25.9 | 37.3 | 39.6 | 43.7 | 31.7 | 54.7 |
| 21.7 | 30.9 | 34.5 | 39.2 | 36.0 | 64.6 |
| 64.7 | 87.3 | 87.9 | 90.2 | 105.3 | 115.2 |

Note:Xiaolingtong (Hand Phone) was included in the mobile phone, not in the category of category of telephone； Bicycles, including electric bicycles.

表14-17

# 分地区每百户农民家庭耐用消费品拥有量(2012年末)
# NUMBER OF DURABLE CONSUMER GOODS OWNED PER 100 RURAL HOUSEHOLDS BY REGION (END OF 2012)

| 耐用消费品 | Durable Consumer Goods | 全 市 Whole Municipality | 市 区 Urban Area | #吴江区 WujiangDistrict | 常 熟 Changshu | 张家港 Zhang jiagang | 昆 山 Kunshan | 太 仓 Taicang |
|---|---|---|---|---|---|---|---|---|
| 洗衣机 (台) | Washing Machine (unit) | 100.3 | 104.6 | 109.3 | 101.3 | 92.0 | 96.7 | 107.0 |
| 电冰箱 | Refrigerator | 103.5 | 108.2 | 112.0 | 99.3 | 94.0 | 105.8 | 118.0 |
| 空调器 | Air Conditioner | 193.7 | 198.0 | 206.7 | 194.7 | 170.0 | 195.0 | 237.0 |
| 抽油烟机 | Smoke Absorber | 73.1 | 79.3 | 75.3 | 72.7 | 62.0 | 75.0 | 76.0 |
| 吸尘器 | Dust Catcher | 21.7 | 28.2 | 23.3 | 18.0 | 12.0 | 11.7 | 45.0 |
| 微波炉 | Microwave Oven | 79.9 | 82.7 | 79.3 | 79.3 | 72.7 | 76.7 | 94.0 |
| 热水器 | Water Heater | 100.8 | 98.6 | 100.0 | 104.0 | 94.0 | 98.3 | 124.0 |
| 自行车 (辆) | Bicycle (coach) | 165.2 | 143.7 | 129.3 | 188.7 | 184.0 | 145.0 | 173.0 |
| 摩托车 | Motorcycle | 56.2 | 53.9 | 74.7 | 64.7 | 40.7 | 45.8 | 103.0 |
| 汽　车 (生活用) | Vehicles (For Living) | 28.5 | 31.8 | 32.7 | 24.0 | 27.3 | 25.0 | 35.0 |
| 电话机 (部) | Telephone (unit) | 98.1 | 101.8 | 102.7 | 101.3 | 84.7 | 99.2 | 108.0 |
| 移动电话 | Mobile Telephone | 253.3 | 247.4 | 242.7 | 266.0 | 240.0 | 245.8 | 292.0 |
| 彩色电视机 (台) | Color TV Set (unit) | 197.5 | 198.8 | 210.7 | 195.3 | 176.7 | 197.5 | 257.0 |
| 黑白电视机 | Black and White TV Set | 1.2 | 1.4 | - | 0.7 | 2.0 | 0.8 | - |
| 摄像机 | Video Camera | 6.4 | 9.2 | 12.7 | 4.7 | 4.0 | 4.2 | 9.0 |
| 影碟机 | Video Disc Player | 37.2 | 47.5 | 55.3 | 45.3 | 19.3 | 27.5 | 33.0 |
| 照相机 | Camera | 35.3 | 37.8 | 33.3 | 30.0 | 31.3 | 36.7 | 47.0 |
| 家用计算机 | Computer | 86.0 | 87.3 | 87.3 | 96.0 | 68.0 | 90.8 | 93.0 |

# 主 要 统 计 指 标 解 释

## 一、城镇住户

**城镇家庭人口** 指居住在一起，经济上合在一起共同生活的家庭成员。凡计算为家庭人口的成员其全部收支都包括在本家庭中。

**城镇就业面** 指就业人口占家庭人口的百分比。

**城镇就业者负担人数** 指家庭人口与就业人口之比。

**城镇家庭总收入** 指家庭成员得到的工薪收入、经营净收入、财产性收入、转移性收入之和，不包括出售财物收入和借贷收入。

**城镇家庭可支配收入** 指家庭成员得到可用于最终消费支出和其它非义务性支出以及储蓄的总和，即居民家庭可以用来自由支配的收入。它是家庭总收入扣除交纳的所得税、个人交纳的社会保障支出以及记账补贴后的收入。计算公式为：

可支配收入=家庭总收入-交纳所得税-个人交纳的社会保障支出-记账补贴

**城镇家庭总支出** 指除借贷支出以外的全部家庭支出。包括消费性支出、购房建房支出、转移性支出、财产性支出、社会保障支出。

**城镇家庭消费性支出** 指家庭用于日常生活的支出，包括食品、衣着、家庭设备用品及服务、医疗保健、交通和通信、娱乐教育文化服务、居住、杂项商品和服务等八大类支出。

**城镇家庭服务性消费支出** 指家庭用于支付社会提供的各种非商品性服务费用。

**城镇家庭收入分组方法** 是将所有调查户按户人均可支配收入由低到高排队，按10%，10%，20%，20%，20%，10%，10%的比例依次分成：最低收入户、低收入户、中等偏下收入户、中等收入户、中等偏上收入户、高收入户、最高收入户等七组。

**恩格尔系数** 指食物支出金额在消费性总支出金额中所占的比例。计算公式为：

$$恩格尔系数=\frac{食品支出金额}{消费性总支出金额}\times 100\%$$

## 二、农村住户

**农村住户** 指农村常住户。农村常住户指长期(一年以上)居住在乡镇(不包括城关镇)行政管理区域内的住户，以及长期居住在城关镇所辖行政村范围内的农村住户。户口不在本地而在本地居住一年及以上的住户也包括在本地农村常住户范围内；有本地户口，但举家外出谋生一年以上的住户，无论是否保留承包耕地都不包括在本地农村住户范围内。

**常住人口** 指全年经常在家或在家居住6个月以上，而且经济和生活与本户连成一体的人口。外出从业人员在外居住时间虽然在6个月以上，但收入主要带回家中，经济与本户连为一体，仍视为家庭常住人口；在家居住，生活和本户连成一体的国家职工、退休人员也为家庭常住人口。但是现役军人、中专及以上(走读生除外)的在校学生、以及常年在外(不包括探亲、看病等)且已有稳定的职业与居住场所的外出从业人员，不算家庭常住人口。家庭常住人口主要作为计算农村住户平均每人收入、消费和积累水平及分析家庭人口状况的依据。

**整、半劳动力** 整劳动力指男子18周岁到50周岁，女子18周岁到45周岁；半劳动力指男子16周岁到17周岁，51周岁到60周岁；女子16周岁到17周岁，46周岁到55周岁，同时具有劳动能力的人。虽然在劳动年龄之内，但已丧失劳动能力的人，不应算为劳动力；超过劳动年龄，但能经常参加劳动，计入半劳动力数内。常住人口中的职工，若这些职工为劳动力，就包括在本户的整半劳动力中。

**总收入** 指调查期内农村住户和住户成员从各种来源渠道得到的收入总和。按收入的性质划分为工资性收入、家庭经营收入、财产性收入和转移性收入。

**工资性收入** 指农村住户成员受雇于单位或个人，靠出卖劳动而获得的收入。

**家庭经营收入** 指农村住户以家庭为生产经营单位进行生产筹划和管理而获得的收入。农村住户家庭经营活动按行业划分为农业、林业、牧业、渔业、工业、建筑业、交通运输业邮电业、批发和零售贸易餐饮业、社会服务业、文教卫生业和其他家庭经营。

**财产性收入** 指金融资产或有形非生产性资产的所有者向其他机构单位提供资金或将有形非生产性资产供其支配，作为回报而从中获得的收入。

**转移性收入** 指农村住户和住户成员无须付出任何对应物而获得的货物、服务、资金或资产所有权等，不包括无偿提供的用于固定资本形成的资金。一般情况下，是指农村住户在二次分配中的所有收入。

**现金收入** 指农村住户和住户成员在调查期内得到以现金形态表现的收入。按来源分成工资性收入、家庭经营现金收入、财产性收入、转移性收入。

**纯收入** 指农村住户当年从各个来源得到的总收入相应地扣除所发生的费用后的收入总和。计算方法：

纯收入=总收入-税费支出-家庭经营费用支出-生产性固定资产折旧-赠送农村亲友支出

纯收入主要用于再生产投入和当年生活消费支出，也可用于储蓄和各种非义务性支出。“农民人均纯收入”按人口平均的纯收入水平，反映的是一个地区或一个农户农村居民的平均收入水平。

**总支出** 指农村住户用于生产、生活和再分配的全部支出。家庭经营费用支出、购置生产性固定资产支出、生产性固定资产折旧、税费支出、生活消费支出、财产性支出和转移性支出。

# EXPLANATORY NOTES ON MAIN STATISTICAL INDICATORS

**I. Urban Households**

**Population of Urban Households** refer to members of households living and sharing economically together in the urban areas. All the income and expenditure of all the members of such households are included in the income and expenditure of the household.

**Proportion of Urban Employment** refers to the proportion of employed population to the population of urban households.

**Number of Dependents per Urban Employee** refers to the ratio between number of persons in an urban household and the number of employed persons.

**Total Income of Urban Households** refers to the sum of wage and salary; net business income; income from properties; and income from transfers of members of the households. Income from selling of properties and income from borrowing are not included.

**Disposable Income of Urban Households** refers to the actual income at the disposal of members of the households which can be used for final consumption, other non-compulsory expenditure and savings. This equals to total income minus income tax, personal contribution to social security and subsidy for keeping diaries in being a sample household. The following formula is used:

Disposable income = total household income - income tax - personal contribution to social security - subsidy for keeping diaries for a sampled household

**Total Expenditure of Urban Households** refers to all expenditure of households except expenditure on lending. It includes expenditure on consumption; on purchasing or building houses; on transfers; on properties; and on social security.

**Consumption Expenditure of Urban Households** refers to total expenditure of households for consumption in daily life, including expenditure on the eight categories of food; clothing; household appliances and services; health care and medical services; transport and communications; recreation, education and cultural services; housing; and miscellaneous goods and services.

**Expenditure of Urban Households on Consumption of Services** refers to expenditure of households on various kinds of non-commercial services provided by society.

**Urban Households by Income Group** All households in the sample are grouped, by per capita disposable income of the household, into groups of lowest income, low income, lower middle income, middle income, upper middle income, high income and highest income, each group consisting of 10%, 10%, 20%, 20%, 20%, 10% and 10% of all households respectively.

**Engel Coefficient** refers to the percentage of expenditure on food in the total consumption expenditure, using the following formula:

$$\text{Engel Coefficient} = \frac{\text{expenditure on food}}{\text{total consumption expenditure}} \times 100\%$$

**II. Rural Household**

**Rural Households** refer to usual resident households in rural areas. Usual resident households in rural areas are households residing on a long term basis (for more than one year) in the areas under the administration of township governments (not including county towns), and in the areas under the administration of villages in county towns. Households residing in the current addresses for over one year with their household registration in other places are still considered as resident households of the locality. For households with their household registration in one place but all members of the households having moved away to make a living in another place for over one year, they will not be included in the rural households of the area where they are registered, irrespective of whether they still keep their contracted land.

**Usual Resident Population** refers to persons staying at home regularly or for over 6 months during a year and integrated with the household economically and in terms of living.. Members of the household staying away from the household for over 6 months but keeping a close economic relation with the household by sending the majority of income to the household are regarded as usual resident of the household. Government staff and workers or retirees living as close members of the household are also considered as usual resident. However, servicemen, students of secondary technical schools or schools of higher education and persons with stable jobs and residence outside the household (excluding those visiting relatives or seeking medical service) are not included as resident population of the household. Resident population is used in calculating income, consumption, accumulation on per capita basis of rural households and in analyzing composition of rural households.

**Full/Semi Labour Force** Full labour force refers to persons capable of work, aged 18-50 for males and 18-45 for females. Semi labour force refers to persons capable of work, aged 16-17 and 51-60 for males and 16-17 and 46-55 for females. Persons at their working ages but not capable of work are not to be included as labour force. Persons not at working ages but participating regularly in work are included in semi labour force. For staff and workers who are usual residents, are included as full or semi labour force of the household if they are in the labour force.

**Total Income** refers to the sum of income earned from various sources by the rural households and their members during the reference period, and is classified as income from wages and salaries, income from household operations, income from properties and income from transfers.

**Income from Wages and Salaries** refers to income from labour earned by the members of rural households employed by other units or individuals.

**Income from Household Operations** refers to income by the rural households as units of production and operation. Operations by rural households are classified according to their economic activities namely agriculture, forestry, animal husbandry, fishery, manufacturing, construction, transportation, post and telecommunications, wholesale, retail and catering, social service, culture, education, health, and other household operations.

**Income from Properties** refers to the income received as returns by owners of financial assets or tangible non-productive assets by providing capitals or tangible non-productive assets to other institutional units.

**Income from Transfers** refers to the receipt by rural households and their members of goods, services, capital or rights of assets without giving or repaying accordingly, excluding capital provided to them for the formation of fixed assets. In general, it refers to all income received by rural households through redistribution.

**Cash Income** refers to income received by rural households and their members in the form of cash during the reference period. It is classified, by source of income, into income from wages and salaries, cash income from household operations, income from properties and income from transfers.

**Net Income** refers to the total income of rural households from all sources minus all corresponding expenses. The formula for calculation is as follows:

Net income = total income - taxes and fees paid - household operation expenses - taxes and fees depreciation of fixed assets for production - gifts to non-rural relatives

Net income is mainly used as input for reinvestment in production and as consumption expenditure of the year, and also used for savings and non-compulsory expenses of various forms. "Per capita net income of farmers" is the level of net income averaged by population, reflecting the average income level of rural households in a given area.

**Total Expenditure** refers to total expenses of rural households on production, consumption and redistribution, including expenditure on household operations,; purchase of productive fixed assets; depreciation of productive fixed assets; taxes and fees; expenses on household consumption; expenses on properties; and expenses on transfers.

# 十五、科 技

# CHAPTER 15
# SCIENCE AND TECHNOLOGY

# 科 技 SCIENCE AND TECHNOLOGY

## 主要统计指标 MAJOR STATISTICAL INDICATORS

| | | | | |
|---|---|---|---|---|
| 2012年市级以上科技进步奖 | Number of Scientific & Technological Prizes Won Over City Level | 158 | 项 | item |
| 2012年专利申请数 | Number of Patent Applications Examined | 139 965 | 件 | unit |
| 比上年增长 | Increase Over Last Year | 37.0 | % | |
| 2012年专利授权数 | Number of Patent Applications Granted | 98 276 | 件 | unit |
| 比上年增长 | Increase Over Last Year | 27.2 | % | |
| 2012年末专业技术人员数 | Number of Scientific & Technical Personnel | 1 099 869 | 人 | person |
| 比上年增长 | Increase Over Last Year | 14.0 | % | |
| 2012年末高级职称专业技术人员数 | Number of Scientific & Technical Personnel with Senior Professional Titles | 46 661 | 人 | person |
| 比上年增长 | Increase Over Last Year | 16.9 | % | |

表15-1

# 部分年份国有事业独立科研机构和人员情况
# STATE-OWNED SCIENCE & RESEARCH INSTITUTIONS AND PERSONNEL OF PARTIAL YEARS

| 项 目 | Item | 1990年 | 2000年 | 2005年 | 2010年 | 2011年 | 2012年 |
|---|---|---|---|---|---|---|---|
| **机构数** (个) | **Number of Institutions** (unit) | | | | | | |
| **全 市** | **Whole Municipality** | **65** | **63** | **46** | **66** | **70** | **75** |
| 市 区 | Urban Area | 48 | 50 | 40 | 54 | 56 | 60 |
| # 吴江区 | Wujiang District | 6 | 3 | 2 | 2 | 2 | 2 |
| 常 熟 | Changshu | 3 | 3 | 2 | 5 | 5 | 6 |
| 张家港 | Zhangjiagang | 5 | 4 | 1 | 2 | 3 | 2 |
| 昆 山 | Kunshan | 7 | 4 | 2 | 3 | 4 | 5 |
| 太 仓 | Taicang | 2 | 2 | 1 | 2 | 2 | 2 |
| **职工人数** (人) | **Number of Staff & Workers** (person) | | | | | | |
| **全 市** | **Whole Municipality** | **3 974** | **3 427** | **3 062** | **6 496** | **6 834** | **8 897** |
| 市 区 | Urban Area | 3 470 | 3 071 | 2 892 | 5 949 | 6 259 | 7 859 |
| # 吴江区 | Wujiang District | 119 | 42 | 25 | 21 | 22 | 22 |
| 常 熟 | Changshu | 129 | 87 | 63 | 106 | 108 | 164 |
| 张家港 | Zhangjiagang | 101 | 106 | 39 | 139 | 150 | 184 |
| 昆 山 | Kunshan | 205 | 93 | 44 | 188 | 201 | 553 |
| 太 仓 | Taicang | 69 | 70 | 24 | 114 | 116 | 137 |
| **专业技术人员数** (人) | **Number of Scientific and Technical Personnel** (person) | | | | | | |
| **全 市** | **Whole Municipality** | | **2 218** | **1 952** | **3 784** | **3 856** | **5 701** |
| 市 区 | Urban Area | | 2 059 | 1 865 | 3 306 | 3 359 | 4 767 |
| # 吴江区 | Wujiang District | | 26 | 18 | 17 | 18 | 20 |
| 常 熟 | Changshu | | 43 | 31 | 98 | 99 | 125 |
| 张家港 | Zhangjiagang | | 46 | 19 | 122 | 130 | 171 |
| 昆 山 | Kunshan | | 52 | 25 | 181 | 191 | 542 |
| 太 仓 | Taicang | | 18 | 12 | 77 | 77 | 96 |

表15-2

# 部分年份分地区专利申请情况
# PATENT APPLICATIONS EXAMINED BY REGION OF PARTIAL YEARS

单位：件 (unit)

| 地 区 | Region | 1985-1994年 | 1995年 | 2000年 | 2005年 | 2010年 | 2011年 | 2012年 |
|---|---|---|---|---|---|---|---|---|
| **全 市** | **Whole Municipality** | **3 405** | **773** | **2 021** | **6 780** | **77 194** | **102 164** | **139 965** |
| 市 区 | Urban Area | 2 345 | 478 | 731 | 3 449 | 38 361 | 55 679 | 76 214 |
| # 吴江区 | Wujiang District | 106 | 82 | 58 | 718 | 19 469 | 28 729 | 38 590 |
| 常 熟 | Changshu | 555 | 98 | 205 | 598 | 12 812 | 16 416 | 15 024 |
| 张家港 | Zhangjiagang | 187 | 105 | 221 | 736 | 7 147 | 7 351 | 9 196 |
| 昆 山 | Kunshan | 213 | 22 | 787 | 1 674 | 14 923 | 17 626 | 31 515 |
| 太 仓 | Taicang | 105 | 70 | 77 | 323 | 3 951 | 5 092 | 8 016 |

表15-3

# 部分年份分地区专利授权情况
# PATENT GRANTED BY REGION OF PARTIAL YEARS

单位：件 (unit)

| 地 区 | Region | 1985-1994年 | 1995年 | 2000年 | 2005年 | 2010年 | 2011年 | 2012年 |
|---|---|---|---|---|---|---|---|---|
| **全 市** | **Whole Municipality** | **2 244** | **415** | **1 922** | **3 315** | **46 109** | **77 281** | **98 276** |
| 市 区 | Urban Area | 1 548 | 244 | 599 | 1 470 | 25 466 | 44 860 | 49 566 |
| # 吴江区 | Wujiang District | 67 | 35 | 38 | 221 | 14 698 | 30 041 | 30 775 |
| 常 熟 | Changshu | 415 | 81 | 159 | 328 | 4 242 | 7 980 | 13 366 |
| 张家港 | Zhangjiagang | 102 | 27 | 136 | 427 | 3 049 | 7 702 | 8 469 |
| 昆 山 | Kunshan | 133 | 30 | 972 | 884 | 10 750 | 12 742 | 20 495 |
| 太 仓 | Taicang | 46 | 33 | 56 | 206 | 2 602 | 3 997 | 6 380 |

表15-4

# 部分年份专利申请和授权分类情况
# PATENT APPLICATIONS EXAMINED AND GRANTED BY TYPE OF PARTIAL YEARS

单位：件 (unit)

| 年份 Year | 申请 Applications Examined | 发明 Inventions | 实用新型 Utility Models | 外观 Designs | 授权 Applications Granted | 发明 Inventions | 实用新型 Utility Models | 外观 Designs |
|---|---|---|---|---|---|---|---|---|
| 1995 | 773 | 47 | 405 | 321 | 415 | 41 | 252 | 122 |
| 2000 | 2 021 | 224 | 927 | 870 | 1 922 | 32 | 1 076 | 814 |
| 2001 | 2 653 | 175 | 1 205 | 1 273 | 1 749 | 33 | 807 | 909 |
| 2002 | 3 109 | 271 | 1 504 | 1 334 | 2 324 | 64 | 1 058 | 1 202 |
| 2003 | 3 780 | 328 | 1 644 | 1 808 | 2 593 | 126 | 1 317 | 1 150 |
| 2004 | 4 687 | 580 | 1 759 | 2 348 | 2 783 | 167 | 1 128 | 1 488 |
| 2005 | 6 780 | 988 | 2 349 | 3 443 | 3 315 | 148 | 1 496 | 1 671 |
| 2006 | 12 874 | 2 002 | 2 841 | 8 031 | 4 855 | 180 | 2 075 | 2 600 |
| 2007 | 33 752 | 4 666 | 4 106 | 24 980 | 9 157 | 292 | 2 948 | 5 917 |
| 2008 | 48 558 | 5 371 | 6 209 | 36 978 | 18 270 | 645 | 4 217 | 13 408 |
| 2009 | 61 336 | 8 281 | 8 972 | 44 083 | 39 288 | 1 030 | 5 585 | 32 673 |
| 2010 | 77 194 | 12 935 | 12 833 | 51 426 | 46 109 | 1 370 | 10 541 | 34 198 |
| 2011 | 102 164 | 21 765 | 19 428 | 60 971 | 77 281 | 2 492 | 14 220 | 60 569 |
| 2012 | 139 965 | 31 984 | 28 778 | 79 203 | 98 276 | 4 309 | 21 577 | 72 390 |

表15-5

# 分地区专利申请和授权分类情况 (2012年)
# PATENT APPLICATIONS EXAMINED AND GRANTED BY TYPE AND REGION (2012)

单位：件 (unit)

| 地区 | Region | 申请 Applications Examined | 发明 Inventions | 实用新型 Utility Models | 外观 Designs | 授权 Applications Granted | 发明 Inventions | 实用新型 Utility Models | 外观 Designs |
|---|---|---|---|---|---|---|---|---|---|
| **全　市** | **Whole Municipality** | **139 965** | **31 984** | **28 778** | **79 203** | **98 276** | **4 309** | **21 577** | **72 390** |
| 市　区 | Urban Area | 76 214 | 17 936 | 16 641 | 41 637 | 49 566 | 2 072 | 12 153 | 35 341 |
| # 吴江区 | Wujiang District | 38 590 | 3 556 | 2 816 | 32 218 | 30 775 | 402 | 2 388 | 27 985 |
| 常　熟 | Changshu | 15 024 | 2 639 | 1 499 | 10 886 | 13 366 | 478 | 1 501 | 11 387 |
| 张家港 | Zhangjiagang | 9 196 | 2 127 | 2 264 | 4 805 | 8 469 | 656 | 1 849 | 5 964 |
| 昆　山 | Kunshan | 31 515 | 7 530 | 6 880 | 17 105 | 20 495 | 884 | 4 907 | 14 704 |
| 太　仓 | Taicang | 8 016 | 1 752 | 1 494 | 4 770 | 6 380 | 219 | 1 167 | 4 994 |

表15-6

# 部分年份科技计划及科技成果获奖情况
# SCIENTIFIC AND TECHNOLOGICAL PLANNING AND PRIZES WON OF PARTIAL YEARS

单位：项 (item)

| 年份 Year | 星火计划 Spark Plan | 火炬计划 Torch Plan | 年末高新技术企业(个) Number of High & New Tech Enterprises at Year-end (unit) | # 当年认定 Certified In this Year | 科技进步奖 Scientific and Technological Progress Prizes 苏州市 Suzhou City | 江苏省 Jiangsu Province | 国家 Nation |
|---|---|---|---|---|---|---|---|
| 1995 | 19 | 24 | 102 | 38 | 137 | 50 | - |
| 2000 | 13 | 37 | 346 | 68 | 162 | 32 | - |
| 2001 | 8 | 39 | 404 | 64 | 153 | 26 | 1 |
| 2002 | 14 | 48 | 484 | 80 | 133 | 23 | - |
| 2003 | 15 | 69 | 555 | 80 | 130 | 17 | - |
| 2004 | 19 | 69 | 622 | 76 | 133 | 20 | 1 |
| 2005 | 12 | 51 | 706 | 103 | 132 | 8 | 3 |
| 2006 | 21 | 110 | 844 | 162 | 114 | 13 | - |
| 2007 | 19 | 125 | 1 430 | 599 | 104 | 11 | 1 |
| 2008 | 22 | 79 | 1 246 | 361 | 103 | 19 | 2 |
| 2009 | 1 | 3 | 680 | 319 | 115 | 15 | 3 |
| 2010 | 36 | 99 | 975 | 297 | 117 | 17 | 4 |
| 2011 | 62 | 96 | 1 345 | 430 | 113 | 16 | 4 |
| 2012 | 61 | 112 | 1 864 | 588 | 122 | 33 | 3 |

注：2008年国家实行高新技术企业新标准认定办法，原认定办法有效期二年，因此，从2009年开始是新标准企业数。
Note: From 2008 the state started to implement the measuring method for the new standards for high-tech enterprises, and the original method was valid for two years, so the number of enterprises beginning from 2009 was that of enterprises of the new standards.

表15-7

# 分地区科技计划及科技成果获奖情况（2012年）
# SCIENTIFIC AND TECHNOLOGICAL PLANNING AND PRIZES WON BY REGION (2012)

单位：项 (item)

| 地区 Region | 星火计划 Spark Plan | 火炬计划 Torch Plan | 年末高新技术企业(个) Number of High & New Tech Enterprises at Year-end (unit) | # 当年认定 Certified In this Year | 科技进步奖 Scientific and Technological Progress Prizes 苏州市 Suzhou City | 江苏省 Jiangsu Province | 国家 Nation |
|---|---|---|---|---|---|---|---|
| **全 市 Whole Municipality** | **61** | **112** | **1 864** | **588** | **122** | **33** | **3** |
| 市 区 Urban Area | 13 | 50 | 1 032 | 322 | 77 | 20 | 1 |
| # 吴江区 Wujiang District | 5 | 9 | 127 | 39 | 6 | 2 | 1 |
| 常 熟 Changshu | 10 | 21 | 144 | 40 | 10 | 2 | 1 |
| 张家港 Zhangjiagang | 13 | 13 | 193 | 54 | 18 | 4 | 1 |
| 昆 山 Kunshan | 17 | 21 | 385 | 135 | 14 | 6 | - |
| 太 仓 Taicang | 8 | 7 | 110 | 37 | 3 | 1 | - |

表15-8

# 大中型工业科技活动企业与机构数（2012年）

# NUMBER OF ENTERPRISES AND INSITITUTIONS OF LARGE & MEDIUM-SIZED INDUSTRIAL ENTERPRISES ON SCIENTIFIC AND TECHNOLOGICAL ACTIVITIES (2012)

单位：个 (unit)

| 项　目 | Item | 企业数 Number of Enterprises | # 有R&D活动企业数 Number of Businesses With R&D Activities | 企业办科技机构数 Number of Science & Technology Institutions Run by Enterprises |
|---|---|---|---|---|
| **总　计** | **Total** | **2 164** | **1 298** | **2 308** |
| **一、按地区分** | **Grouped by Region** | | | |
| 市　区 | Urban Area | 1 034 | 558 | 1 091 |
| # 吴江区 | Wujiang District | 279 | 78 | 294 |
| 常　熟 | Changshu | 265 | 208 | 288 |
| 张家港 | Zhangjiagang | 181 | 156 | 264 |
| 昆　山 | Kunshan | 540 | 296 | 520 |
| 太　仓 | Taicang | 144 | 80 | 145 |
| **二、按登记注册类型分** | **Grouped by Registration Status** | | | |
| 国有企业 | State-owned Enterprises | 16 | 12 | 19 |
| 集体企业 | Collective-owned Enterprises | 2 | 1 | 2 |
| 股份合作企业 | Share-holding Cooperative Enterprises | 8 | 7 | 8 |
| 联营企业 | Joint Ownership Enterprises | 2 | 1 | 2 |
| 有限责任公司 | Limited Liability Corporations | 109 | 86 | 176 |
| 股份有限公司 | Share-holding Corporations Ltd. | 64 | 52 | 105 |
| 私营企业 | Private Enterprises | 491 | 322 | 555 |
| 其他企业 | Other Enterprises | 6 | 3 | 6 |
| 港澳台商投资企业 | Enterprises with Investment from HongKong, Macao and Taiwan | 453 | 272 | 460 |
| 外商投资企业 | Enterprises with Foreign Investment | 1 013 | 542 | 975 |
| **三、按主要行业分** | **Grouped by Sector** | | | |
| **采矿业** | **Mining and Quarrying** | **2** | **2** | **2** |
| 有色金属矿采选业 | Nonferrous Metals Mining and Processing | 1 | 1 | 1 |
| 非金属矿采选业 | Nonmetal Minerals Mining and Dressing | 1 | 1 | 1 |
| **制造业** | **Manufacturing** | **2 145** | **1 288** | **2 293** |
| 农副食品加工业 | Food Processing | 6 | 3 | 6 |
| 食品制造业 | Food Production | 12 | 7 | 12 |
| 酒、饮料和精制茶制造业 | Wine, Beverage and Refined tea manufacturing | 5 | 4 | 5 |
| 纺织业 | Textile Industry | 179 | 103 | 190 |

表15-8 续表 Continued

单位：个 (unit)

| 项 目 | Item | 企业数 Number of Enterprises | # 有R&D活动企业数 Number of Businesses With R&D Activities | 企业办科技机构数 Number of Science & Technology Institutions Run by Enterprises |
|---|---|---|---|---|
| 纺织服装、服饰业 | Garments and Apparel Industry | 154 | 91 | 154 |
| 皮革、毛皮、羽毛及其制品和制鞋业 | Leather, Fur, Wool and Shoes Products | 25 | 10 | 25 |
| 木材加工及木、竹、藤、棕、草制品业 | Wood Processing, Wood, Bamboo, Rattan and Coir Products Straw Products | 8 | 5 | 6 |
| 家具制造业 | Furniture Manufacturing | 23 | 10 | 22 |
| 造纸和纸制品业 | Papermaking and Paper Products | 22 | 14 | 19 |
| 印刷业、记录媒介的复制业 | Printing and Record Medium Reproduction | 30 | 18 | 32 |
| 文教、工美、体育和娱乐用品制造业 | Stationary,Educational,Industrial arts, Sports and Entertainment products | 34 | 23 | 38 |
| 化学原料和化学制品制造业 | Raw Chemical Materials and Chemical Products | 67 | 50 | 100 |
| 医药制造业 | Medical and Pharmaceutical Products | 26 | 15 | 27 |
| 化学纤维制造业 | Chemical Fiber | 36 | 27 | 56 |
| 橡胶和塑料制品业 | Rubber and Plastic Products | 99 | 63 | 99 |
| 非金属矿物制品业 | Nonmetal Mineral Products | 39 | 23 | 41 |
| 黑色金属冶炼和压延加工业 | Smelting and Pressing of Ferrous Metals | 23 | 20 | 22 |
| 有色金属冶炼和压延加工业 | Smelting and Pressing of Nonferrous Metals | 25 | 17 | 26 |
| 金属制品业 | Metal Products | 97 | 60 | 99 |
| 通用设备制造业 | General Equipment Manufacture | 133 | 90 | 148 |
| 专用设备制造业 | For Special Purposes Equipment Manufacturing | 131 | 78 | 150 |
| 汽车制造业 | Automobile Manufacturing | 76 | 53 | 89 |
| 铁路、船舶、航空航天和其他运输设备制造业 | Railway, Ship, Aerospace and other transportation equipment manufacturing | 27 | 14 | 25 |
| 电气机械和器材制造业 | Electric Equipment and Machinery | 179 | 129 | 208 |
| 计算机、通信和其他电子设备制造业 | Computer Telecommunications and Other Electronic Equipment Manufacture | 650 | 336 | 651 |
| 仪器仪表制造业 | Instruments, Meters Machinery | 37 | 25 | 41 |
| 其他制造业 | Other Products Manufacture | 2 | – | 2 |
| **电力、燃气及水的生产和供应业** | **Production and Supply of Electricity, Gas and Water** | **17** | **8** | **13** |
| 电力、热力的生产和供应业 | Production and Supply of Electricity and Thermal Power | 8 | 4 | 5 |
| 燃气生产和供应业 | Production and Supply of Gas | 1 | – | – |
| 水的生产和供应业 | Production and Supply of Water | 8 | 4 | 8 |

表15-9 大中型工业企业科技活动人员情况 (2012年)

## NUMBER OF PERSONS ENGAGED IN SCIENTIFIC & TECHNOLOGICAL ACTIVTIES IN LARGE AND MEDIUM-SIZED INDUSTRIAL ENTERPRISES (2012)

单位：人 (person)

| 项 目 | Item | 研究与试验发展人员 Research and Development Personnel | # 参加项目人员 Present Item Personnel | 企业办科技机构人员 Personnel in Science & Technology Institutions Run by Enterprises |
|---|---|---|---|---|
| **总 计** | **Total** | **91 807** | **85 362** | **122 170** |
| **一、按地区分** | **Grouped by Region** | | | |
| 市 区 | Urban Area | 43 807 | 40 822 | 56 547 |
| # 吴江区 | Wujiang District | 10 662 | 10 106 | 13 980 |
| 常 熟 | Changshu | 8 332 | 7 706 | 11 533 |
| 张家港 | Zhangjiagang | 11 173 | 10 146 | 9 025 |
| 昆 山 | Kunshan | 24 278 | 22 761 | 38 349 |
| 太 仓 | Taicang | 4 217 | 3 927 | 6 716 |
| **二、按登记注册类型分** | **Grouped by Registration Status** | | | |
| 国有企业 | State-owned Enterprises | 636 | 545 | 1 125 |
| 集体企业 | Collective-owned Enterprises | 48 | 46 | 27 |
| 股份合作企业 | Share-holding Cooperative Enterprises | 142 | 135 | 184 |
| 联营企业 | Joint Ownership Enterprises | 16 | 16 | 63 |
| 有限责任公司 | Limited Liability Corporations | 8 298 | 7 561 | 8 242 |
| 股份有限公司 | Share-holding Corporations Ltd. | 6 090 | 5 751 | 6 706 |
| 私营企业 | Private Enterprises | 13 399 | 12 382 | 16 475 |
| 其他企业 | Other Enterprises | 136 | 115 | 261 |
| 港澳台商投资企业 | Enterprises with Investment from Hong Kong, Macao and Taiwan | 18 552 | 17 182 | 26 066 |
| 外商投资企业 | Enterprises with Foreign Investment | 44 490 | 41 629 | 63 021 |
| **三、按主要行业分** | **Grouped by Sector** | | | |
| **采矿业** | **Mining and Quarrying** | **106** | **103** | **148** |
| 有色金属矿采选业 | Nonferrous Metals Mining and Processing | 54 | 52 | 56 |
| 非金属矿采选业 | Nonmetal Minerals Mining and Dressing | 52 | 51 | 92 |
| **制造业** | **Manufacturing** | **91 605** | **85 179** | **121 523** |
| 农副食品加工业 | Food Processing | 33 | 32 | 138 |
| 食品制造业 | Food Production | 174 | 160 | 254 |
| 酒、饮料和精制茶制造业 | Wine, Beverage and Refined tea manufacturing | 95 | 89 | 127 |
| 纺织业 | Textile Industry | 3 338 | 3 014 | 3 872 |

表15-9 续表 Continued

单位：人 (person)

| 项 目 | Item | 研究与试验发展人员 Research and Development Personnel | # 参加项目人员 Present Item Personnel | 企业办科技机构人员 Personnel in Science & Technology Institutions Run by Enterprises |
|---|---|---|---|---|
| 纺织服装、服饰业 | Garments and Apparel Industry | 1 982 | 1 876 | 2 775 |
| 皮革、毛皮、羽毛及其制品和制鞋业 | Leather, Fur, Wool and Shoes Products | 223 | 207 | 591 |
| 木材加工及木、竹、藤、棕、草制品业 | Wood Processing, Wood, Bamboo, Rattan and Coir Products Straw Products | 102 | 95 | 195 |
| 家具制造业 | Furniture Manufacturing | 164 | 158 | 326 |
| 造纸和纸制品业 | Papermaking and Paper Products | 1 723 | 1 628 | 2 323 |
| 印刷业、记录媒介的复制业 | Printing and Record Medium Reproduction | 545 | 518 | 826 |
| 文教、工美、体育和娱乐用品制造业 | Stationary,Educational,Industrial arts, Sports and Entertainment products | 1 428 | 1 328 | 1 956 |
| 化学原料及化学制品制造业 | Raw Chemical Materials and Chemical Products | 2 848 | 2 576 | 3 801 |
| 医药制造业 | Medical and Pharmaceutical Products | 848 | 641 | 1 134 |
| 化学纤维制造业 | Chemical Fiber | 4 858 | 4 415 | 3 377 |
| 橡胶和塑料制品业 | Rubber and Plastic Products | 2 769 | 2 430 | 4 028 |
| 非金属矿物制品业 | Nonmetal Mineral Products | 1 668 | 1 535 | 1 768 |
| 黑色金属冶炼和压延加工业 | Smelting and Pressing of Ferrous Metals | 2 016 | 1 891 | 2 494 |
| 有色金属冶炼和压延加工业 | Smelting and Pressing of Nonferrous Metals | 1 128 | 1 067 | 936 |
| 金属制品业 | Metal Products | 2 445 | 2 302 | 4 067 |
| 通用设备制造业 | General Equipment Manufacture | 6 010 | 5 519 | 7 793 |
| 专用设备制造业 | For Special Purposes Equipment Manufacturing | 7 642 | 7 145 | 10 015 |
| 汽车制造业 | Automobile Manufacturing | 3 417 | 3 127 | 4 625 |
| 铁路、船舶、航空航天和其他运输设备制造业 | Railway, Ship, Aerospace and other transportation equipment manufacturing | 456 | 418 | 1 204 |
| 电气机械及器材制造业 | Electric Equipment and Machinery | 10 906 | 10 130 | 12 093 |
| 计算机、通信和其他电子设备制造业 | Computer Telecommunications and Other Electronic Equipment Manufacture | 33 032 | 31 234 | 48 950 |
| 仪器仪表制造业 | Instruments, Meters Machinery | 1 755 | 1 644 | 1 846 |
| 其他制造业 | Other Products Manufacture | – | – | 9 |
| **电力、燃气及水的生产和供应业** | **Production and Supply of Electricity, Gas and Water** | **96** | **80** | **499** |
| 电力、热力的生产和供应业 | Production and Supply of Electricity and Thermal Power | 50 | 46 | 399 |
| 燃气生产和供应业 | Production and Supply of Gas | – | – | – |
| 水的生产和供应业 | Production and Supply of Water | 46 | 34 | 100 |

表15-10 大中型工业企业科技活动经费支出情况 (2012年)

# EXPENDITURES OF SCIENTIFIC & TECHNOLOGIAL ACTIVITIES OF LARGE & MEDIUM-SIZED INDUSTRIAL ENTERPRISES (2012)

单位：万元 (10 000 yuan)

| 项　目 | Item | R&D经费内部支出合计 Internal Expenditures on Research and Development | # 政府资金 Government Funds | # 企业资金 Enterprises Funds | # 境外资金 Abroad Funds |
|---|---|---|---|---|---|
| **总　计** | **Total** | **2 086 212** | **31 163** | **1 959 209** | **35 223** |
| **一、按地区分** | **Grouped by Region** | | | | |
| 市　区 | Urban Area | 927 294 | 20 411 | 842 803 | 21 058 |
| # 吴江区 | Wujiang District | 189 929 | 14 271 | 173 345 | 224 |
| 常　熟 | Changshu | 241 722 | 2 991 | 233 043 | 1 675 |
| 张家港 | Zhangjiagang | 384 262 | 4 116 | 374 193 | 387 |
| 昆　山 | Kunshan | 414 399 | 3 467 | 395 301 | 8 451 |
| 太　仓 | Taicang | 118 535 | 177 | 113 868 | 3 653 |
| **二、按登记注册类型分** | **Grouped by Registration Status** | | | | |
| 国有企业 | State-owned Enterprises | 11 176 | 537 | 10 639 | – |
| 集体企业 | Collective-owned Enterprises | 970 | 26 | 944 | – |
| 股份合作企业 | Share-holding Cooperative Enterprises | 4 936 | 3 | 4 933 | – |
| 联营企业 | Joint Ownership Enterprises | 130 | – | 130 | – |
| 有限责任公司 | Limited Liability Corporations | 298 918 | 4 384 | 290 097 | 931 |
| 股份有限公司 | Share-holding Corporations Ltd. | 145 398 | 4 513 | 140 042 | 72 |
| 私营企业 | Private Enterprises | 290 406 | 16 109 | 267 787 | 857 |
| 其他企业 | Other Enterprises | 3 079 | – | 1 924 | 62 |
| 港澳台商投资企业 | Enterprises with Investment from Hong Kong, Macao and Taiwan | 394 421 | 1 966 | 377 034 | 9 979 |
| 外商投资企业 | Enterprises with Foreign Investment | 936 779 | 3 625 | 865 678 | 23 322 |
| **三、按主要行业分** | **Grouped by Sector** | | | | |
| **采矿业** | **Mining and Quarrying** | **1 066** | **54** | **1 011** | **–** |
| 有色金属矿采选业 | Nonferrous Metals Mining and Processing | 551 | – | 551 | – |
| 非金属矿采选业 | Nonmetal Minerals Mining and Dressing | 514 | 54 | 460 | – |
| **制造业** | **Manufacturing** | **2 083 342** | **31 108** | **1 956 399** | **35 223** |
| 农副食品加工业 | Food Processing | 856 | – | 856 | – |
| 食品制造业 | Food Production | 5 303 | – | 4 218 | – |
| 酒、饮料和精制茶制造业 | Wine, Beverage and Refined tea manufacturing | 821 | – | 821 | – |
| 纺织业 | Textile Industry | 82 808 | 1 008 | 80 691 | 204 |

表15-10 续表 Continued

单位：万元 (10 000 yuan)

| 项 目 | Item | R&D经费内部支出合计 Internal Expenditures on Research and Development | # 政府资金 Government Funds | # 企业资金 Enterprises Funds | # 境外资金 Abroad Funds |
|---|---|---|---|---|---|
| 纺织服装、服饰业 | Garments and Apparel Industry | 37 147 | 331 | 36 741 | – |
| 皮革、毛皮、羽毛及其制品和制鞋业 | Leather, Fur, Wool and Shoes Products | 4 173 | – | 4 038 | – |
| 木材加工及木、竹、藤、棕、草制品业 | Wood Processing, Wood, Bamboo, Rattan and Coir Products Straw Products | 1 857 | 1 | 1 856 | – |
| 家具制造业 | Furniture Manufacturing | 3 311 | – | 3 311 | – |
| 造纸和纸制品业 | Papermaking and Paper Products | 52 767 | 4 | 52 703 | 60 |
| 印刷业、记录媒介的复制业 | Printing and Record Medium Reproduction | 12 955 | 43 | 11 466 | – |
| 文教、工美、体育和娱乐用品制造业 | Stationary,Educational,Industrial arts, Sports and Entertainment products | 19 776 | 167 | 19 609 | – |
| 化学原料及化学制品制造业 | Raw Chemical Materials and Chemical Products | 89 713 | 1 854 | 83 700 | 1 942 |
| 医药制造业 | Medical and Pharmaceutical Products | 15 888 | 1 362 | 13 801 | 725 |
| 化学纤维制造业 | Chemical Fiber | 133 241 | 1 266 | 131 179 | – |
| 橡胶和塑料制品业 | Rubber and Plastic Products | 49 962 | 356 | 49 317 | – |
| 非金属矿物制品业 | Nonmetal Mineral Products | 35 899 | 91 | 31 371 | 4 437 |
| 黑色金属冶炼和压延加工业 | Smelting and Pressing of Ferrous Metals | 208 330 | 564 | 207 766 | – |
| 有色金属冶炼和压延加工业 | Smelting and Pressing of Nonferrous Metals | 28 874 | 205 | 28 056 | – |
| 金属制品业 | Metal Products | 49 873 | 649 | 48 117 | 62 |
| 通用设备制造业 | General Equipment Manufacture | 130 455 | 1 178 | 122 436 | 2 380 |
| 专用设备制造业 | For Special Purposes Equipment Manufacturing | 95 366 | 1 010 | 90 306 | 2 848 |
| 汽车制造业 | Automobile Manufacturing | 73 813 | 344 | 65 396 | 3 638 |
| 铁路、船舶、航空航天和其他运输设备制造业 | Railway, Ship, Aerospace and other transportation equipment manufacturing | 13 663 | 31 | 13 206 | 427 |
| 电气机械及器材制造业 | Electric Equipment and Machinery | 258 711 | 14 692 | 231 853 | 7 139 |
| 计算机、通信和其他电子设备制造业 | Computer Telecommunications and Other Electronic Equipment Manufacture | 651 088 | 5 070 | 600 095 | 10 049 |
| 仪器仪表制造业 | Instruments, Meters Machinery | 26 696 | 883 | 23 493 | 1 314 |
| 其他制造业 | Other Products Manufacture | – | – | – | – |
| **电力、燃气及水的生产和供应业** | **Production and Supply of Electricity, Gas and Water** | **1 805** | **1** | **1 799** | – |
| 电力、热力的生产和供应业 | Production and Supply of Electricity and Thermal Power | 691 | – | 691 | – |
| 燃气生产和供应业 | Production and Supply of Gas | – | – | – | – |
| 水的生产和供应业 | Production and Supply of Water | 1 113 | 1 | 1 108 | – |

## 表15-11 大中型工业企业自主知识产权情况（2012年）

## SELF-OWNED INTELLECTUAL PROPERTY RIGHTS OF SCIENTIFIC & TECHNOLOGICAL ACTIVITIES OF LARGE & MEDIUM-SIZED INDUSTRIAL ENTERPRISES (2012)

单位：件 (unit)

| 项　　目 | Item | 专利申请数 Patents Submitted for Examination | # 发明专利 Invention | 拥有发明专利数 Owning Inventive Patent |
|---|---|---|---|---|
| **总　　计** | **Total** | **14 762** | **4 948** | **9 396** |
| **一、按地区分** | **Grouped by Region** | | | |
| 市　区 | Urban Area | 6 903 | 2 328 | 5 407 |
| # 吴江区 | Wujiang District | 2 052 | 640 | 1 051 |
| 常　熟 | Changshu | 1 488 | 538 | 764 |
| 张家港 | Zhangjiagang | 2 267 | 623 | 624 |
| 昆　山 | Kunshan | 3 089 | 1 021 | 2 361 |
| 太　仓 | Taicang | 1 015 | 438 | 240 |
| **二、按登记注册类型分** | **Grouped by Registration Status** | | | |
| 国有企业 | State-owned Enterprises | 96 | 46 | 70 |
| 集体企业 | Collective-owned Enterprises | 2 | – | – |
| 股份合作企业 | Share-holding Cooperative Enterprises | 18 | 9 | 14 |
| 联营企业 | Joint Ownership Enterprises | – | – | – |
| 有限责任公司 | Limited Liability Corporations | 1 777 | 724 | 446 |
| 股份有限公司 | Share-holding Corporations Ltd. | 1 342 | 521 | 899 |
| 私营企业 | Private Enterprises | 4 015 | 1 141 | 1 728 |
| 其他企业 | Other Enterprises | 13 | 2 | 33 |
| 港澳台商投资企业 | Enterprises with Investment from Hong Kong, Macao and Taiwan | 3 517 | 975 | 1 385 |
| 外商投资企业 | Enterprises with Foreign Investment | 3 982 | 1 530 | 4 821 |
| **三、按主要行业分** | **Grouped by Sector** | | | |
| **采矿业** | **Mining and Quarrying** | **1** | **1** | **11** |
| 有色金属矿采选业 | Nonferrous Metals Mining and Processing | – | – | – |
| 非金属矿采选业 | Nonmetal Minerals Mining and Dressing | 1 | 1 | 11 |
| **制造业** | **Manufacturing** | **14 749** | **4 947** | **9 383** |
| 农副食品加工业 | Food Processing | 3 | – | 3 |
| 食品制造业 | Food Production | 29 | 11 | 15 |
| 酒、饮料和精制茶制造业 | Wine, Beverage and Refined tea manufacturing | 8 | – | – |
| 纺织业 | Textile Industry | 951 | 161 | 168 |

表15-11 续表　Continued

单位：件　　(unit)

| 项　　目 | Item | 专利申请数 Patents Submitted for Examination | # 发明专利 Invention | 拥有发明专利数 Owning Inventive Patent |
|---|---|---|---|---|
| 纺织服装、服饰业 | Garments and Apparel Industry | 795 | 32 | 175 |
| 皮革、毛皮、羽毛及其制品和制鞋业 | Leather, Fur, Wool and Shoes Products | 10 | 9 | 17 |
| 木材加工及木、竹、藤、棕、草制品业 | Wood Processing, Wood, Bamboo, Rattan and Coir Products Straw Products | 22 | 4 | 1 |
| 家具制造业 | Furniture Manufacturing | 19 | – | 1 |
| 造纸和纸制品业 | Papermaking and Paper Products | 309 | 182 | 39 |
| 印刷业、记录媒介的复制业 | Printing and Record Medium Reproduction | 40 | 20 | 43 |
| 文教、工美、体育和娱乐用品制造业 | Stationary,Educational,Industrial arts, Sports and Entertainment products | 838 | 68 | 302 |
| 化学原料及化学制品制造业 | Raw Chemical Materials and Chemical Products | 311 | 184 | 293 |
| 医药制造业 | Medical and Pharmaceutical Products | 43 | 31 | 52 |
| 化学纤维制造业 | Chemical Fiber | 659 | 236 | 120 |
| 橡胶和塑料制品业 | Rubber and Plastic Products | 286 | 76 | 107 |
| 非金属矿物制品业 | Nonmetal Mineral Products | 435 | 124 | 84 |
| 黑色金属冶炼和压延加工业 | Smelting and Pressing of Ferrous Metals | 398 | 229 | 116 |
| 有色金属冶炼和压延加工业 | Smelting and Pressing of Nonferrous Metals | 47 | 18 | 58 |
| 金属制品业 | Metal Products | 405 | 151 | 354 |
| 通用设备制造业 | General Equipment Manufacture | 1 184 | 414 | 2 716 |
| 专用设备制造业 | For Special Purposes Equipment Manufacturing | 1 014 | 409 | 530 |
| 汽车制造业 | Automobile Manufacturing | 332 | 107 | 172 |
| 铁路、船舶、航空航天和其他运输设备制造业 | Railway, Ship, Aerospace and other transportation equipment manufacturing | 190 | 65 | 48 |
| 电气机械及器材制造业 | Electric Equipment and Machinery | 2 659 | 840 | 1 341 |
| 计算机、通信和其他电子设备制造业 | Computer Telecommunications and Other Electronic Equipment Manufacture | 3 346 | 1 391 | 2 489 |
| 仪器仪表制造业 | Instruments, Meters Machinery | 416 | 185 | 139 |
| 其他制造业 | Other Products Manufacture | – | – | – |
| **电力、燃气及水的生产和供应业** | **Production and Supply of Electricity, Gas and Water** | **12** | **–** | **2** |
| 电力、热力的生产和供应业 | Production and Supply of Electricity and Thermal Power | 12 | – | 1 |
| 燃气生产和供应业 | Production and Supply of Gas | – | – | – |
| 水的生产和供应业 | Production and Supply of Water | – | – | 1 |

表15-12

# 大中型工业企业技术改造及引进、吸收情况（2012年）
# TECHNICAL INNOVATIONS, INTRODUCTION AND ABSORPTION OF LARGE & MEDIUM-SIZED INDUSTRIAL ENTERPRISES (2012)

单位：万元 (10 000 yuan)

| 项　目 | Item | 技术改造经费支出 Expenditure for Technical Innovation | 技术引进经费支出 Expenditure for Technical Innovation | 用于消化吸收经费支出 Expenditure for Technical Absorption | 购买国内技术支出 Purchases of Domestic Technologies |
|---|---|---|---|---|---|
| **总　计** | **Total** | **854 412** | **222 986** | **68 080** | **83 359** |
| **一、按地区分** | **Grouped by Region** | | | | |
| 市　区 | Urban Area | 459 083 | 113 043 | 17 924 | 22 005 |
| # 吴江区 | Wujiang District | 172 730 | 80 542 | 9 719 | 18 390 |
| 常　熟 | Changshu | 169 665 | 5 877 | 1 129 | 8 082 |
| 张家港 | Zhangjiagang | 154 886 | 85 289 | 47 231 | 52 597 |
| 昆　山 | Kunshan | 23 426 | 10 966 | 198 | 90 |
| 太　仓 | Taicang | 47 351 | 7 812 | 1 598 | 584 |
| **二、按登记注册类型分** | **Grouped by Registration Status** | | | | |
| 国有企业 | State-owned Enterprises | 9 254 | – | 30 | 305 |
| 集体企业 | Collective-owned Enterprises | 279 | – | – | – |
| 股份合作企业 | Share-holding Cooperative Enterprises | – | – | – | – |
| 联营企业 | Joint Ownership Enterprises | – | – | – | – |
| 有限责任公司 | Limited Liability Corporations | 160 815 | 94 115 | 48 625 | 54 769 |
| 股份有限公司 | Share-holding Corporations Ltd. | 161 400 | 32 355 | 1 382 | 18 760 |
| 私营企业 | Private Enterprises | 128 448 | 4 989 | 4 216 | 7 049 |
| 其他企业 | Other Enterprises | 1 111 | – | – | 560 |
| 港澳台商投资企业 | Enterprises with Investment from Hong Kong, Macao and Taiwan | 185 812 | 47 612 | 4 150 | 957 |
| 外商投资企业 | Enterprises with Foreign Investment | 207 293 | 43 915 | 9 676 | 958 |
| **三、按主要行业分** | **Grouped by Sector** | | | | |
| **采矿业** | **Mining and Quarrying** | **2 219** | **–** | **–** | **5** |
| 有色金属矿采选业 | Nonferrous Metals Mining and Processing | – | – | – | – |
| 非金属矿采选业 | Nonmetal Minerals Mining and Dressing | 2 219 | – | – | 5 |
| **制造业** | **Manufacturing** | **843 106** | **222 986** | **68 080** | **83 354** |
| 农副食品加工业 | Food Processing | – | – | – | – |
| 食品制造业 | Food Production | 193 | – | – | – |
| 酒、饮料和精制茶制造业 | Wine, Beverage and Refined tea manufacturing | 6 723 | – | – | – |
| 纺织业 | Textile Industry | 17 758 | 6 383 | 2 059 | 6 641 |

表15-12 续表 Continued

单位：万元 (10 000 yuan)

| 项 目 | Item | 技术改造经费支出 Expenditure for Technical Innovation | 技术引进经费支出 Expenditure for Technical Innovation | 用于消化吸收经费支出 Expenditure for Technical Absorption | 购买国内技术支出 Purchases of Domestic Technologies |
|---|---|---|---|---|---|
| 纺织服装、服饰业 | Garments and Apparel Industry | 43 369 | 5 029 | 1 038 | 931 |
| 皮革、毛皮、羽毛及其制品和制鞋业 | Leather, Fur, Wool and Shoes Products | – | – | – | – |
| 木材加工及木、竹、藤、棕、草制品业 | Wood Processing, Wood, Bamboo, Rattan and Coir Products Straw Products | 2 000 | – | – | – |
| 家具制造业 | Furniture Manufacturing | – | – | – | – |
| 造纸和纸制品业 | Papermaking and Paper Products | 52 765 | – | – | – |
| 印刷业、记录媒介的复制业 | Printing and Record Medium Reproduction | 553 | – | – | 960 |
| 文教、工美、体育和娱乐用品制造业 | Stationary,Educational,Industrial arts, Sports and Entertainment products | 2 740 | – | – | 100 |
| 化学原料及化学制品制造业 | Raw Chemical Materials and Chemical Products | 42 820 | 3 100 | 2 515 | 8 645 |
| 医药制造业 | Medical and Pharmaceutical Products | 3 182 | – | 30 | 370 |
| 化学纤维制造业 | Chemical Fiber | 119 369 | 30 714 | 6 342 | 12 688 |
| 橡胶和塑料制品业 | Rubber and Plastic Products | 4 210 | 4 134 | 56 | 95 |
| 非金属矿物制品业 | Nonmetal Mineral Products | 7 119 | 3 623 | 533 | – |
| 黑色金属冶炼和压延加工业 | Smelting and Pressing of Ferrous Metals | 83 923 | 81 929 | 44 148 | 41 972 |
| 有色金属冶炼和压延加工业 | Smelting and Pressing of Nonferrous Metals | 69 109 | 1 120 | 39 | 5 979 |
| 金属制品业 | Metal Products | 4 191 | – | 10 | 598 |
| 通用设备制造业 | General Equipment Manufacture | 50 121 | 1 658 | 5 212 | 1 303 |
| 专用设备制造业 | For Special Purposes Equipment Manufacturing | 22 278 | 1 075 | 46 | 1 151 |
| 汽车制造业 | Automobile Manufacturing | 20 707 | 4 825 | 168 | 169 |
| 铁路、船舶、航空航天和其他运输设备制造业 | Railway, Ship, Aerospace and other transportation equipment manufacturing | – | 1 800 | – | – |
| 电气机械及器材制造业 | Electric Equipment and Machinery | 113 053 | 3 551 | 2 972 | 1 081 |
| 计算机、通信和其他电子设备制造业 | Computer Telecommunications and Other Electronic Equipment Manufacture | 173 198 | 74 045 | 2 911 | 670 |
| 仪器仪表制造业 | Instruments, Meters Machinery | 3 725 | – | – | – |
| 其他制造业 | Other Products Manufacture | – | – | – | – |
| **电力、燃气及水的生产和供应业** | **Production and Supply of Electricity, Gas and Water** | **9 086** | – | – | – |
| 电力、热力的生产和供应业 | Production and Supply of Electricity and Thermal Power | 9 086 | – | – | – |
| 燃气生产和供应业 | Production and Supply of Gas | – | – | – | – |
| 水的生产和供应业 | Production and Supply of Water | – | – | – | – |

表15-13

## 部分年份专业技术人员
## SCIENTIFIC AND TECHNICAL PERSONNEL OF PARTIAL YEARS

单位：人 (person)

| 项　目 | Item | 1990年 | 2000年 | 2010年 | 2011年 | 2012年 |
|---|---|---|---|---|---|---|
| **总　计** | **Total** | **131 812** | **291 199** | **846 564** | **964 505** | **1 099 869** |
| # 高级职称人员 | Personnel with Senior Professional Titles | 5 552 | 13 241 | 34 439 | 39 917 | 46 661 |
| 中级职称人员 | Personnel with Medium Professional Titles | 30 756 | 71 247 | 209 820 | 234 400 | 271 384 |
| 总计中：市　区 | Urban Area | | 170 057 | 339 058 | 417 977 | 501 968 |
| # 吴江区 | Wujiang District | | 24 478 | 114 542 | 129 003 | 143 919 |
| 常　熟 | Changshu | | 38 694 | 131 448 | 141 279 | 163 603 |
| 张家港 | Zhangjiagang | | 35 449 | 111 208 | 130 953 | 150 802 |
| 昆　山 | Kunshan | | 28 835 | 193 336 | 199 107 | 205 859 |
| 太　仓 | Taicang | | 18 164 | 71 514 | 75 189 | 77 637 |

表15-14

## 分经济类型专业技术人员（2012年末）
## SCIENTIFIC AND TECHNICAL PERSONNEL BY SECTOR (END OF 2012)

单位：人 (person)

| 类　型 | Sector | 总　计 Total | # 高级职称 Senior Professional Titles | #中级职称 Medium Professional Titles | #研究生 Postgraduates | #大学本科 University and College | #大学专科 Specialized Institutions of Higher Education |
|---|---|---|---|---|---|---|---|
| **总　计** | **Total** | **1 099 869** | **46 661** | **271 384** | **45 522** | **417 404** | **432 176** |
| 全民事业 | Institutions Owned by the Whole People | 108 294 | 14 515 | 53 744 | 5 202 | 67 728 | 25 910 |
| 国有企业 | State-owned Enterprises | 9 322 | 711 | 2 308 | 688 | 4 725 | 2 910 |
| 部省属 | Province and State Council Department Owned Enterprises | 27 790 | 3 189 | 7 020 | 4 751 | 14 177 | 6 430 |
| 外资及港澳台资企业 | Enterprises with Foreign Investment or Investment from Hongkong, Macao and Taiwan | 503 068 | 14 955 | 111 150 | 21 597 | 167 088 | 217 377 |
| 民营企业 | Enterprises of Private Ownership | 451 395 | 13 291 | 97 162 | 13 284 | 163 686 | 179 549 |

表15-15

# 分地区专业技术人员 (2012年末)
# NUMBER OF SCIENTIFIC AND TECHNICAL PERSONNEL BY REGION (END OF 2012)

单位：人　　(person)

| 地　区 | Region | 总　计 Total | # 女　性 Female | 按职称分 Grouped by Professional Titles # 高级职称人员 Personnel with Senior Professional Titles | # 中级职称人员 Personnel with Medium Professional Titles | # 初级职称人员 Personnel with Junior Professional Titles |
|---|---|---|---|---|---|---|
| **总　计** | **Total** | **1 099 869** | **440 925** | **46 661** | **271 384** | **459 885** |
| 市　区 | Urban Area | 501 968 | 211 247 | 21 297 | 164 360 | 205 651 |
| # 吴江区 | Wujiang District | 143 919 | 72 424 | 4 267 | 16 800 | 22 548 |
| 常　熟 | Changshu | 163 603 | 54 540 | 8 045 | 31 496 | 66 524 |
| 张家港 | Zhangjiagang | 150 802 | 58 964 | 7 162 | 31 546 | 82 151 |
| 昆　山 | Kunshan | 205 859 | 87 553 | 6 361 | 25 968 | 72 154 |
| 太　仓 | Taicang | 77 637 | 28 621 | 3 796 | 18 014 | 33 405 |

表15-15 续表　Continued

单位：人　　(person)

| 地　区 | Region | 按学历分 Grouped by Educational Level 研究生 Postgraduates | 大学本科 University and College | 大学专科 Specialized Institutions of Higher Education | 中　专 Specialized Secondary School | 高中以下 Senior Middle School and below |
|---|---|---|---|---|---|---|
| **总　计** | **Total** | **45 522** | **417 404** | **432 176** | **141 787** | **62 980** |
| 市　区 | Urban Area | 32 322 | 190 259 | 182 660 | 63 523 | 33 204 |
| # 吴江区 | Wujiang District | 2 323 | 48 754 | 55 120 | 30 877 | 6 845 |
| 常　熟 | Changshu | 3 643 | 59 765 | 72 096 | 18 465 | 9 634 |
| 张家港 | Zhangjiagang | 3 613 | 52 719 | 58 524 | 28 289 | 7 657 |
| 昆　山 | Kunshan | 4 233 | 87 498 | 88 001 | 18 598 | 7 529 |
| 太　仓 | Taicang | 1 711 | 27 163 | 30 895 | 12 912 | 4 956 |

# 主要统计指标解释

**专利** 是专利权的简称，是对发明人的发明创造经审查合格后，由专利局依据专利法授予发明人和设计人对该项发明创造享有的专有权。包括发明、实用新型和外观设计。反映拥有自主知识产权的科技和设计成果情况。

**发明（专利）** 指对产品、方法或者其改进所提出的新的技术方案。是国际通行的反映拥有自主知识产权技术的核心指标。

**实用新型（专利）** 指对产品的形状、构造或者其结合所提出的适于实用的新的技术方案。反映具有一定技术含量的技术成果情况。

**外观设计（专利）** 指对产品的形状、图案、色彩或者其结合所作出的富有美感并适于工业上应用的新设计。反映拥有自主知识产权的外观设计成果情况。

**专业技术人员** 指从事专业技术工作的人员以及从事专业技术管理工作且已在1983年以前评定了专业技术职称或在1984年以后聘任了专业技术职务的人员。

专业技术人员具体指工程技术人员、农业技术人员、科研人员(自然科学研究、社会科学研究及实验技术人员)、卫生技术人员、教学人员(含高等院校、中等专业学校、技工学校、中学、小学)、民用航空飞行技术人员、船舶技术人员、经济人员、会计人员、统计人员、翻译人员、图书资料、档案、文博人员、新闻、出版人员、律师、公证人员、广播电视播音人员、工艺美术人员、体育人员、艺术人员及政工人员。

专业技术管理人员具体指企业、事业单位的领导；企业、事业单位下设的职能机构、企业的生产车间和辅助车间(或附属辅助生产单位)中从事生产、技术、经济管理和政治工作人员。

按照公务员管理或参照公务员管理的人员不统计为专业技术人员。

# EXPLANATORY NOTES ON MAIN STATISTICAL INDICATORS

**Patent** is an abbreviation for the patent right and refers to the exclusive right of ownership by the inventors or designers for the creation or inventions, given from the patent offices after due process of assessment and approval in accordance with the Patent Law. Patents are granted for inventions, utility models and designs. This indicator reflects the achievements of S&T and design with independent intellectual property.

**Patented Inventions** refer to new technical proposals to the products or methods or their modifications. This is universal core indicator reflecting the technologies with independent intellectual property.

**Patented Utility Models** refer to the practical and new technical proposals on the shape and structure of the product or the combination of both. This indicator reflects the condition of technological results with certain technical content.

**Designs** refer to the aesthetics and industrially applicable new designs for the shape, pattern and colour of the product, or their combinations. This indicator reflects the appearance design achievements with independent intellectual property.

**Professional Personnel** refers to the persons who are engaged in special professional work or in professional management who got the titles of a professional post before 1983 or who were appointed to professional positions since 1984.

Professional personnel specifically refers to engineering professionals, agricultural professionals, scientific research professionals (natural science researchers, social science researchers and laboratory technicians), health professionals, teaching professionals (including institutions of higher education, specialized secondary schools, technical schools, regular secondary schools, and primary schools), civil aviation professionals, nautical professionals, economic professionals, accounting professionals, statistical professionals, interpretation professionals, library professionals, archives professionals, professionals of culture, arts and cultural relics, newsman and publishing professionals, lawyers, notary professionals, radio and television announcers, industrial arts professionals, sports professionals, artists and political professionals.

Professional management personnel specifically refers to the managers of enterprises and institutions, the personnel engaged in the management of production, technical, economic management and political aspects in the functional departments under the enterprise and institution, production workshops and accessorial workshops (or accessorial production units) under the enterprises.

Professional personnel do not include personnel under or managed according to the system of civil servants.

# 十六、教育 文化

# CHAPTER 16
# EDUCATION AND CULTURE

# 教育　文化 EDUCATION AND CULTURE

## 主 要 统 计 指 标 MAJOR STATISTICAL INDICATORS

| | | | | |
|---|---|---|---|---|
| 2012年各类学校数 | Number of Schools of Various Types | 632 | 所 | unit |
| 高等学校数 | Number of Institutions of Higher Education | 20 | | |
| 中等职业教育学校 | Secondary Vocational Education Schools | 33 | | |
| 技工学校 | Technical Schools | 11 | | |
| 普通中学 | Regular Secondary Schools | 261 | | |
| 小　学 | Primary Schools | 294 | | |
| 特殊教育学校 | Special Education Schools | 13 | | |
| 2012年在校学生数 | Number of Students Enrollment | 989 146 | 人 | person |
| 高等学校 | Institutions of Higher Education | 192 206 | | |
| 中等职业教育学校 | Secondary Vocational Education Schools | 64 706 | | |
| 技工学校 | Technical Schools | 27 244 | | |
| 普通中学 | Regular Secondary Schools | 261 788 | | |
| 小　学 | Primary Schools | 440 400 | | |
| 特殊教育学校 | Special Education Schools | 2 802 | | |
| 2012年毕业生数 | Graduates | 224 189 | | |
| 2012年招生数 | New Student Enrollment | 265 056 | | |
| 2012年幼儿园数 | Number of Kindergartens | 465 | 所 | unit |
| 2012年在园幼儿数 | Number of Enrollment in Kindergartens | 229 746 | 人 | person |
| 2012年艺术表演团体 | Number of Art Troupes | 14 | 个 | unit |
| 2012年末公共图书馆 | Number of Public Libraries (Year-end) | 12 | 个 | unit |
| 2012年末博物馆 | Number of Museums (Year-end) | 36 | 个 | unit |

表16-1

# 历年各类学校及幼儿园数
# NUMBER OF SCHOOLS OF ALL TYPES AND KINDERGARTENS OVER THE YEARS

单位：所 (unit)

| 年 份 Year | 各类学校总 计 Total | 高等学校 Institutions of Higher Education | 中等职业教育学校 Secondary Vocational Education Schools | 技工学校 Technical Schools | 普通中学 Regular Secondary Schools | 小 学 Primary Schools | 特殊教育学校 Special Education Schools | 附:幼儿园 Kindergartens |
|---|---|---|---|---|---|---|---|---|
| 1949 | 1 694 | 2 | 14 | | 60 | 1 617 | 1 | |
| 1952 | 3 272 | 2 | 17 | | 67 | 3 185 | 1 | |
| 1957 | 3 373 | 2 | 14 | | 94 | 3 262 | 1 | |
| 1962 | 3 685 | 4 | 13 | 1 | 164 | 3 502 | 1 | |
| 1965 | 4 472 | 4 | 143 | 1 | 136 | 4 187 | 1 | |
| 1970 | 5 445 | 4 | 1 | 1 | 519 | 4 919 | 1 | |
| 1975 | 4 986 | 4 | 6 | 2 | 606 | 4 365 | 3 | |
| 1978 | 4 392 | 4 | 7 | 6 | 544 | 3 828 | 3 | |
| 1980 | 4 103 | 5 | 19 | 9 | 523 | 3 543 | 3 | |
| 1985 | 3 788 | 10 | 48 | 13 | 544 | 3 169 | 3 | |
| 1990 | 3 276 | 9 | 58 | 17 | 424 | 2 757 | 10 | |
| 1991 | 3 048 | 9 | 58 | 17 | 380 | 2 573 | 10 | |
| 1992 | 2 851 | 9 | 59 | 17 | 341 | 2 413 | 11 | |
| 1993 | 2 716 | 9 | 64 | 17 | 321 | 2 293 | 11 | |
| 1994 | 2 636 | 9 | 67 | 18 | 308 | 2 222 | 11 | |
| 1995 | 2 471 | 8 | 71 | 18 | 302 | 2 061 | 10 | |
| 1996 | 2 234 | 8 | 73 | 20 | 288 | 1 834 | 10 | |
| 1997 | 2 018 | 7 | 72 | 21 | 278 | 1 628 | 11 | |
| 1998 | 1 740 | 7 | 72 | 21 | 262 | 1 366 | 11 | |
| 1999 | 1 542 | 7 | 78 | 21 | 260 | 1 164 | 11 | |
| 2000 | 1 352 | 7 | 69 | 20 | 264 | 980 | 11 | |
| 2001 | 1 151 | 8 | 66 | 19 | 270 | 776 | 11 | |
| 2002 | 1 047 | 9 | 62 | 18 | 268 | 678 | 11 | |
| 2003 | 902 | 12 | 41 | 17 | 270 | 550 | 11 | |
| 2004 | 832 | 13 | 39 | 11 | 268 | 488 | 12 | |
| 2005 | 802 | 16 | 40 | 12 | 270 | 452 | 12 | 347 |
| 2006 | 745 | 17 | 41 | 13 | 265 | 397 | 12 | 357 |
| 2007 | 681 | 18 | 33 | 14 | 260 | 344 | 12 | 368 |
| 2008 | 677 | 18 | 34 | 15 | 261 | 337 | 12 | 389 |
| 2009 | 668 | 19 | 33 | 13 | 257 | 334 | 12 | 385 |
| 2010 | 652 | 20 | 34 | 12 | 257 | 317 | 12 | 411 |
| 2011 | 646 | 20 | 34 | 11 | 263 | 306 | 12 | 444 |
| 2012 | 632 | 20 | 33 | 11 | 261 | 294 | 13 | 465 |

注：1980年至2004年的学校总数中包含1所工读学校。
Note:From 1980 to2004, the total number of schools including a reform school.

表16-2

# 历年在校学生数
# STUDENT ENROLLMENT OVER THE YEARS

单位：人　(person)

| 年　份 Year | 各类学校在校学生总计 Total | 高等学校 Institutions of Higher Education | 中等职业教育学校 Secondary Vocational Education Schools | 技工学校 Technical Schools | 普通中学 Regular Secondary Schools | 小　学 Primary Schools | 特殊教育学校 Special Education Schools | 附:幼儿园在园幼儿数 Number of Enrollment in Kindergartens |
|---|---|---|---|---|---|---|---|---|
| 1949 | 167 633 | 847 | 2 443 | | 15 121 | 149 148 | 74 | |
| 1952 | 339 287 | 2 349 | 8 616 | | 34 028 | 294 220 | 74 | |
| 1957 | 415 729 | 3 251 | 7 738 | | 55 497 | 349 164 | 79 | |
| 1962 | 436 498 | 5 772 | 1 896 | 344 | 58 585 | 369 788 | 113 | |
| 1965 | 560 023 | 2 579 | 12 070 | 515 | 62 397 | 482 322 | 140 | |
| 1970 | 839 053 | 37 | | | 171 242 | 667 632 | 142 | |
| 1975 | 956 704 | 3 922 | 1 309 | 540 | 215 023 | 735 619 | 291 | |
| 1978 | 968 070 | 6 502 | 2 748 | 1 181 | 327 561 | 629 614 | 464 | |
| 1980 | 812 756 | 8 819 | 5 231 | 1 757 | 228 618 | 567 858 | 460 | |
| 1985 | 706 893 | 12 443 | 19 802 | 3 244 | 235 600 | 435 340 | 445 | |
| 1990 | 711 333 | 16 280 | 25 293 | 5 866 | 217 284 | 445 627 | 951 | |
| 1991 | 694 742 | 16 445 | 27 181 | 6 234 | 230 192 | 413 623 | 1 027 | |
| 1992 | 700 882 | 17 045 | 32 014 | 6 417 | 244 981 | 399 231 | 1 158 | |
| 1993 | 730 611 | 20 247 | 40 599 | 6 591 | 251 034 | 410 205 | 1 911 | |
| 1994 | 761 988 | 22 837 | 49 432 | 8 450 | 264 899 | 413 831 | 2 505 | |
| 1995 | 789 526 | 23 182 | 57 999 | 10 844 | 270 832 | 422 643 | 3 993 | |
| 1996 | 822 296 | 25 749 | 63 162 | 13 228 | 260 130 | 455 903 | 4 071 | |
| 1997 | 833 785 | 29 031 | 67 844 | 15 174 | 233 225 | 484 903 | 3 537 | |
| 1998 | 845 618 | 32 375 | 73 606 | 16 442 | 230 019 | 488 831 | 4 312 | |
| 1999 | 860 296 | 39 341 | 68 594 | 14 347 | 263 133 | 470 812 | 4 025 | |
| 2000 | 876 897 | 47 701 | 60 185 | 12 346 | 304 661 | 448 363 | 3 605 | |
| 2001 | 900 019 | 61 165 | 58 273 | 12 783 | 335 136 | 429 066 | 3 552 | |
| 2002 | 918 446 | 69 614 | 69 588 | 15 297 | 360 305 | 400 183 | 3 389 | |
| 2003 | 939 800 | 80 523 | 84 731 | 22 118 | 367 460 | 381 542 | 3 361 | |
| 2004 | 936 782 | 94 960 | 93 708 | 21 206 | 358 882 | 364 951 | 3 060 | |
| 2005 | 956 948 | 113 090 | 115 541 | 27 215 | 338 222 | 359 930 | 2 950 | 141 666 |
| 2006 | 941 320 | 130 622 | 102 737 | 28 875 | 324 690 | 351 549 | 2 847 | 149 387 |
| 2007 | 948 683 | 152 389 | 93 656 | 31 119 | 314 089 | 354 569 | 2 861 | 158 521 |
| 2008 | 961 934 | 166 828 | 94 661 | 33 018 | 300 886 | 363 807 | 2 734 | 174 886 |
| 2009 | 960 812 | 187 678 | 81 493 | 32 627 | 285 990 | 370 224 | 2 800 | 183 467 |
| 2010 | 958 474 | 187 829 | 74 828 | 32 158 | 272 541 | 388 353 | 2 765 | 197 889 |
| 2011 | 972 642 | 188 750 | 71 409 | 29 371 | 265 442 | 414 972 | 2 698 | 209 965 |
| 2012 | 989 146 | 192 206 | 64 706 | 27 244 | 261 788 | 440 400 | 2 802 | 229 746 |

注：1980年至2004年的在校学生数包含1所工读学校学生数。

Note:From 1980 to2004, the number of students in the school include students from a reform school.

表16-3

# 历年毕业生数
# NUMBER OF GRADUATES OVER THE YEARS

单位：人 (person)

| 年份 Year | 全市总计 Total | 高等学校 Institutions of Higher Education | 中等职业教育学校 Secondary Vocational Education Schools | 技工学校 Technical Schools | 普通中学 Regular Secondary Schools | 小学 Primary Schools | 特殊教育学校 Special Education Schools |
|---|---|---|---|---|---|---|---|
| 1949 | 12 766 | 126 | 802 | | 3 919 | 7 919 | |
| 1952 | 21 973 | 140 | 920 | | 4 936 | 15 972 | 5 |
| 1957 | 46 371 | 890 | 2 300 | | 12 572 | 30 609 | |
| 1962 | 55 127 | 1 416 | 879 | 29 | 20 200 | 32 595 | 8 |
| 1965 | 50 427 | 1 280 | 401 | 131 | 15 828 | 32 780 | 7 |
| 1970 | 135 095 | 528 | | | 46 969 | 87 585 | 13 |
| 1975 | 180 176 | 501 | 850 | 368 | 76 247 | 102 189 | 21 |
| 1978 | 262 706 | 1 757 | 83 | 422 | 152 832 | 107 604 | 8 |
| 1980 | 184 353 | 1 260 | 614 | 571 | 90 439 | 91 414 | 55 |
| 1985 | 140 384 | 2 386 | 5 829 | 758 | 65 943 | 65 410 | 54 |
| 1990 | 141 461 | 4 965 | 8 787 | 1 814 | 55 259 | 70 574 | 57 |
| 1991 | 151 203 | 4 888 | 8 438 | 1 931 | 61 993 | 73 877 | 57 |
| 1992 | 159 976 | 4 913 | 7 684 | 2 127 | 66 181 | 78 991 | 55 |
| 1993 | 157 013 | 4 862 | 7 658 | 2 177 | 70 032 | 72 170 | 93 |
| 1994 | 185 068 | 5 266 | 9 657 | 1 971 | 85 474 | 82 515 | 167 |
| 1995 | 181 891 | 7 246 | 12 214 | 2 239 | 83 993 | 76 053 | 134 |
| 1996 | 155 056 | 6 817 | 14 666 | 2 730 | 78 902 | 51 737 | 165 |
| 1997 | 166 338 | 6 791 | 18 346 | 4 231 | 92 661 | 43 866 | 373 |
| 1998 | 189 452 | 6 612 | 21 549 | 4 853 | 91 013 | 65 061 | 312 |
| 1999 | 184 905 | 7 926 | 18 739 | 4 861 | 69 435 | 83 525 | 379 |
| 2000 | 192 596 | 9 094 | 21 331 | 5 818 | 67 780 | 88 191 | 311 |
| 2001 | 213 613 | 9 551 | 22 390 | 4 965 | 88 808 | 87 317 | 533 |
| 2002 | 223 826 | 11 544 | 16 179 | 3 807 | 103 193 | 88 466 | 591 |
| 2003 | 217 663 | 15 187 | 12 434 | 3 014 | 109 347 | 76 964 | 645 |
| 2004 | 231 199 | 18 756 | 17 295 | 4 302 | 117 878 | 72 349 | 571 |
| 2005 | 247 087 | 22 498 | 21 257 | 6 965 | 126 944 | 68 878 | 545 |
| 2006 | 235 206 | 23 236 | 22 050 | 5 953 | 115 345 | 68 092 | 530 |
| 2007 | 236 025 | 30 335 | 23 937 | 7 532 | 108 974 | 64 845 | 402 |
| 2008 | 238 243 | 39 717 | 21 950 | 8 104 | 107 089 | 60 936 | 447 |
| 2009 | 234 727 | 40 995 | 23 992 | 7 387 | 102 375 | 59 494 | 484 |
| 2010 | 241 924 | 54 009 | 22 825 | 8 403 | 98 078 | 58 109 | 500 |
| 2011 | 231 498 | 55 176 | 18 098 | 9 539 | 90 001 | 58 206 | 478 |
| 2012 | 224 189 | 49 652 | 17 726 | 8 651 | 86 898 | 60 769 | 493 |

注：1980年至2004年的毕业生数包含1所工读学校学生数。
Note:From 1980 to2004, the number of graduates in the school include graduates from a reform school.

表16-4

# 历年专任教师数

# NUMBER OF FULL-TIME TEACHERS OVER THE YEARS

单位：人 (person)

| 年　份 Year | 各类学校专任教师总计 Total | 高等学校 Institutions of Higher Education | 中等职业教育学校 Secondary Vocational Education Schools | 技工学校 Technical Schools | 普通中学 Regular Secondary Schools | 小　学 Primary Schools | 特殊教育学校 Special Education Schools | 幼儿园专任教师数 Number of Full-time Teachers in Kindergartens |
|---|---|---|---|---|---|---|---|---|
| 1949 | 6 285 | 86 | 321 | - | 780 | 5 090 | 8 | |
| 1952 | 10 573 | 270 | 485 | - | 1 280 | 8 530 | 8 | |
| 1957 | 12 636 | 513 | 723 | - | 1 876 | 9 516 | 8 | |
| 1962 | 17 518 | 797 | 261 | 51 | 3 194 | 13 201 | 14 | |
| 1965 | 19 512 | 880 | 571 | 46 | 3 289 | 14 706 | 20 | |
| 1970 | | 789 | 86 | 48 | | 20 823 | 21 | |
| 1975 | 35 441 | 886 | 154 | 98 | 9 820 | 24 434 | 49 | |
| 1978 | 40 127 | 1 288 | 264 | 161 | 15 217 | 23 134 | 63 | |
| 1980 | 35 978 | 1 375 | 591 | 167 | 12 570 | 21 209 | 62 | |
| 1985 | 36 103 | 2 358 | 1 432 | 435 | 12 833 | 18 962 | 77 | |
| 1990 | 40 145 | 2 927 | 2 164 | 656 | 14 584 | 19 609 | 192 | |
| 1991 | 40 724 | 2 865 | 2 168 | 762 | 14 995 | 19 717 | 201 | |
| 1992 | 39 771 | 2 739 | 2 244 | 817 | 14 708 | 19 041 | 207 | |
| 1993 | 40 400 | 2 763 | 2 535 | 828 | 15 170 | 18 871 | 221 | |
| 1994 | 41 989 | 2 774 | 2 910 | 1 044 | 15 804 | 19 211 | 229 | |
| 1995 | 44 140 | 2 793 | 3 367 | 1 220 | 16 585 | 19 896 | 265 | |
| 1996 | 45 800 | 2 691 | 3 869 | 1 225 | 17 017 | 20 698 | 273 | |
| 1997 | 45 824 | 2 775 | 3 847 | 1 365 | 17 026 | 20 543 | 247 | |
| 1998 | 46 459 | 2 821 | 4 143 | 1 184 | 17 109 | 20 895 | 285 | |
| 1999 | 47 072 | 2 877 | 3 881 | 1 179 | 17 644 | 21 232 | 238 | |
| 2000 | 47 908 | 3 127 | 3 543 | 824 | 19 023 | 21 122 | 245 | |
| 2001 | 49 736 | 3 461 | 3 324 | 957 | 20 548 | 21 181 | 236 | |
| 2002 | 51 125 | 3 769 | 3 529 | 806 | 21 870 | 20 893 | 238 | |
| 2003 | 53 125 | 4 408 | 3 750 | 655 | 23 366 | 20 671 | 249 | |
| 2004 | 54 324 | 5 435 | 3 024 | 552 | 24 220 | 20 821 | 248 | |
| 2005 | 56 371 | 6 428 | 4 040 | 545 | 24 268 | 20 851 | 239 | 4 963 |
| 2006 | 58 189 | 7 138 | 4 423 | 1 153 | 24 323 | 20 909 | 243 | 5 480 |
| 2007 | 59 898 | 7 762 | 4 563 | 1 351 | 24 614 | 21 353 | 255 | 6 045 |
| 2008 | 61 704 | 8 498 | 4 739 | 1 351 | 24 868 | 21 969 | 279 | 6 988 |
| 2009 | 62 881 | 8 787 | 4 626 | 1 237 | 25 270 | 22 668 | 293 | 7 611 |
| 2010 | 65 174 | 10 104 | 4 680 | 1 411 | 25 295 | 23 375 | 309 | 8 658 |
| 2011 | 66 265 | 9 832 | 4 697 | 1 350 | 25 558 | 24 555 | 273 | 9 702 |
| 2012 | 68 404 | 10 392 | 4 830 | 1 310 | 25 916 | 25 656 | 300 | 11 082 |

注：1980年至2004年的专任教师数包含1所工读学校教师数。

Note:From 1980 to2004, the number of full-time teachers in the school teachers from a reform school.

表16-5

# 分地区各类学校基本情况（2012年）

| 项目 | Item | 全市 Whole Municipality |
|---|---|---|
| **学校数 (所)** | **Number of Schools (unit)** | **632** |
| 高等学校 | Institutions of Higher Education | 20 |
| 中等职业教育学校 | Secondary Vocational Education Schools | 33 |
| 技工学校 | Technical Schools | 11 |
| 普通中学 | Regular Secondary Schools | 261 |
| # 高　中 | Senior | 65 |
| 小　学 | Primary Schools | 294 |
| 特殊教育学校 | Special Education Schools | 13 |
| **招生数 (人)** | **New Student Enrollment (person)** | **265 056** |
| 高等学校 | Institutions of Higher Education | 60 127 |
| 中等职业教育学校 | Secondary Vocational Education Schools | 20 179 |
| 技工学校 | Technical Schools | 11 257 |
| 普通中学 | Regular Secondary Schools | 90 303 |
| # 高　中 | Senior | 26 639 |
| 小　学 | Primary Schools | 82 782 |
| 特殊教育学校 | Special Education Schools | 408 |
| **在校学生数 (人)** | **Student Enrollment (person)** | **989 146** |
| 高等学校 | Institutions of Higher Education | 192 206 |
| 中等职业教育学校 | Secondary Vocational Education Schools | 64 706 |
| 技工学校 | Technical Schools | 27 244 |
| 普通中学 | Regular Secondary Schools | 261 788 |
| # 高　中 | Senior | 84 079 |
| 小　学 | Primary Schools | 440 400 |
| 特殊教育学校 | Special Education Schools | 2 802 |

# BASIC CONDITION OF SCHOOLS BY REGION (2012)

| 市 区<br>Urban Area | # 吴江区<br>Wujiang District | 常 熟<br>Changshu | 张家港<br>Zhangjiagang | 昆 山<br>Kunshan | 太 仓<br>Taicang |
|---|---|---|---|---|---|
| **330** | **71** | **97** | **77** | **78** | **50** |
| 14 | 1 | 1 | 1 | 3 | 1 |
| 18 | 2 | 4 | 6 | 4 | 1 |
| 9 | – | 1 | 1 | – | – |
| 133 | 36 | 41 | 37 | 32 | 18 |
| 39 | 9 | 8 | 9 | 6 | 3 |
| 147 | 31 | 49 | 31 | 38 | 29 |
| 9 | 1 | 1 | 1 | 1 | 1 |
| **151 929** | **24 345** | **34 701** | **29 252** | **34 572** | **14 602** |
| 44 104 | 1 340 | 4 578 | 2 878 | 6 959 | 1 608 |
| 10 580 | 2 157 | 3 393 | 3 045 | 1 959 | 1 202 |
| 9 938 | – | 778 | 541 | – | – |
| 44 643 | 11 693 | 14 400 | 12 722 | 11 863 | 6 675 |
| 14 084 | 4 056 | 4 153 | 3 508 | 3 123 | 1 771 |
| 42 471 | 9 104 | 11 436 | 10 032 | 13 741 | 5 102 |
| 193 | 51 | 116 | 34 | 50 | 15 |
| **551 429** | **94 368** | **140 137** | **118 831** | **121 386** | **57 363** |
| 142 191 | 3 162 | 17 918 | 10 054 | 17 476 | 4 567 |
| 33 631 | 6 272 | 10 992 | 10 412 | 6 364 | 3 307 |
| 22 503 | – | 1 638 | 3 103 | – | – |
| 131 881 | 34 334 | 41 172 | 36 140 | 33 440 | 19 155 |
| 44 683 | 12 882 | 13 121 | 11 276 | 9 730 | 5 269 |
| 219 982 | 50 430 | 67 606 | 58 908 | 63 670 | 30 234 |
| 1 241 | 170 | 811 | 214 | 436 | 100 |

表16-5 续表

| 项　　目 | | Item | | 全　市 Whole Municipality |
|---|---|---|---|---|
| **毕业生数** | (人) | **Graduates** | (person) | **224 189** |
| 高等学校 | | Institutions of Higher Education | | 49 652 |
| 中等职业教育学校 | | Secondary Vocational Education Schools | | 17 726 |
| 技工学校 | | Technical Schools | | 8 651 |
| 普通中学 | | Regular Secondary Schools | | 86 898 |
| #高　中 | | Senior | | 31 525 |
| 小　学 | | Primary Schools | | 60 769 |
| 特殊教育学校 | | Special Education Schools | | 493 |
| **教职工数** | (人) | **Staff and Teachers** | (person) | **79 817** |
| 高等学校 | | Institutions of Higher Education | | 15 556 |
| 中等职业教育学校 | | Secondary Vocational Education Schools | | 5 685 |
| 技工学校 | | Technical Schools | | 1 467 |
| 普通中学 | | Regular Secondary Schools | | 29 514 |
| 小　学 | | Primary Schools | | 27 225 |
| 特殊教育学校 | | Special Education Schools | | 370 |
| **专任教师数** | (人) | **Number of Full-time Teachers** | (person) | **68 404** |
| 高等学校 | | Institutions of Higher Education | | 10 392 |
| 中等职业教育学校 | | Secondary Vocational Education Schools | | 4 830 |
| 技工学校 | | Technical Schools | | 1 310 |
| 普通中学 | | Regular Secondary Schools | | 25 916 |
| #高　中 | | Senior | | 9 163 |
| 小　学 | | Primary Schools | | 25 656 |
| 特殊教育学校 | | Special Education Schools | | 300 |

Continued

| 市 区<br>Urban Area | # 吴江区<br>Wujiang District | 常 熟<br>Changshu | 张家港<br>Zhangjiagang | 昆 山<br>Kunshan | 太 仓<br>Taicang |
|---|---|---|---|---|---|
| **125 598** | **23 299** | **30 849** | **28 132** | **25 766** | **13 844** |
| 36 266 | 1 251 | 3 863 | 2 477 | 5 555 | 1 491 |
| 7 945 | 2 452 | 2 342 | 4 332 | 2 009 | 1 098 |
| 7 106 | - | 614 | 931 | - | - |
| 44 981 | 12 336 | 13 722 | 11 638 | 10 210 | 6 347 |
| 17 247 | 5 224 | 4 654 | 4 281 | 3 516 | 1 827 |
| 29 154 | 7 234 | 10 089 | 8 743 | 7 882 | 4 901 |
| 146 | 26 | 219 | 11 | 110 | 7 |
| **46 451** | **7 662** | **11 023** | **9 124** | **8 895** | **4 324** |
| 12 276 | 198 | 1 106 | 647 | 1 200 | 327 |
| 2 666 | 313 | 1 126 | 1 066 | 631 | 196 |
| 1 121 | - | 179 | 167 | - | - |
| 16 142 | 3 782 | 4 250 | 3 836 | 3 451 | 1 835 |
| 14 011 | 3 338 | 4 319 | 3 375 | 3 568 | 1 952 |
| 235 | 31 | 43 | 33 | 45 | 14 |
| **38 974** | **7 069** | **9 646** | **8 109** | **7 705** | **3 970** |
| 8 131 | 150 | 740 | 472 | 820 | 229 |
| 2 262 | 296 | 961 | 920 | 516 | 171 |
| 1 001 | - | 160 | 149 | - | - |
| 14 058 | 3 411 | 3 736 | 3 396 | 2 998 | 1 728 |
| 5 140 | 1 261 | 1 197 | 1 328 | 1 015 | 483 |
| 13 328 | 3 183 | 4 017 | 3 144 | 3 338 | 1 829 |
| 194 | 29 | 32 | 28 | 33 | 13 |

表16-6

# 高等学校基本情况（2012年）
# CONDITIONS OF INSTITUTIONS OF HIGHER EDUCATION (2012)

单位：人 (person)

| 学校名称 | Schools | 毕业生数 Graduates | 招生数 New Student Enrollment | 在校学生数 Student Enrollment | 专任教师数 Number of Full-time Teachers |
|---|---|---|---|---|---|
| **总　计** | **Total** | **49 652** | **60 127** | **192 206** | **10 392** |
| # 研究生 | Postgraduates | 3 147 | 3 713 | 11 059 | – |
| 苏州大学 | Soochow University | 8 573 | 9 416 | 35 357 | 2 840 |
| 苏州科技学院 | Suzhou Technological College | 3 108 | 4 059 | 14 876 | 943 |
| 常熟理工学院 | Changshu Scienve and Engineering College | 2 782 | 3 398 | 12 615 | 740 |
| 西交利物浦大学 | Xijiao Liverpool University | 643 | 2 289 | 7 226 | 398 |
| 苏州工艺美术职业技术学院 | Suzhou Arts and Handicrafts Technical School | 1 555 | 1 648 | 4 776 | 321 |
| 苏州农业职业技术学院 | Suzhou Agricultural Vocational College | 2 268 | 2 699 | 7 417 | 405 |
| 苏州市职业大学 | Suzhou Vocational College | 4 808 | 4 696 | 13 699 | 683 |
| 沙洲职业工学院 | Shazhou Vocational Institute of Engineering | 1 064 | 1 424 | 3 920 | 215 |
| 苏州工业园区职业技术学院 | Suzhou Industrial Park Vocational College | 1 616 | 1 692 | 5 129 | 211 |
| 苏州市工业职业技术学院 | Suzhou Industry Profession Technology Institute | 1 697 | 2 670 | 7 535 | 346 |
| 苏州市经贸职业技术学院 | Suzhou Economy and Trade Technology Institute | 2 632 | 3 206 | 9 223 | 435 |
| 苏州卫生职业技术学院 | Suzhou Health College | 2 178 | 2 702 | 7 274 | 343 |
| 健雄职业技术学院 | Jianxiong Vocational College | 1 491 | 1 608 | 4 567 | 229 |
| 硅湖职业技术学院 | Silicone Lake Vocational College | 1 519 | 1 459 | 3 407 | 163 |
| 苏州托普信息技术学院 | Suzhou Tuopu Information Technology Institute | 1 153 | 1 358 | 2 208 | 101 |
| 昆山登云科技职业学院 | Kunshan Dengyun Technological COllege | 1 302 | 2 110 | 4 622 | 175 |
| 港大思培科技职业技术学院 | Gangda Technical College | 489 | 368 | 1 251 | 64 |
| 苏州高博软件技术职业学院 | Suzhou Global Institute of Software Technology | 1 283 | 893 | 2 514 | 158 |
| 苏州信息职业技术学院 | Suzhou Institute of Information Technology | 1 251 | 1 340 | 3 162 | 150 |
| 苏州工业园区服务外包职业技术学院 | Suzhou Industrial Park Institute of Sernces Outsourcing | – | 1 682 | 4 378 | 195 |
| *江苏科技大学苏州理工学院 | Suzhou Institute of Technology,Jiangsu University of Science and Technology | 1 413 | 1 454 | 6 134 | 257 |
| *苏大文正学院 | Wenzheng College of Soochow University | 2 098 | 2 345 | 9 344 | 294 |
| *苏大应用技术学院 | Applied Technology School of Soochou University | 1 581 | 2 032 | 7 239 | 381 |
| *苏州科技学院天平学院 | Tianping College of Suzhou University of Science and Technology | 2 067 | 2 399 | 9 030 | 345 |
| *常熟理工学院虞山学院 | Yushan College of Changshu Institute of Technology | 1 081 | 1 180 | 5 303 | – |

注：带"*"号的五所学院为二级学院。 Note: The college With "*" is secondary colleges.

表16-7

## 幼儿园基本情况 (2012年)
## BASIC CONDITION OF KINDERGARTENS (2012)

单位：人　(person)

| 地　区 | Region | 园数 (所) Number of Kindergartens (unit) | 招生数 Number of Newly Enrolled in Kindergartens | 在园幼儿数 Number of Enrollment in Kindergartens | 专任教师 Number of Full-time Teachers |
|---|---|---|---|---|---|
| **全　市** | **Whole Municipality** | **465** | **90 979** | **229 746** | **11 082** |
| 市　区 | Urban Area | 260 | 45 092 | 119 143 | 6 549 |
| # 吴江区 | Wujiang District | 42 | 9 694 | 24 418 | 896 |
| 常　熟 | Changshu | 61 | 11 265 | 30 176 | 1 165 |
| 张家港 | Zhangjiagang | 37 | 11 864 | 28 415 | 984 |
| 昆　山 | Kunshan | 73 | 18 130 | 39 911 | 1 771 |
| 太　仓 | Taicang | 34 | 4 628 | 12 101 | 613 |

表16-8

## 升学率和专任教师合格率 (2012年)
## PERCENTAGE OF GRADUATES ENTERING HIGHER LEVEL SCHOOLS AND RATE OF QUALIFIED FULL-TIME TEACHERS (2012)

单位：%　(%)

| 地　区 | Region | 毕业生升学率 Percentage of Graduates Entering Higher Level Schools | | 专任教师合格率 Rate of Qualified Full-time Teachers in Secondary and Primary Schools | | | | |
|---|---|---|---|---|---|---|---|---|
| | | 小　学 Primary Schools | 初　中 Junior Secondary Schools | 高　中 Senior Secondary Schools | 初　中 Junior Secondary Schools | 中等职业学校 Specialized Secondary Schools | 小　学 Primary Schools | 幼儿园 Kindergartens |
| **全　市** | **Whole Municipality** | **100.00** | **99.70** | **99.50** | **99.43** | **95.59** | **100.00** | **99.99** |
| 市　区 | Urban Area | 100.00 | 99.70 | 99.38 | 99.55 | 95.09 | 100.00 | 100.00 |
| # 吴江区 | Wujiang District | 100.00 | 99.58 | 99.76 | 98.98 | 99.32 | 100.00 | 100.00 |
| 常　熟 | Changshu | 100.00 | 98.14 | 99.67 | 98.90 | 95.21 | 100.00 | 99.91 |
| 张家港 | Zhangjiagang | 100.00 | 99.67 | 99.77 | 99.66 | 96.20 | 100.00 | 100.00 |
| 昆　山 | Kunshan | 100.00 | 99.88 | 99.51 | 99.60 | 96.71 | 100.00 | 100.00 |
| 太　仓 | Taicang | 100.00 | 99.70 | 99.59 | 99.04 | 97.66 | 100.00 | 100.00 |

表16-9

# 部分年份文化事业基本情况
# BASIC STATISTICS ON CULTURAL UNDERTAKINGS OF PARTIAL YEARS

| 项　目 | Item | 1990年 | 2000年 | 2010年 | 2011年 | 2012年 |
|---|---|---|---|---|---|---|
| **机构数** (个) | **Number of Institutions** (unit) | | | | | |
| 1.艺术事业 | Art | 50 | 45 | 15 | 15 | 14 |
| 2.文物事业 | Historical Relics | 18 | 20 | 42 | 45 | 45 |
| 3.图书馆事业 | Libraries | 7 | 11 | 12 | 12 | 12 |
| 4.群众文化事业 | Mass Cultural | 183 | 164 | 107 | 111 | 111 |
| 5.艺术教育事业 | Art Education | 4 | 5 | 3 | 3 | 2 |
| 6.其他文化事业 | Others | 16 | 40 | 12 | 10 | 10 |
| **职工人数** (人) | **Number of Staff and Workers** (person) | | | | | |
| 1.艺术事业 | Art | 1 036 | 914 | 554 | 563 | 557 |
| 2.文物事业 | Historical Relics | 304 | 242 | 671 | 628 | 761 |
| 3.图书馆事业 | Libraries | 180 | 192 | 589 | 667 | 520 |
| 4.群众文化事业 | Mass Cultural | 495 | 853 | 906 | 963 | 846 |
| 5.艺术教育事业 | Art Education | 87 | 94 | 83 | 69 | 73 |
| 6.其他文化事业 | Others | 249 | 360 | 97 | 69 | 70 |
| **主要文化活动** | **Main Culture Activities** | | | | | |
| 艺术表演团体演出场次 (千场次) | Number of Art Performance Troupes' Performers (1 000 show-times) | 17.3 | 16.9 | 13.2 | 17.8 | 17.4 |
| 博物馆参观人数 (千人次) | Number of Visitor to Museums(1 000 person-times) | 387 | 402 | 8 513 | 3 058 | 3 683 |
| 文物保护参观人数 | Number of Visitor to Historical Relics Preservation | 671 | 125 | 110 | 155 | 205 |
| 书刊文献外借人次 | Person-times of Borrowers of Books, Magazines and Documents | 868 | 1 051 | 3 868 | 2 508 | 4 712 |
| 书刊文献外借册次 (千册次) | Number of Books, Magazines and Documents Borrowed by the Readers (1 000 volume-times) | 2 396 | 1 874 | 6 120 | 6 764 | 11 102 |

表16-10

# 艺术表演团体基本情况（2012年）
# BASIC STATISTICS ON ART TROUPES (2012)

| 地 区 | Region | 机构数(个) Number of Institutions (unit) | 从业人员(人) Employed Persons (person) | 演出场次(场次) Number of Performances (show-time) | 观众人次(千人次) Number of Spectators (1 000person-times) | 公用房屋建筑面积(平方米) Floor Space of Public Buildings (sq.m) |
|---|---|---|---|---|---|---|
| **全 市** | **Whole Municipality** | **14** | **557** | **17 381** | **5 162** | **15 459** |
| 市 区 | Urban Area | 9 | 435 | 13 260 | 3 842 | 7 088 |
| # 吴江区 | Wujiang District | 2 | 10 | 590 | 100 | – |
| 常 熟 | Changshu | 2 | 63 | 2 660 | 730 | 2 171 |
| 张家港 | Zhangjiagang | 1 | 59 | 1 461 | 590 | 6 200 |
| 昆 山 | Kunshan | 2 | – | – | – | – |
| 太 仓 | Taicang | – | – | – | – | – |

表16-11

# 艺术表演场馆基本情况（2012年）
# BASIC SITUATION OF PERFORMING ARTS VENUES (2012)

| 地 区 | Region | 机构数(个) Number of Institutions (unit) | 从业人员(人) Employed Persons (person) | 座席数(个) Seating Capacity (set) | 演(映)出场次(场次) Number of Performances (show-time) | 观众人次(千人次) Number of Spectators (1 000person-times) | 公用房屋建筑面积(平方米) Floor Space of Public Buildings (sq.m) |
|---|---|---|---|---|---|---|---|
| **全 市** | **Whole Municipality** | **23** | **653** | **22 516** | **168 827** | **6 336** | **280 103** |
| 市 区 | Urban Area | 12 | 331 | 14 931 | 112 353 | 4 213 | 215 919 |
| # 吴江区 | Wujiang District | 2 | 37 | 2 224 | 7 424 | 206 | 9 731 |
| 常 熟 | Changshu | 1 | 10 | 1 208 | 42 | 4 | 6 627 |
| 张家港 | Zhangjiagang | 6 | 141 | 3 387 | 14 426 | 697 | 46 583 |
| 昆 山 | Kunshan | 4 | 171 | 2 990 | 42 006 | 1 422 | 10 974 |
| 太 仓 | Taicang | – | – | – | – | – | – |

表16-12

# 文化馆、文化站及文物保护基本情况（2012年）

| 指　标 | | Item | | 全　市 Whole Municipality |
|---|---|---|---|---|
| **文化馆** | | **Cultural Centers** | | |
| 机构数 | (个) | Number of Institutions | (unit) | 12 |
| 从业人员 | (人) | Employed Persons | (person) | 254 |
| 举办展览个数 | (个) | Number of Exhibitions | (unit) | 141 |
| 组织文艺活动次数 | (次) | Art Performances and Story-Telling Sessions | (time) | 1 810 |
| 举办训练班班次 | | Number of Training Courses | | 368 |
| 举办训练班培训人次 | (人次) | Number of People Trained in Training Courses | (person-time) | 32 422 |
| 公用房屋建筑面积 | (平方米) | Floor Space of Public Buildings | (sq.m) | 61 322 |
| # 业务用房 | | Space for Business | | 43 295 |
| 群众业余文艺团队 | (个) | Masses' Amateur Arts Teams | (unit) | 403 |
| **文化站** | | **Cultural Stations** | | |
| 机构数 | (个) | Number of Institutions | (unit) | 99 |
| 从业人员 | (人) | Employed Persons | (person) | 846 |
| 举办展览个数 | (个) | Number of Exhibitions | (unit) | 834 |
| 组织文艺活动次数 | (次) | Art Performances and Story-Telling Sessions | (time) | 6 788 |
| 藏　书 | (册) | Collection of Books | (volume) | 2 745 166 |
| 举办训练班班次 | (次) | Number of Training Courses | (time) | 2 763 |
| 举办训练班培训人次 | (人次) | Number of People Trained in Training Courses | (person-time) | 132 062 |
| 公用房屋建筑面积 | (平方米) | Floor Space of Public Buildings | (sq.m) | 480 882 |
| # 文化活动用房 | | Space for Cultural Activities | | 284 290 |
| 村（社区）文化室个数 | (个) | Number of Culture Rooms | (unit) | 2 023 |
| **文物保护** | | **Historical Relics Preservation** | | |
| 机构数 | (个) | Number of Institutions | (unit) | 9 |
| 从业人员 | (人) | Employed Persons | (person) | 70 |
| 文物藏品 | (件) | Number of Collections | (piece) | 10 161 |
| 参观人次 | (千人次) | Number of Visitors | (1 000 person-times) | 205 |
| 公用房屋建筑面积 | (平方米) | Floor Space of Public Buildings | (sq.m) | 15 837 |
| # 展览用房 | | Space for Exhibitions | | 1 841 |

# BASIC SITUATION OF CULTURAL CENTERS, CULTURAL STATIONS AND HISTORICAL RELICS PRESERVATION (2012)

| 市 区<br>Urban Area | # 吴江区<br>Wujiang District | 常 熟<br>Changshu | 张家港<br>Zhangjiagang | 昆 山<br>Kunshan | 太 仓<br>Taicang |
|---|---|---|---|---|---|
| | | | | | |
| 8 | 1 | 1 | 1 | 1 | 1 |
| 110 | 10 | 61 | 51 | 15 | 17 |
| 120 | 2 | 6 | 5 | 5 | 5 |
| 935 | 52 | 110 | 320 | 255 | 190 |
| 177 | 113 | 100 | 80 | 5 | 6 |
| 20 542 | 11 000 | 2 000 | 3 850 | 5 000 | 1 030 |
| 44 283 | 7 600 | 2 000 | 7 600 | 2 593 | 4 846 |
| 28 949 | 7 600 | 2 000 | 5 000 | 2 500 | 4 846 |
| 176 | – | 15 | 99 | 13 | 100 |
| | | | | | |
| 62 | 9 | 10 | 9 | 11 | 7 |
| 471 | 78 | 79 | 61 | 189 | 46 |
| 493 | 73 | 105 | 72 | 112 | 52 |
| 3 560 | 872 | 856 | 993 | 985 | 394 |
| 1 422 503 | 580 038 | 516 794 | 349 218 | 342 713 | 113 938 |
| 1 590 | 166 | 328 | 371 | 315 | 159 |
| 69 758 | 11 100 | 15 430 | 23 994 | 14 150 | 8 730 |
| 287 816 | 149 982 | 40 931 | 84 289 | 44 481 | 23 365 |
| 144 062 | 43 252 | 32 330 | 71 607 | 19 239 | 17 052 |
| 1 056 | 309 | 291 | 262 | 279 | 135 |
| | | | | | |
| 6 | 3 | 1 | 1 | 1 | – |
| 55 | 2 | 5 | 3 | 7 | – |
| 5 393 | – | 1 | 8 | 4 759 | – |
| 205 | – | – | – | – | – |
| 4 640 | – | 10 785 | 116 | 296 | |
| 1 841 | – | – | – | – | – |

表16-13

# 博物馆及公共图书馆基本情况 (2012年)

| 指标 | | Item | | 全市 Whole Municipality |
|---|---|---|---|---|
| **博物馆** | | **Museums** | | |
| 机构数 | (个) | Number of Institutions | (unit) | 36 |
| 从业人员 | (人) | Employed Persons | (person) | 691 |
| 文物藏品 | (件) | Number of Collections | (piece) | 114 020 |
| # 一级品 | | Grade One | | 326 |
| 二级品 | | Grade Two | | 1 951 |
| 参观人次 | (千人次) | Number of Visitors | (1 000 person-times) | 3 683 |
| 公用房屋建筑面积 | (平方米) | Floor Space of Public Buildings | (sq.m) | 154 994 |
| # 展览用房 | | Space for Exhibitions | | 76 578 |
| **公共图书馆** | | **Public Libraries** | | |
| 机构数 | (个) | Number of Institutions | (unit) | 12 |
| 从业人员 | (人) | Employed Persons | (person) | 520 |
| 总藏量 | (册、件) | Total Collections | (volume) | 16 628 581 |
| # 图书 | | Books Published | | 11 414 160 |
| # 古籍 | | Ancient Books | | 454 690 |
| 报刊 | | Newspapers and Magazines | | 428 205 |
| 累计发放有效借书证数 | (个) | Grand Total Number of Valid Library Cards Released | (unit) | 1 179 446 |
| 书刊文献外借人次 | (人次) | Number of Borrowers of Books, Magazines and Documents | (person-time) | 4 711 726 |
| 书刊文献外借册次 | (册次) | Number of Books, Magazines and Documents Borrowed by the Readers | (volume-time) | 11 101 726 |
| 为读者举办各种活动 | (次) | Various Activities Held for Readers | (time) | 1 403 |
| 参加人数 | (人次) | Number of Visitors | (person-time) | 429 371 |
| 公用房屋建筑面积 | (平方米) | Floor Space of Public Buildings | (sq.m) | 153 002 |
| # 书库 | | Stock Rooms | | 12 349 |
| 阅览室 | | Reading Rooms | | 41 084 |
| 阅览室座席数 | (个) | Seating Capacity of Reading Rooms | (set) | 7 584 |
| # 少儿阅览室座席数 | | Seating Capacity of Children's Reading Rooms | | 1 823 |

# BASIC STATISTICS ON MUSEUMS AND PUBLIC LIBRARIES (2012)

| 市 区<br>Urban Area | # 吴江区<br>Wujiang District | 常 熟<br>Changshu | 张家港<br>Zhangjiagang | 昆 山<br>Kunshan | 太 仓<br>Taicang |
|---|---|---|---|---|---|
| | | | | | |
| 20 | 2 | 5 | 1 | 3 | 7 |
| 373 | 40 | 202 | 27 | 19 | 70 |
| 86 009 | 9 349 | 20 392 | 1 860 | 3 344 | 2 415 |
| 254 | 10 | 22 | 1 | 35 | 14 |
| 1 434 | 17 | 291 | 8 | 205 | 13 |
| 2 371 | 120 | 849 | 50 | 187 | 226 |
| 88 302 | 6 515 | 30 596 | 12 060 | 3 626 | 20 410 |
| 38 849 | 3 800 | 17 591 | 4 000 | 3 015 | 13 123 |
| | | | | | |
| 8 | 1 | 1 | 1 | 1 | 1 |
| 257 | 59 | 46 | 77 | 74 | 66 |
| 10 984 767 | 1 438 700 | 1 669 401 | 1 411 665 | 1 756 137 | 806 611 |
| 6 328 951 | 1 283 497 | 1 369 254 | 1 339 369 | 1 683 574 | 693 012 |
| 247 732 | 72 839 | 205 065 | 130 | 130 | 1 633 |
| 276 966 | 15 924 | 70 798 | 44 394 | 10 933 | 25 114 |
| 738 277 | 78 958 | 140 984 | 82 000 | 186 000 | 32 185 |
| 1 641 267 | 600 000 | 391 234 | 521 216 | 1 732 077 | 425 932 |
| 5 664 297 | 1 010 000 | 1 173 703 | 1 585 049 | 1 826 000 | 852 677 |
| 733 | 149 | 74 | 445 | 121 | 30 |
| 228 019 | 83 944 | 38 000 | 77 517 | 65 000 | 20 835 |
| 77 059 | 16 000 | 12 128 | 25 250 | 18 600 | 19 965 |
| 5 408 | 775 | 2 191 | 4 200 | 250 | 300 |
| 21 962 | 3 446 | 3 045 | 6 200 | 4 000 | 5 877 |
| 4 434 | 921 | 356 | 1 620 | 731 | 443 |
| 1 066 | 98 | 200 | 398 | 60 | 99 |

表16-14

# 广播节目播出情况 (2012年)
# BROADCASTING BROADCAST SITUATION (2012)

单位：小时 (hours)

| 地区 | Region | 全年公共广播节目播出时间合计 The Whole year's Public Radio Program Broadcast Time | # 新闻资讯类 News and Information | # 专题服务类 Feature Services | # 综艺益智类 Variety Puzzles | 合计中：自制节目 In Total：Self-made Program |
|---|---|---|---|---|---|---|
| **全　市** | **Whole Municipality** | **60 066** | **9 139** | **20 541** | **16 389** | **51 821** |
| 市　区 | Urban Area | 33 971 | 4 399 | 10 731 | 10 128 | 31 269 |
| # 吴江区 | Wujiang District | 6 023 | 1 228 | 2 555 | 1 510 | 4 563 |
| 常　熟 | Changshu | 8 760 | 1 440 | 3 477 | 1 830 | 7 113 |
| 张家港 | Zhangjiagang | 6 290 | 2 023 | 2 319 | 1 743 | 4 510 |
| 昆　山 | Kunshan | 6 300 | 730 | 912 | 2 140 | 4 550 |
| 太　仓 | Taicang | 4 745 | 548 | 3 102 | 548 | 4 379 |

表16-15

# 电视节目播出情况(2012年)
# TV BROADCAST SITUATION (2012)

单位：小时 (hours)

| 地区 | Region | 全年公共电视节目播出时间合计 The Whole year's Public TV Program Broadcast Time | # 新闻资讯类 News and Information | # 专题服务类 Feature Services | # 影视剧类 Film and Television Drama | 合计中：自制节目 In Total：Self-made Program |
|---|---|---|---|---|---|---|
| **全　市** | **Whole Municipality** | **56 543** | **7 652** | **8 385** | **28 634** | **34 519** |
| 市　区 | Urban Area | 36 374 | 4 998 | 6 389 | 18 200 | 26 388 |
| # 吴江区 | Wujiang District | 6 570 | 912 | 1 261 | 2 185 | 2 725 |
| 常　熟 | Changshu | 5 687 | 438 | 227 | 3 824 | 1 846 |
| 张家港 | Zhangjiagang | 4 161 | 1 085 | 387 | 1 643 | 1 806 |
| 昆　山 | Kunshan | 3 660 | 340 | 105 | 2 175 | 792 |
| 太　仓 | Taicang | 6 661 | 791 | 1 278 | 2 792 | 3 687 |

表16-16

# 广播节目制作情况(2012年)
# BROADCASTING PROGRAMMING SITUATION (2012)

单位：小时 (hours)

| 地 区 | Region | 全年制作广播节目时间 Annual Production of Broadcasting Programs | # 新闻资讯类 News and Information | # 专题服务类 Feature Services | # 综艺益智类 Variety Puzzles | # 广告类 Advertisements |
|---|---|---|---|---|---|---|
| **全 市** | **Whole Municipality** | **44 869** | **6 630** | **18 243** | **11 339** | **1 264** |
| 市 区 | Urban Area | 28 370 | 3 581 | 9 138 | 8 977 | 201 |
| # 吴江区 | Wujiang District | 3 259 | 680 | 1 490 | 1 078 | 11 |
| 常 熟 | Changshu | 6 052 | 1 098 | 3 477 | 1 464 | 12 |
| 张家港 | Zhangjiagang | 3 518 | 1 038 | 1 980 | 350 | 150 |
| 昆 山 | Kunshan | 2 550 | 365 | 545 | – | 780 |
| 太 仓 | Taicang | 4 379 | 548 | 3 103 | 548 | 121 |

表16-17

# 电视节目制作情况 (2012年)
# TV PROGRAMMING SITUATION (2012)

单位：小时 (hours)

| 地 区 | Region | 全年制作电视节目时间 Annual Production of TV Programs | # 新闻资讯类 News and Information | # 专题服务类 Feature Services | # 广告类 Advertisements | 全年购买、交换国内电视节目时间 Purchase and Exchange of Domestic TV Time of The Whole Year |
|---|---|---|---|---|---|---|
| **全 市** | **Whole Municipality** | **16 605** | **5 146** | **4 576** | **2 274** | **21 447** |
| 市 区 | Urban Area | 12 169 | 4 158 | 3 286 | 860 | 9 773 |
| # 吴江区 | Wujiang District | 979 | 332 | 106 | 380 | 3 633 |
| 常 熟 | Changshu | 1 019 | 110 | 62 | 645 | 3 842 |
| 张家港 | Zhangjiagang | 455 | 225 | 73 | 112 | 2 172 |
| 昆 山 | Kunshan | 920 | 288 | 36 | 288 | 2 868 |
| 太 仓 | Taicang | 2 042 | 365 | 1 119 | 369 | 2 792 |

# 主 要 统 计 指 标 解 释

**普通高等学校** 指按照国家规定的设置标准和审批程序批准举办的，通过全国普通高等学校统一招生考试，招收高中毕业生为主要培养对象，实施高等教育的全日制大学、独立设置的学院和高等专科学校、高等职业学校和其他机构。

大学、独立设置的学院主要实施本科层次以上教育，高等专科学校、高等职业学校实施专科层次教育，其他机构是承担国家普通招生计划任务不计校数的机构。包括普通高等学校分校和批准筹建的普通高等学校等。

**文化事业机构** 指从事专业文化工作和为专业文化工作服务的独立建制的单位。不包括这些单位另外举办独立核算的其他机构和各部门的业余文化组织。该指标主要反映文化事业机构发展规模水平。

**艺术表演团体** 指从事戏曲、音乐、舞蹈、杂技等专业艺术表演，有独立帐户的单位，不包括半工半艺、半农半艺和民间职业剧团。该指标主要反映全国专业艺术表演团体发展规模水平。

**艺术表演观众人数(人次)** 指售票、包场演出或民族地区免费演出的艺术表演观众人次数，不包括彩排审查和内部观摩演出的观看人次数。该指标主要反映全国观看专业艺术表演团体演出的效益规模。

# EXPLANATORY NOTES ON MAIN STATISTICAL INDICATORS

**Regular Institutions of Higher Learning** refer to educational establishments set up according to the government evaluation and approval procedures, enrolling graduates from senior secondary schools and providing higher education courses and training for senior professionals. They include full-time universities, colleges, institutions of higher professional education, institutions of higher vocational education and others.

Universities and colleges primarily provide undergraduate courses; institutions of higher professional education and institutions of higher vocational education primarily provide professional trainings; and others refer to educational establishments, which are responsible for enrolling higher education students under the State Plan but not enumerated in the total number of schools, including: branch schools of universities and colleges, and universities and colleges that have been approved and under plan for construction.

**Cultural Institutions** refer to units which have their own organizational system and independent accounting system and specialize in cultural work or service cultural work. They do not include other establishments run by these units with separate accounting system and amateur cultural groups established by various departments. The statistics reflect the scale and level of development of institutions engaged in cultural undertakings.

**Art Troupes** refer to the troupes which are engaged in drama, opera, music, dance, acrobatics or other art performance, have independent accounts with banks and have self-supporting accounting system. Troupes which are engaged partly in industrial or agricultural activities, partly in art performance and the professional troupes organized by the mass are not included. The statistics reflect the scale and level of development of professional art troupes nationally.

**Number of Audience at Art Performance** refers to the number of spectators at commercial shows, privately organized shows or free shows given in ethnic minority areas, and does not include the number of spectators at rehearsals and internal viewings. This indicator mainly reflects the scale and effects of viewing of performances given by professional art troupes across the country.

# 十七、卫生 体育

# CHAPTER 17
# PUBLIC HEALTH AND SPORTS

# 卫生 体育
# PUBLIC HEALTH AND SPORTS

## 主要统计指标
## MAJOR STATISTICAL INDICATORS

| | | | | |
|---|---|---|---|---|
| 2012年末卫生机构数 | Number of Health Institutions | 2 992 | 个 | unit |
| 2012年末卫生机构床位数 | Number of Beds in Health Institutions | 46 070 | 张 | unit |
| 2012年末卫生技术人员 | Number of Medical Technical Personnel | 57 168 | 人 | person |
| # 医生数 | Doctors | 23 194 | 人 | person |
| 注册护士数 | Professional Nurses | 21 943 | 人 | person |
| 2012年按户籍人口计算: | Calculated by Household Population: | | | |
| 每千人拥有卫生机构床位数 | Number of Beds in Health Institutions Per 1 000 Persons | 7.71 | 张 | unit |
| 每千人拥有医院床位数 | Number of Hospital Beds Per 1 000 Persons | 6.01 | 张 | unit |
| 每千人拥有卫生技术人员 | Number of Medical Technical Personnel Per 1 000 Persons | 8.82 | 人 | person |
| 每千人拥有医生数 | Number of Doctors Per 1 000 Persons | 3.58 | 人 | person |
| 每千人拥有注册护士数 | Number of Professional Nurses Per 1 000 Persons | 3.39 | 人 | person |
| 2012年发展二级以上等级裁判员 | Newly-added Number of Referees of Grade II and Above | 471 | 人 | person |
| 2012年发展二级以上等级运动员 | Newly-added Number of Sportsmen of Grade II and Above | 153 | 人 | person |

表17-1

# 历年卫生事业基本情况
# BASIC STATISTICS ON PUBLIC HEALTH OVER THE YEARS

| 年 份 Year | 机构数 (所) Institutions (unit) | # 医 院、卫生院 Hospitals | # 诊所、卫生所、医务室、社区卫生服务站 Clinics | 床位数 (张) Number of Beds (unit) | 人员数 (人) Number of Persons (person) | # 卫生技术人员 Medical Technical Personnel |
|---|---|---|---|---|---|---|
| 1949 | 27 | 12 | 7 | 778 | 3 270 | 3 100 |
| 1952 | 238 | 16 | 163 | 1 372 | 4 908 | 3 256 |
| 1957 | 447 | 16 | 410 | 2 655 | 7 773 | 6 037 |
| 1962 | 683 | 155 | 457 | 6 727 | 9 582 | 7 831 |
| 1965 | 823 | 170 | 549 | 7 661 | 10 891 | 8 862 |
| 1970 | 675 | 169 | 496 | 9 001 | 9 338 | 7 593 |
| 1975 | 806 | 194 | 581 | 13 759 | 14 202 | 11 174 |
| 1978 | 971 | 204 | 714 | 14 470 | 16 465 | 12 902 |
| 1980 | 1 125 | 207 | 864 | 13 720 | 18 752 | 14 514 |
| 1985 | 1 544 | 203 | 1 280 | 15 064 | 24 921 | 19 343 |
| 1990 | 1 537 | 207 | 1 256 | 18 424 | 29 545 | 22 253 |
| 1991 | 1 532 | 207 | 1 248 | 18 622 | 30 505 | 23 067 |
| 1992 | 1 524 | 208 | 1 239 | 18 800 | 30 884 | 23 676 |
| 1993 | 1 485 | 209 | 1 197 | 19 670 | 31 609 | 24 315 |
| 1994 | 1 487 | 210 | 1 197 | 19 680 | 32 170 | 24 769 |
| 1995 | 1 486 | 210 | 1 197 | 19 535 | 33 076 | 25 326 |
| 1996 | 1 485 | 212 | 1 196 | 19 489 | 33 321 | 25 835 |
| 1997 | 1 433 | 212 | 1 143 | 19 747 | 32 669 | 25 070 |
| 1998 | 1 440 | 212 | 1 147 | 19 486 | 32 855 | 25 233 |
| 1999 | 1 466 | 209 | 1 175 | 19 293 | 30 303 | 25 550 |
| 2000 | 1 319 | 197 | 1 045 | 19 504 | 31 793 | 24 881 |
| 2001 | 1 254 | 191 | 986 | 19 791 | 31 559 | 24 706 |
| 2002 | 1 463 | 213 | 1 187 | 19 978 | 31 601 | 24 535 |
| 2003 | 1 450 | 199 | 1 152 | 20 631 | 33 958 | 27 805 |
| 2004 | 1 715 | 207 | 1 392 | 21 662 | 34 970 | 29 069 |
| 2005 | 1 945 | 197 | 1 582 | 26 185 | 38 736 | 32 049 |
| 2006 | 2 285 | 205 | 1 902 | 28 872 | 43 954 | 36 951 |
| 2007 | 2 314 | 214 | 1 901 | 31 261 | 46 952 | 38 091 |
| 2008 | 2 344 | 233 | 1 876 | 33 631 | 50 810 | 40 336 |
| 2009 | 2 524 | 234 | 2 041 | 37 235 | 53 869 | 43 232 |
| 2010 | 2 675 | 216 | 2 152 | 39 204 | 56 910 | 46 507 |
| 2011 | 2 858 | 242 | 2 292 | 42 972 | 63 409 | 50 866 |
| 2012 | 2 992 | 251 | 2 380 | 46 070 | 70 449 | 57 168 |

表17-2

# 部分年份分地区卫生事业基本情况
# BASIC STATISTICS ON PUBLIC HEALTH BY REGION OF PARTIAL YEARS

| 项　　目 | Item | 1985年 | 1990年 | 2000年 | 2010年 | 2011年 | 2012年 |
|---|---|---|---|---|---|---|---|
| **机构数**　（所） | **Institutions** (unit) | **1 544** | **1 537** | **1 319** | **2 675** | **2 858** | **2 992** |
| 市　区 | Urban Area | 939 | 951 | 761 | 1 298 | 1 390 | 1 471 |
| # 吴江区 | Wujiang District | 93 | 62 | 93 | 336 | 348 | 370 |
| 常　熟 | Changshu | 274 | 192 | 159 | 392 | 443 | 453 |
| 张家港 | Zhangjiagang | 113 | 134 | 212 | 422 | 417 | 410 |
| 昆　山 | Kunshan | 83 | 89 | 118 | 393 | 419 | 435 |
| 太　仓 | Taicang | 135 | 171 | 69 | 170 | 189 | 223 |
| **床位数**　（张） | **Beds** (unit) | **15 064** | **18 424** | **19 504** | **39 204** | **42 972** | **46 070** |
| 市　区 | Urban Area | 8 656 | 10 583 | 10 489 | 22 061 | 23 698 | 25 376 |
| # 吴江区 | Wujiang District | 1 359 | 1 669 | 1 698 | 4 536 | 4 714 | 4 661 |
| 常　熟 | Changshu | 2 270 | 3 192 | 3 195 | 4 954 | 5 883 | 6 454 |
| 张家港 | Zhangjiagang | 1 583 | 2 043 | 2 719 | 5 270 | 5 615 | 6 013 |
| 昆　山 | Kunshan | 1 190 | 1 292 | 1 695 | 4 311 | 4 609 | 5 043 |
| 太　仓 | Taicang | 1 365 | 1 314 | 1 406 | 2 608 | 3 167 | 3 184 |
| **卫生技术人员**　（人） | **Medical Technical Personnel** (person) | **19 343** | **22 253** | **24 881** | **46 507** | **50 866** | **57 168** |
| 市　区 | Urban Area | 12 245 | 13 429 | 13 697 | 25 010 | 26 661 | 29 423 |
| # 吴江区 | Wujiang District | 1 561 | 1 659 | 2 167 | 5 225 | 5 218 | 5 351 |
| 常　熟 | Changshu | 2 580 | 3 259 | 3 872 | 5 780 | 6 634 | 7 493 |
| 张家港 | Zhangjiagang | 1 742 | 2 369 | 3 205 | 5 898 | 6 702 | 7 440 |
| 昆　山 | Kunshan | 1 421 | 1 635 | 2 296 | 6 780 | 7 572 | 9 166 |
| 太　仓 | Taicang | 1 355 | 1 561 | 1 811 | 3 039 | 3 297 | 3 646 |
| **医生数** | **Doctors** | **8 461** | **10 895** | **11 594** | **18 156** | **19 518** | **23 194** |
| 市　区 | Urban Area | 5 522 | 6 675 | 6 247 | 9 417 | 9 951 | 11 626 |
| # 吴江区 | Wujiang District | 592 | 693 | 975 | 1 570 | 1 672 | 2 386 |
| 常　熟 | Changshu | 1 002 | 1 595 | 1 909 | 2 466 | 2 635 | 3 193 |
| 张家港 | Zhangjiagang | 677 | 1 059 | 1 504 | 2 322 | 2 712 | 3 062 |
| 昆　山 | Kunshan | 649 | 821 | 1 070 | 2 742 | 2 940 | 3 845 |
| 太　仓 | Taicang | 611 | 745 | 864 | 1 209 | 1 280 | 1 468 |

表17-3

# 分地区卫生机构、人员及床位数 (2012年末)

| 指　　标 | Item | 全　市 Whole Municipality |
|---|---|---|
| **卫生机构数 (个)** | **Number of Health Institutions (unit)** | **2 992** |
| 医　院 | Hospitals | 163 |
| 社区卫生服务中心 | Neighborhood Medical Service Station | 75 |
| 卫生院 | Rural Township Hospitals | 88 |
| 门诊部 | Clinics | 213 |
| 急救中心（站） | First Aide Center | 4 |
| 采供血机构 | Blood Collection and Supply Center | 7 |
| 妇幼保健院（所、站） | Hospitals for Maternity and Child Care | 7 |
| 专科疾病防治院 | Disease Control Center | 7 |
| 疾病预防控制中心 | Disease Prevention Center | 13 |
| 卫生监督所 | Medical Supervision Station | 13 |
| 医学在职培训机构 | On-the-Job Medical Training | 2 |
| 健康教育所（站、中心） | Health Education Station | 3 |
| 其他卫生机构 | Other Health Care Institutions | 17 |
| 诊所、卫生所、医务室、社区卫生服务站 | Clinic, Medical Station, Medical Office and Neighborhood Medical Station | 2 380 |
| **卫生机构人员数 (人)** | **Number of Persons Engaged in Health Institution (person)** | **70 449** |
| # 卫生技术人员 | Medical Technical Personnel | 57 168 |
| # 医　生 | Doctors | 23 194 |
| # 执业医师 | Professional medical worker | 21 104 |
| 执业助理医师 | Professional assistant medical worker | 2 090 |
| 注册护士 | Professional nurse | 21 943 |
| 药师（士） | Apothecary and Assistant Pharmacist | 3 447 |
| 技师（士） | Technician | 2 861 |
| 其　他 | Others | 5 723 |
| 私营卫生机构人员数 | Number of Medical Staff in Privately Owned Medical Institutions | 19 045 |
| # 医　生 | Doctors | 6 215 |
| **卫生机构床位数 (张)** | **Number of Beds in Health Institutions (unit)** | **46 070** |
| 医　院 | Hospitals | 38 954 |
| # 综合医院 | General Hospitals | 23 960 |
| 中医医院 | Hospitals of Chinese Medicine | 3 728 |
| 专科医院 | Disease Control and Prevention Station | 5 651 |
| 卫生院 | Rural Township Hospitals | 4 818 |
| 专科疾病防治院 | Disease Prevention Academy | 50 |
| 其　他 | Others | 2 248 |

# NUMBER OF HEALTH INSTITUTIONS, PERSONS ENGAGED AND BEDS BY REGION (END OF 2012)

| 市 区<br>Urban Area | # 吴江区<br>Wujiang District | 常 熟<br>Changshu | 张家港<br>Zhangjiagang | 昆 山<br>Kunshan | 太 仓<br>Taicang |
|---|---|---|---|---|---|
| **1 471** | **370** | **453** | **410** | **435** | **223** |
| 72 | 8 | 23 | 36 | 25 | 7 |
| 44 | 1 | 5 | 1 | 21 | 4 |
| 32 | 18 | 26 | 8 | 5 | 17 |
| 87 | 18 | 23 | 2 | 82 | 19 |
| 1 | | 1 | | 1 | 1 |
| 2 | 1 | 2 | 1 | 1 | 1 |
| 3 | 1 | 1 | 1 | 1 | 1 |
| 7 | 5 | – | – | – | – |
| 9 | 1 | 1 | 1 | 1 | 1 |
| 9 | 1 | 1 | 1 | 1 | 1 |
| 1 | – | – | 1 | – | – |
| – | – | 1 | – | 1 | 1 |
| 5 | – | 1 | – | 11 | – |
| 1 199 | 316 | 368 | 358 | 285 | 170 |
| **36 549** | **6 423** | **9 561** | **8 909** | **11 109** | **4 321** |
| 29 423 | 5 351 | 7 493 | 7 440 | 9 166 | 3 646 |
| 11 626 | 2 386 | 3 193 | 3 062 | 3 845 | 1 468 |
| 10 804 | 2 148 | 2 820 | 2 585 | 3 594 | 1 301 |
| 822 | 238 | 373 | 477 | 251 | 167 |
| 11 682 | 1 984 | 2 622 | 2 729 | 3 547 | 1 363 |
| 1 821 | 301 | 504 | 426 | 474 | 222 |
| 1 425 | 227 | 398 | 354 | 497 | 187 |
| 2 869 | 453 | 776 | 869 | 803 | 406 |
| 11 077 | 1 178 | 1 175 | 3 381 | 2 866 | 546 |
| 3 447 | 577 | 444 | 1 099 | 1 017 | 208 |
| **25 376** | **4 661** | **6 454** | **6 013** | **5 043** | **3 184** |
| 21 715 | 3 508 | 4 891 | 5 718 | 4 418 | 2 212 |
| 12 222 | 2 683 | 2 996 | 4 214 | 3 212 | 1 316 |
| 1 224 | 420 | 570 | 610 | 844 | 480 |
| 3 681 | 200 | 711 | 481 | 362 | 416 |
| 2 042 | 1 013 | 1 314 | 295 | 344 | 823 |
| 50 | – | – | – | – | – |
| 1 569 | 140 | 249 | – | 281 | 149 |

表17-4

# 卫生机构诊疗基本情况（2012年）

# BASIC STATISTICS OF MEDICAL INSTITUTIONS ON PATIENTS TREATING (2012)

| 地区或类别 | Region and Type | 诊疗总人次（万人次）Total Number of Patients Treated (10 000 person-times) | #门诊 Out-patients | 入院人数（人）Hospital Admissions (person) | 病床使用率（%）Utilization Rate of Beds (%) | 病床周转次数 Bed Turnover |
|---|---|---|---|---|---|---|
| **总　计** | **Total** | **7 324.96** | **6 618.44** | **1 314 076** | **87.83** | **29.8** |
| **一、按地区分** | **Grouped by Region** | | | | | |
| 市　区 | Urban Area | 3 734.56 | 3 369.95 | 626 595 | 90.00 | 30.2 |
| #吴江区 | Wujiang District | 709.77 | 640.84 | 125 307 | 91.58 | 35.4 |
| 常　熟 | Changshu | 989.90 | 904.01 | 215 383 | 91.84 | 30.7 |
| 张家港 | Zhangjiagang | 815.65 | 747.39 | 217 117 | 98.56 | 36.0 |
| 昆　山 | Kunshan | 1 360.67 | 1 221.04 | 156 036 | 87.22 | 32.7 |
| 太　仓 | Taicang | 424.17 | 376.04 | 98 945 | 93.37 | 31.0 |
| **二、按类别分** | **Grouped by Type of Hospital** | | | | | |
| 1. 医　院 | Hospitals | 3 796.13 | 3 410.95 | 1109 129 | 91.42 | 29.5 |
| #综合医院 | General Hospitals | 2 803.55 | 2 509.18 | 843 927 | 94.86 | 36.4 |
| 中医医院 | Hospitals of Chinese Medicine | 619.07 | 553.12 | 141 502 | 100.93 | 38.4 |
| 专科医院 | Disease Control and Prevention Station | 330.65 | 310.19 | 97 797 | 88.85 | 17.9 |
| 儿童医院 | Children's Hospital | 118.97 | 107.34 | 38 306 | 112.92 | 47.9 |
| 传染病院 | Hospitals for Infectious Diseases | 16.10 | 15.60 | 8 027 | 105.06 | 19.5 |
| 精神病院 | Mental Hospitals | 52.95 | 51.20 | 9 413 | 99.89 | 4.2 |
| 口腔医院 | Stomata logical Hospitals | 29.96 | 29.95 | 88 | 3.93 | 3.7 |
| 耳鼻喉科医院 | Otolaryngology Hospitals | 11.94 | 11.87 | 4 728 | 50.36 | 29.3 |
| 其他专科医院 | Other Specialized Hospitals | 100.73 | 94.23 | 37 235 | 61.97 | 20.7 |
| 2. 社区卫生服务中心 | Community Medical Service Station | 1 055.79 | 952.11 | 42 831 | 50.67 | 24.0 |
| 3. 卫生院 | Rural Township Hospitals | 1 348.33 | 1 228.77 | 155 099 | 73.42 | 34.5 |
| 4. 门诊部 | Outpatient Department | 173.50 | 155.18 | – | – | – |
| 5. 妇幼保健院（所、站） | Hospitals for Maternity and Child Care | 35.50 | 30.18 | – | – | – |
| 6. 专科疾病防治院 | Disease Prevention Academy | 30.34 | 14.89 | 507 | 26.72 | 12.2 |
| 7. 其　他 | Others | 885.37 | 826.35 | 6 510 | 75.74 | 37.8 |

注：床位周转次数是指在一定时期内每张床位的病人出院人数，其公式：床位周转次数=出院人数/平均开放床位数。

Note: The bed turnover refers to the number of patients per bed discharged from hospital within a certain period of time, and the formula is: bed turnover times = number of discharged patients / average number of open beds.

表17-5

# 全市前十位疾病死因及比重 (2012年)
# DEATH RATE OF 10 MAJOR DISEASES IN WHOLE MUNICIPALITY (2012)

| 位 次<br>NO. | 死 因 | Cause of Death | 占全部死因比重(%)<br>As % of Total Deaths |
|---|---|---|---|
| | **总 计** | **Total** | **93.73** |
| 1 | 恶性肿瘤 | Malignant Tumor | 29.12 |
| 2 | 脑血管病 | Cerebrovascular Disease | 19.63 |
| 3 | 心脏病 | Heart Trouble | 14.38 |
| 4 | 呼吸系统疾病 | Respiratory Disease | 13.19 |
| 5 | 损伤和中毒外部原因 | Trauma and Toxicosis | 7.34 |
| 6 | 内分泌、营养和代谢的其他疾病 | Endocrine, Nutrition and Metabolic Diseases | 2.98 |
| 7 | 消化系统疾病 | Digestive Disease | 2.59 |
| 8 | 精神障碍 | Mental Disease | 1.97 |
| 9 | 神经系统疾病 | Nervous System Diseases | 1.36 |
| 10 | 泌尿生殖系统疾病 | Urinary Disease | 1.17 |

表17-6

# 体育系统从业人员 (2012年)
# SPORTS SYSTEM EMPLOYEES (2012)

单位：人 (person)

| 人员分类 | Category of Personnel | 总 计<br>Total | #体育行政机关<br>Sports Administration | #运动项目管理部门<br>Sports Management | #体育运动学校<br>Physical Education and Sports Schools | #业余体校<br>Spare-time Sports Schools |
|---|---|---|---|---|---|---|
| **总 计** | **Total** | **1 347** | **820** | **25** | **239** | **263** |
| 公务员 | Orderly | 106 | 106 | – | – | – |
| 教练员 | Coaches | 199 | – | – | 80 | 119 |
| 运动员 | Athletes | 153 | – | – | 41 | 112 |
| 科研人员 | Scientific and Technical Personnel | 9 | – | 9 | – | – |
| 文化教师 | Teachers | 47 | – | – | 47 | – |
| 管理人员 | Administrative Staff | 561 | 483 | 16 | 45 | 17 |
| 其 他 | Others | 272 | 231 | – | 26 | 15 |

表17-7

## 运动员获奖牌情况 (2012年)
## ATHLETES' AWARD-WINNING (2012)

单位：枚 (unit)

| 项目 | Item | 总计 Total | 金牌 Gold Medal | 银牌 Silver Medal | 铜牌 Bronze Medal |
|---|---|---|---|---|---|
| **合计** | **Total** | **774** | **291** | **251** | **232** |
| 世界比赛 | World Competition | 10 | 8 | 2 | - |
| 亚洲比赛 | Asian Competition | 33 | 15 | 12 | 6 |
| 全国比赛 | National Competition | 63 | 40 | 13 | 10 |
| 省内比赛 | Province Competition | 668 | 228 | 224 | 216 |

表17-8

## 分地区体育场馆情况 (2012年)
## CONDITION OF THE STADIUM AND GYMNASIUM BY REGIN (2012)

| 项目 | Item | 全市 Whole Municipality | 市区 Urban Area | # 吴江区 Wujiang District | 常熟 Changshu | 张家港 Zhangjiagang | 昆山 Kunshan | 太仓 Taicang |
|---|---|---|---|---|---|---|---|---|
| **体育场馆数 (个)** | Condition of the Stadium and Gymnasium (unit) | **116** | **84** | **5** | **4** | **15** | **4** | **9** |
| 体育场数 | Condition of the Stadium | 62 | 54 | 2 | 1 | 2 | 1 | 4 |
| 体育馆数 | Condition of the Gymnasium | 54 | 30 | 3 | 3 | 13 | 3 | 5 |
| **体育场馆面积(平方米)** | The Area of Stadium and Gymnasium (sq.m) | **1 496 109** | **947 109** | **204 743** | **100 000** | **132 000** | **134 000** | **183 000** |

表17-9

## 发展等级运动员、裁判员及社会体育指导员认证人数
## NUMBER OF CERTIFIED LEVEL ATHLETES, REFEREES AND COMMUNITY PHYSICAL EDUCATION INSTRUCTORS RECRUITED

单位：人 (person)

| 项目 | Item | 1995年 | 2000年 | 2010年 | 2011年 | 2012年 |
|---|---|---|---|---|---|---|
| **年内发展二级以上等级运动员** | **Newly-added Number of Sportsmen of Grade II and Above** | **47** | **86** | **222** | **126** | **153** |
| 运动健将 | Master of Sports | - | - | - | - | - |
| 一级 | First Grade | 3 | 9 | - | - | - |
| 二级 | Second Grade | 44 | 77 | 222 | 126 | 153 |
| **年内发展二级以上等级裁判员** | **Newly-added Number of Referees of Grade II and Above** | **42** | **49** | **303** | **362** | **471** |
| 国家(际)级 | National (International) Referees | - | 1 | - | - | - |
| 一级 | First Grade | 23 | 15 | - | - | - |
| 二级 | Second Grade | 19 | 33 | 303 | 362 | 471 |
| **年末社会体育指导员认证总人数** | **Total Number of certified Community Physical Education Instructors by the End of the Year** | | | **15 677** | **14 689** | **21 002** |

# 主 要 统 计 指 标 解 释

**卫生机构** 包括医疗机构、疾病预防控制中心(防疫站)、采供血机构、卫生监督及监测(检验)机构、医学科研和在职培训机构、健康教育所等。

**医疗机构** 包括医院、社区卫生服务中心(站)、疗养院、卫生院、门诊部、诊所(卫生所、医务室)、妇幼保健院(所、站)、专科疾病防治院(所、站)、急救中心(站)和临床检验中心。医疗机构分为非赢利性医疗机构和赢利性医疗机构。

**医院** 包括综合医院、中医医院、中西医结合医院、民族医院、各类专科医院和护理院。

**卫生技术人员** 指卫生机构中医生、护理人员 、药剂人员、检验人员等卫生技术人员。

**医生** 指在医疗、预防保健机构工作且取得《执业医师证书》的执业医师和执业助理医师。

**等级运动员人数** 指经考核正式批准授予等级运动员称号的人数。运动员等级分为国际级运动健将、运动健将、一级运动员、二级运动员、三级运动员、少年级运动员。

**等级裁判员人数** 指经考核正式批准授予等级裁判员称号的人数。裁判员等级分为国际裁判、国家级裁判、一级裁判、二级裁判、三级裁判。

**体育场馆** 体育场指有400米跑道（中心含足球场）、有固定道牙、跑道6条以上并有固定看台的室外田径场地；体育馆指有固定看台、可供篮球、排球、羽毛球、乒乓球、体操等项目训练比赛活动用的室内运动场地。

# EXPLANATORY NOTES ON MAIN STATISTICAL INDICATORS

**Health Care Institutions** include: medical institutions, disease prevention and control centres (epidemic prevention stations), blood gathering and supplying institutions, health supervision and inspection (check up) institutions, medicinal scientific research and on-job training institutions, health education centres and so on.

**Medical Organizations** include: hospitals, health service centres (stations) in communities, sanatoria, health centres, outpatient clinics, clinics (health stations and infirmaries), maternity and child care agencies (centres and stations), special disease prevention and curing agencies (centres and stations), first aid centres (stations) and clinical inspection centres. Medical organizations are grouped by two types: profit-making and non-profit-making medical organizations.

**Hospitals** include: polyclinics, traditional Chinese medical hospitals, hospitals integrating traditional Chinese therapeutics and western therapeutics, ethnic hospitals, various specialist hospitals and nursing homes.

**Medical Technical Personnel** refers to doctors, nurses, pharmacists and laboratory technicians working in medical institutions.

**Doctors** refer to certified physicians and certified assistant physicians with certifications working in medical and health care and prevention agencies.

**Number of Athletes in Grades** refers to the number of athletes who have been given titles through examination. The titles of athletes include international masters of sports, masters of sports, first-grade, second-grade and third-grade sportsmen and young athletes.

**Number of Referees in Grades** refers to the number of referees who have been given titles after examination. They are classified as international referees, national referees and referees of the first, second and third grades.

**Stadiums and Gymnasiums** a stadium refers to an outdoor track and field space with a 400-meter runway (including a central football field), fixed road teeth, an above-6-track runway and fixed bleachers. a gymnasium refers to an indoor sports venue with fixed stands, and used for training and competition activities of basketball, volleyball, badminton, table tennis and gymnastics.

# 十八、民政 司法

## CHAPTER 18
## CIVIL ADMINISTRATION, JUDICIARY

# 民政 司法
# CIVIL ADMINISTRATION, JUDICIARY

## 主 要 统 计 指 标
## MAJOR STATISTICAL INDICATORS

| | | | | |
|---|---|---|---|---|
| 2012年末社会福利院数 | Number of Social Welfare Homes | 7 | 个 | unit |
| 2012年末社会福利医院数 | Number of Social Welfare Hospitals | 1 | 个 | unit |
| 2012年末养老机构 | Number of Old-age Care Institutions | 205 | 个 | unit |
| 2012年末社会福利院床位数 | Number of Beds in Social Welfare Homes | 3 255 | 张 | unit |
| 2012年末社会福利医院床位数 | Number of Beds in Social Welfare Hospitals | 1 930 | 张 | unit |
| 2012年末养老机构床位数 | Number of Beds in Old-age Care Institutions | 46 223 | 张 | unit |
| 2012年末律师事务所 | Number of Law Offices | 194 | 所 | unit |
| 2012年末专职律师数 | Number of Full-time Lawyers | 2 292 | 人 | person |
| 2012年末人民调解委员会数 | Number of People's Mediation Committees | 5 379 | 个 | unit |
| 2012年调解纠纷总数 | Number of Disputes Mediated | 89 317 | 起 | case |

表18-1

# 部分年份民政事业基本情况
# BASIC STATISTICS ON CIVIL ADMINISTRATION OF PARTIAL YEARS

| 指　　标 | | Item | | 1990年 | 2000年 | 2010年 | 2011年 | 2012年 |
|---|---|---|---|---|---|---|---|---|
| **社会福利院** | | **Social Welfare Homes** | | | | | | |
| 院　数 | (个) | Number of Homes | (unit) | 6 | 6 | 9 | 7 | 7 |
| 职工人数 | (人) | Number of Staff and Workers | (person) | 268 | 410 | 576 | 506 | 511 |
| 床位数 | (张) | Number of Beds | (unit) | 845 | 1 315 | 3 046 | 2 477 | 3 255 |
| 在院人数 | (人) | Number of Persons Housed | (person) | 561 | 971 | 2 493 | 1 901 | 2 260 |
| **社会福利医院** | | **Social Welfare Hospitals** | | | | | | |
| 院　数 | (个) | Number of Hospitals | (unit) | 5 | 4 | 1 | 1 | 1 |
| 职工人数 | (人) | Number of Staff and Workers | (person) | 282 | 302 | 216 | 177 | 177 |
| 床位数 | (张) | Number of Beds | (unit) | 524 | 694 | 1 930 | 1 930 | 1 930 |
| 在院人数 | (人) | Number of Persons Housed | (person) | 399 | 390 | 1 712 | 1 720 | 1 712 |
| **养老机构** | | **Old-age Care Institutions** | | | | | | |
| 院　数 | (个) | Number of Homes | (unit) | 169 | 181 | 162 | 179 | 205 |
| 职工人数 | (人) | Number of Staff and Workers | (person) | 921 | 938 | 2 325 | 3 065 | 4 677 |
| 床位数 | (张) | Number of Beds | (unit) | 4 135 | 5 400 | 25 455 | 30 809 | 46 223 |
| 在院人数 | (人) | Number of Persons Housed | (person) | 3 133 | 3 391 | 16 035 | 19 369 | 32 500 |
| **社会福利企业** | | **Welfare Enterprises Run by Communities** | | | | | | |
| 单位数 | (个) | Number of Units | (unit) | 611 | 1 020 | 369 | 378 | 363 |
| 职工人数 | (人) | Number of Staff and Workers | (person) | 57 933 | 70 398 | 43 895 | 44 927 | 43 307 |
| 纳税总额 | (万元) | Tax Paid | (10 000 yuan) | - | 41 993 | 78 347 | 78 787 | 63 132 |

表18-2

# 分地区民政事业基本情况 (2012年末) BASIC STATISTICS ON CIVIL ADMINISTRATION BY REGION (END OF 2012)

| 地　区 | Region | 院　数 (个) Number of Homes (unit) | 职工人数 (人) Number of Staff and Workers (person) | 床位数 (张) Number of Beds (unit) | 在院人数 (人) Number of Persons Housed (person) |
|---|---|---|---|---|---|
| **社会福利院** | **Social Welfare Homes** | | | | |
| **全　市** | **Whole Municipality** | **7** | **511** | **3 255** | **2 260** |
| 市　区 | Urban Area | 4 | 270 | 1 242 | 1 060 |
| # 吴江区 | Wujiang District | 1 | 11 | 60 | 40 |
| 常　熟 | Changshu | 1 | 58 | 352 | 210 |
| 张家港 | Zhangjiagang | – | – | – | – |
| 昆　山 | Kunshan | 1 | 153 | 1 141 | 690 |
| 太　仓 | Taicang | 1 | 30 | 520 | 300 |
| **社会福利医院** | **Social Welfare Hospitals** | | | | |
| **全　市** | **Whole Municipality** | **1** | **177** | **1 930** | **1 712** |
| 市　区 | Urban Area | 1 | 177 | 1 930 | 1 712 |
| # 吴江区 | Wujiang District | – | – | – | – |
| 常　熟 | Changshu | – | – | – | – |
| 张家港 | Zhangjiagang | – | – | – | – |
| 昆　山 | Kunshan | – | – | – | – |
| 太　仓 | Taicang | – | – | – | – |
| **养老机构** | **Old-age Care Institutions** | | | | |
| **全　市** | **Whole Municipality** | **205** | **4 677** | **46 223** | **32 500** |
| 市　区 | Urban Area | 116 | 2 617 | 21 292 | 18 166 |
| # 吴江区 | Wujiang District | 31 | 240 | 5 390 | 3 700 |
| 常　熟 | Changshu | 23 | 397 | 8 163 | 5 650 |
| 张家港 | Zhangjiagang | 36 | 920 | 7 432 | 5 200 |
| 昆　山 | Kunshan | 13 | 367 | 5 021 | 354 |
| 太　仓 | Taicang | 17 | 376 | 4 315 | 3 130 |

表18-3

# 社会办福利企业情况（2012年）
# STATISTICS ON SOCIAL WELFARE ENTERPRISES RUN BY COMMUNITIES (2012)

单位：万元 (10 000 yuan)

| 地 区 | Region | 单位数（个）Number of Units (unit) | 职工人数（人）Number of Staff and Workers (person) | 退税总额 Tax Exempted | 纳税总额 Tax paid | 利润额 Profits |
|---|---|---|---|---|---|---|
| **全 市** | **Whole Municipality** | **363** | **43 307** | **46 115** | **63 132** | **47 178** |
| 市 区 | Urban Area | 99 | 13 161 | 14 848 | 22 279 | 20 685 |
| # 吴江区 | Wujiang District | 75 | 10 669 | 12 500 | 16 100 | 11 360 |
| 常 熟 | Changshu | 41 | 2 891 | 2 586 | 3 832 | 219 |
| 张家港 | Zhangjiagang | 92 | 13 119 | 12 902 | 17 640 | 6 351 |
| 昆 山 | Kunshan | 97 | 11 062 | 11 946 | 14 401 | 14 576 |
| 太 仓 | Taicang | 34 | 3 074 | 3 833 | 4 980 | 5 347 |

表18-4

# 社区服务中心情况（2012年）
# BASIC STATISTICS OF COMMUNITY SERVICE ENTERPRISES (2012)

| 地 区 | Region | 单位数（个）Number of Units (unit) | 职工人数（人）Number of Staff and Workers (person) | 收 入（万元）Total Incomes (10 000yuan) | 社区其他服务设施（个）Other Community Service Facilities (units) |
|---|---|---|---|---|---|
| **全 市** | **Whole Municipality** | **135** | **1 154** | **5 674** | **3 634** |
| 市 区 | Urban Area | 63 | 703 | 2 827 | 2 812 |
| # 吴江区 | Wujiang District | 10 | 239 | 1 451 | 975 |
| 常 熟 | Changshu | 13 | 81 | 319 | 333 |
| 张家港 | Zhangjiagang | 30 | 240 | 1 080 | 89 |
| 昆 山 | Kunshan | 20 | 79 | 1 158 | 87 |
| 太 仓 | Taicang | 9 | 51 | 290 | 313 |

表18-5

# 自然灾害情况(2012年)
# STATISTICS ON NATURAL DISASTERS (2012)

| 地区 | Region | 农作物受灾面积(公顷) Area of Farm Crops Affected (hectare) | # 风雹灾 Winds and Hails | 农作物绝收面积(公顷) Area of Farm Crops Without Harvest (hectare) | # 风雹灾 Winds and Hails | 直接经济损失(万元) Direct Pecuniary Losses (10 000 yuan) |
|---|---|---|---|---|---|---|
| **全市** | **Whole Municipality** | **17 012** | **189** | **1 306** | **1** | **102 144** |
| 市区 | Urban Area | 3 871 | – | 172 | – | 64 712 |
| # 吴江区 | Wujiang District | 1 490 | – | – | – | 19 474 |
| 常熟 | Changshu | 5 580 | – | 733 | – | 18 158 |
| 张家港 | Zhangjiagang | 210 | 23 | – | – | 1 328 |
| 昆山 | Kunshan | 519 | – | – | – | 4 230 |
| 太仓 | Taicang | 6 833 | 166 | 401 | 1 | 13 716 |

表18-6

# 救灾救济情况(2012年)
# STATISTICS ON RELIEF AND ALMSGIVING (2012)

| 地区 | Region | 需救济人口(人) Population Needing Disaster Relief (person) | 已救济人口(人) Population Provided with Relief Funds (person) | 已安排救济款(万元) Relief Payment Arranged (10 000 yuan) | 救灾救济资金投入(万元) Disaster Relief Fund Investment (10 000 yuan) |
|---|---|---|---|---|---|
| **全市** | **Whole Municipality** | **25 145** | **25 145** | **2 310** | **6 435** |
| 市区 | Urban Area | 5 098 | 5 098 | 554 | 3 689 |
| # 吴江区 | Wujiang District | 1 027 | 1 027 | 412 | 1 852 |
| 常熟 | Changshu | 8 883 | 8 883 | 523 | 630 |
| 张家港 | Zhangjiagang | 136 | 136 | 514 | 884 |
| 昆山 | Kunshan | 2 593 | 2 593 | 444 | 580 |
| 太仓 | Taicang | 8 435 | 8 435 | 275 | 653 |

表18-7

# 社会救济和最低生活保障情况（2012年）
# SOCIAL RELIEF AND HOUSEHOLD SUPPORT TO THE RESIDENTS COVERED BY LOWEST WELFARE (2012)

单位：人 (person)

| 地　区 | Region | 社会救济对象总人数 Total Number of People Receiving Social Welfare | 城乡传统救济对象人数 Number of Traditional Urban and Rural Relief Receivers | # 农村居民 Number of Rural Residents | 城乡居民最低生活保障已保总人数 Number of Urban and Rural Residents Covered by Lowest Welfare | 城镇居民 Number of Urban Residents | 农村居民 Number of Rural Residents |
|---|---|---|---|---|---|---|---|
| **全　市** | **Whole Municipality** | **57 617** | **1 798** | **1 798** | **55 819** | **21 631** | **34 188** |
| 市　区 | Urban Area | 29 225 | 95 | 95 | 29 130 | 15 092 | 14 038 |
| # 吴江区 | Wujiang District | 9 290 | - | - | 9 290 | 1 089 | 8 201 |
| 常　熟 | Changshu | 7 927 | 929 | 929 | 6 998 | 700 | 6 298 |
| 张家港 | Zhangjiagang | 8 033 | 508 | 508 | 7 525 | 1 986 | 5 539 |
| 昆　山 | Kunshan | 9 208 | - | - | 9 208 | 2 916 | 6 292 |
| 太　仓 | Taicang | 3 224 | 266 | 266 | 2 958 | 937 | 2 021 |

表18-8

# 城乡服务网络情况（2012年末）
# STATISTICS ON URBAN AND RURAL SOCIAL SERVICE NETWORKS (END OF 2012)

单位：个 (unit)

| 地　区 | Region | 建立社会保障服务网络镇街 Number of Towns and Subdistrict with the Network Established | 社区服务机构 Number of Urban Welfare Facilities | # 社区服务中心 Urban and Town Community Service Centers | 便民利民服务网点 Convenience Stations |
|---|---|---|---|---|---|
| **全　市** | **Whole Municipality** | **95** | **1 248** | **135** | **4 957** |
| 市　区 | Urban Area | 59 | 502 | 63 | 2 305 |
| # 吴江区 | Wujiang District | 9 | 54 | 10 | 975 |
| 常　熟 | Changshu | 11 | 327 | 13 | 780 |
| 张家港 | Zhangjiagang | 8 | 97 | 30 | 770 |
| 昆　山 | Kunshan | 10 | 160 | 20 | 760 |
| 太　仓 | Taicang | 7 | 162 | 9 | 342 |

表18-9

# 部分年份律师、公证工作情况
# STATISTICS ON LAWYERS AND NOTARIZATION OF PARTIAL YEARS

| 指　　标 | | Item | | 1990年 | 2000年 | 2010年 | 2011年 | 2012年 |
|---|---|---|---|---|---|---|---|---|
| **律师工作情况** | | **Lawyers** | | | | | | |
| 律师事务所 | (所) | Number of Law Offices | (unit) | 14 | 73 | 171 | 180 | 194 |
| 律师事务所人员 | (人) | Personnel of Law Offices | (person) | 185 | 784 | 1 823 | 2 107 | 2 330 |
| # 女律师 | | Female | | – | 73 | 405 | 488 | 492 |
| # 专职律师 | | Full-time Lawyers | | 66 | 482 | 1 788 | 2 042 | 2 792 |
| 兼职律师 | | Part-time Lawyers | | 15 | 42 | 35 | 34 | 38 |
| 义务法律咨询服务件数 | (件) | Agent of Voluntary Legal Advisory Services | (case) | – | 27 156 | 11 785 | 22 313 | 15 551 |
| 参加义务法律咨询律师人次 | (人次) | Number of Lawyers Participating in Voluntary Legal Advisory Services | (person-time) | – | 11 946 | 1 403 | 1 482 | 1 960 |
| 担任法律顾问 | (家) | Number of Units with Permanent Legal Advisors | (unit) | 1 083 | 2 947 | 8 538 | 9 919 | 10 426 |
| 刑事诉讼辩护及代理 | (件) | Defender and Agent of Criminal Cases | (case) | 1 478 | 1 752 | 5 531 | 5 032 | 4 514 |
| 民事案件诉讼代理 | | Agent of Civil Cases | | 1 436 | 4 933 | 24 060 | 25 886 | 29 493 |
| 经济案件诉讼代理 | | Agent of Economic Cases | | 1 006 | 4 049 | – | – | – |
| 非诉讼法律事务 | | Agent of Non-litigious Legal Affairs | | 292 | 3 116 | 3 720 | 2 983 | 5 064 |
| 涉外及涉港澳台 | | Agent of Foreign-related, Hong Kong, Macao & Taiwan Legal Affairs | | – | 228 | – | – | – |
| 经济案件索回赔欠款 | (万元) | Debt and Indemnity Claimed in Economic Cases | (10 000 yuan) | – | 106 466 | – | – | – |
| **公证工作情况** | | **Notarization** | | | | | | |
| 公证处 | (所) | Number of Notary Offices | (unit) | 8 | 12 | 11 | 12 | 12 |
| 公证处人员 | (人) | Notarial Personnel | (person) | 63 | 79 | 130 | 137 | 158 |
| # 公证员 | | Notaries | | 33 | 59 | 60 | 65 | 67 |
| 办理公证总数 | (件) | Number of Notarial Documents Issued | (case) | 23 414 | 47 159 | 109 379 | 106 988 | 108 892 |
| # 国内民事 | | Domestic Civil Relations | | 9 391 | 14 787 | 66 284 | 65 611 | 68 003 |
| 国内经济 | | Domestic Economic Affairs | | 10 597 | 14 258 | 15 772 | 12 978 | 10 759 |
| 涉外及涉港澳台 | | Foreign-related, Hong Kong, Macao & Taiwan Legal Affairs | | 3 426 | 18 114 | 27 323 | 28 399 | 30 130 |

表18-10 分地区律师、公证工作情况（2012年）

| 指标 | | Item | | 全市 Whole Municipality |
|---|---|---|---|---|
| **律师工作情况** | | **Lawyers** | | |
| 律师事务所 | (所) | Number of Law Offices | (unit) | 194 |
| 律师事务所人员 | (人) | Personnel of Law Offices | (person) | 2 330 |
| # 女律师 | | Female | | 492 |
| # 专职律师 | | Full-time Lawyers | | 2 292 |
| 兼职律师 | | Part-time Lawyers | | 38 |
| 义务法律咨询服务件数 | (件) | Agent of Voluntary Legal Advisory Services | (case) | 15 551 |
| 参加义务法律咨询律师人数 | (人次) | Number of Lawyers Participating in Voluntary Legal Advisory Services | (person-time) | 1 960 |
| 担任法律顾问 | (家) | Number of Units with Permanent Legal Advisors | (unit) | 10 426 |
| 刑事诉讼辩护及代理 | (件) | Defender and Agent of Criminal Cases | (case) | 4 514 |
| 民事案件诉讼代理 | | Agent of Civil Cases | | 29 493 |
| 非诉讼法律事务 | | Agent of Non-litigious Legal Affairs | | 5 064 |
| **公证工作情况** | | **Notarization** | | |
| 公证处 | (所) | Number of Notary Offices | (unit) | 12 |
| 公证处人员 | (人) | Notarial Personnel | (person) | 142 |
| # 公证员 | | Notaries | | 60 |
| 办理公证总数 | (件) | Number of Notarial Documents Issued | (case) | 108 892 |
| # 国内民事 | | Domestic Civil Relations | | 68 003 |
| 国内经济 | | Domestic Economic Affairs | | 10 759 |
| 涉外及涉港澳台 | | Foreign-related, Hong Kong, Macao & Taiwan Legal Affairs | | 30 130 |

# STATISTICS ON LAWYERS AND NOTARIZATION BY REGION (2012)

| 市 区<br>Urban Area | # 吴江区<br>Wujiang District | 常 熟<br>Changshu | 张家港<br>Zhangjiagang | 昆 山<br>Kunshan | 太 仓<br>Taicang |
|---|---|---|---|---|---|
| | | | | | |
| 135 | 12 | 10 | 10 | 30 | 9 |
| 1 610 | 131 | 149 | 159 | 329 | 83 |
| 307 | 25 | 28 | 36 | 98 | 23 |
| 1 576 | 131 | 145 | 159 | 329 | 83 |
| 34 | – | 4 | – | – | – |
| 10 362 | 1 570 | 875 | 620 | 3 355 | 339 |
| 1 285 | 113 | 137 | 159 | 281 | 98 |
| 5 858 | 858 | 1 124 | 765 | 1 761 | 918 |
| 2 551 | 430 | 279 | 251 | 1 093 | 340 |
| 15 485 | 1 774 | 2 053 | 3 586 | 6 535 | 1 834 |
| 2 187 | 279 | 336 | 127 | 870 | 1 544 |
| | | | | | |
| 7 | 1 | 1 | 1 | 2 | 1 |
| 78 | 16 | 12 | 17 | 25 | 10 |
| 33 | 7 | 6 | 5 | 11 | 5 |
| 71 948 | 5 633 | 8 480 | 8 757 | 16 698 | 3 009 |
| 45 684 | 2 414 | 4 000 | 5 208 | 11 958 | 1 153 |
| 6 908 | 1 317 | 684 | 1 342 | 1 275 | 550 |
| 19 356 | 1 902 | 3 796 | 2 207 | 3 465 | 1 306 |

表18-11

# 分地区人民调解基层司法工作情况 (2012年)

| 指　　标 | | Item | | 全　市 Whole Municipality |
|---|---|---|---|---|
| 人民调解委员会 | (个) | Number of People's Mediation Committees | (unit) | 5 379 |
| 调委会人员数 | (人) | Number of Mediators | (person) | 24 139 |
| 调解纠纷总数 | (起) | Number of Disputes Mediated | (case) | 89 317 |
| # 婚姻家庭 | | Marriage and family | | 4 425 |
| 邻里纠纷 | | Neighbor Disputes | | 6 126 |
| 调解纠纷成功数 | | Number of Disputes Successful Mediated | | 89 091 |
| 防止民间纠纷引起自杀 | (件) | Prevention of Suicide Due to Civil Disputes | (case) | - |
| | (人) | | (person) | - |
| 防止民间纠纷转化为刑事案件 | (件) | Prevention of Civil Disputes from Turning into Criminal Cases | (case) | 32 |
| | (人) | | (person) | 89 |
| 宣讲法律 | (场) | Lectures on Law | (time) | 6 613 |
| 受教育人数 | (万人次) | Number of Persons Receiving Law Education | (10 000 person-times) | 101 |
| 为基层政府提供司法建议 | (条) | Providing Legal Advice for Local Governments | (piece) | 101 |
| 协助基层政府处理社会矛盾纠纷 | (件) | Helping Local Government on Social Conflicts | (case) | 1 018 |
| 代理诉讼事务 | | Service as legal representative | | 8 469 |
| 代理非诉讼事务 | | Service not as legal representative | | 2 866 |
| 担任法律顾问 | (家) | Number of Units with Legal Advisors | (unit) | 1 197 |
| 避免、挽回经济损失 | (万元) | Economic Loss Avoided and Reclaimed | (10 000 yuan) | 47 108 |

# STATISTICS ON PEOPLE'S MEDIATION AND BASIC-LEVEL JUDICIAL WORK BY REGION (2012)

| 市 区 Urban Area | # 吴江区 Wujiang District | 常 熟 Changshu | 张家港 Zhangjiagang | 昆 山 Kunshan | 太 仓 Taicang |
|---|---|---|---|---|---|
| 3 068 | 689 | 655 | 561 | 806 | 289 |
| 12 646 | 3 121 | 2 631 | 3 292 | 4 352 | 1 218 |
| 44 769 | 8 340 | 7 147 | 10 054 | 21 021 | 6 326 |
| 2 536 | 1 048 | 326 | 343 | 1 106 | 114 |
| 3 296 | 856 | 450 | 403 | 1 909 | 68 |
| 44 583 | 8 268 | 7 118 | 10 052 | 21 013 | 6 325 |
| – | – | – | – | – | – |
| – | – | – | – | – | – |
| 2 | – | 26 | – | 4 | – |
| 5 | – | 75 | – | 9 | – |
| 3 687 | 258 | 505 | 885 | 1 349 | 187 |
| 22 | 1 | 8 | 51 | 18 | 2 |
| 42 | 17 | 2 | 48 | 8 | 1 |
| 205 | 18 | – | 97 | 496 | 220 |
| 2 641 | 1 499 | 1 175 | 3 200 | 519 | 934 |
| 1 340 | 648 | 375 | 1 027 | 25 | 99 |
| 287 | 203 | 218 | 278 | 216 | 198 |
| 9 748 | 2 188 | 1 247 | 24 835 | 5 975 | 5 304 |

表18-12

# 部分年份人民调解基层司法工作情况
# STATISTICS ON PEOPLE'S MEDIATION AND BASIC-LEVEL JUDICIAL WORK OF PARTIAL YEARS

| 指　标 | Item | 1995年 | 2000年 | 2010年 | 2011年 | 2012年 |
|---|---|---|---|---|---|---|
| 人民调解委员会 (个) | Number of People's Mediation Committees (unit) | 6 966 | 5 717 | 3 794 | 3 738 | 5 379 |
| 调委会人员数 (人) | Number of Mediators (person) | 98 289 | 53 801 | 26 800 | 26 541 | 24 139 |
| 调解纠纷总数 (起) | Number of Disputes Mediated (case) | 18 762 | 16 981 | 40 865 | 59 544 | 89 317 |
| # 婚姻家庭 | Marriage and family | – | – | 4 130 | 4 186 | 4 425 |
| 邻里纠纷 | Neighbor Disputes | – | – | 5 686 | 7 331 | 6 126 |
| 调解纠纷成功数 | Number of Disputes Successful Mediated | 18 362 | 16 747 | 40 561 | 59 223 | 89 091 |
| 防止民间纠纷引起自杀 (件) | Prevention of Suicide Due to Civil Disputes (case) | 72 | 88 | 11 | 14 | – |
| (人) | (person) | 74 | 100 | 11 | 15 | – |
| 防止民间纠纷转化为刑事案件 (件) | Prevention of Civil Disputes from Turning into Criminal Cases (case) | 226 | 167 | 90 | 101 | 32 |
| (人) | (person) | 338 | 310 | 359 | 617 | 89 |
| 宣讲法律 (场) | Lectures on Law (time) | – | 1 415 | 3 652 | 5 348 | 6 613 |
| 受教育人数 (万人次) | Number of Persons Receiving Law Education (10 000 person-times) | – | 51 | 92 | 90 | 101 |
| 为基层政府提供司法建议 (条) | Providing Legal Advice for Local Governments (piece) | – | – | 90 | 88 | 101 |
| 协助基层政府处理社会矛盾纠纷(件) | Helping Local Government on Social Conflicts (case) | – | – | 948 | 639 | 1 018 |
| 代理诉讼事务 | Service as legal representative | – | – | 7 144 | 10 779 | 8 469 |
| 代理非诉讼事务 | Service not as legal representative | – | – | 1 744 | 2 795 | 2 866 |
| 担任法律顾问 (家) | Number of Units with Legal Advisors (unit) | 4 163 | 4 026 | 1 756 | 1 553 | 1 197 |
| 避免、挽回经济损失 (万元) | Economic Loss Avoided and Reclaimed (10 000 yuan) | – | – | 29 394 | 45 888 | 47 108 |

表18-13

# 道路、船舶交通事故及火灾情况（2012年）
# STATISTICS ON HIGHWAY，WATERWAY TRAFFIC ACCIDENTS AND FIRES (2012)

| 地　区 | Region | 起数(起) Number of Traffic Accidents (case) | 死亡(人) Number of Deaths (person) | 伤人(人) Number of Injuries (person) | 损失折款(万元) Losses Converted into Cash (10 000 yuan) |
|---|---|---|---|---|---|
| **道路交通事故** | **Road Accidents** | | | | |
| **全　市** | **Whole Municipality** | **2 827** | **629** | **2 688** | **2 689** |
| 市　区 | Urban Area | 1 006 | 272 | 934 | 1 191 |
| # 吴江区 | Wujiang District | 462 | 91 | 432 | 243 |
| 常　熟 | Changshu | 700 | 118 | 694 | 663 |
| 张家港 | Zhangjiagang | 465 | 91 | 408 | 238 |
| 昆　山 | Kunshan | 353 | 86 | 337 | 261 |
| 太　仓 | Taicang | 303 | 62 | 315 | 337 |
| **船舶交通事故** | **Waterway Accidents** | | | | |
| **全　市** | **Whole Municipality** | **16** | **6** | **6** | **56** |
| 市　区 | Urban Area | 15 | 6 | 6 | 51 |
| # 吴江区 | Wujiang District | 6 | 1 | – | 25 |
| 常　熟 | Changshu | 1 | – | – | 5 |
| 张家港 | Zhangjiagang | – | – | – | – |
| 昆　山 | Kunshan | – | – | – | – |
| 太　仓 | Taicang | – | – | – | – |
| **火　灾** | **Fires** | | | | |
| **全　市** | **Whole Municipality** | **544** | **11** | **6** | **2 555** |
| 市　区 | Urban Area | 276 | 9 | 5 | 1 073 |
| # 吴江区 | Wujiang District | 72 | – | – | 263 |
| 常　熟 | Changshu | 89 | – | – | 678 |
| 张家港 | Zhangjiagang | 63 | – | – | 237 |
| 昆　山 | Kunshan | 100 | 1 | 1 | 400 |
| 太　仓 | Taicang | 16 | 1 | – | 167 |

# 主 要 统 计 指 标 解 释

**社会福利事业单位** 指集中收养社会孤老、残、幼的机构，包括由民政部门管理的社会福利院、儿童福利院、精神病人福利院和城镇集体举办的福利院及农村集体举办的敬老院以及优抚医院和具有收养能力的社区服务中心等。该指标主要反映我国社会福利性单位的投入水平。

**社会福利事业单位收养人数** 包括民政部门管理和城镇、农村集体举办的社会福利事业单位中收养的老人、少年儿童、缺乏生活自理能力的残疾人员和精神病人。该指标主要反映收养性社会福利单位的收养能力。

**社会福利企业单位** 指以安置城镇有一定劳动能力的盲、聋、哑和肢体残疾人员就业为目的，享受国家减免税待遇的国有或集体企业。包括福利工厂、福利商业和服务业、假肢厂和安置农场等单位。该指标主要反映我国对残疾人照顾的特殊政策。

**律师** 指依法取得律师执业证书，担任法律顾问，民事(刑事、行政)案件代理人、刑事案件辩护人、办理非诉讼业务，解答法律询问，代写法律事务文书等，为社会提供法律服务的人员。

**公证人员** 指在公证处工作的人员总称，包括公证处主任、副主任、公证员、公证员助理(助理公证员)和其他从事辅助性工作的人员。

**公证文书** 指公证处根据当事人申请，依照事实和法律，按照法定程序制作的，具有法律效力的司法证明文书。根据公证书用途和使用地，公证书分为国内公证书、国内经济公证书、涉外民事公证书、涉外经济公证书四类。

**调解员** 指在人民调解委员会担负调解民间纠纷工作的人员，包括调解委员会的委员和调解小组的调解员。该指标主要反映从事人民调解工作的人员数量。

**调解民间纠纷** 指调解委员会按照法律规定，根据自愿原则，用说服教育的方法调解民间发生的有关民事权利和义务争执的件数，包括调解成功数和调解未成功数。该指标主要反映人民调解委员会的工作量。

# EXPLANATORY NOTES ON MAIN STATISTICAL INDICATORS

**Social Welfare Institutions** refer to institutions taking care of old people without children, handicapped people and orphans. They include social welfare institutions run by civil affairs departments, children welfare institutions, social welfare institutions for mental patients, collective-owned old people's homes in rural areas, convalescent homes and community service centers with the capacity of receiving those people. This indicator reflects the input in social welfare institutions.

**Number of People Accommodated by Social Welfare Institutions** refers to the number of old people, children, totally dependent handicapped people and mental patients Accommodated by social welfare institutions run by civil affairs departments and those run by collective units in urban and rural areas. This indicator reflects the capacity of social welfare institutions.

**Social Welfare Enterprises** are collective-owned enterprises which employ the blind, deaf-mute, and physically disabled people who are able to work in cities and towns and enjoy exemption from State taxes. They include welfare plants, welfare commercial services, artificial limb plants and farms, etc. This indicator reflects the preferential policies toward disabled persons.

**Lawyers** are certified legal workers according to law, and who are employed by legal counselling firms to act as legal advisers; agents in criminal or civil lawsuits; and defenders in criminal lawsuits; or to handle non-litigious legal affairs, to advise on matters of law or to write legal papers for others and provide service to the public.

**Notary Personnel** refers to people working for notary offices including: directors, deputy directors, notaries, assistant notaries and other people providing assistance.

**Notary Documents** refer to the judicial notary documents drawn up at the request of the interested party and are in accordance with facts and the law and following certain legal proceedings. According to usage and locality, notary documents are divided into the following 4 types: domestic notary documents, domestic economic notary documents, foreign-related civil notary documents and foreign-related economic notary documents.

**Mediators** refer to workers on people's mediation committees responsible for mediating in civil disputes and cases of slight infraction of the law. They include members of the mediation committees and mediators of mediation groups. This indicator reflects the number of people engaged in mediation.

**Mediation of Civil Disputes** refers to number of cases made by mediation committees in mediating in civil disputes concerning civil rights and duties through persuasion and education in accordance with the provisions of law on a voluntary basis, so as to solve disputes by helping the parties involved come to an agreement and understanding, including those unsuccessful ones. This indicator reflects the workload of the mediation committees.

# 十九、城市建设 环境保护

# CHAPTER 19
# URBAN CONSTRUCTION AND ENVIRONMENTAL PROTECTION

# 城市建设　环境保护
# URBAN CONSTRUCTION AND ENVIRONMENTAL PROTECTION

## 主要统计指标
## MAJOR STATISTICAL INDICATORS

| | | | | |
|---|---|---|---|---|
| 2012年市区建成区面积 | Build up Area of Urban District | 436.53 | 平方公里 | sq.km |
| 2012年市区人均拥有道路面积 | Per Capita Roads Area of Urban District | 31.39 | 平方米 | sq.m |
| 2012年市区人均公园绿地面积 | Per Capita Park Green Space of Urban District | 17.41 | 平方米 | sq.m |
| 2012年市区建成区绿化覆盖率 | Coverage Rate of Green Areas in Developed Areas of Urban District | 41.89 | % | |
| 2012年市区污水处理率 | Treatment Rate of Urban District | 91.85 | % | |
| 2012年市区供水总量 | Total Water Supply of Urban District | 79 575 | 万立方米 | 10 000 cu.m |
| 2012年市区煤气供气总量 | Total Coal Gas Supply of Urban District | 4 449 | 万立方米 | 10 000 cu.m |
| 2012年市区天然气供气总量 | Total Natural Gas Supply of Urban District | 90 312 | 万立方米 | 10 000 cu.m |
| 2012年市区液化石油气供气总量 | Total Liquefied Petroleum Gas Supply | 62 000 | 吨 | ton |

表19-1

## 分地区城市设施水平 (2012年)
## URBAN FACILITY CONDITION BY REGION (2012)

| 地　区 | Region | 人均日生活用水量(升) Per Capita Daily Consumption of Tap Water for Residential Use (liter) | 人均拥有道路面积(平方米) Per Capita Area of Roads (sq.m) | 人均公园绿地面积(平方米) Per Capita Park Green Areas (sq.m) | 建成区绿化覆盖率(%) Coverage Rate of Green Areas in Developed Areas (%) | 污水处理率(%) Treatment Rate of Sewage (%) |
|---|---|---|---|---|---|---|
| **全　市** | **Whole Municipality** | **293.95** | **31.29** | **17.17** | **42.58** | **91.87** |
| 市　区 | Urban Area | 318.58 | 31.39 | 17.41 | 41.89 | 91.85 |
| #吴江区 | Wujiang District | 163.71 | 42.48 | 16.64 | 39.03 | 91.95 |
| 常　熟 | Changshu | 215.63 | 31.04 | 19.77 | 44.62 | 90.12 |
| 张家港 | Zhangjiagang | 239.20 | 28.42 | 14.35 | 43.64 | 91.73 |
| 昆　山 | Kunshan | 315.18 | 29.26 | 16.12 | 43.54 | 93.50 |
| 太　仓 | Taicang | 197.81 | 40.61 | 16.24 | 41.76 | 90.82 |

表19-2

## 分地区城市建设用地 (2012年末)
## LAND USE OF URBAN CONSTRUCTION BY REGION (END OF 2012)

单位：平方公里 (sq.km)

| 地　区 | Region | 建成区面积 Build up Area | 城市建设用地面积 Urban Construction Areas | # 居住用地 Residential | 公共管理与服务用地 Public Administration and Service Land | 工业用地 Industrial | 交通设施用地 Traffic Facilities Land | 绿　地 Green Land |
|---|---|---|---|---|---|---|---|---|
| **全　市** | **Whole Municipality** | **719.94** | **678.67** | **208.33** | **40.33** | **189.00** | **85.34** | **82.26** |
| 市　区 | Urban Area | 436.53 | 433.46 | 122.41 | 27.45 | 131.16 | 59.54 | 52.15 |
| #吴江区 | Wujiang District | 86.59 | 84.02 | 22.51 | 7.16 | 35.62 | 8.67 | 7.28 |
| 常　熟 | Changshu | 98.00 | 84.18 | 34.27 | 2.73 | 18.37 | 7.15 | 5.49 |
| 张家港 | Zhangjiagang | 67.41 | 64.94 | 23.63 | 4.15 | 18.03 | 6.74 | 7.66 |
| 昆　山 | Kunshan | 72.00 | 50.09 | 15.24 | 4.61 | 9.94 | 6.37 | 7.95 |
| 太　仓 | Taicang | 46.00 | 46.00 | 12.78 | 1.39 | 11.50 | 5.54 | 9.01 |

表19-3

# 分地区城市供水情况 (2012年)
# URBAN WATER SUPPLY BY REGION (2012)

| 地区 | Region | 水厂综合生产能力(万立方米/日) General Production Capacity (10 000 cu.m/day) | 全年供水总量(万立方米) Total Annual Volume of Water Supply (10 000 cu.m) | | | 供水管道长度(公里) Length of Water Supply Pipelines (km) |
|---|---|---|---|---|---|---|
| | | | | #生产运营用水量 For Productive Use | 居民家庭用水量 For Residential Use | |
| **全市** | **Whole Municipality** | **688.59** | **114 213** | **55 169** | **34 401** | **11 544** |
| 市区 | Urban Area | 348.89 | 79 575 | 39 007 | 24 220 | 7 611 |
| #吴江区 | Wujiang District | 106.89 | 14 763 | 10 273 | 2 467 | 1 209 |
| 常熟 | Changshu | 87.50 | 8 821 | 4 441 | 2 493 | 1 692 |
| 张家港 | Zhangjiagang | 65.00 | 5 286 | 1 079 | 2 480 | 792 |
| 昆山 | Kunshan | 150.00 | 14 172 | 6 663 | 3 881 | 845 |
| 太仓 | Taicang | 37.20 | 6 359 | 3 979 | 1 327 | 604 |

表19-4

# 分地区城市人工煤气供气情况(2012年)
# URBAN COAL GAS SUPPLY BY REGION(2012)

| 地区 | Region | 供气总量(万立方米) Total Gas Supply (10 000 cu.m) | | 用气户数(户) Total Number of Residents with Access to Gas (household) | | 供气管道长度(公里) Total Length of Gas Pipelines (km) |
|---|---|---|---|---|---|---|
| | | | # 家庭用量 Consumption for Residential Use | | # 家庭用户 Residential Households | |
| **全市** | **Whole Municipality** | **4 449** | **3 524** | **79 710** | **79 539** | **568** |
| 市区 | Urban Area | 4 449 | 3 524 | 79 710 | 79 539 | 568 |
| #吴江区 | Wujiang District | – | – | – | – | – |
| 常熟 | Changshu | – | – | – | – | – |
| 张家港 | Zhangjiagang | – | – | – | – | – |
| 昆山 | Kunshan | – | – | – | – | – |
| 太仓 | Taicang | – | – | – | – | – |

表19-5

## 分地区城市天然气供气情况（2012年）
## URBAN NATURAL GAS SUPPLY BY REGION (2012)

| 地 区 | Region | 供气总量（万立方米）Total Gas Supply (10 000 cu.m) | # 家庭用量 Consumption for Residential Use | 用气户数(户) Total Number of Residents with Access to Gas (household) | # 家庭用户 Residential Households | 供气管道长度（公里）Total Length of Gas Pipelines (km) |
|---|---|---|---|---|---|---|
| **全 市** | **Whole Municipality** | **229 211** | **35 221** | **1 347 000** | **1 339 430** | **10 399** |
| 市 区 | Urban Area | 90 312 | 14 405 | 754 651 | 750 592 | 4 624 |
| #吴江区 | Wujiang District | 16 000 | 843 | 56 866 | 56 290 | 430 |
| 常 熟 | Changshu | 31 422 | 1 415 | 104 965 | 104 150 | 1 307 |
| 张家港 | Zhangjiagang | 34 300 | 1 461 | 85 391 | 85 000 | 864 |
| 昆 山 | Kunshan | 51 717 | 15 930 | 341 103 | 340 040 | 2 543 |
| 太 仓 | Taicang | 21 460 | 2 010 | 60 890 | 59 648 | 1 061 |

表19-6

## 分地区城市液化石油气供气情况（2012年）
## URBAN LIQUEFIED PETROLEUM GAS SUPPLY BY REGION (2012)

| 地 区 | Region | 供气总量（吨）Total Gas Supply (ton) | # 家庭用量 Consumption for Residential Use | 用气户数(户) Total Number of Residents with Access to Gas (household) | # 家庭用户 Residential Households | 供气管道长度（公里）Total Length of Gas Pipelines (km) |
|---|---|---|---|---|---|---|
| **全 市** | **Whole Municipality** | **155 390** | **112 028** | **319 700** | **286 227** | **45** |
| 市 区 | Urban Area | 62 000 | 53 800 | 60 997 | 60 847 | - |
| #吴江区 | Wujiang District | 9 000 | 8 800 | 54 247 | 54 147 | - |
| 常 熟 | Changshu | 14 128 | 12 026 | 66 090 | 65 498 | 26 |
| 张家港 | Zhangjiagang | 34 675 | 22 540 | 79 500 | 78 800 | 19 |
| 昆 山 | Kunshan | 27 650 | 17 328 | 79 863 | 54 372 | - |
| 太 仓 | Taicang | 16 937 | 6 334 | 33 250 | 26 710 | - |

表19-7

# 分地区城市市政设施情况 (2012年末)
# URBAN CIVIL FACILITIES BY REGION (END OF 2012)

| 地 区 | Region | 实有道路长度(公里) Length of Roads (km) | 实有道路面积(万平方米) Area of Roads (10 000 sq.m) | 路灯数(盏) Number of Street Lights (unit) | 桥梁数(座) Number of Bridges (unit) | 排水管道长度(公里) Length of Drainage Pipelines (km) |
|---|---|---|---|---|---|---|
| **全 市** | **Whole Municipality** | **5 672** | **11 924** | **520 225** | **3 408** | **11 534** |
| 市 区 | Urban Area | 3 571 | 7 698 | 371 425 | 2 577 | 7 321 |
| #吴江区 | Wujiang District | 586 | 1 425 | 44 618 | 347 | 1 489 |
| 常 熟 | Changshu | 640 | 1 265 | 46 903 | 311 | 1 771 |
| 张家港 | Zhangjiagang | 451 | 1 101 | 25 756 | 66 | 901 |
| 昆 山 | Kunshan | 670 | 1 097 | 36 995 | 178 | 791 |
| 太 仓 | Taicang | 340 | 763 | 39 146 | 276 | 751 |

表19-8

# 已建成城市轨道交通情况 (2012年末)
# URBAN RAIL TRANSIT CONDITION THAT HAS BEEN BUILT (END OF 2012)

| 地 区 | Region | 线路条数(条) Number of Routes(line) | 轻轨运营线路总长度(公里) Total Length of Light Rail Transit Operating Routes (km) | 配置车辆数(辆) The number of configured vehicles (cars) | 运营里程(万列公里) Operating mileage (ten thousand km/ train) | 客运量(万人次) Passenger Traffic (10 000 Person-Times) | 从业人员(人) Number of Employed Persons (person) |
|---|---|---|---|---|---|---|---|
| **全 市** | **Whole Municipality** | **1** | **25.2** | **96** | **143.3** | **2 594.8** | **1 671** |
| 市 区 | Urban Area | 1 | 25.2 | 96 | 143.3 | 2 594.8 | 1 671 |

表19-9

# 分地区城市公共交通和出租汽车情况 (2012年末)
# URBAN PUBLIC TRANSIT AND TAXI BY REGION (END OF 2012)

| 地 区 | Region | 公共汽车营运线路网长度(公里) Length of Bus Routes (km) | 公共汽车营运车辆(辆) Operating Bus (coach) | 公共汽车客运总量 (万人次) Number of Passengers Carried by Bus (10 000 person-times) | 公共汽车运营里程 (万公里) Length of Bus Operating (10 000 kms) | 出租汽车营运车辆(辆) Operating Taxis (coach) |
|---|---|---|---|---|---|---|
| **全 市** | **Whole Municipality** | **11 624** | **6 306** | **91 246** | **44 434** | **8 132** |
| 市 区 | Urban Area | 8 054 | 4 389 | 69 714 | 31 576 | 5 048 |
| #吴江区 | Wujiang District | 1 566 | 563 | 7 126 | 3 900 | 745 |
| 常 熟 | Changshu | 769 | 463 | 4 740 | 3 060 | 709 |
| 张家港 | Zhangjiagang | 610 | 319 | 2 889 | 1 994 | 557 |
| 昆 山 | Kunshan | 1 820 | 1 039 | 13 082 | 7 213 | 1 390 |
| 太 仓 | Taicang | 371 | 96 | 821 | 591 | 428 |

表19-10

## 分地区城市园林绿化情况（2012年末）

## URBAN PARKS，GARDENS & GREEN AREAS BY REGION (END OF 2012)

单位：公顷 (hectare)

| 地区 | Region | 绿化覆盖面积 Coverage Space of Green Areas | # 建成区 Build up Area | 绿地面积 Total Area of Green Areas | # 建成区 Build up Area | 公园绿地面积 Total Area of Park Green Areas |
|---|---|---|---|---|---|---|
| **全　市** | **Whole Municipality** | **40 906** | **30 657** | **33 738** | **27 885** | **6 542** |
| 市　区 | Urban Area | 26 114 | 18 286 | 20 904 | 16 499 | 4 271 |
| #吴江区 | Wujiang District | 9 510 | 3 491 | 6 248 | 3 380 | 558 |
| 常　熟 | Changshu | 4 734 | 4 373 | 4 425 | 4 057 | 806 |
| 张家港 | Zhangjiagang | 3 236 | 2 942 | 2 747 | 2 667 | 556 |
| 昆　山 | Kunshan | 3 714 | 3 135 | 3 363 | 2 852 | 604 |
| 太　仓 | Taicang | 3 108 | 1 921 | 2 299 | 1 810 | 305 |

表19-11

## 分地区城市清洁卫生情况（2012年）

## URBAN ENVIRONMENT SANITATION BY REGION (2012)

| 地区 | Region | 道路清扫保洁面积(万平方米) Area under Cleaning Program (10 000sq.m) | 生活垃圾清运量(万吨) Volume of Residential Garbage Disposed (10 000tons) | 生活垃圾无害化处理量(万吨) Volume of No Harm Dispasal of Garbage (10 000tons) | 粪便清运量(万吨) Volume of Excrement and Urine Disposal (10 000tons) | 公共厕所(座) Number of Public Lavatories (unit) |
|---|---|---|---|---|---|---|
| **全　市** | **Whole Municipality** | **11 828** | **325.50** | **325.50** | **12.71** | **1 280** |
| 市　区 | Urban Area | 8 648 | 182.91 | 182.91 | 3.02 | 793 |
| #吴江区 | Wujiang District | 1 215 | 35.41 | 35.41 | 1.82 | 105 |
| 常　熟 | Changshu | 995 | 38.50 | 38.50 | 4.50 | 251 |
| 张家港 | Zhangjiagang | 560 | 15.72 | 15.72 | 2.40 | 58 |
| 昆　山 | Kunshan | 861 | 61.77 | 61.77 | 1.83 | 104 |
| 太　仓 | Taicang | 764 | 26.60 | 26.60 | 0.96 | 74 |

表19-12

## 分地区城市房屋概况 (2012年末)
## OVERVIEW OF URBAN HOUSING BY REGION (END OF 2012)

| 地 区 | Region | 实有房屋建筑面积 (万平方米) Total Floor Space of Buildings(10 000sq.m) | # 住 宅 Residential Buildings | 年末成套住宅建筑面积 (万平方米) Building Area of Residential Housing In Sets by The End of The Year(10 000sq.m) | 住宅成套率 (%) Rate For Residential Housing In Sets (%) |
|---|---|---|---|---|---|
| **全 市** | **Whole Municipality** | **69 153** | **26 717** | **25 505** | **95.5** |
| 市 区 | Urban Area | 34 475 | 13 950 | 12 946 | 92.8 |
| #吴江区 | Wujiang District | 8 662 | 2 811 | 2 642 | 94.0 |
| 常 熟 | Changshu | 9 440 | 3 165 | 3 096 | 97.8 |
| 张家港 | Zhangjiagang | 7 781 | 2 408 | 2 401 | 99.7 |
| 昆 山 | Kunshan | 13 627 | 5 887 | 5 848 | 99.3 |
| 太 仓 | Taicang | 3 830 | 1 306 | 1 215 | 93.0 |

注：该表统计范围为国有土地上的房屋。 Note:The range of statistics of the table was the housing on state-owned land.

表19-13

## 分地区城市房屋登记情况 (2012年末)
## REGISTRATION OF URBAN HOUSING BY REGION (END OF 2012)

单位：万平方米 (10 000 sq.m)

| 地 区 | Region | 已登记国有土地上房屋建筑面积 Registered Housing Construction Area on The State-owned Land | # 住 宅 Residential Buildings | # 办公楼 Office Buildings | # 商业营业用房 Commercial Buildings | 已登记集体土地上的房屋建筑面积 Registered Housing Construction Area on The Collective Land |
|---|---|---|---|---|---|---|
| **全 市** | **Whole Municipality** | **65 665** | **25 383** | **2 409** | **5 483** | **6 089** |
| 市 区 | Urban Area | 32 887 | 13 522 | 863 | 1 875 | 2 760 |
| #吴江区 | Wujiang District | 7 948 | 2 565 | 435 | 1 117 | 2 542 |
| 常 熟 | Changshu | 8 219 | 2 291 | 154 | 704 | 466 |
| 张家港 | Zhangjiagang | 7 355 | 2 390 | 677 | 458 | - |
| 昆 山 | Kunshan | 13 551 | 5 887 | 618 | 934 | 1 082 |
| 太 仓 | Taicang | 3 654 | 1 292 | 97 | 1 511 | 1 780 |

表19-14

# 分地区环境保护情况 (2012年)

| 指　　标 | | Item | | 全　市 Whole Municipality |
|---|---|---|---|---|
| 工业废水排放量 | (万吨) | Volume of Industrial Wastewater Discharged | (10 000 tons) | 70 754 |
| 工业废水处理量 | | Volume of Treated Industrial Wastewater | | 73 790 |
| 工业废气排放总量 | (亿立方米) | Total Volume of Industrial Waste Gas Emission | (100 million cu.m) | 14 821 |
| 工业二氧化硫产生量 | (吨) | Volume of Sulphur Dioxide Produced | (ton) | 582 531 |
| 工业二氧化硫排放量 | | Volume of Sulphur Dioxide Emission | | 183 401 |
| 化学需氧量排放量 | | Volume of COD Emission | | 93 880 |
| # 工业化学需氧量排放量 | | Industrial Volume of COD Emission | | 46 741 |
| 氨氮排放量 | | Volume of Ammonia Nitrogen | | 16 458 |
| # 工业氨氮排放量 | | Industrial Volume of Ammonia Nitrogen | | 3 622 |
| 氮氧化物排放量 | | Volume of Nitrogen Oxides | | 276 946 |
| # 工业氮氧化物排放量 | | Industrial Volume of Nitrogen Oxides | | 210 598 |
| 工业烟（粉）尘产生量 | | Volume of Industrial Smoke (Powder) Dust Produced | | 6 305 869 |
| 工业烟（粉）尘排放量 | | Volume of Industrial Smoke (Powder) Dust Emission | | 56 065 |
| 工业固体废物产生量 | (万吨) | Volume of Industrial Solid Wastes Produced | (10 000 tons) | 2 214 |
| 工业固体废物处置量 | | Volume of Industrial Solid Wastes Treated | | 35 |
| 工业固体废物综合利用量 | | Volume of Industrial Solid Wastes Utilized in a Comprehensive Way | | 2 179 |
| 环境污染治理本年投资总额 | (万元) | Investment For Environmental Pollution Abatement in 2012 | (10 000 yuan) | 2 573 610 |
| 环境噪声达标区总面积 | (平方公里) | The Total Area of the Areas Reaching the Eenvironmental Noise Standards | (sq km) | 466 |
| 空气质量达标（API<100）天数 | (天) | The number of days reaching the air quality standards (API <100) | (days) | 356 |
| 工业锅炉 | (台) | Industrial Boilers | (unit) | 1 701 |
| | (蒸吨) | | (ton) | 56 285 |
| 工业炉窑 | (台) | Industrial Furnaces & Kilns | (unit) | 592 |

# ENVIRONMENTAL PROTECTION BY REGION (2012)

| 市 区<br>Urban Area | # 吴江区<br>Wujiang District | 常 熟<br>Changshu | 张家港<br>Zhangjiagang | 昆 山<br>Kunshan | 太 仓<br>Taicang |
|---|---|---|---|---|---|
| 37 689 | 13 230 | 11 711 | 9 362 | 7 124 | 4 868 |
| 34 590 | 8 785 | 9 464 | 15 644 | 9 094 | 4 998 |
| 2 160 | 469 | 1 034 | 9 044 | 1 290 | 1 293 |
| 136 549 | 42 059 | 138 101 | 110 130 | 24 959 | 172 792 |
| 53 427 | 23 653 | 37 609 | 51 152 | 13 830 | 27 382 |
| 43 907 | 23 090 | 14 382 | 16 362 | 7 238 | 11 990 |
| 22 175 | 8 646 | 7 982 | 6 195 | 5 611 | 4 777 |
| 9 892 | 2 927 | 1 745 | 1 932 | 1 624 | 1 266 |
| 1 509 | 502 | 550 | 409 | 673 | 481 |
| 103 380 | 28 697 | 64 491 | 44 807 | 23 651 | 40 616 |
| 64 562 | 23 423 | 56 537 | 37 085 | 16 140 | 36 274 |
| 1 515 098 | 329 390 | 987 468 | 1 238 290 | 372 201 | 2 192 811 |
| 15 598 | 8 101 | 11 427 | 21 131 | 2 156 | 5 753 |
| 292 | 80 | 288 | 1 310 | 59 | 264 |
| 9 | 5 | 4 | 7 | 12 | 3 |
| 283 | 74 | 285 | 1 303 | 47 | 261 |
| 1 089 517 |  | 360 212 | 498 345 | 452 355 | 173 182 |
| 246 | 16 | 80 | 31 | 87 | 22 |
| 339 | 361 | 362 | 363 | 362 | 351 |
| 793 | 300 | 337 | 118 | 296 | 157 |
| 16 600 | 4 576 | 10 374 | 8 372 | 2 562 | 18 377 |
| 150 | 9 | 93 | 149 | 177 | 23 |

# 主要统计指标解释

**供水综合生产能力** 指按供水设施取水、净化、送水、出厂输水干管等环节设计能力计算的综合生产能力。包括在原设计能力的基础上，经挖、革、改增加的生产能力。计算时，以四个环节中最薄弱的环节为主确定能力。

**年末供水管道长度** 指从送水泵至用户水表之间所有管道的长度。不包括新安装尚未使用、水厂内以及用户建筑物内的管道。

**全年供水总量** 指报告期供水企业(单位)供出的全部水量。包括有效供水量和漏损水量。

**生活用水量** 包括公共服务用水和居民家庭用水。公共服务用水指为城市社会公共生活服务的用水。包括行政事业单位、部队营区和公共设施服务、社会服务业、批发零售贸易业、旅馆饮食业以及其他公共服务业等单位的用水。居民家庭用水指城市范围内所有居民家庭的日常生活用水。包括城市居民、农民家庭、公共供水站用水。

**用水普及率** 指城市用水人口数与城市人口总数的比率。计算公式：

$$\text{用水普及率}=\frac{\text{城市用水人口数}}{\text{城市人口总数}}\times 100\%$$

**人工煤气生产能力** 指报告期末人工煤气生产厂制气、净化、输送等环节的综合生产能力，不包括备用设备能力。一般按设计能力计算，如果实际生产能力大于设计能力时，应按实际测定的生产能力计算。测定时应以制气、净化、输送三个环节中最薄弱的环节为主。

**供气管道长度** 指报告期末从气源厂压缩机的出口或门站出口至各类用户引入管之间的全部已经通气投入使用的管道长度。不包括煤气生产厂、输配站、液化气储存站、灌瓶站、储配站、气化站、混气站、供应站等厂(站)内的管道。

**全年供气总量** 指全年燃气企业(单位)向用户供应的燃气数量。包括销售量和损失量。

**燃气普及率** 指报告期末使用燃气的城市人口数与城市人口总数的比率。计算公式为：

$$\text{燃气普及率}=\frac{\text{城市用气人口数}}{\text{城市人口总数}}\times 100\%$$

**年末道路长度** 指年末道路长度和与道路相通的桥梁、隧道的长度，按车行道中心线计算。在统计时只统计路面宽度在3.5米(含3.5米)以上的各种铺装道路，包括开放型工业区和住宅区道路在内。

**城市桥梁** 指为跨越天然或人工障碍物而修建的构筑物。包括跨河桥、立交桥、人行天桥以及人行地下通道等。按使用年限分为永久性桥和半永久性桥。

**城市排水管道长度** 指所有排水总管、干管、支管、检查井及连接井进出口等长度之和。

**城市污水日处理能力** 指污水处理厂(或污水处理装置)每昼夜处理污水量的设计能力。

**年末运营车数** 指年末城市用于公共交通运营业务的全部车辆数。新购、新制和调入的运营车辆，自投入之日起开始计算；调出、报废和调作他用的运营车辆，自上级主管机关批准之日起不再计入。

**园林绿地面积** 指报告期末用作园林和绿化的各种绿地面积。包括公园绿地、生产绿地、防护绿地、单位附属绿地、防护绿地、生产绿地、道路绿地和风景林地面积。

**公园绿地** 城市中向公众开放的以游憩为主要功能，有一定的游憩设施和服务设施，同时兼有健全生态、美化景观，防灾减灾等综合作用的绿化用地。包括综合公园，社区公园、专类公园、带状公园和街旁绿地。其中综合公园、专类公园和带状公园面积之和为公园面积。

**每万人拥有公共交通车辆** 指报告期末城区内每万人平均拥有的公共交通车辆标台数。计算公式：

$$每万人拥有公共交通车辆=\frac{公共交通运营车标台数}{城市人口总数}$$

**工业废水排放量** 指经过企业厂区所有排放口排到企业外部的工业废水量。包括生产废水、外排的直接冷却水、超标排放的矿井地下水和与工业废水混排的厂区生活污水，不包括外排的间接冷却水(清污不分流的间接冷却水应计算在内)。

**工业废水排放达标量** 指报告期内废水中各项污染物指标都达到国家或地方排放标准的外排工业废水量，包括未经处理外排达标的，经废水处理设施处理后达标排放的，以及经污水处理厂处理后达标排放的。

**工业废水排放达标率** 指工业废水排放达标量占工业废水排放量的百分率，计算公式为：

$$工业废水排放达标率=\frac{工业废水排放达标量}{工业废水排放量}\times100\%$$

**生活污水排放量** 指城镇居民每年排放的生活污水。用人均系数法测算。测算公式为：

$$\begin{matrix}生活污水\\排放量\end{matrix}=\begin{matrix}城镇生活污水\\排放系数\end{matrix}\times\begin{matrix}市镇非\\农业人口\end{matrix}\times365$$

**工业废气排放量** 指报告期内企业厂区内燃料燃烧和生产工艺过程中产生的各种排入大气的含有污染物的气体的总量，以标准状态(273K，101325Pa)计算。测算公式为：

$$\begin{matrix}工业废气\\排放量\end{matrix}=\begin{matrix}燃料燃烧过程\\中废气排放量\end{matrix}+\begin{matrix}生产工艺过程\\中废气排放量\end{matrix}$$

**工业二氧化硫（$SO_2$）排放量** 指报告期内企业在燃料燃烧和生产工艺过程中排入大气的$SO_2$总量，计算公式为：

$$\begin{matrix}工业SO_2\\排放量\end{matrix}=\begin{matrix}燃料燃烧过程\\中SO_2排放量\end{matrix}+\begin{matrix}生产工艺过程\\中SO_2排放量\end{matrix}$$

**工业烟尘排放量** 指企业厂区内燃料燃烧过程中产生的烟气中夹带的颗粒物排放量。

**工业粉尘排放量** 指企业在生产工艺过程中排放的能在空气中悬浮一定时间的固体颗粒物排放量。如钢铁企业的耐火材料粉尘、焦化企业的筛焦系统粉尘、烧结机的粉尘、石灰窑的粉尘、建材企业的水泥粉尘等。不包括电厂排入大气的烟尘。

**工业固体废物产生量** 指报告期内企业在生产过程中产生的固体状、半固体状和高浓度液体状废弃物的总量，包括危险废物、冶炼废渣、粉煤灰、炉渣、煤矸石、尾矿、放射性废物和其他废物等；不包括矿山开采的剥离废石和掘进废石(煤矸石和呈酸性或碱性的废石除外)。酸性或碱性废石指采掘的废石其流经水、雨淋水的pH值小于4或pH值大于10.5者。

**工业固体废物综合利用量** 指报告期内企业通过回收、加工、循环、交换等方式，从固体废物中提取或者使其转化为可以利用的资源、能源和其他原材料的固体废物量(包括当年利用往年的工业固体废物贮存量)，如用作农业肥料、生产建筑材料、筑路等。综合利用量由原产生固体废物的单位统计。

**工业固体废物综合利用率** 指工业固体废物综合利用量占工业固体废物产生量(包括综合利用往年贮存量)的百分率。计算公式为：

$$\begin{matrix}工业固体废物\\综合利用率\end{matrix}=\frac{\begin{matrix}工业固体废物\\综合利用率\end{matrix}}{\begin{matrix}工业固体废物产生量+\\综合利用往年贮存量\end{matrix}}\times100\%$$

**工业固体废物处置量** 指报告期内企业将固体废物焚烧或者最终置于符合环境保护规定要求的场所，并不再回取的工业固体废物量(包括当年处置往年的工业固体废物贮存量)。处置方式有填埋(其中危险废物应安全填埋)、焚烧、专业贮存场(库)封场处理、深层灌注、回填矿井及海洋处置(经海洋管理部门同意投海处置)等。

**工业固体废物排放量** 指报告期内企业将所产生的固体废物排到固体废物污染防治设施、场所以外的数量，不包括矿山开采的剥离废石和掘进废石(煤矸石和呈酸性或碱性的废石除外)。

**“三废”综合利用产品产值** 指报告期内利用“三废”作为主要原料生产的产品价值(现行价)；已经销售或准备销售的应计算产品价值，留作生产自用的不应计算产品价值。

# EXPLANATORY NOTES ON MAIN STATISTICAL INDICATORS

**Production Capacity of Water Supply** refers to the designed overall production capacity of water facilities, covering the four segments of water collection, purification, conveyance, and outflow through trunk pipelines. Increased capacity through transformation and innovation projects is included as well. The capacity is determined mainly on the weakest of the above-mentioned four segments.

**Length of Water Supply Pipelines at the Year-end** refers to the total length of all the pipelines between the water pumps and the user water meters, excluding pipelines newly installed but not used yet, pipeline in the water factory,and pipeline in the user's buildings.

**Annual Volume of Water Supply** refers to the total volume of water supplied by water-works (units) during the reference period, including both the effective water supply and loss during the water supply.

**Consumption of Water for Residential Use** refers to water consumption of households for daily life and water consumption of public service facilities. The latter refers to water consumption for urban public services, including the consumption of government agencies and public institutions, military barracks, public facilities, wholesale and retail outlets, restaurants, hotels, and other units providing public services. Household water consumption refers to consumption of water for daily life of all households within the boundary of cities, including households of urban residents and farmers, and public water supply stations.

**Coverage Rate of Urban Population with Access to Tap Water** refers to the ratio of the urban population with access to tap water to the total urban population. The formula is:

$$\text{Coverage of urban population with access to tap water} = \frac{\text{Urban population with access to tap water}}{\text{Urban population}} \times 100\%$$

**Production Capacity of Gaswork Gas** refers to the overall production capacity of the urban gasworks in gas generation, purification and delivery at the end of the reference period, excluding capacity of the reserved facilities. In general, it is determined by the designed capacity, and when actual production capacity is larger than the designed capacity, the capacity is determined by the actual measurement on the weakest segment in the production, purification and delivery.

**Length of Gas Pipelines** refers to the total length of pipelines in use between the outlet of the compressor of gas-work or outlet of gas stations and the leading pipe of users, excluding pipelines within gasworks, delivery stations, LPG storage stations, refilling stations, gas-mixing stations and supply stations.

**Volume of Gas Supply** refers to the total volume of gas provided to users by gas-producing enterprises (units) in a year, including the volume sold and the volume lost.

**Coverage Rate of Urban Population with Access to Gas** refers to the ratio of the urban population with access to gas to the total urban population at the end of the reference period. The formula is:

$$\text{Coverage rate of urban population with access to gas} = \frac{\text{Urban population with access to gas}}{\text{Urban population}} \times 100\%$$

**Length of Paved Roads at Year-end** refers to the length of roads with paved surface including bridges and tunnels connected with roads by the end of the year. Length of the roads is measured by the central lines for vehicles for paved roads with a width of 3.5 meters and over, including roads in open-ended factory compounds and residential quarters.

**Urban Bridges** refer to bridges built to cross over natural or man-made barriers, including bridges over rivers, overpasses for traffic and for pedestrians, underpasses for pedestrians, etc. Both permanent and semi-permanent bridges are included.

**Length of Urban Sewage Pipes** refers to the total length of general drainage, trunks, branch and inspection wells, connection wells, inlets and outlets, etc.

**Daily Disposal Capacity of Urban Sewage** refers to the designed 24-hour capacity of sewage disposal by the sewage treatment works or facilities.

**Number of Vehicles under Operation at Year-end** refers to the total number of vehicles under operation by public transport enterprises (units) at the end of the year, based on the records of operational vehicles by the enterprises (units).

**Area of Gardens and Green Areas** refers to the total area occupied for green projects at the end of the reference period, including park green land, residential area green land, subsidiary green land of the units, protection green land, production green land, roadside green land and scenic forest land.

**Park Green Area** refers to green areas open to the public for amusement and rest with the facilities of amusement, rest and services. Its function includes perfecting ecology, beautifying landscape, and preventing and reducing disaster. Park green areas include comprehensive park, community park, topic park, belt-shaped park and green area nearby street. Total areas of comprehensive park, topic park and belt-shaped is the area of park.

**Public Transportation Vehicles per 10000 Population** refers to the number of public transportation vehicles, at the end of the reference period, per 10000 population in the city district. The formula for calculation is:

$$\frac{\text{Public Transportation Vehicles}}{\text{per 10000 Population}} = \frac{\text{Number of Public Transportation Vehicles}}{\text{City District Population}}$$

**Waste Water Discharged by Industry** refers to the volume of waste water discharged by industrial enterprises through all their outlets, including waste water from production process, directly cooled water, groundwater from mining wells which does not meet discharge standards and sewage from households mixed with waste water produced by industrial activities, but excluding indirectly cooled water discharged (It should be included if the discharge is not separated from waste water).

**Industrial Waste Water Meeting Discharge Standards** refers to volume of industrial waste water discharge which, with or without treatment, reaches national or local standards with regard to all pollutants.

**Ratio of Industrial Waste Water Meeting Discharge Standards** refers to percentage of industrial waste water meeting discharge standards over total industrial waste water discharge. It is calculated as:

$$\frac{\text{Ratio of industrial waste water}}{\text{meeting discharge standards}} = \frac{\text{industrial waste water meeting discharge standards}}{\text{total industrial waste water discharge}}$$

**Urban Non-industrial Waste Water Discharge** refers to annual discharge of non-industrial waste water by urban households. It is estimated by per capita coefficient using the formula:

$$\frac{\text{Urban non - industrial}}{\text{waste water discharge}} = \frac{\text{urban non - industrial waste}}{\text{water discharge coefficient}} \times \frac{\text{urban non - agricultural}}{\text{population}} \times 365$$

**Industrial Waste Air Emission** refers to the discharge into atmosphere of waste air containing pollutants generated from fuel burning and production processes in enterprises within a given period of time. It is calculated at standard status (273K, 101325Pa) as:

$$\frac{\text{Industrial waste}}{\text{air emission}} = \frac{\text{emission through}}{\text{fuel burning}} + \frac{\text{emission through}}{\text{production process}}$$

**$SO_2$ Emission through Industrial Activities** refers to volume of sulphur dioxide emission from fuel burning and production process by enterprises during a given period of time. It is calculated as:

$$\text{SO}_2\text{ emission through industrial activities} = \frac{\text{SO}_2\text{ emission from}}{\text{fuel burning}} + \frac{\text{SO}_2\text{ emission from}}{\text{production process}}$$

**Industrial Soot Emission** refers to the volume of soot in smoke emitted in the process of fuel burning in the premises of enterprises.

**Industrial Dust Emission** refers to volume of dust emitted by production process of enterprises and suspended in the air for a given period of time, including dust from refractory material of iron and steel works, dust from coke-screening systems and sintering machines of coke plants, dust from lime kilns and dust from cement production in building material enterprises, but excluding soot and dust emitted from power plants.

**Industrial Solid Wastes Produced** refers to total volume of solid, semi-solid and high concentration liquid residues produced by industrial enterprises from production process in a given period of time, including hazardous wastes, slag, coal ash, gangue, tailings, radioactive residues and other wastes, but excluding stones stripped or dug out in mining - gangue and acid or alkaline stones not included (a stone is acid or alkaline according to the pH value of the water being below 4 or above 10.5 when the stone is in, or soaked by water).

**Industrial Solid Wastes Utilized** refers to volume of solid wastes from which useful materials can be extracted or which can be converted into usable resources, energy or other materials by means of reclamation, processing, recycling and exchange (including utilizing in the year the stocks of industrial solid wastes of the previous year). Examples of such utilizations include fertilizers, building materials and road materials. The information shall be collected by the producing units of the wastes.

**Rate of Utilization of Industrial Solid Wastes** refers to the percentage of industrial solid wastes utilized over industrial solid wastes produced (including stocks of the previous years). It is calculated as:

$$\text{Rate of utilization of industrial solid wastes} = \frac{\text{volume of industrial solid wastes utilized}}{\text{industrial solid wastes produced + stock of previous years}} \times 100\%$$

**Industrial Solid Wastes Disposed** refers to the quantity of industrial solid wastes which are burnt or placed ultimately in the sites meeting the requirements for environmental protection and not salvaged or recycled (including disposition in the year of those wastes of previous years). The disposition includes landfill (Safe landfills should be conducted for hazardous wastes), incineration, containment spaces, deep underground disposal, backfill in mining pits and disposal at sea.

**Industrial Solid Wastes Discharged** refers to the volume of industrial solid wastes discharged by producing enterprises to disposal facilities or to other sites. The wastes exclude stones stripped or dug from mining (gangue and acid or alkaline waste stones not included).

**Output Value of Products Made from Waste Gas, Waste Water and Solid Wastes** refers to the current value of products with waste gas, waste water and solid wastes as main materials of production. Products sold and ready to sell shall be included while those produced for own use shall not be included.

# 二十、城市比较

## CHAPTER 20
## CITIES COMPARE

# 城市比较
# CITIES COMPARE

## 全国副省级城市
## CITIES UNDER PROVINCIAL LEVELS

| 沈 阳 | 哈尔滨 | 厦 门 | 武 汉 | 西 安 | 深 圳 | 成 都 | 济 南 |
|---|---|---|---|---|---|---|---|
| Shenyang | Haerbin | Xiamen | Wuhan | Xi'an | Shenzhen | Chengdu | Jinan |
| 大 连 | 宁 波 | 青 岛 | 广 州 | 南 京 | 长 春 | 杭 州 | |
| Dalian | Ningbo | Qingdao | Guangzhou | Nanjing | Changchun | Hangzhou | |

## 全国首批沿海开放城市
## FIRST BATCH OF OPEN COASTAL CITIES

| 大 连 | 秦皇岛 | 烟 台 | 连云港 | 宁 波 | 福 州 | 湛 江 |
|---|---|---|---|---|---|---|
| Dalian | Qinhuangdao | Yantai | Lianyungang | Ningbo | Fuzhou | Zhanjiang |
| 天 津 | 青 岛 | 南 通 | 上 海 | 温 州 | 广 州 | 北 海 |
| Tianjin | Qingdao | Nantong | Shanghai | Wenzhou | Guangzhou | Beihai |

## 全国首批历史文化名城
## FIRST BATCH OF HISTORICAL AND CULTURAL CITIES

| 北 京 | 大 同 | 苏 州 | 杭 州 | 泉 州 | 曲 阜 |
|---|---|---|---|---|---|
| Beijing | Datong | Suzhou | Hangzhou | Quanzhou | Qufu |
| 承 德 | 南 京 | 扬 州 | 绍 兴 | 景德镇 | 洛 阳 |
| Chengde | Nanjing | Yangzhou | Shaoxing | Jingdezhen | Luoyang |
| 开 封 | 长 沙 | 桂 林 | 遵 义 | 大 理 | 西 安 |
| Kaifeng | Changsha | Guilin | Zunyi | Dali | Xi'an |
| 江 陵 | 广 州 | 成 都 | 昆 明 | 拉 萨 | 延 安 |
| Jiangling | Guangzhou | Chengdu | Kunming | Lasa | Yanan |

表20-1

# 全国部分大中城市主要经济指标 (2012年)

单位：亿元

| 城　市 | City | 土地面积 (平方公里) Area of Land (sq.km) | 年末户籍总人口 (万人) Year-end Household Population (10 000 persons) | 地区生产总值 Gross Domestic Product | 第一产业 Primary Industry | 第二产业 Secondary Industry | 第三产业 Tertiary Industry | 按常住人口人均地区生产总值(元) Resident Population Per-capitaGDP (yuan) |
|---|---|---|---|---|---|---|---|---|
| 苏　州 | Suzhou | 8 488 | 647.81 | 12 011.65 | 195.08 | 6 502.25 | 5 314.32 | 114 029 |
| 南　京 | Nanjing | 6 587 | 638.48 | 7 201.57 | 185.06 | 3 170.78 | 3 845.73 | 88 525 |
| 无　锡 | Wuxi | 4 627 | 470.07 | 7 568.15 | 137.22 | 4 012.03 | 3 418.90 | 117 357 |
| 常　州 | Changzhou | 4 372 | 364.77 | 3 969.87 | 126.37 | 2 100.76 | 1 742.74 | 85 040 |
| 上　海 | Shanghai | 6 341 | 1 426.93 | 20 101.33 | 127.80 | 7 912.77 | 12 060.76 | 85 033 |
| 北　京 | Beijing | 16 411 | 1 297.50 | 17 801.00 | 150.30 | 4 058.30 | 13 592.40 | 87 091 |
| 天　津 | Tianjin | 11 917 | 993.20 | 12 885.18 | 171.54 | 6 663.68 | 6 049.96 | 93 110 |
| 重　庆 | Chongqing | 82 269 | 3 343.44 | 11 459.00 | 940.01 | 6 172.33 | 4 346.66 | 39 083 |
| 杭　州 | Hangzhou | 16 596 | 700.52 | 7 803.98 | 255.93 | 3 626.88 | 3 921.17 | 88 985 |
| 宁　波 | Ningbo | 9 816 | 577.71 | 6 524.70 | 269.97 | 3 516.73 | 2 738.02 | 85 475 |
| 温　州 | Wenzhou | 11 784 | 800.21 | 3 650.06 | 112.90 | 1 843.06 | 1 694.10 | 39 894 |
| 嘉　兴 | Jiaxing | 3 915 | 344.52 | 2 884.94 | 150.05 | 1 620.82 | 1 114.07 | 63 580 |
| 湖　州 | Huzhou | 5 820 | 261.38 | 1 661.97 | 123.31 | 888.20 | 650.46 | 57 270 |
| 福　州 | Fuzhou | 11 968 | 655.27 | 4 218.29 | 367.64 | 1 916.99 | 1 933.65 | 58 304 |
| 厦　门 | Xiamen | 1 573 | 190.92 | 2 817.07 | 25.21 | 1 374.01 | 1 417.85 | 77 392 |
| 广　州 | Guangzhou | 7 434 | 822.30 | 13 551.21 | 220.72 | 4 713.16 | 8 617.33 | 105 909 |
| 深　圳 | Shenzhen | 1 997 | 287.62 | 12 950.08 | 5.56 | 5 737.64 | 7 206.88 | 123 247 |
| 珠　海 | Zhuhai | 1 724 | 106.55 | 1 503.81 | 38.84 | 796.28 | 668.70 | 95 474 |
| 汕　头 | Shantou | 2 064 | 532.86 | 1 415.01 | 82.18 | 728.78 | 604.05 | 26 047 |
| 海　口 | Haikou | 2 305 | 161.59 | 820.58 | 57.74 | 201.67 | 561.17 | 38 719 |
| 济　南 | Jinan | 8 177 | 609.21 | 4 812.68 | 252.92 | 1 938.14 | 2 621.62 | 69 574 |
| 青　岛 | Qingdao | 11 282 | 769.56 | 7 302.11 | 324.41 | 3 402.23 | 3 575.47 | 82 680 |
| 威　海 | Weihai | 5 797 | 253.57 | 2 337.86 | 180.11 | 1 249.30 | 908.45 | 83 516 |
| 秦皇岛 | Qinhuangdao | 7 802 | 291.22 | 1 139.17 | 147.58 | 447.68 | 543.90 | 37 797 |
| 烟　台 | Yantai | 13 746 | 650.29 | 5 281.38 | 377.31 | 2 985.09 | 1 918.98 | 75 672 |
| 沈　阳 | Shenyang | 12 860 | 724.79 | 6 606.80 | 315.20 | 3 389.10 | 2 902.50 | 80 532 |
| 大　连 | Dalian | 12 574 | 590.30 | 7 002.80 | 451.40 | 3 634.80 | 2 916.70 | 102 216 |
| 长　春 | Changchun | 20 604 | 756.90 | 4 456.60 | 317.10 | 2 291.90 | 1 847.70 | 58 691 |
| 吉　林 | Jilin | 27 120 | 430.80 | 2 430.00 | 242.70 | 1 207.50 | 979.80 | 56 408 |
| 武　汉 | Wuhan | 8 494 | 821.71 | 8 003.82 | 301.21 | 3 869.56 | 3 833.05 | 79 482 |
| 成　都 | Chengdu | 12 121 | 1 173.35 | 8 138.94 | 348.07 | 3 790.62 | 4 000.25 | 57 624 |
| 西　安 | Xi'an | 10 108 | 795.98 | 4 369.37 | 195.59 | 1 893.79 | 2 279.99 | 51 205 |
| 哈尔滨 | Haerbin | 53 068 | 993.50 | 4 550.10 | 506.80 | 1 638.90 | 2 404.40 | 45 810 |

# MAJOR ECONOMIC INDICATORS OF MAIN LARGE AND MEDIUM-SIZED CITIES (2012)

(100 million yuan)

| 农林牧渔业总产值 Gross Output Value of Farming, Forestry, Animal Husbandry and Fishery | 规模以上工业企业 Industry Enterprises Above Designated Size | | | | 全社会用电量 (亿千瓦时) Electricity Consumption of the Whole Society (100 million kwh) | |
|---|---|---|---|---|---|---|
| | 总产值 Gross Output Value | 主营业务收入 Major Business Revenue | 利税总额 Total Tax and Profits | # 利润总额 Total Profits | | # 工 业 Industry |
| 337.72 | 28 745.54 | 28 998.80 | 1 816.35 | 1 251.57 | 1 189.93 | 982.66 |
| 318.54 | 11 437.80 | 11 283.26 | 1 372.78 | 604.44 | 424.96 | 265.64 |
| 224.15 | 14 446.85 | 14 191.69 | 1 261.48 | 878.69 | 578.01 | 464.51 |
| 219.58 | 8 970.30 | 9 097.95 | 730.30 | 443.77 | 351.51 | 277.88 |
| 320.76 | 31 548.41 | 33 738.32 | 3 768.61 | 2 131.33 | 1 353.45 | 786.25 |
| 395.70 | 15 405.80 | 16 851.20 | 1 962.50 | 1 216.60 | 874.30 | 298.10 |
| 375.62 | 23 250.54 | 23 570.38 | 2 962.23 | 1 939.96 | 722.49 | 510.21 |
| 1 402.03 | 13 104.02 | 12 715.72 | 1 187.77 | 608.29 | 723.03 | 469.39 |
| 384.34 | 12 884.26 | 12 404.24 | 1 289.93 | 751.75 | 591.72 | 396.19 |
| 420.50 | 12 155.08 | 11 795.98 | 1 112.86 | 553.21 | 514.09 | 384.59 |
| 185.11 | 4 166.68 | 3 890.61 | 330.46 | 191.22 | 326.95 | 210.51 |
| 253.85 | 6 004.13 | 5 606.55 | 432.13 | 255.91 | 351.42 | 289.23 |
| 208.48 | 3 396.26 | 3 341.76 | 256.69 | 158.79 | 165.84 | 126.50 |
| 624.93 | 5 890.58 | 5 389.24 | 591.34 | 380.83 | 322.56 | 196.39 |
| 41.29 | 4 430.79 | 4 405.18 | 366.67 | 227.81 | 182.89 | 101.52 |
| 379.73 | 16 066.43 | 15 728.35 | 1 594.64 | 825.60 | 694.13 | 358.95 |
| 14.86 | 20 883.90 | 20 395.87 | 1 608.66 | 1 064.77 | 722.10 | 423.24 |
| 69.80 | 3 035.45 | 3 444.23 | 231.35 | 148.73 | 117.47 | 72.58 |
| 148.85 | 2 111.54 | 2 072.74 | 234.53 | 164.88 | 154.36 | 94.01 |
| 91.14 | 516.02 | 505.80 | 73.96 | 39.99 | 52.67 | 14.49 |
| 451.86 | | 5 032.40 | 420.60 | 176.90 | 253.60 | 248.90 |
| 566.52 | 14 426.08 | 13 751.98 | 1 255.28 | 670.73 | 318.00 | 200.00 |
| 351.36 | 5 626.87 | 5 569.03 | 496.83 | 308.11 | 97.50 | 66.80 |
| 273.95 | 1 495.09 | 1 541.05 | 49.55 | 10.13 | 159.72 | 119.54 |
| 674.75 | 12 596.55 | 12 627.04 | 1 274.38 | 971.15 | 353.81 | 280.36 |
| 603.33 | 12 858.35 | 12 582.35 | 1 099.75 | 716.05 | 270.00 | 141.20 |
| 823.60 | 10 331.10 | 9 720.00 | 855.60 | 349.40 | 287.30 | 188.10 |
| 562.50 | 8 262.60 | 8 595.10 | 1 083.10 | 623.20 | 179.00 | 100.50 |
| 424.10 | 3 019.40 | 3 019.90 | 242.20 | 62.60 | 152.40 | 122.40 |
| 476.04 | 9 018.88 | 9 448.74 | 1 029.79 | 361.75 | 403.26 | 230.13 |
| 577.84 | | 7 611.10 | 1 148.80 | 581.30 | 411.80 | 209.87 |
| 308.60 | 4 023.19 | 3 529.20 | 251.90 | 132.80 | 235.26 | 93.26 |
| 991.20 | 2 775.20 | 2 427.20 | 287.00 | 103.20 | 191.50 | 92.50 |

表20-1 续表

单位：亿元

| 城　市 | City | 进出口总额(亿美元) Total Imports and Exports (USD 100 million) | # 出口总额 Total Exports | 外商及港澳台商投资企业(亿美元) Enterprises with Investment from Foreign ,Hong Kong,Macao and Taiwan (USD 100 million) 合同外资金额 Contractual Foreign Investment | 实际利用外资 Amount of Foreign Capital Actually Used | 全社会固定资产投资额 Total Investment in Fixed Assets | # 房地产开发 Real Estate Development |
|---|---|---|---|---|---|---|---|
| 苏　州 | Suzhou | 3 056.92 | 1 746.89 | 151.68 | 91.65 | 5 266.49 | 1 263.36 |
| 南　京 | Nanjing | 552.35 | 319.01 | 61.66 | 41.30 | 4 010.03 | 871.43 |
| 无　锡 | Wuxi | 707.72 | 413.13 | 43.31 | 40.10 | 3 618.07 | 974.37 |
| 常　州 | Changzhou | 290.28 | 199.60 | 54.20 | 33.61 | 2 760.14 | 597.01 |
| 上　海 | Shanghai | 4 367.58 | 2 068.07 | 223.38 | 151.85 | 5 254.38 | 2 381.36 |
| 北　京 | Beijing | 4 079.20 | 596.50 | 113.50 | 80.40 | 6 462.81 | 3 153.40 |
| 天　津 | Tianjin | 1 156.23 | 483.14 | 185.85 | 150.16 | 8 871.31 | 1 260.00 |
| 重　庆 | Chongqing | 532.04 | 385.71 | 72.62 | 105.33 | 9 380.00 | 2 508.35 |
| 杭　州 | Hangzhou | 616.83 | 412.62 | 82.65 | 49.61 | 3722.75 | 1 597.36 |
| 宁　波 | Ningbo | 965.73 | 614.45 | 53.13 | 28.53 | 2901.43 | 884.35 |
| 温　州 | Wenzhou | 204.38 | 176.96 | 5.92 | 3.98 | 2 357.11 | 687.50 |
| 嘉　兴 | Jiaxing | 287.44 | 196.03 | 28.14 | 17.82 | 1 642.31 | 415.88 |
| 湖　州 | Huzhou | 87.37 | 73.96 | 16.87 | 10.26 | 970.73 | 211.17 |
| 福　州 | Fuzhou | 310.60 | 211.31 | 20.56 | 13.39 | 3 266.49 | 972.27 |
| 厦　门 | Xiamen | 744.91 | 454.02 | 18.28 | 15.95 | 1 332.64 | 518.88 |
| 广　州 | Guangzhou | 1 171.31 | 589.12 | 69.31 | 47.43 | 3 758.39 | 1 370.45 |
| 深　圳 | Shenzhen | 4 667.85 | 2 713.70 | 62.62 | 52.29 | 2 314.43 | 1 046.62 |
| 珠　海 | Zhuhai | 456.69 | 216.31 | 21.90 | 14.47 | 787.62 | 242.08 |
| 汕　头 | Shantou | 88.02 | 61.63 | 1.57 | 1.31 | 611.72 | 83.35 |
| 海　口 | Haikou | 42.15 | 17.98 | 0.20 | 4.53 | 510.38 | 175.55 |
| 济　南 | Jinan | 91.50 | 57.20 | 16.20 | 12.20 | 2 186.10 | 663.30 |
| 青　岛 | Qingdao | 732.08 | 408.20 | 60.02 | 46.00 | 4 153.90 | 930.10 |
| 威　海 | Weihai | 135.59 | 84.54 | 9.10 | 8.00 | 1 595.45 | 366.19 |
| 秦皇岛 | Qinhuangdao | 44.12 | 24.88 | 4.29 | 6.23 | 739.30 | 213.32 |
| 烟　台 | Yantai | 478.02 | 283.59 | 24.34 | 14.10 | 3 043.92 | 573.52 |
| 沈　阳 | Shenyang | 127.48 | 59.65 | 29.92 | 58.04 | 5 625.40 | 1 942.96 |
| 大　连 | Dalian | 641.10 | 346.80 | 91.60 | 123.50 | 5 654.10 | 1 396.50 |
| 长　春 | Changchun | 196.80 | 29.00 | 8.50 | 36.80 | 3 172.90 | 649.70 |
| 吉　林 | Jilin | 11.50 | 4.90 | 7.10 | 1.78 | 1 954.40 | 248.80 |
| 武　汉 | Wuhan | 203.54 | 107.48 |  | 44.44 | 5 031.25 | 1 574.86 |
| 成　都 | Chengdu | 475.39 | 303.61 | 39.50 | 85.90 | 5 890.10 | 1 890.00 |
| 西　安 | Xi'an | 130.14 | 72.99 | 36.03 | 24.78 | 4 243.43 | 1 281.90 |
| 哈尔滨 | Haerbin | 53.30 | 18.60 | 6.50 | 19.00 | 3 950.00 | 772.00 |

Continued

(100 million yuan)

| 社会消费品零售总额 Total Retail Sales of Consumer Goods | 地方公共财政预算收入 General Budgetary Revenue | 地方公共财政预算支出 General Budgetary Expenditure | 城乡居民储蓄存款余额 Urban and Rural Savings Deposits | 市区居民消费价格总指数(%) General Consumer Price Index (%) | 城镇居民人均可支配收入(元) Per Capita Disposable Income of Town Residents (yuan) | 农民人均纯收入(元) Per Capita Net Income of Rural Residents (yuan) |
|---|---|---|---|---|---|---|
| 3 240.97 | 1 204.33 | 1 113.47 | 5 787.75 | 102.7 | 39 079 | 19 396 |
| 3 103.82 | 733.02 | 769.66 | 4 465.37 | 102.7 | 35 092 | 14 786 |
| 2 443.24 | 658.03 | 648.61 | 3 731.83 | 102.5 | 35 663 | 18 509 |
| 1 413.33 | 378.99 | 391.22 | 2 473.27 | 102.5 | 33 326 | 16 737 |
| 7 387.32 | 3 743.71 | 4 184.02 | 19 506.70 | 102.8 | 40 188 | 17 401 |
| 7 702.80 | 3 314.90 | 3 685.30 | 21 419.30 | 103.3 | 36 469 | 16 476 |
| 3 921.43 | 1 760.02 | 2 143.21 | 7 055.38 | 102.7 | 29 626 | 13 571 |
| 3 961.19 | 1 703.49 | 3 046.36 | 8 472.51 | 102.6 | 22 968 | 7 383 |
| 2 944.63 | 859.99 | 786.28 | 6 022.08 | 102.5 | 37 511 | 17 017 |
| 2 329.26 | 725.50 | 828.44 | 4 175.96 | 101.7 | 38 043 | 18 475 |
| 1 929.29 | 279.01 | 387.79 | 3 616.96 | 102.3 | 34 820 | 14 719 |
| 1 083.74 | 257.73 | 260.70 | 2 144.49 | 102.2 | 35 696 | 18 636 |
| 703.87 | 138.55 | 167.51 | 1 078.46 | 102.0 | 32 987 | 17 188 |
| 2 319.82 | 382.01 | 409.37 | 2 939.46 | 102.2 | 29 399 | 11 492 |
| 881.91 | 422.91 | 462.69 | 1 680.19 | 102.1 | 37 576 | 13 455 |
| 5 977.27 | 1 102.25 | 1 343.76 | 11 310.69 | 103.0 | 38 054 | 16 788 |
| 4 008.78 | 1 482.08 | 1 565.71 | 8 389.06 | 102.8 | 40 742 | – |
| 635.20 | 162.60 | 212.15 | 1 216.75 | 102.8 | 32 978 | 13 399 |
| 1 029.82 | 96.34 | 173.28 | 1 534.46 | 102.6 | 20 024 | 9 032 |
| 436.26 | 71.17 | 113.85 | 952.15 | 103.3 | 22 331 | 8 134 |
| 2 323.60 | 380.80 | 465.70 | 2 888.70 | 102.4 | 29 505 | 11 786 |
| 2 564.50 | 670.18 | 765.98 | 3 757.60 | 102.7 | 32 145 | 13 990 |
| 953.87 | 158.40 | 244.31 | 1 205.74 | 101.8 | 28 630 | 13 962 |
| 453.81 | 108.66 | 199.97 | 1 150.19 | 103.1 | 21 919 | 8 315 |
| 1 859.82 | 357.36 | 476.87 | 2 767.33 | 101.8 | 30 045 | 13 298 |
| 2 802.20 | 715.00 | 765.10 | 4 318.80 | 103.0 | 26 431 | 13 045 |
| 2 224.00 | 750.10 | 891.00 | 4 160.50 | 103.4 | 27 539 | 15 990 |
| 1 739.60 | 340.80 | 555.51 | 2 767.30 | 102.3 | 22 970 | – |
| 935.60 | 259.60 | 284.90 | 1 148.50 | 102.3 | 22 068 | 9 224 |
| 3 432.43 | 828.58 | 874.78 | 4 728.66 | 102.8 | 27 061 | 11 190 |
| 3 317.70 | 780.90 | 983.85 | 7 060.00 | 103.0 | 27 194 | 11 501 |
| 2 236.06 | 396.96 | 597.49 | 4 787.03 | 102.8 | 29 982 | 11 442 |
| 2 394.60 | 354.70 | 643.60 | 3 320.70 | 103.2 | 22 499 | 11 443 |

表20-2

# 全省各省辖市主要经济指标 (2012年)

| 城市 | City | 土地面积 (平方公里) Area of Land (sq.km) | 年末户籍人口 (万人) Year-end Household Population (10 000 persons) | 年末常住人口 (万人) Year-end Resident Population (10 000 persons) | 地区生产总值 (亿元) Gross Domestic Product (100 million yuan) | | |
|---|---|---|---|---|---|---|---|
| | | | | | | 第一产业 Primary Industry | 第二产业 Secondary Industry |
| **江苏省** | **Jiangsu Province** | **102 658** | **7 553.43** | **7 920.00** | **54 058.22** | **3 418.29** | **27 121.95** |
| 南京市 | Nanjing City | 6 587 | 638.48 | 816.10 | 7 201.57 | 185.06 | 3 170.78 |
| 无锡市 | Wuxi City | 4 627 | 470.07 | 646.55 | 7 568.15 | 137.22 | 4 012.03 |
| 徐州市 | Xuzhou City | 11 259 | 990.53 | 856.41 | 4 016.58 | 382.46 | 1 968.52 |
| 常州市 | Changzhou City | 4 372 | 364.77 | 468.68 | 3 969.87 | 126.37 | 2 100.76 |
| **苏州市** | **Suzhou City** | **8 488** | **647.81** | **1 054.91** | **12 011.65** | **195.08** | **6 502.25** |
| 南通市 | Nantong City | 8 001 | 765.20 | 729.73 | 4 558.67 | 319.09 | 2 414.11 |
| 连云港市 | Lianyungang City | 7 615 | 510.99 | 440.69 | 1 603.42 | 232.40 | 736.14 |
| 淮安市 | Huaian City | 10 072 | 546.81 | 480.30 | 1 920.91 | 247.98 | 889.20 |
| 盐城市 | Yancheng City | 16 972 | 822.40 | 721.63 | 3 120.00 | 456.13 | 1 472.87 |
| 扬州市 | Yangzhou City | 6 591 | 458.42 | 446.72 | 2 933.20 | 205.19 | 1 554.46 |
| 镇江市 | Zhenjiang City | 3 847 | 271.40 | 315.48 | 2 630.42 | 115.77 | 1 419.54 |
| 泰州市 | Taizhou City | 5 787 | 506.35 | 462.98 | 2 701.67 | 191.75 | 1 434.53 |
| 宿迁市 | Suqian City | 8 555 | 560.26 | 479.80 | 1 522.03 | 226.80 | 716.85 |

# MAJOR ECONOMIC INDICATORS OF THE PROVINCIAL CITIES OF JIANGSU PROVINCE (2012)

| 第三产业 Tertiary Industry | 按常住人口人均地区生产总值(元) Resident Population Per-capitaGDP (yuan) | 农林牧渔业总产值(亿元) Gross Output Value of Farming,Forestry,Animal Husbandry and Fishery (100 million yuan) | 粮食产量 (万吨) Total of Grain (10 000 tons) | 棉花产量 (万吨) Total of Cotton (10 000 tons) | 油料产量 (万吨) Total of Oil-bearing Crops (10 000 tons) | 牛奶产量 (万吨) Total of Cow Milk (10 000 tons) |
|---|---|---|---|---|---|---|
| **23 517.98** | **68 347** | **5 808.81** | **3 372.48** | **22.04** | **146.95** | **61.30** |
| 3 845.73 | 88 525 | 318.54 | 117.50 | 0.41 | 10.63 | 8.25 |
| 3 418.90 | 117 357 | 224.15 | 81.65 | – | 0.87 | 3.17 |
| 1 665.60 | 46 877 | 712.55 | 471.73 | 3.67 | 10.63 | 26.78 |
| 1 742.74 | 85 040 | 219.58 | 114.80 | 0.05 | 3.77 | 2.40 |
| **5 314.32** | **114 029** | **337.72** | **116.46** | **0.13** | **2.59** | **9.25** |
| 1 825.47 | 62 506 | 548.86 | 332.97 | 5.53 | 39.20 | 2.56 |
| 634.88 | 36 470 | 426.24 | 361.35 | 0.28 | 11.78 | 2.48 |
| 783.73 | 39 992 | 456.18 | 456.11 | 0.05 | 9.95 | 3.29 |
| 1 191.00 | 43 172 | 925.20 | 672.71 | 10.92 | 30.94 | 5.60 |
| 1 173.55 | 65 691 | 369.08 | 308.35 | 0.47 | 7.41 | 0.99 |
| 1 095.11 | 83 651 | 176.49 | 125.66 | 0.19 | 5.66 | 2.31 |
| 1 075.39 | 58 378 | 322.11 | 323.77 | 1.55 | 11.63 | 4.23 |
| 578.38 | 31 827 | 415.98 | 388.75 | 0.24 | 4.75 | 2.43 |

表20-2 续表 1

| 城　市 | City | 肉类产量(万吨) Total of Meat (10 000 tons) | 水产品产量(万吨) Total of Aquatic Products(10 000 tons) | 规模以上工业企业(亿元) Industrial Enterprises Above | | |
|---|---|---|---|---|---|---|
| | | | | 总产值 Total Output Value | 应收账款净额 Net Account Receivable | 主营业务收入 Major Business Revenue |
| **江苏省** | **Jiangsu Province** | **396.52** | **493.74** | **120 124.91** | **13 263.73** | **117 774.29** |
| 南京市 | Nanjing City | 12.42 | 20.75 | 11 437.80 | 1 331.13 | 11 283.26 |
| 无锡市 | Wuxi City | 10.95 | 12.61 | 14 446.85 | 2 377.47 | 14 191.69 |
| 徐州市 | Xuzhou City | 97.14 | 18.14 | 8 882.29 | 616.18 | 8 837.26 |
| 常州市 | Changzhou City | 14.32 | 18.12 | 8 970.30 | 1 187.05 | 9 097.95 |
| **苏州市** | **Suzhou City** | **14.21** | **28.84** | **28 745.54** | **4 588.02** | **28 998.80** |
| 南通市 | Nantong City | 48.11 | 84.81 | 9 890.12 | 822.21 | 9 690.95 |
| 连云港市 | Lianyungang City | 29.55 | 70.13 | 3 413.38 | 207.77 | 3 346.45 |
| 淮安市 | Huaian City | 32.03 | 25.17 | 3 952.61 | 185.60 | 3 953.91 |
| 盐城市 | Yancheng City | 88.94 | 106.11 | 5 554.35 | 307.49 | 5 561.88 |
| 扬州市 | Yangzhou City | 19.11 | 39.20 | 7 198.48 | 533.76 | 7 037.79 |
| 镇江市 | Zhenjiang City | 8.49 | 8.92 | 6 105.69 | 589.61 | 5 975.34 |
| 泰州市 | Taizhou City | 25.63 | 35.91 | 7 127.29 | 558.68 | 6 918.60 |
| 宿迁市 | Suqian City | 36.65 | 24.97 | 2 248.28 | 104.59 | 2 213.14 |

Continued 1

| Designated Size (100 million yuan) | | 规模以上固定资产投资(亿元) Fixed Assets Investment above Designated Size (100 million yuan) | 全社会用电量(亿千瓦时) Electricity Consumption of the Whole Society (100 million kwh) | | 社会消费品零售总额(亿元) Total Retail Sales of Consumer Goods (100 million yuan) | 进出口总额(亿美元) Total Imports and Exports (USD 100 million) | |
|---|---|---|---|---|---|---|---|
| 利润总额 Total Profits | 利税总额 Total Tax and Profits | | | # 工业 Industry | | | # 出口 Exports |
| **7 250.20** | **11 934.34** | **31 706.58** | **4 580.90** | **3 562.48** | **18 331.30** | **5 480.93** | **3 285.38** |
| 604.44 | 1 372.78 | 4 558.49 | 424.96 | 265.64 | 3 103.82 | 552.35 | 319.01 |
| 878.69 | 1 261.48 | 3 618.07 | 578.01 | 464.51 | 2 443.24 | 707.72 | 413.13 |
| 743.38 | 1 319.96 | 2 685.89 | 318.57 | 246.08 | 1 312.50 | 83.27 | 62.88 |
| 443.77 | 730.30 | 2 621.56 | 351.51 | 277.88 | 1 413.33 | 290.28 | 199.60 |
| **1 251.57** | **1 816.35** | **5 142.51** | **1 189.93** | **982.66** | **3 240.97** | **3 056.92** | **1 746.89** |
| 786.59 | 1 160.15 | 2 886.47 | 301.79 | 222.96 | 1 719.27 | 263.01 | 187.86 |
| 273.20 | 423.96 | 1 280.88 | 115.97 | 75.91 | 575.49 | 80.02 | 36.01 |
| 209.13 | 378.48 | 1 247.99 | 134.78 | 95.50 | 633.24 | 42.38 | 33.64 |
| 396.91 | 690.89 | 1 940.89 | 225.31 | 164.49 | 1 023.20 | 57.54 | 34.65 |
| 498.81 | 865.25 | 1 783.65 | 173.63 | 123.20 | 973.97 | 101.73 | 81.72 |
| 363.11 | 567.37 | 1 500.67 | 193.47 | 151.62 | 766.46 | 114.13 | 77.37 |
| 538.06 | 900.98 | 1 454.59 | 211.31 | 164.81 | 737.57 | 103.67 | 69.45 |
| 250.83 | 346.38 | 1 025.56 | 114.34 | 79.90 | 388.23 | 27.93 | 23.18 |

表20-2 续表 2

| 城　市 | City | 实际利用外资(亿美元) Foreign Capital Actually Utilized (USD 100 million) | 地方公共财政预算收入(亿元) General Budgetary Revenue (100 million yuan) | 地方公共财政预算支出(亿元) General Budgetary Expenditure (100 million yuan) | 金融机构人民币存款余额(亿元) RMB Deposits Balance of National Banking System (100 million yuan) | # 储蓄存款 Saving Deposits of Urban and Rural Residents |
|---|---|---|---|---|---|---|
| **江苏省** | **Jiangsu Province** | **357.60** | **5 860.69** | **7 027.67** | **75 481.51** | **30 057.19** |
| 南京市 | Nanjing City | 41.30 | 733.02 | 769.66 | 16 131.41 | 4 465.37 |
| 无锡市 | Wuxi City | 40.10 | 658.03 | 648.61 | 10 293.40 | 3 731.83 |
| 徐州市 | Xuzhou City | 17.00 | 366.76 | 530.05 | 3 364.47 | 1 794.72 |
| 常州市 | Changzhou City | 33.61 | 378.99 | 391.22 | 5 604.90 | 2 473.27 |
| **苏州市** | **Suzhou City** | **91.65** | **1 204.33** | **1 113.47** | **17 663.50** | **5 787.75** |
| 南通市 | Nantong City | 22.05 | 419.72 | 513.01 | 6 297.19 | 3 588.06 |
| 连云港市 | Lianyungang City | 7.34 | 208.94 | 312.55 | 1 503.66 | 723.59 |
| 淮安市 | Huaian City | 21.21 | 233.61 | 339.86 | 1 502.79 | 806.86 |
| 盐城市 | Yancheng City | 21.11 | 312.78 | 473.48 | 2 699.33 | 1 519.33 |
| 扬州市 | Yangzhou City | 21.38 | 225.00 | 284.80 | 3 310.84 | 1 697.51 |
| 镇江市 | Zhenjiang City | 22.14 | 215.48 | 235.25 | 2 850.51 | 1 301.36 |
| 泰州市 | Taizhou City | 14.50 | 223.62 | 300.90 | 3 032.63 | 1 546.53 |
| 宿迁市 | Suqian City | 4.52 | 158.13 | 272.40 | 1 226.87 | 621.02 |

Continued 2

| 金融机构人民币贷款余额(亿元) RMB Loans Balance of National Banking System (100 million yuan) | 在岗职工平均工资(元) Average Wage of Staff and Workers (yuan) | 城镇居民人均可支配收入(元) Per Capita Disposable Income of Town Residents(yuan) | 城镇居民人均消费性支出(元) Per Capita Living Expenditure for Consumption of Town Resident s(yuan) | 农民人均纯收入(元) Per Capita Net Income of Rural (yuan) | 农民人均消费性支出(元) Per Capital Living Expenditure of Rural (yuan) | 市区居民消费价格总指数(%) General Consumer Price Index(%) |
|---|---|---|---|---|---|---|
| **54 412.30** | **51 279** | **29 677** | **18 825** | **12 202** | **8 655** | **102.6** |
| 12 314.41 | 60 404 | 35 092 | 22 446 | 14 786 | 11 114 | 102.7 |
| 7 467.03 | 56 883 | 35 663 | 23 000 | 18 509 | 12 795 | 102.5 |
| 2 047.23 | 44 070 | 21 716 | 13 730 | 10 762 | 6 742 | 102.6 |
| 3 832.80 | 55 764 | 33 326 | 20 918 | 16 737 | 12 027 | 102.5 |
| **13 626.86** | **57 622** | **39 079** | **25 157** | **19 396** | **14 381** | **102.7** |
| 3 832.14 | 49 399 | 28 292 | 17 858 | 13 231 | 9 839 | 102.5 |
| 1 196.58 | 44 124 | 20 816 | 12 726 | 9 589 | 6 210 | 102.3 |
| 1 173.18 | 41 966 | 20 950 | 14 458 | 9 838 | 6 493 | 102.4 |
| 1 831.44 | 40 357 | 21 941 | 15 430 | 11 898 | 6 998 | 102.8 |
| 2 006.50 | 44 689 | 25 712 | 16 492 | 12 686 | 8 714 | 102.6 |
| 2 073.29 | 47 626 | 30 045 | 17 897 | 14 518 | 10 530 | 102.4 |
| 2 007.97 | 42 985 | 26 574 | 16 499 | 12 493 | 8 990 | 101.7 |
| 1 002.86 | 36 624 | 16 991 | 11 864 | 9 495 | 6 594 | 102.8 |

表20-3

# 全省分县(市)主要经济指标 (2012年)

| 市县名称 | City and County | 年末户籍人口(万人) Year-end Household Population (10 000 persons) | 地区生产总值(亿元) Gross Domestic Product (100 million yuan) | 第一产业 Primary Industry | 第二产业 Secondary Industry | 第三产业 Tertiary Industry |
|---|---|---|---|---|---|---|
| **南京市** | **Nanjing** | | | | | |
| 溧水县 | Lishui County | 41.88 | 369.38 | 29.33 | 222.11 | 117.94 |
| 高淳县 | Gaochun County | 43.26 | 365.27 | 30.29 | 193.31 | 141.67 |
| **无锡市** | **Wuxi** | | | | | |
| 江阴市 | Jiangyin City | 121.07 | 2 535.38 | 47.69 | 1 443.91 | 1 043.78 |
| 宜兴市 | Yixing City | 107.73 | 1 085.98 | 47.68 | 581.22 | 457.08 |
| **徐州市** | **Xuzhou** | | | | | |
| 丰 县 | Feng County | 116.62 | 228.73 | 46.39 | 103.82 | 78.52 |
| 沛 县 | Pei County | 128.67 | 431.30 | 67.91 | 203.81 | 159.58 |
| 睢宁县 | Suining County | 137.36 | 302.45 | 57.18 | 132.34 | 112.93 |
| 新沂市 | Xinyi City | 107.15 | 350.16 | 47.91 | 149.44 | 152.81 |
| 邳州市 | Pizhou City | 179.86 | 513.49 | 79.32 | 223.64 | 210.53 |
| **常州市** | **Changzhou** | | | | | |
| 溧阳市 | Liyang City | 78.99 | 559.20 | 39.02 | 306.58 | 213.60 |
| 金坛市 | Jintan City | 55.31 | 373.81 | 27.64 | 197.80 | 148.37 |
| **苏州市** | **Suzhou** | | | | | |
| 常熟市 | Changshu City | 106.78 | 1 870.19 | 37.02 | 996.95 | 836.22 |
| 张家港市 | Zhangjiagang City | 91.02 | 2 050.58 | 27.53 | 1 175.51 | 847.54 |
| 昆山市 | Kunshan City | 73.76 | 2 725.32 | 24.46 | 1 631.25 | 1 069.61 |
| 太仓市 | Taicang City | 47.26 | 955.12 | 33.61 | 520.36 | 401.15 |

# MAIN ECONOMIC INDICATORS OF COUNTRIES (CITIES) OF THE PROVINCE (2012)

| 粮食产量 (万吨) Total of Grain (10 000 tons) | 地方公共财政预算收入(亿元) Budgetary Revenue (100 million yuan) | 社会消费品零售总额(亿元) Total Retail Sales of Consumer Goods (100 million yuan) | 工业用电量 (亿千瓦时) Electricity Consumption of Industry (100 million kwh) | 出口总额 (亿美元) Total Exports (USD 100 million) | 实际利用外资 (亿美元) Foreign Capital Actually Utilized (USD 100 million) | 农民人均纯收入 (元) Per Capita Net Income of Rural (yuan) |
|---|---|---|---|---|---|---|
| | | | | | | |
| 24.46 | 29.20 | 103.18 | 10.36 | 3.17 | 1.51 | 14 356 |
| 18.70 | 22.00 | 120.07 | 3.21 | 3.12 | 0.81 | 14 816 |
| | | | | | | |
| 20.35 | 167.19 | 515.48 | 205.88 | 105.15 | 7.98 | 19 660 |
| 48.72 | 78.38 | 371.28 | 70.66 | 31.89 | 4.70 | 16 862 |
| | | | | | | |
| 52.89 | 24.92 | 68.58 | 9.61 | 1.71 | 0.69 | 9 783 |
| 61.17 | 38.96 | 124.42 | 21.32 | 3.69 | 1.70 | 11 351 |
| 91.62 | 25.56 | 85.22 | 13.10 | 4.89 | 1.29 | 9 541 |
| 65.69 | 32.85 | 83.06 | 28.03 | 2.51 | 1.85 | 9 808 |
| 82.77 | 42.12 | 114.06 | 18.31 | 14.02 | 1.80 | 11 282 |
| | | | | | | |
| 54.52 | 40.50 | 198.26 | 50.54 | 8.55 | 4.05 | 15 261 |
| 28.26 | 23.11 | 156.73 | 31.17 | 13.65 | 2.51 | 15 608 |
| | | | | | | |
| 32.22 | 128.15 | 499.54 | 123.65 | 129.21 | 9.56 | 19 467 |
| 28.05 | 149.61 | 370.73 | 246.75 | 128.11 | 9.52 | 19 460 |
| 12.42 | 220.28 | 493.62 | 146.47 | 555.17 | 17.54 | 19 563 |
| 21.48 | 90.15 | 195.07 | 68.79 | 56.60 | 8.11 | 19 411 |

表20-3 续表 1

| 市县名称 | City and County | 年末户籍人口 (万人) Year-end Household Population (10 000 persons) | 地区生产总值 (亿元) Gross Domestic Product (100 million yuan) | | | |
|---|---|---|---|---|---|---|
| | | | | 第一产业 Primary Industry | 第二产业 Secondary Industry | 第三产业 Tertiary Industry |
| **南通市** | **Nantong** | | | | | |
| 海安县 | Haian County | 93.87 | 480.14 | 47.69 | 246.30 | 186.15 |
| 如东县 | Rudong County | 104.60 | 478.00 | 56.56 | 243.03 | 178.41 |
| 启东市 | Qidong City | 112.38 | 589.14 | 61.48 | 306.09 | 221.57 |
| 如皋市 | Rugao City | 142.50 | 590.17 | 52.77 | 318.49 | 218.90 |
| 海门市 | Haimen City | 99.97 | 663.10 | 46.50 | 377.60 | 239.00 |
| **连云港市** | **LianyunGang** | | | | | |
| 赣榆县 | Ganyu County | 115.58 | 331.36 | 50.46 | 166.07 | 114.83 |
| 东海县 | Donghai County | 118.02 | 277.30 | 51.02 | 127.37 | 98.91 |
| 灌云县 | Guanyun County | 102.01 | 220.29 | 50.34 | 102.23 | 67.72 |
| 灌南县 | Guannan County | 78.73 | 210.47 | 39.39 | 105.28 | 65.80 |
| **淮安市** | **Huaian** | | | | | |
| 涟水县 | Lianshui County | 111.39 | 228.64 | 45.01 | 93.66 | 89.97 |
| 洪泽县 | Hongze County | 38.59 | 155.09 | 25.17 | 66.89 | 63.03 |
| 盱眙县 | Xuyi County | 78.30 | 221.88 | 40.49 | 96.50 | 84.89 |
| 金湖县 | Jinhu County | 35.71 | 142.39 | 22.94 | 58.42 | 61.03 |
| **盐城市** | **Yancheng** | | | | | |
| 响水县 | Xiangshui County | 61.48 | 181.35 | 35.58 | 89.85 | 55.92 |
| 滨海县 | Binhai County | 120.05 | 267.69 | 49.70 | 117.89 | 100.10 |
| 阜宁县 | Funing County | 110.88 | 274.99 | 46.34 | 131.61 | 97.04 |
| 射阳县 | Sheyang County | 96.66 | 320.31 | 69.59 | 129.38 | 121.34 |

Continued 1

| 粮食产量(万吨) Total of Grain (10 000 tons) | 地方公共财政预算收入(亿元) Budgetary Revenue (100 million yuan) | 社会消费品零售总额(亿元) Total Retail Sales of Consumer Goods (100 million yuan) | 工业用电量(亿千瓦时) Electricity Consumption of Industry (100 million kwh) | 出口总额(亿美元) Total Exports (USD 100 million) | 实际利用外资(亿美元) Foreign Capital Actually Utilized (USD 100 million) | 农民人均纯收入(元) Per Capita Net Income of Rural (yuan) |
|---|---|---|---|---|---|---|
| | | | | | | |
| 63.29 | 37.53 | 181.98 | 30.61 | 12.79 | 2.52 | 12 663 |
| 91.89 | 32.17 | 202.18 | 27.88 | 9.99 | 3.20 | 12 156 |
| 26.39 | 52.21 | 228.73 | 15.96 | 14.43 | 2.39 | 14 127 |
| 74.02 | 53.60 | 229.85 | 31.02 | 23.72 | 2.14 | 11 663 |
| 18.43 | 51.61 | 237.12 | 22.36 | 12.38 | 1.22 | 15 162 |
| | | | | | | |
| 56.47 | 29.21 | 108.28 | 19.48 | 2.79 | 1.30 | 10 310 |
| 114.33 | 27.46 | 107.89 | 10.79 | 2.12 | 1.39 | 9 910 |
| 80.49 | 25.86 | 78.69 | 5.20 | 2.15 | 0.55 | 8 929 |
| 62.90 | 25.59 | 54.01 | 15.14 | 1.34 | 0.23 | 8 472 |
| | | | | | | |
| 90.84 | 21.62 | 64.48 | 8.26 | 3.04 | 2.10 | 9 185 |
| 42.06 | 17.10 | 58.88 | 11.81 | 1.36 | 2.25 | 10 838 |
| 97.20 | 23.15 | 62.52 | 8.81 | 3.97 | 2.80 | 10 031 |
| 50.67 | 15.35 | 55.75 | 7.30 | 3.04 | 2.00 | 10 624 |
| | | | | | | |
| 53.17 | 19.73 | 42.18 | 28.44 | 3.53 | 1.32 | 9 861 |
| 91.16 | 24.94 | 69.98 | 16.01 | 1.95 | 1.50 | 10 429 |
| 92.25 | 25.48 | 82.09 | 20.48 | 1.45 | 1.68 | 10 545 |
| 107.93 | 20.80 | 110.00 | 9.90 | 1.82 | 1.60 | 11 726 |

表20-3 续表 2

| 市县名称 | City and County | 年末户籍人口 (万人) Year-end Household Population (10 000 persons) | 地区生产总值 (亿元) Gross Domestic Product (100 million yuan) | 第一产业 Primary Industry | 第二产业 Secondary Industry | 第三产业 Tertiary Industry |
|---|---|---|---|---|---|---|
| 建湖县 | Jianhu County | 80.41 | 324.47 | 42.13 | 154.35 | 127.99 |
| 东台市 | Dongtai City | 113.59 | 506.69 | 78.33 | 231.89 | 196.47 |
| 大丰市 | Dafeng City | 72.53 | 393.36 | 63.34 | 173.82 | 156.20 |
| **扬州市** | **Yangzhou** | | | | | |
| 宝应县 | Baoying County | 90.31 | 323.03 | 55.43 | 151.85 | 115.75 |
| 仪征市 | Yizheng City | 56.24 | 370.27 | 19.30 | 212.86 | 138.11 |
| 高邮市 | Gaoyou City | 81.74 | 336.00 | 55.96 | 156.05 | 123.99 |
| **镇江市** | **Zhenjiang** | | | | | |
| 丹阳市 | Danyang City | 81.17 | 830.51 | 44.79 | 447.76 | 337.96 |
| 扬中市 | Yangzhong City | 28.09 | 360.20 | 11.50 | 202.69 | 146.01 |
| 句容市 | Jurong City | 58.84 | 336.86 | 31.71 | 177.89 | 127.26 |
| **泰州市** | **Taizhou** | | | | | |
| 兴化市 | Xinghua City | 157.28 | 512.36 | 81.54 | 222.50 | 208.32 |
| 靖江市 | Jingjiang City | 66.66 | 600.85 | 18.88 | 335.88 | 246.09 |
| 泰兴市 | Taixing City | 119.83 | 543.55 | 42.80 | 291.15 | 209.60 |
| 姜堰市 | Jiangyan City | 79.31 | 405.86 | 31.68 | 210.80 | 163.38 |
| **宿迁市** | **Suqian** | | | | | |
| 沭阳县 | Shuyang County | 186.82 | 480.50 | 71.76 | 220.49 | 188.25 |
| 泗阳县 | Siyang County | 103.60 | 273.74 | 46.21 | 137.97 | 89.56 |
| 泗洪县 | Sihong County | 105.45 | 264.63 | 49.17 | 111.14 | 104.32 |

Continued 2

| 粮食产量 (万吨) Total of Grain (10 000 tons) | 地方公共财政预算收入(亿元) Budgetary Revenue (100 million yuan) | 社会消费品零售总额（亿元） Total Retail Sales of Consumer Goods (100 million yuan) | 工业用电量 (亿千瓦时) Electricity Consumption of Industry (100 million kwh) | 出口总额 (亿美元) Total Exports (USD 100 million) | 实际利用外资 (亿美元) Foreign Capital Actually Utilized (USD 100 million) | 农民人均纯收入 (元) Per Capita Net Income of Rural (yuan) |
|---|---|---|---|---|---|---|
| 69.19 | 32.94 | 108.32 | 10.50 | 2.81 | 1.60 | 11 705 |
| 91.13 | 43.67 | 158.09 | 27.03 | 4.10 | 3.10 | 13 647 |
| 77.64 | 40.01 | 108.80 | 28.02 | 4.68 | 3.10 | 13 517 |
| | | | | | | |
| 91.13 | 20.71 | 105.35 | 8.95 | 4.72 | 1.00 | 11 670 |
| 33.71 | 24.66 | 114.75 | 23.79 | 4.53 | 3.52 | 12 244 |
| 86.04 | 21.72 | 110.57 | 12.07 | 3.01 | 0.98 | 11 828 |
| | | | | | | |
| 50.48 | 50.09 | 202.38 | 46.70 | 21.84 | 4.76 | 15 171 |
| 10.78 | 22.57 | 90.32 | 9.99 | 3.63 | 1.67 | 16 631 |
| 34.77 | 25.02 | 93.31 | 13.80 | 4.45 | 4.26 | 13 235 |
| | | | | | | |
| 139.31 | 29.46 | 112.69 | 46.08 | 4.65 | 1.35 | 11 827 |
| 33.53 | 44.01 | 123.25 | 27.15 | 23.44 | 2.61 | 13 715 |
| 69.43 | 32.61 | 142.95 | 39.16 | 10.77 | 2.52 | 12 505 |
| 54.78 | 23.54 | 122.15 | 20.17 | 6.32 | 1.12 | 12 228 |
| | | | | | | |
| 131.84 | 48.79 | 108.34 | 22.48 | 4.76 | 1.01 | 9 557 |
| 60.59 | 21.76 | 63.58 | 7.57 | 5.78 | 0.64 | 9 541 |
| 102.79 | 19.76 | 65.24 | 6.19 | 3.42 | 0.64 | 9 327 |

# 风采集萃

## COLLECTION OF ENTERPRISES' VISUALIZE

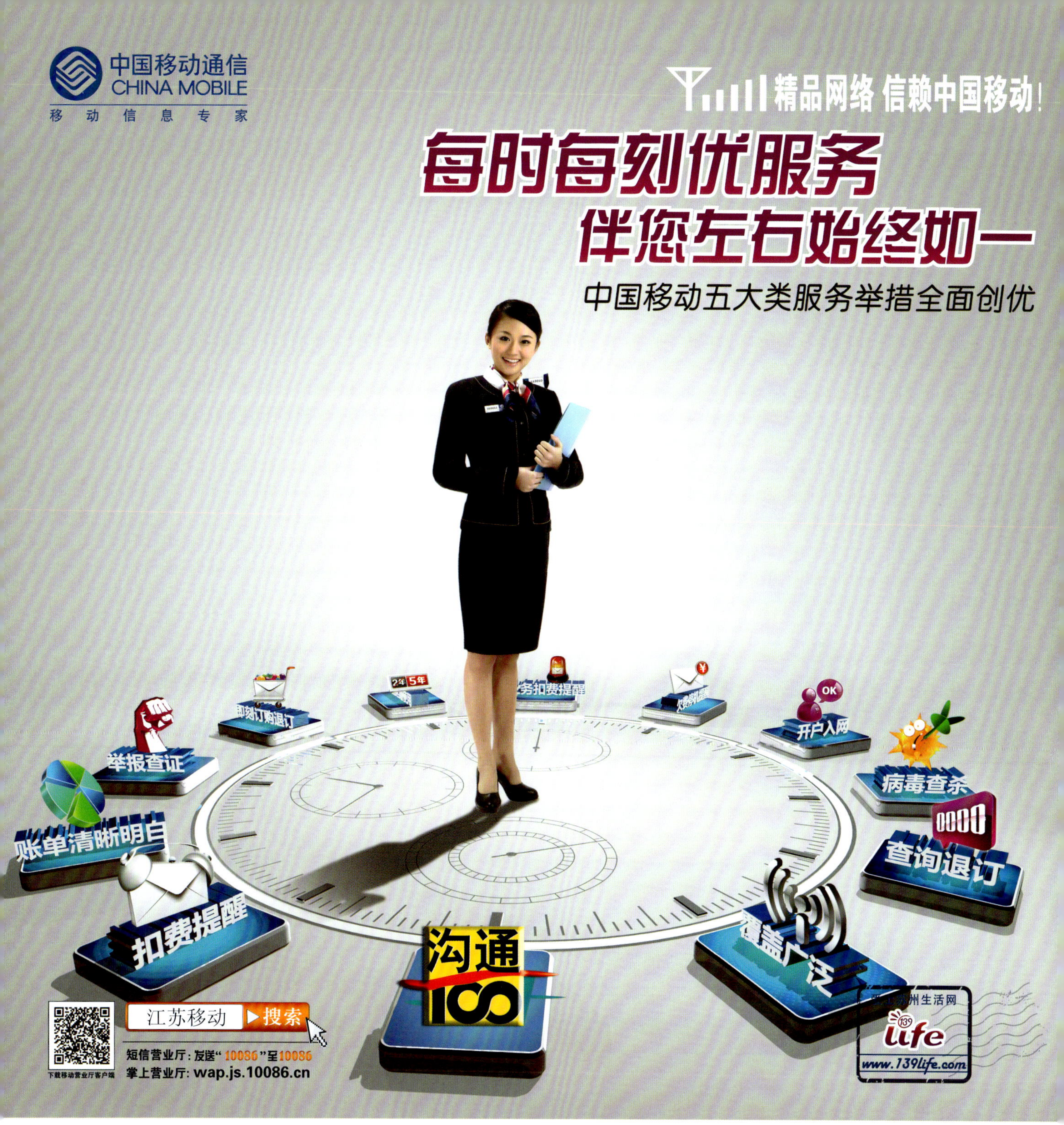

中国移动通信 CHINA MOBILE
移动信息专家

精品网络 信赖中国移动！

# 每时每刻优服务 伴您左右始终如一

中国移动五大类服务举措全面创优

账单清晰明白 举报查证 即刻订购退订 扣费提醒 沟通100 覆盖广泛 查询退订 病毒查杀 开户入网

江苏移动 搜索
下载移动营业厅客户端
短信营业厅：发送“10086”至10086
掌上营业厅：wap.js.10086.cn

www.139life.com

为了您的每一分满意，我们坚持一心一意，以百分努力和全心专注，每分每秒时刻相伴，为您提供20年始终如一的优品质服务。中国移动五大类二十多项服务新举措先行升级，为您全方位开启移动互联优生活！

**“优服务”五大类服务举措**

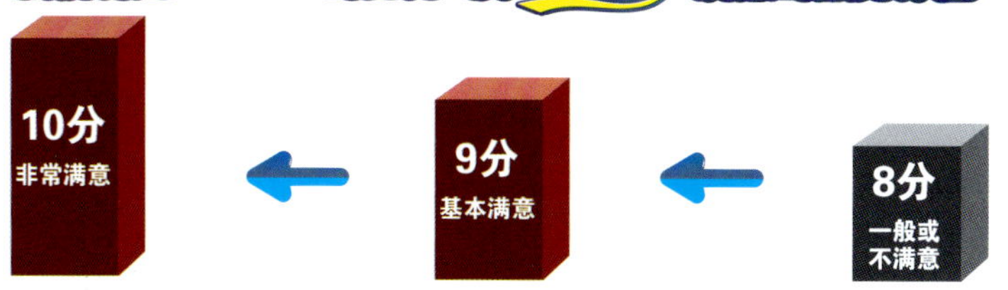

◎优质网络 覆盖广泛 ◎信息安全 通信保障 ◎资费优惠 全面惠民

◎透明消费 多重提醒 ◎窗口服务 优质高效

# 苏州二建建筑集团有限公司

苏州二建建筑集团有限公司成立于 1952 年，是江苏省内大型建筑施工企业。公司具有国家房屋建筑工程施工总承包特级资质和对外工程承包资格。公司主营业务包括房屋建筑施工、勘察设计、市政公路、地基基础、钢结构、装饰装修、设备安装、消防、园林古建、建筑幕墙等，是一家集设计、施工、房地产开发、教育培训、建材经营、设备租赁、公路、水利水电、铁路、化工石油设备管道安装、管道、桥梁、隧道、环保和物业管理为一体的大型建筑施工单位。

公司注册资金 30280 万元，年完成企业总产值 100 亿元，公司以服务社会、诚信经营为原则，各项工作争创一流，连续多年被评为江苏省最佳建筑企业，位居苏州市建筑业首强，2011 年入围“中国建筑业竞争力百强企业”。公司也被评为江苏省纳税百强民营企业，荣列全国“阳光财富企业榜”，并连续三年入围“ENR 中国承包商 60 强”。 公司董事长宫长义先生为江苏省有突出贡献建筑业企业家、全国优秀施工企业家，并获江苏省劳动模范称号。

公司于 2002 年率先通过 ISO9001：2000 质量管理体系、ISO14001：2004 环境管理体系、GB/T28001-2001 职业健康安全管理体系的一体化认证，使企业综合管理水平上了台阶。多年来，公司依靠科技进步、强化管理，坚持“优质高速，信誉至上”的企业宗旨，屡创佳绩，信誉卓著。

承建的工程中获部、省、市优质工程 100 多项，获省市级文明工地 100 余项。共荣获 6 项“鲁班奖”（其中参加一项），4 项“国家优质工程奖”。

公司坚持把“信为本、诚为基、德为源”作为发展理念，把“胸怀企业兴衰，心系员工冷暖，牢记社会责任”作为对全体员工的共同要求，紧紧依靠职工，团结拼搏，开拓创新，全面致力于做大做强、做实做优企业的各项工作，为企业持续、健康、和谐发展不懈努力。

# 苏州统计服务
Suzhou Statistical Services

苏州统计服务品牌的主题:
统计求实　服务创优

标识图案由两只抽象的鸿雁组成，形象地表示“苏州统计服务”英文首位字母3个“S”，象征着苏州社会经济发展空间的无限延伸；折起而变化的线条好似跳动的数字，上下中间的红色和绿色则喻示着发展变化和数字升降；两只抽象的鸿雁形成相拥之势，喻意社会发展需要相互包容，相互支持，相互依赖，相互服务。图案之中还隐含着国家统计局统计标识的图形和内涵，便于识记。

## 最新图书简目

以最后出书为准）

**2013年市（县）级综合统计年鉴系列**

天津滨海新区 石家庄 唐山 邯郸 太原 大同 长治 阳泉 晋城 朔州 晋中

运城 忻州 临汾 呼和浩特 包头 通辽 沈阳 大连 长春 吉林市 四平 哈尔滨 黑龙江垦区

上海浦东新区 南京 苏州 无锡 常州 徐州 南通 盐城 镇江 宿迁 泰州 连云港 江阴 丹阳

杭州 宁波 绍兴 台州 温州 金华 嘉兴 衢州 福州 福州经济技术开发区

厦门经济特区 宁德 南昌 上饶 济南 青岛 潍坊 郑州 洛阳 三门峡 南阳 武汉 宜昌

十堰 荆州 咸宁 长沙 广州 东莞 惠州 深圳 桂林 南宁 柳州 来宾 河池 海口 成都 绵阳

贵阳 昆明 庆阳 西安 兰州 银川 乌鲁木齐

**2010年人口普查资料系列**

中国2010年人口普查资料 北京 天津 河北 山西 内蒙古 辽宁 吉林 黑龙江 上海 江苏

浙江 安徽 福建 江西 山东 河南 湖北 湖南 广东 广西 海南 重庆 四川 贵州 云南

西藏 陕西 甘肃 青海 宁夏 新疆 新疆生产建设兵团 河南省各市2010年人口普查资料丛书

中国分县2010年人口普查资料 中国分乡镇、街道2010年人口普查资料 中国分民族2010年人口普查资料

**“十一五”规划教材**

统计学（“十二五”规划，黄良文） 抽样调查理论与实践（“十二五”规划，冯士雍）

统计学（“十二五”规划，单徽） 试验设计（“十二五”规划，茆诗松） 贝叶斯统计（“十二五”规划，茆诗松）

统计学：从数据到结论（十二五规划，吴喜之） 医学统计学（陆守曾）

非参数统计（吴喜之） 概率论与数理统计（茆诗松） 现代金融投资统计分析（李腊生）

多元统计分析（任雪松） 应用时间序列分析（王振龙） 统计指数理论及应用（徐国祥）

经济计量学教程（贺铿） 质量管理统计方法 （茆诗松） 统计实验系列教材（许涤龙）

社会统计学（蒋萍） 市场调查与预测（蒋志华） 统计学原理（非统计专业用，朱胜）

国民经济核算教程(杨灿) 概率论与数理统计(经济、管理类专业使用，朱胜)

**重点图书**

挑大学选专业2013—高考志愿填报指南 挑大学选专业2013—考研择校指南

中国统计出版社发行部电话：（010）63376907,63376908 同楫行书店电话：68783171,68783172

通讯地址：北京市西城区三里河月坛南街57号 邮政编码：100826

网址：http://csp.stats.gov.cn

## 中国统计出版社

（仅供参考，

### 统计资料

中国统计年鉴-2013
中国统计摘要-2013
国际统计年鉴-2013
2013中国发展报告
中国第三产业统计年鉴-2013
中国区域经济统计年鉴-2013
中国劳动统计年鉴-2013
中国社会统计年鉴-2013
中国城市统计年鉴-2013
中国建筑业统计年鉴-2013
中国人口和就业统计年鉴-2013
中国工业经济统计年鉴-2013
中国商品交易市场统计年鉴-2013
中国房地产统计年鉴-2013
中国能源统计年鉴-2013
中国民政统计年鉴-2013
中国贸易外经统计年鉴-2013
2013中国地区经济监测报告
中国科技统计年鉴-2013
中国农村统计年鉴-2013
中国农产品价格调查年鉴-2013
中国高技术产业统计年鉴-2013
中国教育经费统计年鉴-2013
中国农村贫困监测报告-2013
全国农产品成本收益资料汇编-2013
中国科学技术协会统计年鉴-2013
工业企业科技活动资料-2013
大中型批发零售和住宿餐饮企业统计年鉴-2013
中国价格统计年鉴-2013
第二次全国R&D资源清查资料汇编－工业企业卷
中国住户调查年鉴-2013
中国县域统计年鉴-2013
中国农村全面建设小康监测报告-2013
第二次全国R&D资源清查资料汇编－综合卷
中国人才资源统计报告-2011
中国民族统计年鉴-2013
中国零售和餐饮连锁企业统计年鉴-2013
2010年中国第六次人口普查公报

### 2013年省级综合统计年鉴系列

北京 天津 河北 山西 内蒙古
辽宁 吉林 黑龙江 上海 江苏
浙江 安徽 福建 江西 山东
河南 湖北 湖南 广东 广西
海南 重庆 四川 贵州 云南
西藏 陕西 甘肃 青海 宁夏
新疆 新疆生产建设兵团

# 工商银行苏州分行

工商银行苏州分行成立于1984年，目前在苏州辖内拥有11个一级支行、210多个营业网点、4000多名员工。工行苏州分行在公司业务、个人业务、资金业务、电子银行业务以及国际业务等各类金融业务方面齐头并进、协调发展，并始终以真诚的服务与专业的能力帮助客户管理资产、创造价值。

在二十多年的发展历程中，苏州分行依托苏州区域经济的快速腾飞，始终坚持改革创新，全面确立“以市场为导向，以客户为中心”的现代商业银行经营理念，新业务、新产品层出不穷，市场领域不断拓展，服务质量持续提升，为满足现代社会的多元化金融需求和地方经济的快速发展提供了强有力的金融支撑。苏州分行坚持“工于至诚、行以致远”的企业文化理念，把培育特色鲜明的企业“家园文化”，作为造就良好经营发展环境，实现企业与员工共同成长与和谐发展的强大动力。

2012年，苏州分行抢抓机遇，着力推进经营结构转型，努力践行改革创新，切实加强风险防控，全行经营管理呈现出“规模效益攀升、经营转型显效、同业位次与市场竞争力提升、管理氛围和企业文化建设稳健和谐”的良好局面。

当前及今后一个时期，苏州分行将在市委、市政府的领导下，以科学发展观为统领，积极支持地方经济建设，履行工商银行应尽的社会责任，围绕“高标、高效、高质”的“三高”标准和“业绩好、氛围好、口碑好”的“三好”要求，为建设“同业争先、系统进位，加快实现苏州地区最优、最强银行”而奋发努力。